JOHN NEWBERY

AND HIS

SUCCESSORS

1740-1814

A BIBLIOGRAPHY

Half-tone reproduction, printed in five colours, of a piece of Dutch floral paper in the possession of S. Roscoe. For details of the original manufacture of this paper see Appendix 2.

JOHN NEWBERY

AND HIS

SUCCESSORS

1740-1814

A BIBLIOGRAPHY

BY

S. ROSCOE

FIVE OWLS PRESS LTD

Published by Five Owls Press Ltd
67 High Road, Wormley, Hertfordshire EN10 6JJ

© S. ROSCOE 1973

ISBN: 0 903838 00 1

Printed in Great Britain
at the University Printing House, Cambridge
Brooke Crutchley, University Printer

CONTENTS

PREFACE

For want of a better name I call this work a Bibliography, though I designed it to be no more than an annotated catalogue. And basically it remains a catalogue, though the volume of the notes in the Juvenile section has grown substantially. The non-Juvenile section (lettered 'A') is an expanded short title catalogue.

But I had also designed that this catalogue should set out the names of the publishers and printers appearing in the imprint of each book, as I wanted to show with whom the Newbery family co-operated in their publishing business. In the event, and largely for reasons of space, it has been possible to set out only in the majority of the Juveniles the names in the imprints. To compensate in some measure for this imperfection the Index of Publishers, Printers and Booksellers will show what books any particular publisher, printer or seller was concerned with, in both sections 'J' and 'A'.

I have not gone out of my way to look for variant issues, though I have noted all that came along. Particularly in the field of the Juveniles variants are legion. For instance, I have recorded four such issues of the undated edition of *Prince Lee Boo* and there are copies in at least nine libraries remaining unchecked. Almost certainly further variants will be found there. There are at least five variant printings of Elizabeth Newbery's *Prettiest Book for Children*. The further I go the more it becomes clear that, particularly as regards Elizabeth's more successful juvenile productions, reprintings were very frequent – almost annual, it may be – and from new settings of type. Dr d'Alté Welch out of his great experience of these juveniles could say 'I am now more than ever convinced that we know little about the vast horde of Newbery variants. Every book I pick up seems to be a variant. It is the exception to the rule that two Newbery items are identical if they are undated'. The difficulties in the way of distinguishing copies (one, say, in Bodley, the other in a private collection in the U.S.A.) may be almost insuperable. Particulars sent to me or given in catalogues are, more often than not, too vague and imprecise to enable one copy to be distinguished from the other. And to get further and better details is not always possible, though photo-copying has proved an immense help. For these reasons my lists of locations may need drastic revision as and when located copies come to be more carefully analysed.

Then there are the bibliographically complex works such as *She stoops to conquer* or the *World displayed*; here I have made no attempt at a detailed analysis. That is a matter for the specialist, who will also give his mind to *Prince Lee Boo* and the problems to be found in the publishing history of the *Royal Primer* and Dr James's *Medicinal Dictionary*.

My full notes on the Juvenile books are more detailed than the notes in the non-Juvenile section. These (the non-Juvenile notes) will be available for inspection by anyone interested on application to me. And it is intended that ultimately they will (by permission of the Committee of the Library) be lodged in the Oxford English Faculty Library at Manor Road, Oxford, where they will be available on application to the Librarian.

I am acutely aware of the many faults and imperfections in this book. With greater energy and persistence I could no doubt have gathered in much more information than is here recorded. And the mass of detail to be dealt with must inevitably throw up gruesome errors, undetected to the end. I ask forbearance for these errors; I also ask the kindly reader to write and tell me of them.

DUNSMORE   S.R.
SOUTH HILL AVENUE
HARROW, MIDDLESEX

March 1973

NOTE ON THE COPIES OF BOOKS EXAMINED

It has not been possible to examine all copies noted in the location lists. In particular I have not been able to visit the great collections across the Atlantic, therefore Part II, the non-Juveniles, is rather inadequate in this respect. For the Juveniles I have been helped by many kind friends in the U.S.A. and Canada, whose names are recorded in the lists of Acknowledgements; and there the trans-Atlantic locations are fuller.

These location lists (where there are any) are at the end of each note, preceded by a square bracket [. They must not be regarded as in any way censuses of holdings.

In each case the details given in the notes are based on the copy (or copies) indicated in the following ways:

As to the Juveniles (Part I), except where otherwise stated, the note is based on the copy or copies of which the dimensions are given in the location list, they having been examined by me. In cases noted as '(Communicated)' or where no dimensions of any copy are given, I have not seen a copy of the book.

In the non-Juveniles (Part II) the note is based on the first copy or copies in the list except where recorded as '(Communicated)' or 'Not seen'.

ACKNOWLEDGEMENTS

My foremost debt, expressed in my *Provisional Check-list*, and now repeated as many times multiplied, is to my old friend Miss M. J. P. Weedon, Librarian of the Oxford English Faculty Library. Miss Weedon has read and criticised much of what I have written, has contributed a vast deal of information from her own great store of learning, and while often enough finding it needful to rebuke me for sins of omission and commission has cheered me on with words of comfort in many moments of weariness and frustration.

The late Dr d'Alté Welch, of Cleveland Heights, Ohio, Bibliographer Royal of American early children's books, whose tragic death we mourn most deeply, put all his great knowledge at my disposal and opened for me the huge collections of children's books in his country; I should have been lost without him. To his memory go my heartfelt thanks. And so also to Miss Judith St John, of the Toronto Public Library, author of the Catalogue of the Osborne Collection there, who has kept me advised of new acquisitions to that wonderful library; and Mr Wilbur Smith, Head of Special Collections at the University of California at Los Angeles, for detailing for me the rich collection of 'Newberys' there (over one hundred and forty of them).

So many others, too, librarians, collectors, booksellers, have helped, each according to his or her ability. I have tried to name them all in the lists that follow. If I have forgotten any I ask forgiveness. To all I say 'Thank you for all the help and encouragement you have given me. You are all part-authors of this book'.

Miss R. E. Adomeit, of Cleveland, Ohio; Dr Robin C. Alston, of Leeds University; Miss Elisabeth Ball, of Muncie, Indiana; Dr L. G. E. Bell, of Southampton; Dr Frank B. Fieler, for very full notes on books in the McKell Collection; Mr Richard Freeman, of University College, London; Mr Frederick R. Gardner, of New York; Mr and Mrs Alan Grant, of Toorak, Victoria; Mrs J. E. I. Grey, of Hitchin (who has ferreted out so many books which I should have missed); Mrs Linda Hannas, of Bromley, Kent; Mr W. N. H. Harding, of Chicago; Dr C. W. J. Higson, of the University of Leicester School of Education; Professor P. C. G. Isaac, of Newcastle University; Mrs Linda F. Lapides, of Baltimore; Miss C. M. Legg (Mrs Dowden) for permission to quote from her *Bibliography of Books printed in Reading in the 18th Century*; Mrs M. Moon, of Chardstock, Devon; Mr Percy H. Muir, of Bishops Stortford; Mr and Mrs Peter Opie, of West Liss, Hants; Dr J. H. P. Pafford, formerly Goldsmith Librarian in the University of London; Mr and Mrs D. Parkinson, of Taverham, Norwich; Miss M. Pollard, of Dublin; Mr Harry W. Pratley, of Tunbridge Wells; Miss Joan Pressler, of Pittsburgh, Penn.; Messrs Bernard Quaritch Ltd, of London; Mr Eric S. Quayle, of Zennor; Mr Herbert Reichner, of Stockbridge, Mass.; Mr and Mrs F. G. Renier, of Barnes, London; the late Mr Ludwig Ries, of New York; Mr and Mrs George Shiers, of Santa Barbara, Cal.; Mr Stanley C. Smith, of the Marchmont Bookshop, London; Miss Rita F. Snowden, of Auckland, N.Z.; Mrs M. Suffolk, of Lower Brailes, Oxon; Mrs M. F. Thwaite, of Hertford; Mr C. W. Traylen, of Guildford; Mr Peter J. Wallis, of the University of Newcastle.

And the following University and other Libraries and Institutions:

The American Antiquarian Society (and their Librarian, Mr. M. A. McCorison); City of Bath Municipal Libraries (and their Director, Mr Peter Pagan); Bedford College of Education, Bedford (and the Principal, Mr H. H. Humphrey and the Librarian, Mrs Boggis); Birmingham Public Library (and their Librarian, Mr W. A. Taylor); Birmingham University Library; Bishop Lonsdale College of Education; the Curators of the Bodleian Library; the Boston, Massachusetts, Public Library (and Mr John Alden, Keeper of Rare Books); the Bridewell Museum at Norwich (and Miss R. M. R. Young, the Assistant Director); the British Museum; Cambridge University Library; the College of Arms, London; Edinburgh University Library; Exeter City Library; the Guildhall Library, City of London; Haverford College, Haverford, Penn.; Hertford County Library (and Miss L. V. Paulin, its Librarian); Hull University Institute of Education (and its Librarian, Mr C. B. Freeman); the Institute of Chartered Accountants, London; the John Johnson Collection of the Oxford University Press, now lodged in the Bodleian (and Mr Harry Carter and Mrs Thrussell); the John Rylands Library; the Library Company of Philadelphia; the London Borough of Wandsworth (and Mrs D. Aubrey, Senior Children's Librarian); the London Museum (and Mrs S. Kington, the Librarian); London University and Miss Legg (for permission to quote from her *Bibliography of Books printed in Reading in the 18th Century*); Manchester Public Libraries (and Miss H. M. McGill, Great Hall Librarian); the Medical Society of London; Melbourne University, Victoria (and Miss M. Lugton, Reference Librarian, the Baillieu Library); Miami University (and Mr L. S. Dutton, Director of Libraries); the National Library of Australia (and Mr Ivan Page); the National Library of Scotland; Newcastle upon Tyne Public Library; the University of New South Wales; Nottingham University (and Mr R. S. Smith, Librarian); the Oxford English Faculty Library; the Peabody Institute, Baltimore; the Pharmaceutical Society, London (and Miss D. Jones, Assistant Librarian, for their search for the bust of John Newbery); the Pierpont Morgan Library (and Mr Herbert Cahoon); Reading Public Library; Reading University Library; the Royal College of Physicians, London; the Royal College of Surgeons, London; the Royal College of Veterinary Surgeons, London; the Royal Horticultural Society; the Royal Institution of Chartered Surveyors, London; the Royal Institution of Great Britain; the Royal Society of Medicine, London; the Royal Veterinary College, London; the St Bride Printing Library, London (and its Librarian, Mr James Mosley); the Society of Friends, London (and Mr E. H. Milligan, its Librarian); the Somerset County Library at Bridgwater; the Worshipful Company of Stationers, London (for permission to quote from Richard Johnson's Day-Books and to examine their collection of Almanacks); University

College, London (and Mr Joseph Scott, the Librarian); the Wellcome Historical Medical Library, London (and Dr F. N. L. Poynter); Whitelands College, Putney, London (and Miss C. S. Ker, the Librarian); the Zoological Society, London.

I also acknowledge with gratitude the courtesy of the owners, libraries and private collectors, listed below, who have allowed me to reproduce pages from their books. The Trustees of the British Museum: Figures 3, 4, 11, 12, 13, 17, 18a–d, 20, 21, 23, 27, 28, 33; Plates 2, 6, 8, 10, 11, 17, 21, 24, 25, 27, 28, 29, 33, 34, 35. The Curators of the Bodleian Library: Figures 6, 7, 24; Plates 1, 9, 12, 13, 14, 16, 18, 20, 30, 31. The Trustees of the National Library of Scotland: Plate 32. Dr L. G. E. Bell: Plate 7. Miss E. Ball and the Pierpont Morgan Library: Figure 22. The St Bride Printing Library, St Bride Institute: Figure 25; Plates 5, 15. Miss M. J. P. Weedon: Figures 8, 15, 16. The Guildhall Library, London: Figure 2. The London Library: Plate 23. The Stationers' Company: Plate 22. The following are reproduced from copies in my collection: Figures 5, 9, 10, 14, 16, 19, 26, 29, 30, 31, 32, 34, 35; Plates 3, 4, 22, 26.

Finally I must express my gratitude, first to Mr and Mrs Brian Alderson who rescued me from the slough of despond at a time when, after more than ten years of work, I was minded to give the whole thing up, sought out the printer, undertook the businesses and worries of publication and got the whole thing moving forward smoothly and efficiently. Secondly to Mr Alan Spilman of Cambridge, who has laboured to prepare my much-amended manuscript for the printer, and seen it through the press, correcting my text, as too often was necessary. Also to my sister Phoebe, who spent many hours reading the proofs, hours which could have been spent more comfortably elsewhere.

But for the help of these kind people the book would not have been possible in its present form, if indeed at all.

I exonerate them from any responsibility for the errors and omissions the book contains. Responsibility for them is mine, and mine alone.

LIST OF ILLUSTRATIONS

Frontispiece   Reproduction of a piece of Dutch floral paper, as used by John Newbery and his contemporaries and successors.

PLATES

BETWEEN PAGES 128–9 AND 288–9

FIGURES

ABBREVIATIONS

a	and.
advtd, adv.	advertised, advertisement.
advert[s.]	advertisement[s].
a s	and sold.
a s b	and sold by.
b	by.
B & S	Bible & Sun.
bd	bound.
bds	boards.
bk[s]	book[s].
BL	Black Letter.
BM	British Museum.
BMQ	*British Museum Quarterly.*
BUCM	*British Union Catalogue of Early Music.*
BUCOP	*British Union Catalogue of Periodicals.*
C	Thomas Carnan.
C & N	Carnan and Francis Newbery the son in partnership.
cat.	catalogue.
CBEL	*Cambridge Bibliography of English Literature,* 1940 (1st edn unless otherwise stated).
CL	County Library.
colln, coll.	collection, collected.
Communicated	Indicates information supplied by the owner.
d	double.
D.f.	Dutch floral.
D.f.b.	Dutch floral boards.
d.p.rule	double plain rule.
d.rule	decorative rule.
d.s.rule	decorative swelled rule.
DNB	*Dictionary of National Biography.*
ed.[d.]	edition[s], edited.
EN	Elizabeth Newbery.

ENC	*Newbery's Catalogue of Instructive & Amusing Publications for Young Minds*, 1800.
engvd	engraved.
engvg[s]	engraving[s].
et al.	and another [others].
ex exc	except.
FN jr	Francis Newbery the son of John Newbery.
FN(N)	Francis Newbery the nephew of John Newbery.
FN(S)	Francis Newbery the son.
FN*	Either Francis the son or the nephew, not known which.
FP	Frontispiece.
GA	*General Advertiser.*
GEP	*General Evening Post.*
GM	*Gentleman's Magazine.*
Gum	Gumuchian's *Livres d'Enfance (n.d.).*
H&L	Halkett and Laing, *Dictionary of Anonymous and Pseudonimous English Literature.*
illustration	Usually used where no information as to whether woodcut or metal engraving, etc.
Jag.	W. Jaggard, *Shakespeare Bibliography*, 1911.
JN	John Newbery.
LC	*London Chronicle.*
LM	*London Magazine.*
MC&LA	*Morning Chronicle and London Advertiser.*
ML	Municipal Library.
N & C	Francis Newbery the son and Carnan in partnership.
NBL	National Book League.
n.d.	No date, undated.
N&Q	*Notes and Queries.*
N(S)	Francis Newbery the son.
Newbery*	Not known which of the Newberys.
ornam., orn.	ornamental, ornament.
p. pp.	page, pages.
PA	*Public Advertiser.*
PL	*Public Ledger.*

PL	Public Library.
PNR	Pater Noster Row (with or without hyphens).
pr	printed.
pr a s b	printed and sold by.
pr b	printed by.
pr b a f	printed by and for.
pr f	printed for.
pr f a s b	printed for and sold by.
prtr	printer.
p.rule	plain rule.
p.s.rule	plain swelled rule, tapering rule.
pt[s]	part[s].
pubd b	published by.
publr	publisher.
s	sold.
s b	sold by.
sgd	signed.
SPCY	St Paul's Church Yard (with or without hyphens).
specification	So far as not otherwise stated implies the format, collation and contents of a book.
TC	Thomas Carnan.
t.d.a.p.	this day are published.
t.d.i.p.	this day is published.
t.d.w.p.	this day was published.
TLS	*Times Literary Supplement.*
TP	title-page.
trans.	translated, translation.
UL	University Library.
UM	*Universal Magazine.*
unsgd	unsigned.
vell.	vellum.
vso	verso.
w.b.p.	will be published.
wct[s]	woodcut[s].
wmk	watermark.

LIBRARIES, COLLECTORS
AND THEIR SYMBOLS

Actuaries	The Institute of Actuaries, London.
AdE	Advocates' Library, Edinburgh.
Adm	The Admiralty, London.
Adomeit	Miss R. E. Adomeit, Cleveland, Ohio.
Algar	The late F. Algar, of Ilford, Essex.
Babson	The Grace K. Babson Collection of Works of Sir Isaac Newton, Babson Park, Mass.
Ball	Miss Elisabeth Ball, Muncie, Indiana (Collection now in course of transfer to Pierpont Morgan Library).
BAS	Basle, Oeffentliche Bibliothek der Universität.
Bath	City of Bath, Municipal Library and Victoria Art Gallery, Somerset.
BCE	Bedford College of Education, Bedford (the Hockliffe Collection).
BEK	Berkeley, University of California.
Bell	Dr L. G. E. Bell, Highfield, Southampton.
BFBS	British and Foreign Bible Society, London.
BGu	Bologna, Biblioteca Universitaria.
Bi	Birmingham University, School of Education.
Birchenough	C. Birchenough.
Bishop Lonsdale	Bishop Lonsdale College of Education, Mickleover, Derby.
BM	British Museum, London.
BM(NH)	British Museum, Natural History, London.
BmPL	Birmingham Public Library.
BmU	Birmingham University Library.
BmU(Wigan)	Birmingham University Library, Wigan (Bewdley) Collection.
Bo. Bodley	Bodleian Library, Oxford.
Bowe	Forrest Bowe, New York City, N.Y.
BPL(S)	Birmingham Public Library (Shakespeare Memorial Library).
Brayshaw	Mrs C. Brayshaw, Withington, Manchester.
Brimmell	R. A. Brimmell, Hastings, Sussex.
Bristol	Bristol Public Library.

BrUL	Bristol University Library.
BRW	Bowdoin College, Brunswick, Maine.
CA	The Institute of Chartered Accountants in England and Wales.
CA(Sc)	The Institute of Chartered Accountants of Scotland.
CambFL	Cambridge Free Library.
CCamarSJ	St John's Seminary, Camarillo (Doheny Collection), U.S.A.
CHH	University of North Carolina, Chapel Hill.
CKC	Cambridge, King's College.
CLU (also UCLA)	University of California at Los Angeles.
CLU-C	the same, William Andrews Clark Memorial Library.
Coons	Mrs Lamont K. Coons, New Haven, Conn. (now in CtNSCSC).
CQC	Cambridge, Queens' College.
CSJC	Cambridge, St John's College.
CtHi	Connecticut Historical Society, Hartford.
CtNSCSC	Southern Connecticut State College, the Carolyn Sherwin Bailey Historical Collection of Children's Books.
CTrC	Cambridge, Trinity College.
CtY	Yale University, New Haven.
CUL (also ULC)	Cambridge University Library.
CVh	Cleveland, Ohio, Western Reserve.
D (also TCD)	Trinity College, Dublin.
DES	Department of Education and Science, London.
DLC	U.S. Library of Congress.
DNS	Nichol Smith Collection, National Library of Australia, Canberra.
DTPL	Detroit, Michigan, Public Library.
DWL	Dr Williams' Library, London.
Edison	Julian I. Edison, St Louis, Missouri.
EdUL	Edinburgh University Library.
Exeter	City Library, Exeter, Devon.
Fox	C. A. O. Fox, Oldbury, Warley, Worcs.
Freeman	R. Freeman, University College, London.
Friends	The Library of the Society of Friends, London.
Gabrielson	Prof. Arvid Gabrielson, Stockholm.
Gardner	Frederick R. Gardner, Amityville, N.Y.

GeoM	Geological Museum, London.
GlaPL	Glasgow Public Library.
GlaUL	Glasgow University Library.
GOB	Göteborg, Sweden, Universitetsbiblioteket.
Grant	Mr and Mrs Alan Grant, Toorak, Victoria, Australia.
Grey	Mrs J. E. I. Grey, Hitchin, Herts.
HammPL	Hammersmith Public Library, London.
HAN	Hanover, Dartmouth College, New Hampshire.
Hannas	Mrs L. Hannas, Bromley, Kent.
Harding	W. N. H. Harding, Chicago.
HeCL	Hertfordshire County Library.
HU	University of Hull, Institute of Education.
HuPL	Hull Public Library.
ICU	University of Chicago (Friedman, Encyclopaedia Britannica Collection).
ICU-J	University of Chicago, Judd Library.
INC	Newberry Library, Chicago.
ITH	Cornell University, Ithaca.
IU	University of Illinois, Urbana.
KE	University of Keele, Institute of Education.
Kent	Kent County Library, Maidstone.
Knaster	Roland Knaster, London.
KU	University of Kansas, Lawrence.
Lambeth	Lambeth Palace Library, London.
Lapides	Mrs L. F. Lapides, Baltimore, Maryland.
LCA	College of Arms, London.
LEB	Brotherton Library, Leeds University.
LEE	University of Leeds, Institute of Education.
LEI	University of Leicester, School of Education.
LEIU(Phys.)	Physical Society Library, University of Leicester.
LGL	City of London, Guildhall Library.
LI	University of Liverpool, School of Education.
Lisney	The late A. A. Lisney (see Bibliographical References, pt I, no. 31).
LKC	King's College, London.
LKePL	Kensington Public Library, London.
LL	London Library.
LOU	University of London, Institute of Education.
Loveday	The late Dr T. F. Loveday, of Banbury (present location of Collection not known).

LScM	Science Museum, London (also ScM).
LUL	London University Library.
LWaPL	Wandsworth Public Library, London.
Lyon	The late H. M. Lyon, of the Court Bookshop, Holborn, London (collection now in BM).
Madison	University of Wisconsin, Madison.
Marchmont Bookshop	The Marchmont Bookshop, Bruton St, London.
MB	Boston Public Library, Boston, Mass.
MBAt	Boston Athenaeum, Boston, Mass.
MBSPNEA	Society for the Preservation of New England Antiquities, Boston, Mass.
McKell	Collection of the late Col. David McKell of Chillicothe, Ohio, now owned by Ross County (Ohio) Historical Society.
MdBJ	Johns Hopkins University, Baltimore.
MdBP	Peabody Institute, Baltimore.
Melbourne	The Morgan Collection, Baillieu Library, University of Melbourne, Victoria.
Melcher	Daniel Melcher, U.S.A.
MH	Harvard University, Cambridge, Mass.
MiDW	Wayne State University, Detroit.
MiU	University of Michigan, Ann Arbor.
MNS	Smith College Library, Northampton, Mass.
MnU	University of Minnesota, Minneapolis.
Moon	Mrs M. Moon, Chardstock, Devon.
MOWl	Moscow, Lenin State Library.
MPL	Manchester Public Library.
MPlyA	Plymouth Atheneum, Plymouth, Mass.
MSaE	Essex Institute, Salem, Mass.
MSL	Medical Society of London.
MTLs	Montreal, Bibliothèque Saint-Sulpice.
Muir	P. H. Muir, Bishops Stortford, Herts.
MWA	American Antiquarian Society, Worcester, Mass.
NB	Brooklyn Public Library (Vail Collection), N.Y.
NBuG	Grosvenor Reference Library, Buffalo.
NjP	Princeton University, New Jersey.
NLA	National Library of Australia, Canberra.
NLSc	National Library of Scotland, Edinburgh.
NLWa	National Library of Wales, Aberystwyth.
NMM	National Maritime Museum, Greenwich.
NN	New York Public Library.
NN-C	Children's Room, N.Y. Public Library, N.Y.

NNC	Columbia University, N.Y.
NNC-Pl	Columbia University, N.Y., Plimpton Collection.
NNC-T	the same, Teacher's College Library.
NorBM	Norwich, Bridewell Museum.
NoU	University of Nottingham, Briggs Collection.
NOUL	University of Nottingham Library.
NPV	Vassar Collection, Poughkeepsie, N.Y.
NRU	University of Rochester, Rochester, U.S.A. (Davis Collection).
NSWPL	Public Library of New South Wales, Sydney, N.S.W.
NSWU	University of New South Wales, Kensington, N.S.W.
NUCC-IAU	National Union Card Catalogue, Library of Congress, Washington, D.C.
NUTP	Newcastle upon Tyne Public Library, Pease Collection.
NUTPL	Newcastle upon Tyne Public Library.
NUTU	Newcastle upon Tyne University Library.
NWebyC	Children's Library, Westbury, Long Island, N.Y.
OB	Oberlin College, Oberlin, Ohio.
OClW-LS	Western Reserve University Library School, Cleveland, Ohio.
OEFL	Oxford English Faculty Library, Oxford.
OMHS	Oxford Museum of the History of Science.
OOxM	Miami University, Oxford, U.S.A. (E. W. King Collection).
Opie	Mr and Mrs Peter Opie, West Liss, Hants.
Oppenheimer	Collection of the late Edgar S. Oppenheimer.
Osborne	The Osborne Collection of Early Children's Books, Toronto Public Library, Toronto, Canada.
Osborne*	the same, but the book not in the 1958 printed Catalogue. (A revised edition is in progress.)
Oup	Oxford University Press, the John Johnson (Constance Meade) Collection, Oxford (now in Bodley).
OxPL	Oxford City Public Library, Oxford.
Parkinson	Bibliothèque Nationale, Paris.
Parkinson	E. and D. Parkinson, Taverham, Norwich.
PHC	Haverham College, Haverford, Penn.
PL	The Public Ledger, the Patent Office, London.
Platt	M. H. Platt, Canonbury, London.
Pollard	Miss M. Pollard, Dublin.
PP	Free Library of Philadelphia (Rosenbach and Elkins Collection), Penn.
PPiU	University of Pittsburgh, Penn.

PPL	Library Co. of Philadelphia, Penn.
Pratley	Harry W. Pratley, Tunbridge Wells, Kent.
Preston	The Spencer Collection, Harris Public Library, Preston, Lancs.
PU	University of Pennsylvania, Philadelphia.
Pv	Bibliothèque Nationale de Versailles.
Quaritch	Messrs Bernard Quaritch Ltd, London.
Quayle	Eric Quayle, Zennor, Cornwall
RAS	Royal Astronomical Society.
RCP	Royal College of Physicians, London.
RCS	Royal College of Surgeons, London.
RCVS	Royal College of Veterinary Surgeons, London.
Reichner	Herbert Reichner, private collection, Stockbridge, Mass.
Renier	Mr and Mrs F. G. Renier, Barnes, London (in course of transfer to V&A).
RePL	Reading Public Library, Berks.
ReU	Reading University Library, Berks.
RHS	Royal Horticultural Society, London.
RI	Royal Institution of Great Britain, London.
RIBA	Royal Institute of British Architects, London.
Richnell	D. T. Richnell, formerly Reading University Library, now LUL.
RICS	Royal Institution of Chartered Surveyors, London.
Ries	The late Ludwig Ries, Forest Hills, New York.
RMO	Ontario Royal Museum.
RMS	Royal Microscopical Society, London.
Roscoe	S. Roscoe, Harrow, Middlesex.
Rosenberg	Mrs Vera Rosenberg, U.S.A.
RP	Providence Public Library, Providence, U.S.A.
RReN	Redwood Library Co., Newport, Rhode Island.
RS	Royal Society, London.
RSM	Royal Society of Medicine, London.
RVC	Royal Veterinary College, London.
RYLANDS	The John Rylands Library, Manchester.
St Bride	St Bride Printing Library, St Bride Institute, London.
Schiller	Justin G. Schiller, Ltd, N.Y.
Schuman	Madame H. Schuman, New York.
ScM	Science Museum, London (also LScM).
Shiers	Mr and Mrs George Shiers, Santa Barbara, Cal.
Sion	Sion Collection, London.
Snowden	Miss Rita F. Snowden, Auckland, N.Z.

SomCL	Somerset County Library, Bridgwater, Somerset.
SPT	Southport Public Library, Southport, Lancs.
Stationers	The Worshipful Company of Stationers and Newspaper Makers, Stationers' Hall, London.
STF	Stanford, California, University Library.
Stone	The late Wilbur Macey Stone (collection dispersed and location unknown).
Suffolk	Mrs M. Suffolk, Lower Brailes, Banbury, Oxon.
SUT	Sutro, California State Library.
SWN	Swansea Public Library, Swansea, Glam.
TCD	Trinity College, Dublin (also D).
Temperley	David Temperley, King's Heath, Birmingham.
Tighe	Benjn Tighe, Bookseller, Athol, Mass.
Traylen	C. W. Traylen, Guildford (private collection).
Tudor	P. Tudor, Glasgow University Library.
UCL	University College, London.
UCLA (also CLU)	University of California at Los Angeles.
ULC (also CUL)	Cambridge University Library.
V&A	Victoria and Albert Museum, London.
V&A(GL)	the same, Guy Little collection.
Vi	Virginia State Library, Richmond, Virginia.
ViU	University of Virginia, Charlottesville, U.S.A.
Walcott	Mrs E. S. Walcott, Brattleboro, Vermont, U.S.A.
Wallis	The late Alfred Wallis, F.R.S.L., of Exeter.
Wallis, Peter	Peter Wallis, The University, Newcastle upon Tyne.
Weedon	Miss M. J. P. Weedon, Oxford.
Welch	The late Dr d'Alté A. Welch, Cleveland Heights, Ohio (Mrs Welch has bequeathed her husband's collection to UCLA).
Wellcome	The Wellcome Historical Medical Library, London.
Wheeler	Wheeler Collection, Engineering Society Library, New York.
Whitelands	Whitelands Collection, West Hill, Putney, London.
Wigan	Wigan Public Library, Lancs.
WRPL	Worcester (England) Public Library.
ZSL	Zoological Society, London.

BIBLIOGRAPHICAL REFERENCES

I. AUTHORITIES REFERRED TO IN THE TEXT

1 Alston   R. C. Alston, *A Bibliography of the English Language from the Invention of Printing to the Year 1800*. Printed for the Author, 1965 (and in progress).

2 Babson   *Descriptive Catalogue of the Grace K. Babson Collection of the Works of Sir Isaac Newton . . . in the Babson Institute Library*, N.Y., 1950.

3 Blagden   Cyprian Blagden, *Thomas Carnan and the Almanack Monopoly* (in *Studies in Bibliography*, Papers of the Bibliographical Society of the University of Virginia, vol. 14, 1961). A full account of the fight between Carnan and the Stationers' Co. over the right to print Almanacks. See Introduction at pp. 22–4.

3A BMECBs   *An Exhibition of Early English Children's Books*, British Museum, 1968.

4 *BMQ*   *British Museum Quarterly.*

5 *BUCM*   *British Union Catalogue of Early Printed Music.*

6 *BUCOP*   *British Union Catalogue of Periodicals.*

6A Cameron & Carroll   *Short Title Catalogue of Books printed in the British Isles... 1701–1800, held in the Libraries of the Australian Capital Territory*, Canberra, 1966. Ed. by W. J. Cameron and Diana J. Carroll.

7 *CBEL*   *Cambridge Bibliography of English Literature*, 1st ed., 1940.

8 Chapman   *Johnsonian Bibliography. A Supplement to Courtney*, by R. W. Chapman (Oxford Bibliographical Society, vol. 5, 1940, pp. 119–66).

9 Courtney   W. P. Courtney, *Bibliography of Samuel Johnson* (revised D. Nicol Smith), Clarendon Press, 1915.

10 Darton   F. J. Harvey Darton, *Children's Books in England*, 2nd ed., Cambridge, 1958.

11 D&M   T. H. Darlow and H. F. Moule, *Historical Catalogue of the Printed Editions of Holy Scripture in the Library of the British and Foreign Bible Society, 1903–1911* (see also no. 22A).

12 *DNB*   *Dictionary of National Biography.*

13 ENC   *Newbery's Catalogue of Instructive and Amusing Publications for young Minds, sold at the Corner of St Paul's Church-Yard*, 1800. A bookseller's catalogue, put out by Elizabeth

Newbery, contains many items not published by her (see p. 31).

14 English Children's Books	Catalogue of an Exhibition of Children's Books, 1563–1900, at the Times Bookshop, 1960.
15 Evans	See no. A606.
16 Fordham 1	Sir Herbert G. Fordham, '*Paterson's Roads*'. *Daniel Paterson his Maps and Itineraries, 1738–1825*, Oxford, 1925.
17 Fordham 2	Sir H. G. Fordham, *The Road-Books and Itineraries of Gt Britain 1570 to 1850. A Catalogue*, Cambridge, 1924.
18 Fussell	G. E. Fussell, *More Old English Farming Books . . . 1731–1793*, 1950.
19 Gray	C. J. Gray, 'Biblio. of the Writings of C... S...'. See no. A546.
19A Grey, J. E.	Mrs J. E. Grey, 'The Lilliputian Magazine—a Pioneering Periodical?' (*Journal of Librarianship*, vol. 2, no. 2, April 1970, pp. 107–15).
19B Grey, J. E.	Mrs J. E. Grey, 'The Strahan Archives' (*The Book Collector*, Summer 1970, note 330, pp. 241–3).
20 Gum.	*Les Livres de l'Enfance due XVe au XIXe Siecle . . . en vente à la Librairie Gumuchian et Cie*, 2 vols, [?1930].
21 H&L	Halkett and Laing, *Dictionary of Anonymous and Pseudonimous English Literature*.
22 Heal	Ambrose Heal, *English Writing Masters, 1570–1800*, 1931.
22A Herbert	A. S. Herbert, *Historical Catalogue of printed Editions of the English Bible, 1525–1961*, 1968. (A revision of no. 11.)
23 Higgs	H. Higgs, *Bibliography of Economics, 1751–75*, Cambridge, 1935.
24 Higson	C. W. J. Higson, *Sources for the History of Education*, Library Association, 1967.
24A Howard-Hill	*Bibliography of British Literary Bibliographies*, Oxford, 1969.
25 Hugo	Rev. Thomas Hugo, *The Bewick Collector*, vol. I, 1866; vol. II (supplement), 1868.
26 IAW	Iolo A. Williams, *Seven XVIII Century Bibliographies*, 1924.
27 Isham	*Catalogue of the Collection of Works of Oliver Goldsmith formed by Lt. Col. Ralph Isham . . . sold at Sotheby's on 16.6.1930*.
28 Jag.	Jaggard, *Shakespeare Bibliography*, 1911.
28A Johnson, Richard	Richard Johnson's Day-Book, see Weedon.
29 Kress	*The Kress Library of Business and Economics*, Boston [1940].
30 Legg	C. M. Legg, *Bibliography of Books printed in Reading in the 18th Century* (University of London, Dipl. Library, 1961). Very full bibliographical notes and transcripts of TPs.

31 Lisney	A. A. Lisney, *Bibliography of British Lepidoptera 1608–1799*, Chiswick Press, 1960. Invaluable as a catalogue and includes many books having little to do with butterflies and moths. But weak in its bibliographical notes.
32 Maxwell	W. H. and L. F. Maxwell, *Legal Bibliography of the British Commonwealth*, 2nd ed., 1955.
33 Moule	T. Moule, *Bibliotheca Heraldica Magnae Britanniae*, 1822.
34 Muir	Percy Muir, *English Children's Books, 1600 to 1900*, 1954.
35 *N&Q*	*Notes and Queries*.
36 NBL	*Children's Books of Yesterday*. A Catalogue (prepared by Mr Percy Muir) of an Exhibition of Children's Books at the National Book League, London, in 1946.
37 Nicoll	Allardyce Nicoll, *History of English Drama, 1660–1900* (vol. III unless otherwise stated).
37A NUTP Cat.	B. Anderton and W. H. Gibson, *Catalogue of the Bewick Collection (Pease Bequest)*, Newcastle upon Tyne, 1904.
38 Opie	I. and P. Opie, *Oxford Dictionary of Nursery Rhymes*, Oxford, 1951.
39 Osborne	*The Osborne Collection of Early Children's Books 1566–1910. A Catalogue* (prepared by Miss Judith St John), Toronto, 1958. The collection is constantly being added to and consequently many books in the collection and noted in part I of the bibliography are not in this catalogue. In such cases the reference is 'Osborne*'. A 2nd ed. has, I understand, been published.
40 Oxford, A. W.	A. W. Oxford, *English Cookery Books to 1850*, 1913.
41 Pierpont Morgan Cat.	*Children's Literature. Books and Manuscripts. An Exhibition November 19, 1954 through February 28, 1955*, The Pierpont Morgan Library, N.Y., 1954.
42 Pressler	Miss Joan Pressler, *A Select List of Newbery Imprints in University of Chicago Libraries*, 1965 (a typescript).
43 Preston	*Catalogue of the Spencer Collection of Early Children's Books and Chapbooks presented to the Harris Public Library by J. H. Spencer*, 1967.
44 Rothschild	*The Rothschild Library. A Catalogue*, 2 vols, Cambridge, 1954.
45 S&W Cat.	A Catalogue of books issued by Simmons and Waters of 10 Spencer St, Leamington, n.d. (*ca.* 1903).
46 Sabin	Joseph Sabin, *Dictionary of Books relating to America*, N.Y., 1868–1936.
47 Scott	J. N. Isaacs, *Oliver Goldsmith bibliographically and biographically considered. Based on the Collection of Material in the Library of W. M. Elkins. By Temple Scott.* N.Y., 1928.

48 Smith, Elva S.	*The History of Children's Literature*, American Library Association, Chicago, 1937. Valuable as a bibliography of N & C, especially at pp. 61–70.
48A Spence	S. A. Spence, *Captain James Cook, R.N. A Bibliography*, 1960.
49 Stone	W. M. Stone, *The History of Little Goody Two-Shoes*. See no. J167, general note.
50 Teerink	H. Teerink, *Bibliography of Writings of Jonathan Swift*, 2nd ed. (rev. Scouten), Philadelphia, 1963.
51 Thwaite	Introduction by Mrs M. F. Thwaite to reprint of *A Little Pretty Pocket-Book, 1767*, Oxford 1966; American ed. 1967.
52 Weedon	Miss M. J. P. Weedon, *Richard Johnson and the Successors to John Newbery*, Bibliographical Society, London, 1949. See no. J191, general note.
53 Welch	d'Alté A. Welch, *A Bibliography of American Children's Books Printed Prior to 1821*. Reprinted from the *Proceedings of the American Antiquarian Society*, 6 vols, 1963–8. English editions of American books are noted here in fuller detail than in the one-volume reprint published by the American Antiquarian Society in 1972.
54 Welsh	Charles Welsh, *A Bookseller of the last Century*, 1885. See Introduction at p. 2 *et passim*.
55 Williams, Iolo A.	See IAW, above.

II. OTHER WORKS

Bibliographical studies dealing solely or principally with the publishing activities of the Newbery family are few. Welsh did his poor best to cover the whole ground. My *Provisional Check-list* of 1966 (now superseded by the present work) dealt only with Juvenile and Educational books. Nos. 3, 49, 51 and 52 listed above deal bibliographically with specialised aspects of the main subject.

On the other hand, much has been written about early children's books; and here the Newberys and Carnan figure largely, as they should. But for the most part the bibliographical aspect is ignored or entirely subordinated to the literary, social, educational or artistic claims of the books. No one except Welsh has tried to deal at length with the whole corpus of the Newbery–Carnan–Power output, non-juvenile as well as juvenile. This is understandable. Juvenile books are, nowadays, in high favour with collectors and educationalists. They have a common nexus in their subject matter – the entertainment or the education of youth – and they can be studied as a single subject. The only nexus for the non-juveniles is the fact of their bearing in the title-page imprints the name of a member of the Newbery family. There is no other connection between the *Vicar of Wakefield* and Dr William Rowley's *Essay on the Cure of Ulcerated Legs*.

The following works can be consulted with a greater or less measure of profit:

Charles Knight, *Shadows of the Old Booksellers* (1865 and modern reprints), chap. XI.

Forster's *Life of Goldsmith*, 6th ed. 1877.

The Newbery House Magazine, 1889, vol. 1, pp. 1ff. and 1890, vol. 3, pp. 599–613 has articles by Charles Welsh, but they add little to what he had already said.

Articles (again by Welsh) on John Newbery and his son in *DNB*, 1894. They add nothing new.

A. W. Tuer, *Pages and Pictures from forgotten Children's Books*, 1898–9.

Arthur Le Blanc Newbery, *Records of the House of Newbery from 1274 to 1910*, 1911. Useful for biographical facts.

F. V. Barry, 'The Lilliputian Library' (in *A Century of Children's Books*, 1923, pp. 58–84, and Appendix A, pt III).

F. A. Mumby, *Publishing and Bookselling*, 1949, pp. 185–9.

M. F. Thwaite, *From Primer to Pleasure*, Library Association, 1953, pp. 40–51 *et passim*, and comprehensive bibliography at pp. 263–79. A new ed. has, I understand, been published (1973).

K. G. Burton, *Early Newspaper Press in Berkshire (1723–1855)*, Reading, 1954 (typed thesis), pp. 104–8.

Virginia Haviland, *Children's Literature. A Guide to Reference Sources*. Library of Congress, 1966.

M. F. Thwaite, 'John Newbery. Publisher and Bookseller, 1713–1767', in *The Private Library*, vol. 8, no. 3, 1967.

Christopher Devlin, *Poor Kit Smart*, 1961, and

Arthur Sherbo, *Christopher Smart: Scholar of the University*, Michigan State University Press, 1967, deal with John Newbery and Carnan in relation to Smart. The latter book is fuller and more detailed.

T. H. Howard-Hill, *Bibliography of British Literary Bibliographies*, Oxford, 1969. Bibliography of 'Children's Literature' at nos. 1552–1573a.

Wm Noblett, 'Publisher Extraordinary', article in *History Today*, April 1972, at pp. 265ff.

INTRODUCTION

I

This Bibliography is concerned with the books published under the imprints of members of the Newbery family[1] in the years 1740–1814; it includes a few books written by Francis Newbery the son of John and published elsewhere.[2] The names in these imprints may stand alone, as in many of the juvenile books, or may be found in a conger of forty or more, as in Johnson's *Lives*.

The 'Newbery family' consisted, for present purposes, of John Newbery, his son Francis, his nephew Francis, his nephew's wife Elizabeth, his step-son Thomas Carnan and his grandson Francis Power. They are the subjects of the brief biographies at pp. 34–5.

There were other Newbery names appearing in imprints in this period – a B. Newbery and a T. Newbery, whom I shall mention later; also there was a Theo. Carnan who in 1751 published, with others, Wm Kenrick's *So much talked of and expected Old Woman's Dunciad*.[3] The name of J. (or John) Carnan (usually '& Co') occurs from time to time. He was Thomas's brother and worked in Reading.

It is not possible to say with any precision how many books (including new editions and reprints) the family put out between them. The chronological list (see pp. 400–42) of dated and datable books names about 2080;[4] in addition there are about 170 recorded undated books (say 30 in the non-juveniles, 140 in the juveniles); there are those known only through advertisements or book-lists and whose dates cannot be established, and those known to have been published but not traced in advertisements or elsewhere. For a total one might hazard a round figure of 2400.

---

[1] The name was often spelt 'Newbury' or 'Newberry', especially in the newspaper advertisements and in the later years. JN would not have approved.

[2] Nos. A240, A382, A383.

[3] On this book see A. Sherbo, *Christopher Smart: Scholar of the University*, 1967, p. 72. Sherbo describes the book as 'printed actually or only nominally by Carnan, whom Smart, as Mrs Midnight, had designated as his sole printer in the future' (a designation not adhered to). Was 'Theo.' a misprint for 'Thos.'? If so, was it a genuine error? The vigilant eye of John Newbery, Thomas Carnan's master at this time, would surely have noted it. If it was deliberate, to what purpose? To hoodwink Smart, who would not perhaps have approved of the Newbery–Carnan house publishing anything by his satirical critic? A very feeble device. The book is expressed to be 'Printed for Theo. Carnan, and sold by F. Stamper in Pope's Head Alley, Cornhill, J. Robinson at the Golden Lion, Ludgate Street, R. Wilson in Pall-Mall; and at all the pamphlet-shops'. I have not met Stamper and Wilson elsewhere as concerned with books in the Newbery–Carnan canon.

[4] In this count each edition is a separate book; but a book in more than one volume counts as one only.

II

The publishing history of the Newbery family can be divided into four clear-cut periods. In the first, 1740–67, John Newbery reigned supreme. The second, 1768–80, following John's death, was marked by schism and quarrelling between the rival establishments of Francis Newbery the son and Carnan on the one hand and Francis the nephew on the other, but also by a greatly increased output. This period ended with the retirement from active publishing of Francis the son in 1779–80, and the death of Francis the nephew in 1780. The third period ended with Carnan's death in 1788 and seems to have been a time of comparative calm between the rivals, Carnan and Elizabeth. Output continued at a high level, but with Carnan more concerned with his Almanacks than with printed books. Elizabeth dominated the fourth and last period (though possibly, as I shall mention, the real motive power may have come from her managers Badcock and Harris). Francis Power put out a few books under his imprint, but was no serious rival to Elizabeth, who retired in 1802, bought out by Harris.

III

For an account of the founding and early years of John Newbery's publishing and bookselling career it is still necessary to turn to Charles Welsh's *Bookseller of the last Century*. 'Welsh' is erratic, unreliable and very incomplete. Unfortunately it came to achieve a measure of biblical authority: as late as 1925 the late Wilbur M. Stone, collector of early children's books and bibliographer of *Goody Two-Shoes* and Boreman's *Gigantick Histories*, could speak of Welsh as containing 'a very complete bibliography'.[1] In point of fact, on a rough computation it would be found that Welsh records perhaps three out of every five known titles bearing the Newbery–Carnan–Power imprints; and these figures exclude almost entirely the four hundred and more items in the 'Almanack' Class (A7). Such records as he has of the various editions and issues of titles are haphazard and casual in the extreme.

Welsh published his book in 1885; he had access to papers no longer available, in particular Newbery's 'Private Memorandum Book'.[2] He quotes liberally from this and from what he calls the 'Newberry MSS'. For all his faults he remains indispensable. Later writings on this subject (lives of John Newbery and his son Francis in *DNB*, articles in the *Newbery House Magazine* and so forth) add nothing to what he wrote in 1885. No serious study of Newbery's early years has appeared since then.

The MSS referred to by Welsh, and now generally known as the 'Newbery-Goldsmith [or 'Goldsmith-Newbery'] Papers' were acquired by the late W. M.

---

[1] Article: 'John Newbery Printer for Children' in *Publisher's Weekly*, vol. 108, 1925, pp. 1391–5. [2] Welsh, pp. 8, 12–18.

Fig. 1. No. 20 Ludgate Street – 'The Corner of St Paul's Church Yard'. From a periodical of 1817 (enlarged). The firm of Harris continued the business begun by John Newbery.

Elkins and are now in the Free Library of Philadelphia.[1] In number about three dozen, they are almost entirely confined to Newbery's dealings with Goldsmith, and comprise promissory notes and receipts for money paid to Goldsmith, a few letters dealing with the edition of *Plutarch's Lives*, statements of account and receipts in respect of literary work and translations undertaken by Goldsmith to Newbery's order, statements of sums owing to Newbery, Mrs Elizabeth Fleming's accounts for Goldsmith's board and lodging at Canonbury (settled by Newbery), a washing bill, and a copy of the auction particulars of Goldsmith's effects after his death in 1774. These papers have been fully investigated by 'Temple Scott'[2] who states (pp. 112ff): 'In the Elkins Collection is preserved the entire series of what have been called the Goldsmith-Newbery Papers, those oft-consulted documents and receipts which John Murray, their one-time owner, placed at the services of Prior and Forster when these biographers were engaged in writing their "Lives" of Oliver Goldsmith . . .' The authority for the words 'the entire series' is not revealed.

[1] The Library has kindly permitted me to use, in writing this note, a microfilm of the papers which is in the possession of Miss Weedon, to whom also my grateful thanks are due.

[2] I.e. no. 47 in the list of authorities on p. xxix, above.

IV

John Newbery's earliest trading efforts, while in Reading, were tentative and exploratory.

He seems to have bought or noted the prices of anything and everything he thought he could sell. Memoranda of cutlery and haberdashery of all sorts, and medicines of various kinds, books, stationery, bought and to buy, occur frequently [in his private Memorandum Book], and wherever he went his mind appears to have been constantly on his business.[1]

There are also many notes in the 'Memorandum Book' about books to be read or published or reprinted.[2] Most of these were of the heaviest sort, Theology, History, Philosophy, Law, 'A Body of Divinity, compiled from Usher Fiddes, and Stackhouse's Bodys of Divinity'; 'Puffendorff's Law of Nature and Nations'; Erasmus; Bishop Thomas Sherlock, the 'Alcoran'; 'Cockman's Tully's Offices'. Mercifully we get a glimpse of his lighter side, such as permitted him, in later years, to publish Smart's *Nonpareil* and *Midwife*:

Print (Price 6*d*.) A collection of curious mottos from Greek, Latin, French, and English Authors, for the use of Poets and Puppeys, by Lawrence Likelihood, Esq; also, The Norfolk Dumplins.

His mind was moving towards books and medicines, the latter having pride of place. Indeed it would probably be true to say that, so far as money-making was concerned, medicines were at all times John Newbery's chief concern, though his heart may have been in his books.

John's first publications were in 1740 from his Reading place of business, the Bible and Crown, in the Market Place, *A Defence of the Author of the Whole Duty of Man*, printed by him and Micklewright of Reading, sold by J. Roberts of London and J. Wimpey of 'Newbery' (i.e. Newbury); *Miscellaneous Works, Serious and Humerous*, printed by J. Carnan of Reading, sold by R. Ware of London, Newbery and Wimpey, this book a crudely printed affair; and John Wallis's *Duty of Seeking all Men's Salvation*, printed by J. Carnan, sold by Newbery and six others as far apart as Newbury, Oxford, Gosport, Havant, Penrith, Kirk-Oswald in Cumberland, and Kirkhaugh near Hexham.

I speak of these books and the others of the first years as 'Newbery's Publications', though how much, and what, active part (if any) he took in their production it is impossible to say. He may have been no more than one of the financial backers, though a more executive role seems probable.

In 1741 the Newbery imprint appeared on only one book, Knapp's *Psalm-Tunes*, 2nd edition, a vile piece of book-production (see Plate 32). But by 1742 he was more determined and active, and six books bore his imprint,[3] all but one

---

[1] Welsh, p. 13.   [2] Welsh, pp. 14–18.
[3] Dated books, that is; the possibility of undated books cannot be ruled out.

(A276) in co-operation with Micklewright. The year 1743 showed only two, in the same co-operation, in 1744 there were three, as well as the advertisement for what seems undoubtedly the first of the Newbery books truly designed for the pleasure of children, the *Little Pretty Pocket-Book*, and very probably that book itself.[1] In this early period he was still running side-lines: Martin's *Micrographia Nova*, 1742 and *Course of Lectures in Philosophy*, 1743 advertised that the microscopes referred to and illustrated with engravings by Emanuel Bowen in those books were sold by Newbery.

At the end of 1743 or early in 1744 he took the decisive step of moving to London,[2] a step which was ultimately to put him well up in the ranks of booksellers and publishers in a period when few, if any, provincial towns (except perhaps Newcastle upon Tyne) stood high in the book trade. In London he set up at the Bible and Crown near Devereux Court without Temple Bar, and in 1745 put out five books from that address.[3] An advertisement in the *Penny London Post* for 12–14 August 1745 shows that by that date he had transferred to his new premises, the Bible and Sun (afterwards No. 65) in St Paul's Church Yard. (The advertisement makes it clear that medicines were then still his main trade.) These new premises were to remain his place of business for the next twenty-two years; on his death they passed under his will to his wife Mary during her life and after her death to his son Francis. Even after Francis had retired from active participation in the book trade into the more lucrative business of selling nostrums in 1779–80, No. 65 continued to be used for the book business by Carnan until his death in 1788; and it was Francis Power's address in the short of period his publishing and bookselling activity up to 1793.

Having moved to the Church Yard Newbery put out five books from there in this same year.[4] Ten books published in the one year, six of them under his sole imprint;[5] clearly by now he was beginning to feel secure in the book world (along with the medicines) and able to operate independently of other publishers. And he was now able to go ahead with the little volumes of the *Circle of the Sciences* and to put out the *Accomplished Housewife*, and *Universal Harmony* (a new edition of the *English Orpheus*) with its songs and music by Arne and Handel and charming engraved head-pieces – a very different story from the grim lists of his early planning – Law, Theology, Philosophy, the Classics.

The year 1746 saw the appearance of seven books and the shortlived *Mercurius Latinus* (. . . *prostat pariter apud Joannem Newbery, ad Insigne Bibliorum & Solis*,

[1] The question of the dating of this book I have mentioned in the note on newspaper advertisements in Appendix 1.

[2] Mrs M. F. Thwaite tells me that the Rate Books in respect of the Devereux Court premises to which Newbery moved from Reading show that he paid rates for them from December 1743 to September 1745.   [3] Nos. A115, 157, 357, 585, 598(1).

[4] Nos. J64(1), J71, J85A(2), A1, A184.

[5] Nos. J64(1), J71, J85A(2), A1, A184, A598(1).

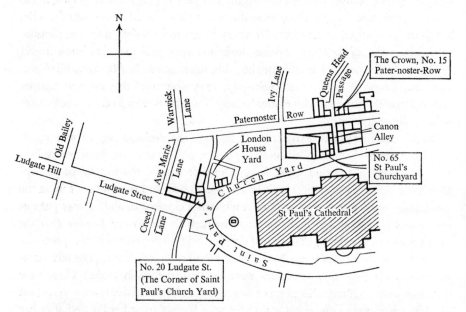

The Devereux Court premises, occupied in 1744–5, were half a mile to the west of the Cathedral, near Temple Bar in Fleet St.

Fig. 2. The premises occupied by the Newbery–Carnan publishing houses in the years 1745–1802. From R. Horwood's map dated 24 May 1799. (Much reduced.)

in Coemeterio sancti Pauli.), this, so far as I know, the first newspaper he was to touch, apart, possibly, from the well-established *Reading Mercury*. In 1747 there was a falling-off to three due, it has been suggested, to the general slump following 'the forty-five'.[1] The year 1748 was largely given up to the *Circle of the Sciences*, the first volumes of which had appeared in 1745 and 1746, very possibly by way of a trial run. Another poor year was 1749, showing only one new edition, one book published by a conger of seven and a broadsheet. But thereafter progress was steady, if slow.

The move to St Paul's Church Yard was wise. Throughout the whole of the second half of the eighteenth century, and indeed through the nineteenth and into the twentieth, there was a greater concentration of the book-trade in Pater Noster Row and its immediate neighbourhood than in any other part of London, and the Bible and Sun was within a stone's throw of Pater Noster Row. The Map above shows the position of the Bible and Sun (No. 65), of Francis the nephew's premises at The Crown in Pater Noster Row in the period before his uncle's death, and of his later premises at 'The Corner of St Paul's Church Yard' (No. 20 Ludgate

[1] Welsh, p. 33.

Street), where his branch of the business was carried on from 1768 until Elizabeth Newbery retired in 1802 and thereafter by John Harris and his successors Grant & Griffith, Griffith & Farran, Griffith Farran Okeden & Welsh, Griffith Farran Browne & Co, until the closing years of the nineteenth century.[1] And in Appendix 3 are set out the names of some of the publishers, booksellers and printers in this neighbourhood in the second half of the eighteenth century, all in, or within a few minutes walk of, Pater Noster Row, over sixty in that street, nearly two dozen in the Church Yard, thirty or so in Ludgate Street and Ludgate Hill (both now Ludgate Hill) and Stationers' Court, nearly a dozen in Ave Maria Lane.[2]

V

It was commonly stated in the past and is still widely believed that John Newbery was the true originator – the inventor – of books for children expressly designed to give real pleasure as well as instructing, and consequently the *Little Pretty Pocket-Book* was (and is) regarded as the very first of such books. Even as late as 1967 the fourth edition of the *Oxford Companion to English Literature* could say that Newbery 'originated the publication of children's books'.[3] This may very well have been the result of Welsh's obscure and erroneous statement (at p. 91), 'Newbery was the first publisher who introduced the regular system of a Juvenile Library, and gave children books in a more permanent form than the popular chapbooks of the period'. But in his Preface, Welsh was nearer the mark in describing Newbery as 'The first bookseller who made the issue of books, specially intended for children, a business of any importance'; and in his article on Newbery in *DNB* he says that Newbery was the first to make the issue of children's books 'an important branch of a publishing business'. That is even better, and he should have left it at that.

Thomas Boreman had put out his set of miniature books, the *Gigantick Histories*, in 1740–3 (they average about $2\frac{1}{4}$ by $1\frac{5}{8}$ inches), and it seems probable that these had set the fashion for this form of juvenile book, a form cheerful and attractive both as to size and colour. They were bound in the bright Dutch floral boards so much favoured by Newbery and his successors, and at a later date by Marshall of Aldermary Church Yard and other publishers. But the idea of a book containing matter to amuse children is far older than Boreman. T.W's *Little Book for Little*

---

[1] From the researches of the late Mr Algar.

[2] Of the names listed it will be true to say that a certain number were not professional booksellers or publishers at all, merely acting as such *ad hoc*, in respect of a book of importance to them in their main line of business, e.g. Whittell and Duncombe's *Treatise on the Dendrometer*, 1768, where two of the sellers named in the imprint, J. Bennett and B. Cole, were 'Instrument Makers'.

[3] Valiant attempts to scotch this lie have been made in recent years, notably by Mr Percy Muir (*English Children's Books*, 1954, p. 61), and Mrs M. F. Thwaite (*From Primer to Pleasure*, 1963, pp. 40ff). But it persists.

Children, with its famous 'A was an Archer and shot at a frog' and the splendid opening lines 'I saw a Peacock with a fiery Tail, I saw a Blazing Star that dropt down Hail', is generally dated *ca.* 1712.

Other publishers followed Boreman: a second edition of the *Child's New Plaything*, published by T. Cooper, was advertised in February 1743, and in the same year Collins of Salisbury put out the first edition of *A Pretty Book for Children*, with a second in 1746; Newbery was one of the publishers of the third edition in 1748. *Tommy Thumb's Song Book*, sold by M. Cooper, was advertised in March 1744, *Nancy Cock's Song Book, being a Companion to Tommy Thumb*, by Nurse Lovechild, in June 1744, in which month was also advertised the *Toy for Miss Thumb to learn A.B.C.*, 'neatly bound and gilt and decorated with above three score pictures neatly engraved', published by C. Corbett. And in the line of religious books in a form attractive to children Wilkin's *Biblia* had appeared as long before as 1727–8, a book considerably more miniature than Boreman: of two copies in my possession the 'taller' measures one and a half by one inches. One may suppose that, in this respect, Boreman had copied Wilkin. It is rather surprising that John Newbery never used this miniature book form; it makes no appearance in the Newbery canon until Elizabeth Newbery's *Bible in Miniuture [sic]* of 1780, a book averaging one and nine-sixteenths by one and three-sixteenths inches, which copied closely earlier *Bibles in Miniature*, by W. Harris in 1771, 1774 and 1775, and J. Harris[1] in 1778, they in turn copying Wilkin.

Mr Percy Muir, in his *English Children's Books* (at pp. 58ff) has dealt at length with the early history of the child's book and stresses Boreman's priority over Newbery. But on some points I must join issue with him. He says, at p. 61:

...not more than half a dozen titles of a purely entertaining or recreational kind for children are credited to John Newbery in his own lifetime. This excludes such titles as the *Circle of the Sciences*, and the history and natural history books, for, although expressly prepared for children, and showing much of the new spirit, they are definitely instructional in nature.

Did John Newbery publish any child's book 'of a *purely* entertaining or recreational kind' (my italics)? I cannot be certain, but in all I have looked into the element of 'improvement' or 'instruction' is present in greater or less degree. On this basis I would give him at least sixteen books[2] in which the element of entertainment or recreation predominates, many of these going through several editions in his lifetime. I have no record of natural history books published by John Newbery, unless *Tommy Trip* is such a one.

John Newbery's achievement was not to invent these juvenile books, not even

---

[1] One may suppose this Harris to have been a relation of, if not identical with, the John Harris who became Elizabeth Newbery's manager and successor, and who, according to *DNB*, was born in 1756.

[2] Nos. J7A, 9, 21, 74, 110, 167, 190B, 219, 225, 253, 267, 308, 309, 336, 346, 358.

to start a fashion for them, but so to produce them as to make a permanent and profitable market for them, to make them a class of book to be taken seriously as a recognised and important branch of the book-trade.

His views on the need for these books – or at all events a view which he deemed appropriate to lay before the public – are expressed in an address 'To the PARENTS, GUARDIANS, and GOVERNESSES of Great Britain and Ireland' introducing a list of his books running to fourteen pages in the 1761 edition of Tom Telescope's *Newtonian System of Philosophy*:

At a time when all complain of the Depravity of Human Nature, and the corrupt Principles of Mankind, any Design that is calculated to remove the Evils, and inforce a contrary Conduct, will undoubtedly deserve the Attention and Encouragement of the Publick.

It has been said, and said wisely, that the only way to remedy these Evils, is to begin with the rising Generation, and to take the Mind in its infant State, when it is uncorrupted and susceptible of any Impression; To represent their Duties and future Interest in a Manner that shall seem rather intended to amuse than instruct, to excite their Attention with Images and Pictures that are familiar and pleasing; To warm their Affections with such little Histories as are capable of giving them Delight, and of impressing on their tender Minds proper Sentiments of Religion, Justice, Honour, and Virtue.

Claims have been made from time to time that Newbery was not alone in the production of his books for children. Welsh, at p. 45, quotes from Nichols's *Literary Anecdotes*:

It is not, perhaps, generally known that to Mr Griffith Jones and a brother of his, Mr Giles Jones, in conjunction with Mr John Newbery, the publick are indebted for the origin of those numerous and popular little books for the amusement and instruction of children, which have been ever since received with universal approbation...

Nichols took this from Stephen Jones's *New Biographical Dictionary* (1st edition 1794 – see no. A279). As Stephen Jones was the son of Giles Jones the claim must be taken seriously. And yet its vagueness makes one wonder if Stephen Jones really knew the facts – or was he merely repeating a family tradition, handed down over half a century without much in the way of detail to support it? The tangled questions involved, the authorship of *Goody Two-Shoes*, *Giles Gingerbread*, *Tommy Trip* and so on, and the part played in their production by the brothers Jones, will very possibly never now be answered.

VI

In 1750 appeared three books under the sole imprint of Thomas Carnan, John Newbery's step-son, the *Journal or Narrative of the Boscawen's Voyage to Bombay*, Burton's *Attempt towards the Eulogium of Dr Conyers Middleton* and the first issue of that splendid best-seller the *Ladies Compleat Pocket-Book* which ran from this year until 1789. In addition the early part-issues of Smart's *The Midwife* were published in this year under Carnan's imprint. He is described in the imprints to these books as 'at J. Newbery's, the Bible and Sun', 'in St Paul's Church Yard' and 'over against the North Door of St Paul's' (i.e. at the Bible and Sun), so it is clear he was working under his step-father's eye. What was behind this arrangement we do not know. Welsh (p. 34) suggested that Newbery 'did not wish his name, which was becoming widely known as a publisher of books for children, to be associated with such a production' (i.e. *The Midwife*, alleged to contain some mild improprieties). This will not do. Up to 1750 Newbery's only major publication for children was the *Circle of the Sciences*; he did not get into his stride as a publisher of children's books (apart from a few of a purely educational nature) until after 1750. So far as is known Carnan was born between 1732 and 1737;[1] so at best he was still in his teens in 1750, and presumably working as an apprentice or assistant. It is to be noted that of the fourteen books put out under his imprint in the period 1751–60 nine were the work of Christopher Smart, whom Anna Maria Carnan, Thomas Carnan's sister, had been misguided enough to marry. From 1760 there were no Carnan imprints until he set up in partnership with Francis the son, after John's death in 1767.

VII

The period 1755–67 was John Newbery's busiest time, his output of books increasing steadily with the years; in 1755 it was fourteen, in the year of his death over forty-five.[2] For the fifteen-year period 1740–54 the total output was about 135, for the following thirteen years about 390, averaging nine a year against thirty.

In addition to books, Newbery was becoming concerned with the launching and conduct of periodicals and newspapers, undiscouraged (it seems) by the early demise of *Mercurius Latinus* in 1746: the *Universal Chronicle, or, Weekly Gazette* (1758), the *Public Ledger* (1760), the *British Magazine* (1760), *Museum Rusticum et Commerciale* (1763). Of these only the *Public Ledger* was to survive. He may very well also have been concerned with the launching, if not the actual conduct, of the *Literary Magazine, or, Universal Review* (1756–8) and the *London Chronicle* (1757). I have found no direct evidence as to the *Chronicle*; but it was his most frequent and regular advertising medium for both books and nostrums, and it so continued for his successors up to the end of the century. He had a financial interest in it,

---

[1] Plomer, *Dictionary*, p. 43, gives the date 1737; the late Mr Algar recorded that he died aged 55, which would give a birth-year 1732–3. The Somerset House records do not reveal his age.

[2] The figures quoted here and generally in these notes are based on the chronological list and are of dated and datable books only. In the result they will fall somewhat short of the true figures which must include the 170 or so undated books. The figures given include second and later editions.

specifically bequeathed by his will along with his interests in *Lloyd's Evening Post*,[1] the *Public Ledger*, '*Owen's Chronicle or the Westminster Journal*'[1] and the '*Sherborn and Yeovill Mercury*'.[1] It seems to have been his policy to keep his name out of these affairs, at all events in the early issues. Did he choose not to let his name be published until the concern had proved itself a success?

He also owned, from at least 1755, according to A. Le Blanc Newbery's *Records of the House of Newbery*, a one-twelfth share in the *Gentleman's Magazine*. This is not mentioned in the list of his newspaper and periodical holdings in his will, and I am inclined to suspect that A. Le Blanc Newbery founded his statement on a mis-reading of the footnote at p. 84 of Welsh, to the effect that B. Collins of Salisbury bought a twelfth share in the *Magazine* in 1755 and afterwards sold it to 'F. Newbery'.

VIII

Mr Julian Roberts, in his article on the first edition of *Goody Two-Shoes* (in *BMQ*, summer 1965) speaks of Newbery's 'misleading practices in advertising his books' and says 'the weight of evidence suggests ... that Newbery made a practice of publicizing, no doubt for sound commercial reasons, books of which he may have already possessed the author's copy, but had printed no edition.' He instances three books listed with others in the 1765 edition of *Goody Two-Shoes* as 'The BOOKS usually read by the Scholars of Mrs TWO SHOES' when (so he suggests) not in existence at all, or certainly not ready for publication: *Giles Gingerbread* '(in fact published in 1766)', the *Whitsuntide Gift* and the *Twelfth-Day Gift* '(both published in 1767)'; though quite properly he adds 'It is possible, though unlikely, that Newbery had published earlier editions of all three books'. Since Mr Roberts wrote his article copies of *Giles Gingerbread* and the *Whitsuntide Gift*, both dated 1764, have come to light, in the Bridewell Museum at Norwich. These were advertised in the *London Chronicle* in December 1764, along with *The Fairing* (of which there was a 'New Edition' in 1767), as books Mr Newbery intended to publish on 1 January. So far as regards the *Twelfth-Day Gift* no edition earlier than 1767 has come to light as yet. It was included in the book-list in the *Pleasant and Useful Companion to the Church of England* which is dated 1764, its first known edition 1767, its second edition (so called in the title-page) 1770, its third 1774 and so on. This does look like a case of the very advance publicity which Mr Roberts had in mind: advertising in 1764 a book which did not appear till 1767. But some other explanation is possible. On the whole, I submit that the available evidence is inconclusive to establish that Newbery made long-in-advance publicity a regular practice; he used it (if at all) only occasionally. Mrs M. F. Thwaite has wisely remarked 'It is hardly likely that such an astute business man [as Newbery] would create a demand for something he could not supply, as a regular practice'.

[1] Welsh, p. 336.

On the other hand there is no doubt whatever that Newbery blew (or caused his authors to blow) his own trumpet, straight into the ears of his readers. There is the often-quoted passage from the *Vicar of Wakefield* about the 'Philanthropic Bookseller' who 'has written so many little books for children'. The title-page to *Six-Pennyworth of Wit* advises its little readers that when they had read that book 'You would do well to buy Twelve-Pennyworth of Wisdom, which is much better, and may be had at the place where this is sold' (i.e. the Bible and Sun). In Allen's *Polite Lady*, 1760, the writer of the Letter on 'Writing' says 'I have sent you Newbery's Dictionary, to assist you in spelling'. (Of course this might be an 'unsolicited testimonial'.) Welsh, at pp. 109–10, quotes some ten instances of other such puffs; but he slips in quoting at length one from the *Blossoms of Morality*, a work which did not appear until more than twenty years after John Newbery's death.[1] Another form of 'puff' was used for the *Little Pretty Pocket-Book*, where a newspaper printed a letter ostensibly from a grateful and admiring parent, one 'A.Z.', who ordered a dozen copies 'bound in calf and gilt' (see the note to J225).

Newbery advertised his books widely and consistently in the newspapers, particularly, as I have mentioned above, in the *London Chronicle*. Dr d'Alté Welch records[2] that he also advertised his juvenile books in American newspapers. And many of his books contain carefully and fully annotated and priced book-lists: the *Compendious History of England*, 1758, lists twenty-nine books described in ten pages, *Utopia*, 1753, lists thirteen books in eight pages, and the *Newtonian System*, 1761, thirty-seven books in fifteen pages.

Newbery also sought, on occasion, to distinguish in his book-lists between 'Children' and 'Young Gentlemen and Ladies'. The *Mosaic Creation* (J248(2)) has a list for 'Children' and another for 'Young Gentlemen and Ladies'; but the compiler of the lists was a bit hazy as to where the dividing line lay, for the last item in the children's list was the *Lilliputian Magazine, or Young Gentleman and Lady's Golden Library*, while the first in the young gentleman's list was the *New Testament, adapted to the Capacities of Children*. And a book or two will slip into these lists which are not juvenile at all: the *Newsreader's Pocket-Book: or, A Military Dictionary. Explaining the most difficult terms made use of in Fortification . . .* crops up several times in juvenile lists; and Dodd's *Familiar Explanation of the Poetical Works of Milton* was no. 59 in the list of 'Books for the Instruction and Amusement of Children' in the *Newtonian System*, 1770.

Mr Muir (*English Children's Books*, p. 68) would have it that these so well

---

[1] Many years later Elizabeth Newbery used this means of advertising: in the *Blossoms*, mentioned above, at p. 22 of the 1796 edition; and in the *Toy Shop*, where the *Looking-Glass for the Mind* is lauded by the Toyman, who also produces for inspection the *Adventures of a Silver Penny*, *Juvenile Rambles*, the *Little Wanderers* and the *Little Moralists*. The passage in the *Toy Shop* is quoted at length by Weedon, p. 38.

[2] Introduction to his *Bibliography of American Children's Books*, p. 144.

advertised children's books 'were of a rather inferior order, not very well constructed, and heavily overlaid with moral lessons. An excellent example is afforded by the most successful of them all – *Goody Two-Shoes.*' Well – perhaps; tastes differ. To moralise was the custom of the age; and by the standards of Elizabeth Newbery at the end of the century, and even more under the fierce scrutiny of Mrs Trimmer and Mrs Sherwood, these books would have been considered regrettably lax in moral tone.

Whatever we of this present century may think of them, there is no doubt that Newbery's children's books suited the eighteenth century; they sold well and, presumably, paid well. Sixpence or a shilling each (say at least 25 or 50 pence in today's values) for little books of eighty to 150 pages, was a fairly stiff price in an age when the wages of a skilled workman were seldom more than 7s 6d a week and often as low as 5s. Yet buyers in plenty there must have been – of the middle and upper classes. Newbery knew his market and he knew how to feed it. He died, so it appears, a very 'warm man', though we do not know how much of his estate derived from his publishing, how much from the medicines; one may suspect the latter as by much the greater profit maker. Nor do we know what proportion of his profits came from the juveniles and educational books as against the non-juveniles, or which were the most paying, the juveniles for pleasure (*Goody Two-Shoes*) as against the educational and instructional books (Cordier's *Colloquia*). So much has been written about the books for children (the pleasure-giving ones, mostly) and so little about the others (apart from the famous names, Goldsmith, Smart and so on) that it is not generally realised how small a proportion of John Newbery's total output was of the juvenile class: somewhere about one in five. With a handful of exceptions, the non-juvenile stuff is of very little value, scarcely known, even more scarcely read outside antiquarian and specialist fields of study. Of works still of general interest I would instance a few bibles, some of Christopher Smart, *Utopia*, Goldsmith, plays by Colman the elder and Isaac Bickerstaffe, some of Dr Johnson; not a large showing for twenty-seven years of publishing.

IX

Carnan's sister, Anna Maria, married Christopher Smart the poet. The younger daughter of that marriage was Elizabeth Anne who married a French refugee, Jean Baptiste Le Noir de la Brosse, in 1795. A letter from her dated Reading, 14 April 1830, to E. H. Barker Esq says:[1]

The old Magpye and the true, was named John and lived at No. 65 opposite the North door of St Pauls This John brought up a Nephew, first as apprentice and afterwards

---

[1] Bodley MS S.C. 28,723, fos 163–5. I am indebted to the Curators of Bodley for permission to quote from the letter. Barker was, among other things, a publisher in a small way. He put out reprints of the *Toy Shop* and *Juvenile Rambles* in 1830.

established a Bookseller in Pater Noster Row, where he married the Daughter of Bryant the Trunk Maker at the [? Corner] so often toasted. This Nephews name was Francis – He was doing very well in a snug way – till a dashing shop on the Ludgate Hill Corner roused his ambition to a rivalry with his Uncle and benefactor for this ingratitude, he had not even the excuse of a family – the rent was double that wh he quitted – however it answered his purpose; he was not an author himself, but employed others, and very soon [? outsoared] his benefactor. Mr. J. Newberys only son was unfortunately called Francis; thus the House was mistaken for [? ever] after. The business at No. 65 was carried on after the death of my Grand father, by his Son in law, whose name was Carnan Mr F. Newbery his own Son, having the half property of James's powder and a pretty good fortune, that it had produced, purchased on the East Side of the Church and erected there a handsome House remarkable for a bust of Dr James...

Why did Mrs Le Noir, whose writing was so bad that publishers and printers protested (see *DNB*), call her grandfather 'the old Magpye'? One might suppose that the acquisitive habits of that bird were reflected in John Newbery's flair for picking up for publication matter of seemingly little value; or perhaps the bird's rapid flight suggested the erratic movements of 'Jack Whirler' as described by Dr Johnson. We shall never know for sure. It may have been the family nickname for the founder of their fortunes.

Mrs Le Noir's letter would imply that the nephew moved to 'the Corner' because of his desire to rival his uncle. This may be so. If it was, the move would seem to have taken place quite soon before the uncle's death. But it is not clear what really happened. The only imprint in 1767 I have found giving the nephew's address as 'the Corner' is in the title-page for the 1767 *Gentleman's Magazine* (vol. XXXVII), which would have been issued at or after the end of the year, to complete the volume. Welsh, at p. 205, prints an advertisement, dated 11 December 1767, of no. 1 of Dodd's *Commentary on the New Testament*, subscriptions for which were taken in by (among others) 'F. Newbery, in Ludgate Street'. But against this must be set another advertisement of this no. 1, in the *London Chronicle* for 17–19 December 1767 (at p. 591) which gives the nephew's address as Pater Noster Row, as do all other of the nephew's imprints in that year. On the whole it looks as if John Newbery's death on 22 December and his nephew's move to Ludgate Street happened to coincide closely, he (the nephew) having just moved, or being about to move when the death took place. Of course the nephew may have had his eye on the premises at 'the Corner' for some time; they were most eligible, right on the busy main road and Church Yard, far more desirable than The Crown, tucked away out of sight in Pater Noster Row.

But the letter goes far towards settling the identity of that Francis Newbery whose business address in the period 1765–7 was The Crown, and under whose imprint the *Vicar of Wakefield* appeared in 1766. Forster's *Life of Goldsmith*, after quoting Boswell's account of Johnson's story of selling the MS of *The Vicar*, says that Johnson 'went with it [the MS] to Francis Newbery the nephew'. Neither

Boswell, Sir John Hawkins nor Mrs Piozzi say to whom Johnson took it. Later writers, discussing the still unfinished story of the sale of the MS, do not deal with the identity of Francis the publisher of the book at all. Most of them seem not to have realised there were two Francises. In the event Forster seems right.

The letter underlines the depth of animosity between the two branches of the family. Mrs Le Noir, of the Francis-the-son branch, has, even after seventy years, no good to say of the nephew. Born in 1754, she may well have remembered quite clearly the family feud in the years after 1765. Whether and how far her unpleasant remarks were justified remains an open question.

But why was it the nephew whom John Newbery set up in business rather than his own son? He, the son, was born in 1743, so by 1765 was old enough. Almost certainly the reason was that his father had higher ambitions for him: the nephew could be taught to earn his living by 'trade'; the son was 'papa's blue-eyed boy' and was to enjoy the leisured life of an Oxford undergraduate 'where he read occasionally English, but the classics were altogether neglected'.[1] (We are told that he never graduated, either there or after migrating to Cambridge.) All which would be a cause of further discord in the family, as would the provisions of John's will and codicil which, as I shall show, gave his son large and lucrative benefits, the nephew getting, by comparison, a very thin slice. But it may well be that, in setting him up in the publishing trade John, as an uncle, had done all that was required of him.

It seems certain that in publishing *The Vicar* the nephew was no more than a nominee for his uncle; indeed, the 2nd edition of Byron's *Voyage round the World*, 1767 ('printed for J. Newbery...and F. Newbery, in Paternoster Row', no. A71(2)), lists *The Vicar* as 'printed for and sold by' John Newbery alone. And very probably this applied also to the majority of the other books under the nephew's imprint in the years 1765–7. For instance, John Potter's *Words of the Wise* (no. J304) was 'Printed for F. Newbery in Pater-Noster Row'. But the Dedication is dated Jan. 1768 – after John's death – and the book was advertised in the *London Chronicle* for 17–19 March 1768 as printed for Francis the son and Carnan. This indicates that the nephew, having no proprietory interest in the book, was obliged to hand it over to the beneficiaries entitled to the publishing rights under John's will, of whom the nephew was not one.

Of the books bearing the nephew's imprint[2] without that of his uncle, but sometimes jointly with others, there were about twenty in all. In addition the nephew became the producer, either real or ostensible, of the *Public Ledger* in 1766, and his name appears as the seller of the *Gentleman's Magazine* in 1767. It seems unlikely that this output would have been possible without John's experience and financial backing. Mrs Le Noir's letter, on the other hand, indicates a state of

[1] Welsh, pp. 67–70 and 126ff.
[2] Occasionally uncle and nephew published jointly, e.g. no. A71(1).

affairs hardly consistent with smooth working between principal and nominee. And certainly there was a small group of books put out by the nephew in this period of which the later editions continued to appear under his name: the three translations of German classics, Gessner's *Abel*, Klopstock's *Messiah*, and Bodmer's *Noah*, together with Harper's *Accomptant's Companion*. Seemingly these were books to which John Newbery could make no claim, and may evidence the rivalry of which Mrs Le Noir speaks.

X

John Newbery died on 22 December 1767. An announcement appeared in the *London Chronicle* for the same day – 'died this morning'. He had made his will on the previous 21 October; a codicil dated 27 November made substantial alterations in the disposition of his residuary estate.[1]

The following is a brief analysis of the relevant provisions of the will and codicil:

By his Will:

1. He gave his house in St Paul's Church Yard to his wife Mary for her life and after her death to his son Francis.

2. He gave his newspaper interests, named as the *London Chronicle, Lloyds Evening Post*, the *Public Ledger*, '*Owens Chronicle* or the *Westminster Journal*' and 'the *Sherborn and Yeovill Mercury*' [but not the newspaper at Reading] to his wife for life and after her death to his daughter, his 'son-in-law' [i.e. step-son] Thomas Carnan and his son and nephew Francis in equal shares. [As to the nephew's interest see note on no. A430.]

3. He gave all his interest and rights in 'all Copys of Books and Pamphletts' in equal fourth shares between his wife, his son, his daughter and Carnan. [This disposition would appear to deal with his publishing rights and book-trade interests generally; but if it did not those matters would have been disposed of according to the directions of the Codicil as to his residuary estate under which his son and Carnan would each have taken a one fifth share.]

4. He gave his interest in the Reading newspaper, his house there and 'all my printing utensils and [with some exceptions] other goods' in that house as to half to 'my son in law John Carnan' [Thomas's brother] and as to the other half to his son upon trust for his step-daughter Anna Maria Smart.

5. He gave his son all his interest in the medicine business, out of the profits of which the son was to pay half a dozen trifling annuities.

6. The provisions as to the residue of his estate were revised by the Codicil (see below).

By his Codicil:

1. He directed his son, Thomas Carnan and his nephew (or such of them as should agree to do so) to carry on 'my Business in my said Dwelling House for their Joint Interest and Benefit and if any of them shall refuse or decline to carry on such Business there then it is my desire that such Business shall be carried on by such of them as shall be desirous to engage therein', and they were to pay to his wife 'such Annual Rent for

---

[1] Welsh's transcript of the will and codicil is reasonably accurate. The note at the head of the transcript 'Date, 1763' is nonsense.

my said House as shall be thought adequate and reasonable...' ['My Business' would seem to refer to the publishing and book-trade, not to the medicines, which had been effectively disposed of by the Will. But at a later date Carnan seems to have been concerned with the medicines, as I shall mention hereafter.]

2. He revoked the provisions of his Will as to his residuary estate and directed that it be divided into five equal parts, one for his wife, one for his son, one for his daughter, one for Thomas Carnan, the remaining fifth to be divided into two equal parts, one for John Carnan, one upon trust for Anna Maria Smart. [There were provisions to prevent her unhappy husband getting control of her share.]

It is very noticeable that Francis the nephew took, under the will, no more than a reversionary interest in one fourth of his uncle's newspaper interests. Francis the son, on the other hand, did extremely well, taking, apart from all else, what was probably his father's most valuable asset, the interests in the medicine business, subject only to his paying out of its profits annuities amounting in all to £65 5s. (For an advertisement of these medicines see Plate 1.) Subsequent history shows that whereas both the nephew and Carnan worked hard and industriously until their deaths in 1780 and 1788, the son really did very little in the way of the book-business, leaving the bulk of the work to his partner Carnan, himself reaping the profits from the quack medicines[1] and, in 1779–80, withdrawing from publishing almost entirely, and in due course setting up in a fine way as a country gentleman and landed proprietor. Paterson's *Roads* had, as I shall mention presently, come into his possession, probably after Carnan's death in 1788, and the 11th (1796) edition of that work contrived to show him in the most flattering circumstances (column 277, lines 11 and 32):

Beyond Cross-in-Hand Turnpike, on r. Heathfield Park, heretofore Bailey Park, so changed in Honour of the late gallant Lord Heathfield, its late owner, now Francis Newbery, Esq....At Heathfield Park, the seat of Francis Newbery, Esq. is a Tower built in Honour of the late Lord Heathfield, the gallant Defender of Gibraltar (*sic*); whence is a most rich, beautiful, and extensive View, as well over the Sea as the surrounding Country.

XI

It must be confessed that some members of John Newbery's family – his son, his nephew and his step-son Thomas Carnan – were not, from what we know of them, entirely amiable characters. The son, one gathers, tended to be 'too big for his boots' and a very superior person in his own eyes; the nephew was quarrelsome enough on occasion and (at all events according to Mrs Le Noir) most ungrateful

[1] He is reputed to have died almost a millionaire. Mention of his activities in this line is made in an article in *The Chemists' Assistant*, vol. 1, no. 1, March 1900, at pp. 9–10, 'Stories of successful Businesses. Francis Newbery and Sons'. The article says that the 'Medical Warehouse' on the north-west corner of St Paul's was still there in 1900 and contained the busts of Johnson, Goldsmith and John Newbery. The Pharmaceutical Society kindly undertook an exhaustive search for Newbery's bust, but without success.

for his uncle's help in setting him up in the world (he is a shadowy figure of whom little is recorded); Carnan, litigious, cantankerous, a born rebel and fighter against the 'establishment', but brave and tenacious of purpose in a high degree, 'a most impracticable man, and at variance with all his bretheren (*sic*)'.[1] Welsh says of Carnan that he 'thought he was hardly treated by the elder Newbery's will, and that he ought to have had a larger share in the business which he had so greatly helped to make...'. But he really did not do so badly: he took a reversionary interest in a quarter of the newspaper interests, a quarter in the 'Books and Pamphletts', and, under the codicil, a one fifth share in the residuary estate. But it must be admitted that if, as Welsh asserts, he had 'so greatly helped to make' his step-father's business, his share was meagre indeed compared with that of Francis the son who, by all accounts, never did a hand's turn of work to help his father. It is not surprising that all three of them, son, step-son and nephew failed to hit it off.

XII

So on the death of John Newbery at the end of 1767 the son and Carnan took over the book business, operating in partnership from No. 65 in the Church Yard, and the nephew (removed from The Crown in Pater Noster Row) was settling in at 'the dashing shop on the Ludgate Hill Corner' (*alias* No. 20 Ludgate Street, *alias* No. 20 St Paul's Church Yard), handing over to his rivals any matter dealt with by him as agent or nominee for his uncle. The nephew was already, at the time of his uncle's death, concerned in the *Gentleman's Magazine*; the volume for 1767 (no. XXXVII) appeared under the imprint 'Printed for D. Henry; sold by F. Newbery, at the Corner...'. Welsh records (p. 84, second footnote) that 'F. Newbery' bought an interest in the *Magazine* from B. Collins of Salisbury, apparently a one twelfth share which Collins had bought in 1755 from David Henry and R. Cave for £333 6s 8d. It seems most probable that this F. Newbery was the nephew. Presumably he declined the partnership provided for by the codicil; it would have been a fiasco.

But the partnership between the son and Carnan was no easy affair. It ended in open quarrelling in 1779 when it was terminating. The *London Chronicle* for 10–12 August in that year carried an announcement that the son had removed the sale of James's Powder, the Analeptic Pills and other medicines to his new warehouse at No. 45, at the east end of St Paul's (the 'handsome house' built by him referred to by Mrs Le Noir), as he had 'totally withdrawn this business from his old ware-house [No. 65]' and he requested that all orders be addressed to No. 45. To this Carnan retorted with a statement in the *Chronicle* for 24–6 August that these medicines *were* to be sold at No. 65 and 'the sale of the medicines is not removed,

[1] Malone, in a letter to Bishop Percy of 28 September 1786 (letter no. x in vol. 1 of *The Percy Letters*, ed. A. Tillotson, 1944, p. 31).

as has been asserted; and all orders addressed to T. Carnan at No. 65...will be supplied with the genuine sorts'. How this squares with the terms of John Newbery's will is not apparent. But the claim is supported by an advertisement in the *London Chronicle* for as long before as 31 December 1768–3 January 1769 (at p. 3) which says that Dr James's Powder for the Fevers was 'sold wholesale and retail only by Newbery and Carnan at the Bible and Sun...Price 2s 6d the Paper', and another advertisement to the like effect on 3–5 January 1769 (at p. 12) as to Greenough's Lozenges of Tolu. There must have been some arrangement between the son and Carnan, but of a terminable nature.

So far as regards the book-business the partnership started off in 1768 with some two dozen or so titles as against the nephew's thirteen.[1] But of these two dozen more than half were new editions or reprints of books previously put out by John Newbery. The majority of the nephew's thirteen on the other hand were new matter. The partners had all the stock and goodwill of the old business to work on, the nephew had to start almost from scratch. In addition the son put out in 1768 a few books under his sole imprint, ignoring Carnan, or with the imprint 'F. Newbery & Co' or simply 'Newbery & Co'. If this was an attempt by the son to dominate the partnership, as it well may have been, it failed; it was Carnan who took the lead in the end. In 1768 the great majority of the books were under the imprint of Newbery and Carnan (in that order), only two in the reverse. In 1769 four were by 'Carnan and Newbery' and there were only a possible two in which Carnan's name did not appear. In 1770 six had the 'Newbery & Carnan' imprint, twenty-five or so 'Carnan & Newbery', and Carnan put out five books under his sole imprint. In the period 1771–80 there were only half a dozen or so under the imprint of 'Newbery & Carnan', two or three under the imprint of the son without Carnan. The chronological list, on the other hand, shows the very large number put out by Carnan without mention of the son. Yet, to confuse the issue, a book published under the imprint of, say, Carnan alone will be found advertised under both names (e.g. Griffin's *Interest Tables*, 1775); and the *London Cries* of 1770 was printed for Carnan but contains a list of books printed for Carnan and Newbery; and so on, in other cases. By the early seventies Carnan had engaged T. Wilson of York to act as his selling-agent for the north country. Reproductions of two lists of books (incomplete), are in my possession. One list gives full details of five non-juvenile books (one not published by Carnan), the other nine juveniles (one not published by Carnan). All but two of these were under Carnan's imprint and advertised as sold by Wilson.

Newspaper advertisements in the eighteen months or so following John Newbery's death mention repeatedly as 'printed for' the partnership books previously put out by John. More often than not what was being advertised was stock in hand of the earlier editions, though there may have been cases where old

---

[1] Approximate figures only – see footnote 2, p. 10, above.

sheets were issued with a new title-page. The first edition of du Martre's *Elements of Heraldry* was published by John in 1765 and listed in 1768 as 'printed for and sold by Newbery and Carnan'. The second edition appeared in 1771. So also with *The Idler*, the third edition of which was published by John and others in 1767; it was listed as by the partners in 1768, but the fourth edition did not appear till 1783.

A matter on which we have no information is how the shares in the publishing business held by Mary the widow of John and Mary Power his daughter were dealt with. It will be remembered that under John's will the 'Books and Pamphletts' passed to the widow, the daughter, the son and Carnan.[1] One may suppose that either the partners bought out the widow and daughter or accounted to them periodically for their shares in the profits. In the note on James's *Medicinal Dictionary* I indicate the possibility of the partners having bought from Mrs Newbery and Mrs Power their shares in that work. It may well be that they did so on other occasions. The question remains open.

XIII

It is not correct to say, as is sometimes done, that the nephew published his uncle's books; he may have done so on one occasion[2] but we do not know the facts of the case. He certainly did not make a practice of it. But he did manage to capture what must have been a most profitable venture – the publication of *She Stoops to Conquer*. It would be most interesting to know how he managed this, seeing that all other work of Goldsmith, his uncle's protégé, which was published by the Newbery family prior to 1780 appeared under the imprints of John Newbery or his son or Carnan. And he tried, as I shall show, to rival the *Ladies Complete Pocket-Book*, started by John and continued by the partners, and he most certainly copied his uncle's ideas about children's books and how they should be made acceptable to their readers in size, binding, subject matter and so forth; all to the understandable indignation of his rivals who, having inherited John's literary and publishing rights, no doubt felt they had similar rights in his 'sales promotion' ideas. Francis the nephew's new establishment was but a few minutes' walk from No. 65 in the Church Yard. Daily, though involuntary, contact, face to face in the street and the shops must have been inevitable. It is not surprising that in such an atmosphere bitterness and jealousy throve.

The *Morning Chronicle and London Advertiser* for 10 June 1772 advertised a number of books published by the nephew, with a concluding note:

[1] Or possibly, under the codicil, to those four and John Carnan and Anna Maria Smart.

[2] Welsh, p. 239, records the 15th edition of Hoyle's *Games Improved* as printed for John Newbery and others about 1760. Later editions, from 1775 onwards, were under the imprints of Francis the nephew and others, and thereafter of Elizabeth and others.

The Public are desired to observe, that T. Carnan, near the Bar in St Paul's Church Yard, has not the least concern in any of the above new entertaining instructive little books for Children; and to prevent paltry compilations being obtruded on them under the sanction of his being one of the successors to my late uncle, Mr John Newbery, they are requested to be particularly careful to apply for them to F. Newbery, at the Corner of St Paul's Church Yard and Ludgate Street.

On 19–21 November in the same year Carnan advertised in the *London Chronicle* his *Ladies Complete Pocket-Book* for 1773 with a *Nota Bene*:

The Pocket Book intended to be obtruded on Public (*sic*) by F. Newbery, at the Corner of Ludgate-Street, is printed on a much worse Writing Paper, and does not contain so much matter by a Sheet and a Half, or 36 Pages.

Carnan was referring to the nephew's *Newbery's Ladies Pocket-Book for 1773* (no. A7(274)). The nephew's riposte (*Morning Chronicle*, 21 November) was swift, personal and vicious:

The well-known malignity of Mr T. Carnan's natural disposition, and his professed inveteracy to me, have been hitherto, and I doubt not will continue, a sufficient antidote against his FOOLISH and IMPOTENT attempts to injure me in my business – the Nota Bene subjoined to his advertisement, asserting, that I have endeavoured to obtrude my Pocket Book on the public as his publication, is an impudent falsehood, and is clearly refuted by my book, which has not the most distant similitude to his; and the very rapid sale with which mine has already been favoured, is a convincing proof, that the Ladies in general justly consider a few additional pages of useless nonsense as an encumbrance rather than a recommendation.

Let the nephew say what he will, his *Newbery's Ladies Pocket-Book*, and its predecessor the *Ladies most elegant and convenient Pocket-Book* (A7(158Aff)) were deliberate attempts to outbid the *Ladies Complete Pocket-Book* which had been running since 1750 and was to continue until the year after Carnan's death in 1788. They even aped John Newbery's slogan that he published 'at the request of several Ladies, eminent for their Oeconomy' with a feeble 'Compiled at the Request of several Ladies of Quality'.

Carnan resorted to heavy sarcasm (*London Chronicle*, 26–8 November):

Mr F. Newbery, at the Corner of St Paul's Church-Yard, having had the Honesty to pirate the whole Memorandum Book Part of the above work [Carnan's *Ladies Complete Pocket-Book*] has also the modesty to assert, that there is not the most distant Similitude between the above Title and NEWBERY'S LADIES POCKET BOOK, though he knows that the latter, which he has assumed, was the Title by which this Book was enquired for and sold almost twenty years, during the time it was published by the late Mr John Newbery. The Ladies are desired to observe, that the book which he wants to obtrude upon them, is printed on a much worse Writing Paper, and does not contain so much Matter by a Sheet and a Half, or 36 Pages, which is above a fifth Part of the Work.

The reading public was also reminded of the iniquities of the nephew in the books themselves, in a paragraph usually appearing on the verso of the title-leaf.[1]

[1] See nos. J27(10 and 11), J167(7), J186(7), J190B(6), J258(8).

Each side accused the other of 'obtruding paltry compilations', which must have been rather confusing for the public; one wonders which of them invented the formula.

The Public are desired to observe, that F. Newbery, at the Corner of St Paul's Church Yard, has not the least concern in any of the late Mr John Newbery's Entertaining Books for Children; and to prevent having paltry compilations obtruded on them, instead of Mr John Newbery's useful Publications, they are desired to be particularly careful to apply for them to T. Carnan and F. Newbery, jun, (Successors to the late Mr John Newbery) at No. 65, near the Bar in St Paul's Church Yard.

A shorter formula was used in title-page imprints:[1]

Printed for T. Carnan and F. Newbery, Junior, at No. 65, in St Paul's Church Yard, (but not for F. Newbery, at the Corner of Ludgate-Street, who has no share in the late Mr John Newbery's Books for Children).

XIV

Carnan's quarrels extended beyond his partner and the nephew. In 1781 he found himself defendant in proceedings by Eyre & Strahan, the King's Printers, who were successful in having him restrained from printing the *Form of Prayer to be used on the General Fast Day* – see the note to A162.

In 1785 he took proceedings against Daniel Paterson and Carington Bowles in the Court of Chancery, claiming that he had purchased the copyright in Paterson's *Roads* and that a rival production by the defendants, Paterson's *British Itinerary*, was in breach of that copyright.[2] Whatever the result of this litigation may have been he, and after him Francis Power, continued to publish the *Roads*.

But his greatest fight of all, an achievement by which he is best remembered in the history of publishing, was with the Stationers' Company to abolish their monopoly to print almanacks. In brief,[3] in 1773 the Company, alarmed by the success of Carnan's almanacks, and finally goaded to action by his publication of Reuben Burrow's *Diary for the Year 1774* (no. A7(20)), tried to buy him out. This failing, they moved in 1774 for an injunction to stop him. Carnan, in his defence, maintained that this monopoly, granted by James I, on which the Company relied, was void, the Crown having no power to make such a grant. And in May 1775 the Court of Common Pleas handed down a judgement supporting Carnan's defence, thus finally abolishing the monopoly.

In spite of this judgement the war continued, the Stationers struggling to bear

---

[1] See, e.g. *The Infant Tutor*, 1776, no. J186(7).
[2] See Weedon, pp. 31–2, for an account of these proceedings.
[3] The story was told by the late Cyprian Blagden in his paper *Thomas Carnan and the Almanack Monopoly* read before the Bibliographical Society in London and published in *Studies in Bibliography*, vol. 14, 1961. I am indebted to this paper for the facts set out in my summary.

up against Carnan's competition. Their indignation and alarm (for the effect on their sales was catastrophic) at being suddenly deprived of what they had for so long thought to be their own absolute property,[1] and their determination to 'down' Carnan by any legal means, is entirely understandable. Plate 2 shows a page from the *London Chronicle* for 21–3 November 1775 (some months after the judgement in Carnan's favour) in which, cheek by jowl, are advertised the almanacks for 1776 published by the Company and by Carnan. Many of them have identical titles; the confusion for the almanack-buying public must have been considerable. Carnan's advertisement goes on, in most ungentlemanly fashion, to taunt the Company with his victory:

The above Almanacks are not printed for the Company of Stationers, but for T. Carnan and G. Robinson; who dispossessed the Stationers' Company of the exclusive privilege of printing Almanacks, which they enjoyed 170 years, (to the discouragement of genius, and the great prejudice of the Booksellers throughout the kingdom) in consequence of a patent obtained from King James the First, which his Most Sacred Majesty had no right to grant. (See Plate 21.)

This triumphant paean Carnan frequently also printed in the almanacks themselves in one form or another, sometimes with offensive additions: Reuben Burrow's *Diary for the Year 1778* was declared to be printed in 'the Third Year of Almanacks being restored to Freedom from Tyranny and Dullness'. And as late as 1784, in spite of the set-back about to be mentioned, he was still exulting. Francis Moore's *Vox Stellarum* for that year was

Printed for T. Carnan...who, after an expensive suit in law and equity, by the unanimous opinion of the Right Hon. Sir Wm de Grey, Sir Henry Gould, Sir Wm Blackstone, and Sir George Nares, Knts. Judges of the Court of Common Pleas, dispossessed the Stationer's Company of their pretended privilege of printing Almanacks, which they had usurped for two centuries; a convincing proof that no unjust monopoly will ever stand the test of an English Court of Justice.

The Stationers tried to get passed into law a Bill which would have restored to them their monopoly. In this they failed; but they did much to injure Carnan's trade by getting the stamp duty on sheet almanacks (a large part of his output) doubled. Carnan petitioned the Commons against this increase on 21 April 1781 (see no. A75), and the *London Chronicle* for 15–18 December 1781 contained an advertisement of the *Middlesex, Essex and Hertfordshire Almanack* for 1782

Printed for T. Carnan...Who presented a Memorial to both Houses of Parliament, against the additional Duty which was laid on Sheet Almanacks last Sessions (*sic*), a copy of which may be had gratis at his shop. The Stationers Company gave their utmost assistance for the additional duty by which the price of Sheet Almanacks is raised two-pence.

[1] But one wonders if they did not perhaps have some doubts. If they really believed in their absolute right why did they not go for an injunction straight away, instead of negotiating for a cash settlement?

He petitioned in vain. And it seems doubtful if he benefited financially to any extent by the victory of 1775. After his death the Stationers bought his almanack interests from his administrators Francis Newbery the son and Anna Maria Smart for £1500[1] and, it appears, suppressed them all.

Another quarrel arose out of the negotiations with the Stationers in their attempt to settle with Carnan for cash, this time with George Robinson, who had been joint publisher with Carnan of a number of his almanacks, and had intervened on his behalf in these negotiations. The two parted company and Robinson announced in the Press[2] that it was he, not Carnan, who had had the idea of challenging the Stationers by publishing a rival almanack.[3] The claim seems unlikely.

Francis the nephew also found himself involved in litigation. He published David Henry's *Historical Account of all the Voyages round the World*, 1774–3. The proprietors or publishers of Hawkesworth's *Voyages*, 1773, had instituted proceedings in the High Court against him and had obtained an interim injunction holding up the publication of his edition, no doubt on the ground of alleged breach of copyright. Advertisements in the *London Chronicle* for 6–8 December 1774 and 25–8 February 1775 announced that the injunction had been dissolved, 'this performance [i.e. Newbery's edition] having undergone the strictest examination by a Master in Chancery and by the Right Hon the Lord Chancellor himself'. The absence of any advertisement of Newbery's edition before December 1774 is, no doubt, accounted for by these proceedings.

Francis the son is reported (Welsh, p. 143) to have taken legal proceedings against Benjamin Collins of Salisbury, manufacturer of the Cordial Cephalic Snuff as well as publisher. Welsh does not say what the proceedings were about; probably the snuff, of which Francis had the selling rights.

XV

The third period in the history of the family, 1780–8, terminating with Carnan's death, seems to have been one of comparative calm, Carnan and Elizabeth Newbery going their respective ways without treading on each other's toes. In this period Carnan was the more prolific publisher, but his output was more of almanacks than of books proper. Of these latter he published two for every five of the almanack class; while for every seven publications by Carnan (books and almanacks combined) Elizabeth put out about three.

Carnan's output of pocket-books, almanacks and other such ephemera was large. The following are some of them (I give the dates of first recorded issues; most of them endured till 1788): *Ladies Complete Pocket-Book*, 1750; *Baldwin's Daily Journal*, 1777; *Goldsmith's Almanack*, 1776; *Ladies Diary*, 1780; various

---

[1] Blagden, p. 37.   [2] *London Evening Post*, 19–22 November 1776.
[3] Blagden, pp. 28–30.

London Almanacks and *Kalendars*, *Moore's Almanack*, 1776 (ancestor of the present-day *Old Moore*); *Poor Robin's Almanack*, 1776; *Rider's Almanack*, 1776; *Vincent Wing's Sheet Almanack*, 1776. In addition there was Carnan's series of County almanacks,[1] beginning in 1778 and mostly, like the others, continuing till 1788. These ultimately covered all the counties of England, plus Monmouth, though the counties more remote from London got but scant and infrequent attention. Probably most, if not all, of these County almanacks were in single-sheet form, printed on one side only and often in black and red, measuring on an average 22 by 18 inches, to hang on the wall. They sold at 6*d*, 7*d* or 8*d*.

This almanack business must have been a heavy undertaking, operated, as it seems to have been, judging by the imprints, mostly by Carnan alone; in 1775–6 he co-operated with George Robinson, but contrived to quarrel with him, as I have mentioned; issues for 1784 were printed for Carnan, sold by Stockdale and one M. Sprag, and Cain Jones's *Welsh Almanack*, 1776 (no. A7(95)) was advertised merely as 'sold by' (not 'printed for') Carnan. The total numbers of copies of all sorts – diaries, pocket-books, almanacks and so on – must have been immense; yet, out of about 155 recorded issues of the County almanacks I have only traced some two dozen copies; and of other ephemera there are equally few. But this is not really surprising: of the tens of thousands of tradesman's calendars now sent out every year, how many are preserved? And how many of us keep our old pocket-books and diaries?

A curious point concerning Carnan is the continued appearance of his name in imprints after his death in 1788. I have noted the following: *Rhetorick* (in the *Circle of the Sciences*), 5th edition and *The Rambler*, 11th edition, both 1789 (these may well have been in the press when Carnan died), Lockman's *New Roman History*, 11th edition, 1791, Locke's *Essay concerning Human Understanding*, 1795, and an edition dated 1795 of Goldsmith's *Abridgement of the History of England*. For these books dated 1791–5 I can only suggest an unexplained mistake. The Lockman of 1791 was advertised in the *London Chronicle* for 5–7 July 1792, p. 18, as printed for E. Newbery and others, without mention of Carnan. That there were two in 1795 may be no more than a coincidence; the Goldsmith was printed by S. Hazard at Bath for W. Johnson, E. Bathurst and Carnan; apart from Carnan's none of these names is in the imprint to Locke's *Essay*.

The only productions of the genus 'Ephemera' with which Elizabeth Newbery was concerned, so far as I know, were the *Housekeeper's Accompt Book* for 1781–95 (no. A242) and the *Ladies most elegant and convenient Pocket-Book* (no. A7), of which I have noted issues by her for 1783, 1784, 1789, 1790 and 1804.

[1] Nos. A7(31)–(43), (44)–(54), (58)–(61A), (62)–(65A), (66)–(69), (90)–(94), 95, (96)–(104), (176)–(179), (180)–(190), (231)–(241), (275)–(285), (286)–(291), (292)–(297), (298)–(301), (371)–(374), (377)–(387), (388)–(393), (395)–(398), (400)–(405), (413)–(416), (432)–(442).

This latter was in continuation of *Pocket Books* published by her husband (nos. A7(159–60) and (409–12)). Whether Elizabeth's *Pocket Book* was issued annually is not apparent; it can hardly have been otherwise, but the absence of advertisements of it in the usual newspapers is remarkable.

Elizabeth's name had first appeared in the imprint to the *Middlesex Journal*, numbers 587–91, in 1772–3. I have not met her again until the year of her husband's death. Title-page imprints indicate that she continued in business at No. 20 in Ludgate Street during the whole of her twenty-two years' reign, except for the brief interval in 1786–7 when following the fire at No. 20, she operated from No. 37 in Ludgate Street. Yet Pendred's *Vade Mecum*, 1785, under the heading 'Stationers, Bookbinders, Booksellers...' lists, 'Newbery, Bookseller, 80 St Paul's Church Yard'. No such address was used by Elizabeth or any other Newbery in any imprint I know of.

Mrs Le Noir, in her letter of 14 April 1830, records that Elizabeth married again:

F. Newbery dying, left a widow who was E. Newbery She married, and changed her name, but continued the business, and retained on the shop and title Pages, the name that had been to her so prosperous I think this conspicuous Corner is at present more remarkable for patent medicines than books for Children – or so it seemed to me when last I past that wellknown Clustering Corner.

The selling of medicines at No. 20 may have been a development since Elizabeth's day, though it seems possible that Francis the nephew may have dabbled in that trade: as far back as 1772 he was handing out 'gratis' a *Short Tract on Worms* (no. A641) which was also to be had of Robert Witch, Chemist, No. 17 Haymarket, where, presumably, the worm-killer was to be had.

There is some evidence that by the eighties of the century the name of Newbery was highly regarded and a valuable commodity, and was on occasion used without justification, just as, at a later date, 'With engravings by Bewick' was used quite unscrupulously for sales promotion purposes. The name 'B. Newbery' of St Paul's Church Yard occurs on the engraved title-page to a 1780 edition of Goldsmith's *Poems and Plays*, jointly with the name of one T. Johnson, whom I have not met elsewhere.[1] This looks like a deliberate attempt to get as close as possible to names well thought of in the trade, without copying them letter for letter: in this case F. (or E.) Newbery and J[oseph] Johnson. Another case in point is *A Voyage round the World: in His Majesty's Ships, The Centurion and Gloucester by Commodore Anson...Printed for T. Newbery, MDCCLXXXVI*.[2] This is a book of 216 pages, approximately 16·0 by 10·0 cm, in chap-book form on rough, coarse paper with blue wrappers, a most un-Newberish practice; nor would a member of the Newbery family have omitted the address in a one-name imprint. More

---

[1] Copies in BM and CUL.
[2] Copy in Mr Traylen's private collection.

than the Goldsmith, this indicates a deliberate use of the valuable Newbery name by an 'outsider'. An S. Johnston appears in 1797, no address beyond 'London' given. See J212(5A).

XVI

The fourth and last period in the family history began with Carnan's death in 1788 and ended when Elizabeth finally sold out to her manager John Harris in 1802.[1] But her retirement was not complete, for in 1804 she published under her sole name the issue for that year of her *Ladies most elegant and convenient Pocket Book* and in 1810 she was joint publisher of the 15th edition of the *New Oxford Guide*. But these were exceptions.

She dominated this period, with Francis the son occasionally dabbling in the publishing business and Francis Power's name appearing in imprints a number of times between 1789 and 1792. Francis Newbery's name appears in the imprints of only one or two works after 1780,[2] but he published two books on the new Income Tax: *Thoughts on Taxation*, 1799 (printed and sold by D. Holt, sold also by H. D. Symonds), and *Observations on the Income Tax Act*, 1801 (printed by W. Bulmer & Co for G. & W. Nicol), a volume of his own very indifferent verses *Donum Amicis...by Francis Newbery, Esquire*, 1815 (printed for the Author), and *A Translation of the second Epistle of the first Book of Horace, to Lollius; by F.N. when at Merchant Taylor's School, in 1762...Printed at the Request of some Friends...*, 1800 (printed by W. Bulmer & Co).

It would seem also that the copyright in Paterson's *Roads* (no. A399) had come into his hands. Miss Weedon, at p. 33, quotes from the 'Advertisement' to the 13th (1803) edition of the *Roads* in which Francis explains that he 'became possessed of the Copy Right, by the death of a relation, who had originally purchased the Work'; and he (being now in his own eyes too superior a person to be named in the imprint) 'determined to continue the publication, through the medium of Messrs. Longman of Paternoster-Row'. After Carnan's death there were 8th and 9th editions of the *Roads* (1789 and 1792) put out by Francis Power, nephew of Francis Newbery the son and probably on his instructions, and a

---

[1] Harris had started publishing on his own account in 1801; in that year he put out the *Dog of Knowledge* (copy in V&A(GL)) and, jointly with John Wallis, George Fox's *New moral and entertaining Game of the Reward of Merit*. His name also appears in that year in the *Gentleman's Magazine* and the *Beauties of England and Wales*. An undated edition by Elizabeth Newbery of Winlove's *Approved entertaining Stories* (J381(9)), which can be dated 1801–2, refers to Harris's *Juvenile Library*. By 1802 he was going strong. Mrs Moon has sent me a preliminary list of not less than ten titles published by him in that year; there were probably more; Harris was bad about dating his books. He was also acting as general bookseller, as Elizabeth Newbery had done before him (though very possibly at his instigation). A list of his publications, of *ca.* 1802–3, says that at his premises (No. 20 Ludgate Street) 'a general Assortment of Books, in all Branches of Polite Literature, may be either seen or procured at the shortest Notice'.

[2] In J231(9) and (10), and possibly in A255, A273(6), A301A.

re-issue of the 9th edition with a cancel title-page, also dated 1792, by Longman, who published the subsequent editions, certainly up to the 18th (*ca.* 1832). The 'relation' from whom Francis the son acquired the copyright was undoubtedly Carnan.[1]

Again, Francis the son seems to have been at the back of two publications bearing Francis Power's imprint, the *Adventures of a Bee* (Weedon 3) and *A Fortnight's Tour* (Weedon 26). Both of these were produced by Richard Johnson and recorded in his day-book under the date July 1789 'Mess. Newbery and Co. To writing...'. While 'Mess. Newbery and Co' could, in theory, be either Francis or Elizabeth Newbery, it is more than unlikely that Johnson would have ledgered Elizabeth under this appellation. Except for one entry in the day-book in 1785, the *New History of the Grecian States* (Weedon 68), ledgered as compiled 'for Mrs Newbery' (but noted as paid for by Badcock), all the day-book entries against Elizabeth after 1780 stand in the name of Badcock, her manager. I think we may assume that this was another case in which Francis the son was dabbling in the book-business while keeping his name off the record. And he appears yet again in Weedon 55, the *Life of George the Third*, ledgered by Johnson under date 1 January 1789 'Mr Newbery and Co. To writing the Life...'; though there is no evidence that this was ever published, at all events under that title.

Of Power it is recorded that he became 'an eminent wine merchant',[2] and the indications are that after 1792 he gave up the book trade. Certainly there is nothing in his brief career as a publisher/bookseller to indicate that he had inherited his ancestors' flair for that line of business. One Francis Power, Merchant, was at 44 Lime Street, in The City, in 1820,[3] and at 35 Essex Street, Strand, in 1826.[4]

Power is named in title-page imprints and advertisements some forty or so times in the period 1789–92,[5] where he is variously named 'Power & Co', 'F. Power & Co', 'F. Power & Co, Successors to the late Mr T. Carnan' and 'Francis Power (Grandson to the late Mr J. Newbery), & Co'. Welsh records (p. 7) that Michael and Mary Power, Francis's parents, 'left a numerous family, some of whom were afterwards connected with the business in St Paul's Churchyard'. Perhaps this accounts for the '& Co'. No other Power is named.

---

[1] Carnan died intestate, a bachelor; so Francis Newbery probably took a share in his estate. Certainly 'became possessed ... by the death of a relation' sounds more like an inheritance than a purchase from Carnan's administrators.

[2] Wm West, *Fifty Years' Recollections of an old Bookseller*, 2nd ed, 1837, pp. 21–2. Power's father was a Spanish merchant, a trade no doubt including the import of wine.

[3] Kent's *London Directory*, 1820, p. 270.

[4] Pigot's *London and Provincial Commercial Directory, 1826–7*. I am indebted to the late Mr Algar for information about Power.

[5] Possibly 1787–93. His name is in an edition of Boyse's *New Pantheon* of (doubtfully) 1787 (no. A51(6)), and a variant or re-issued 12th edition of the *Museum for Young Gentlemen* dated 1793 (no. J253(16)).

Of the books bearing the Power imprint only three can be said, with any certainty, to be first editions: the *Adventures of a Bee*, 1790, *A Lecture upon Games and Toys*, by Christopher Comical, 1789, and *A Fortnight's Tour*, 1790. All other books had appeared previously in one form or another. The *Adventures of a Bee* and *A Fortnight's Tour* I have already mentioned as having been published by Power under the direction of Francis Newbery the son.

It seems that Power was also a bookseller, at all events of books previously put out by Carnan. The *Mother Goose's Melody* published under Power's imprint in 1791 has a list of some sixty juvenile books (and a few others) all, but for two or three, previously published by Carnan, and none, but for the three named above, known to have been published under Power's imprint. The list is headed 'The following CHILDREN'S BOOKS are sold by FRANCIS POWER...'. This was a bookseller's catalogue, not a publisher's.

Welsh, at pp. 87–8, says that

after he [Francis the son] went to his new house at the north-east end of St Paul's in 1779...by some means or other, either by transfer or purchase, or revival of lapsed books, all the old publications of Newbery [the son] subsequently passed into the hands of Elizabeth (his cousin's widow) and to Harris and his successors.

An examination of all the juvenile books and all the dated and datable non-juveniles published by Elizabeth shows that her name appears in the following books previously published by Francis the son or other members of his branch of the family: *Museum for young Gentlemen...*, 19th edition, *ca.* 1800, jointly with three others, and Lockman's *New History of England*, 24th edition, 1801, jointly with thirteen others. In addition six books,[1] previously so published, of which I have seen no copies, were advertised or listed as printed for Elizabeth. Perhaps she bought up the whole remaining stock of these and sold them off without revising the title-pages. The available evidence cannot support Welsh's statement, at all events so far as regards Elizabeth; I cannot speak as to Harris. Perhaps Welsh was muddling up the two Francises; Elizabeth certainly took over her husband's publishing rights, and operated on them for a period of twenty-two years.

Elizabeth published books for children and young people in preference to all others. Her output of dated books was, in round figures, three hundred and ten juveniles and two hundred and ten of all other sorts; and of the juveniles rather more than three out of every four were under her sole imprint. Of the non-juveniles there were about ten published by her jointly with others as against every three under her imprint alone. And of those published jointly a large number were by congers of not less than nine or so names, and up to fifty or more,[2] books in the production of which Elizabeth presumably took no practical part beyond her financial backing.

[1] Nos. J294(4), J301(2), J307(9), J348(8), J377(3), A222(19).
[2] In, for example, the 1801 edition of Johnson's *Lives*.

29

NEWBERY's New Publications.

Sold by E. Newbery, at the *Corner of St. Paul's Church-yard*, London; where may be had the greatest Variety of Books, together with Diffected Maps of all Countries, Geographical Paftimes, Diffected Tables of the Englifh and Roman Hiftories, and every Article for the Inftruction and Amufement of young People.

	£.	s.	d.
Chronological Tables of the Englifh Hiftory, 4s. 6d. on a Sheet.—Diffected	0	10	6
Chronological Tables of the Roman Hiftory, 4s. 6d. on a Sheet.—Diffected	0	10	6
Youthful Recreations, or the Amufements of a Day	0	0	6
Life and Adventures of a Fly	0	0	6
Triumph of Good Nature	0	0	6
The Youthful Jefter, or Repofitory of Wit	0	0	6
Anecdotes of a Little Family	0	1	0
The Entertaining and Affecting Hiftory of Prince Lee Boo, a Native of the Pelew Iflands	0	1	6
The Hiftory of North America, by the Rev. Mr. Cooper	0	1	6
The Hiftory of South America, by the fame Author	0	1	6
The Bloffoms of Morality, by the Editor of the Looking Glafs for the Mind	0	2	6
Holiday Entertainment, or the Good Child's Fairing	0	0	1
Hiftory of the little Boy found under a Hay-cock.	0	0	1
Hermit of the Foreft and the Wandering Infants.	0	0	1
Foundling, or the Hiftory of Lucius Stanhope.	0	0	1
Rural Felicity, or the Hiftory of Tommy and Sally.	0	0	1
Lovechild's Golden Prefent, to all little Mafters and Miffes.	0	0	1
The Royal Alphabet, or Child's beft Inftructor.	0	0	1
The Father's Gift, or the way to be Wife and Happy.	0	0	1
The Sifter's Gift, or the Naughty Boy Reformed.	0	0	1
The Brother's Gift, or the Naughty Girl Reformed.	0	0	1
Hiftory of Tommy Carelefs, or the Misfortunes of a Week.	0	0	1
The Holiday Spy.	0	0	1
Hiftory of Tommy Titmoufe.	0	0	2
The Flights of a Lady-Bird	0	0	2
The Village Tattlers, or Anecdotes of the Rural Affembly	0	0	2
The Fortune Teller, by the renowned Dr. Hurlothrumbo	0	0	2
The Hiftory of Little King Pippin, to which is added the Story of the Children in the Wood	0	0	2
Virtue and Vice	0	0	2
The Entertaining Traveller	0	0	2
Tom Thumb's Exhibition	0	0	2
The Hobby Horfe; or Chriftmas Companion	0	0	2
Robin Goodfellow, a Fairy Tale, written by a Fairy	0	0	2
Little Moralifts, or the Hiftory of Amintor and Florella	0	0	3
Little Wanderers	0	0	3
The Mountain Piper	0	0	3
Falfe Alarms	0	0	3
The Adventures of Mafter Headftrong and Mifs Patient	0	0	3
The Juvenile Biographer	0	0	3
A Bag of Nuts ready cracked, by Thomas Thumb, Efq.	0	0	3
The Puzzling Cap; being a choice Collection of Riddles, in familiar Verfe;	0	0	3
Juvenile Rambles through the Paths of Nature	0	0	6
Adventures of a Silver Penny	0	0	6

Fig. 3. A price-list of books sold by Elizabeth Newbery (after 1780).

She also operated a general bookshop. Her *Catalogue of Instructive and Amusing Publications for young Minds, sold at the Corner of St Paul's Church-Yard*, 1800,[1] includes a considerable number of titles of which there is no evidence that she was publisher, either solely or jointly. It will be noted that she only describes it as a catalogue of books *sold* at her premises. It comprises among other items a list of forty-eight 'French Books', a 'Catalogue' of about 190 titles grouped under prices from 1*d* up to 6*s* (most of which did bear her imprint), a list of 'Useful and Amusing Games, &c', priced from 1*s* 6*d* to 10*s* 6*d*, and a priced 'List', in alphabetical order, of about 213 additional titles, very few indeed of which are known to bear her imprint. This 'List' is headed by a note:

The following further List of AMUSING and INSTRUCTIVE BOOKS for YOUNG MINDS, is merely subjoined as a Guide to those Persons who have not leisure to select them at E. NEWBERY's, where a complete Assortment, together with DISSECTED MAPS, and a Variety of Schemes in the form of GAMES, calculated to make the Road to Knowledge pleasant and easy, are always ready for Inspection.

Whether some of the items in the list, e.g. Bonhote's *Parental Monitor* (4 vols, 14*s*), Genlis's *Theatre of Education* (4 vols, 12*s*), 'Knox on Education' (2 vols, 8*s*), Lemprière's *Classical Dictionary* (10*s* 6*d*) were proper to be described as 'amusing and instructive books for young minds' is open to question.

In the field of the juveniles it is noticeable that as the century drew to a close Elizabeth came to co-operate frequently with Vernor and Hood. Many of the books so published had book-lists headed 'Printed for Vernor & Hood and E. Newbery', of which books the majority, on examination, are found to have appeared under the imprint of Vernor and Hood alone. Here they seem to have been in control. She also co-operated with John Wallis in producing instructional table games, perhaps a new venture for the Newbery family.[2] Such were the *New Game of Human Life*, 1790 (NBL 934 and 934a – sets in the Hannas and Grant collections), the *Royal Genealogical Pastime of the Sovereigns of England*, 1791 (Oup and Hannas), and *A new geographical Game exhibiting a complete Tour through Scotland and the Western Isles*, 1792 (Hannas). These were sheet games. Closely allied were nos. J57–9 (the *Chronological Tables*) which, it appears from the advertisements, could be had and used either as sheet games or as dissected (jig-saw) puzzles. With some of these EN may not have been concerned as publisher. Another line of hers not, so far as I know, previously worked by the family, was the Harlequinade.[3] I can record under her imprint three of these (there may well have been others, but this form of book is, by its very nature, more than normally frail and short-lived):

[1] BM, 11901.aa.27(1).

[2] But the 'Set of Fifty-Six Squares, and directions for playing with them' mentioned by Welsh (p. 219) and recorded by him as advertised by John Newbery as early as 21 March 1744 seems, from the description of it, to have been a form of educational table game.

[3] *Harlequinades* – see Muir, pp. 204–10 and plates 91–3, and items 1558 and 1566 in Howard-Hill.

Mother Shipton and *A New Book of Emblems*, both dated 1800 and published by her jointly with I. Strutt and E. Burns, and a much earlier one, *Sister Witches*, 1782.

It is pertinent, at this point, to add one more to the long list of unanswered questions raised in this Introduction. I have spoken of Elizabeth doing this and that. But was she really the master and active director of her publishing and book-selling business? Or did she only lend her name (a valuable one in the trade, we may be sure, after all those years), leaving the practical conduct of affairs in the active hands of her manager Abraham Badcock,[1] and after him John Harris? I have already mentioned that Richard Johnson, in his dealings with Elizabeth's firm after 1780, on all occasions but one (the *New History of the Grecian States* in 1785) ledgered each item of work done by him against 'Mr Badcock'. The *Grecian States* was ledgered as compiled 'for Mrs Newbery' but later marked as paid for by Badcock. Of these ledger entries, all between 1785 and 1792, there are about thirty-seven. Clearly a substantial measure of the work of Elizabeth's firm was in Badcock's hands, if not under his ultimate control. Johnson died in 1793, Badcock in 1797, and I have no evidence as to the role of Harris in the conduct of the firm's affairs in the years leading up to Elizabeth's retirement.

The difference between the moral and didactic tone of many of Elizabeth's juveniles at the end of the century and John Newbery's in the fifties and sixties is striking. John had published books designed primarily to give pleasure, both as to content and outward form, though, as I have said before, moral teaching was not absent. Elizabeth still produced some of the little juveniles priced from one penny to sixpence, in their bright floral paper wrappers. But she initiated a new class, larger, much more expensive (Mitchell's *Tales of Instruction*, 2 vols, cost 6s, Pilkington's *Historical Beauties* 3s 6d), bound in calf or plain boards and paper back-strip, in which moral inculcation dominated, zeal for 'improvement', spiritual, moral and social – above all social[2] – overcoming the desire to give genuine pleasure. By the standards of Mrs Trimmer (grim editor of the *Guardian of Education*) and of Mrs Sherwood (author of the *Fairchild Family*, with its afternoon walk to show the children the corpse on the gibbet, all for moral uplift) Elizabeth's views on education and training for life were no doubt deplorable; but to the reader of the present day the didactic element in such books as the *Mirror for the female Sex*, the *Looking-Glass for the Mind* or the *Blossoms of Morality* is sometimes quite overwhelming. And it is permissible to think that John Newbery might have been of somewhat the same opinion. But at least Elizabeth had the saving grace, denied, it seems, to Mrs Trimmer and her kind, of an appreciation of the

---

[1] On Badcock see Weedon, at pp. 34–5.

[2] These books were to the address of the children of the upper and middle classes. The 'poor' only figure in them in order to be patronised and 'done good to'. How very comfortably off are the papas and mamas, how beautifully dressed the young ladies and gentlemen.

commercial value – if not the aesthetic worth – of John Bewick's exquisite little woodcuts which turn some of these books into things of delight, saving them from the oblivion to which their written contents must surely have condemned them. And it must be supposed that Elizabeth Newbery studied her market, as John had done before her, and designed her books to meet the views of the parents and teachers of her age; and that they too, while no doubt admiring the Reverend Mr Sherlock's flatulent discourse on Female Courage,[1] could also appreciate John Bewick's picture of that pompous cleric and his admiring circle of young ladies, and the delicious head-piece to 'The Sparrow's Nest', than which John Bewick did nothing better.[2]

The world of children's books after the turn of the century was not really so gloomy as Charles Lamb would have us believe:

Mrs Barbauld's stuff has banished all the old classics of the nursery, and the shopman at Newbery's hardly deign'd to reach them off an old exploded corner of a shelf, when Mary ask'd for them. Mrs B's and Mrs Trimmer's nonsense lay in piles about... Science has succeeded to Poetry no less in the little walks of children than with men. Is there no possibility of averting this sore evil?[3]

There were good things to be had at that time, and more to come. *Original Poems for Infant Minds* appeared in 1804. John Harris was publishing fast, soon to win to his zenith with the *Butterfly's Ball*; John Marshall and John Wallis were putting out their sets of miniature books in gaily decorated wooden boxes, and in a few years Lumsden of Glasgow was to publish the halfpenny, one-penny, two-penny and six-penny books for children – *Robinson Crusoe*, *Captain Gulliver*, *Goody Two-Shoes*, *Giles Gingerbread* – excellently printed, illustrated with engravings in coloured ink or hand-coloured woodcuts. John Newbery would have approved; Poetry was not dead. The trade he had put on a sound business footing half a century before – the trade in books to please children – was flourishing. Mrs Trimmer was to lose the fight.

[1] *Blossoms of Morality*, 1796, p. 128.
[2] *Looking-Glass for the Mind*, 1794, p. 138.
[3] Letter to Coleridge, 23 October 1802 (Lucas, *Life of Lamb*, I, 232).

BRIEF BIOGRAPHIES

JOHN NEWBERY. Born 1713 at Waltham St Lawrence, Berks, s. of Robert N.
In 1730 employed by Wm Carnan of Reading (d. 1737), proprietor and editor of
the *Reading Mercury* whose widow, Mary, he married. She had, by her first
marriage, sons Thomas and John and daughter Anna Maria (b. 26 Jan. 1732; m.
Christopher Smart the poet 1752; one of her daughters Elizabeth Anne (b. 27 Oct.
1754) m. Jean Baptiste Le Noir de la Brosse in 1795 – see Introduction, p. 13).
By his wife Mary John N. had three children, Mary (b. 1740, m. Michael Power
10 April 1766, d. 13 May 1792); John (b. 1741, d. 1752); Francis (see below).
First books to bear his imprint 1740. Moved from Reading to London end of 1743
or early 1744 and in business (medicines and publishing) at the Bible and Crown
near Devereux Court without Temple Bar. Moved to the Bible and Sun (afterwards No. 65) in St Paul's Church Yard about July 1745 where he remained till
his death 22 Dec. 1767. No contemporary portrait of him traced as now extant.
A 'likeness' of him faces p. 5 of A. le B. Newbery's *Records of the House of
Newbery*, 1911, but whether authentic or imaginary is not stated.

FRANCIS NEWBERY, son of John N. and his wife Mary. Born 1743, m.
1770 Mary Raikes, sister of Robert Raikes of Gloucester, promoter of Sunday
schools and proprietor of the *Gloucester Journal*. In partnership in the publishing
business after his father's death in 1767 with his half-brother Thomas Carnan.
Retired from that in favour of the medicines in 1779–80. Moved to No. 45 in
St Paul's Church Yard in 1779. Purchased Heathfield House and Park in Sussex
in 1795. Wrote pamphlets on taxation and income tax 1799–1801 (A382, 383) and
is there described as 'A Commissioner of Taxes' and 'One of the Commissioners
of Appeal for the County of Sussex'. Pricked for High Sheriff. D. 1818, having
made a fortune out of patent medicines. Portraits of him and wife in *Records of the
House of Newbery* (above).

FRANCIS NEWBERY, nephew of John N. Acted as nominee for his uncle who
set him up in the publishing business at the Crown in Pater Noster Row. His first
imprint 1765. On John N.'s death in 1767 set up as publisher on his own account
at No. 20 Ludgate Street (afterwards Ludgate Hill), *alias* 'The Corner of St Paul's
Church Yard', *alias* No. 20 St. Paul's Church Yard. Quarrelled bitterly with his
cousin Francis and Thomas Carnan. M. Elizabeth Bryant. D. 1780.

ELIZABETH NEWBERY, widow of Francis, nephew of John N., *née*
Bryant. Carried on her husband's business at the same address. Remarried but
continued to use in business the name of Newbery. Burned out in 1786 and

temporarily at No. 37 in Ludgate Street, but soon back at 'the Corner'. Her manager was Abraham Badcock up to 1797 and then John Harris (1756–1846) who bought her out in 1801–2, and continued the business at the same address. Her name in the imprints of a few books up to 1814. D. 1821.

THOMAS CARNAN, step-son of John N. Born between 1732 and 1737 (see Introduction, pp. 9–10). Employed by John N. in the publishing business; his first imprint in 1750, apparently as nominee for his step-father. On John N.'s death in 1767 in partnership with Francis the son at No. 65 in the Church Yard, a very uneasy affair. Gradually assumed control over the business as the more active partner. Specialised in almanacks. Successful litigation with the Stationers' Co over the Almanack Monopoly (see Introduction, pp. 22–4). D. 29 July 1788 in Hornsey Lane, London, intestate, a bachelor.

FRANCIS POWER, son of Mary (*née* Newbery, daughter of John N. – see above) and Michael Power (a Spanish Merchant, in business as John and Michael Power in 1775 at No. 1, New Court, Crutched Friars; he d. 5 Jan. 1800); publisher and bookseller for a brief period up to 1792 or 1793, at No. 65 in St Paul's Church Yard. Left the book trade and became a wine merchant. The name Francis Power appears in London Directories as a Merchant, in 1826 and earlier.

PART I

BOOKS FOR THE ENTERTAINMENT
INSTRUCTION AND EDUCATION
OF CHILDREN AND YOUNG PEOPLE
LETTERED 'J'

ACCOMPTANT'S COMPANION. See Harper, Thos.

J1. ACCOUNT OF THE CONSTITUTION AND PRESENT
STATE OF GREAT BRITAIN, AN.
(1) An edition of 1759 or before. Pr f JN. Price 2s. Listed *LM* May 1759. Welsh
233.

Engvd title: AN ACCOUNT OF THE | CONSTITUTION | AND | PRESENT
STATE OF | GREAT BRITAIN, | TOGETHER | WITH A VIEW OF ITS TRADE, |
POLICY, AND INTEREST, | [5 lines] | [d.p.rule] | LONDON. | PR F J. NEWBERY,
AT THE BIBLE | AND SUN IN SPCY.

In 6's. 148 leaves+9 insets. Pp. iv+291[292]. Engvd FP sgd 'Boitard del'
'Boyce sculp'. Engvd TP and 7 other engvd leaves. Advert. on p. [292].
[BM, 13·5×8·0 cm; Bodley; CUL; LUL; RePL; Renier; Osborne*; Shiers;
NLA; McKell; DLC; MH; CtY.
(2) An undated edition, not before 1768. Pr f C & N. NBL 135 (dates '*ca.* 1765'
in error).

Engvd title as for no. (1) with *imprint*: PR F NEWBERY AND CARNAN, | NO.
65 THE NORTH SIDE OF SPCY.

Pp. iv+284. Engvd FP and TP and 7 other engvd leaves. (Communicated.)
[UCLA; DLC; NNC; CHH.
(3) Second edition, 'corrected'. Pr f C & N. Price 2s in the vell. manner. Adv.
LC 6–8.3.70, p. 231. Perhaps = no. (2).
(4) An edition of 1779 or after. Pr f TC. Price 2s 6d. There is reference at p. 222
to 'this time, 1779'.

Engvd TP as for no. (1). *Imprint*: PR F THOMAS CARNAN. | NO. 65 THE
NORTH SIDE OF SPCY.

In 6's. 144 leaves+9 insets as in no. (1). Pp. iv+284. Speckled bds, vell. backstrip.
[BM, 13·8×8·5 cm.

J2. ADVENTURES OF A BEE, THE, 1790. Pr f Power & Co. Price 4d.
Weedon 3. Richard Johnson's Day-book records: *1789 July. Mess. Newbery and
Co.---To writing The Adventures of a Bee---£3. 3s.* [*Paid by Power Aug. 31.*]
One of the three juveniles with Power's imprint not known to have been previously
published. The other two are J75 and J140. It is to be noted that although be-
spoken by 'Mess. Newbery & Co' (i.e. EN) Johnson's account was discharged by
Power. So also in the case of J140.

THE | ADVENTURES | OF | A BEE, | WHO INVITES | ALL HIS LITTLE
FRIENDS | TO | SIP HIS HONEY, | AND | AVOID HIS STING. | [p.rule] |
EMBELLISHED WITH CUTS. | LONDON, | PR F F. POWER, (GRANDSON TO |
THE LATE MR. J. NEWBERY) AND CO. | NO. 65, NEAR THE BAR, SPC- | Y, 1790. |
[PRICE FOUR PENCE.]

Pp. 92. Wcts. Bk-list at end. D.f.b. (Communicated.)
[Ball; Snowden; UCLA.

J3. ADVENTURES OF A SILVER PENNY, THE. Adv. *LC* 26–8.12.86, p. 620, as 'just published'. Welsh 306 and 168; NBL 434; *CBEL*, II, 563 (dates [1787]); Weedon 4 and p. 35, note 6. Richard Johnson's Day-book records: *1786 June 9. Mr Badcock——To writing The Adventures of a Silver Penny——5 Half Sheets, 32°——£5. 5s.* An edition was listed in *Flights of a Lady-Bird,* 1794.

(1) An undated edition, having an unsgd wct FP, measuring approx. 7·2×4·5 cm. Pr f EN. Price 6*d.*

Title and *imprint* approx. as for no. (2). 8°. 64 leaves. Pp. 126[127]. Last leaf a paste-down. Wcts in text as for no. (2). Bk-list on p. [127].

[BM, 10·9×7·3 cm; Welch; UCLA.

(2) Another undated edition having a wct FP sgd 'Bwk' (= John Bewick) measuring approx. 8·6×6·0 cm. Pr f EN. Price 6*d.*

See Plate 3.

In 8's. 64 leaves. Pp. 126. Wct FP and 12 wcts in text, probably the work of John Bewick and/or Lee. D.f.b.

[BM, 10·9×7·3 cm; CUL; Roscoe; Osborne*; Ball.

(3) An edition of 1800. Pr f EN. Price 6*d.*

Title approx. as for no. (2). *Imprint:* PR F E. NEWBERY, THE CORNER OF | SPC-Y; | BY J. CROWDER, WARWICK-SQUARE, 1800. | [PRICE SIX-PENCE.]

Pp. 126. Wct FP sgd 'Bwk' and 12 wcts in text. D.f.b.; also yellow bds printed with title etc. (Communicated.)

[UCLA; Sotheby 5.2.68, lot 64, 10·6×7·5 cm; Bondy, Cat. 77 [1969] item 102; Maxwell Hunley, Cat. 48 [winter 1969] item 8.

ADVENTURES OF A SILVER THREE-PENCE. See 'Truelove, Mr'.

J4. ADVENTURES OF BILLY BOOTS. Pr f FN(N). Price 6*d.* Listed in *Cries of London,* 1775. No copy traced.

J5. ADVENTURES OF CAPTAIN GULLIVER, THE. Welsh 312.

(1) Adv. *MC&LA* 10.6.72 as 'to be had of' FN(N) price 6*d.* Also adv. *LC* 9–12.1.73, p. 34, as one of 'Newbery's Little Books for Children' sold at the Corner of SPCY.

(2) Adv. *LC* 30.12.81–1.1.82, p. 7, as 'to be had of' EN, price 6*d,* and thereafter in many lists up to and including ENC (p. 6).

(3) An edition in S&W Cat., dated '(1787)'. EN. Described as 24mo. D.f.b.

(4) An undated edition, not before 1790. Pr f EN. Price 6*d.* Teerink 329c.

THE | ADVENTURES | OF | CAPTAIN GULLIVER, | IN A | VOYAGE | TO THE ISLANDS OF | LILLIPUT AND BROBDINGNAG. | ABRIDGED FROM THE WORKS OF | THE CELEBRATED DEAN SWIFT. | ADORNED WITH CUTS. | [p.rule] | LONDON: | PR F E. NEWBERY, AT THE CORNER OF | SPC-Y. | (PRICE SIX-PENCE.)

In 8's. 64 leaves. Pp. 123+iv. 19 wcts in text. List of bks pr f EN on last 4 pp. Floral design in green impressed on D.f.b.

[Hannas (imperf.), 10·7×7·2 cm; MiU; MWA; Roscoe (photocopy selected leaves MWA copy).

(5) Another undated edition. Pr f EN. Price 6d.

Title and *imprint* as for no. (4). Signed in 8's, gathered in 16's. Should be 64 (?68) leaves. Pp. 126 (?128). bk-list at end. 19 wcts in text.

[Hannas, 9·7×6·4 cm (imperf.).

(6) Copies in Ball, NRU, CtY, MnU, Ries (imperf.), can be either (4) or (5) or yet another undated edd.

J6. ADVENTURES OF MASTER HEADSTRONG AND MISS PATIENT, THE. Except for the variants (4) and (5), all the following may relate to the same ed.

(1) An edition adv. *LC* 19–21.12.80, p. 589, as to be pubd by EN in the Christmas Holidays, price 3d. D.f.b. There was a French ed. of 1786, *Les Aventures de Monsieur Tetu et de Miss Patience, dans leur Voyage vers la Terre du Bonheur* . . . [Paris, chez Lormel] – copy in R. Hatchwell's Malmesbury Miscell. no. 13 [1966], item 4.

(2) An undated edition. Pr f EN, recorded by Hugo, II, 325, item 37. Pp. 94.

(3) An edition of [?1789] recorded by *CBEL*, II, 563. Welsh's entry at p. 168 is obscure.

(4) An undated edition, Pr f EN. Price 3d.

THE | ADVENTURES | OF | MASTER HEADSTRONG, | AND | MISS PATIENT, | IN THEIR JOURNEY TOWARDS THE LAND | OF HAPPINESS. | CONTAINING, | AN ACCOUNT OF THE VARIOUS DIFFICULTIES | THAT MASTER HEADSTRONG EXPERIENCED, | BY LISTENING TO PASSION, LEAVING MISS | PATIENT, AND NOT CONSENTING THAT | REASON, WHOM THEY MET ON THEIR ROAD, | SHOULD ALWAYS DIRECT HIS COURSE. | [p.s.rule 4·0 cm] | LONDON: | PR F E. NEWBERY, THE COR (*sic*) | OF SPC-Y. | [PRICE THREE-PENCE.]

Pp. 94. Wct FP. ?other wcts. (Communicated.)

[Ball; Welch.

(5) A variant issue of (4), the rule on the TP being 1·4 cm long. (Communicated.)

[Ball.

ADVENTURES OF MUSUL. See Kendall, E. A.

J7. AESOP'S FABLES. The *Fables* will be found in bk-lists and adverts. under titles making it impossible to link them with certainty with known edd. For instance, (3) or (4) below might refer to no. (2).

(1) AESOP'S FABLES, adorned with a great Variety of beautiful Cuts, 6d, adv. in *GM* May 1774, as pr f FN(N).

(1A) A NEW AND BEAUTIFUL EDITION OF AESOP'S FABLES, WITH INSTRUCTIVE MORALS, ADORNED WITH CUTS. Price 6d. So described in bk-list in J53(2), 1777 as pr f FN(N). Welsh 168.

(2) An undated edition. Pr f EN. Price 6d.

SELECT FABLES OF AESOP AND OTHERS, WITH INSTRUCTIVE APPLICA-

TIONS. EMBELLISHED WITH NUMEROUS CUTS. LONDON: PR F F. NEWBERY, AT THE CORNER OF SPC-Y. [PRICE SIX-PENCE.]

Pp. vi+[7]–127. 13 wcts in text. D.f.b. (Communicated.)

[Adomeit; Ball; McKell.

(3) AESOP'S FABLES. Pr f EN. Price 6d. Listed in J328, 1795. One of the 10 vols forming *The Lilliputian Library* (no. J218), 'compiled' by Richard Johnson and first pubd by W. Domville et al. See Weedon 57.

(4) FABLES OF THE WISE AESOP. Price 6d. Listed in ENC, p. 7.

AESOP'S FABLES. See also Croxall, Saml; Richardson, Saml; *Fables in Verse*, J108; 'Aesop, Abraham'.

J7A. 'AESOP, Abraham'. FABLES IN VERSE. This has been attributed to one John Oakman on the strength of an article in *GM* for Dec. 1793, p. 1081, sgd H.L. All the article says is: 'In imitation of the celebrated Fables of Mr Gay, he [Oakman] also published a collection in Mr Newbery's shop, among which are some of considerable merit.' As Oakman was, according to *DNB*, born in ?1748, and the first ed. of 'Abraham Aesop' was dated 1757, the attribution seems more than unlikely, unless *DNB* has erred. *CBEL*, II, 561. Darton, p. 20.

(1) First edition, 1757. Pr f the Booksellers of all Nations . . . Price 6d bd and gilt.

FABLES IN VERSE | FOR THE IMPROVEMENT OF THE | YOUNG AND THE OLD. | BY | ABRAHAM AESOP, ESQ; | TO WHICH ARE ADDED, | FABLES IN VERSE AND PROSE, | WITH THE | CONVERSATION OF BIRDS AND BEASTS, | AT THEIR SEVERAL MEETINGS, | ROUTS AND ASSEMBLIES. | BY | WOGLOG THE GREAT GIANT: | ILLUSTRATED WITH A VARIETY OF CURIOUS CUTS, | BY THE BEST MASTERS. | AND AN ACCOUNT OF THE LIVES OF THE | AUTHORS. | [rule] | [3 lines quote] | [rule] | LONDON: | PR F THE BOOKSELLERS OF ALL NATIONS, AND SOLD AT | THE BIBLE AND SUN IN SPCY. | MDCCLVII. (PR. 6d. BOUND.)

In 6's. 72 leaves. Pp. xxxvi+37–144. 38 wcts. List of Newbery bks on pp. 138–44. D.f.b. (Communicated.)

[Bell; UCLA.

(2) Second edition, 1758. Pr f the Booksellers . . . Price 6d. Welsh 215.

Title and *imprint* approx. as for no. (1), with THE SECOND EDITION and date MDCCLVIII.

In 6's. 72 leaves. Pp. 144. 38 half-page wcts. List of bks pubd by 'Mr New-berry' on pp. 139–44. D.f.b.

[BM (imperf.), 10·9×7·0 cm.

(3) Third edition, 1760. Pr f the Booksellers . . . Price 6d.

Title and *imprint* approx. as for no. (1), with THE THIRD EDITION and date MDCCLX.

In 6's. 72 leaves. Pp. vi+7–144. 38 wcts in text. Bk-list on pp. 138–44. D.f.b. (Communicated.)

[Osborne*, 10·8×7·4 cm.

(4) Fourth edition, 1763. Pr f the Booksellers . . . Price 6*d.*

Title and *imprint* approx. as for no. (1), with THE FOURTH EDITION and date 1763.

In 6's. 72 leaves. Pp. 144. 38 half-page wcts as before. A number of ornamental tail-pieces. List of bks pubd by JN on pp. 138–44. D.f.b.

[NorBM, 11·0×7·5 cm.

(5) Fifth edition, 1765. Pr f the Booksellers . . . Price 6*d.* Welsh 215–16.

Title and *imprint* approx. as for no. (1), with THE FIFTH EDITION and date 1765.

In 6's. 72 leaves. Pp. vi+7–144. 38 half-page wcts. List of bks pubd by JN on pp. 138–44.

[BM, 10·6×7·2 cm; Bodley; CUL (mutilated).

(6) Sixth edition, 1768. Pr f the Booksellers . . . Price 6*d.*

Title and *imprint* approx. as for no. (1), with THE SIXTH EDITION, date 1768 and 'No 65' in place of 'The Bible and Sun'.

In 6's. 72 leaves. Pp. vi+7–138[144]. 38 half-page wcts. List of bks pr f a s b N & C on pp. 138–44. D.f.b.

[St Bride, 11·1×7·5 cm; Welch; RP.

(7) An edition of 1772. Pr f the Booksellers . . . and sold at The Bible and Sun, Number 65 . . . Price 6*d.*

[Ball; Gardner; Hodgson's, 8.5.53, lot 561.

(8) An edition of 1774. 'Pr f Mr Newbery'. Janet Adam Smith, *Children's Illustrated Books*, 1948, p. 9.

(9) An edition of 1777. Pr f the Booksellers . . . Price 6*d.*

Title and *imprint* approx. as for no. (6), with date 1777.

In 6's. 72 leaves. Pp. vi+7–138[144]. 38 half-page wcts. List of bks pr f C & N on pp. 138–44.

[Schiller (imperf.), 11·1×7·2 cm; UCLA.

(10) An edition of 1783. Pr f the Booksellers . . . Price 6*d.*

Title and *imprint* approx. as for no. (6), with date 1783.

72 leaves. Pp. vi+7–138[144]. 38 half-page wcts. List of bks pr f TC on pp. 138–44. D.f.b.

[BM, 11·5×7·7 cm; Ball.

J8. ALLEN, Charles. THE POLITE LADY. Sometimes listed as PORTIA, the signatory to the letters forming the book. The authorship of Allen has not yet found its way into catalogues and bibliographies. See *European Magazine* Jan.–June 1792, p. 159, where it is recorded that Allen died in Jan. 1792, aged 63, 'author of Female Preceptor, Polite Lady &c'. Welsh 288.

(1) First edition, 1760. Pr f JN. Price 2*s* 6*d* sewed in bds, 3*s* in calf.

THE | POLITE LADY: | OR A COURSE OF | FEMALE EDUCATION. | IN A | SERIES OF LETTERS, | FROM A MOTHER TO HER DAUGHTER. | [3 lines quote] | [ornamental design] | LONDON: | PR F J. NEWBERY AT THE BIBLE AND | SUN IN SPC-Y. | MDCCLX.

12mo. 150 leaves+engvd FP sgd 'Le Pautré sculp'. Pp. xii+288.
[BM, 16·0×9·5 cm; Bodley; Renier; Hannas; Osborne.*

(2) Second edition, 1769. Pr f N & C. Price 3s in the vell. manner. *CBEL*, II, 122.

Title approx. as for no. (1), with THE SECOND EDITION CORRECTED. *Imprint:* PR F NEWBERY AND CARNAN, NO. 65, | THE NORTH SIDE OF SPC-Y. | MDCCLXIX.

12mo. 144 leaves+engvd FP as in (1). Pp. xii+276. Pink bds, green vell. spine.
[BM, 16·4×10·0 cm; Bodley; Oup; LI; HU; LEI; Weedon, 16·7×10·2 cm; Osborne*; UCLA.

(3) Third edition, 1775. Pr f C & N. Price 3s.

Title approx. as for no. (1), with THIRD EDITION. *Imprint:* PR F T. CARNAN, AND F. NEWBERY, JUNIOR, | AT NUMBER 65, SPC-Y. | MDCCLXXV.

12mo. 144 leaves+engvd FP as in (1). Pp. xii+276.
[BM, 17·8×10·5 cm; CUL; Opie.

(4) Fourth edition, 1785. Pr f TC. Price 3s.

Title approx. as for no. (1), with FOURTH EDITION. *Imprint:* PR F THOMAS CARNAN, IN SP | C-Y. | MDCCLXXXV.

12mo. 144 leaves+engvd FP. Pp. xii+276. A new FP is used.
[BM, 17·4×9·9 cm; Grant.

ALMANACK. For an Almanack for the use of schools, see no. A7(70).

J9. ALPHABET ROYAL, OU GUIDE COMMODE & AGRÉABLE DANS L'ART DE LIRE.

(1) An undated edition adv. in *GEP* 1.8.50. Pr f JN et al. Price 6d. Welsh 169 and 295.

See Fig. 4.

In 8's. 36 leaves. Pp. 72. 26 small wcts. Text in French. Drab bds, large wct on each cover; also D.f.b. One of the bks put out by JN as 'introductory' to the *Circle of the Sciences* series.
[BM, 9·4×6·4 cm; Opie.

(2) Advertised as pr f C & N in *LC* 11–14.4.72, p. 359. Price 6d.

(3) Listed as pr f TC in *Newtonian System*, 1787. Price 6d.

J10. AMASIS, OR THE MANNERS OF THE ANCIENT GAULS.
Listed in Kendall's *Adventures of Musul*, 1800 as one of 'the Books of Vernor and Hood and E. Newbery lately published'. Many books in such lists as this prove to have been published under the imprint of Vernor and Hood alone, and this was probably the case here.

J11. AMIABLE TUTORESS, THE, 1801. S b EN. Price 2s neatly bd in vell.
THE | AMIABLE TUTORESS: | OR, | THE HISTORY | OF | MARY AND JANE HORNSBY. | [d.p.rule] | A TALE | FOR | YOUNG PERSONS. | [d.p.rule] | LONDON: | PR F T. HURST, | NO. 32, P-N-R; | A S B E. NEWBERY, CORNER OF SPC-Y. | [p.rule] | J. CUNDEE, PRINTER, IVY-LANE. | [d.p.rule] | 1801.

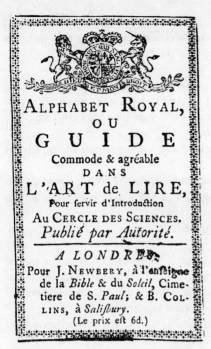

ALPHABET ROYAL,
OU
GUIDE
Commode & agréable
DANS
L'ART de LIRE,
Pour servir d'Introduction
Au CERCLE DES SCIENCES.
Publié par Autorité.

A LONDRES,
Pour J. NEWBERY, à l'enseigne
de la *Bible* & du *Soleil*, Cime-
tiere de S. *Paul*; & B. COL-
LINS, à *Salisbury*.
(Le prix est 6d.)

(2)
Deux bons Enfants, Fille & Garçon,

Chacun après sa leçon.
QUI néglige son *A, B, C,*
Est toujours Animal chaussé ;
Mais qui se plaît à sa leçon,
Fera bientôt grosse maison.

COMME l'Ozier prend le pli
qu'on lui donne ;
Ainsi l'Enfant que l'on façonne
Dès l'ongle tendre aux bonnes mœurs,
Conservera cette couronne,
Et se verra comblé d'honneurs.

Fig. 4. Title-page and page 2 of J9(1).

In 6's. 90 leaves+engvd FP. Pp. 169[175]. Half-title. Adv. of bks pubd by
Hurst on Q2ʳ–Q4ʳ.

[BM, 13·6×8·4 cm; Ball; UCLA.

AMUSING AND INSTRUCTIVE TALES FOR YOUTH. See J391(2).

J12. AMUSING INSTRUCTOR, THE.
(1) An edition of 1777. Pr f FN(N). Price 2s. Welsh 169; NBL 446; *CBEL*, II,
562.

THE | AMUSING INSTRUCTOR: | OR, | TALES AND FABLES | IN | PROSE
AND VERSE, | FOR THE | IMPROVEMENT OF YOUTH. | [6 lines] | LONDON, |
PR F F. NEWBERY, AT THE CORNER OF S | PC-Y, 1777.

12mo. 102 leaves+10 insets. Pp. 198. K4 a blank. Engvd FP sgd 'Simpson sc',
11 other engvgs, 2 wcts.

[BM, 12·8×7·7 cm; DES; Welch; UCLA; Maxwell Hunley, Cat. 48 [winter
1969] item 15.
(2) Listed as pr f EN in Chesterfield's *Maxims*, 1786. Price 2s.

J13. ANCHORET, THE, A MORAL TALE, IN A SERIES OF
LETTERS. Adv. as pubd by FN(N), 3 vols, price 7s 6d sewed, in *LC* 3–5.12.72,
p. 540. There was another *Anchoret* dated 1776, pubd by Murray and Creech.

J14. ANECDOTES OF A LITTLE FAMILY. No dated edn recorded; listed in *Prince Lee Boo*, 1789. A copy in the Welch colln, lacking title-leaf, has wmk 1796 at pp. 20–1. Welsh 169; Gum 353; *CBEL*, II, 563.

(1) An edition pr f EN. Price 1*s*.

ANECDOTES | OF A | LITTLE FAMILY, | INTERSPERSED WITH | FABLES, STORIES, AND ALLEGORIES, | [4 lines] | [p.s.rule] | EMBELLISHED WITH CUTS. | [p.s.rule] | LONDON: | PR F E. NEWBERY, THE CORNER OF | SPC-Y. | [p.rule] | [PRICE ONE SHILLING BOUND.]

In 6's. 83 leaves+6 insets. Pp. 170. Engvd FP and 5 other engvd leaves. List of bks pr f EN on pp. 157–70. D.f.b.

In this ed. PREFACE on A2^r is 5·6 cm long and is followed by a p.s.rule 3·6 cm long. On p. [1] ANECDOTES is 4·9 cm long. On p. 156 FINIS is approx. 4·7 cm below last line of text.

[BM, 11·6×7·6 cm; V&A(GL) (imperf.); Ball.

(2) Another edition. Pr f EN. Price 1*s*.

TP and specification approx. as for no. (1). In this ed. PREFACE on A2^r is 4·4 cm long and is followed by a d.p.rule 2·3 cm long. On p. [1] ANECDOTES is 4·3 cm long. On p. 156 FINIS is approx. 2·7 cm below last line of text. (Communicated.)

[Welch (formerly Tighe); Roscoe (photocopied selected leaves).

(3) Copies in Osborne*; NNC-T (Darton Coll.); CLU; Elkin Mathews, Cat. 163 [1965] item 41, not identified.

ANECDOTES OF MARY. See S., H.

J15. 'ANGELO, Master Michael'. DRAWING SCHOOL, THE, FOR LITTLE MASTERS AND MISSES. Weedon 20. Richard Johnson's Day-book records: *1772 Nov. 16. Delivered to Mr Carnan The Drawing School for Little Masters and Misses. Value Five Guineas.* [*Received 1773 Feb. 1.*]

(1) First edition, 1773. Pr f TC. Price 6*d*. NBL 653; Pressler, p. 3.

Engvd TP: See Fig. 5.

In 6's. 56 leaves+2 insets; last leaf a blank. Pp. iv+[5]–106. Engvd FP sgd 'W. Walker sculp'; engvd TP; 53 wcts of birds, heads, feet etc. The cuts of the birds are remarkable for their high standard. D.f.b.

[Roscoe, 11·3×7·2 cm; V&A(GL); Opie; ICU-J; UCLA.

(2) Second edition, 1774. Pr f TC. Price 6*d*. Welsh 207.

Engvd title and *imprint* approx. as for no. (1), with date MDCCLXXIIII. and price at foot.

In 6's. 54 leaves+2 insets. Pp. 106. Slight revisions in wcts. Buff or white bds, black impress; also D.f.b.

[BM, 11·0×7·5 cm; V&A(GL); BCE; Renier; CLU; Ball; Lapides; Sotheby, 5.2.1945 (the Bussell sale) Cat. 125.

(3) Third edition, 1777. Pr f TC. Price 6*d*. Gum 2744.

Engvd title and *imprint* approx. as for no. (1), with date MDCCLXXVII. and price at foot.

THE

DRAWING SCHOOL

FOR
LITTLE MASTERS AND MISSES:

CONTAINING

The moſt eaſy and conciſe Rules

FOR

LEARNING TO DRAW,

Without the Aſſiſtance of a TEACHER.

Embelliſhed with a great Variety of FIGURES
curiouſly deſigned.

To which are added,

The whole Art of KITE MAKING;

AND

The AUTHOR's new Diſcoveries in the
Preparation of WATER COLOURS.

By Maſter MICHAEL ANGELO.

LONDON:

Printed for T. CARNAN, at Number 65,
in St. Paul's Church Yard.

———————
MDCC LXXIII.

Fig. 5. Frontiſpiece and title-page of J15(1).

In 6's. 54 leaves+2 insets. A different engvd FP. Pp. [7]–108. Wcts as before
with slight revision. D.f.b.; also buff bds with black or red pictorial impress.
[Schiller, 11·6×7·6 cm; V&A(GL) (imperf.); Brayshaw; Opie; Welch; UCLA.

J16. 'ANGELO, Master Michel'. JUVENILE SPORTS. Weedon 43.
Richard Johnson's Day-book records: *1773 June 14. Left with Mr Carnan for
Inspection Juvenile Sports and Pastimes———£5. 5s. [Received 1776 Jan. 3.] 1775
Aug. Corrected Juvenile Sports and Pastimes, for Mr Carnan———10s. 6d. [Received
1776 Jan. 5.]*
(1) First edition, ?1773 or 1774. Pr f TC. Price 6d. Adv. *LC* 1–4.1.74, p. 11.
(2) Second edition, 1776. Pr f TC. Price 6d. Welsh 244–5; *CBEL*, II, 562.
JUVENILE SPORTS | AND | PASTIMES. | TO WHICH ARE PREFIXED, |
MEMOIRS OF THE AUTHOR: | INCLUDING A NEW MODE OF | INFANT
EDUCATION. | [p.rule] | BY MASTER MICHEL ANGELO, | AUTHOR OF | THE
DRAWING-SCHOOL FOR LITTLE | MASTERS AND MISSES. | [p.rule] | THE
SECOND EDITION. | [p.rule] | LONDON: | PR F T. CARNAN, AT NUMBER 65,
IN S | PC-Y. PRICE SIX-PENCE. | MDCCLXXVI.
In 6's. 54 leaves. Pp. 104. 22 wcts. D.f.b.

47

[Bodley, 11·2×7·4 cm.

(3) An edition of 1780. Pr f TC. Price 6d. Welsh 244–5; *CBEL*, II, 562; Gum 2764.

    Title and *imprint* approx. as for no. (2), with date MDCCLXXX.

    In 6's. 54 leaves. Pp. 108. 22 wcts. D.f.b.

    [Bodley, 11·2×7·1 cm; Ball.

ANNOTATIONS ON ST JOHN. See Merrick, J243A and B.

ARITHMETIC MADE FAMILIAR. See J61.

ART OF ARITHMETIC. See J61.

ART OF POETRY MADE EASY. See J68.

J16A. ART OF POETRY ON A NEW PLAN, THE. Usually ascribed to JN as author – but on what authority? (*CBEL*, II, 27). (To be distinguished from the *Art of Poetry* vols in the *Circle of the Sciences*.) Welsh, p. 287, says there were 'four editions with different titles before 1776'. Probably he was dragging in the *Circle* volumes.

(1) An edition by JN, 1761, recorded by Welsh 286–7, who also records another ed. or issue of vol. I, dated 1762. The 1761 ed. is probably a ghost: copies seen have, for vol. I, date MDCCLXII, for vol. II date MDCCLXI, seemingly a misprint for MDCCLXII.

(2) An edition of 1762. Pr f JN. 2 vols, price 6s. *CBEL*, II, 27 and 641; IAW p. 122; H&L, I, 145–6; *N&Q*, 3rd ser, IV, 61; Scott 81–3.

    THE | ART | OF | POETRY | ON A | NEW PLAN: | ILLUSTRATED WITH A GREAT VARIETY OF | EXAMPLES FROM THE BEST ENGLISH POETS; | [7 lines] | [p.rule] | VOL. I. [II.] | [d.p.rule] | LONDON: | PR F J. NEWBERY, AT THE BIBLE AND SUN | IN SPC-Y. | MDCCLXII. [MDCCLXI].

    Vol. I: 12mo. 139 leaves. Pp. viii[xxiv], vi+[7]–252. Engvd FP sgd 'Ant. Walker del et sculp.'

    Vol. II: 12mo. 191 leaves. Pp. 382. For the date see no. (1).

    [BM, 16·9×9·9 cm; Bodley; CUL; LUL; OOxM; CLU-C; DNS; Sotheby, 30.6.69, lot 251, and 8.3.71, lot 212.

(3) Listed various dates up to 1786 as by N & C or TC.

(4) Listed in Smart's *Poems*, 1791, as s b F. Power & Co.

ART OF RHETORICK. See J69.

ART OF WRITING. See J72.

ASIATIC PRINCESS. See Pilkington, M. (H).

ATLAS MINIMUS. See Gibson, John.

J17. AULNOY, Marie Catherine de la Mothe, Comtesse d'. MOTHER
BUNCH'S FAIRY TALES. Welsh 272; *CBEL*, II, 565.
(1) An edition of 1773 ? the first. Pr f FN(N). Price 9*d* bd and gilt. Muir, plate 16.
MOTHER BUNCH'S | FAIRY TALES. | PUBLISHED FOR THE | AMUSEMENT
| OF ALL THOSE | LITTLE MASTERS AND MISSES | WHO, | BY DUTY TO THEIR
PARENTS, AND OBEDIENCE | TO THEIR SUPERIORS, | AIM AT BECOMING |
GREAT LORDS AND LADIES. | ADORNED WITH COPPER-PLATE CUTS. |
LONDON: | PR F F. NEWBERY, AT THE | CORNER OF SPC-Y. | MDCCLXXIII.
| PRICE NINE-PENCE.
In 8's. 96 leaves. Pp. 191[192]. Engvd FP and 10 other engvd leaves. Bk-list on
p. [192]. D.f.b.
[NorBM, 10·1×6·3 cm; Welch; Ball.
(1A) An edition of 1776. Pr f EN. Price 9*d*.
Title and *imprint* approx. as for no. (1).
In 8's. [A]-[M8]. 96 leaves+engvd FP and 10 or 11 other engvd leaves. Pp. 191.
D.f.b.
[Sotheby, 14.3.72, 9·6×6·6 cm.
(2) An edition of 1784. Pr f EN. Price 9*d*.
Title approx. as for no. (1). *Imprint:* PR F E. NEWBERY, AT THE | CORNER
OF SPC-Y. | MDCCLXXXIV. | [PRICE NINE-PENCE.]
D.f.b. gilt. (Communicated.)
[Opie.
(3) An edition of 1790. Pr f EN. [Ball.
(4) An edition of 1795. Pr f EN. [Ball.
(5) An edition of 1799. Pr f EN. Price 9*d*.
Title approx. as for no. (1). *Imprint* approx. as for no. (2), with date MDCCXCIX.
Pp. 192. Engvd FP and 11 other engvd leaves. D.f.b. (Communicated.)
[Ball; Welch.

J18. AVIARY, THE, 1800. Pr f EN. Price 1*s* 6*d*, 'a few copies coloured' 2*s* 6*d*.
THE | AVIARY; | OR, | GRAND ASSEMBLAGE | OF | THE FEATHERED
TRIBES. | COMPRISING NEAR | ONE HUNDRED FIGURES, | ACCURATELY
ENGRAVED ON COPPER-PLATES. | [5 lines] | [d.p.rule] | LONDON: | PR F E.
NEWBERY, | CORNER OF SPC-Y; | BY J. CUNDEE, IVY-LANE. | [p.rule] | 1800.
In 6's. 18 leaves+19 leaves of engvd figures. Pp. 36. Half-title. The 19 engvd
leaves, comprising *ca.* 79 figures of birds, are grouped together at end of text. Stiff
marbled paper covers, blue back-strip, blue oval label on upper cover. Stabbed.
[Roscoe, 14·1×7·4 cm; Welch.

BAG OF NUTS READY CRACKED. See 'Thumb, Thomas'.

J18A. BARNARD, Sir John. PRESENT FOR AN APPRENTICE.

Tenth edition listed in *Newtonian System*, 1770 and 1779, as pr f C & N, price 1*s*. An undated 10th ed. (copy in LGL) was by J. Fletcher and B. Collins.

J19. BATTLEDORE. THE BRITISH BATTLEDORE.

Recorded by Welsh, p. 172, without date or publisher; price 4*d* plain, 6*d* coloured. Stated to consist of an Alphabet, one Spelling Lesson, the Arabic Numerals and 8 wcts of animals.

J20. BATTLEDORE. THE IMPERIAL BATTLEDORE.

Recorded by Welsh, p. 172, without date or publisher; price 4*d* plain, 6*d* coloured. Stated to consist of two short Spelling Lessons, the Lord's Prayer, the Arabic Numerals and 6 small wcts.

J21. BATTLEDORE. THE ROYAL BATTLEDORE.

It may be questioned whether there were not two productions under this title: no. (1) below (advtd as a *First Book for Children*), i.e. a book of more than two leaves, or no. (4), a true battledore, a single card sheet. On the whole it seems more likely there was only one – the battledore proper; for the advertised description and price of no. (1) fits no. (4) precisely. To refer to a battledore as a 'book' is correct usage – see *OED*, sense 3. Welsh 172.

(1) (*Advtd title*) THE ROYAL BATTLEDORE; OR FIRST BOOK FOR CHILDREN TO LEARN THEIR LETTERS AND FIGURES; ADORNED WITH TWENTY FOUR CUTS, AND EXPLANATIONS. Pr f JN, J. Hodges and B. Collins. Price 2*d* neatly glazed and gilt. Adv. *PA* 1.1.53 as *a new edition*.

(2) Frequently listed as pr f JN up to 1765. Price 2*d*.

(3) Listed as pr f a s b JN in *Little Pretty Pocket-Book*, 1767 under the title THE ROYAL BATTLEDORE; OR, FIRST BOOK FOR CHILDREN. Price 2*d* neatly gilt and glazed.

(3A) An undated edition. Pr b JN et al. Price 2*d*.

THE ROYAL BATTLEDORE: BEING THE FIRST INTRODUCTORY PART OF THE | CIRCLE OF THE SCIENCES, &C. PUBLISH'D BY THE KING'S AUTHORITY. | LONDON: PR BY J. NEWBERY, IN SPC-Y, AND B. COLLINS, IN SARUM, PR 2*d*. | ALSO THE ROYAL PRIMER, OR SECOND BOOK FOR CHILDREN, PRICE 3*d*. BOUND, ADORN'D WITH CUTS.

Reproduced as a facsimile 'Horn-Book' in Tuer's *History of the Horn Book*. The location of the original is not stated. A single card sheet, folded once, with wct alphabet. The Tuer facsimile is bound in D.f. paper.

(4) An undated edition. Pr b N & C et al. Price 2*d*. *N&Q*, ser VI, vol. 7, 336.

See Figure 6. A yellow single sheet card, folded once, D.f. paper on vso. The wcts for the alphabet had been used in no. (3A), and are, with the exception of those for H, J, N, R, U and Y, used in reverse, and in a much cruder cutting, in the *New Invented Horn Book* usually, though without good reason, attributed to the young Thomas Bewick, and assigned by Hugo (no. 2) to 1770-1.

Fig. 6. *The Royal Battledore.* J21(4) (slightly reduced).

He that ne'er learns his A B C,   For ever, will a Blockhead be.

a b c d e f g h i j k l m n o p q
r ſ s t u v w x y z.

A B C D E F G H I J K L M N
O P Q R S T U V W X Y Z.

ſt ſi ſſ ff ſl fl ſſi ffi ffl & &.

Douce   a e i o u y. Ad l. 316

ab eb ib ob ub	ba be bi bo bu
ac ec ic oc uc	ca ce ci co cu
ad ed id od ud	da de di do du

IN the Name of the Fa-ther, and of the Son, and of the Ho-ly Ghoſt. *A-men.*

I Pray God to bleſs my Fa-ther and Mo-ther, Bro-thers and Siſ-ters, and all my good Friends, and my E-ne-mies. *A-men.*

OUR Fa-ther, which art in Hea-ven, hal-low-ed be thy Name; thy King-dom come; thy Will be done on Earth as it is in Hea-ven. Give us this Day our dai-ly Bread; and for-give us our Treſ-paſ-ſes, as we for-give them that treſ-paſs a-gainſt us; and lead us not in-to Temp-ta-tion, but de-li-ver us from E-vil; for thine is the King-dom, the Pow-er and the Glo-ry, for e-ver and e-ver. *A-men.*

Figures, 1 2 3 4 5 6 7 8 9 0.

But he that learns theſe Letters fair,   Shall have a Coach to take the Air.

Douce Ad.. 316

a Apple
b Bull
c Cat
d Dog
e Egg
f Fiſh
g Goat
h Hog
j Judge
k King
l Lion
m Mouſe
n Nag
o Owl
p Peacock
q Queen
r Robin
ſ Squirrel
t Top
v Vine
w Whale
x Xerxes
y young Lamb
z Zani

[Bodley, approx. 12·0 × 14·3 cm.
(5) Listed with title as in no. (3) between 1770 (no. J348(4)) and 1787 (no. J348(7)) as pr f C & N or TC. Price 2d.

BEAUTIES OF HISTORY. See Dodd, Wm.

J21A. BEES. A SHORT HISTORY OF BEES; IN TWO PARTS, COMPREHENDING THE NATURAL HISTORY OF BEES; WITH THE MANAGEMENT OF THEM &c. ALSO, AN ENIGMA-TICAL ACCOUNT OF THEIR QUEEN, HER PALACES, ATTEN-DANTS &c. BY A LADY. So advert. in *LC* 5–7.5.1801, p. 439, as pr f Vernor and Hood and EN. Price 2s. Recorded by Lyon as dated 1800. Also listed in Smythies' *History of a Pin*, 1801, as pr f EN.

BE MERRY AND WISE. See 'Trapwit, Tommy'.

J22. BERNARDIN DE SAINT-PIERRE, JACQUES HENRI. PAUL ET VIRGINIE, and PAUL AND VIRGINIA (trans. Helen M. Williams). Frequently listed as pr f a s b EN and Vernor and Hood; all copies seen were by Vernor and Hood alone. No ed. with EN's name recorded in Toinet's Bibliography.

J23. BERQUIN, Arnaud. FAMILY BOOK, THE, 1798. Pr f [E.]N. et al. This, and the French ed. (no. J24) were adv. *LC* 8–10.1.99, p. 39, as two of 'Newbery's New Publications', price 3*s* 6*d* for the English ed., 3*s* for the French. Stockdale put out edd. of this work under almost identical titles in 1798 and 1799.

THE | FAMILY BOOK; | OR | CHILDREN'S JOURNAL. | CONTAINING | MORAL AND AMUSING TALES, | WITH | INSTRUCTIVE DIALOGUES | UPON SUBJECTS WHICH GENERALLY OCCUR IN | FAMILIAR SOCIETY. | [d.p.rule] | TRANSLATED FROM THE FRENCH OF | MONS. BERQUIN. | [d.p.rule] | [3 lines quote] | [d.p.rule] | LONDON: | PR F VERNOR AND HOOD, NO. 31, POULTRY; | T. BOOSEY, NO. 4, OLD BROAD-STREET; | NEWBERY, SPCY; AND | DARTON AND HARVEY, GRACECHURCH-STREET. | [p.rule] | 1798.

12mo. 138 leaves. Pp. 267[272]. List of bks pr f EN et al. on last 3 pp. Engvd FP. (Communicated.)

[Pollard; Brimmell, Cat. 67 [1970] item 15; Platt.

J24. BERQUIN, Arnaud. LE LIVRE DE FAMILLE, 1798. EN et al. Price 3*s*. For the English trans. see no. J23.

LE LIVRE DE FAMILLE, | OU | JOURNAL DES ENFANS; | CONTENANT DES | HISTORIETTES MORALES ET AMUSANTES, | [3 lines] | AVEC FIGURES. | [d.rule] | PAR M. BERQUIN. | [d.p.rule] | [4 lines] | [d.p.rule] | A LONDRES: | DE L'IMPRIMERIE DE BAYLIS, | ET SE TROUVE CHEZ E. NEWBERY, SP- | C-Y; VERNOR & HOOD, POULTRY; | BOOSEY, OLD BROAD-STREET, PRÈS DE LA BOURSE- | ROYALE; & DARTON & HARVEY, GRACE-CHURCH- | STREET. ——1798.

In 6's. 170 leaves. Pp. 337.

[Weedon, 13·5 × 8·0 cm.

J25. BERQUIN, Arnaud. LOOKING-GLASS FOR THE MIND, THE. Weedon 62; Welsh 259; *CBEL*, II, 566.

Richard Johnson had a hand in this production, but exactly how or what is uncertain – see Miss Weedon's note. His Day-book records: *1787 March. Mr Badcock——To compiling The Looking Glass——18 Half Sheets——£18. 18s. 1792 March. Mr Badcock——To writing Heads to The Looking-Glass——£1. 11s. 6d.* This is one of the books ascribed to 'the Rev. Mr Cooper' in *The Oriental Moralist*, 1791/2.

(1) First [English] edition, 1787. Pr f EN. Price 2*s* 6*d*.

THE | LOOKING-GLASS | FOR THE | MIND; | OR, | INTELLECTUAL MIRROR. | BEING AN ELEGANT COLLECTION | OF THE | MOST DELIGHTFUL LITTLE STORIES | [2 lines] | CHIEFLY TRANSLATED FROM THAT MUCH ADMIRED

WORK, | L'AMI DES ENFANS, | [2 lines] | [p.s.rule] | LONDON: | PR F E.
NEWBERY, THE CORNER OF SP | C-Y. 1787.

In 6's. 108 leaves+engvd FP inset. Pp. 212.

[BM, 16·7×9·8 cm; V&A(GL); Weedon; Renier; Osborne*; Welch; Gardner;
UCLA; Sotheby, 5.2.68, lot 3; Maxwell Hunley, Cat. 48 [winter 1969] item 30.

(2) An edition of 1789. Recorded *CBEL*. Not traced.

(3) A new edition, 1792. Pr f EN. Price 3*s*. NUTP Cat. no. 57 (wrongly describes
as 1st ed.). Hugo 66. Title begins approx. as for no. (1); continues: A NEW
EDITION, | WITH SEVENTY-FOUR CUTS, DESIGNED AND | ENGRAVED ON
WOOD | BY BEWICK. | LONDON: | PR B J. CROWDER, | FOR E. NEWBERY,
THE CORNER OF | SPC-Y. | MDCCXCII.

In 6's. 140 leaves+inset engvd FP. Pp. 271. 37 wct headpieces, 37 wct tailpieces, most, if not all, the work of John Bewick.

[BM, 17·0×10·1 cm; Bodley; NUTP; DLC; UCLA.

(4) A new edition, 1794. Pr f EN. Price 3*s*.

Title and *imprint* approx. as for no. (3), with date MDCCXCIV. Specification
approx. as for no. (3). Mavor's *Juvenile Olio*, 1796, lists either this ed. or no. (5),
adding that 'At the particular request of several admirers of Mr Bewick's engravings, a few copies are printed on a superfine, wove, hot-pressed paper, price 4*s*.
in boards, or elegantly bound, 6*s*'.

[V&A; Roscoe, 16·7×10·2 cm; Renier; Osborne*; Welch; CLU; Elkin
Mathews, Cat. 163 [1965] item 53.

(5) An edition of 1796 (?5th). Pr f EN. Price 3*s*. Gum 580.

Title approx. as for no. (1) down to 'Des Enfans'; then read: | WITH SEVENTY-
FOUR CUTS, DESIGNED AND | ENGRAVED ON WOOD BY | [wct vignette engvd
with the name I. BEWICK] | [d.p.rule] | LONDON: | PR B J. CROWDER, | FOR
E. NEWBERY, THE CORNER OF SP | C-Y. | [p.s.rule] | MDCCXCVI.

In 6's. 140 leaves. Pp. 271. 37 wct headpieces, 38 wct tailpieces as in no. (3).

[BM, 16·7×9·9 cm; Bodley; Roscoe; Renier; A. R. Heath, Cat. 22 [1972] item
19.

(6) Sixth edition not traced.

(7) Seventh edition, 1798. Pr f EN. Price 3*s* 6*d*. Hugo 4098; NBL 456.

Title as for no. (5), continuing after the vignette: THE SEVENTH EDITION. |
LONDON: | PR B J. CROWDER, | FOR E. NEWBERY, THE CORNER OF SP | C-Y.
| MDCCXCVIII. | [PRICE THREE SHILLINGS AND SIX PENCE.]

In 6's. 140 leaves. Pp. 271. 37 wct headpieces, 39 wct tailpieces as in no. (3).

[Weedon, 16·2×9·7 cm; NNC-Pl; UCLA.

(8) Eighth edition, 1800. Pr f EN.

Title and *imprint* approx. as for no. (7), with THE EIGHTH EDITION and
date 1800. Specification approx. as for no. (7). Details taken from the CUL
copy.

[CUL; Osborne, Cat. p. 233; NNC-T (Darton Coll.); CtNSCSC.

J26. BERQUIN, Arnaud. MOUNTAIN PIPER, THE. Welsh 273; *CBEL*, II, 563; Weedon 66 and p. 35, note 6.

Richard Johnson's Day-book records: *1787 June 22. Mr Badcock——To writing The Mountain Piper——£3. 3s.* The bk was adv. *LC* 27–9.12.87, p. 619, as for sale in the Christmas holidays. It is a rather free version of the *Mountain Piper*, a tale in the 19th vol. of Berquin's *Children's Friend*, 1786–7. In that tale there is no mention of Edgar and Matilda, and other names differ. The author of *A Journey to London* is not known; it could well have been Johnson himself.

(1) An undated edition. Pr f EN. 1787 or after. Price 3*d*.

THE | MOUNTAIN PIPER; | OR, THE | HISTORY | OF EDGAR AND MATILDA. | TO WHICH IS ADDED, | A JOURNEY TO LONDON, | A MORAL TALE. | [p.rule] | EMBELLISHED WITH CUTS. | [d.p.rule] | LONDON: | PR F E. NEWBERY, THE CORNER | OF SPC-Y. | (PRICE 3*d*.)

In 8's. 48 leaves. Pp. 96. 12 wcts in the manner of Lee, or possibly by John Bewick. First leaf a FP or blank. D.f.b. On the TP 'Embellished with Cuts' is in Roman type and followed by a thick and thin rule; on p. [7] line 10 reads 'you here see.'; on p. 96 last line reads 'country.'.

[BM (imperf.), 10·0×6·3 cm; ? UCLA.

(2) Another undated edition. Pr f EN. 1787 or after. Price 3*d*.

Wct FP. Wcts in text. Pp. 96. On TP 'Embellished with Cuts' is in italics and followed by a single rule; on p. [7] line 9 reads 'him, as you here see.'; on p. 96 last line reads 'the country.'. Not seen.

[Welch. (Welch and Roscoe have photocopied selected leaves.)

(3) Unverified copies in Bowe, Harding, MiDW.

J27. BIBLE. HOLY BIBLE ABRIDGED, THE.

(1) An edition of 1757 (probably the 1st). Pr f JN. Price 6*d* bd and gilt. Presumably the ed. adv. *PA* 31.12.56.

THE | HOLY BIBLE | ABRIDGED: | OR, THE | HISTORY | OF THE | OLD AND NEW TESTAMENT. | ILLUSTRATED WITH NOTES, | AND | ADORNED WITH CUTS. | FOR THE USE OF CHILDREN. | [p.rule] | SUFFER LITTLE CHILDREN TO COME UNTO ME, AND | FORBID THEM NOT. LUKE XVIII. 16. | [p.rule] | LONDON: | PR F J. NEWBERY, AT THE BIBLE AND SUN | IN SPC-Y. 1757. | [PRICE SIX-PENCE BOUND.]

In 8's. 96 leaves. Pp. vii[xv]+176. Should be 91 wcts in text.

[Roscoe (imperf., cropped), 9·3×5·7 cm; Welch.

(2) Listed in J76(1), 1758 as pr f a s b JN. Price 6*d*. Welsh 173. ? = no. (1).

(3) Third edition, 1760. Pr f JN. Price 6*d* bd. *Title* (THE THIRD EDITION added), *imprint* (with date 1760), and specification approx. as for no. (1). D.f.b. (Communicated.)

[UCLA.

(4) Fourth edition not traced.

(5) Fifth edition, 1764. Pr f JN. Price 6*d* bd.

Title (THE FIFTH EDITION added) and *imprint* (with date 1764) approx. as for no. (1).

In 8's. 96 leaves. Pp. vii[xv]+176. 60 wcts in text. D.f.b.

[BFBS, 9·0×6·0 cm; NorBM, 9·9×6·5 cm.

(6) Sixth edition, 1764. Pr f JN. Price 6*d*.

THE | HOLY BIBLE | ABRIDGED: | OR, THE | HISTORY | OF THE | OLD AND NEW TESTAMENT. | ILLUSTRATED | WITH NOTES, AND ADORNED WITH CUTS, | FOR THE USE OF CHILDREN. | [rule] | SUFFER LITTLE CHILDREN TO COME UNTO ME, AND FORBID | THEM NOT. LUKE XVIII 16. | [rule] THE SIXTH EDITION. | [rule] | LONDON: | PR F J. NEWBERY, AT THE BIBLE AND SUN | IN SPC-Y. 1764. | PRICE SIX-PENCE BOUND.

16mo. Pp. vii[xv or xvi]+176. D.f.b. (Communicated.)

[Schiller.

(7) Seventh edition, 1768. Pr f N & C. Price 6*d* bd.

Title approx. as for no. (1) with THE SEVENTH EDITION. *Imprint:* PR F NEWBERY AND CARNAN, AT THE | BIBLE AND SUN, NO. 65, THE NORTH SIDE OF S | PC-Y. 1768. | [PRICE SIX-PENCE BOUND.]

In 8's. 96 leaves. Pp. 176. 61 wcts in text. D.f.b.

[St Bride, 9·8×6·5 cm.; NorBM.

(8) An edition of 1770. Pr f C & N. Price 6*d* bd and gilt.

Title and *imprint* approx. as for no. (7) (no ed. stated), with date 1770.

In 8's. 96 leaves. Pp. vii[xvi]+176. 61 wcts in text. D.f.b.

[BM, 9·8×5·9 cm; V&A(GL).

(9) An edition of 1772. Pr f C & N. Price 6*d*. (Communicated.)

[Opie.

(10) An edition of 1775. Pr f C & N. Price 6*d* bd.

Title approx. as for no. (1). *Imprint:* PR F T. CARNAN AND F. NEWBERY, | JUNIOR, NO. 65, IN SPC-Y; | BUT NOT FOR F. NEWBERY AT THE CORNER OF | LUDGATE STREET, WHO HAS NO SHARE IN THE LATE | MR. JOHN NEWBERY'S BOOKS FOR CHILDREN. | 1775. [PRICE SIX PENCE BOUND.]

In 8's. 96 leaves. Pp. vii[xv]+176. *ca.* 61 wcts in text. On the vso of the TP is the diatribe by C & N against FN(N)'s 'paltry Compilations'.

[BM, approx. 9·4×6·6 cm; Welch; McKell; MiDW; NLA.

(11) An edition of 1778. Pr f C & N. Price 6*d* bd.

Title approx. as for no. (1). *Imprint* approx. as for no. (10), with date 1778.

In 8's. 96 leaves. Pp. vii[xv]+176. 61 wcts in text. Diatribe against FN(N) as in no. (10). The wcts are those used in no. (1). White or cream bds, with wct ornamental designs impressed in black.

[Roscoe, 9·5×6·4 cm (imperf.); CUL; DES.

(12) An edition of 1782. Pr f TC. Price 6*d* bd. Welsh 173.

Title approx. as for no. (1). *Imprint:* PR F T. CARNAN, | SUCCESSOR TO MR. J. NEWBERY, | IN SPC-Y. 1782. | [PRICE SIX-PENCE BOUND.]

In 8's. 96 leaves. Pp. 176. 61 wcts in text. White or cream bds, impressed illustrations in black (Fox and Grapes, Fox and Crow).

[Bodley; CUL, 9·7×6·4 cm (imperf.); Bell.

(13) An edition of 1786. Pr f TC. Price 6*d*. Welsh 173.

Title and *imprint* approx. as for no. (12) with date 1786.

In 8's. 96 leaves. Pp. vii[xv]+176. 61 wcts in text. D.f.b.

[BM, 9·4×5·9 cm; SomCL, 9·8×6·5 cm; Welch.

(14) An edition of 1791. Pr f F. Power '(grandson of the late J. Newbery) and Co', 65 SPCY. Price 6*d*. Pink bds, gilt, impressed with 'snow crystals' in black. (Communicated.)

[Opie.

J28. BIBLE. BIBLE IN MINIUTURE, 1780. Pr f EN. Price 1*s* calf, 2*s* morocco.

Of all miniature Bibles this is at the present time the one most easy to come by; it cannot be described as 'rare'. The number of copies printed off must have been immense. Originally appearing in 1780, it was still being listed as for sale in 1800, at the original published price of 1*s*.

There were three issues in respect of the printer's imprint on the last page, two issues of the engraved TP, copies appeared on a heavily ribbed bluish paper, there was an unknown number of re-settings of the type. And the tiny engraved plates were re-worked again and again.

The book was in fact only a new edition (the type re-set) of that put out by J. Harris of Leadenhall St in 1778. EN followed this almost word for word in her edition, with the same number of pages, engravings of the same subjects, and closely similar TP and fly-title at p. 149. J. Harris's edition in its turn followed earlier ones by W. Harris of 70 St Paul's Church Yard in 1771, 1774 and 1775,

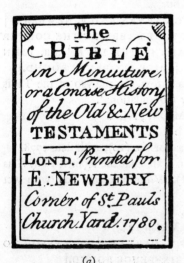
(*a*)

(*b*)

Fig. 7. J28. The title-page, enlarged approximately four times, showing (*a*) the early, and (*b*) the re-engraved states. In (*b*) the first letter 'u' in 'Miniuture' has been altered to 'a'.

56

the text of which followed that used in Wilkin's *Biblia* of 1727/8. Welsh 173; Gum 6251; Spielmann, *Miniature Books* (1961), no. 17 (and references cited there).

See Figure 7 for the original and amended TPs (enlarged about four times).

In 8's. ?64mo. A–[Q8]. 128 leaves+16 insets. Pp. 256. The inset leaves are usually on a rather stouter paper, and comprise engvd TP and fly-title to the New Testament, and 14 engvd plates.

The principal issues and variants:

(1) *Imprint* at foot of p. 256: HEMSTED, PRINTER.

[BM; Roscoe; Osborne*; Adomeit; CLU; Maxwell Hunley, Cat. 48 [winter 1969] item 32.

(2) *Imprint* at foot of p. 256: CROWDER & HEMSTED, | PRINTERS, | WAR-WICK-SQUARE.

[Roscoe; CLU; Adomeit; Rosenberg; Walcott.

(3) No imprint at p. 256.

[BM; Bodley; Roscoe; Bath; Preston; Hannas; Welch; CLU; Edison; NN; Wightman; Adomeit; Ries; Shiers; Gardner; Grant.

(4) In its first state the engvd TP reads MINIUTURE in 3rd line. The re-engraved state reads MINIATURE, a very feeble effort.

[Roscoe (both states); Ries (re-engraved).

(5) Many resettings of type.

(6) Engvd plates reworked, or new plates used, e.g. the plate of Adam and Eve to face p. 25: in most cases there are many apples on the tree, in varying degrees of distinctness; but in one copy (in which also the TP has been reworked to read MINIATURE, see no. (4) above) the tree has been entirely redrawn without any apples.

(7) Copies on bluish paper.

[Roscoe; Adomeit.

Copies vary in size: an average would be about 4·0×2·7 cm. They were issued in plain calf; crimson morocco with gilt tooling and a central onlay in black or dark green, bearing the sacred monogram (the most frequently found); black morocco with gilt tooling and central onlay in crimson with the monogram; green morocco with gilt tooling and crimson central onlay with the monogram.

J29. BIBLE. BIBLE IN MINIATURE, 1786. The copy in Bodley (Arch. Ag 19(3)) used to be recorded in the catalogue as of that date. I am almost sure this is a misreading for 1780. There is a mark over the O in the engvd TP date which might conceivably be an attempt to alter it to 6.

BIBLE. NEW HISTORY OF THE HOLY BIBLE. BY A CLERGY-MAN. See A34(7).

J30. BIBLE. POCKET BIBLE FOR LITTLE MASTERS AND MISSES.

(1) An edition of 1772. Pr f FN(N). Price 6*d*.

Engvd title: See Fig. 8.

32mo in 8's. 74 leaves. Pp. [7]–143. 1st and last leaves paste-downs. Engvd FP and *ca.* 22 wcts in text. D.f.b.

[Weedon, 8·1 × 5·2 cm.

(2) Adv. *LC* 30.12.81–1.1.82, p. 7, as to be had of EN, price 6*d*. Listed in various bks by EN up to 1789, and possibly later. Welsh 173.

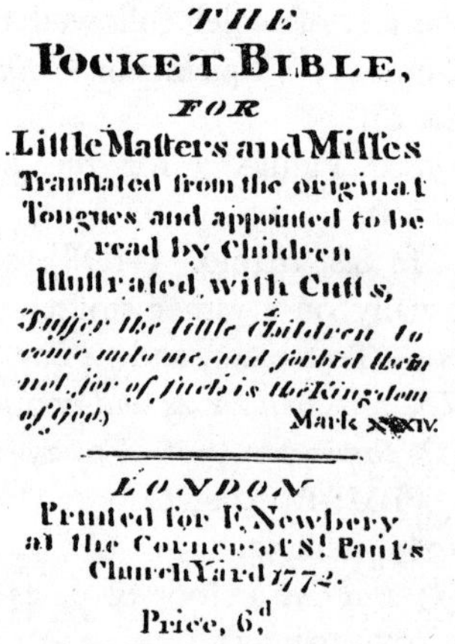

THE

POCKET BIBLE,

FOR

Little Masters and Misses

Translated from the original Tongues, and appointed to be read by Children

Illustrated with Cuts,

Suffer the little Children to come unto me, and forbid them not, for of such is the Kingdom of God)

Mark x.xiv.

LONDON

Printed for E. Newbery at the Corner of S! Paul's Church Yard 1772.

Price, 6.^d

Fig. 8. Title-page of J30(1).

J31. BIBLE. NEW TESTAMENT...ABRIDGED AND HARMONIZED..., 1764. Pr f JN. Price 1*s*. Adv. *LC* 27–9.12.64, p. 623, as being vol. 1 of the *Young Christian's Library* (no. J392A).

THE | NEW TESTAMENT | OF OUR | LORD AND SAVIOUR | JESUS CHRIST, | ABRIDGED AND HARMONIZED IN THE | WORDS OF THE EVANGELISTS, | AND ADORNED WITH CUTS. | FOR THE USE OF CHILDREN. | [5 lines] | LONDON: | PR F J. NEWBERY, AT THE BIBLE | AND SUN IN SPC-Y. | MDCCLXIV.

In 8's. 160 leaves+8 insets. Pp. xv[xvi]+17–311[320]. Engvd FP and 7 engvd plates. Bk-list on last 8 pp. D.f.b.

[BM; St Bride, 9·8 × 6·4 cm; Exeter.

J32. BIBLE. NEW TESTAMENT ADAPTED TO THE CAPACITIES OF CHILDREN: OR, THE FOUR GOSPELS HARMONIZED.

(1) Listed as pr f JN in *Newtonian System*, 1766, price 1*s*.

(2) Listed in *Newtonian System*, 1770, as pr f C & N. Price 1*s*.

This and later lists give the following title: *The New Testament adapted to the Capacities of Children: or, the Four Gospels Harmonized, and adorned with Copper Plate-Cuts. To which is prefixed a Preface, setting forth the Nature and Necessity of the Work.*

(3) Listed in *Newtonian System*, 1787, as pr f TC. Price 1*s*.

J33/4. Entries deleted.

J35. BIBLE. NEW TESTAMENT ADAPTED TO THE CAPACITIES OF CHILDREN. TO WHICH IS ADDED, AN

HISTORICAL ACCOUNT OF THE LIVES...OF THE
APOSTLES...
(1) An edition of 1755. Pr f JN. Price 2s 6d neatly bd in red. Welsh 276; D&M
837; Pressler, p. 1.

THE | NEW TESTAMENT | ADAPTED TO THE | CAPACITIES OF CHILDREN.
| TO WHICH IS ADDED, AN | HISTORICAL ACCOUNT | OF THE | LIVES,
ACTIONS, TRAVELS, SUFFERINGS, | AND DEATH | OF THE | APOSTLES
AND EVANGELISTS. | VIZ. | [parallel columns of 9 and 8 lines] | [4 lines] |
DESIGNED BY THE CELEBRATED RAPHAEL, | AND ENGRAVED BY MR.
WALKER. | [d.p.rule] | LONDON: | PR F J. NEWBERY, AT THE BIBLE AND
SUN IN | SPC-Y. MDCCLV.

In 12's. 150 leaves +8 insets. Pp. xi[xii]+288. Engvd FP sgd 'Walker sculp',
7 leaves of engvd plates 'after Raphael' sgd by Walker.

[BM, 14·5×8·2 cm; V&A(GL); Opie; BFBS; Osborne*; ICU-J.
(2) Listed in *Newtonian System*, 1770, as pr f C & N. Price 2s 6d.

J36. Entry deleted.

BIOGRAPHY FOR GIRLS. See Pilkington, M. (H).

J37. BISSET, James. JUVENILE REDUPLICATIONS, 1800. S b [E]N
et al. *CBEL*, II, 560.

JUVENILE REDUPLICATIONS: | OR, | THE NEW | "HOUSE THAT JACK
BUILT." | A PARODY. | WITH APPROPRIATE CUTS AND EXPLANATORY
NOTES. | BY J. BISSET, | AUTHOR OF | THE ORPHAN BOY; THE FLIGHTS OF
FANCY; | [3 lines] | [1 line quote] | [d.p.rule] | [ENTERED AT STATIONERS
HALL.] | [d.p.rule] | BIRMINGHAM: | PR B GRAFTON & REDDELL, NO. 10,
HIGH-STREET, | FOR THE AUTHOR; | S B NEWBERY, SPC-Y; T. HEPTINSTALL,
| HOLBORN; AND T. HURST, PN R; | LONDON. | [d.p.rule] | 1800.

Pp. iv+[5]–34[36]. Engvd FP sgd 'J.B.' (i.e. James Bisset) and 'F. Eginton
sc'. 12 wcts in text. Pink paper wrappers. (Communicated.)

[Osborne*; Welch; Shiers; NoU; McKell; Bondy, Cat. 70 [1967] item
136.

J38. BISSET, James. ORPHAN BOY, THE. Welsh 280; *CBEL*, II, 560.
(1) An undated edition (before Jan. 1800). Pr f EN. Price 6d (MS note in BM copy).

THE | ORPHAN BOY, | [d.p.rule] | BY J. BISSET. | [d.p.rule] | [1 line quote] |
[p.s.rule] | [ENTERED AT STATIONERS' HALL.] | [d.p.rule] | BIRMINGHAM: |
PR B SWINNEY & HAWKINS; FOR E. NEWBERY, | SPC-Y, | LONDON.

8 unsgd leaves. Pp. 15.
[BM, 12·7×9·0 cm.
(2) Sixth edition, n.d. [1800]. S b EN.

THE ORPHAN BOY A PATHETIC TALE FOUNDED ON FACT BY J. BISSET
SIXTH EDITION BIRMINGHAM S B E. NEWBERY.

Pp. 14[16]. Engvd FP sgd 'I-B Museum Birm.' and 'F. Eginton sc'. Notices of bks by Bisset on pp. [15–16]. (Communicated.) 'I-B' was, it seems, J. Bisset. ⌈Ries.

(3) Ninth edition, n.d. (? *ca.* 1802). S b EN. Described in R. Gilbertson Cat. Autumn 1965, item 181, as THE ORPHAN BOY: A PATHETIC TALE. Birmingham, pr b Grafton & Reddell for the Author. S b EN. Sanguine tinted FP. (Communicated.)

BLIND CHILD, THE. See Pinchard, Mrs E.

J39. BLOSSOMS OF MORALITY, THE. Welsh 175; *CBEL*, II, 558; Weedon 13. Richard Johnson's Day-book records: *1788 Dec. Mr Badcock——— To writing The Blossoms of Morality———£16. 16s.*

(1) First edition, 1789. Pr f EN. Price 2*s* 6*d.*

Engvd TP: THE | BLOSSOMS | OF | MORALITY. | INTENDED FOR THE | AMUSEMENT & INSTRUCTION | OF | YOUNG LADIES & GENTLEMEN. | BY THE EDITOR OF | THE LOOKING-GLASS FOR THE MIND. | [p.s.rule] | [engvd vignette] | [p.s.rule] | LONDON: | PR F E. NEWBERY, THE CORNER OF | SPCY. | MDCCLXXXIX.

In 6's. 108 leaves+2 insets. Pp. 212. Engvd FP and TP. No wcts.

⌈BM, 17·2×10·2 cm; Bell; BmPL; Grant; Sotheby, 5.2.1945 (the Bussell sale), lot 74.

(2) Second edition, 1796. Pr f EN. Price 3*s* 6*d.* Hugo no. 87; ENC, p. 10; NUTP Cat. no. 75.

THE | BLOSSOMS | OF | MORALITY. | INTENDED FOR THE | AMUSEMENT AND INSTRUCTION | OF | YOUNG LADIES AND GENTLEMEN. | BY THE EDITOR OF | THE LOOKING-GLASS FOR THE MIND. | WITH FORTY-SEVEN CUTS, | DESIGNED AND ENGRAVED | BY | I. BEWICK [in white on a wct vignette] | LONDON: | PR F E. NEWBERY, THE CORNER | OF SPC-Y. | MDCCXCVI.

In 6's. 116 leaves. Pp. x+221. 23 wct headpieces, 24 wct tailpieces, the work of John Bewick.

⌈BM; Bodley; CUL; Roscoe, 17·0×9·9 cm; Bell; LI; V&A(GL); NUTP; NoU; Osborne*; NNC-T (Darton Coll.); NLA.

(3) Second edition, 1796, a large paper issue. A copy in LL measures 19·8×11·2 cm in untrimmed state, in marbled bds (possibly the original). A heavy cream-white wove paper, with occasional thin sheets.

⌈LL; Knaster; NorBM.

(4) Third edition, 1801. Pr f EN. Price 2*s* 6*d* (*per* Welsh). Hugo II, no, 4126.

Title approx. as for no. (2). *Imprint:* THE THIRD EDITION. | [d.p.rule] | LONDON: | PR B J. CROWDER, WARWICK-SQUARE; | FOR E. NEWBERY, THE CORNER OF SPC-Y. | [p.s.rule] | 1801.

In 6's. 116 leaves. Pp. x+221. 23 wct headpieces as in no. (2), wct tailpieces as in no. (2) with the omission of that at p. 42.

⌈Bodley, 16·8×9·9 cm; CUL; NorBM, 17·5×10·1 cm; Sotheby, 24.3.72, lot 355;

BmPL; Osborne, Cat. p. 268; Welch; UCLA; Maxwell Hunley, Cat. 48 [winter 1969] item 173.

J40. BOOK OF COMMON PRAYER, THE. AN EXPOSITION OF...PLEASANT AND USEFUL COMPANION TO THE CHURCH OF ENGLAND, A. Forms vol. v of the *Young Christian's Library* (no. J392A).
(1) An edition of 1764. Pr f JN. Price 1*s*.

A PLEASANT AND USEFUL COMPANION TO THE | CHURCH OF ENGLAND: | OR, A | SHORT, PLAIN, AND PRACTICAL | EXPOSITION | OF THE | BOOK OF COMMON-PRAYER. | CONTAINING | [15 lines] | [p.rule] | [3 lines quotes] | [p.rule] | LONDON: PR F J. NEWBERY, AT THE BIBLE | AND SUN, IN SPCY. 1764.

In 8's. 116 leaves+8 insets. Pp. 228[232]. Engvd FP and 7 engvd leaves in text. List of bks pr f JN at pp. [229–31]. List of medicines at pp. [231–2]. D.f.b.; also blue bds, paper back-strip.

[Bodley, 9·7×6·4 cm; St Bride; BCE; Ball; McKell.
(2) Listed as by C & N in 1769–70. Price 1*s*. Welsh 289–90.
(3) Listed as pr f TC in *Newtonian System*, 1787, price 1*s*, under the title *A Plain and Concise Exposition of the Book of Common Prayer; with an Account of the Feasts and Festivals...*

J41. BOREMAN, Thomas. DESCRIPTION OF THREE HUNDRED ANIMALS, A. This work is ascribed to Boreman on the strength of a ms note on the TP to the BM copy of the 1st ed. For a full bibliography see Lisney, pp. 86–110.

Of the figures in the 'Beasts' section (which includes the crocodile, the 'cameleon' and two lizards) about fifty-five derive from Topsell's *Beasts* (1607 and 1658). Of these fifty-five Topsell copied forty-five from Gesner's *Historiae Animalium* (1st ed. 1551–87) and *Icones Animalium* (1553). Gesner again copied the rhinoceros from Dürer's wct, while the ancestors of his ape and camelopardal will be found in Breydenbach's *Peregrinationes* (German ed., Mainz 1488, recto of last leaf). A few of the 'serpents' and 'insects' (these include the two winged dragons) also derive from Gesner via Topsell's *History of Serpents* (1608 and 1658) and Moffett's *Insectorum...Theatrum* (1634 and 1658). The golden eagle is after Gesner. I have not traced the ancestors (if any) of the figures of other birds.

This work was one of Thomas Bewick's earliest readings in natural history ('a wretched composition called the *History of three hundred Animals*'). Speaking both as artist and naturalist he was justified in his condemnation.

(1) Eleventh edition, 1774. Pr f FN(N) et al. Price 2*s* 6*d*. Lisney 137, who reckons it as the 12th ed. But as there were two edd. of the 9th ed. (1762 and 1763, the latter not known to Lisney) it should, strictly, be the 13th.

Title in black and red: A | DESCRIPTION | OF THREE HUNDRED |

And God said, Let us make man in our image, after our
likeneß: and let them have dominion over ỹ fish of the
sea, and over ỹ fowl of ỹ air, and over ỹ cattle, & over
all ỹ earth & over every creeping thing ỹ creeps upon ỹ earth

Fig. 9(a). Frontispiece to J41(3).

ANIMALS, | VIZ. | [left column] BEASTS, | BIRDS, | FISHES, | [right column]
SERPENTS, | AND | INSECTS, | WITH | A PARTICULAR ACCOUNT OF THE
MANNER OF | THEIR CATCHING WHALES IN GREENLAND. | [2 lines] |
ILLUSTRATED WITH COPPER-PLATES, | [3 lines] | [p.rule] | THE ELEVENTH
EDITION, | CAREFULLY CORRECTED AND AMENDED. | [p.rule] | [4 lines
quote] | [d.p.rule] | LONDON: PR F J. AND F. RIVINGTON, HAWES, CLARKE |

A

DESCRIPTION

OF THREE HUNDRED

ANIMALS,

V I Z.

BEASTS,	SERPENTS,
BIRDS,	AND
FISHES,	INSECTS.

W I T H

A particular Account of the Manner of
their Catching *Whales* in GREENLAND.

Extracted from the best AUTHORS, and
adapted to the Use of all Capacities.

Illustrated with COPPER-PLATES,
whereon-is curiously engraven every BEAST,
BIRD, FISH, SERPENT, and INSECT,
described in the whole BOOK.

A NEW EDITION,
CAREFULLY CORRECTED AND AMENDED.

PSALM l. 10, 11.
*For every Beast of the Forest is mine, and the Cattle
upon a thousand Hills. I know all the Fowls of the
Mountains, and the wild Beasts of the Field are mine.*

L O N D O N:
PRINTED FOR J. F. AND C. RIVINGTON, B. LAW,
G. G. J. AND J. ROBINSON, T. CARNAN, R.
BALDWIN, AND E. NEWBERY.

M.DCC.LXXXVI.

Fig. 9(*b*). Title-page of J41(3).

AND COLLINS, T. CASLON, S. CROWDER, B. LAW, | F. NEWBERY, G.
ROBINSON AND H. BALDWIN. | MDCCLXXIV. [PR. 2s. 6d.]

12mo in 6's. 60 leaves+*ca.* 61 insets. Pp. 212. Engvd FP, *ca.* 59 other engvd
leaves and one folding engvd leaf 'The Greenland Whale Fishery'. The 59 engvd
leaves are included in the pagination. List of bks on A2^v.

[BM(NH), 16·6×9·6 cm; Freeman; Sotheby, 13.3.72, lot 170.
(2) 'Twelfth edition' (not mentioned as such by Lisney) adv. t.d.w.p. in *LC*

15–17.12.85, p. 579, as pr f J. F. and C. Rivington, B. Law, T. Carnan, G. G. and J. Robinson, R. Baldwin, J. Bew and E. Newbery. Price 3s. Probably = the ed. of 1786, Lisney 139.

(3) A 'new edition', 1786. Pr f TC, EN et al. Lisney 139, who reckons it as the 14th; should be 15th – see no. (1) above.

Title approx. as for no. (1). *Imprint:* PR F J. F. AND C. RIVINGTON, B. LAW, | G. G. J. AND J. ROBINSON, T. CARNAN, R. | BALDWIN, AND E. NEWBERY. | MDCCLXXXVI. See Figs. 9(*a*) and (*b*).

12mo in 6's. 60 leaves+54 inset engvd leaves. Pp. 213. The inset leaves are paginated in sequence with the text on those sides which bear engvgs; they comprise FP and 53 leaves of figures, some figures on both sides of the leaf, some on one only. ? Folding leaf as in no. (1).

[Bodley; Roscoe, 17·0×9·9 cm; Lisney; Weedon; Osborne, Cat. pp. 197–8; UCLA.

(4) A 'new edition', 1791. Pr f EN, F. Power & Co et al. Price 3s. Lisney, p. 142, who calls it the 17th ed.; should be 18th – see no. (1) above.

Title approx. as for no. (1). *Imprint:* PR F J. F. AND C. RIVINGTON, B. LAW, | G. G. J. AND J. ROBINSON, S. BLADON, R. BALD- | WIN, E. NEWBERY, SCATCHERD AND WHITAKER, | G. AND T. WILKIE, AND F. POWER & CO. | MDCCXCI.

12mo. 60 leaves+*ca.* 6 inset engvd leaves (including the folding leaf) as in no. (1). Pp. 212.

[BM(NH), 17·1×10·3 cm.

J41A. BRAYLEY, E[? dward] W[? edlake]. THE GRAND ALPHABET OF ALPHABETS, 1800. Listed in *Monthly Mag.* June 1800, p. 473, as by EN et al. Price 6d, under the following title:

THE GRAND ALPHABET OF ALPHABETS: BEING AN ENGRAVED SERIES OF RUNNING HAND, EVERY LINE OF WHICH CONTAINS ALL THE LETTERS OF THE ENGLISH LANGUAGE. COMPOSED BY E. W. BRAYLEY.

J42. BREWER, George. LIFE OF ROLLA, THE, 1800. Pr f EN et al. Welsh 301.

THE | LIFE OF ROLLA: | A | PERUVIAN TALE. | WITH MORAL INCULCATIONS FOR YOUTH. | INCLUDING, | A DESCRIPTION OF THE TEMPLE OF THE SUN. | [7 lines] | WITH A FRONTISPIECE, ... | [1 line] | [p.rule] | [1 line quote] | [p.rule] | BY THE AUTHOR OF THE SIAMESE TALES. | [d.p.rule] | TO WHICH ARE ADDED, SIX PERUVIAN FABLES: | [4 lines in 2 parallel columns] | BY THE SAME AUTHOR. | [p.s.rule] | LONDON: PR F E. NEWBERY, CORNER OF | SPC-Y; AND VERNOR | AND HOOD, POULTRY. | 1800.

12mo. 72 leaves+engvd FP sgd 'R. K. Porter del'. Pp. xii+132. Half-title. D.f.b.; also marbled bds.

[UCLA, 13·7×8·5 cm; NNC-T (Darton Coll., Cat. item 28); Osborne*; Bondy, Cat. 73 [1967] item 561.

J43. BREWER, George. SIAMESE TALES. Listed in Palmer's *Letters*, 1797 (J273) as pr f EN, price 2s 6d. Also listed as pr f EN in Trimmer's *Silver Thimble*, 1799 and 1801. There is an ed. of 1796 in BM by Vernor and Hood and Champante and Whitrow. Welsh 306.

J44. BROTHER'S GIFT, THE; OR THE NAUGHTY GIRL REFORMED. Welsh 179.
(1) An edition of 1770, probably the 1st Pr f FN(N). Price 1d.

THE | BROTHER'S GIFT; | OR THE | NAUGHTY GIRL REFORMED. | PUBLISHED FOR | THE ADVANTAGE OF THE RISING GE- | NERATION. | [6 lines quote] | [p.rule] | LONDON: | PR F F. NEWBERY, AT THE CORNER | OF SPC-Y. 1770. | PRICE ONE PENNY.

In 8's. 16 leaves, first and last pastedowns. Pp. 31. Wct FP with 4 lines of verse, 8 wcts in text. D.f. paper wrappers, sewed.

[NorBM, 9·1×6·2 cm.
(2) A 'new edition', 1777. Pr f FN(N). Price 1d. *CBEL*, II, 562.

THE | BROTHER'S GIFT, | OR THE | NAUGHTY GIRL REFORMED. | PUBLISHED FOR | THE ADVANTAGE OF THE RISING | GENERATION. | [7 lines quote] | A NEW EDITION. | LONDON: | PR F F. NEWBERY, AT THE CORNER | OF SPC-Y. 1777. | [PRICE ONE PENNY.]

A single gathering of 16 leaves, sgd [A]–[B8], first and last pastedowns. Pp. 29[31]. 9 wcts. List of bks pr f a s b FN(N) on last 2 pp. Hand-coloured paper wrappers.

[V&A, 9·9×6·4 cm.
(3) A 'new edition', 1781. Pr f EN. Price 1d.

Title approx. as for no. (2). *Imprint:* PR F E. NEWBERY, | AT THE CORNER | OF SPC-Y. 1781. | [PRICE ONE PENNY.]

Pp. 29. Wcts. D.f.b. (Communicated.)

[MWA, 10·5 cm; CtHi.
(4) An edition of 1787. Pr f EN. Pp. 29[31]. Bk-lists on last 2 pp. D.f.b. (Communicated.)

[Platt.
(5) Frequently listed and adv. up to 1800, price 1d.

J44A. BROWNE, Thomas. NEW CLASSICAL DICTIONARY FOR THE USE OF SCHOOLS, 1797. Pr f EN et al. Price 5s in bds. Welsh 179.

A NEW | CLASSICAL DICTIONARY, | FOR THE | USE OF SCHOOLS, | CONTAINING | UNDER ITS DIFFERENT HEADS, | EVERY THING ILLUSTRA- TIVE AND EXPLANATORY | OF THE | MYTHOLOGY, HISTORY, GEOGRAPHY, MANNERS, CUSTOMS, &C | OCCURRING IN THE GREEK AND ROMAN AUTHORS, | [5 lines] | [d.p.rule] | BY THOMAS BROWNE, A.B. | [d.p.rule] | LONDON: | PR F G. G. AND J. ROBINSON, PATERNOSTER ROW; | AND E. NEWBERY, CORNER OF ST. PAUL'S. | [p.rule] | 1797.

In 8's. 231 leaves. Pp. vii (remainder unnumbered). Half-title. Bd sheep. [BM, 12·7×10·3 cm.

J45. BUCHANAN, James. NEW POCKET-BOOK FOR YOUNG GENTLEMEN AND LADIES; OR A SPELLING DICTIONARY OF THE ENGLISH LANGUAGE.
Listed as pr f C & N in *World Displayed*, vol. XVII, 1778. Price 2*s*. There was an ed. of 1757 by R. Baldwin (copy in Bodley); Alston, IV, 674.

J46. BUDGET, THE, 1799. Pr f EN. Price 1*s* 6*d*. Welsh 180.
THE | BUDGET, | OR | MORAL AND ENTERTAINING | FRAGMENTS. | REPRESENTING | THE PUNISHMENT OF VICE, | AND | THE REWARD OF VIRTUE. | [d.p.rule] | LONDON: | PR F E. NEWBERY, THE CORNER OF SP | C-Y, | BY G. WOODFALL, NO. 22, PATERNOSTER ROW. | [p.s.rule] | 1799.
In 6's. 90 leaves+1 inset. Pp. 175. Engvd FP. Marbled bds, green vell. spine with label.
[BM, 13·6×8·4 cm; MH.

J47. BUNYAN, John. THE PILGRIM'S PROGRESS.
(1) Entry deleted.
(2) Pts I, II and III. EN. Price 9*d* [? each]. Hugo, II, 311.
(3) Pts I, II and III. EN. Price 6*d* [? each]. Hugo, II, 310.
(4) Pts I and II. EN. Price 6*d* each. Welsh 180. Listed in S.J.'s *Life of a Fly* (not before 1787).
(5) Listed as pr f EN in *Prince Lee Boo*, 1789.

J48. 'BUNYANO, Don Stephano'. THE PRETTIEST BOOK FOR CHILDREN; BEING THE HISTORY OF THE ENCHANTED CASTLE. Welsh 210. Usually described in bk-lists as the *History of the Enchanted Castle*.
(1) An edition of 1772. FN(N). 12° NBL 598, which incorrectly describes this as 1st ed., there was an ed. of 1770 by J. Coote. Adv. *MC&LA* 10.6.72. Price 6*d*.
(2) Listed in *Cries of London*, 1784, as pr f EN, price 6*d*.
(3) An edition listed in S&W Cat. as by EN, and given the (unreliable) date '(1788)'. Described as 24mo, with rude wood engvgs. D.f.b.
(4) An undated edition by EN. Price 6*d*.
THE | PRETTIEST BOOK | FOR | CHILDREN; | BEING THE | HISTORY | OF THE | ENCHANTED CASTLE; | SITUATED IN ONE OF THE | FORTUNATE ISLES, | AND GOVERNED BY THE | GIANT INSTRUCTION. | WRITTEN FOR THE ENTERTAINMENT OF | LITTLE MASTERS AND MISSES. | BY DON STEPHANO BUNYANO. | UNDER-SECRETARY TO THE AFORESAID GIANT. | [d.p.rule] | LONDON: | PR F E. NEWBERY, AT THE CORNER OF SP | C-Y. | [d.p.rule] | [PRICE SIX-PENCE.]
In 8's. 64 leaves. Pp. 122[128]. Wct FP portrait of Don Stephano Bunyano; 15

wcts in text. List of bks pr f EN on pp. [123–8]. D.f.b. No. 1 in the bk-list at p. [123] is *Holiday Entertainment*. There are d.p.rules on TP immediately preceding the imprint and after 'Church-Yard'. Three lines of text between these rules.

⌈Bodley, 10·7×7·3 cm.

(4A) Another undated edition. Pr f EN. Price 6*d*. *Title* and *imprint* approx. as for no. (4).

In 8's. 64 leaves. Pp. 122[128]. Wct FP and 14 wcts in text. List of bks pr f EN on pp. [123–8]. No rules on TP and the imprint (excluding the price) is of 2 lines. The 1st bk in the list at p. [123] is the *Holiday Spy*. D.f.b.

⌈V&A(GL), 10·1×7·0 cm.

(5) Another undated edition or variant issue by EN. Probably before 1798. No. 1 in the bk-list is *Mrs Lovechild's Golden Present*. (Communicated.)

⌈Ball.

(6) Another undated edition or variant issue by EN, *ca.* 1798. No. 1 in the bk-list is *Holiday Entertainment*. ? = no. (4). (Communicated.)

⌈Photocopy in Welch.

(7) Another undated edition or variant issue by EN. 1799 or before (ms sig. and date 1799). No. 1 in the bk-list is *Holiday Entertainment*. Printer's ornaments differ from those in no. (6). (Communicated.)

⌈Ball.

(8) Copies of editions by EN, undated, in Osborne*, and Bondy, Cat. 79 [1970] item 141. Not seen.

J48A. BUTCHER, Rev. Edmund. MORAL TALES, 1801. S b EN.

MORAL TALES: | DESIGNED | TO AMUSE THE FANCY AND IMPROVE THE HEARTS | OF THE | RISING GENERATION. | [p.s.rule] | BY | THE REV. EDMUND BUTCHER. | [d.p.rule] | [4 lines quote] | [d.p.rule] | TO WHICH IS ADDED, BY A LADY, | THE UNHAPPY FAMILY; | OR, | THE DREADFUL EFFECTS OF VICE. | A TALE. | [p.s.rule] | LONDON: | PR B J. CUNDEE, IVY-LANE, | FOR VERNOR AND HOOD, POULTRY, | AND S B E. NEWBERY, CORNER OF | SPC-Y. | [p.rule] | 1801.

In 6's. 108 leaves. Pp. v+210. Engvd FP. Marbled bds, vell. spine with label. Details taken from the BCE copy.

⌈BCE; Shiers, 13·4×8·8 cm.

J49. CAMPE, Joachim Heinrich. THE NEW ROBINSON CRUSOE. Weedon 70. Richard Johnson's Day-book records: *1790 Mr Badcock——To translating The New Robinson Crusoe——£5. 5s.*

(1) An edition of 1790. Pr f EN. Price 6*d*. NBL 621.

THE NEW | ROBINSON CRUSOE, | DESIGNED FOR THE | AMUSEMENT AND INSTRUCTION | OF THE | YOUTH OF BOTH SEXES. | TRANSLATED FROM THE ORIGINAL GERMAN. | [p.s.rule] | EMBELLISHED WITH CUTS. | [p.s.rule] | LONDON, | PR F E. NEWBERY, AT THE CORNER OF | SPC-Y, 1790. | [PRICE SIX-PENCE.]

16mo. 64 leaves. Pp. 128. Wct FP and 13 wcts in text. D.f.b. (Communicated.)
[McKell (imperf.), 10·7×7·1 cm.
(2) An edition of 1797. Pr f EN. Price 6d. Rothschild 612.
Title and *imprint* approx. as for no. (1) with date 1797. Specification as for no.
(1). (Communicated.)
[McKell, 11·0×7·7 cm.

CANARY BIRD, THE. See Kendall, E. A.

J49A. CATECHISM. Wm Strahan's Ledger for Nov. 1759 records the
printing of 2000 copies of a Catechism of 5 sheets for JN. (J. E. Grey, *The Strahan
Archives*, p. 243.)

J49B. CEBES. THE CIRCUIT OF HUMAN LIFE.
(1) First edition, 1774. Pr f TC. Price 1s.
THE | CIRCUIT OF HUMAN LIFE: | A VISION. | IN WHICH ARE ALLEGO-
RICALLY DESCRIBED, | THE VIRTUES AND VICES. | TAKEN FROM THE
TABLATURE OF CEBES, | A DISCIPLE OF SOCRATES. | FOR THE INSTRUC-
TION OF YOUTH. | LONDON: | PR F T. CARNAN, AT NUMBER 65, | IN SPC-Y.
1774. | [PRICE ONE SHILLING.]
In 6's. 60 leaves. Pp. 115[116]. Engvd FP sgd 'W. Walker sculp'. List of bks
pr f TC on last page.
[BM, 15·0×8·8 cm; Bodley.
(2) Second edition, n.d. Pr f TC. Price 1s. Hugo, II, 320–1 dates 'about 1783'.
(Communicated.)
[Harding.

J50. CERVANTES. DON QUIXOTE, ABRIDGED.
(1A) An edition listed in Chesterfield's *Maxims*, 1777, as THE ADVENTURES OF
DON QUIXOTE, ABRIDGED, ADORNED WITH COPPER-PLATES. Pr f FN(N).
Price 1s.
(1B) An edition of 1778. Pr f FN(N). Price 3s.
THE | LIFE AND EXPLOITS | OF THE | INGENIOUS GENTLEMAN | DON
QUIXOTE, DE LA MANCHA. | WITH THE | HUMOROUS CONCEITS | OF HIS |
FACETIOUS SQUIRE | SANCHO PANCA. | ABRIDGED. | [d.p.rule] | LONDON:
| PR F F. NEWBERY, THE CORNER OF | SPC-Y. | MDCCLXXVIII.
12mo. 138 leaves+6 insets. Pp. xi+263. Engvd FP sgd 'Royce sc', 5 other
engvd leaves by Royce.
[BM, 17·5×10·1 cm; Weedon; Opie; Schiller; Osborne*.
(2) An edition by EN described as ADVENTURES OF DON QUIXOTE ABRIDGED,
price 1s. Listed in Chesterfield's *Maxims*, 1786. Welsh 183.
(3) An edition pr f EN, described as HISTORY OF DON QUIXOTE ABRIDGED,
price 3s. Listed in *Anecdotes of Mary*, 1795 and *Joseph Andrews*, 1799.

CHARACTERS

OF THE

KINGS AND QUEENS

OF

ENGLAND;

SELECTED FROM

THE BEST HISTORIANS.

To which is added,

A TABLE of the Succeſſion of each, from ALFRED to
the preſent Time.

With Heads, by T. BEWICK, Newcaſtle.

LONDON:

Printed for E. NEWBURY, St. Paul's Church-yard;
and VERNOR and HOOD, Birchin Lane, Cornhill.

1795.

Fig. 10. Title-page to J51.

J51. CHARACTERS OF THE KINGS AND QUEENS OF
ENGLAND, 1795. Pr f E. Newbury (*sic*) et al. Price 2*s*. Welsh 185 (*sub nom.*
'Chronicles of the Kings...').

See Fig. 10.

12mo. 108 leaves+1 inset. Pp. viii+204[207]. Engvd FP portrait of George III,
sgd 'Hall sculp'. Wct on TP and 33 wct bust portraits of monarchs in text. List
of bks by Vernor and Hood on last 3 pages. The statement on TP that the 'Heads'
are by T. Bewick cannot be accepted. One hesitates to attribute them to his
brother John, even to his workshop. The bk is a series of extracts from Hume,
Smollett and one or two other historians, lifted bodily from J. Holt's *Characters of
the Kings of England*, Dublin, 1789. It is no more than a boiled-down ed. of that
work, omitting all the voluminous notes and many extracts. The tables of the
Succession of Monarchs at the end follow Holt almost word for word; no
acknowledgement is made. The only original element in the 1795 bk is the
wcts.

[NUTP; Roscoe, 13·3×7·8 cm; A. W. Laywood, Grantham, Cat. 22 [1972] item 250; Osborne, Cat. p. 168.

J52. 'CHATTER, Charly'. THE LILLIPUTIAN AUCTION. Welsh 183.

(1) An edition by TC, adv. *LC* 2–5.1.73, p. 12, price 1*d*, bd and gilt.
(2) An edition of 1777. S b TC. Price 1*d*. *CBEL*, II, 562.

THE | LILLIPUTIAN | AUCTION. | TO WHICH | ALL LITTLE MASTERS AND MISSES | ARE INVITED, BY | CHARLY CHATTER. | WALK IN, | YOUNG GENTLEMEN AND LADIES, | A GOING, A GOING, A GOING. | [p.rule] | [3 lines] | [p.rule] | LONDON: | S B T. CARNAN, IN SP | C-Y. MDCCLXXVII. | [PRICE ONE PENNY.]

A single gathering of 16 leaves, sgd [A]–[B8]. Pp. 31; first and last leaves pastedowns. Wct FP and 7 wcts in text. Buff paper wrappers, with impressed pictorial designs.

[V&A, 9·8×6·4 cm.

(3) An edition of 1783. S b TC. Price 1*d*.

Title and *imprint* approx. as for no. (2), with date MDCCLXXXIII. Specification approx. as for no. (2). Paper wrappers printed in red. (Communicated.)

[MWA.

J53. CHESTERFIELD, Philip Dormer Stanhope, Lord. MAXIMS. S. L.

Gulick, *Chesterfield Bibliography to 1800* (in *Papers of Bibliographical Society of America*, vol. 29, 1935).

(1) An edition of 1774 (perhaps the first). Pr f FN(N). Price 1*s*. Described in *N&Q* by Col. W. F. Prideaux (ser. VII, 1 (1886), p. 503). Gulick no. 114; who knew of no extant copy, made no mention of the *N&Q* article, and dated this edition 1775 in reliance on an advert. in *LC* for 14–16.2.75, where it is described as t.d.w.p.

LORD CHESTERFIELD'S | MAXIMS; | OR, | A NEW PLAN OF EDUCATION, | ON THE PRINCIPLES OF | VIRTUE AND POLITENESS. | IN WHICH IS CONVEYED, | SUCH INSTRUCTION AS CANNOT FAIL TO FORM | THE MAN OF HONOUR, THE MAN OF | VIRTUE, AND THE ACCOMPLISHED | GENTLE-MAN. | BEING | THE SUBSTANCE OF THE EARL OF CHESTERFIELD'S | LETTERS, TO HIS SON, PHILIP STANHOPE, ESQ; | [d.p.rule] | LONDON: | PR F F. NEWBERY, THE CORNER OF S | PC-Y, IN LUDGATE STREET. | MDCCLXXIV.

In 6's. 48 leaves+1 inset. Pp. xii+90[95]. Five-page list of bks pr f FN(N) at end. Engvd FP portrait of Lord Chesterfield sgd 'J June sculp'. D.f.b.

[NorBM, 13·2×8·5 cm; McKell; Ball.

(2) An edition of 1777. Pr f FN(N). Welsh 183; Gulick 115.

LORD CHESTERFIELD'S MAXIMS: | OR, A | NEW PLAN OF EDUCATION, | ON THE PRINCIPLES OF | VIRTUE AND POLITENESS. | IN WHICH | THE EXCEPTIONABLE PARTS OF THAT NOBLE LORD'S | LETTERS TO HIS SON

ARE CAREFULLY REJECTED, AND | SUCH ONLY ARE PRESERVED AS CANNOT FAIL TO FORM | THE MAN OF HONOUR, | THE MAN OF VIRTUE, | AND THE | ACCOMPLISHED GENTLEMAN. | [d.p.rule] | LONDON: PR F F. NEWBERY, THE CORNER OF SP | C-Y, IN LUDGATE-STREET. | 1777.

In 4's (?4°). 56 leaves. Pp. xvii+96. Engvd FP as in no. (1). List of bks pr f FN(N) on last 4 pages. Details taken from the Opie copy.

⌈Opie; NoU; MdBJ; Melbourne.

(3) A 'new edition', 1786. Pr f EN. Gulick 116.

Title approx. as for no. (2), with A NEW EDITION. *Imprint:* PR F E. NEWBERY, THE CORNER OF SP | C-Y. | 1786.

In 6's. 66 leaves+1 inset. Pp. xii+116. Engvd FP portrait as in no. (1). Marbled bds, green vell. spine. List of bks pr f EN on last 2 pages.

⌈BM, 16·4×10·4 cm; Oup; INC.

(4) A 'new edition', 1793. Pr f EN. Price 1s 6d. Not in Gulick.

Title and *imprint* approx. as for no. (3), with date 1793.

In 6's. 66 leaves+1 inset. Pp. 118[120] (error for 130[132], all pages after 48 misnumbered). Engvd portrait FP as in no. (1). List of bks pr f EN on last 2 pages. Marbled bds, green vell. spine.

⌈Bodley, 16·8×10·3 cm; Brimmell, List [summer 1968] item 52.

CHILDREN'S JOURNAL, THE. See Berquin, A., J23.

CHILD'S GRAMMAR. See Fenn, Lady E.

J54. CHILD'S GUIDE TO POLITE LEARNING. ? JN. Welsh 183. Not identified.

CHOICE COLLECTION OF RIDDLES. See 'Puzzlewell, Peter'.

CHOICE EMBLEMS. See Wynne, J. H., J389.

J55. CHOICE SCRAPS. Welsh 183; *CBEL*, II, 564; NBL 141; Weedon 19. Richard Johnson's Day-book records: *1790 Jan. Mr Badcock——To writing Choice Scraps——£10. 10s.*

(1) An undated edition. Pr f E. Newfery (*sic*). Price 1s.

CHOICE SCRAPS, | HISTORICAL AND BIOGRAPHICAL, | CONSISTING OF | PLEASING STORIES | AND | DIVERTING ANECDOTES, | MOST OF THEM SHORT TO PREVENT THEIR BEING | TIRESOME. | COMPREHENDING MUCH USEFUL INFORMATION | AND INNOCENT AMUSEMENT. | FOR | YOUNG MINDS. | [p.s.rule] | EMBELLISHED WITH COPPER-PLATE CUTS. | [p.s.rule] | LONDON: | PR F E. NEWFERY, AT THE CORNER | OF SPC-Y. | [PRICE ONE SHILLING.]

In 6's. 72 leaves+4 insets. Pp. 142[144]. Four engvd leaves. List of bks pr f EN on last 2 pages. D.f.b.

[BM, 11·2×7·6 cm; Osborne, Cat. pp. 166 and 278; Ball.

(2) Another undated edition. Pr f EN. Price 1s.

Title and *imprint* approx. as for no. (1), but 'Newbery' spelt correctly, a p.rule above 'Embellished with...', a d.p. rule below.

In 6's. 90 leaves+5 insets. Pp. 178, 2. Engvd FP and 4 engvd leaves in text. List of bks pr f EN on last 2 pages.

[Bodley, 11·1×6·9 cm; Grant.

(2A) An undated edition. Pr f EN. Price 1s. May be identical with (2), but has no bk-list at end. Not later than 1793 (the MH copy has ms inscription with date 'Saturday Decr. 21 93').

[MH.

(3) An edition of 1801. EN. Romer's list 27, item 14.

J56. CHRISTIAN'S NEW-YEAR'S GIFT, THE. BY A CLERGYMAN OF THE CHURCH OF ENGLAND. (This should probably not have been classed as a Juvenile.)

(1) An edition pr f JN, price 2s. Adv. *LC* 24–7.12.63, p. 613, as 'Monday next w.b.p.'. Welsh 185.

(2) Frequently listed as by C & N between 1769 and 1773. Price 2s.

(3) Listed as s b TC in Goldsmith's *History of England*, 1786, vol. 2 (no. J147(9)). Price 2s.

CHRISTMAS AMUSEMENT. See 'Puzzlebrains, Peregrine'.

CHRONICLE OF THE KINGS OF ENGLAND. See Dodsley, Robt.

CHRONOLOGICAL ABRIDGMENT OF THE LIFE...OF HENRY IV OF FRANCE. See J158.

J57. CHRONOLOGICAL TABLES OF ENGLISH HISTORY FOR THE INSTRUCTION OF YOUTH. Listed in Mavor's *Juvenile Olio*, 1796, as to be had of EN, price 4s 6d on a sheet, or neatly dissected in a mahogany box 10s 6d. This could be either a sheet game or a dissected puzzle. Sets in the Hannas collection are dated 1788, published by John Wallis, sold by John Binns, Leeds and Lewis Bull, Bath; and 1799, published by Wallis alone.

J58. CHRONOLOGICAL TABLES OF ROMAN HISTORY FROM THE FOUNDATION OF THE CITY TO THE AUGUSTAN AGE. Listing and prices as for no. J57. A sheet game or dissected puzzle. A set in the Hannas collection was published 20 October 1789 by Wallis and EN.

J59. CHRONOLOGICAL TABLES OF THE HISTORY OF FRANCE, FROM PHARAMOND, FIRST KING, TO LOUIS XVI.

A sheet game or dissected puzzle. Listing and prices as for no. J57. EN may not have been concerned with the publication of this.

CHRONOLOGY MADE FAMILIAR. See J62.

CHURCH OF ENGLAND. See J40.

J60. CIRCLE OF THE SCIENCES, THE. Welsh 186–92; Thwaite, pp. 160–3.

The *Penny London Post* for 14–16 January 1745 announced that *The Circle* was 'in the Press and speedily will be published'. 'This work', it said, 'is in great Forwardness, and for the Sake of those who can't afford to lay out much Money at a Time will be published in little Volumes, bound, at Six-pence, each'.

An advertisement in the twenty-third issue of *Mercurius Latinus* (16 August 1746) reported that seven volumes of *The Circle*, issued under royal privilege and licence dated 8 December 1744, had by then been published; and that a further six subjects 'are in the Press, and will be publish'd with all expedition'. See Figures 11 and 12. Those already published were:

Vol. I. EASY AND ENTERTAINING SPELLING BOOK. No copy seen.

Vol. II. COMPENDIOUS GRAMMAR OF THE ENGLISH TONGUE. 1st edition 1745 under the title EASY INTRODUCTION TO THE ENGLISH LANGUAGE; OR A COMPENDIOUS GRAMMAR... Continued in later editions as GRAMMAR MADE FAMILIAR, the first volume in the series.

Vol. III. [EASY] SPELLING DICTIONARY, ON A NEW PLAN. 1st edition 1745. Removed from *The Circle* and continued as an independent publication (nos. J268 (1ff)).

Vol. IV. THE ART OF WRITING. 1st edition 1746, 2nd 1748; apparently no further editions, though listed in *Tom Thumb's Folio*, 1768.

Vol. V. THE ART OF ARITHMETIC. 1st edition 1746. Continued in later editions as ARITHMETIC MADE FAMILIAR, vol. II of the series.

Vol. VI. THE ART OF RHETORICK. 1st edition 1746. Continued thereafter as RHETORICK MADE FAMILIAR, vol. III of the series.

Vol. VII. THE ART OF POETRY. 1st edition 1746. Continued thereafter as POETRY MADE FAMILIAR, vol. IV of the series.

Those 'to be publish'd with all expedition' were:

ART OF LOGIC. 1st edition 1748, under the title LOGIC MADE FAMILIAR, vol. V of the series.

CRITICISM. Not traced.

GEOGRAPHY. 1st edition 1748, vol. VI of the series.

CHRONOLOGY. 1st edition 1748, vol. VII of the series.

HISTORY. Not traced.

PHILOSOPHY. Not traced.

Whether the volumes on Criticism, History and Philosophy were ever published I cannot say for certain – most probably not: I have found no trace of them in advertisements or bk-lists. And the statement that they were 'in the Press' need not be taken seriously; frequently the expression meant no more than that a work was under consideration as a possibility.

In 1776 C & N were to produce the two composite volumes in the series: *Grammar and Rhetoric* and *Logic, Ontology and the Art of Poetry*.

Several other works put out by JN were described in advertisements, or in their titles, as being 'introductory' parts of *The Circle*. Seemingly this was by way of puff, in the usual Newbery manner. When listed or advertised these books appear quite separate from, and in no way connected with, *The Circle*. They are: *The Infant Tutor...designed as an introductory Part to The Circle...* (1753 or before – no. J186), *Alphabet Royal, ou Guide Commode...pour servir d'Introduction au Cercle...* (no. J9(1)), the single sheet *Royal Battledore; being the first Introductory Part of the Circle...* (n.d. – no. J21(3A and 4)), the second (1748) edition of the *Art of Writing* (no. J72(2)) and later editions of the *Spelling Dictionary* (no. J268).

The seven volumes which finally constituted *The Circle* – Arithmetic, Chronology, Geography, Grammar, Logic, Poetry, Rhetorick – were not usually republished *en bloc*, but, it seems, as and when new supplies of a particular volume were called for. Thus, e.g. *Arithmetic* appeared in 1746, 1748, 1769, 1777 and 1788, *Grammar* in 1745, 1748, 1755, 1769, 1776 and 1787, *Logic* in 1748, 1755, 1769, 1777 and 1789. And there was revision in the titles of individual volumes, some volumes were dropped and others added.

Note on prices and bindings. The seven orthodox volumes were to be had as a set for 7s, individual ones at 1s, except *Grammar* which cost only 6d, the same for the *Spelling Book* of 1745–6, and 1s 6d for the *Geography*. In 1755 *The Circle* was being advertised at 7s, 'neatly bound in red'. I have not seen this binding. Original bindings seen are noted below.

J61. CIRCLE OF THE SCIENCES. ARITHMETIC.

(1) See Fig. 11(*a*).

  In 8's. 105 leaves. Pp. 200.

  [BM, 9·6×6·0 cm.

(2) See Fig. 11(*b*).

  In 8's. 105 leaves. Pp. 200.

  [BM, 9·7×5·7 cm; Oup; MPL; Renier; BCE; MNS; NNC-Pl; ICU-J.

(3) See Fig. 11(*c*).

  In 8's. 106 leaves. Pp. 200[202]. List of bks pr f N & C on last leaf. Green vell. spine, blue bds.

  [BM, 9·9×6·4 cm; BCE; Pollard; Welch; McKell; Sotheby, 13.3.72, lot 127.

(4) Fourth edition, 1777. Pr f C & N.

  In 8's. 104 leaves. Pp. vi+198. Blue bds, green vell. spine, with label; also marbled bds.

  [BM, 10·0×6·3 cm; Welch; NNC-Pl; McKell; NSWPL; UCLA.

(5) Fifth edition, 1788. Pr f TC.

  In 8's. 104 leaves. Pp. 198. Blue bds, green vell. spine.

  [BM, 10·3×6·3 cm; LUL; Whitelands; UCLA.

THE
A R T
OF
ARITHMETICK
M A D E
Familiar and eaſy to every
Capacity.
Being the
FIFTH VOLUME
OF THE
Circle of the *Sciences*, &c.

By the KING's *Authority*.

LONDON:
Printed for J. NEWBERY, at the *Bible*
and *Sun*, in St. *Paul*'s Church-Yard.
MDCCXLVI.

(*a*)

Arithmetic
Made familiar and eaſy to
Young *Gentlemen* and *Ladies*.
Being the
SECOND VOLUME.
OF THE
Circle of the *Sciences*, &c.

Publiſhed by the KING's *Authority*.

The SECOND EDITION.

LONDON:
Printed for J. NEWBERY, at the *Bible*
and *Sun*, in St. *Paul*'s Church-Yard.
MDCCXLVIII.

(*b*)

ARITHMETIC
Made familiar and eaſy to
Young *Gentlemen* and *Ladies*.
Being the
SECOND VOLUME
OF THE
Circle of the Sciences, *&c.*

Publiſhed by the KING's *Authority*.

The THIRD EDITION.

LONDON:
Printed for NEWBERY and CARNAN,
No. 65, the North Side of St. Paul's
Church-yard.
MDCCLXIX.

(*c*)

Fig. 11. Title-pages of the first three editions of J61.

J62. CIRCLE OF THE SCIENCES. CHRONOLOGY.
(1) First edition, 1748. Pr f JN.

CHRONOLOGY | MADE FAMILIAR AND EASY TO | YOUNG GENTLEMEN
AND LADIES. | TO WHICH IS ADDED, | A TABLE OF THE MOST MEMO- |
RABLE EVENTS FROM THE BE- | GINNING OF THE WORLD TO THE | YEAR
1747. | BEING THE | SEVENTH VOLUME | OF THE | CIRCLE OF THE SCIENCES,
&C. | [p.rule] | PUBLISHED BY THE KING'S AUTHORITY. | [p.rule] | LONDON:
| PR F J. NEWBERY, AT THE BIBLE | AND SUN, IN SPC-Y. | MDCCXLVIII.

In 8's. 145 leaves. Pp. xvi+272.

[BM, 9·7×5·8 cm; Oup; Roscoe; CUL; Osborne, Cat. p. 132; NNC-Pl.
(2) Second edition. Adv. *GA* 14.4.48 as s b JN, R. Baldwin and W. Owen, and
3.1.49 as s b JN and R. Baldwin.
(3) Third edition, 1770. Pr f N & C.

In 8's. 144 leaves. Pp. xvi+272. Blue bds, green vell. spine with label.

[BM, 9·7×6·3 cm; Bodley; LUL; BmPL; Osborne, Cat. pp. 132–3; Pollard;
NNC-T (Darton Coll.); McKell; Sotheby, 19.4.71, lot 117.
(4) Fourth edition, 1778. Pr f C & N.

In 8's. 144 leaves. Pp. xvi+272. Marbled bds, green vell. spine with label.

[BM, 9·9×6·2 cm; Weedon; Whitelands; Welch; McKell; UCLA.
(5) Fifth edition not traced.

J63. CIRCLE OF THE SCIENCES. GEOGRAPHY.
(1) First edition, 1748. Pr f JN.

GEOGRAPHY | MADE FAMILIAR AND EASY TO | YOUNG GENTLEMEN
AND LADIES. | BEING THE | SIXTH VOLUME | OF THE | CIRCLE OF THE
SCIENCES, &C. | [p.rule] | PUBLISHED BY THE KING'S AUTHORITY. | [p.rule]
| LONDON: | PR F J. NEWBERY, AT THE BIBLE | AND SUN, IN SPC-Y. |
MDCCXLVIII.

In 8's. 170 leaves+inset engvd folding map by E. Bowen. Pp. xv+319.

[BM (imperf.); Oup, 10·0×5·9 cm; BmPL; LEI; Renier; ICU-J; Sotheby,
19.4.71, lot 119.
(2) Second edition, 1748. Pr f JN. Adv. *GA* 14.4.48 and 3.1.49.

[? MNS; ? NNC-Pl.
(3) Third edition, 1769. Pr f N & C.

In 8's. 174 leaves. ? a map. Pp. 319[328]. List of bks pr f N & C on last 9 pages.
Blue bds, green vell. spine with label.

[BM, 9·8×6·3 cm; LUL; Weedon; BCE; Pollard; Osborne, Cat. p. 133;
ICU-J.
(4) Fourth edition, 1776. Pr f C & N.

In 8's. 176 leaves. ? a map. Pp. 319[332]. List of bks pr f C & N on last 13 pages.
Blue bds, green vell. spine with label.

[BM, 10·0×6·5 cm; Bell; MPL; McKell; Sotheby, 16.3.70, lot 47.
(5) Fifth edition, 1783. Pr f TC. Welsh 190 records another 5th ed. of 1793
by Darton and Harvey.

In 8's. 176 leaves. Pp. 319[332]. List of bks pr f TC on last 13 pages. Marbled bds.

⌈Whitelands, 9·8×6·7 cm; Welch; UCLA.

CIRCLE OF THE SCIENCES. EASY INTRODUCTION TO THE ENGLISH LANGUAGE. See J64(1).

J64. CIRCLE OF THE SCIENCES. GRAMMAR. *CBEL*, II, 931 listed as written by JN.

(1) First edition, 1745. Pr f JN. Alston, I, 91.

AN EASY | INTRODUCTION | TO THE | ENGLISH LANGUAGE; | OR, A COMPENDIOUS | GRAMMAR | FOR THE USE OF | YOUNG GENTLEMEN, LADIES, | AND FOREIGNERS. | BEING THE | SECOND VOLUME | OF THE | CIRCLE OF THE SCIENCES, &C. | [p.rule] | BY THE KING'S AUTHORITY. | [p.rule] | LONDON: | PR F J. NEWBERY, AT THE BIBLE | AND SUN, IN SPC-Y. | MDCCXLV.

In 8's. 82 leaves. Pp. xvi+144. *GEP* for 26–9.10.45 adv. both *An Easy Introduction to the English Language* and an *English Grammar*, as separate works. Probably a compositor's error, but the *Grammar* might have been the *Easy and Entertaining Spelling Book* (no. J70).

⌈BM, 9·5×6·0 cm.

(2) Second edition, 1748. Pr f JN. Alston, I, 92.

Title and *imprint* approx. as for no. (3).

In 8's. 82 leaves. Pp. xvi+144.

⌈BM, 9·7×5·8 cm; MPL; MH; ICU.

(3) Third edition, 1755. Pr f JN. Alston, I, 94.

GRAMMAR | MADE FAMILIAR AND EASY TO | YOUNG GENTLEMEN, LADIES, | AND FOREIGNERS. | BEING THE | FIRST VOLUME | OF THE | CIRCLE OF THE SCIENCES. | [p.rule] | PUBLISHED BY THE KING'S AUTHORITY. | [p.rule] | THE THIRD EDITION. | [p.rule] | LONDON: | PR F J. NEWBERY, AT THE BIBLE | AND SUN, IN SPC-Y. | MDCCLV.

In 8's. 82 leaves. Pp. xv+144.

⌈Oup, 9·9×5·9 cm; LUL; Renier; DLC; Welch; MNS; Sotheby, 19.4.71, lot 120.

(4) Third edition, with additions, 1769. Pr f N & C. Alston, I, 95.

In 8's. 88 leaves. Pp. xvi+152. Last 3 leaves blanks, last a pastedown. Blue bds, green vell. spine with label.

⌈BM, 9·7×6·5 cm; LUL; Weedon; BCE; Pollard; Welch; McKell; Madison; Osborne, Cat. p. 133; Grant.

(5) Fourth edition, 1776. Pr f C & N. Alston, I, 98.

In 8's. 88 leaves. Pp. xvi+152[156]. List of bks pr f C & N on last 4 pages. Marbled bds, vell. spine with label; also blue bds, green vell. spine with label.

⌈BM, 9·9×6·6 cm; Roscoe; Renier; MH; CLU.

(6) Fifth edition, 1787. Pr f TC. Alston, I, 99; Gum 2790.

In 8's. 96 leaves. Pp. xvi+152[172]. List of bks s b TC on pp. [153–72]. Marbled bds, green vell. spine.

[Whitelands, 9·9×6·4 cm; Osborne*; Welch; UCLA.

J65. CIRCLE OF THE SCIENCES. GRAMMAR AND RHETORICK, 1776. Pr f C & N. Price 3s in the vell. manner. *CBEL*, II, 232 and 931; Alston, I, 97.

GRAMMAR | AND | RHETORICK, | BEING THE FIRST AND THIRD VOLUMES | OF THE | CIRCLE OF THE SCIENCES. | CONSIDERABLY EN-LARGED, AND GREATLY IMPROVED. | [d.p.rule] | LONDON, | PR F T. CARNAN AND F. NEWBERY, JUN. AT | NUMBER 65, IN SPCY. | MDCCLXXVI.

In 6's. 116 leaves. Pp. vi+221[222]. Half-title. List of bks pr f C & N on last page.

[BM, 17·6×10·1 cm; NLSc; Weedon; NNC; ICU; BRW; Sotheby, 5.2.68, lot 19.

J66. CIRCLE OF THE SCIENCES. LOGIC.

(1) First edition, 1748. Pr f JN. Alston, VII, 225.

LOGIC | MADE FAMILIAR AND EASY TO | YOUNG GENTLEMEN AND LADIES. | TO WHICH IS ADDED, A | COMPENDIOUS SYSTEM | OF | META-PHYSICS, | OR | ONTOLOGY. | BEING THE | FIFTH VOLUME | OF THE | CIRCLE OF THE SCIENCES, &c. | [p.rule] | PUBLISHED BY THE KING'S AUTHORITY. | [p.rule] | LONDON: | PR F J. NEWBERY, AT THE BIBLE | AND SUN, IN SPC-Y. | MDCCXLVIII.

In 8's. 153 leaves. Pp. xxxix+264.

[BM, 9·9×5·9 cm; MPL; NNC-T (Darton Coll.); ICU-J.

(2) Second edition, 1755. Pr f JN. Alston, VII, 226.

In 8's. 152 leaves. Pp. xxxviii+264.

[Oup, 9·9×6·0 cm; Osborne, Cat. p. 133; Renier; MNS.

(3) Third edition, 1769. Pr f N & C. Alston, VII, 227.

In 8's. 152 leaves. Pp. 264. Blue bds, green vell. spine with label.

[BM, 9·8×6·2 cm; LUL; Weedon; HeCL; BCE; Pollard; Welch; McKell; NNC-T (Darton Coll.); Osborne, Cat. p. 133.

(4) Fourth edition, 1777. Pr f C & N. Alston, VII, 230.

In 8's. 152 leaves. Pp. xl+264. Blue bds, green vell. spine with label; and marbled bds.

[BM, 10·0×6·5 cm; CUL; Whitelands; Welch; McKell; UCLA.

(5) Fifth edition, 1789. 'Pr f Francis Power & Co. Grandson to the late Mr J. Newbery', No. 65, SPC-Y. Alston, VII, 231.

In 8's. 152 leaves. Pp. xl+264. Marbled bds, green vell. spine with label. Details taken from the Brimmell copy.

[Brimmell; UCLA.

J67. CIRCLE OF THE SCIENCES. LOGIC, ONTOLOGY, AND THE ART OF POETRY, 1776. Pr f C & N. Price 5s in the vell. manner. *CBEL*, II, 232; Welsh 190; Alston, VII, 229.

LOGIC, ONTOLOGY, | AND THE | ART OF POETRY; | BEING THE | FOURTH AND FIFTH VOLUMES | OF THE | CIRCLE OF THE SCIENCES. | CONSIDERABLY ENLARGED, AND GREATLY IMPROVED. | [d.p.rule] | LONDON, | PR F T. CARNAN, AND F. NEWBERY, JUNIOR, AT | NUMBER 65, IN SPCY. | MDCCLXXVI.

12mo. 246 leaves. Pp. xii+473[480]. List of bks 'Pr f a s b J. Newbery' (*sic*) on last 7 pages. (JN had died in 1767.)

[BM, 17·9×10·2 cm; CUL; Schiller.

J68. CIRCLE OF THE SCIENCES. POETRY. (Ascribed to JN as author.)

(1) See Fig. 12(*a*). *CBEL*, II, 27.
In 8's. 114 leaves. Pp. [7]–224.
[BM, 9·4×6·1 cm.

(2) See Fig. 12(*b*). *CBEL*, II, 27.
In 8's. 114 leaves. Pp. [7]–224.
[BM, 9·6×5·8 cm; Oup; MPL; Renier; NNC-T (Darton Coll.); MNS; ICU-J.

(3) See Fig. 12(*c*). *CBEL*, II, 27.
In 8's. 114 leaves. Pp. vi+7–224. Blue bds, green vell. spine with label.
[BM, 9·9×6·5 cm; LUL; Pollard; BCE; Osborne, Cat. pp. 133–4; Melbourne; McKell; UCLA.

(4) Fourth edition, 1776. Pr f C & N. *CBEL*, II, 231; Alston, VI, 572.
In 8's. 144 leaves. Pp. vi+7–281[284]. List of bks s b C & N on last 3 pages. Blue bds, green vell. spine with label.
[BM, 10·0×6·5 cm; Weedon; Welch; MH; McKell; UCLA.

(5) Fifth edition, 1788. Pr f TC. Gum 4590.
In 8's. 144 leaves. Pp. vi+7–281[284]. List of bks s b TC on last 3 pages. Marbled bds, green vell. spine.
[Whitelands, 9·6×8·4 cm; Opie; Suffolk; UCLA.

J69. CIRCLE OF THE SCIENCES. RHETORICK.

(1) First edition, 1746. Pr f JN. Alston, VI, 182.
THE | ART | OF | RHETORICK | LAID DOWN IN | AN EASY ENTERTAINING MANNER. | [5 lines] | BEING THE | SIXTH VOLUME | OF THE | CIRCLE OF THE SCIENCES &c. | [p.rule] | BY THE KING'S AUTHORITY. | [p.rule] | LONDON: PR F J. NEWBERY, | AT THE BIBLE AND SUN, IN SP | C-Y. MDCCXLVI.

In 8's. 143 leaves. Pp. 276.
[BM, 9·6×5·9 cm.

(2) Second edition, 1748. Pr f JN. Alston, VI, 183.
RHETORIC | MADE FAMILIAR AND EASY TO | YOUNG GENTLEMEN AND

THE

A R T

OF

P O E T R Y

Made eafy,

A N D

Embellifh'd with great Variety
of the moft fhining *Epigrams*,
Epitaphs, Songs, Odes, Paftorals,
&c. from the beft Authors.

Being the

SEVENTH VOLUME

OF THE

Circle of the *Sciences*, &c.

―――――――――――――

By the K I N G's *Authority.*

L O N D O N:

Printed for J. NEWBERY, at the *Bible*
and *Sun*, in St. *Paul's* Church-Yard.

MDCCXLVI.

(*a*)

𝕻𝖔𝖊𝖙𝖗𝖞

Made familiar and eafy to

'Young *Gentlemen* and *Ladies*,

A N D

Embellifh'd with a great Variety of the moft fhining *Epigrams*,
Epitaphs, Songs, Odes, Paftorals,
&c. from the beft Authors.

Being the

FOURTH VOLUME

OF THE

Circle of the *Sciences*, &c.

―――――――――――――

Publifhed by the K I N G's *Authority.*

THE SECOND EDITION.

L O N D O N:

Printed for J. NEWBERY, at the *Bible*
and *Sun*, in St. *Paul's* Church-Yard.

MDCCXLVIII.

(*b*)

P O E T R Y

Made familiar and eafy to

Young Gentlemen and Ladies,

A N D

Embellifhed with a great Variety of the moft
fhining EPIGRAMS, EPITAPHS, SONGS,
ODES, PASTORALS, &c. from the beft
Authors.

Being the

FOURTH VOLUME

OF THE

CIRCLE of the SCIENCES.

―――――――――――――

Publifhed by the KING's *Authority.*

THE THIRD EDITION.

L O N D O N,

Printed for NEWBERY and CARNAN,
No. 65, the North Side of St. *Paul's*
Church-Yard.

MDCCLXIX.

(*c*)

Fig. 12. Title-pages of the first three editions of J68.

LADIES, | [5 lines] | BEING THE | THIRD VOLUME | OF THE | CIRCLE OF THE SCIENCES, &c. | [p.rule] | PUBLISHED BY THE KING'S AUTHORITY. | [p.rule] | THE SECOND EDITION. | [p.rule] | LONDON: | PR F J. NEWBERY, AT THE BIBLE | AND SUN, IN SPC-Y. | MDCCXLVIII.

In 8's. 143 leaves. Pp. 276. Wct tailpiece on vso of last leaf is 4 small ornaments forming a square.

[BM, 9·8×5·9 cm; MPL; MNS (imperf.); UCLA; Sotheby, 5.2.68, lot 35; Bondy, Cat. 77 [1969] item 174.

(3) Second edition, 1748, a variant issue. Alston, VI, 183. The type of quire S has been reset, with a tailpiece on vso of last leaf showing a human face within a circular frame, a cornucopia on either side. Which is the earlier issue is not apparent.

[BM, 9·7×6·2 cm; CUL; Oup; Osborne, Cat. p. 134; ICU-J.

(4) Third edition, 1769. Pr f N & C. Alston, VI, 185.

In 8's. Pp. x+11–286[288]. List of bks pr f N & C on last leaf. Blue bds, green vell. spine with label.

[BM, 9·9×6·4 cm; Pollard; Melbourne; McKell; NNC-T (Darton Coll.); Sotheby, 19.4.71, lot 203.

(5) Fourth edition, 1777. Pr f C & N. Alston, VI, 187.

In 8's. 144 leaves. Pp. x+11–280[282]. List of bks pr f C & N on last 2 pages. Blue bds, green vell. spine with label; also marbled bds.

[BM, 9·9×6·1 cm; Welch; McKell; UCLA.

(6) Fifth edition, 1789. Pr f TC. Alston, VI, 188.

In 8's. 144 leaves. Pp. x+11–286[288]. List of bks pr f TC on last 2 pages. Marbled bds.

[Whitelands, 9·6×6·5 cm; Welch; UCLA.

J70. CIRCLE OF THE SCIENCES. SPELLING BOOK. AN EASY AND ENTERTAINING SPELLING BOOK was adv. *Mercurius Latinus* 16.8.46 as 'now [i.e. "already"] publish'd', being vol. I of *The Circle*. Price 6*d*. No copy located; and there is no trace of a 2nd ed., but the book was adv. in *GA* for 14.4.48, as one of the 'Introductory Parts' to *The Circle*. This work is not to be confused with the *Easy Spelling Dictionary*, vol. III in the series, also adv. as then issued in *Mercurius Latinus* (see General Note in J60).

J71. CIRCLE OF THE SCIENCES. EASY SPELLING DICTIONARY. First edition, 1745. Pr f JN. Price 1*s*. Described as the third volume of *The Circle*, but afterwards discontinued as part of the series and became an independent publication under the title *A Spelling Dictionary of the English Language on a New Plan*, and described in the TP as an 'Introductory Part' to *The Circle*. See nos. J268(1ff.). Alston, IV, 561.

AN EASY | SPELLING-DICTIONARY | OF THE | ENGLISH LANGUAGE, | ON A NEW PLAN; | FOR THE USE OF | YOUNG GENTLEMEN, LADIES, | AND FOREIGNERS. | BEING THE | THIRD VOLUME | OF THE | CIRCLE OF THE

SCIENCES, &c. | [p.rule] | BY THE KING'S AUTHORITY. | [p.rule] | LONDON: PR F J. NEWBERY, AT THE BIBLE | AND SUN, IN SPC-Y. | MDCCXLV.

In 8's or 8°. 142 leaves, first 2 and last 2 blanks. No pagination. (Communicated.) [PHC, 9·6×6·1 cm, heavily cropped; BM (photocopy); UCLA.

J72. CIRCLE OF THE SCIENCES. WRITING.
(1) First edition, 1746. Pr f JN. Price 1s.

THE | ART OF WRITING, | ILLUSTRATED WITH | COPPER-PLATES: | TO WHICH IS ADDED, | A | COLLECTION | OF | LETTERS, AND DIRECTIONS | FOR | ADDRESSING PERSONS OF DISTINCTION | EITHER IN WRITING OR DISCOURSE. | BEING THE | FOURTH VOLUME | OF THE | CIRCLE OF THE SCIENCES, &c. | [p.rule] | BY THE KING'S AUTHORITY. | [p.rule] | LONDON: | PR F J. NEWBERY, AT THE BIBLE | AND SUN, IN SPC-Y. | MDCCXLVI.

In 8's. 66 leaves+8 insets. Pp. 130. The 8 inset engvd leaves of lettering follow C8.

[BM, 9·4×6·0 cm.

(2) Second edition, 1748. Pr f JN. Though called 'the second edition' in the TP it was no longer treated as part of *The Circle* proper, being now classed among the 'Introductory' vols.

THE | ART OF WRITING, | ILLUSTRATED [as in no. (1) down to] DIS-COURSE. | BEING AN | INTRODUCTORY PART | OF THE | CIRCLE OF THE SCIENCES, &c. | [p.rule] | PUBLISHED BY THE KING'S AUTHORITY. [p.rule] | THE SECOND EDITION. | [p.rule] | [Imprint as for (1) with date MDCCXLVIII.]

In 8's. 66 leaves+8 insets as in no. (1), inserted following A8. Pp. 130. Blue bds, green vell. spine (probably a rebound copy, in or after 1768).

[BM, 9·7×6·3 cm; CUL.

(3) Listed in *Tom Thumb's Folio*, 1768, price 1s. But no copy later than (2) traced.

CIRCUIT OF HUMAN LIFE. See Cebes.

COLLECTION OF JESTS AND MAXIMS. See J358(1).

J72A. COLLECTION OF LETTERS FROM EMINENT AUTHORS. Pr f C & N. Adv. *LC* 11–14.4.72, p. 359. Price 1s. Presumably an ed. of Newbery's *Letters* (J266).

J73. COLLECTION OF PIECES IN PROSE AND VERSE. Pr f C & N. Listed in J219(6). Not identified.

J74. COLLECTION OF PRETTY POEMS FOR THE AMUSEMENT OF CHILDREN SIX FOOT HIGH. Welsh 294–5.
(1) An edition of 1757. Pr f the Booksellers of Europe...[i.e. JN]. Price 1s bd. *PA* for 26.11.56 announced that the work was in the press and that 'two hundred thousand are printed for the present'. Welsh 294–5.

Frontispiece.

Vim Viron
Last Week
Private Letters
Pound Rates

Nor Weath nor Honours this great Child regards
But Whimpers Still for Horse's, Cocks & Cards.

A
COLLECTION
O F
PRETTY POEMS
For the Amusement of
CHILDREN Six Foot High.

INTERSPERSED

With a Series of LETTERS
·FROM·
Cousin Sam· to Cousin Sue,

On the Subjects of
CRITICISM, POETRY, and POLITICS.

With Notes *Variorum.*

Calculated with a Design to do Good.

Adorned with Variety of Copper-Plate Cuts, designed and engraved by the best Masters.

Virginibus Puerisque canto.	Hor.
Vice, if it e'er can be abash'd, Must be, or *ridicul'd,* or *lash'd.*	Swift.

L O N D O N:
Printed for the Booksellers of *Europe, Asia, Africa* and
America; and sold at the *Bible* and *Sun* in *St. Paul's
Church-Yard.* [Price 1s. bound.]

Fig. 13. Frontispiece and title-page of J74(3).

A | COLLECTION | OF | PRETTY POEMS | FOR THE AMUSEMENT OF |
CHILDREN SIX FOOT HIGH. | INTERSPERSED | WITH A SERIES OF LETTERS
| FROM | COUSIN SAM TO COUSIN SUE, | ON THE SUBJECTS OF | CRITICISM,
POETRY AND POLITICS. | WITH NOTES VARIORUM. | [3 lines] | [p.rule] | [3
lines quotes] | [p.rule] | LONDON: | PR F THE BOOKSELLERS OF EUROPE,
ASIA, AFRICA AND | AMERICA; AND SOLD AT THE BIBLE AND SUN IN SP |
C-Y, 1757. PRICE 1s. BOUND.

Pp. x[xii]+144. Engvd FP and 8 other engvd leaves. D.f.b. (Communicated.)
[Ball; Melcher.

(2) Listed frequently as pr f JN between 1758 and 1765.

(3) An undated edition (BM dates ?1760). See Fig. 13. *CBEL*, II, 219.
Title and *imprint* approx. as for no. (1).

In 6's. 78 leaves+9 insets. Pp. x[xii]+142[144]. Engvd FP as in no. (1), and
8 other engvd leaves. List of bks 'just pubd by JN' on last 2 pages.
[BM, 11·6×7·6 cm.

(4) Sixth edition, n.d. Pr f JN. Price 1s bd. The date [?1770] assigned by BM and
CBEL, II, 227 is too late: JN died 1767.

Title approx. as for no. (1), THE SIXTH EDITION added. *Imprint:* PR F J. NEWBERY, AT THE BIBLE AND SUN, IN S | PC-Y; A S B THE BOOKSELLERS OF | EUROPE, ASIA, AFRICA AND AMERICA. PRICE 1*s*. BOUND.

In 6's. 73 leaves+9 insets. Pp. viii[x]+136. Engvd FP and 8 other engvd leaves as before. D.f.b.

[BM, 11·6×7·6 cm; Bodley.

(5) Seventh edition, n.d. Pr f 'the Booksellers of Europe...'. BM and *CBEL*, II, 230 date [?1775].

Title approx. as for no. (1), THE SEVENTH EDITION added. *Imprint* approx. as for no. (1).

In 6's. 72 leaves+9 insets (as before). Pp. viii[x]+134. D.f.b.

[BM, 11·8×7·9 cm; Opie.

(6) Listed in *Newtonian System*, 1770, as pr f C & N, price 1*s*.

(7) An edition of 1779. Pr f the Booksellers...S b C & N. Price 1*s* bd.

Title approx. as for no. (1). *Imprint:* PR F THE BOOKSELLERS OF EUROPE, ASIA, AFRICA, | AND AMERICA; A S B T. CARNAN AND F. | NEWBERY, JUN. AT NUMBER 65, IN SP | C-Y. PRICE ONE SHILLING BOUND. | MDCCLXXIX.

Engvd FP and 8 other engvd leaves. (Communicated.)

[Ball; Melcher.

(8) Listed in *Newtonian System*, 1787, as pr f TC, price 1*s*.

(9) An edition of 1789 [?1779, i.e. no. (7)] C & N.

[CCamarSJ, Cat. 1940, p. 211.

COLLECTION OF PRETTY POEMS FOR THE AMUSEMENT OF CHILDREN THREE FOOT HIGH. See 'Tagg, Tommy'.

COLLECTION OF RIDDLES... See 'Puzzlewell, Peter'.

COLLECTION OF THE MOST APPROVED ENTERTAINING STORIES. See 'Winlove, Solomon'.

COLLOQUIA SELECTA. See Cordier, Maturin.

J75. 'COMICAL, Christopher'. LECTURE UPON GAMES AND TOYS, A. Presumably the work listed in no. J250(2), 1791, as *Lecture upon Toys*, 2 vols, price 6*d* each.

(1) Part I, 1789. Elva Smith, p. 67.

(2) Part II, 1789. Pr f Francis Power & Co. Price 6*d*.

A | LECTURE | UPON | GAMES AND TOYS, | FOR THE AMUSEMENT OF | GOOD GIRLS AND BOYS. | [p.rule] | BY CHRISTOPHER COMICAL, | MASTER OF THE REVELS OF THE KING | OF FUNNYLAND, AND POET LAUREAT (*sic*) | TO THE LILLIPUTIANS. | [p.rule] | [3 lines quote] | [p.rule] | IN TWO PARTS. | PART II. | [d.p.rule] | LONDON: PR F FRANCIS POWER, (GRANDSON | TO THE LATE MR. J. NEWBERY,) AND CO. | NO. 65, SPCY, 1789.

44 leaves. Pp. 86. Wct FP and 16 wcts in text. Orange bds impressed with gold stars and dots. (Communicated.)

[Adomeit, 11·2×7·7 cm.

J76. COMPENDIOUS HISTORY OF ENGLAND, A. Welsh 211.
(1) First edition, 1758. Pr f JN. Price 2*s*.

A COMPENDIOUS | HISTORY | OF | ENGLAND, | FROM | THE INVASION BY THE ROMANS, | TO | THE PRESENT TIME. | ADORNED WITH | A MAP OF GREAT BRITAIN AND | IRELAND, COLOUR'D; | AND EMBELLISHED WITH | THIRTY-ONE CUTS OF ALL THE KINGS AND QUEENS | [3 lines] | [p.rule] | [4 lines quote] | [p.rule] | LONDON: | PR F J. NEWBERY, AT THE BIBLE AND SUN | IN SPC-Y. MDCCLVIII. | [PRICE BOUND TWO SHILLINGS.]

In 6's. 144 leaves+1 inset. Pp. [i]–iv, [v–xii], i–viii+9–266[276]. Folding engvd map of the British Isles by Emanuel Bowen, 31 wct whole-length figures of sovereigns, most sgd JB. List of bks pr f a s b JN on pp. [267–76].

[Roscoe, 13·9×8·5 cm; UCLA; Sotheby, 16.3.70, lot 2.
(2) Second edition. Adv. *LC* 30.6.–2.7.1768, p. 2, as pr f N & C, price 2*s* in the vell. manner.
(3) Third edition. Adv. *LC* 20–3.6.72, p. 599, as pr f C & N, price 2*s* in the vell. manner.
(4) Fourth edition not traced.
(4A) An edition of 1780. Pr f TC. Price 2*s*.

Title and *imprint* approx. as for no. (6) except for date MDCCLXXX and (PRICE TWO SHILLINGS BOUND) at foot of imprint. Specification approx. as for no. (6).

[Grey, 13·6×8·5 cm.
(5) Adv. *LC* 14–16.6.81, p. 574, as to be had of TC, price 2*s*. Probably = no. (4A).
(6) An edition of 1784. Pr f TC. Price 2*s*.

A COMPENDIOUS | HISTORY | ... | TO THE | ACCESSION OF HIS PRESENT MAJESTY; | WITH A | MAP... | LONDON: | PR F T. CARNAN, IN SPC-Y. | MDCCLXXXIV.

In 6's. 144 leaves+1 inset. Pp. iv[xii], viii+9–272[276]. Engvd folding map as in (1), 31 wct figures as in (1) except figures of Henry V and Henry VII redrawn, and initials JB removed from all blocks. List of bks pr f TC on last 4 pages.

[BM, 13·1×8·3 cm.
(7) The bk was pubd by G. G. and J. Robinson in or before 1792 and again in 1794, bringing the work down to the latter year.

J77. COMPENDIOUS HISTORY OF THE WORLD, A. Frequently advertised under the title *A Taste of Ancient Times, or a Compendious History...* written by JN, according to an advert. in an 1805 ed. of Wakefield's *Juvenile Travels*.
(1) An edition of 1763 (? the first). Pr f JN. 2 vols, price 1*s* 6*d* in embossed paper, 2*s* bd and gilt. Welsh 276; NBL 134.

Engvd title: A COMPENDIOUS | HISTORY | OF THE | WORLD | FROM THE CREATION TO YE DISSOLUTION | OF THE ROMAN REPUBLIC. | COMPILED

FOR THE USE OF YOUNG | GENTLEMEN & LADIES | BY THEIR OLD FRIEND MR. NEWBERY. | EMBELLISHED | WITH VARIETY OF COPPER PLATES. [d.p.rule] | VOL. I [II.] | [p.rule] | LONDON PR F J. NEWBERY AT THE | BIBLE & SUN IN SPCY 1763.

Vol. I. In 8's. 92 leaves+8 insets. Pp. viii+176. Engvd FP and TP and 6 other engvd leaves.

Vol. II. In 8's. 76 leaves+8 insets. Pp. 152. Engvd FP and TP and 6 other engvd leaves.

D.f.b., also blue bds, green vell. spine.

[BM; St Bride, vol. I 9·8×6·4 cm, vol. II 10·0×6·3 cm; NorBM; Opie; Pollard; Ball; NNC-T (Darton Coll. vol. II only).

(2) An edition adv. *LC* 27–9.12.70 as s b C & N, price 1*s* 6*d*.

(3) An edition listed in *Newtonian System*, 1787, as pr f TC, 2 vols, price 1*s* 6*d* in the vell. manner.

(4) An edition of 1788. Pr f TC. 2 vols. Marbled bds, green vell. spine. (Communicated.)

[Opie; Ball.

J77A. COMPENDIUM OF BIOGRAPHY, A.

Under this heading *LC* for 6–9 March 1762 (at p. 229) had the following advertisement: 'Mr Newbery begs Leave to offer to the young Gentlemen and Ladies of these Kingdoms, A COMPENDIUM OF BIOGRAPHY: Or, an History of the Lives of these great Personages, both Ancient and Modern, who are most worthy of Esteem and Imitation. This Work will begin with a Compendium of the Lives recorded by Plutarch, and be continued down to modern Times... The whole embellished with Cuts, will be printed in small Pocket Volumes, and delivered Monthly at Mr Newbery's House in St Paul's Church-yard, at the easy Price of Eighteen-Pence each Volume. Vol. I will be published on the first of May next; and the subsequent Volumes the first of each Month...' It looks as though the work never got further than the seven volumes of the Plutarch (no. J294). Newbery perhaps conceived of this series as a rival to the *British Plutarch, or, Biographical Entertainer* which Dilly was putting out at this time.

See R. M. Wardle, *Oliver Goldsmith*, 1957, p. 133.

COMPLETE COURSE OF GEOGRAPHY. See Gaultier, A. E. C.

COMPLETE ENGLISH EXPOSITOR. JN. Listed *LM* April 1753, p. 198. = no. J295(1).

COMPLETE ENGLISH GRAMMAR ON A NEW PLAN. See Wiseman, Chas.

J78. COMPLETE HISTORY OF ENGLAND WITH HEADS OF 30 KINGS AND QUEENS. Adv. *MC&LA* 10.6.72 as to be had of FN(N), price 1*s* 6*d*.

J78A. COMPLETE HISTORY OF ENGLAND, A. Price 1s. Adv. in *GM* May 1774, as pr f FN(N). Not identified.

J79. COMPLETE HISTORY OF ENGLAND WITH HEADS OF 36 KINGS AND QUEENS. Listed in *Clarissa...abridged*, n.d., no. J315(2), as pr f EN, price 1s 6d. Possibly = J51, 1795; but that has only 34 heads.

J80. CONSTANTIO AND SELIMA, 1795. Pr f EN. Price 1s 6d.
CONSTANTIO | AND | SELIMA. | [d.p.rule] | A FAIRY TALE. | [d.p.rule] | [wct vignette] | [d.s.rule] | SALISBURY: | PR B J. EASTON; | FOR E. NEWBERY, THE CORNER OF SP | C-Y, LONDON. | [d.p.rule] | 1795.
In 12's. 42[?44] leaves. Pp. [?viii]+76. Marbled bds, green vell. spine, oval label on upper cover.
[Weedon (lacks one or more leaves of prelims), 16·4×9·8 cm.

CONSTITUTION AND PRESENT STATE OF GREAT BRITAIN. See ACCOUNT OF THE CONSTITUTION...

CONVERSATIONS AND AMUSING TALES. See English, Harriet.

J81. COOPER'S NEW JUVENILE ENGLAND, 1794. EN. Price 1s. Welsh 194. Probably the 9th (1794) ed. of Cooper's *New History of England*, no. J84(7), priced 1s 6d. Welsh's information appears to be second-hand; the bk should have been listed at p. 345 had he seen it.

J82. COOPER, The Rev. Mr, *alias* The Rev. J., *alias* The Rev. Samuel.
Miss Weedon, in her *Richard Johnson and the Successors to John Newbery*, discusses in some detail, at pp. 35–7, the books purporting to have been written by the Rev. Mr Cooper or the Rev. Mr J. Cooper, and concludes 'there seems to be a case for suggesting [Richard] Johnson as author or compiler of all the works attributed to the Reverend Mr Cooper with the exception of the *New History of England* and part of *The History of France*'. On the facts cited this conclusion appears to be amply justified, except only that I doubt (with great respect to Miss Weedon) the justification for the word 'author'.
The following are the books attributed to 'Cooper', with the authority for each attribution:
New Roman History, 1770, no. J263(1). Weedon no. 71. Attributed to Cooper in the bk-list in the *Oriental Moralist*, 1791/2.
New History of England, 1775, no. J84(1). Title-page.
History of France, 1786, no. J83(1). *Oriental Moralist.*
New History of the Grecian States, 1786, no. 261(1). Weedon no. 68. *Oriental Moralist.*
Looking-Glass for the Mind, 1787. Weedon no. 62. *Oriental Moralist.*
Blossoms of Morality, 1789. Weedon no. 13. *Oriental Moralist.*

History of North America, 1789. Weedon no. 35. Title-page.
History of South America, 1789. Weedon no. 37. Title-page.
Oriental Moralist, 1791/2. Weedon no. 75. Title-page.
Poetical Blossoms, 1793. Weedon no. 77. Title-page.

The author of the *New History of England* is stated, in an advertisement of its 1775 ed. in vol. III of Ward's *Modern System of Natural History*, 1775, to be 'The Rev. Samuel Cooper'. But in the TP to the 1780 ed. he is merely 'The Rev. Mr Cooper'. Welsh, p. 195, gives 'the Rev. S. Cooper' as the author of the *Oriental Moralist*.

The available evidence, such as it is, certainly points to the three Coopers being one and the same person, that is to say (with the exceptions mentioned) Richard Johnson. These exceptions I deal with below, under the name 'Cooper'; all other works appearing under his name or ascribed to him are listed under the true author or under the title.

J83. 'COOPER, Rev. Mr'. HISTORY OF FRANCE, FROM THE EARLIEST PERIOD...
(1) First edition, 1786. Pr f EN. Price 1*s* 6*d*. Welsh 194; Weedon 32; NBL 138. Richard Johnson's Day-book records: *1786 Jan. 23. Mr Badcock——To writing Part of the History of France 4 Sheets——£6. 6s. 1792 July. Mr Badcock——To improving The History of France——£4. 4s.*

THE | HISTORY | OF | FRANCE, | FROM | THE EARLIEST PERIOD TO | THE PRESENT TIME. | [5 lines] | [p.s.rule] | EMBELLISHED WITH | COPPER-PLATE CUTS. | [p.s.rule] | [2 lines] | [d.p.rule] | LONDON: | PR F E. NEWBERY, THE CORNER OF | SPC-Y. | [p.rule] | MDCCLXXXVI.

In 6's. 124 leaves+6 insets. Pp. xv+228. Engvd FP and 5 other engvd leaves. Marbled bds, green vell. spine.

[BM, 13·7×8·2 cm; Weedon; Opie; MPL; Brimmell, List (summer 1968) item 39; Osborne, Cat. p. 166; UCLA; McKell.

(2) Second edition, 1792. Pr f EN. Price 1*s* 6*d*. Welsh 194; Weedon 32; Gum 1854.

Title and *imprint* approx. as for no. (1), with THE SECOND EDITION and date MDCCXCII.

18mo. 90 leaves+6 insets. Pp. 172. Engvd FP and 5 other engvd leaves. Marbled bds, green vell. spine with label.

[BM, 13·7×8·5 cm; Weedon; Roscoe; Traylen; Osborne, Cat. p. 167; UCLA; Shiers; Bondy, Cat. 77 [1969] item 156; Elkin Mathews, Cat. 163 [1965] item 199.

J84. 'COOPER, Rev. Samuel'. NEW HISTORY OF ENGLAND, A, FROM THE EARLIEST PERIOD TO THE PRESENT TIME.
Weedon, p. 46 footnote, and p. 36. As to 'Samuel Cooper' see J82.
(1) An edition of 1775 (? the first). Pr f FN(N). Price 1*s* 6*d*. Welsh 193.

A | NEW HISTORY | OF | ENGLAND. | FROM THE | EARLIEST PERIOD TO THE PRESENT TIME. | ON A PLAN RECOMMENDED BY | THE EARL OF

CHESTERFIELD. | EMBELLISHED WITH COPPER-PLATES, ELEGANTLY | ENGRAVED FROM THE DESIGNS OF MR. WALE. | [p.rule] | BY THE REVEREND MR. COOPER. | [p.rule] | [3 lines quote] | LONDON: | PR F F. NEWBERY, THE CORNER OF SP | C-Y, IN LUDGATE-STREET. 1775.

In 6's. 78 leaves+6 insets. Pp. xii+[13]–156. Engvd FP and 5 other engvd leaves. Blue bds, green vell. spine. Details taken from the Marchmont copy.

⌈Opie; UCLA; Marchmont Bookshop, Cat. 26 [1967] item 88; Ries.

(2) A 'New Edition', 1780. Pr f FN(N).

Title and *imprint* approx. as for no. (1), with 'A New Edition' following the quotation, and date 1780.

In 6's. 79 leaves+6 insets. Pp. xii+[13]–156. Engvd FP and 5 other engvd leaves. Marbled bds, green vell. spine. (Communicated.)

⌈HU; Osborne, Cat. p. 162.

(3) A 'New Edition', 1785. Pr f EN.

Title approx. as for no. (2). *Imprint:* PR F E. NEWBERY, THE CORNER OF SP | C-Y. 1785.

In 6's. 90 leaves+6 insets. Pp. xii+[13]–180. Engvd FP and 5 other engvd leaves. Marbled bds, green vell. spine with label.

⌈BM, 13·8×8·3 cm; HeCL.

(4) An edition of 1786. Pr f EN.

⌈M. G. Atkins' Book-list CHI/13 [Oct. 1964] item 2.

(5) A 'New Edition', 1788. Pr f EN. Price 1s 6d. Welsh 193.

Pp. xii+[13]–177[180]. Engvd FP and 5 other engvd leaves. 3 pp. list of bks pr f EN at end. Marbled bds, green vell. spine with label. (Communicated.)

⌈Opie; CLU; Grant; Bondy, Cat. 73 [1967] item 512.

(6) Eighth edition, 1791. Pr f EN.

Title (with THE EIGHTH EDITION) approx. as for no. (1). *Imprint* (with date 1791) and specification as for no. (3). Marbled bds, green vell. spine with label.

⌈Weedon, 13·7×8·4 cm; CUL; ReU; Opie.

(7) Ninth edition, 1794. Pr f EN. Price 1s 6d.

Title (with THE NINTH EDITION) approx. as for no. (1). *Imprint* (with date 1794) and specification approx. as for no. (3). Marbled bds, green vell. spine with label.

⌈Bell; BCE, 13·9×8·7 cm; Elkin Mathews, Cat. 163 [1965] item 200.

(8) Tenth edition, 1798. Pr f EN. Price 1s 6d. Welsh 193.

Title (with THE TENTH EDITION) approx. as for no. (1). *Imprint* (with date 1798) approx. as for no. (3).

In 6's. 93 leaves+6 insets. Pp. xii+[13]–186. Engvd FP and 5 other engvd leaves. Marbled bds, green vell. spine with label.

⌈BM, 13·2×8·3 cm.

(9) Eleventh edition, 1801. Pr f EN. Price 2s. Welsh 193.

A | NEW HISTORY | OF | ENGLAND; | FROM THE | EARLIEST PERIOD, TO THE PRESENT TIME. | ON A PLAN RECOMMENDED BY | THE EARL OF CHESTERFIELD. | [p.s.rule] | BY THE REVEREND MR. COOPER; | [1 line] |

[p.s.rule] | [3 lines quote] | [d.p.rule] | THE ELEVENTH EDITION; | WITH CONSIDERABLE ADDITIONS. | [d.p.rule] | LONDON: | PR F E. NEWBERY, THE CORNER OF SP | C-Y.——1801. | [PRICE TWO SHILLINGS.] | T. DAVISON, LOMBARD-STREET, FLEET-STREET.

In 6's. 110 leaves+1 inset. Pp. xii+13–220. Engvd FP. Marbled bds, green vell. spine, label.

[V&A(GL), 13·5×8·2 cm; RP.

J85. 'COOPER, Rev. Samuel'. NOUVELLE HISTOIRE D'ANGLETERRE, 1788. Imprimé pour EN. Price 1s 6d. Welsh 194.

NOUVELLE HISTOIRE | D'ANGLETERRE. | DEPUIS | LES PREMIERS PERIODES, | JUSQU'AU TEMPS PRESENT. | SUR UN PLAN RECOMMANDÉ PAR LE | COMTE DE CHESTERFIELD. | ENRICHI DE FIGURES EN TAILLE DOUCE, SOIG- | NEUSEMENT GRAVÉES D'APRÈS LES DESSEINS | DE MR. WALE. | [p.rule] | TRADUIT DE L'ANGLOIS DU REV. MR. COOPER, | PAR LE S.L.B. DE ST. AMAND. | [p.rule] | [4 lines quote] | [d.p.rule] | LONDRES: | IMPRIME POUR E. NEWBERY, AU COIN DU | CIMETIERE DE ST. PAUL. 1788.

Pp. xii+[13]–208. Engvd FP and 4 other engvd leaves. Marbled bds, green vell. spine. (Communicated.)

[Welch; UCLA.

COPY BOOK FOR YOUTH. See Webb, Benjn.

J85A. CORDIER, Maturin. COLLOQUIA SELECTA (Loggon's ed.). The work was popularly known in the schools as 'the Cordery'.

(1) First edition, ?1744. Pr a s b JN and C. Micklewright, at Reading. Price 1s 6d; 15s a dozen 'to school-masters or those who take quantities'. Adv. *Penny London Morning Advertiser*, 21-3.3.44. Welsh 195.

(2) Second edition, 1745. Pr f JN. Price 1s. Welsh 195; Legg, no. 124.

Title and *imprint* approx. as for no. (4), with THE SECOND EDITION IMPROV'D and date MDCCXLV.

In 6's. 84 leaves. Pp. vi+7–168.

[DES, 16·0×9·3 cm (imperf.).

(3) Third edition. Adv. *PA* 2.10.55 as pr f JN, price 1s.

(4) Fourth edition, 1759. Pr f JN.

MATHURINI CORDERII COLLOQUIA | SELECTA: | OR, | SELECT COLLOQUIES | OF | MATHURIN CORDIER: | BETTER ADAPTED TO THE CAPACITIES OF YOUTH, AND | FITTER FOR BEGINNERS IN THE LATIN TONGUE, | [3 lines] | [12 lines in 2 parallel columns] | [p.rule] | BY SAMUEL LOGGON, M.A. | [p.rule] | FOR THE USE OF SCHOOLS. | [p.rule] | THE FOURTH EDITION IMPROV'D. | [p.rule] | LONDON: | PR F J. NEWBERY, AT THE BIBLE AND SUN, IN SP | C-Y. MDCCLIX.

12mo in 6's. 84 leaves. Pp. vi+7–168.

[BM, approx. 16·4×9·3 cm.

(5) Fifth edition, ?1768. Pr f N & C. Price 1s. Adv. *LC* 11–13.10.68, p. 357 and 14–17.1.69, p. 51. The latter advert. sets out the notice about bks 'bound in linen and sewed in bands' which I quote at p. 397.

(6) Sixth edition. Not traced.

(7) Seventh edition, 1776. Pr f C & N.

Imprint: PR F T. CARNAN AND F. NEWBERY, JUN. AT | NUMBER 65, IN SPC-Y. | MDCCLXXVI.

12mo. 84 leaves. Pp. vi+7–168.

[Marchmont Bookshop [1963], 17·0×9·9 cm.

(8) An edition of 1783. Pr f TC.

Title approx. as for no. (4). *Imprint:* PR F T. CARNAN, IN SPC-Y. | [MDCCLXXXIII].

12mo. 84 leaves. Pp. vi+7–168. Bound in linen (see no. (5)).

[BM, 16·7×10·0 cm.

(9) Intermediate edd. not traced.

(10) Twelfth edition, 1790. Pr f F. Power & Co.

Title approx. as for no. (4), with THE TWELFTH EDITION. *Imprint:* LONDON: | PR F F. POWER AND CO. (SUCCESSOR TO THE LATE MR. | T. CARNAN) IN SPC-Y. MDCCXC.

12mo. 84 leaves. Pp. vi+7–168.

[BM, 16·7×10·1 cm.

COURS DE LECTURES. See Gaultier, A. E. C., nos. J143 and J143A.

CRESTED WREN, THE. See Kendall, E. A.

J86. CRIES OF LONDON, THE.

(1) An edition adv. *LC* 8–10.1.71, p. 39, as to be had of FN(N), price 6*d*.

(2) An edition of 1775. Pr f FN(N). Price 6*d*. TP reproduced in Muir, pl. 32. Pierpont Morgan, Cat. no. 281.

Title approx. as for no. (3). *Imprint:* PR F F. NEWBERY, AT THE CORNER OF | SPC-Y. 1775. | [PRICE SIX-PENCE.]

In 8's. 72 leaves. Pp. v+6–133[139]. Wct FP and 61 wcts in text. List of bks pr f FN(N) on pp. [134–9].

[Bell, 10·0×6·5 cm; Osborne*; Ball; Oppenheimer; McKell.

(3) An edition of 1784. Pr f EN. Price 6*d*. Welsh 196; NBL 679.

THE | CRIES OF LONDON, | AS | THEY ARE DAILY EXHIBITED IN THE STREETS; | WITH AN EPIGRAM IN VERSE, | ADAPTED TO EACH. | EMBEL-LISHED WITH SIXTY-TWO ELEGANT CUTS. | TO WHICH IS ADDED, | A DESCRIPTION OF THE METROPOLIS | IN VERSE. | [printer's ornament] | LONDON: | PR F E. NEWBERY, AT THE CORNER OF | SPC-Y. 1784. | [PRICE SIX-PENCE.]

In 8's. 72 leaves. Pp. v+6–133[139]. Last leaf a paste-down. Wct FP and 61 whole page wcts in text. List of bks pr f EN on pp. [134–9]. D.f.b.

[Bodley, 10·1×6·5 cm; Ball.
(4) An edition of 1791. EN.
[ICU.
(5) An edition of 1796. Pr f EN. Price 6*d.* Bk-list at end.
[Harding.
(6) An edition of 1799. EN. Price 6*d.* NBL 743.
[Oppenheimer; UCLA.
(7) A copy lacking TP, EN. Pp. v+133. Wcts. List bks pr f EN at end.
[SomCL, 9·6×6·0 cm.

CRITICAL SPELLING BOOK. See Lowe, Solomon.

J87. CROXALL, Samuel. FABLES OF AESOP. It seems that the experts have never settled whether the cuts to the Fables were on wood or soft metal: Linton (*Masters of Wood-Engraving*, p. 132) and Basil Gray (*The English Print*, p. 61) favour soft metal, Bliss (*History of Wood-Engraving*, p. 5) is for wood.
(1) Ninth edition, 1770. Pr f FN(?N) et al. Price 3*s.*

Title approx. as for no. (2). *Imprint:* LONDON: | PR F W. STRAHAN, J. AND F. RIVINGTON, | J. HINTON, HAWES, CLARKE AND COLLINS, | T. CASLON, S. CROWDER, T. LONGMAN, B. LAW, | J. D. CORNISH, T. CADELL, G. PEARCH, | F. NEWBERY, T. DAVIES, | T. LOWNDES, AND | E. REEVE. | [p.rule] | MDCCLXX.

12mo. 186 leaves+1 inset. Pp. 329[336]. Engvd FP. About 196 cuts to the fables.
[BM, 17·8×10·4 cm; Bodley.
(2) Tenth edition, 1775. Pr f FN(N) et al. Listed as pr f FN(N) in *Cries of London*, 1775.

FABLES | OF | ÆSOP | AND | OTHERS: | TRANSLATED INTO ENGLISH. | WITH | INSTRUCTIVE APPLICATIONS; | AND A PRINT BEFORE EACH FABLE. | BY SAMUEL CROXALL, D.D. | LATE ARCHDEACON OF HEREFORD. | THE TENTH EDITION, | CAREFULLY REVISED, AND IMPROVED. | [d.p.rule] | LONDON, | PR F W. STRAHAN, J. AND F. RIVINGTON, J. HINTON, | HAWES, CLARKE AND COLLINS, R. HORSFIELD, T. CASLON, | S. CROWDER, T. LONGMAN, B. LAW, J. D. CORNISH, | T. CADELL, F. NEWBERY, T. DAVIES, T. LOWNDES, | W. GOLDSMITH, T. BECKET, G. ROBINSON, J. JOHNSON, | AND B. COLLINS. | [p.rule] | MDCCLXXV.

12mo. 186 leaves +1 inset. Pp. 329[335]. Engvd FP. Ornamental wct head-pieces. About 196 cuts to the fables.
[Roscoe, 17·1×9·6 cm.
(3) Eleventh edition not traced.
(4) Twelfth edition, 1782. Pr f EN et al. Price 3*s.* NUTP Cat. no. 146.

Title approx. as for no. (2). *Imprint:* LONDON: | PR F W. STRAHAN, J. F. AND C. RIVINGTON, T. CASLON, | S. CROWDER, T. LONGMAN, B. LAW, C. DILLY, T. CADELL, | J. BEW, T. LOWNDES, R. BALDWIN, W. GOLDSMITH,

G. | ROBINSON, J. JOHNSON, E. NEWBERY, W. GINGER, AND | B. COLLINS.
| MDCCLXXXII.

12mo. 186 leaves+1 inset. Pp. 329[336]. Engvd FP and cuts as before.

[NUTP (details taken from the NUTP copy); Hodgson's, 28.7.1965, lot 19.

(5) Thirteenth edition, 1786. Pr f EN et al. Price 3s. Welsh 168.

Title approx. as for no. (2). *Imprint:* LONDON: | PR F J. F. AND C. RIVINGTON,
T. | LONGMAN, B. LAW, C. DILLY, J. JOHNSON, | G. G. J. AND J. ROBINSON,
T. CADELL, R. | BALDWIN, J. BEW, W. GOLDSMITH, W. GIN- | GER, A.
STRAHAN, W. LOWNDES, SCATCHERD | AND WHITAKER, W. BENT,
E. NEWBERY, AND | B. C. COLLINS. 1786.

12mo. 186 leaves+1 inset. Pp. 329[336]. Engvd FP and cuts as before.

[BM, 16·9×10·0 cm.

(6) Fourteenth edition, 1788. Pr f EN et al. Price 3s.

Adv. *LC* 3–6.1.89, p. 19, as pr f J. F. and C. Rivington, T. Longman, B. Law,
J. Johnson, G. G. J. & J. Robinson, T. Cadell, R. Baldwin, J. Bew, W. Goldsmith, W. Lowndes, Scatcherd & Whitaker, W. Bent, E. Newbery & C. Stalker.

(7) Fifteenth edition, n.d. (1795 or before). Pr f EN et al. Price 3s.

Title approx. as for no. (2). *Imprint:* LONDON: | PR F T. LONGMAN, B. LAW
AND SON, C. DILLY, | J. JOHNSON, G. G. AND J. ROBINSON, W. GINGER, |
T. CADELL, R. BALDWIN, J. BEW, F. AND | C. RIVINGTON, W. GOLDSMITH,
W. LOWNDES, | SCATCHERD AND WHITAKER, W. BENT, E. NEW- | BERY,
AND G. AND T. WILKIE.

12mo. 186 leaves. Pp. 329[336]. Engvd FP and cuts as before.

[BM, 16·5×9·7 cm.

(8) Sixteenth edition, 1798. Pr f EN et al. Price 3s.

Title approx. as for no. (2). *Imprint:* PR F C. DILLY, J. JOHNSON, G. G.
AND J. | ROBINSON, W. GINGER AND SON, R. BALDWIN, F. AND | C.
RIVINGTON, W. LOWNDES, J. SCATCHERD, W. BENT, | E. NEWBERY,
G. WILKIE, CADELL AND DAVIES, T. N. | LONGMAN, C. LAW, B. CROSBY,
AND LEE AND HURST. | [d.s.rule] | MDCCXCVIII.

12mo. 186 leaves. Pp. xxiv[xxxvi]+329[336]. Wct FP, a copy of the earlier
engvd FP, sgd 'C. Nesbit'. Cuts to the Fables as before.

[BM, 17·7×10·3 cm; CUL.

J88. CURIOSITIES OF LONDON AND WESTMINSTER
DESCRIBED, THE. Sold at 2s the set of 4 vols, or 6d each vol. bd and gilt.
Welsh 258.

There were a number of edd. (how many cannot be said with certainty) up to
1799, possibly later. The earliest traced, and probably the first, is that of 1770.
The 4-vol. set of that year, and the set of 1771, are the only uniform and complete
sets traced. Other sets have been made up from vols of different years, and it
seems quite possible that complete sets were not issued after 1771, but that new
individual vols were put out as and when required.

As a rule vols were issued in D.f.b., but a set of the 4 vols of the 1771 ed. in

THE
CURIOSITIES
O F
London and Weftminfter
D E S C R I B E D :

I N F O U R V O L U M E S.

Embellifhed with elegant Copper Plates.

VOLUME II.

Containing a Defcription of

Guildhall	The Eaft India Houfe
Guildhall Chapel	St Stephen's Walbrook
The Bank of England	St Mary le Bow
St Thomas's Hofpital	Bridewell Hofpital
The Manfion Houfe	Chrift's Hofpital, and
Foundling Hofpital	London Stone.

L O N D O N,
Printed for F. Newbery, at the Corner of St.
Paul's Church Yard. 1770.
(Price Sixpence.)

Fig. 14. Title-page of J88(1).

the writer's possession is bd in 2 vols, in the vell. manner, blue bds and green vell. spine with white spine label lettered DESCRIPTION | OF | LONDON. | VOL. I. [11.], the price apparently still 2s.

The same subjects in the engvd plates (frequently and much reworked or entirely re-engraved) are used in all edd. seen. The plate of the House of Lords between pp. 102 and 103 in vol. IV of the 1770 ed. is sgd 'J. June sculp'; all the plates may well be his work. (For June see *DNB*.)

(1) Edition of 1770. Pr f FN(N). 4 vols. The TPs follow the layout and wording shown in Figure 14 except as to the lists of contents, which are set out in the notes on vols I, III and IV.

Vol. I. *Contents:* Tower of London, Monument, London Bridge, Custom House, Royal Exchange, Bethlem Hospital, St Luke's Hospital, The Magdalen House, Gresham College, Sion College, The South Sea House.

In 8's. 65 leaves+6 engvd plates. Pp. 125[128]. List of bks pubd by FN(N) on last 3 pages.

Vol. II. See Figure 14. In 8's. 65 leaves+6 engvd plates. Pp. 125[128]. List of bks as in vol. I. Whole page wcts of Gog and Magog on pp. 10–11.

Vol. III. *Contents:* St Paul's Cathedral, Black Friars Bridge, British Museum,

94

The Temple, Temple Bar, St Bartholomew's Hospital, Northumberland House, Charing Cross, Lincoln's Inn.

In 8's. 65 leaves+6 engvd plates. Pp. 124[127]. List of bks as in vol. I.

Vol. IV. *Contents:* Westminster-Abbey, Westminster-Bridge, Westminster-Hall, House of Lords, House of Commons, Buckingham House, or the Queen's Palace, Banquetting House, Horse Guards, Admiralty Office.

In 8's. 65 leaves+6 engvd plates. Pp. 125[128]. List of bks as in vol. I. Engvg of House of Lords facing p. 103 sgd 'J. June sculp'.

[Roscoe, average 10·2×6·7 cm; NorBM (vols. II and IV).

(2) Edition of 1771. Pr f FN(N). 4 vols. TPs, lists of contents and engvd plates as in no. (1). No bk-lists.

Vol. I. In 8's. 64 leaves+6 engvd plates. Pp. 126 (LGL copy). Pp. 125 (Roscoe copy).

Vol. II. In 8's. 64 leaves+6 engvd plates. Wcts of Gog and Magog on pp. 10–11.

Vol. III. In 8's. 64 leaves+6 engvd plates. Pp. 126. Last leaf a blank.

Vol. IV. In 8's. 65 leaves+6 engvd plates. Pp. 125.

[LGL; Roscoe (bd in 2 vols, see General Note, above), approx. 10·2×6·4cm; BmPL (vol. I); Opie (vols. I and II); Hannas (vols. I and II); UCLA (vol. II); LEI (vols. III and IV).

(3) A set of 4 vols, 1786, 1783, 1784, 1782. Pr f EN. D.f.b. New plates engvd for vol. I; for the rest the old plates are used, but very worn and thin. TPs and contents lists as before.

Vol. I, 1786. In 8's. 64 leaves+6 engvd plates. Pp. 126[128]. List of bks pr f EN on last leaf. 10·3×6·8 cm.

Vol. II, 1783. In 8's. 64 leaves+6 engvd plates. Pp. 127. Wcts of Gog and Magog at pp. 12–13. 10·1×6·0 cm.

Vol. III, 1784. In 8's. 64 leaves+6 engvd plates. Pp. 126. Last leaf a pastedown. 10·4×6·2 cm.

Vol. IV, 1782. In 8's. 64 leaves+6 engvd plates. Pp. 125. 10·3×6·5 cm.

[Roscoe; V&A (vol. I); Renier (vol. II); BCE (vol. I green bds, vol. III marbled bds, green vell. spine, label); Welch (vol. I, D.f.b.); Schiller (1970) (vol. I, green vell. spine, papered bds).

(4) Vol. II, 1786. Pr f EN. In 8's. 64 leaves+6 engvd plates. Wcts of Gog and Magog at pp. 12–13. Pp. 127. D.f.b.

[LGL (imperf.), 10·3×6·1 cm; LUL; Weedon; SomCL; Welch.

(4A) Vol. IV, 1788. EN.

[NNC-T (Darton Coll.); Schiller (1970).

(4B) Vol. II, 1788. EN.

[Exhibited Victoria Art Gallery, Bath, Nov. 1944, Cat. item 126.

(4C) Vol. II, 1793. Pr f EN. Collates [A]-H8. Pp. 127. 6 engvd plates. (Communicated.)

[Schiller (1970).

(5) Vol. IV, 1793. Pr f EN. Welsh 258. In 8's. 64 leaves+6 engvd plates. Pp. 126[128]. List of bks pr f EN on last 2 pages.

[Oup, 9·7×6·2 cm; Welch (bd with no. (6), marbled bds, vell. spine).
(6) Vol. III, n.d. (? *ca.* 1793). Pr f EN. In 8's. 63 leaves+3 plates (should be 64+6). Pp. 126.
[Oup, 9·7×6·2 cm (imperf.); NNC-T (Darton Coll.); Welch (bd with no. (5)), marbled bds, vell. spine; also D.f.b.
(6A) Vol. I, 1796. Pr f EN. In 8's. 64 leaves+5 (?6) engvd plates. Pp. 127[128]. List of bks pr f EN on p. [128]. D.f.b.
[BmPL, 10·1×6·4 cm; Schiller (1970).
(7) Vol. IV, 1797. Pr f EN. In 8's. 64 leaves+6 engvd plates. Pp. 126[128]. List of bks pr f EN on last 2 pages. D.f.b.
[Bell, 10·2×6·4 cm; Weedon.
(8) Vol. II, 1798. Pr f EN. In 8's. 64 leaves+6 engvd plates. Pp. 127. Wcts of Gog and Magog on pp. 12–13.
[LGL, 10·1×6·2 cm; BmPL; Welch (bd with a copy of no. (9), marbled bds, green vell. spine).
(9) Vol. I, 1799. Pr f EN. In 8's. 64 leaves+6 engvd plates. Pp. 127[128]. List of bks pr f EN on last page.
[Weedon, 9·9×5·8 cm; Welch (bd with a copy of no. (8), marbled bds, green vell. spine).
(10) Vol. I, n.d. Pr f EN. Specification as before, but lacks engvd plates. D.f.b. Copy examined.
[NorBM.

J89. CURIOUS COLLECTION OF VOYAGES AND TRAVELS, PERFORMED BY ILLUSTRIOUS ADVENTURERS, n.d. (Listed in *Anecdotes of Mary*, 1795.) Pr f EN. Price *6d.* One of the 10 vols forming the *Lilliputian Library* originally 'compiled' by Richard Johnson and pubd by W. Domville. See Weedon 57 and no. J218. Composed of the sheets of the Domville ed. with a cancel title-leaf, the FP and pp. iv–v removed.

A | CURIOUS COLLECTION | OF | VOYAGES AND TRAVELS | PERFORMED BY | ILLUSTRIOUS ADVENTURERS. | [p.s.rule] | ADORNED WITH A GREAT VARIETY OF | DESCRIPTIVE CUTS. | [p.s.rule] | LONDON: | PR F E. NEWBERY, AT THE CORNER OF SP | CY. | [PRICE SIX-PENCE.]

Pp. viii+[9]–120. Cancel TP. There is a wct FP in the Domville ed. 12 wcts in text. D.f.b. (Communicated.)
[Ball.

J89A. CUZ'S CHORUS, THE, SET TO MUSIC. TO BE SUNG BY CHILDREN... Recorded by Welsh, 196, who gives neither date, publisher nor place. Price *3d.*

DAVENPORT FAMILY, HISTORY OF THE. See S., H.

J90. Entry deleted.

J91. DAVIS, Mr. SHORT AND EASY INTRODUCTION TO ENGLISH GRAMMAR, A. Pr f EN. Price 1s. Listed in Palmer's *Letters*, 1797.

J92. DAY, Thomas. HISTORY OF SANDFORD & MERTON, ABRIDGED. Welsh 197; Weedon 36. The abridgment seems to have been done by Richard Johnson, whose Day-book records: *1790 April. Mr Badcock* ——*To writing the History of Sandford and Merton*——*£10. 10s.*
(1) Second edition, n.d. (not before 1794 – wmk). Pr f EN et al. Price 2s.

THE | HISTORY | OF | SANDFORD AND MERTON. | ABRIDGED | FROM THE ORIGINAL. | [d.p.rule] | EMBELLISHED WITH ELEGANT PLATES. | [d.p.rule] | [8 lines of verse] | [p.s.rule] | THE SECOND EDITION. | [d.p.rule] | LONDON: | PR F J. WALLIS, NO. 16, LUDGATE-STREET; AND | E. NEWBERY, THE CORNER OF SPC-Y. | [PRICE TWO SHILLINGS.]

In 6's. 90 leaves+6 insets. Pp. 173. Engvd FP and 5 other engvd leaves. Marbled bds, green vell. spine with label.

[BM, 13·7×8·8 cm; LUL; Bell; Osborne, Cat. p. 243; UCLA; NNC-PL.
(2) Third edition, n.d. J. Wallis & EN. Price 2s. NBL 475. Marbled bds, green vell. spine.

[Opie.
(3) Listed in *Anecdotes of Mary*, 1795, Trimmer's *Silver Thimble*, 1799 and ENC, p. 9. Price 2s.

J93. DEFOE, Daniel. THE WONDERFUL LIFE & SURPRISING ADVENTURES OF...ROBINSON CRUSOE.
(1) An undated edition. 'Pr f the Inhabitants of his Island'. JN or N & C. *Pierpont Morgan Cat.*, item 200, describes as '[London: Newbery. 1760]' but quotes no authority. Because of absence of earlier publicity, I incline to date this ed. not before 1768. The BM Cat. gives the title: *The wonderful Life and surprising Adventures of that renowned Hero Robinson Crusoe. Printed for the Inhabitants of his Island.*

[Oppenheimer; CtHi.
(1A) An undated edition. 'Pr f the Inhabitants...' [N & C]. Price 6d. Perhaps the ed. listed in *Goody Two-Shoes*, 1768; and perhaps = no. (1).

Engraved title: THE WONDERFUL | LIFE | AND SURPRISING | ADVEN-TURES | OF THAT RENOWNED HERO | ROBINSON CRUSOE. | WHO LIVED TWENTY EIGHT YEARS, | ON AN UNINHABITED ISLAND, | WHICH HE AFTERWARDS COLONISED. | [p.rule] | PR F THE INHABITANTS OF | HIS ISLAND, AND S B ALL THE | BOOKSELLERS IN THE WORLD. | PRICE SIXPENCE BOUND.

In 8's. 80 leaves+engvd FP and TP and 5 other engvd leaves. Pp. 150[160]. List of bks pr f N & C on pp. [151–60]. D.f.b.

[NorBM, 9·8×6·4 cm.
(1B) An undated edition, 1783 or before. S b TC. Price 6d. Welsh 197. On

the cover of the Osborne copy is a ms signature 'Watkin Griffith, May 25, 1783'.

THE | WONDERFUL LIFE, | AND | SURPRISING ADVENTURES | OF THAT RENOWNED HERO, | ROBINSON CRUSOE, | WHO LIVED TWENTY-EIGHT YEARS | ON AN | UNINHABITED ISLAND. | WHICH HE AFTERWARDS COLO-NISED. | [p.rule] | LONDON: | PR F THE INHABITANTS OF HIS ISLAND, AND | S B T. CARNAN, IN SPC | Y. | [PRICE SIX-PENCE BOUND.]

In 8's. 80 leaves. Pp. 160. Wct FP of Crusoe, and 3 or 4 whole page wcts in the text. White or buff bds, black impressed pictorial design within a frame on each cover.

[Osborne*.

(2) An edition of 1784. S b TC. Price 6d bd.

Title and *imprint* approx. as for no. (1B), with date 1784. Pp. 160. ? wct FP. Wcts in text. White or buff bds, 2 wcts in red on upper and lower. (Communicated.)

[SomCL, 9·6×6·2 cm; DLC.

(3) Entry deleted.

(4) An edition of 1789. Pr f F. Power & Co. Price 6d bd.

Title approx. as for no. (1B). *Imprint:* PR F THE INHABITANTS OF THE ISLAND: | A S B F. POWER AND CO. (GRANDSON OF THE | LATE MR. JOHN NEWBERY) AT NO. 65, IN S | PC-Y. | [PRICE SIXPENCE BOUND.] MDCCLXXXIX.

12mo. Pp. 132. Wct FP and whole-page wcts in text. D.f.b.

[MiU; Welch; Sotheby, 24.2.69, lot 161.

(5) Editions of 1794 and 1798 with imprint: PR B ASSIGNMENT OF F. POWER AND CO...AND S B DARTON AND HARVEY.

[Hannas (1794); Oup; Ball (1798).

J93A. DESCRIPTION OF LONDON IN TWO POCKET VOLUMES. Pr f EN. Price 2s. Listed in J362(1), 1799. Almost certainly a set of J88 bd in 2 vols.

DESCRIPTION OF LONDON AND WESTMINSTER, in 4 vols. The 4-vol. set of J88 is sometimes so adv. or listed.

DESCRIPTION OF THE GUILDHALL...WITH A HISTORY OF THE GIANTS = vol. II of J88.

DESCRIPTION OF THE TOWER OF LONDON, THE WILD BEASTS... = vol. I of J88.

DESCRIPTION OF 300 ANIMALS. See Boreman, Thos.

DESCRIPTION OF WESTMINSTER ABBEY, WITH A PARTICULAR ACCOUNT OF THE MONUMENTS = vol. IV of J88.

DICK THE LITTLE PONY. See MEMOIRS OF DICK...

J94. DODD, William. BEAUTIES OF HISTORY, THE. The 1st ed. was compiled [? by Stephen Jones] from Dodd's *Sermons to young Men*. For the enlarged 2nd ed. Jones added much from Wm Seward's *Anecdotes of some distinguished Persons*, 1795, and other sources. But nowhere is it acknowledged that Dodd's work is really based on L. M. Stretch's *Beauties of History* (1st ed. 1770, 7th ed. 1787), from which Jones from time to time lifted appropriate passages. Possibly the words 'considerably enlarged' in the title to the 1st ed. of Dodd are an oblique reference to Stretch. It is difficult to know to what else they could refer.
(1) First edition, 1795. Pr f EN et al.
THE | BEAUTIES OF HISTORY; | OR, | PICTURES OF VIRTUE AND VICE: | DRAWN FROM | EXAMPLES OF MEN EMINENT FOR THEIR VIRTUES, | OR INFAMOUS FOR THEIR VICES. | [4 lines] | [d.p.rule] | BY THE LATE W. DODD, LL.D. | [d.p.rule] | CONSIDERABLY ENLARGED. | [d.p.rule] | LONDON: | PR F VERNOR AND HOOD, BIRCHIN LANE, CORNHILL, | AND E. NEWBERY, CORNER OF SPC-Y. | 1795.
12mo. 144 leaves+1 inset. Pp. 2+ii+300+4. Engvd FP as in no. (2) but before signatures. Wct tailpiece at p. 300 in the Bewick manner. Advert. on a2ʳˑᵛ. Bk-list on last 4 pages.
[BM, 15·6×9·4 cm; EdUL.
(2) Second edition, 1796. Pr f EN et al. Price 3s sewed, a few copies at 3s 6d 'on a fine cream-coloured paper'. Hugo 88; Gum 2231.
TP approx. as for no. (1), continuing: THE SECOND EDITION, | WITH CONSIDERABLE ADDITIONS AND IMPROVEMENTS, AND | ORNAMENTED WITH VIGNETTES BY BEWICK. | [d.p.rule] | [vignette by John Bewick] | [d.p.rule] | LONDON: | PR F VERNOR AND HOOD, BIRCHIN-LANE, | CORN- HILL; E. NEWBERY, CORNER OF S | PC-Y, AND DARTON | AND HARVEY, GRACE-CHURCH- | STREET. 1796.
12mo. 162 leaves+inset engvd FP. Pp. xviii+300[306]. FP sgd 'Stothard del' 'E. Thomson sculp'. 29 wct vignettes, the work of John Bewick, all used in Berquin's *Looking-Glass* of 1796. Bk-list on last 6 pages. The copy in the writer's possession on a greenish paper.
[BM, 17·4×9·7 cm; CUL; NoU; Renier; Opie; Roscoe; NLA; Oppenheimer.
(3) Third edition, 1800. Pr f EN et al. Price 3s 6d in bds, 4s 6d bd. Welsh 201; Hugo II, 4104.
TP approx. as for no. (1), continuing: THE THIRD EDITION. | ORNAMENTED WITH UPWARDS OF THIRTY ENGRAVINGS, | BEAUTIFULLY CUT ON WOOD. | [d.p.rule] | [vignette] | [d.p.rule] | LONDON: | PR B T. MAIDEN, SHERBOURN- LANE, | FOR VERNOR AND HOOD, E. NEWBERY, J. CUTHELL, | DARTON

AND HARVEY, J. SCATCHERD, | LACKINGTON, ALLEN & CO. | AND J. WALKER. | 1800.

12mo. 156 leaves+inset engvd FP. Pp. xxiv+288. The FP is that of no. (2), the plate reworked. About 51 wct head- and tailpieces, many in the Bewick manner or aping him. Many may be the work of W. M. Craig.

[BM, 17·0×10·0 cm; V&A(GL); Roscoe; Ries; Oppenheimer.

J95. DODSLEY, Robert. CHRONICLE OF THE KINGS OF ENGLAND, THE.

(1) A 'new edition', 1799. Pr f EN et al. Price 2s.

THE | CHRONICLE | OF THE | KINGS OF ENGLAND, | FROM THE | NORMAN CONQUEST TO THE | PRESENT TIME. | [p.s.rule] | BY R. DODSLEY. | [p.s.rule] | A NEW EDITION ENLARGED. | [d.p.rule] | [wct vignette] | [d.p.rule] | LONDON: | PR F VERNOR AND HOOD, POULTRY; | E. NEWBERY, SPC-Y; DARTON AND HARVEY, | GRACECHURCH-STREET; LACKINGTON, ALLEN AND CO. | MOORFIELDS; AND C. CAWTHORNE, STRAND. | [p.rule] | 1799.

12mo. 72 leaves. Pp. iv+140. Wct on TP; 33 wct oval bust portraits of sovereigns. The vignette and portraits had been used in *Characters of the Kings and Queens of England*, 1795 (J51), but without the frames of lines. 18 wct tail-pieces, many of the Bewick workshop or school, and used in other books of this period. The *Characters* of 1795 claims that the 'heads' were by 'Bewick'. At most, they were the work of pupils, or possibly done by John Bewick when working in London (1786–95).

[BM, 12·7×7·6 cm.

(2) A 'new edition, enlarged', undated. Pr f EN et al. ? Hugo 3772.

THE | CHRONICLE | OF THE | KINGS | OF | ENGLAND, | FROM | THE NORMAN CONQUEST UNTO | THE PRESENT TIME. | [p.rule] | BY R. DODSLEY. | [p.rule] | A NEW EDITION ENLARGED. | [p.rule] | [oval wct] | LONDON | PR F VERNOR AND HOOD, BIRCHIN LANE; | AND E. NEWBERY, SPCY.

In 12's. 80 leaves. Pp. ii+156. Wcts (probably as in (1)). Marbled bds, green vellum spine.

[Osborne*, 12·3×7·7 cm.

DRAMATIC DIALOGUES. See Pinchard, Mrs E.

DRAWING SCHOOL FOR LITTLE MASTERS... See 'Angelo, Master Michel'.

J96. DUCRAY-DUMENIL, Francois Guillaume. THE LITTLE MOUNTAINEERS OF AUVERGNE, 1801. S b EN. Price 4s. Welsh 257.

THE LITTLE | MOUNTAINEERS | OF | AUVERGNE; | OR, | THE ADVEN-TURES | OF | JAMES AND GEORGETTE. | [p.s.rule] | ALTERED FROM THE FRENCH, AND ADAPTED TO THE | PERUSAL OF YOUTH. | [d.p.rule] | [orna-ment] | LONDON: | PR F R. AND L. PEACOCK, | THE JUVENILE LIBRARY,

NO. 259, OXFORD-STREET; | VERNOR AND HOOD, POULTRY; | A S B | E. NEWBERY, CORNER OF SP. | [p.rule] | J. CUNDEE, PRINTER, IVY-LANE. | [d.p.rule] | 1801.

In 12's. 120 leaves+1 inset. Pp. viii+232. Engvd FP sgd 'Corbould del', 'C. Pye sct'. 11 wct tailpieces. Half-title.

The adaptation from Ducray-Dumenil's *Petit Jacques et Georgette, ou les petits Montagnards Auvergnats* has been attributed to both Lucy Peacock and Elizabeth Sandham. Miss Judith St John of Toronto has adduced weighty reasons against the latter.

[BM, 17·2×10·1 cm; Traylen; Preston, Cat. p. 118; UCLA; Muirhead, Cat. 31 [1967] item 111; Schiller, Cat. 26 (1971) item 395.

J97. EASTER-GIFT, THE.
(1) Adv. *LC* 27–9.12.64, p. 619: 'Mr Newbery intends to publish on 1st January.' Price 2*d*. Probably = no. (1A).
(1A) An edition of 1764 (very probably the 1st). Pr f JN. Price 2*d*.

Title approx. as for no. (3). *Imprint:* PR F J. NEWBERY, AT THE BIBLE AND | SUN IN SPC-Y. 1764. | [PRICE TWO PENCE BOUND.]

A single gathering of 32 leaves, sgd [A]–[D8]. Pp. 58[63]. First and last leaves pastedowns. List of bks 'sold at Mr Newbery's' at pp. [59–62]. The text, with a wct, continues at p. [63]. 19 wcts in text, mostly by the hand that did the *Goody Two-Shoes* cuts. D.f. paper wrappers.

[NorBM, 9·6×6·5 cm.
(2) An edition listed in *Newtonian System*, 1770, as pr f C & N. Price 2*d*. 'Bd, gilt & adorned with cuts'.
(3) An edition of 1781. Pr f TC. Price 2*d*. *CBEL*, II, 563.

THE | EASTER-GIFT; | OR, | THE WAY TO BE VERY GOOD. | A BOOK VERY MUCH WANTED, AND WHICH | OUGHT TO BE READ BY THE PARENTS AS | WELL AS CHILDREN. | FOR IN IT THEY MAY CHANCE TO FIND | SOMETHING TO MEND THE HEART AND MIND. | WOGLOG. | [p.rule] | ADORNED WITH CUTS. | [d.p.rule] | LONDON: | PR F T. CARNAN, IN S | PC-Y. 1781. | [PRICE TWO PENCE BOUND.]

Pp. 59[63]. Wct FP and wcts in text. Advert. on p. 59. Bk-list on pp. 60[62]. Wct and 4 lines verse on p. [63]. 'Illustrated paper covers'. (Communicated.)
[Welch.
(4) An edition of 1785. TC. Welsh 208. The copy in the S&W Cat. is described as having 'a white cover, with 4 curious woodcuts (2 on either side), printed in red'.
[Ball.

EASY AND ENTERTAINING SPELLING BOOK. See CIRCLE OF THE SCIENCES, No. J70.

J98. EASY GUIDE TO THE ENGLISH LANGUAGE, AN.
(1) Adv. *LC* 27–9.12.68, p. 623, as pr f N & C, price 1*s*. 'Bound in Linen and sewed

in Bands, by which method it will last ten Times as long as the Spelling Books, which are bound in the common Manner.'

(2) An edition listed as pr f TC in *Abraham Aesop*, 1783, and in *Newtonian System*, 1787, price 1*s*. Welsh 213.

EASY INTRODUCTION TO THE ENGLISH LANGUAGE. See CIRCLE OF THE SCIENCES, no. J64(1).

J99. EASY SPELLING DICTIONARY FOR THOSE WHO WOULD WRITE CORRECTLY, AN. Adv. *LC* 6–8.1.63, p. 28, as to be had of JN, price 1*s*. Perhaps J268(9), 1763.

EASY SPELLING DICTIONARY ON A NEW PLAN, AN.
Newbery's *Spelling Dictionary...on a New Plan*, J268, is frequently so listed or adv. Welsh 200.

EDWARD BARNARD. See Pilkington, M. (H.).

ELMINA; OR, THE FLOWER THAT NEVER FADES. See Masson, C. F. P.

ENCHANTED CASTLE, HISTORY OF THE. See J48.

J100. ENCHANTED MIRROR, THE.
(1) An edition of 1799. S b E. Newberry (*sic*). Price 1*s* 6*d* sewed.

THE | ENCHANTED MIRROR, | A | MOORISH ROMANCE. | [d.p.rule] | [ornam. wct design] | [d.p.rule] | SALISBURY: | PR A S B J. EASTON, SOLD ALSO BY E. NEWBERRY, | SPC-Y, LONDON. | [p.s.rule] | 1799. | [PRICE 1*s* 6*d*. SEWED.]

12mo. 66 leaves. Pp. iv[vi]+123[124]. Last leaf a blank. A number of small wct tailpieces. Bk-list on vso of last leaf.

[BM (imperf.), 17·8×10·1 cm; Bodley.
(2) Second edition, 1800. S b E. Newberry (*sic*) et al. Price 1*s* 6*d*.

THE | ENCHANTED MIRROR, | A | MOORISH ROMANCE. | [d.s.rule] | SECOND EDITION. | [d.p.rule] | [wct ornamental design] | [d.p. rule] | SALISBURY: | PR A S B J. EASTON, HIGH-STREET. SOLD ALSO BY | E. NEWBERRY, SPC-Y, LONDON. | [p.s.rule] | 1800.

Pp. viii+[9]–110. Half-title. Marbled bds, green vell. spine. (Communicated.)
[Welch, 14·0 cm.

J101. ENGLISH, Harriet. CONVERSATIONS AND AMUSING TALES, 1799. S b E. Newberry (*sic*) et al.

CONVERSATIONS | AND | AMUSING TALES. | OFFERED | TO THE PUBLICK | FOR THE | YOUTH OF GREAT BRITAIN. | [p.rule] | [11 lines quotes] | [d.p.rule]

| LONDON: | PR F THE AUTHOR, | BY CHARLES CLARKE, NORTHUMBERLAND COURT, STRAND. | PUBLISHED BY HATCHARD, PICCADILLY; | A S B CADELL AND DAVIES, STRAND; EGERTON, WHITE HALL; | FAULDER, NEW BOND STREET; PEACOCK, OXFORD STREET; | NEWBERRY, SPCY; AND DARTON | AND HARVEY, GRACECHURCH STREET. | [p.s.rule] | 1799.

4°. 202 [?203] leaves+15 insets. Pp. xi[xiv]+385[392]. Engvd FP sgd 'W. Hamilton R.A. pinxt', 'F. Bartolozzi sculpt'; 12 leaves of mezzotints; 2 folding leaves of music; 9 ornam. wct tailpieces; engvd coat-of-arms at head of a1^r. ? Half-title.

[BM, 25·4×19·1 cm; Bodley (thick paper); Osborne*; CUL; LI; KE; Grant; Brimmell, Cat. 67 (1970) item 16; A. R. Heath, Cat. 22 (1972) item 16.

J102. ENGLISH, Harriet. THE FAITHFUL MIRROR, 1799. S b EN et al.

THE | FAITHFUL MIRROR. | INSCRIBED | TO HER ROYAL HIGHNESS | PRINCESS CHARLOTTE AUGUSTA OF | WALES. | [p.rule] | [6 lines quote] | [d.p.rule] | LONDON: | PR F THE AUTHOR: | S B E. NEWBERY, THE CORNER OF SPC | Y; AND J. HATCHARD, PICCADILLY. | [p.rule] | 1799.

In 8's. 28 leaves. Pp. vii[viii]+[9]-56. 14 small wct tailpieces.

[BM, 12·3×9·0 cm; MSaE.

J102A. ENTERTAINING AND REMARKABLE HISTORY OF ROBIN HOOD. An undated ed. was 'Pr b Assignment of T. Carnan, by P. Norbury' (copy in CLU). It is likely enough that TC also put out an ed. For another such 'Assignment' see J384.

J103. ENTERTAINING FABLES FOR THE INSTRUCTION OF CHILDREN.

(1A) Listed as pubd for a s b JN in *Mosaic Creation*, 1766, or before (J248(3)).
(1B) Listed in *Goody Two-Shoes*, 1768, as s b N & C; and in *LC* 3–5.8.69. Price 1*d*.
(2) An edition of 1770. Pr f C & N. Price 1*d*.

ENTERTAINING | FABLES | FOR THE | INSTRUCTION OF | CHILDREN. | EMBELLISHED WITH CUTS. | [d.p.rule] | LONDON: | PR F T. CARNAN AND F. NEW- | BERY, JUN, AT NO. 65, IN SP | CY. 1770 | [PRICE ONE-PENNY.]
Pp. vii+21[22]. 18 wcts in text. D.f. paper wrappers. (Communicated.)
[Opie.
(2A) An undated edition. Pr f C & N. Pp. [vii]+21[24]. D.f. wrappers. (Not seen.)
[Maxwell Hunley, Cat. 48 [winter 1969] item 100, 9·2×6·5 cm.
(3) Listed in *Newtonian System*, 1787, as pr f TC. Price 1*d*. Welsh 215.
(4) An undated edition. Pr f TC. Specification as for (2). (Communicated.)
[UCLA.

J104. ENTERTAINING MEDLEY, THE, n.d. Pr f EN. Listed in *Anecdotes of Mary*, 1795. Weedon 57, IX. One of the 10 vols forming the *Lilliputian*

Library 'compiled' by Richard Johnson (see J218). It has not been possible to compare EN's ed. with Domville's, but, by analogy with nos. J89 and J217, it will probably be found to consist of the sheets of Domville, less one leaf of quire A, with a cancel TP.

THE | ENTERTAINING MEDLEY; | CONTAINING THE | HISTORY OF PRINCE CHERY | AND | PRINCESS FAIR STAR; | AND THE | STORY OF THE PIGEON AND DOVE. | [p.s.rule] | ADORNED WITH CUTS. | [p.s.rule] | LONDON: | PR F E. NEWBERY, AT THE CORNER OF SP | CY. | [PRICE SIX-PENCE.]

In 12's. 59 leaves+13 insets. Cancel TP. Pp. 120. Wct FP and 12 wcts in text. D.f.b.

[Bell, 10·0×8·3 cm.

J105. ENTERTAINING TRAVELLER, THE. Welsh 319; Weedon 22. Adv. *LC* 19–21.12.80 as for publication in the Christmas holidays. Richard Johnson's Day-book records: *1780 Oct. 2.——Delivered to* [*M*ʳˢ *Newbery*] *Journey to the Island of Wisdom——£2. 2s.*

(1) An edition of ?1780–81. Pr f EN. Price 2*d* bd and gilt.

THE | ENTERTAINING TRAVELLER; | GIVING A | BRIEF ACCOUNT | OF THE | VOYAGES AND TRAVELS | OF | MASTER TOMMY COLUMBUS, | IN SEARCH OF THE | ISLAND OF WISDOM; | WITH A | DESCRIPTION OF THAT ISLAND; | AS ALSO OF THE | ROCK OF CURIOSITY, THE COURT OF AM- | BITION, THE FIELD OF LUXURY, AND | THE DESERT OF FAMINE. | [d.p.rule] | LONDON: | PR F E. NEWBERY, AT THE CORNER | OF SPCY. | [PRICE TWO PENCE BOUND AND GILT.]

In 16's. 32 leaves. Collates [A]–[B16]. Pp. 63. First and last leaves pastedowns. Wct FP and 14 wcts in text. D.f. paper wrappers.

[Weedon, 10·0×6·4 cm; Sotheby, 16.3.70, lot 100.

(2) Another edition of ?1780–81. Pr f EN. Price 2*d* bd and gilt.

Title and *imprint* as for no. (1) except in line 16 read DESART. Collates [A]–[D8]. 32 leaves. Pp. 63. First and last leaves pastedowns. Wct FP and 14 wcts in text. Pink floral impress on grey paper wrappers.

[Bell, 10·2×5·8 cm.

(3) Copies in MSaE and MWA not checked.

(4) Listed in ENC, p. 5. Price 2*d*.

EVERY YOUNG MAN'S COMPANION. See Gordon, W.

EXPOSITION OF THE COMMON PRAYER BOOK. See no. J40.

J106. FABLES FOR YOUTH.

(1) An edition of 1777. Pr f TC. Price 2*s*.

FABLES | FOR | YOUTH. | EMBELLISHED WITH | COPPER-PLATE CUTS. | LONDON: | PR F T. CARNAN, AT NUMBER 65, | IN SPC-Y. | [p.rule] | MDCCLXXVII.

In 12's. 74 leaves+17 insets. Pp. vi+[3]–144. Engvd FP and 16 other engvd leaves.

⌊BM, 10·5 × 8·6 cm.

(2) An edition quoted by Welsh 215: 'From Carnan's List, 1789'. Price 2s.

J107. FABLES FOR YOUTH. TO WHICH IS ADDED A FABLE ON LIBERTY, WRITTEN BY THAT FRIEND OF FREEDOM, HIS MAJESTY OF PRUSSIA. Pr f TC. Price 2s in the vell. manner. Adv. *LC* 21–4.12.76, p. 603.

This is no. J106, the 'Fable on Liberty' being that no. XVII, 'The Bullfinch and the Sparrow. By the King of Prussia'.

FABLES IN VERSE. See 'Aesop, Abraham'.

J108. FABLES IN VERSE; WITH THE LIFE OF AESOP, AND THE CONVERSATION OF BIRDS AND BEASTS, n.d. Pr f the Booksellers of all Nations...(probably EN, with Darton and Harvey, who were at 55 Gracechurch Street from about 1785). Price 6d.

FABLES | IN VERSE; | WITH THE | LIFE OF ÆSOP, | AND THE | CONVER-SATION OF BIRDS AND BEASTS; | WITH A VARIETY OF | CUTS FOR CHILDREN. | [rule] | BY THEIR OLD FRIEND, JOHN NEWBERRY (sic). | [d.p.rule] | LONDON: | PR F THE BOOKSELLERS OF ALL NATIONS, AND | SOLD AT THE CORNER OF SPC-Y, | AND AT NO. 55, GRACECHURCH-STREET. | [PRICE SIX-PENCE.]

Pp. 84. (Communicated.)

⌊Ball, 12·5 cm; MiDW.

FABLES OF FLOWERS. See Wynne, J. H.

J109. Entry deleted.

FACILE INTRODUCTION A LA CONNOISSANCE DE LA NATURE...DES SAINTES ECRITURES. See Trimmer, Sarah.

J110. FAIRING, THE; OR, A GOLDEN TOY; FOR CHILDREN.
(1) Adv. *LC* 27–9.12.64, p. 619: 'On 1st January Mr. Newbery intends to publish...'. Price 6d.
(2) A 'new edition' of 1767. ?JN.
⌊St Bride (missing).
(3) An edition of 1768. Pr f N & C. Price 6d bd and gilt.

THE | FAIRING: | OR, A | GOLDEN TOY; | FOR | CHILDREN | OF ALL | SIZES AND DENOMINATIONS. | IN WHICH THEY MAY SEE ALL THE FUN OF THE FAIR, | AND AT HOME BE AS HAPPY AS IF THEY WERE THERE. | ADORNED WITH VARIETY OF CUTS, FROM | ORIGINAL DRAWINGS. |

[d.p.rule] | LONDON: | PR F NEWBERY AND CARNAN, AT | NO. 65, THE NORTH SIDE OF SP | C-Y, 1768. | PRICE SIX-PENCE BOUND AND GILT.

FP and illustrations in the text. 3 pages of adverts. at end. (Communicated.)

[Ball; Sotheby, 5.2.1945 (the Bussell sale), lot 100.

(4) An edition of 1777. (? N & C).

[Sotheby, 5.2.1945 (the Bussell sale), lot 145.

(4A) An edition of 1780. Pr f TC. Price 6*d*.

Title approx. as for no. (3). *Imprint:* PR F T. CARNAN, IN SP | C-Y. | MDCCLXXX. | (PRICE SIXPENCE.)

In 8's. 69[+?] leaves. Pp. vi+7–138[+?]. 32[+?] wcts. Black wcts on white or buff bds.

[Bath, 9·4×6·4 cm (imperf.); Gardner (formerly Tighe); UCLA.

(5) An edition of 1784. Pr f TC. Price 6*d*.

Title approx. as for no. (3). *Imprint:* PR F T. CARNAN, SUCCESSOR TO MR | J. NEWBERY, IN SPC-Y. | MDCCLXXXIV. | (PRICE SIX-PENCE.)

32mo. 72 leaves. Pp. vi+7–141[144]. List of bks pr f TC on last 3 pages. Wct FP and many wcts in text. D.f.b. (Communicated.)

[McKell, 9·5×6·5 cm; Ball.

(6) One or more edd. mentioned in Welsh 216 (Carnan's List, 1787); *CBEL*, II, 563 (*ca.* 1787); Gum 2460 (*ca.* 1786); Gum 2461 (1787); and listed in *Newtonian System*, 1787, pr f TC. Price 6*d*.

Gum's 2461 lacks TP and it is not apparent on what authority that copy is dated 1787. All these references may be to the same ed., and perhaps identical with no. (5).

FAITHFUL MIRROR, THE. See English, Harriet.

J111. FALSE ALARMS. Weedon 24. Recorded in Richard Johnson's Day-book as: *1787 June 15. Mr Badcock——To writing False Alarms——£.3. 3s.*

(1) An edition of 1770 by JN is recorded by A. W. Tuer (*Stories from Old-fashioned Children's Books*); this is repeated by *CBEL*, II, 562. But JN had died in 1767. Weedon, probably rightly, considers 1770 an 'erroneous date': see the date in Johnson's Day-book entry (though Johnson may not have been the real author).

(2) An edition of 1787–8. Pr f EN. Price 3*d*. Adv. *LC* 27–9.12.87, p. 619, as 'In the Christmas holidays will be published'. Welsh 216.

(3) An edition of 1796. Pr f EN.

Title approx. as in no. (5). 13 cuts. Coloured floral wrappers.

[Elkin Mathews, Cat. 163 [1965] item 227.

(4) An edition of 1799. Hugo 3779 gives an abbreviated transcription of the title, with *imprint* PR F F. NEWBERY AT THE CORNER...1799. PRICE THREE PENCE.

FP and 12 wcts, 'apparently by John Bewick'.

Is the misprint 'F. Newbery' in Hugo or in the bk itself?

(5) An edition of 1799. Pr f EN. Price 3*d.*

FALSE ALARMS; | OR, THE | MISCHIEVOUS DOCTRINE | OF | GHOSTS AND APPARITIONS, | OF | SPECTRES AND HOBGOBLINS, | EXPLODED FROM THE | MINDS OF EVERY MISS AND MASTER. | [d.p.rule] | TO WHICH IS ADDED, | THE LITTLE PRISONER, | A MORAL TALE. | [d.p.rule] | LONDON: | PR F E. NEWBERY, AT THE CORNER | OF SPC-Y. | [p.rule] | 1799. | PRICE THREE PENCE.

In 8's. 48 leaves. Pp. 96. Wct FP and 12 wcts in text. Green paper wrappers, impressed with floral design, gilt.

[NorBM, 9·8×6·1 cm; Ball.

(6) An undated edition by EN.

[MWA; MSaE.

FAMILY AT SMILEDALE, HISTORY OF THE. See M., A.

FAMILY BOOK, THE. See Berquin, A.

J112. FATHER'S GIFT, THE.
(1) Adv. *LC* 3–5.1.75, p. 11, as pr f FN(N). Price 1*d.* Welsh 216.
(2) Listed in J88(3), vol. I, 1786, as pr f EN, price 1*d.*
(3) See Plate 4.

A single gathering of 16 leaves, sgd [A]–[B8]. First and last leaves pastedowns. Pp. 29[31]. Wct FP and 11 wcts in text. List of bks pr f EN on pp. [30–1]. D.f. paper wrappers.

[Roscoe, 9·6×6·3 cm; Sotheby, 5.2.1945 (the Bussell sale), lot 135.

(4) One or more edd. referred to in Welsh 216 ('E. Newbery's List, 1796'); Hugo II, 308; ENC, p. 5. Price 1*d.*
(5) Listed as pr f EN in *The Menagerie*, 1800. Price 1*d.*

J113. FENELON, Francois de Salignac de la Mothe. **TELEMAQUE.** (Juvenile edd.) Welsh 217.

(1) AVANTURES DE TELEMAQUE, CORRIGEE PAR N. WANOSTRACHT, LL.D. Listed in Pilkington's *Obedience rewarded*, 1797, as pr f a s b EN and Vernor and Hood. Price 3*s.* The ed. of 1796 was by Vernor and Hood, Ogilvy and Speare, and T. Boosey (copy in CLU).

(2) ADVENTURES OF TELEMACHUS, ABRIDGED, THE, 1770. Pr f TC. Price 2*s* 6*d* in the vell. manner. Richard Johnson had a hand in this, but in what way is not clear. His Day-book records *1770 March 16. Delivered The Adventures of Telemachus.——Twenty Guineas. [Paid by Carnan.]* See Weedon 5.

Engraved TP: THE | ADVENTURES | OF | TELEMACHUS, | THE | SON OF ULYSSES. | ABRIDGED FROM THE FRENCH | OF THE | ARCHBISHOP OF CAMBRAY. | [p.s.rule] | LONDON | PR F T. CARNAN, | IN SPCY | MDCCLXX.

In 6's. 168 leaves+2 insets. Pp. x, viii+315. Engvd FP sgd 'W. Walker' and TP. 24 wcts in text. Blue bds, green vell. spine, label.

[Bodley, 13·4×8·0 cm; LUL; Renier.

(3) Many listings and adverts. of the work as by TC or C & N between 1773 and 1777. Price 2s 6d.

(4) ADVENTURES OF TELEMACHUS, ABRIDGED, THE, 1781. Pr f TC. Price 2s 6d. Weedon 5.

Engraved TP approx. as for no. (2), with date MDCCLXXXI.

In 6's. 162 leaves+2 insets. Pp. 305[308]. Engvd FP sgd 'W. Walker sculp' and TP. 24 oval wcts by the hand that produced the cuts in Wynne's *Choice Emblems.* List of bks pr f TC on pp. [306–8]. Bds, red vell. spine.

[Weedon, 13·8×8·7 cm; V&A(GL); Tudor.

J114. FENN, Lady Ellenor (or Eleanor) is generally credited with being the authoress of books by 'Mrs Lovechild'. This attribution is supported by BM General Cat. and *DNB.* The late Alfred Wallis, on the other hand, asserted that 'this good creature [Lady Fenn] did not pose as Mrs Lovechild but preferred to rank with the other sex, as "Solomon Lovechild"'. At present there seems no convincing evidence, one way or the other; and Wallis is too pugnacious to be taken very seriously.

Welsh, at p. 218, lists the following as by Fenn, 'under pseudonym of Mrs Lovechild': *Child's Grammar, Mother's Do., Parsing Lessons for elder Pupils; Do. Do. Young Persons; Grammatical Amusements in a Box; Sunday Miscellany; Short Sermons for Young Persons; Short Introduction to Geography,* 22nd ed. The *Geography* was in fact written by Mr Newcombe, of Hackney (see no. J268A). It may be that Lady Fenn edited or re-wrote it. On the other hand the identity of Lady Fenn with 'Mrs Teachwell' seems reasonably established. The 2nd ed. of her *Rational Dame* (J. Marshall, n.d.) lists a 'complete Set of Mrs Teachwell's Works' (this must be a fairly early list): *Cobwebs to catch Flies, Fables in Monosyllables, Fables, in which the Morals are drawn incidentally..., Juvenile Correspondence, Rational Sports, School Occurrences, School Dialogues for Boys, The Female Guardian, A Spelling Book.* And see *CBEL,* II, 557.

J115. FENN, Lady Ellenor. CHILD'S GRAMMAR, by 'Mrs Lovechild'.
(1) Listed as pubd by EN in Fenn's *Parsing Lessons for elder Pupils,* 1798. Price 6d. Listed elsewhere at 8d.
(2) Listed in ENC, p. 22. Price 8d.

J116. FENN, Lady Ellenor. FRIEND OF MOTHERS, THE, 1799. Adv. as by 'Mrs Lovechild'. Pr f EN. Price 1s. Alston, I, 524.

THE | FRIEND OF | MOTHERS: | DESIGNED TO | ASSIST THEM IN THEIR ATTEMPTS | TO INSTIL THE | RUDIMENTS | OF | LANGUAGE AND ARITH-METIC, | AT AN EARLY AGE, | AND IN A | MANNER AGREEABLE TO THEIR CHILDREN. | [d.p.rule] | LONDON: | PR F E. NEWBERY, CORNER OF S | PC-Y. | [p.s.rule] | 1799.

Pp. vi+83+3 blanks. Lists of books and other educational matter s b EN on pp. 79–83. Stiff salmon-pink wrappers, oval label on upper. (Communicated.)

⸢Shiers, 13·3×8·6 cm.

J116A. FENN, Lady Ellenor. INFANT'S DELIGHT, THE, 1797. Pr f EN. Price 1s 6d.

THE | INFANT'S | DELIGHT. | [line of 8 stars] | LONDON: | PR F E. NEWBERY, s | PC-Y. | [p.rule] | 1797.

A single gathering of 7 unsigned and unnumbered leaves, the fourth an inset, unbound. Accompanying the pamphlet are 6 cards, each showing 6 etchings by G. Quinton of common objects (Fir, Boy, Oak etc.) each etching being numbered and titled, the whole in a cardboard slip-case, 14·0×9·0 cm, with label THE INFANT'S DELIGHT. (Communicated.)

⸢Melbourne, 11·2 cm.

J117. FENN, Lady Ellenor. INFANT'S FRIEND, THE. PART I. SPELLING BOOK. By 'Mrs Lovechild'. 1797. Pr f EN. Price 8d and 'a few copies on fine paper, neatly bound in red' price 1s and 1s 6d. Welsh 218 and 260. Alston, IV, 923 and Plate XCIX.

THE | INFANT'S FRIEND. | [d.p.rule] | PART I. | [d.p.rule] | A SPELLING BOOK. | BY MRS. LOVECHILD. | [wct ornamental device] | LONDON: | PR F E. NEWBERY, AT THE CORNER | OF SPC-Y. | [p.rule] | 1797.

In 6's. 54 leaves. Pp. xii+92[93]. Wct FP. Advert. of Pt II of the bk on last leaf. Blue bds, with label on upper.

⸢BM, 13·8×8·6 cm; Opie; Pollard; NNC-T (Darton Coll.); McKell.

J118. FENN, Lady Ellenor. INFANT'S FRIEND, THE. PART II. READING LESSONS. By 'Mrs Lovechild'. 1797. Pr f EN. Price 1s and 'a few copies on fine paper, neatly bound in red, 1s 6d'. Welsh 218 and 260; Alston, IV, 923.

THE | INFANT'S FRIEND. | [d.p.rule] | PART II. | [d.p.rule] | READING LESSONS. | BY MRS. LOVECHILD. | [Vignette] | LONDON: | PR F E. NEWBERY, AT THE CORNER | OF SPC-Y. | 1797.

Pp. xii+163[168]. ? A wct FP. Adverts. on last 4 pages. (Communicated.)

⸢Pollard; UCLA; (imperf.); NNC-T (Darton Coll.).

J119. FENN, Lady Ellenor. INFANT'S FRIEND, THE. PART III. READING LESSONS. By 'Mrs Lovechild'. Listed in Trimmer's *Silver Thimble*, 1799, as pr f EN. Price 1s.

J119A. FENN, Lady E. INFANT'S PATH STREWED WITH FLOWERS, THE. Listed in Fenn's *Friend of Mothers*, 1799, as s b EN, price 5s.

J120. FENN, Lady Ellenor. MOTHER'S GRAMMAR, THE. Listed as by 'Mrs Lovechild'. Listed in Fenn's *Parsing Lessons for young Children*, 1798, and in ENC, as s b EN. Price 6*d*. Alston, 1, 518.

J121. FENN, Lady Ellenor. MRS LOVECHILD'S GOLDEN PRESENT. Welsh 218.
(1) An edition adv. *LC* 27–9.12.68, p. 619, among bks 'prepared as proper presents' by FN(N). Price 1*d*. Perhaps = no. (2).
(2) An undated edition (1770 or before). Pr f FN(N). Price 1*d* bd and gilt. (Ms inscription in the CLU copy 'Calvin Ward 1770'.)
    MRS. LOVECHILD'S | GOLDEN PRESENT, | TO ALL THE LITTLE | MASTERS AND MISSES, | OF | EUROPE, ASIA, AFRICA, AND AMERICA. | THE SEEDS OF VIRTUE, VIRTUOUS DEEDS PRODUCE. | LONDON, | PR F A S B F. NEWBERY, THE | CORNER OF SPC-Y. | [PRICE ONE PENNY, BOUND AND GILT.]
    Pp. 31. First and last leaves pastedowns. Wct FP and 25 wcts in text. (Communicated.)
    [UCLA, 10·0×6·5 cm.
(3) An edition listed as pr f a s b FN(N) in *Brother's Gift*, 1777. Price 1*d*.
(4) Listed in J88(3), vol. 1, 1786, as pr f EN. Price 1*d*.
(5) Listed in *Flights of a Lady-Bird*, 1794, as pr f EN, and in ENC. Price 1*d*.

J122. FENN, Lady Ellenor. PARSING LESSONS FOR ELDER PUPILS, 1798, by 'Mrs. Lovechild'. Pr f EN. Price 1*s* 3*d*. Alston, 1, 520.
    PARSING LESSONS | FOR | ELDER PUPILS: | RESOLVED INTO | THEIR ELEMENTS. | FOR THE | ASSISTANCE | OF | PARENTS AND TEACHERS. | BY | MRS. LOVECHILD. | [d.p.rule] | LONDON: | PR F E. NEWBERY, THE CORNER | OF SPC-Y. | [p.rule] | 1798.
    In 6's. 72 leaves. Pp. xii+127[131]. Lists of bks pubd by EN on final pages. Blue stiff paper wrappers, oval white label on upper.
    [BM, 14·1×8·8 cm.

J123. FENN, Lady Ellenor. PARSING LESSONS FOR YOUNG CHILDREN, 1798, by 'Mrs. Lovechild'. Pr f EN. Price 9*d*. Alston, 1, 519.
    PARSING LESSONS | FOR | YOUNG CHILDREN: | RESOLVED INTO | THEIR ELEMENTS, | FOR THE | ASSISTANCE | OF | PARENTS AND TEACHERS. | BY | MRS. LOVECHILD. | [d.p.rule] | LONDON: | PR F E. NEWBERY, THE CORNER | OF SPC-Y. | [p.rule] | 1798.
    In 6's. 36 leaves. Pp. xiv+56[58]. List of bks s b EN on pp. [57–8].
    [BM, 13·1×7·9 cm; Melbourne.

J124. ? FENN, Lady Ellenor. RATIONAL DAME, THE; OR, HINTS TOWARDS SUPPLYING PRATTLE FOR CHILDREN. Listed in

Fenn's *Parsing Lessons for elder Pupils*, 1798, as a bk which 'may be had' at Mrs Newbery's. Price 1s 6d. But all edd. seen are by J. Marshall. ENC, p. 19; *CBEL*, II, 557.

FENN, Lady Ellenor. READING LESSONS = *The Infant's Friend*, Pts II and III.

J125. FENN, Lady Ellenor. SHORT HISTORY OF INSECTS, A; CONTAINING RUDIMENTS OF THAT BRANCH OF NATURAL HISTORY: DESIGNED AS AN INTRODUCTION TO THE STUDY, AND AS A POCKET COMPANION TO THOSE WHO VISIT MUSEUMS. Listed in Trimmer's *Silver Thimble*, 1799 and 1801, as pr f EN. Price 3s 6d uncoloured and sewed. *CBEL*, II, 557; ENC, pp. 10 and 23.

The bk was pubd by Stevenson and Matchett, of Norwich in [1797] and [?1800] (copies in BM).

J126. ? FENN, Lady Ellenor. SHORT HISTORY OF QUADRUPEDS, A, EXTRACTED FROM AUTHORS OF CREDIT; CONTAINING A GREAT NUMBER OF PLATES; THE ANIMALS ARRANGED SYSTEMATICALLY, AGREEABLE TO PENNANT. 2 vols.

Listed in Fenn's *Parsing Lessons for elder Pupils*, 1798, as a book to be had of Mrs Newbery. Price 5s. ENC, p. 23.

J127. Entry deleted.

J128. FENN, Lady Ellenor. SUNDAY MISCELLANY, THE, IN PROSE AND VERSE, FOR YOUNG PERSONS. Pr f EN. Price 1s. Listed in J122, 1798 and J362(1), 1799. Welsh 312.

J129. FENN, Lady Ellenor. TOILES D'ARAIGNÉES POUR ATTRAPER LES MOUCHES, 1799. Chez EN et al. Price 1s 6d.
TOILES D'ARAIGNÉES | POUR ATTRAPER | LES MOUCHES, | OU | COURTS DIALOGUES | POUR | L'INSTRUCTION DES ENFANS, | DEPUIS L'ÂGE DE TROIS ANS, | JUSQU'À CELUI DE HUIT. | [d.p.rule] | EN DEUX VOLUMES. | [d.p.rule] | VOL. I | [p.s.rule] | À LONDRES: | DE L'IMPRIMERIE DE BAYLIS, GREVILLE-STREET, | HATTON GARDEN, | ET SE TROUVE CHEZ T. HURST, NO. 32. PATERNOSTER-ROW; | ET E. NEWBERY, AU COIN DE ST. PAUL'S CHURCH-YARD. | [p.rule] | 1799.
Divisional title for vol. II *at G4*: TOILES D'ARAIGNÉES | POUR ATTRAPER | LES MOUCHES, | OU | DIALOGUES | À | L'USAGE DES ENFANS, DEPUIS L'ÂGE DE TROIS ANS, | JUSQU'À CELUI DE HUIT. | [d.p.rule] | VOL. II. | [d.p.rule].

In 6's. 72 leaves. Pp. xvi+[17]–141[142]; the pagination is continuous through vols I and II. Marbled bds, green vell. spine, label on upper cover. No wcts.

The first ed., with the English title *Cobwebs to catch Flies* and text, was pubd by John Marshall from his address at 4 Aldermary Church Yard. The Dedication is dated 15 July 1783. It was in 2 vols, 12 wcts in vol. I, 15 in vol. II; these wcts are some of the most delightful in any book by Marshall. There were a number of later English edd. by Marshall, one (in the writer's possession) not before 1812; all had the wcts. How EN came to issue this rather dreary ed. with French text of one of Marshall's very successful publications is not apparent; it has no wcts, the 2 vols are run into one. As compared with Marshall's edd., it makes a very poor showing. EN listed it in *LC* for 21–4.12.99 as one of her publications for the Christmas holidays; but it does not appear in her 1800 Catalogue (ENC), though Harris listed it in his *Dog of Knowledge*, 1801, at 1s 6d.

[BCE, 13·9×8·5 cm.

J130. ? FENN, Lady Ellenor. VILLAGE MATRON, THE, A MISCELLANEOUS WORK FOR YOUNG PERSONS. Pr f EN. Price 1s. Listed in J362(1), 1799. Welsh 325. The attribution to Fenn is by Algar.

J130A. FENNING, Daniel. THE YOUNG ALGEBRAIST'S COMPANION. Adv. *GEP* 11.5.50 as s b JN et al. according to Welsh 218–19. There were edd. of 1750, 1751 and later, but I have traced none under a Newbery imprint.

FESTIVAL HYMNS. See Merrick, John.

J131. FIELDING, Henry. HISTORY OF JOSEPH ANDREWS... ABRIDGED.
(1) An edition of 1769. Pr f FN(N). Price 1s.
THE | HISTORY | OF THE | ADVENTURES | OF | JOSEPH ANDREWS, | AND HIS FRIEND | MR. ABRAHAM ADAMS. | ABRIDGED | FROM THE WORKS OF H. FIELDING, ESQ; | [device] | [d.p.rule] | LONDON: | PR F F. NEWBERY, AT THE CORNER OF | SPC-Y. | [p.rule] | MDCCLXIX.

In 6's. 82 leaves+6 insets. Pp. 149. Last leaf a blank. Engvd FP and 5 other engvd plates. List of children's bks s b FN(N) on A5ᵛ–A6ᵛ. D.f.b.
[BM, 11·2×7·2 cm.
(1A) Listed in Chesterfield's *Maxims*, 1777, as pr f FN(N). Price 1s.
(2) An edition of 1784. Pr f EN. Price 1s. Welsh 219; Gum 2522.

Title as for no. (1). *Imprint:* PR F E. NEWBERY, AT THE CORNER | OF SPC-Y. PRICE 1s. | [p.rule] | MDCCLXXXIV.

In 6's. 87 leaves+6 insets. Pp. 163. Engvd FP and 5 other engvd plates. D.f.b.
[BM, 11·0×7·6 cm; Bell; Ball; Osborne*.
(3) An edition of 1793. Pr f EN. Price 1s. Gum 2523.

Title and *imprint*, with date 1793, approx. as for no. (2). Pp. 180. FP and other plates as for no. (2). D.f.b. (Communicated.)

⌐Ball.

(4) An edition of 1799. Pr f EN. Price 1*s*.

THE | HISTORY | AND | ADVENTURES | OF | JOSEPH ANDREWS, | AND HIS FRIEND | MR. ABRAHAM ADAMS. | ABRIDGED | FROM THE WORKS OF H. FIELDING, ESQ. | [d.p.rule] | LONDON: | PR F E. NEWBERY, THE CORNER OF SP | C-Y. | BY G. WOODFALL, NO. 22, PN-R. | 1799. | [p.s.rule] | PRICE ONE SHILLING.

In 6's. Pp. 136[144]. Engvd FP sgd 'Scott sculp'. List of bks pr f EN on pp. [137–44]. Blue wrappers, label on upper. (Communicated.)

⌐Shiers, 13·8 × 8·5 cm.

J132. FIELDING, Henry. HISTORY OF TOM JONES... ABRIDGED.

(1) Adv. *LC* 27–9.12.68, p. 619, as pr f FN(N), and 'in a few days w.b.p.'. Price 1*s*. Also listed in Winlove's *Moral Lectures*, 1769.

(1A) Listed in Chesterfield's *Maxims*, 1777, as pr f FN(N). Price 1*s*.

(2) An edition of 1784. Pr f EN.

THE | HISTORY | OF | TOM JONES, | A | FOUNDLING. | ABRIDGED FROM THE WORKS OF | HENRY FIELDING, ESQ. | [d.p.rule] | LONDON: | PR F E. NEWBERY, THE CORNER | OF SPCY. | [p.rule] | MDCCLXXXIV.

Pp. 194[207]. Engvd FP sgd 'J. Lodge sculp'. Engvd plates in text. Bk-list on pp. [195–207]. D.f.b. (Communicated.)

⌐Ball; UCLA.

(3) Listed in *Anecdotes of Mary*, 1795 and *Joseph Andrews*, 1799 as pr f EN. Price 1*s*.

J133. FIELDING, Sarah. THE GOVERNESS; OR, THE LITTLE FEMALE ACADEMY. Listed in Wynne's *Tales for Youth*, 1794, as pr f EN, and in ENC, price 1*s* 6*d*. Listed in *Anecdotes of Mary*, 1795, price 1*s*. Welsh 232; J. E. Grey, *Sarah Fielding. The Governess* (London, 1968), pp. 72 and 358–9 [no. 22].

J134. FILIAL DUTY, RECOMMENDED AND ENFORC'D. *CBEL*, II, 564.

(1) An edition of 1770 recorded by Lyon. FN(N).

(2) An undated edition, probably not before 1777 (bk-list includes edd. of nos. J12 (1777) and J50 (1777, 1778)). Pr f FN(N). Price 1*s*.

A NEW BOOK FOR THE IMPROVEMENT OF YOUNG | GENTLEMEN AND LADIES. | FILIAL DUTY, | RECOMMENDED AND ENFORC'D, | BY A VARIETY OF INSTRUCTIVE AND | ENTERTAINING STORIES, | OF | CHILDREN WHO HAVE BEEN REMARKABLE FOR | AFFECTION TO THEIR PARENTS; | [7 lines] | [p.s.rule] | LONDON: | PR F F. NEWBERY, THE CORNER OF | SPCY.

In 6's. 88 leaves+7 insets. Pp. viii+165[171]. Engvd FP sgd 'Royce Fecit' and 6 other engvd plates (one duplicate). List of bks pr f FN(N) on last 6 pages. D.f.b. (Communicated.)

[Osborne, Cat. p. 254, 11·2×7·1 cm. ? NNC-T (Darton Coll.).

(2A) Adv. *LC* 31.12.78–2.1.79, p. 4, as t.d.w.p. Price 1*s*. Probably = no. (2).

(3) An undated edition. Pr f EN.

Title approx. as for no. (2). *Imprint:* PR F E. NEWBERY THE CORNER OF S | PCY.

In 6's. 90 leaves+6 insets. Pp. viii+160[170]. Last leaf a blank, a pastedown. Engvd FP as in no. (2), 5 other engvd plates. List of bks pr f EN on pp. [161–70]. D.f.b.

[Roscoe, 11·5×8·0 cm; Ball; Osborne* (imperf.).

(4) Another undated edition. Pr f EN. Welsh 219–20.

Title approx. as for no. (2). *Imprint:* PR F E. NEWBERY, THE CORNER OF | SPCY

In 6's. 90 leaves+6 insets. Pp. viii+164[172]. FP as in no. (2) and 5 other engvd plates. List of bks pr f EN on last 8 pages. D.f.b.

[BM, Ch. 780/20; Roscoe, 11·5×7·6 cm.

(5) Another undated edition, 1798 or after. Pr f EN. Price 1*s* 6*d*. Welsh 219–20.

The *title* omits the first 2 lines (A NEW BOOK...LADIES.); otherwise approx. as for no. (2). *Imprint:* PR F E. NEWBERY, THE CORNER OF | SPC-Y.

In 6's. 90 leaves+engvd FP sgd 'Eckstein delt', 'J. Scott sculp' and publicn date 25.3.98. Pp. vi+174. Marbled bds, green vell. spine with label. Not in ENC.

[BM, 13·7×8·6 cm; Weedon; Roscoe (photocopied selected leaves); MB; Welch.

J135. FIRST BOOK FOR CHILDREN, BEING AN ATTEMPT TO MAKE THE ART OF READING BOTH EASY AND PLEASANT, BY ADAPTING THE MATTER AND MANNER OF EXPRESSIONS TO THE CAPACITIES OF CHILDREN. This title is quoted from Welsh (p. 220) who takes it from an EN list of 1789. Elsewhere the title is given as THE FIRST BOOK FOR CHILDREN; OR, READING MADE EASY.

(1) Adv. *LC* 30.12.81–1.1.82, p. 7, as to be had of EN, price 6*d*.

(2) Listed as pr f EN up to 1795 (no. J328). Price 6*d*.

FIRST COPY BOOK FOR YOUTH. See J378.

J135A. FIRST INTRODUCTION TO GEOGRAPHY. Pr f FN(N). Price 6*d*. Listed in *Cries of London*, 1775. Probably = Newcombe's *Short Introduction to Geography* (J268A).

J136. FLIGHTS OF A LADY-BIRD, THE. Weedon 25 (only records a Harris ed. of 1804). Richard Johnson's Day-book records: *1786 July.* M*ͬ*

Badcock——*To writing The Flights of a Lady-Bird. 2 Half Sheets. 32°. £2. 2s.*
The Dedication is signed R.J.

(1) Adv. *LC* 26–8.12.86, p. 620, as one of EN's New Publications for the Christmas Holidays 'just published', price 2*d*. Probably = no. (2).

(2) An edition of 1787. EN. Price 2*d*. Welsh 251. S&W Cat. D.f.b.

[Ball.

(3) An edition of 1794. Pr f EN. Price 2*d*.

Title and *imprint* approx. as for no. (4), with date 1794.

32mo in 16's. 32 leaves. Pp. 61[64]. Wct FP and 12 wcts in text. First and last leaves pastedowns. List of bks pubd by EN on last 2 pages. Pink and green wrappers with figures of St Petrus and St Paulus. (Communicated.)

[McKell, 9·9×6·4 cm.

(4) An edition of 1799. Pr f EN. Price 2*d*.

THE FLIGHTS | OF A | LADY-BIRD; | OR, THE | HISTORY | OF THE | WINGED RAMBLER: | [d.p.rule] | EMBELLISHED WITH CUTS. | [d.p.rule] | LONDON: | PR F E. NEWBERY, THE CORNER OF | SPC-Y. | 1799. | [PRICE TWO-PENCE.]

In 8's. 32 leaves. Pp. 61[63]. First and last leaves pastedowns. Wct FP and 12 wcts in the text. List of bks pr f EN on pp. [62–3]. Paper wrappers with green impressed floral design.

[Bodley, 9·9×6·1 cm; McKell.

FLORA; OR, THE DESERTED CHILD. See Somerville, Elizabeth.

J137. FLORIAN, Jolly B. GUIDE TO THE STUDY OF THE HISTORY OF ENGLAND, n.d. Pr f EN. Price 1*s*. Welsh 212; ENC, p. 8. Adv. *LC* t.d.i.p. 8–10.1.99, p. 39.

A | GUIDE | TO THE | STUDY | OF THE | HISTORY OF ENGLAND. | IN A SERIES OF QUESTIONS UPON | GOLDSMITH'S ABRIDGEMENT. | [p.s.rule] | COMPOSED FOR THE USE OF THE YOUNG LADIES AT ASSEMBLY-HOUSE | BOARDING SCHOOL, LAYTONSTONE, ESSEX. | [d.p.rule] | BY M. FLORIAN. | [d.p.rule] | LONDON: | PR F | E. NEWBERY, THE CORNER OF SPCY.

In 6's. 43 leaves. Pp. iv+80. Brown canvas school binding.

[Traylen, 16·7×10·2 cm.

J138. FLORIST, THE; OR, POETICAL NOSEGAY. Pr f EN. Price 1*s*.

Listed in *Anecdotes of Mary*, 1795. Welsh, p. 221, describes '*The Florist, or Poetical Nosegay and Drawing Book*, Containing 24 Copper Plates…with a descriptive Moral Poem to each…with full directions for colouring them… E. Newbery's List, c. 1800. Pp. 64…No place nor publisher nor date.' Copies of such an ed. are in BM and CUL, but whether identical with the ed. listed in *Anecdotes of Mary* is not apparent.

FOOD FOR THE MIND. See 'John-the-Giant-Killer'.

J139. FORCE OF EXAMPLE, THE, 1797. Pr f EN. Price 2s. Attributed by Algar to Mrs Pilkington. Welsh 221; Gum 2590; *CBEL*, II, 564.

THE | FORCE OF EXAMPLE; | OR, | THE HISTORY OF | HENRY AND CAROLINE: | WRITTEN FOR THE INSTRUCTION AND AMUSEMENT | OF YOUNG PERSONS. | [d.p.rule] | LONDON: | PR F E. NEWBERY, CORNER OF SP | C-Y. | [p.rule] | 1797.

12mo. 81 leaves+engvd FP sgd 'Kirk del', 'Scott sc.'. Pp. 159.

[Bodley; Roscoe, 17·2×10·3 cm; V&A(GL); Renier; Schiller; Preston, Cat. p. 111; UCLA; Ball; Shiers; NNC-T (Darton Coll.).

J140. FORTNIGHT'S TOUR, A, 1790. Pr f F. Power & Co. Price 4d. Welsh 222; Weedon 26. Richard Johnson's Day-book records: *1789 July. Mess. Newbery and Co.——To writing A Fortnight's Tour——£.3. 3s. [Paid Aug. 31 by Power]*.

One of the three known juvenile bks with Power's imprint not recorded as previously pubd. See also nos. J2 and J75. It is to be noted that Johnson's Day-book records he 'wrote' the bk to the order of 'Mess. Newbery and Co' (i.e. FN(S)), but that it was paid for by Power. See the Introduction at p. 28.

A | FORTNIGHT'S TOUR | THROUGH | DIFFERENT PARTS OF THE COUNTRY, | BY | MASTER TOMMY NEWTON; | INCLUDING | ORIGINAL ANECDOTES | OF SEVERAL | LITTLE MISSES AND MASTERS. | [p.rule] | EMBELLISHED WITH CUTS. | [d.p.rule] | LONDON, | PR F F. POWER, (GRANDSON TO | THE LATE MR. J. NEWBERY) AND CO. | NO. 65, NEAR THE BAR, SPC- | Y, 1790. | [PRICE FOUR-PENCE.]

In 8's. 50 leaves. Pp. 89[92]. Wct FP and 12 wcts in text. List of bks s b Power on last 3 pages. (Communicated.)

[Osborne, Cat. pp. 269–70; Ball; RP.

J141. FORTUNE-TELLER, THE, BY THE RENOWNED DR. HURLOTHRUMBO.

(1) The edition of 1769 not by a Newbery or TC.

(1A) Adv. as pr f FN(N) in *GM*, May 1774. Price 2d.

(2) Listed in *Cries of London*, 1775, as pr f FN(N). Price 2d.

(3) Listed in *Cries of London*, 1784, as pr f EN. Price 2d.

(4) An edition of 1785. Pr f EN.

[MSaE.

(5) Listed as pr f EN in *The Menagerie*, 1800. Price 1d.

J142. FOUNDLING, THE; OR, THE HISTORY OF LUCIUS STANHOPE. Weedon 27. Richard Johnson's Day-book records:

1787 July. Mr Badcock——To writing The Hermit of the Forest |
—— —— ——*The Foundling——* | £2. 2s.

(1) An edition of 1787. Pr f EN. Price 1*d*. Welsh 222; Gum 2602; *CBEL*, II, 563.
Title and *imprint* approx. as for no. (2), with date 1787. Pp. 31. Illustrations. (Communicated.)

⌈Ball.

(2) An edition of 1794. Pr f EN. Price 1*d*.

THE | FOUNDLING; | OR, THE | HISTORY | OF | LUCIUS STANHOPE. | [p.rule] | EMBELLISHED WITH CUTS. | [d.p.rule] | LONDON: | PR F E. NEWBERY, AT THE CORNER OF | SPC-Y. 1794. | [PRICE ONE PENNY.]

A single gathering 'A' of 16 leaves, first and last pastedowns. Pp. 31. Wct FP and 7 wcts in text. Green paper wrappers, blind embossed; pink paper wrappers embossed with grey floral design.

⌈Bell, 10·3×6·5 cm; Opie.

J142A. FRAGMENTS. Listed in *Joseph Andrews*, 1799, as pr f EN, price 1*s* 6*d*. Not identified, if the price stated is correct. *Instructive Fragments* was listed at 6*d*, in line with the other *Lilliputian Library* bks.

FRENCH SHEET ALMANACK FOR...1773 PARTICULARLY CALCULATED FOR THE USE OF SCHOOLS. See A7(70).

FRIEND OF MOTHERS. See Fenn, Lady E.

J142B. GAULTIER, Aloisius Edouard Camille. COMPLETE COURSE OF GEOGRAPHY, A, 2nd edition. PART I. 1795. S b EN et al. Price £1 1*s* and 10*s* 6*d* for the counters. Part II has not come to light.

A | COMPLETE COURSE | OF | GEOGRAPHY, | BY MEANS OF | INSTRUCTIVE GAMES. | INVENTED BY | THE ABBÉ GAULTIER. | [p.s.rule] | THE SECOND EDITION, | [1 line] | [p.s.rule] | PART I. | CONTAINING | THE GAME OF SIMPLE GEOGRAPHY. | [7 lines] | [p.s.rule] | [5 lines] | [p.rule] | LONDON: | PR F THE AUTHOR: | A S B P. ELMSLEY, IN THE STRAND; E. HARLOW, IN PALL-MALL; E. NEWBERY, THE CORNER OF | SPC-Y: T. BOOSEY, NO. 4, OLD BROAD-STREET, NEAR THE ROYAL EXCHANGE; AND | AT MR. DE POGGI'S NEW ROOM, NO. 91, NEW BOND-STREET, NEAR OXFORD-ROAD. | [d.p.rule] | MDCCXCV.

Pp. viii+12; xii+46+1 leaf (an Atlas etc.), +4 coloured inset folding maps+8 uncoloured, +1 coloured 'plain map'. The maps are engvd, some by Neele, Wm Foden, Robert Sayer, Laurie and Whittle, some unsgd. Engvd FP (a 'Table of general Questions'). The Preface explains that the 'game' is to be played with a bag of balls, each marked with a geographical name, and a set of counters. Marbled bds, ¼ bd. (Communicated.)

⌈Shiers, 36·0×23·7 cm.

J143. GAULTIER, Aloisius Edouard Camille. COURS DE LECTURES GRADUÉES POUR LES ENFANS. PREMIER COURS. COURS

DE LECTURES GRADUÉES POUR LES ENFANS DE TROIS, QUATRE, ET CINQ ANS, 1796. S b EN et al. 3 vols, price 6s 6d.
(1) Vol. I.

Half-title at A8ʳ: [d.p.rule] | LECTURES | POUR | LES ENFANS | DE | TROIS ANS. | [d.p.rule].

Title (within an ornamental rectangular frame): COURS | DE | LECTURES GRADUÉES | POUR | LES ENFANS | DE | TROIS, QUATRE, ET CINQ ANS. | [p.rule] | PAR M. L'ABBÉ GAULTIER. | [p.rule] | VOL. I. | [d.p.rule] | LONDRES. | [p.rule] | 1796.

Imprint on vso of title leaf: CET OUVRAGE SE VEND CHEZ MM. ELMSLEY | & BREMNER, STRAND; & E. NEWBERY, | SPC-Y.

Half-title at A1ʳ: LECTURES GRADUÉES | POUR | LES ENFANS. | [d.p.rule] | PREMIER COURS. | [d.p.rule] | EN TROIS VOLUMES.

43[?44] leaves+1 inset. Pp. xxiv[xxviii]+58[?60]. Inset engvd FP: in the Ries copy a portrait of the Abbé by Anthony Carden; in the Herts C.L. copy a mother seated at a round table teaching three small children, lettered 'Pubd for the Abbe Gaultier by A. C. de Poggi, No. 91 New Bond Street Feb [   ] 179[   ]'. Divisional titles at A14ʳ and B14ʳ.

[For locations see no. (3).

(2) Vol. II.

Half-title: [d.p.rule] | LECTURES | POUR | LES ENFANS | DE | QUATRE ANS. | [d.p.rule].

Title not seen.

In 16's. 112 (or more) leaves. Pp. 223 (?+). Wcts at pp. 5 and 69.

[For locations see no. (3).

(3) Vol. III.

Half-title: [d.p.rule] | LECTURES | POUR | LES ENFANS | DE | CINQ ANS. | [d.p.rule].

Title: as for vol. I, with VOL. III. Imprint on vso of title as for vol. I.

In 16's. 149 leaves. Pp. 285[298]. Wcts at pp. 5, 77, 151.

[HeCL (imperf.), 11·0×8·0 cm; Rics; M. G. Atkins, List CHI/11 [1964] item 122.

(4) Vol. III. An imperfect copy in CUL (10.e.34), lacking title-leaf, a wct at p. 5. May = no. (3).

J143A. GAULTIER, Aloisius Edouard Camille. COURS DE LECTURES GRADUÉES POUR LES ENFANS. SECOND COURS. COURS DE LECTURES GRADUÉES POUR LES ENFANS DE SIX, SEPT, ET HUIT ANS. S b EN et al.

I have traced no obviously complete set of this 'Second Cours'; indeed, on present evidence it is impossible to be sure what a complete set would consist of. Reference is made to the 9 vols of the set (see no. (8) below – 3 in the 'Premier Cours', no. J143, 6 in the 'Second Cours'), and to the 10th vol. (see no. (9) below), but this ignores the extra vol. no. (6) below. The 6 vols cost 14s 6d.

In some of the following items the name of EN appears as a seller; in others there is no name of publisher or seller. But all the vols are similar in type and general layout; and it seems more than probable that EN was in fact one of the sellers of all the vols ('on peut se procurer séparément chacun des deux cours, chez...E. Newbery...'). Accordingly the following items include all vols in this 'Second Cours', whether or not EN is named.

The two major holdings are in HeCL and CUL (10.e.28–33, 34), both of which I have examined. The latter set is very carelessly made up: the vol numbered II comprises the text of an ed. of vol. IV, the vol. numbered III has a half-title to vol. VI and the text of an ed. of vol. II, the vol. numbered VII comprises an ed. of vol. III of the 'Premier Cours', no. J143(4).

(1) Vol. I, 1798. No sellers' or publishers' names.

COURS | DE | LECTURES GRADUÉES | POUR | LES ENFANS | DE | SIX, SEPT, ET HUIT ANS. | [p.rule] | PAR M. L'ABBÉ GAULTIER. | [p.rule] | VOL. I. | [d.p. rule] | (CE PREMIER VOLUME EST LE QUATRIEME DE | TOUT L'OUVRAGE.) | [d.p.rule] | LONDRES, 1798. (The whole within an ornamental rectangular frame.)

Half-title: [d.p.rule] | LECTURES | POUR | LES ENFANS | DE | SIX ANS. | [d.p.rule].

In 8's. 134 leaves. Pp. 255.

[CUL; HeCL, 11·3×8·2 cm (imperf.).

(2) Vol. II, 1798. EN et al.

Half-title (following the title-leaf): [d.p.rule] | LECTURES | POUR | LES ENFANS | DE | SIX ANS. | [d.p.rule].

Title (within an ornamental rectangular frame): COURS | DE | LECTURES GRADUÉES | POUR | LES ENFANS | DE | SIX, SEPT, ET HUIT ANS. | [p.rule] | PAR M. L'ABBÉ GAULTIER. | [p.rule] | VOL. II. | [d.p.rule] | (CE SECOND VOLUME EST LE CINQUIÈME DE | TOUT L'OUVRAGE.) | [d.p.rule] | LONDRES. 1798.

Imprint on vso of title-leaf: ON PEUT SE PROCURER SÉPARÉMENT CHACUN | DES DEUX COURS,

CHEZ { MM. ELMSLEY & BREMNER, STRAND; E. NEWBERY, SPC-Y; T. BOOSEY, BROAD-STREET, &c.

Half-title (preceding the title-leaf): LECTURES GRADUÉES | POUR | LES ENFANS. | [d.p.rule] | SECOND COURS. | [d.p.rule] | EN SIX VOLUMES.

In 8's. 112 leaves. Pp. 201[204]. List of bks by Gaultier on last 2 pages.

[HeCL, *ca.* 11·3×8·2 cm.

(2A) Vol. II, 1798. A copy without TP, half-title reads LECTURES | POUR | LES ENFANS | DE | SIX ANS, followed by text of vol. II, pp. 201. May be identical with no. (2).

[CUL.

(3) Vol. III, 1798. No sellers' or publishers' names apparent.

COURS | DE | LECTURES GRADUÉES | POUR | LES ENFANS | DE | SIX, SEPT, ET HUIT ANS. | [p.rule] | PAR M. L'ABBÉ GAULTIER. | [p.rule] | VOL. III. | [d.p.rule] | (CE TROISIÈME VOLUME EST LE SIXIÈME DE | TOUT L'OUVRAGE.) | [d.p.rule] | LONDRES, 1798.

The title-leaf transcribed here is tipped in to the CUL copy of vol. II, no. (2A) above.

(4) Vol. IV, 1798. EN et al.

Half-title (on [a3^r], following the title leaf): [d.p.rule] | LECTURES | POUR | LES ENFANS | DE | SEPT ANS. | [d.p.rule].

Title (on [a2^r]) as for no. (2), except VOL. IV and (CE QUATRIÈME VOLUME EST LE SEPTIÈME DE | TOUT L'OUVRAGE.)

Half-title (on [a1^r]), preceding the title-leaf, as in no. (2); on the vso is the imprint of EN et al. as in no. (2). 'Table des matières' on 4th–6th leaves.

In 8's. 220 leaves. Pp. 428. 6 leaves of prelims.

[HeCL, *ca.* 11·3×8·2 cm (imperf.); Grey.

(4A) Vol. IV, a copy with text of pp. 448. Title of vol. II tipped in. Half-title.

[CUL (in vol. numbered II).

(5) Vol. IV, 1798, another issue. No sellers' or publishers' names. Identical with no. (4) except as to the prelims: no half-title following the title-leaf; no imprint on [a1^v]; 'Table des Matières' on 3rd and 4th leaves; 4 leaves of prelims. 181 leaves in all.

[Bodley (30999.f.169^d), 11·4×7·8 cm.

(5A) Vol. IV, 1798. A copy with title, and half-title following the title-leaf (with imprint of EN et al.) as in no. (4). Pp. 426. Possibly identical with no. (4).

[CUL (in vol. numbered IV).

(6) An undated vol., without name of publisher or seller.

LECTURES | POUR | LES ENFANS | DE | SEPT ANS. | [d.p.rule] | SUBSTANTIF, | PREMIÈRE PARTIE DU DISCOURS. | [d.p.rule] | EXEMPLES | ET EXERCISES. (The whole within an oval orn. frame.)

In 8's. 118 leaves. Pp. 236. The layout of the TP corresponds to that of the divisional title at p. [325] of no. (4).

[Bodley (30999.f.169^g), 11·5×7·9 cm.

(7) Vol. V, 1799. EN et al.

Half-title (following the title-leaf): [d.p.rule] | LECTURES | POUR | LES ENFANS | DE | HUIT ANS. | [d.p.rule].

Title as for no. (2), except VOL. V, and (CE CINQUIÈME VOLUME EST LE HUITIÈME DE | TOUT L'OUVRAGE.), and date 1799.

Half-title (preceding title-leaf): as in no. (2); on the vso is the *Imprint* as on vso of title-leaf in no. (2).

In 8's. 183 leaves. Pp. 358. Divisional titles at K4^r and O4^r.

[HeCL, *ca.* 11·3×8·2 cm; CUL.

(8) Vol. VI, 1799. EN et al.

Half-title (following the title-leaf): [d.p.rule] | LECTURES | POUR | LES ENFANS | DE | HUIT ANS. | [d.p.rule].

Title as for no. (2), except VOL. VI, and (CE SIXIÈME VOLUME EST LE NEUVIÈME DE | TOUT L'OUVRAGE.), and date 1799.

Half-title (preceding the title-leaf): as in no. (2); on the vso is the *Imprint* as on vso of title-leaf to no. (2).

In 8's. 72 leaves+2 insets. Pp. 42, [66 unnumbered], 26[28]. A folding leaf relating to 'La Particule'; another being a 'Tableau d'Analyse de Grammaire'. Divisional titles at A1ʳ, C6ʳ and G6ʳ. List of Gaultier's bks on last 2 pages.

[HeCL, *ca.* 11·3 × 8·2 cm; Traylen.

(9) An undated vol., without name of publisher or seller.

LECTURES | POUR | LES ENFANS | DE | HUIT ANS. | [d.p.rule] | INTER-JECTION, | DIXIÈME & DERNIÈRE PARTIE DU | DISCOURS. | [d.p.rule] | EXEMPLES | ET EXERCISES. (The whole within an oval orn. frame.)

In 8's. 134 leaves. Pp. 42, [64], [ii], 26. Divisional titles at [C6ʳ] and [G6ʳ].

[CUL.

J144. GAULTIER, Aloisius Edouard Camille. JEU DES FAUTES, 1796. Chez EN et al. Price 2*s.*

JEU | DES | FAUTES | QUE LES ENFANS & LES JEUNES GENS | COMMET-TENT LE PLUS ORDINAIREMENT | CONTRE | LA BONNE ÉDUCATION | ET CONTRE | LA POLITESSE. | [d.p.rule] | PAR M. L'ABBÉ GAULTIER. | [d.p.rule] | [3 lines quote] | [d.p.rule] | CET OUVRAGE FAIT PARTIE DU COURS DES JEUX, INVENTÉS | PAR L'AUTEUR POUR L'INSTRUCTION DE LA JEUNESSE. | [d.p.rule] | A LONDRES: | CHEZ P. ELMSLEY, DANS LE STRAND; & CHEZ | E. NEWBERY, SPC-Y. | [p.rule] | MDCCXCVI.

In 6's. 60 leaves. Pp. xii+106[108]. List of 'Jeux Instructifs...par L'Abbé Gaultier' on last 2 pages.

[BM, 16·0 × 8·7 cm.

J145. GENTLEMAN AND LADY'S KEY TO POLITE LITERATURE, THE. Welsh 247. All edd. have an engvd title, pulled from the same plate, only the imprint being revised for each successive ed. See Figure 15 for the title to no. (5).

(1) An edition of 1761 or before. Pr f JN. Price 2*s.* Listed in *Newtonian System*, 1761.

The engvd title-page imprint reads LONDON, | PR F J. NEWBERY AT THE BIBLE AND SUN | IN SPCY.

In 6's. 126 leaves+2 insets (engvd FP and TP, the former sgd 'Le Pautre sculp'). No pagination.

[Bodley, 13·5 × 7·9 cm; CUL; NoU; Ries; MdBP; UCLA.

(2) Frequently adv. in *LC* and elsewhere, and mentioned in bk-lists, from 1763 onwards; and there may well have been edd. put out in the period 1764–75 not here recorded.

(3) An edition of 1776. Pr f C & N.

Imprint: PR F T. CARNAN & F. NEWBERY JUNR. | AT NO. 65, SPCY. MDCCLXXVI

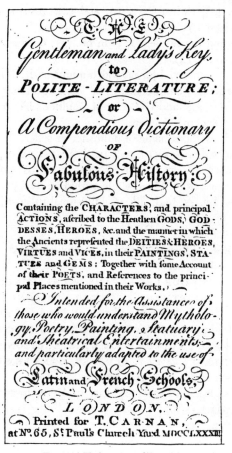

Fig. 15. Title-page of J145(5).

Specification as for no. (1). No pagination.

[LUL; Roscoe, 13·7×8·1 cm; NjP; Latvian State Lib. A. R. Heath, Cat. 22 (1972) item 85.

(4) An edition of 1780. Pr f TC.

Imprint: PR F T. CARNAN, | AT NO. 65, SPCY MDCCLXXX

Specification as for no. (1). No pagination.

[BM, 14·0×8·2 cm; Bodley.

(5) An edition of 1783. Pr f TC.

See Figure 15. Specification as for no. (1). No pagination.

[BM; Weedon, 13·8×8·7 cm; Opie; Osborne, Cat. p. 10; Hannas, Cat. 25 [1968] item 306.

(6) An edition of 1788. Pr f TC.

Imprint as for no. (5), with date '1788'. Specification as for no. (1). No pagination.

[Bodley (Vet A 5 f 215), 13·8×8·4 cm; Welch; BEK; UCLA.

(7) Another edition of 1788. Pr f TC. Type reset with slight variations, otherwise identical with no. (6). Last page, last line, last word 'year.'; in (6) the full-stop after 'year' is under righthand side of 'e' in 'are' in line above; in (7) the stop is just to right of shank of 'r' in 'are'.

[BM, 13·5 × 8·2 cm; Bodley (Vet A 5 1654).

GEOGRAPHY FOR CHILDREN. See Lenglet du Fresnoy, N.

GEOGRAPHY FOR CHILDREN, BY QUESTION AND ANSWER. Welsh 224. = Lenglet du Fresnoy's *Geography for Children*.

GEOGRAPHY MADE FAMILIAR. See CIRCLE OF THE SCIENCES, J63.

J146. GEOGRAPHY REFORMED; OR, A NEW SYSTEM OF GENERAL GEOGRAPHY ACCORDING TO AN ANALYSIS OF THE SCIENCE... Third edition. Pr f FN(N). Price 3s 6d. Adv. *LC* 26–9.10.71, p. 411. An unspecified ed. listed in *Cries of London*, 1775. Welsh 225.

J146A. GIBSON, John. ATLAS MINIMUS. Welsh 170–1.
(1) First edition, 1758, first issue. Pubd a s b JN. Price 4s calf, 5s 6d with the maps coloured.
Engraved title: ATLAS MINIMUS, | OR A NEW SET OF | POCKET MAPS | OF THE SEVERAL EMPIRES, | KINGDOMS AND STATES | OF THE KNOWN | WORLD, | WITH HISTORICAL EXTRACTS RELATIVE TO EACH. | DRAWN AND ENGRAV'D | BY J. GIBSON | FROM THE BEST AUTHORITIES | REVIS'D, COR-RECTED AND IMPROV'D, | BY EMAN: BOWEN | GEOGRAPHER TO HIS MAJESTY. | [p.rule] | PUBLISH'D ACCOR^G TO ACT OF PARL^T JAN^Y 2^D 1758. & S B | J. NEWBERY AT Y^E BIBLE AND SUN IN S^T PAULS CH: YARD, LONDON.
58 unsgd and unnumbered leaves, all blank on vso, comprising FP, TP, preface, index, 52 leaves of maps, 1 advert. leaf, 1 blank. All text and maps engraved.
In this issue, at the foot of the index page is the text: ERRATA, | IN THE MAP OF AFRICA, READ 4850 M^{ls} IN LENGTH, 3960 IN BREADth And the engvd text on map no. 4 (Africa) reads: ...IS 900 MILES IN LENGTH, 290 IN BREADTH...
[BM, Maps, C.7.a.20 (uncoloured), 11·1 × 8·4 cm; Weedon (coloured); Osborne (coloured, Cat. p. 178).
(2) First edition, 1758, second issue (see Fig. 16). Identical with the first issue except:
(1) The errata note has been removed from the index page.
(2) The text on map 4 reads: ...IS 4850 MILES IN LENGTH, 3690 IN BREADTH...
(3) The presence of an advert. leaf is uncertain, though that, or a second blank, is called for.

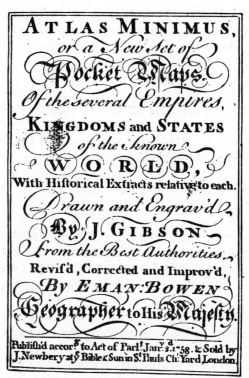

Fig. 16. Title-page of J146A(2).

[Bodley (coloured); Roscoe (coloured), 11·0×7·9 cm; Bell (coloured); McKell.
(3) Listed in *Newtonian System*, 1770, as pr f C & N, price as before. Probably
sheets of the 1758 ed.; a revised TP is unlikely.
(4) An edition of 1774. Pr f C & N. Price 4*s*, 4*s* 6*d* bd in the vell. manner, 5*s* 6*d*
with the maps coloured.

ATLAS MINIMUS | ILLUSTRATUS: | CONTAINING | FIFTY-TWO POCKET
MAPS | OF THE WORLD. | DRAWN AND ENGRAVED BY J. GIBSON; |
REVISED, CORRECTED, AND IMPROVED, | BY E. BOWEN, GEOGRAPHER TO
HIS MAJESTY. | TO WHICH ARE ADDED | [8 lines] | [d.p.rule] | LONDON: |
PR F T. CARNAN AND F. NEWBERY, JUNIOR, | AT NUMBER 65, IN SPC-Y. |
MDCCLXXIV.

110 unsgd and unnumbered leaves, comprising engvd FP, TP and preface
printed from type, engvd index, 54 leaves of descriptive text printed from type,
52 leaves of engvd maps. The maps are on a much heavier paper than the printed
text, and, generally, are identical with those in the first ed., 2nd issue, except for
occasional reworkings of the plates, e.g. engvd text top left corner map 1 revised;
in map 6 the names of York Isle and Trinity Isle in lower left corner re-engraved.
Wallis recorded that the ed. was issued in limp vell. with a flap.

[Roscoe, uncoloured, 10·4×7·3 cm.

(5) An edition of 1779. Pr f C & N. Price 4s bd in the vell. manner. Chubb: *Printed Maps of the Atlases of G.B. and Ireland*, 1927, no. CCXIVa.

Title and *imprint* approx. as for no. (4), with date MDCCLXXIX. 109 unsgd and unnumbered leaves. TP and 55 leaves of text, 52 maps. Engvd contents leaf; all other matter printed from type. Marbled bds, green vell. spine with label.

[Bodley, 11·0×8·2 cm; BCE, 10·9×8·4 cm; McKell.

(6) An edition of 1792 by C. D. Piguenit.

[Roscoe.

GIBSON, John. POCKET MAPS OF THE WORLD = ATLAS MINIMUS.

GILES GINGERBREAD. See J267.

J147. GOLDSMITH, Oliver. HISTORY OF ENGLAND, AN, IN A SERIES OF LETTERS FROM A NOBLEMAN TO HIS SON. *CBEL*, II, 641; Scott, 119–20, and 123–4.

(1) First edition, 1764. Pr f JN. 2 vols, price 6s. Welsh 228; IAW 130; Isham 10; Rothschild 1023.

AN | HISTORY | OF | ENGLAND, | IN A | SERIES OF LETTERS | FROM A | NOBLEMAN TO HIS SON. | VOL. I. [II.] | [2 lines quote] | LONDON, | PR F J. NEWBERY, AT THE BIBLE AND SUN, | SPC-Y. | MDCCLXIV.

Vol. I. 12mo. 157 leaves. Pp. 2+309.

Vol. II. 12mo. 145 leaves. Pp. 286[288]. List of bks pr f JN on last 2 pages of each vol.

Minor variations are to be found in the collations and TP imprints.

[BM, 16·9×9·9 cm; Bodley; CUL; LUL; MPL; Opie; Osborne*; UCLA; Grant; Sotheby, 8.4.68, lot 93; Hannas, Cat. 15 [1963] item 506; Bishop Percy's Lib. (Sotheby, 23.6.69, lot 206), 10.11.69, lot 86, and 8.3.71, lot 213.

(2) An edition of 1769. Pr f N & C. 2 vols, price 6s in the vell. manner.

Title approx. as for no. (1). *Imprint:* PR F NEWBERY AND CARNAN, NO. 65, THE | NORTH SIDE OF SPC-Y. | MDCCLXIX.

Vol. I. 12mo. 158 leaves. Pp. 309. Last leaf a blank.

Vol. II. 12mo. 129 leaves. Pp. 254[256]. List of bks pr f N & C on last 2 pages.

[Bodley, 17·0×9·9 cm.

(3) An edition of 1770. Pr f C & N. 2 vols, price 6s in the vell. manner, 7s in calf.

Title approx. as before. *Imprint:* PR F CARNAN AND NEWBERY, AT NO. 65. | IN SPC-Y. | MDCCLXX.

Vol. I. 12mo. 156 leaves. Pp. 312.

Vol. II. 12mo. 144 leaves. Pp. 280[287]. List of bks s b C & N on pp. [281–7].

[Bodley, 17·0×10·0 cm; DNS.

(4) An edition of 1772. Pr f C & N. 2 vols, price 6s. Welsh 228.

Title and *imprint* approx. as for no. (3), with date MDCCLXXII.

Vol. I. 12mo. 156 leaves. Pp. 312.

Vol. II. 12mo. 144 leaves. Pp. 280[288]. List of bks s b C & N on pp. [281–8].

[BM, 17·9×10·0 cm; Bodley; CUL; Osborne, Cat. p. 165; UCL; NoU; RP; NLA.

(5) Fourth edition. Adv. *LC* 17–19.2.74, p. 171, as pr f C & N. Price 6*s* calf in 2 vols, 5*s* for the 2 vols in one, in the vell. manner. An ed. of 1774 is listed in *CBEL*, II, 641.

(6) Fifth edition, 1776. Pr f C & N. Price for the 2 vols in calf 7*s*, for the 2 vols in one in the vell. manner 5*s*.

Title and *imprint* (with date MDCCLXXVI & FIFTH EDITION) approx. as for no. (1). Specification as for no. (4).

[CUL; Roscoe, 17·0×10·3 cm; UCLA.

(7) Sixth edition, 1780. Pr f TC. 2 vols. Welsh 228; Gum 2747.

Title (with SIXTH EDITION) approx. as for no. (1). *Imprint:* PR F T. CARNAN, IN SPC-Y. | MDCCLXXX.

Vol. I. 12mo. 156 leaves. Pp. 312.

Vol. II. 12mo. not seen.

[BM (vol. I), 17·5×10·3 cm; Hannas, Cat. 32 [1970] item 170.

(8) An edition of 1783. Pr f TC. 2 vols.

Title approx. as for no. (1). *Imprint* (with date MDCCLXXXIII) approx. as for no. (7).

Vol. I. In 12's. 156 leaves. Pp. 312.

Vol. II. In 12's. 144 leaves. Pp. 280[288]. List of bks s b TC on pp. [281–8].

[CUL; Marchmont Bookshop (1965), 17·3×10·0 cm; A. R. Heath, Cat. 20 [1971] item 207.

(9) An edition of 1786. Pr f TC. 2 vols.

Title approx. as for no. (1). *Imprint* (with date MDCCLXXXVI) approx. as for no. (7).

Both vols 12mo, otherwise specifications approx. as for no. (8). The 2 vols in one bd marbled bds, green vell. spine with label LETTERS | ON | ENGLAND

[OEFL, approx. 17·1×10·0 cm; Schiller.

(10) An edition of 1790. Pr f F. Power & Co. Price 6*s*, 2 vols.

Title approx. as for no. (1). *Imprint:* PR F F. POWER AND CO. SUCCESSORS TO THE LATE | MR. T. CARNAN, NO. 65, SPC-Y. | [p.rule] | MDCCXC.

Both vols 12mo, otherwise specifications approx. as for no. (8). List of bks s b Power on last 8 pages of vol. II.

[Weedon, 17·2×10·6 cm; UCLA.

J148. GOLDSMITH, Oliver. HISTORY OF THE LIVES...OF THE...MARTYRS, AND PRIMITIVE FATHERS. Welsh 216 and 230. See R. W. Seitz, 'Goldsmith's Lives of the Fathers', in *Modern Philology*, vol. 26 (1928–9), pp. 295ff.

(1) An edition of 1764 (probably the first). Pr f JN. Price 1*s*. This formed vol. IV of the *Young Christian's Library* (no. J392A). *CBEL*, II, 641; NBL 124.

AN HISTORY | OF THE LIVES, ACTIONS, TRAVELS, SUFFERINGS, | AND DEATHS OF THE MOST EMINENT MARTYRS, | AND PRIMITIVE FATHERS OF

THE CHURCH, | IN THE FIRST FOUR CENTURIES; VIZ. | [3 parallel columns of 12 lines each] | [5 lines] | EXTRACTED FROM THE HOLY SCRIPTURES, AND THE | BEST ECCLESIASTICAL HISTORIANS. | ADORNED WITH VARIETY OF COPPER-PLATE CUTS. | LONDON: | PR F J. NEWBERY, AT THE BIBLE AND | SUN, IN SPC-Y. 1764.

In 8's. 120 leaves+8 insets. Pp. 228. Engvd FP and 7 other engvd leaves. D.f.b.

⌈St Bride, 9·8×6·4 cm; Ball.

(2) Frequently listed in 1769–70 as pr f N & C. Price 1s. Probably only stock in hand inherited from JN.

(3) An edition of 1774, by C & N, adv. *Morning Chronicle* 1.7.74, price 1s. Very doubtful.

IAW, pp. 166–7, quotes Prior for the statement that the *Life of Christ* and the *Lives of the Fathers* were repubd by C & N in 1774 'with Goldsmith's name in separate form' (whatever that may mean). IAW doubts 'whether Goldsmith's name actually was on the pamphlets, and was not merely inferred by Prior from an advertisement. Otherwise it seems strange that they have disappeared, as they appear to have done'. Why 'Pamphlets'? It looks as though IAW had never seen copies of the books. And there is nothing whatever strange in such disappearance; it is 'strange' when these little books survive at all. IAW is also wrong in his statement that there is no copy of the *Morning Chronicle* in BM. The copy is in Burney 611b. But he is justified in doubting the existence of this ed. of Goldsmith.

(4) Listed in *Newtonian System*, 1787, as pr f TC. Price 1s.

GOODY TWO-SHOES. See HISTORY OF LITTLE...

J148A. GORDON, W. (? Wm Gordon of Glasgow, author of the *Universal Accomptant and complete Merchant*). EVERY YOUNG MAN'S COMPANION. Welsh 356.

(1) First edition, 1755. Pr f J. & J. Rivington, JN, R. Baldwin, B. Collins, and R. Williamson of Liverpool. 12mo. Pp. [12]+456. Price 2s 6d. Alston, IV, 624. (Communicated.)

⌈Opie; GOB.

(2) Second edition, 1757. Pr f JN et al. Price 2s 6d. Alston, IV, 625.

Title approx. as for no. (3), continuing: THE SECOND EDITION, CORRECTED | WITH LARGE ADDITIONS. *Imprint:* PR F J. HODGES NEAR LONDON-BRIDGE; J. RIVINGTON | AND J. NEWBERY IN SPC-Y; J. RIVINGTON | AND J. FLETCHER, R. BALDWIN, S. CROWDER AND | H. WOODGATE IN P-NR; AND B. COLLINS IN | SALISBURY. MDCCLVII.

In 12's. 228 leaves+engvd FP sgd 'A. Walker del et sculpt'. Pp. 444. Numerous wct diagrams and figures. Wct of a gauger at p. 333.

CUL, 17·0×9·8 cm; MB (imperf.).

(3) Third edition, 1759. Pr f JN et al. Alston, IV, 626.

EVERY | YOUNG MAN'S COMPANION: | CONTAINING | [parallel columns of

27 and 26 lines] | TOGETHER WITH | A GREAT VARIETY OF CUTS AND TABLES, | [2 lines] | [p.rule] | BY W. GORDON, | TEACHER OF MATHEMATICS. | [p.rule] | THE THIRD EDITION, CORRECTED, | [1 line] | [d.p.rule] | LONDON: | PR F J. RIVINGTON AND J. NEWBERY, IN SPC- | Y; S. CROWDER AND CO...; J. RIVINGTON | AND J. FLETCHER, R. BALDWIN, AND H. WOODGATE,... | ...; AND B. COLLINS, IN SALISBURY. | MDCCLIX.

In 6's. 228 leaves. Pp. 444. Numerous wct diagrams and figures; wct of a gauger at p. 333.

[BM, 16·6×9·7 cm.

(4) Fourth edition, 1765. Pr f JN et al. Price 2s 6d. Alston, IV, 627.

EVERY | YOUNG MAN'S COMPANION. | CONTAINING | [34 and 33 lines in parallel columns] | TOGETHER WITH | A GREAT VARIETY OF CUTS AND TABLES. | [p.rule] | BY W. GORDON, | TEACHER OF THE MATHEMATICKS. | [p.rule] | THE FOURTH EDITION, CORRECTED. | WITH LARGE ADDITIONS, AND GREAT IMPROVEMENTS. | [d.p.rule] | LONDON: | PR F J. RIVINGTON, H. WOODFALL, J. NEWBERY, | R. BALDWIN, S. CROWDER, T. CASLON, B. LAW, | M. RICHARDSON, AND B. COLLINS, IN SALISBURY. | MDCCLXV.

In 6's. 228 leaves+inset engvd FP. Pp. 443[444]. Numerous wct diagrams and figures in text. Wct of a gauger at p. 374.

[V&A, 16·5×9·4 cm; CUL; LUL; Renier; Opie; NN.

(5) Fifth edition, 1769. Pr f N & C et al. Alston, IV, 628.

Pr f H. Woodfall, J. Rivington, R. Baldwin, Newbery and Carnan et al. 12mo. Pp. 443[444].

[LUL; MB (imperf.).

(6) Sixth edition, 1777. Pr f N & C. Alston, IV, 629.

EVERY | YOUNG MAN'S COMPANION. | CONTAINING | [31 lines in 2 parallel columns] | [2 lines] | [p.rule] | BY W. GORDON, | [1 line] | [p.rule] | THE SIXTH EDITION, CORRECTED. | [1 line] | [d.p.rule] | LONDON: | PR F H. WOODFALL, J. RIVINGTON, R. BALDWIN, T. CAS- | LON, S. CROWDER, G. ROBINSON, T. LOWNDES, F. NEWBERY | AND T. CARNAN, AND B. COLLINS, IN SALISBURY. | MDCCLXXVII.

12mo. 228 leaves. Pp. 443[444]. A number of wcts and wct diagrams. Bk-lists on A6ᵛ and U6ᵛ.

[Bodley, 17·0×10·0 cm; BM.

J149. GOVERNESS, THE; OR, EVENING AMUSEMENTS, 1800. S b EN et al. Price 2s.

THE GOVERNESS: | OR, | EVENING AMUSEMENTS, | AT | A BOARDING SCHOOL. | [wct vignette] | [d.p.rule] | LONDON: | PR F VERNOR AND HOOD, POULTRY, | A S B | E. NEWBERY, SPC-Y; | BY TEGG AND DEWICK, | WESTMORELAND BUILDINGS, ALDERSGATE STREET. | [p.rule] | 1800.

Mixed format. 114 leaves+1 inset. Pp. iv+119[122]. Last leaf a blank. Engvd FP. List of bks on O3ʳ·ᵛ. Marbled bds, green vell. spine with label.

[BM, 12·9×8·6 cm; V&A(GL); Renier; A. R. Heath, Cat. 22 [1972] item 91.

Pl. 1. Advertisement of medicines sold by Francis Newbery, the son, at St Paul's Church Yard, not later than August 1779. (Reduced.)

Of whom may be had,

Proposals for the work both in volumes and weekly numbers; and the first number of the work as a specimen, on return, if not approved of.

N. B. The Subscribers In volumes are desired to send for this, or any of the former volumes, to George Keith, in Gracechurch-street, where they are ready to be delivered according to the proposals.

Where may be had handsome new editions of

1. Dr. Gill's Exposition of the Canticles, in 122 Sermons, price 12s.
2. ——— Cause of God and Truth, in 4 parts, price 15s.
3. ——— Sermons and Tracts, 2 vols. price 30s.
4. ——— on the Hebrew language, letters, vowel points, and accents, price 5s.

And the Author's other works.

This Day were published,

THE following A L M A N A C K S, For the Y E A R 1776,

Printed for the COMPANY of STATIONERS, And sold by George Hawkins, at their Hall, in Ludgate-street;

And may be had of all the Country Booksellers:

The Free-Masons' Calendar, | Parker's Ephemeris,
The Gentleman's Diary, | Poor Robin's Almanack,
The Ladies' Diary, | Saunder's English Apollo,
Francis Moore's Almanack, | Season on the Seasons,
John Partridge's Almanack, | Tycho Wing's Almanack,
 | White's Coelestial Atlas;
 | or, New Ephemeris.

All the above price 9 d. each stitched.

Cardanus Rider's British Merlin, price 9 d. stitched.

Goldsmith's Almanack, price 8 d. stitched.

Wing's Sheet Almanack, price 6 d.

Cambridge Sheet Almanack, price 6 d.

London Sheet Almanack, on a copper-plate, price 6 d.

Cardanus Rider's Sheet Almanack, price 6 d. which may be bound up with the Court and City Register and Royal Kalendar, or put into Memorandum or Pocket Books.

Stationers' Hall. At a Court of Assistants held the 17th day of November, 1775:

An advertisement for the publication of certain Almanacks for the Year 1776, inserted in many of the country news-papers, being produced and read at this Court, in which are the following words: "The proposals made by the Worshipful Company for an ignominious compromise were treated with the utmost contempt by T. Carnan, who was the defendant in the suit."

This Court doth hereby declare, that this assertion is totally groundless, no proposal for any compromise, or offer of compromise, directly or indirectly, having been made, by or on the behalf of this Company, to the said T. Carnan, or to any other person,

... of the Court,

PARTRIDGE, Clerk.

Canada. XIII. An account of New Britain, or Terra de Labradore and Hudson's Bay. XIV. The history of Nova Scotia.

Printed for T. Becket, corner of the Adelphi, in the Strand.

This Day were published,

THE following A L M A N A C K S, For the Y E A R 1776.

1. A Diary, or Sheet Almanack, on an improved plan of more utility than any hitherto published, by Reuben Burrow, late Assistant Astronomer to the Royal Observatory.
2. A Sheet Almanack on the same plan as that formerly published by Vincent Wing.
3. A Cambridge Sheet, on the same plan as that formerly published under that title.
4. A New London Sheet, printed on Pearl Letter, more distinct than the Copper-plate Sheet, and containing a variety of useful articles never inserted in the London Sheet of the Stationers' Company.
5. Rider's Almanack, on an improved plan, compiled by the Rev. Mr. Rider, Sur-master of St. Paul's School.
6. Goldsmith's Almanack, on an improved plan. All the above Almanacks, price 6d. each.
7. Ladies and Gentleman's Diary or Royal Almanack, containing a variety of enigmas, rebusses, &c. by Reuben Burrow, late Assistant Astronomer at the Royal Observatory.
8. Vox Stellarum, or a Loyal Almanack, by Francis Moore.
9. Poor Robin's Almanack, by Reuben Robins.
10. Parker's Ephemeris. Improved by Charles Vyse.

The last four Almanacks, price 9d. each.

Printed for T. Carnan, at No. 65, in St. Paul's Church-yard: and G. Robinson, at No. 25, in Pater-noster-row.

††† The above Almanacks are not printed for the Company of Stationers, but for T. Carnan and G. Robinson; who dispossessed the Stationers' Company of the exclusive privilege of printing Almanacks, which they enjoyed 170 years, (to the discouragement of genius, and the great prejudice of the Booksellers throughout the kingdom) in consequence of a patent obtained from King James the First, which his Most Sacred Majesty had no right to grant.

Reply to the Advertisement from Stationers' Hall, dated Nov. 17:

May 29, 1775, after the Judges of the Court of Common Pleas had certified their opinion to the Court of Chancery, William Waller, Esq; of Lincoln's Inn, came to and offered T. Carnan Ten Thousand Pounds, if he would not move the Court of Chancery to dissolve the injunction; and he said, In that case if any other person should print an Almanack, that the Stationers' Company would directly file a Bill in Chancery against him.

Nov. 20, 1775. THOMAS CARNAN, St. Paul's Church-yard.

(partial column, cut off at right edge:)

fold by

The 1776,

JOH

Bound prin muc kine

TH for th plain a monies in the Toget alphab Londo numbe table o interes Coach and to Pri yard.

Th Emb

TE casting month sun's r An in the rem writin ruled receive ladies Madar quy. tunate daught Wine. New f

Pri No. 6 R. Bal Salisbu

** for th a num encou partic Pocke has no

Pl. 2. A page from the *London Chronicle* for 21–3 November 1775, p. 500. Almanacks advertised by the Stationers' Company (*left*) and T. Carnan (*right*). (Reduced.)

THE

ADVENTURES

OF A

SILVER PENNY.

INCLUDING

MANY SECRET ANECDOTES

OF

LITTLE MISSES AND MASTERS

BOTH

GOOD AND NAUGHTY.

Embellished with CUTS.

LONDON:

Printed for E. Newbery, at the Corner of St. Paul's
Church-Yard.

[Price Six-pence.]

WISDOM and VIRTUE presenting
the SILVER PENNY.

Pl. 3. Frontispiece and title-page of J3(2). (Slightly reduced.)

Hear the Instruction of thy
FATHER, and forget not the
Law of thy MOTHER.

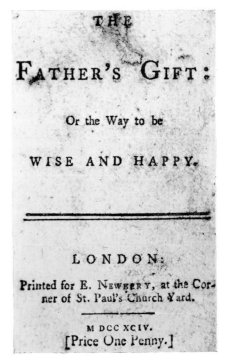

THE

FATHER'S GIFT:

Or the Way to be

WISE AND HAPPY.

LONDON:

Printed for E. NEWBERY, at the Corner of St. Paul's Church Yard.

M DCC XCIV.
[Price One Penny.]

Pl. 4. Frontispiece and title-page of J112(3).

Little Goody Two-Shoes.

THE
HISTORY
OF
Little Goody Two-Shoes;
Otherwise called,
Mrs. Margery Two-Shoes.
WITH
The Means by which fhe acquired her
Learning and Wifdom, and in confe-
quence thereof her Eftate ; fet forth
at large for the Benefit of thofe,

Who from a State of Rags and Care,
And having Shoes but half a Pair ;
Their Fortune and their Fame would fix,
And gallop in a Coach and Six.

See the Original Manufcript in the *Vatican*
at *Rome*, and the Cuts by *Michael Angelo.*
Illuftrated with the Comments of our
great modern Critics.

The FOURTH EDITION.

LONDON:
Printed for J. NEWBERY, at the Bible and
Sun in St. Paul's Church-yard, 1767.

[Price Six-pence.]

Pl. 5. Frontispiece and title-page of J167(4).

Frontispiece

God is the Fountain of all Goodness.

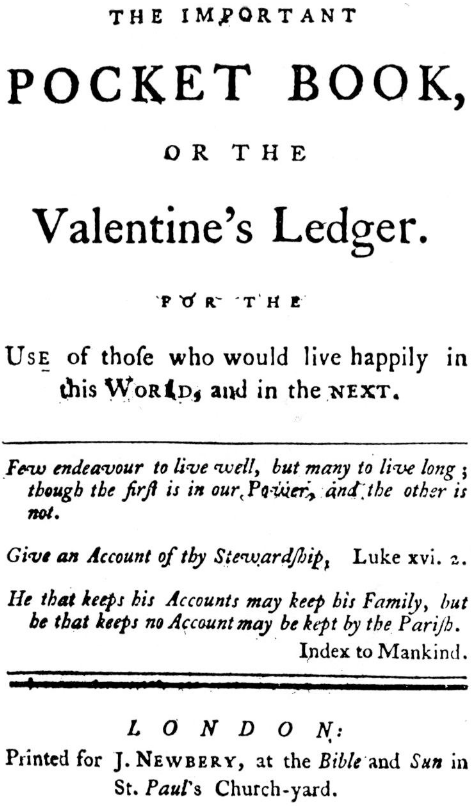

THE IMPORTANT

POCKET BOOK,

OR THE

Valentine's Ledger.

FOR THE

Use of thofe who would live happily in
this World, and in the NEXT.

---

*Few endeavour to live well, but many to live long ;
though the firft is in our Power, and the other is
not.*

Give an Account of thy Stewardfhip, Luke xvi. 2.

*He that keeps his Accounts may keep his Family, but
he that keeps no Account may be kept by the Parifh.*
Index to Mankind.

L O N D O N:
Printed for J. NEWBERY, at the *Bible* and *Sun* in
St. *Paul's* Church-yard.

Pl. 6. Frontispiece and title-page of J185(1).

THE
Lilliputian Letter-Writer,
CONTAINING A
Variety of Pleafing and Interefting
EPISTLES
FROM
YOUNG PEOPLE
TO
EACH OTHER,
And to their
PARENTS and FRIENDS.

ADORNED WITH CUTS.

LONDON :
rinted for E. NEWBERY, at the Corner of St. Paul's
Church Yard.
[Price Six-pence.]

Pl. 7. Frontispiece and title-page of J217. (Slightly reduced.)

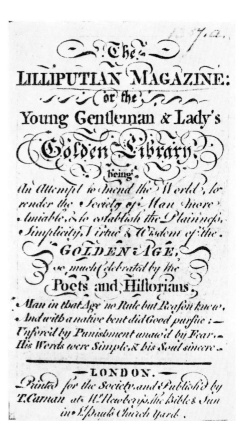

Pl. 8. Frontispiece and title-page of J219(2). (See also Fig. 18(a)–(d).)

A LITTLE
LOTTERY-BOOK
FOR
CHILDREN:
CONTAINING

A *new* Method of *playing* them into a
Knowledge of the
LETTERS, FIGURES, &c.

Embellished with above FIFTY CUTS,

AND

Published with the Approbation of the
Court of *Common Sense*.

The SIXTH EDITION.

L O N D O N:
Printed for all the Booksellers, and sold
at the B I B L E and S U N in *St. Paul's
Church-Yard.* 1767.
[Price 3*d.* bound and gilt.]

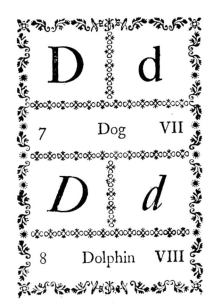

D	d
7 Dog	VII
D	*d*
8 Dolphin	VIII

Dŏg.

Dŏl-phin.

Pl. 9. Title-page and a page-opening from J223(2).

Delectando monemus.
Instruction with Delight.

Pocket Book

A Little Pretty
POCKET-BOOK,
Intended for the
Instruction and *Amusement*
OF
LITTLE MASTER *TOMMY*,
AND
PRETTY MISS *POLLY*:
With Two Letters from
JACK the GIANT-KILLER;
AS ALSO
A BALL and PINCUSHION;
The Use of which will infallibly make
Tommy a good Boy, and *Polly* a good Girl.

The TENTH EDITION.

To which is added,
A LITTLE SONG-BOOK,
BEING
A *New Attempt* to teach Children the Use of
the *English Alphabet*, by way of Diversion.

LONDON: Printed for J. NEWBERY,
in *St. Paul's Church-Yard.* 1760.
[Price *Six-pence*, bound.]

Pl. 10. Frontispiece and title-page of J225(6).

Pl. 11. The upper cover of J253(13), with picture and borders printed in maroon. The lower cover is identical. (See also Appendix 2.)

Old *Gaffer Gingerbread.*

Tom *Trip* to his *Companions.*

Old Gingerbread, with Wifdom found,
Sells ufeful Knowledge by the Pound,
And feeds the little Folks, who're good,
At once with Learning and with Food.
What fay you Friends—Shall we go buy?
Aye, Aye!—Who's firft then, you or I?
And away they ran for a Book.

Lydia

Donce Adds 302

HISTORY

Lydia OF *Heaton*

Giles Gingerbread:

Febuary 4: 1770

Little Boy who lived upon Learning.

LONDON:

Printed for NEWBERY and CARNAN,
No. 65, the North Side of St. *Paul's*
Church-yard, 1769.

[Price One Penny.]

Donce Adds 302

Pl. 12. Frontispiece and title-page of J267(4).

Drawings by Mr. Ritson

Come hither pretty little Boy,
Come learn of me your A, B, C;
And you fhall have my dapper Nag,
To gallop round the Country.

CHRISTMAS-BOX:

OR, THE

GOLDEN PLAY-THING

FOR

LITTLE CHILDREN.

By which they may learn the Letters as foon as they can fpeak,
and know how to behave fo as
to make every body love them.

Adorned with Thirty CUTS.

Printed for the AUTHOR, and Sold by
Carnan, and Newbery at Nº. 65, in
St. Paul's Church-Yard, London.

(Price One Penny.)

Pl. 13. Frontispiece and title-page of J269(5).

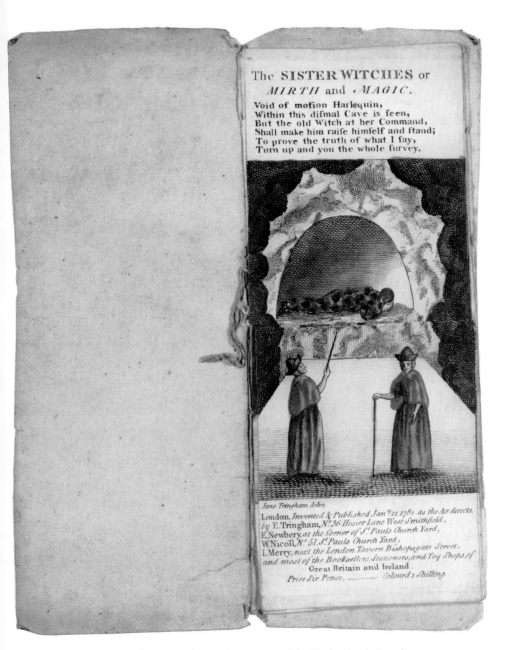

Jane Tringham delin.

London, *Invented & Published Jan^ry 22 1782. as the Act directs,* by E.Tringham, N.º 36 Hosier Lane West Smithfield, E.Newbery, *at the Corner of S.t Pauls Church Yard,* W.Nicoll, N.º 51.S.t Pauls Church Yard, I.Merry, *next the London Tavern Bishopsgate Street,* and most of the Booksellers, Stationers, and Toy Shops, of Great Britain and Ireland. Price Six Pence, ——— Coloured 1 Shilling.

Pl. 14. Title-page and inner front cover of the Harlequinade J334A.

The Merry PHILOSOPHER.

Do you bite your Thumb at us, Sir?

Shakespeare.

Six-Pennyworth of WIT;
OR,

Little Stories for Little Folks,
Of all Denominations.

Adorned with CUTS.

Unhappy Wit, like most mistaken Things,
Atones not for the Envy which it brings.

So singeth that excellent Poet Master *Pope*;
and therefore, when you have read this
Six-pennyworth of WIT, you would do
well to buy *Twelve-pennyworth* of WIS-
DOM, which is much better, and may
be had at the Place where this is sold.——
Wit and *Wisdom* should always be blended
together; for, as Mrs. *Margery Two-
Shoes* observes, WIT is FOLLY, *unless*
a wise Man hath the keeping of it.

LONDON:
Printed for J. NEWBERY, at the Bible and
Sun, in St. Paul's Church Yard; and sold
by all the Booksellers in the World.
[Price Six pence bound and gilt.]

Pl. 15. Frontispiece and title-page of J336(1).

HIS ROYAL HIGHNESS PRINCE FREDERICK. BISHOP OF OSNABRUG.

H Y M N S
Lydia FOR THE *Heaton*

A M U S E M E N T

OF

C H I L D R E N.

By CHRISTOPHER SMART, M.A.

THIRD EDITION.

LONDON:
Printed for T. CARNAN, at Number 65,
in St. Paul's Church-yard. Price 6d.

MDCCLXXV.

Pl. 16. Frontispiece and title-page of J338(3). (Reduced.)

Pl. 17. The lower cover of J348(6), boards, with the woodcuts printed in red and signed
'J. Bell Sc.'. (See also Appendix 2.)

Tom Thumb's *Maxim in* Trade *and* Politics.

He who buys this Book for a *Penny,* and lays it up till it is worth *Two-pence,* may get an Hundred *per Cent.* that is, One half, by the Bargain: But let him take Care that he gets Money honeftly; *for he that cheats another, cheats himfelf, and inftead of gaining fhall lofe double.*

There is no Treasure *like* Honefty, *and no* Gain *like a good* Confcience.

TOM THUMB's FOLIO;
OR, A NEW
PENNY PLAY-THING
FOR
LITTLE GIANTS,
To which is prefixed,
An ABSTRACT of
The LIFE of Mr. THUMB,
AND
An Hiftorical ACCOUNT of the
WONDERFUL DEEDS he performed.
Together with
Some ANECDOTES refpecting
GRUMBO the Great GIANT.

LONDON:
Printed for the People of all Nations; and fold by T. CARNAN, Succeffor to Mr. J. NEWBERY, in St. Paul's Church-Yard, 1786.
[Price One Penny.]

Pl. 18. Frontispiece and title-page of J356(3).

The Valentines.

THE

VALENTINE's GIFT:

O R,

A PLAN to enable CHILDREN
of all SIZES and DENOMINATIONS

To behave with

HONOUR, INTEGRITY, and HUMANITY.

Very neceſſary in a Trading Nation.

To which is added,

Some Account of OLD ZIGZAG, and of
the Horn which he uſed to underſtand
the Language of *Birds, Beaſts, Fiſhes,*
and *Inſcás.*

The LORD *who made thee, made the Crea-
tures alſo; thou ſhalt be merciful and kind
unto them, for they are thy Fellow-Te-
nants of the Globe.*   ZOROASTER.

L O N D O N:

Printed for T. CARNAN and F. NEWBERY, Jun,
at Number 65, in St. Paul's Church-yard.

MDCCLXXVII.

[Price SIX-PENCE bound.]

Pl. 19. Frontispiece and title-page of J368(4).

The little *wise* Man.

I will sing unto the Lord a new Song, and praise him for all his Mercies.

He hath taught me to walk in his Ways with a benevolent Heart and contented Mind, and therefore am I happy.

The benevolent Man is a Partner with all the World: he rejoiceth at the Prosperity of all Men, and hath therefore a Share of all the Satisfaction which Fortune, Wealth, and Power can produce.

THE
Whitfuntide-Gift:
Peggy   OR,   *Haskell*

The WAY to be very HAPPY.

A Book neceffary for all Families, and intended to be read by *Parents,* as well as *Children* of all Denominations.

Let thofe who cannot read learn, that they may be WISE *and* HAPPY.   PLATO.

Adorned with Cuts.

LONDON:

Printed for J. NEWBERY, at the *Bible* and *Sun* in St. *Paul's Church-yard,* 1767.

[Price *Two-Pence* bound.]

Pl. 20. Frontifpiece and title-page of J380(2).

GOVERNESS, THE; OR, LITTLE FEMALE ACADEMY. See Fielding, Sarah.

GRAMMAR AND RHETORICK. See CIRCLE OF THE SCIENCES, J65.

GRAMMAR MADE FAMILIAR. See CIRCLE OF THE SCIENCES, J64.

GRAND ALPHABET OF ALPHABETS. See Brayley, E. W.

GUIDE TO THE STUDY OF THE HISTORY OF ENGLAND. See Florian, Jolly B.

GUILDHALL, DESCRIPTION OF, WITH THE HISTORY OF THE GIANTS = vol. II of no. J88.

J150. GULLIVER'S INSTRUCTIVE LESSONS. Pr f EN. Price 6*d*. See Weedon 57, x. Perhaps = some ed. of no. J152.

J151. GULLIVER'S LECTURES, WITH THE FAIRY TALES OF PRINCE CHERI. Pr f EN. Price 6*d*. Listed in *Anecdotes of Mary*, 1795. See Weedon 57, 1. One of the 10 vols of the *Lilliputian Library* 'compiled' by Richard Johnson (no. J218).

J152. 'GULLIVER, Lilliputius'. INSTRUCTIVE LESSONS CONVEYED TO THE YOUTHFUL MIND. Weedon 57, x. But not, it seems, one of the *Lilliputian Library* series. *pace* Weedon, who equates it with *Instructive Fragments*, 1800.
(1) An edition of 1800. Pr f EN. Price 6*d*. Hugo, II, 325.
    INSTRUCTIVE LESSONS | CONVEYED TO THE | YOUTHFUL MIND | THROUGH THE | MEDIUM | OF | TALE AND DIALOGUE. | [d.p.rule] | BY | LILLIPUTIUS GULLIVER. | [d.p.rule] | LONDON: | PR F E. NEWBERY, AT THE CORNER OF SP | C-Y. | 1800.
    In 8's. 64 leaves. Pp. 128. ? a wct FP. Wcts in text. Black floral impress on orange bds. Details taken from the Osborne copy.
    [Osborne*; Grant; UCLA; Maxwell Hunley, Cat. 48 [winter 1969] item 165.
(2) An undated ed. recorded by Lyon. [?E].N.

J153. HAMLAIN; OR, THE HERMIT OF THE BEACH, 1799. Pr f EN. Price 1*s* 6*d*. *CBEL*, II, 564. Noticed in *Young Gentleman's and Lady's Magazine*, no. XII, 1800.
    HAMLAIN; | OR, | THE HERMIT OF THE BEACH. | A | MORAL REVERIE. | CALCULATED FOR THE | INSTRUCTION AND AMUSEMENT | OF | YOUTH. |

[d.p.rule] | LONDON: | PR F E. NEWBERY, THE CORNER OF SP | C-Y, | BY G. WOODFALL, NO. 22, PN-R. | [p.s.rule] | 1799.

In 6's. 99 leaves+engvd FP. Pp. 198. Marbled bds, green vell. spine.

⌈Traylen, 13·2×9·4 cm; BCE; Welch; McKell; UCLA; NSWU.

HAPPY FAMILY AT EASON HOUSE, THE. See Sandham, Eliz.

HARLEQUINADES. See J250A, J254A, J334A.

J153A. HARPER, Thomas. ACCOMPTANT'S COMPANION, THE. (1) Second edition. Pr f FN(N) in PNR and H. Webley in Holborn. Price 1s 6d. Adv. *LC* 7–10.9.65, p. 244.
(2) Third edition not traced.
(3) Fourth edition, 1770. S b FN(N) et al.

THE | ACCOMPTANT'S COMPANION: | OR, THE | YOUNG ARITHMETI-CIAN'S GUIDE. | BEING | [19 lines] | [p.rule] | THE FOURTH EDITION. | [p.rule] | BY THOMAS HARPER, | [1 line] | [d.p.rule] | LONDON: | PR F A S B R. HARPER, AT THE ABOVE | ACADEMY; ALSO BY F. NEWBERY, THE CORNER OF | SPCY, AND H. WEBLEY IN HOLBORN. | MDCCLXX.

In 6's. 102 leaves+engvd FP (portrait of Harper). Pp. vi[viii]+192.

⌈RICS, 17·1×10·2 cm.

HARRIS'S JUVENILE LIBRARY. See 'Winlove, S.' *Collection of entertaining Stories*, J381(9).

J154. Entry deleted.

J155. HELME, Elizabeth. INSTRUCTIVE RAMBLES IN LONDON. Welsh 236; *CBEL*, III, 399.
(1) An edition of 1798. Pr f EN et al. Price 6s, 2 vols.

INSTRUCTIVE RAMBLES | IN LONDON, | AND | THE ADJACENT VILLAGES. | [2 lines] | [d.p.rule] | BY ELIZABETH HELME. | [d.p.rule] | [5 lines quote] | IN TWO VOLUMES. | VOL. I. [11.] | [p.s.rule] | LONDON: | PR F T. N. LONGMAN, PATERNOSTER ROW; | AND E. NEWBERY, SPC-Y. | 1798.

Vol. I. 12mo. 101 leaves+1 inset. Pp. xii+189. Engvd FP sgd 'R. K. Porter 1798' and 'T. Cook sc'. Half-title.

Vol. II. 12mo. 90 leaves+1 inset. Pp. viii+169[172]. Engvd FP sgd as in vol. I. List of bks on last 3 pages. Half-title.

⌈BM, 17·0×10·0 cm; HammPL; BI (vol. I); Renier; Osborne, Cat. p. 183; UCLA (vol. I).
(2) An edition of 1799. EN. Recorded by Lyon.
(3) An edition of 1800. Pr f EN et al. Price 4s in 1 vol. Gum 2969.

Title approx. as for no. (1). *Imprint:* PR F T. N. LONGMAN, AND O. REES, PN R; | AND E. NEWBERY, SPC-Y. | [p.s.rule] | 1800.

In 6's. 149 leaves+2 insets. Pp. xii+284[286]. Engvd FP as in vol. 1 of no. (1); engvd leaf as FP to vol. II of no. (1). Half-title. List of bks on last page.

[BM, 17·5 × 10·3 cm; Bodley; UCLA; Ball; NNC-T; A. W. Laywood, Cat. 21 [1972] item 161.

J156. HELME, Elizabeth. INSTRUCTIVE RAMBLES EXTENDED IN LONDON, 1800. S b EN. 2 vols, price 5s sewed, also 6s. *CBEL*, III, 399.

INSTRUCTIVE RAMBLES | EXTENDED | IN | LONDON, | AND | THE ADJACENT VILLAGES. | [2 lines] | [d.p.rule] | BY ELIZABETH HELME. | [d.p.rule] | [3 lines quote] | IN TWO VOLUMES. | VOL. I. [11.] | [p.s.rule] | LONDON: | PR B A F | SAMPSON LOW, BERWICK STREET, SOHO: | A S B | E. NEWBERY, SPC-Y. | [p.s.rule] | 1800.

Vol. I. 12mo. 99 leaves+1 inset. Pp. ii, iv+187. Engvd FP sgd 'R. K. Porter delt' and 'J. Mitan sculp'. Half-title.

Vol. II. 12mo. 101 leaves+1 inset. Pp. iv+194. Engvd FP sgd 'Thurston del' and 'Mitan sculp'. Bk-list on p. 194. Half-title.

[BM, 16·7×9·8 cm; V&A(GL); SomCL; Bell; Osborne, Cat. p. 183; Ball; UCLA.

HELME, Elizabeth, Junr, *alias* Elizabeth Somerville. FLORA; OR, THE DESERTED CHILD. See Somerville, Eliz., J342A.

J157. HELME, Elizabeth, Junr, *alias* Elizabeth Somerville. JAMES MANNERS. *CBEL*, II, 560. As to the authorship – Helme junr or Somerville – the evidence of the TP transcribed below is good enough; yet the TPs to the 1800 and 1806 edd. of *Flora* (no. J342A) state that work to be 'By Elizabeth Somerville, author of "James Manners, Little John, and their Dog Bluff," &c &c'. One is forced to the conclusion that Somerville and Helme junr were one and the same person, notwithstanding that they seem to have continued after 1800 to produce books under both names; see *CBEL*, III, 399 and 570 (but this fails to distinguish between Helme and Helme junr – if there is a distinction).
(1) First edition, 1799. S b EN et al. Price 1s 6d.

JAMES MANNERS, | LITTLE JOHN, | AND THEIR | DOG BLUFF. | [d.p.rule] | [3 lines quote] | [d.p.rule] | BY | ELIZABETH HELME, JUN. | [d.p.rule] | LONDON: | PR F THE PROPRIETORS; | A S B DARTON AND HARVEY, GRACE- | CHURCH STREET; AND E. NEWBERY, | SPCY. | 1799.

In 6's. 71 leaves. Pp. iv+137[140]. List of 'Books for Youth' on pp. [139–40]. Marbled bds, green vell. spine.

[BM, 14·5×8·7 cm; NorBM; NNC-T.
(2) Second edition, 1801. EN, and Darton and Harvey.
Pp. 137. Engvd plates and wcts. D.f.b. (Communicated.)

[M. Reissman; Victoria Book Shop, N.Y. Cat. 9, item 310; UCLA.

J158. HENRY IV OF FRANCE. A CHRONOLOGICAL ABRIDGMENT OF THE LIFE AND REIGN OF.
(1) An undated edition, pr f FN(N). Price 2*s*. Not later than 1780 or 1781, *pace* BM Gen. Cat.

A | CHRONOLOGICAL ABRIDGMENT | OF THE | LIFE AND REIGN | OF | HENRY IV. SURNAMED THE GREAT; | LXIId. KING OF FRANCE: | EXHIBIT-ING A CONCISE VIEW | OF | THE STATE OF EUROPE, | FROM 1553 TO 1610. | [4 lines] | [d.p.rule] | LONDON: | PR F F. NEWBERY, THE CORNER OF SP | C-Y.

In 6's. 99 leaves [? a final blank]. Pp. 198.
[BM, 12·9 × 8·1 cm.
(2) An edition by EN, price 2*s*, mentioned by Welsh at p. 236, as from a list of *ca.* 1798.

J159. HENRY IV OF FRANCE, LIFE OF. Adv. *LC* 19–21.12.80, p. 589, as one of EN's new publications, price 2*s*. Perhaps an ed. of no. J158.

J160. HENRY IV OF FRANCE, THE LIFE OF. An edition, price 1*s* 6*d*, listed as pr f EN in *History of Prince Lee Boo*, 1789. Welsh 236. Perhaps an ed. of no. J158.

HERMIT OF THE BEACH. See HAMLAIN; OR, THE HERMIT...

J161. HERMIT OF THE FOREST, THE. Weedon 29. Richard Johnson's Day-book records:

1787 July. M *Badcock——To writing The Hermit of the Forest*⎱
—— —— The Foundling ⎰ £ 2. 2*s*.

(1) An edition of 1788. Pr f EN. Price 1*d*. Welsh 236.
[Sotheby, 5–6 Feb. 1945 (the Bussell sale), lot 135.
(2) An edition of 1794. Pr f EN. Price 1*d*.

THE | HERMIT OF THE FOREST, | AND THE | WANDERING INFANTS. | A | RURAL FRAGMENT. | [p.s.rule] | EMBELLISHED WITH CUTS. | [d.p.rule] | LONDON: | PR F E. NEWBERY, THE CORNER OF | SPCY. 1794. | [PRICE ONE PENNY.]

Pp. 31. Wct FP and wcts in text. D.f.b. (Communicated.)
[Welch.
(3) An edition of 1799. EN. Pp. 31. Flowered paper. (Communicated.)
[NNC-Pl; UCLA; Maxwell Hunley, Cat. 48 [winter 1969] item 172, 8·9 × 5·7 cm.

HISTOIRE NATURELLE. See no. J238.

HISTORICAL BEAUTIES FOR YOUNG LADIES. See Pilkington, M. (H).

HISTORIES OR TALES OF PAST TIMES TOLD BY MOTHER
GOOSE. See Perrault, C.

J162. HISTORY OF A DOLL, THE. CONTAINING ITS
ORIGIN AND PROGRESS THROUGH LIFE, WITH THE
VARIOUS CALAMITIES THAT BEFELL IT. BY NANCY
MEANWELL. [Title taken from an ed. by J. Harris, Gum 142.] Pr f EN. Price
1*d*. Weedon 31.

Richard Johnson's Day-book records, under date 30 Oct. 1780, the delivery
to Mrs Newbery of the *History of a Doll*, priced £1. 1*s*. This entry has been struck
out, but after Johnson's death the work was sold to Badcock for 1 gn.

Listed in *The Menagerie*, 1800, as pr f EN, price 1*d*.

J163. HISTORY OF A LITTLE BOY FOUND UNDER A
HAYCOCK, THE, CONTINUED FROM THE FIRST PART.
Weedon 34. Richard Johnson's Day-book records: *1786 July. M*ʳ* Badcock——*
To writing The History of a Little Boy found under a Haycock——Half a Sheet.
32°. ——£1. 1s.

'The First Part' referred to in the title seems undoubtedly to be the earlier
instalment of the Little Boy's career which had appeared in the *Royal Alphabet...
to which is added, the History of a Little Boy found under a Haycock* (no. J322).
There is no record of Johnson having written the earlier instalment.

(1) Adv. *LC* 26–8.12.86, p. 620, as 'just pubd' by EN. Price 1*d*. This may =
no. (2).

(2) An edition of ?1786–7. Pr f EN. Price 1*d* bd and gilt.

THE | HISTORY | OF | A LITTLE BOY | FOUND UNDER A HAYCOCK, |
CONTINUED FROM THE FIRST PART, | GIVEN IN THE | ROYAL ALPHABET;
| OR, | CHILD'S BEST INSTRUCTOR. | [p.s.rule] | EMBELLISHED WITH CUTS.
| [p.s.rule] | LONDON: | PR F E. NEWBERY, THE CORNER OF | SPC-Y. | [PRICE
ONE PENNY, BOUND AND GILT.]

A single gathering 'A' of 16 leaves, first and last pastedowns. Pp. 31. Wct FP
and 8 wcts in text. Advert. of *Royal Alphabet* on A2ᵛ. Orange D.f.b., also purple
wrappers with grey floral impress.

[Bell, 10·2×6·5 cm; Welch.

(3) Listed as pr f EN in *The Menagerie*, 1800. Price 1*d*.

HISTORY OF A PIN. See Smythies, Miss.

J164. HISTORY OF A SCHOOL BOY. WITH OTHER PIECES.
Adv. *LC* 14–16.6.88, p. 612, as pr f Stockdale and EN, price 1*s*. But only Stockdale's name in the imprint of the BM copy.

HISTORY OF A SILVER THIMBLE. See J362.

J165. HISTORY OF A SILVER THREEPENCE. Probably =
ADVENTURES OF A SILVER THREEPENCE, J364.

HISTORY OF ENGLAND IN A SERIES OF LETTERS. See
Goldsmith, Oliver, J147.

J165A. HISTORY OF ENGLAND, A, IN QUESTION AND
ANSWER. 11th ed. ?1762. See IAW 125–6 and *CBEL*, ii, 645. Probably the
11th ed. of Lockman's *New History of England, by Question and Answer.*

HISTORY OF FRANCE, FROM THE EARLIEST PERIOD. See
'Cooper, Rev. Mr', J83.

J165B. HISTORY OF GREECE, THE, BY WAY OF QUESTION
AND ANSWER.
　　Probably inspired by Lockman's immensely successful *New History of England
by Question and Answer* and *New Roman History by Question and Answer.* There is
nothing to indicate that Lockman was concerned with this *History of Greece*; but
it is to be noted that the conger which produced no. (1) below is identical with
that which produced the 6th, 1762, ed. of Lockman's *Roman History.* Whether the
New History of Greece by Question and Answer (no. J260) is related to the present
work will only be known if and when a copy turns up.
(1) An edition of 1761. Pr f JN et al.
　　THE | HISTORY | OF | GREECE. | BY WAY OF | QUESTION AND ANSWER.
| IN THREE PARTS. | I. A GEOGRAPHICAL DESCRIPTION... | [3 lines] | II.
A SHORT HISTORICAL ACCOUNT... | [2 lines] | III. OF THE RELIGION,
LAWS, CUSTOMS... | [7 lines] | [p.rule] | FOR THE USE OF SCHOOLS. | [p.rule]
| LONDON: | PR F C. HITCH AND L. HAWES, H. WOODFALL, | J. RIVINGTON,
J. NEWBERY, R. BALDWIN, W. | JOHNSTON, J. RICHARDSON, S. CROWDER
AND CO. | B. LAW AND CO. T. CASLON, R. WITHY, AND M. | COOPER.
MDCCLXI.
　　In 12's. 113 leaves. Pp. 219.
　　[Traylen, 16·6×9·8 cm; Osborne*.
(2) Listed in T.G.'s *Description of Thanet,* 1765, as pr f JN, price 2s 6d.

J166. HISTORY OF JACKY IDLE AND DICKY DILIGENT,
THE, 1797. Pr f EN. Price 2d. Weedon 33. Richard Johnson's Day-book
records: *1790. Mr Badcock——To writing The History of Jacky Idle and Dicky
Diligent.——£2. 2s.*
　　THE | HISTORY | OF | JACKY IDLE, | AND | DICKY DILIGENT, | EXHIBIT-
ING A | STRIKING CONTRAST BETWEEN THE | DIFFERENT CONSEQUENCES
| ARISING FROM | INDOLENT INATTENTION, AND | LAUDABLE PERSE-
VERANCE. | [rule] | EMBELLISHED WITH CUTS. | [rule] | LONDON: | PR F E.
NEWBERY, THE CORNER OF S | PC-Y. | 1797. | (PRICE TWO PENCE.)

Pp. 61[62ff]. First and last leaves pastedowns. Bk-list following p. 61. Wct FP and 12 other wcts in text. D.f.b. (Communicated.)

[UCLA; Lapides.

J167. HISTORY OF LITTLE GOODY TWO-SHOES, THE. Welsh 231–2; *CBEL*, II, 561; W. M. Stone, 'The History of little Goody Two-Shoes', in *Proc. of American Antiquarian Soc.*, N.S. vol. 49 (Oct. 1939). Welch no. 427.1 (at pp. 587–9) has a very full list of English edd.

A ms note by Winter Jones in a 1796 ed. of the bk in BM (C.45.a.23) says that it was written by Giles Jones (Winter Jones's grandfather) who was 'an intimate friend of John Newbery'. See further about this in an article in *N&Q* by 'G.T.S.', 16 Dec. 1871, p. 510, and an article by Edwin Pearson (himself a most unreliable authority) in *N&Q* for 6 Jan. 1872. Winter Jones's reply to Pearson, in violent contradiction, is written in the BM copy mentioned above. Also ascribed to John Newbery. See also Harvey Darton, pp. 130–5, Muir *passim*, and Welsh's Introduction to his facsimile of the 3rd ed. Few writers (if any) on children's bks fail to mention *Goody Two-Shoes*, but the authorship remains undecided.

(1) First edition, 1765. Pr f JN. Price 6d. R. Julian Roberts, 'The 1765 Edition of Goody Two-Shoes', in *BMQ*, Summer 1965, pp. 67–70, and plate XVII. It is to be noted that Mr Roberts, with perhaps almost too much scholarly caution, will not say outright that the copy of which he writes, recently acquired by BM, is the 1st ed. (though he evidently thinks that it is); it is only 'almost certainly this edition'.

THE | HISTOR[Y] | OF | LITTLE GOODY TWO-SHOES; | OTHERWISE CALLED, | MRS. MARGERY TWO-SHOES. | WITH | THE MEANS BY WHICH SHE ACQUIRED HER | LEARNING AND WISDOM, AND IN CONSE- | QUENCE THEREOF HER ESTATE; SET FORTH | AT LARGE FOR THE BENEFIT OF THOSE | [4 lines of verse] | SEE THE ORIGINAL MANUSCRIPT IN THE VATICAN | [3 lines] | [p.rule] | LONDON: | PR F J. NEWBERY, AT THE BIBLE AND | SUN IN SPC-Y, 1765. | [PRICE SIX-PENCE.] (See Plate 5.)

32mo. 72 leaves+engvd FP. Pp. 140[144]. Wcts. List of bks 'usually read by the Scholars of Mrs. Two Shoes', and of medicines, on last two leaves.

[BM.

(2) A 'new edition, corrected', 1766. Pr f JN. Price 6d. NBL 629. *Festival of Britain, Exhib. of Bks*, 1951, no. 47. *Pierpont Morgan Cat.* item 192.

Title and *imprint* approx. as for no. (1), with date 1766. Engvd FP. Wcts. (Communicated.)

[Opie; Oppenheimer.

(3) Third edition, 1766. Pr f JN. Price 6d. Facsim. copy ed. by C. Welsh, Griffith and Farran, 1881.

Title and *imprint* approx. as for no. (1), with THE THIRD EDITION and date 1766.

In 8's. 80 leaves+engvd FP. Pp. 156[160]. 35 wcts. List of 'The BOOKS usually read by the Scholars of Mrs 'Two-Shoes...sold at Mr. Newbery's' at pp. [157–9]. List of medicines at p. [160].

⌈BM (imperf.), 9·6×6·2 cm; Edison; formerly Stone. The copy recorded by Stone as in the 'South Kensington Museum' (i.e. the V&A) cannot now be traced.

(4) See Plate 5. Gum 2753.

Title and *imprint* approx. as for no. (1), with THE FOURTH EDITION and date 1767. Specification as for no. (3). D.f.b.

⌈St Bride, 9·5×6·5 cm; Osborne* (imperf.); CCamarSJ.

(5) Fifth edition, 1768. Pr f N & C. Price 6*d*. Gum 2755.

Title approx. as for no. (1), with THE FIFTH EDITION. *Imprint:* PR F NEWBERY AND CARNAN, AT | NO. 65, THE NORTH SIDE OF SP | C-Y, 1768. | [PRICE SIX-PENCE.]

32mo in 8's, list of bks s b N & C; otherwise specification as for no. (3). D.f.b.

⌈Bodley, 9·4×6·4 cm; NorBM; Welch; Ball.

(6) An edition of 1770. Pr f C & N. Price 6*d*. NBL 633.

Title approx. as for no. (1). *Imprint:* PR F T. CARNAN AND F. NEWBERY, | JUN. AT NO. 65, IN SPC- | Y. 1770. [PRICE SIX-PENCE.]

In 8's. All copies seen and recorded were imperfect.

⌈BM, 9·7×6·4 cm; Ball; Welch; UCLA; formerly Stone.

(7) An edition of 1772. Pr f C & N. Price 6*d*. The TP has the usual diatribe against FN(N) and his 'paltry compilations'. (Communicated.)

⌈Ball.

(8) An edition of 1773. TC. Stone records as 'In the Owen list'. Welch thinks this is an error for '1783', i.e. no. (13).

(8A) Seventh edition, 1774. Pr f N & C; and Dublin reprinted. Price 'a British Six Pence'. Unknown to Stone and Welch.

Title approx. as for no. (1), with THE SEVENTH EDITION. *Imprint:* LONDON: | [p.rule] | PR F NEWBERY AND CARNAN: AND | DUBLIN, RE-PRINTED BY THOMAS | WALKER, IN DAME-STREET, 1774. | (PRICE A BRITISH SIX PENCE.)

In 8's. 80 leaves+engvd FP. Pp. 156[160]. 33 wcts in text. List of bks s b Thomas Walker on pp. [157–60]. Probably a piracy; the wcts are poor copies after those in the London edd. A different setting of type. D.f.b.

⌈CUL, 9·5×6·0 cm.

(9) An edition of 1775. Pr f C & N. Price 6*d* bd and gilt. *English Children's Books*, 1563–1900, no. 12.

Title approx. as for no. (1). *Imprint:* PR F T. CARNAN AND F. NEWBERY | JUNR AT NO. 65 IN SPC-Y. | MDCCLXXV. | (PRICE SIXPENCE, BOUND AND GILT.)

In 8's. Pp. 156[160]. ? engvd FP. 34 wcts in text. Bk-list on last 2 leaves. D.f.b. (Communicated.)

⌈Pratley, 9·6×6·6 cm. Welch (2 copies).

(10) An edition of 1777. Pr f C & N. Price 6*d*. Rothschild 608.

Title approx. as for no. (1). *Imprint* approx. as for no. (9), with date MDCCLXXVII.

16mo in 8's. Engvd FP. Wcts in text. 'Black & white paper bds, decorated with vignette illustns of the story' (Rothschild).

⌜Ball; MiDW; formerly Stone.

(11) An undated edition (dated *ca.* 1780 by Stone). 'Pr f The Proprietors and sold by all Booksellers'. Is probably a piracy. Sold in the Harmsworth sale in 1939.

(12) An edition of 1780. Pr f C & N. Price 6*d.* Scott, pp. 357–8.

Title approx. as for no. (1). *Imprint* approx. as for no. (6), with date MDCCLXXX.

In 8's. Pp. 156[160]. Engvd FP. Wcts. (Communicated.)

⌜Osborne*; CLU; PP; NRU; Welch (imperf.).

(13) An edition of 1783. Pr f TC. Price 6*d.* Gum 2756; NBL 635; Hugo, II, 321, no. 5.

Title approx. as for no. (1). *Imprint:* PR F T. CARNAN, | SUCCESSOR TO MR. J. NEWBERY, IN SP | C-Y. MDCCLXXXIII.

In 8's. 80 leaves. Pp. 158[160]. Wct FP and wcts in text. List of bks pr f TC on pp. [159–60]. White bds, impressed with pictorial designs in black.

⌜BM, 9·6×6·0 cm (imperf.); Traylen; Ball; Welch. Copy at Sotheby, 9.11.64, lot 124, was either of this ed. or no. (14). The copy reported by Stone to be in the V&A cannot now be traced.

(14) Another edition of 1783. Recorded by Stone as by Newbery & Carnan, and sold at Sotheby's in 1930. Very doubtful: I know of no other case of co-operation between EN & FN(S) after 1780, except as members of a conger.

(15) An undated edition (Stone dates *ca.* 1784). Pr f TC. Price 6*d.*

Title approx. as for no. (1). *Imprint:* PR F T. CARNAN, SUCCESSOR TO MR J. | NEWBERY, AT NO. 65, NEAR THE BAR, IN S | PC-Y. | [PRICE SIX-PENCE, BOUND.]

In 6's. 62 leaves. Pp. 124. Wct FP and 32 wcts in text. D.f.b.; also green flowered bds.

In this ed. the traditional form of the bk, 8° or 8's, running to *ca.* 160 pp., which had been followed from the first ed., is abandoned. There are larger type and type-area, and the wcts are now surrounded by borders of printer's ornaments; the 'Appendix' is omitted.

⌜BM (imperf.), 11·5×7·7 cm; Roscoe; MWA.

J168. HISTORY OF LITTLE KING PIPPIN, THE. Welsh 247.
(1) Adv. *LC* 3–5.1.75, p. 11, as one of FN(N)'s new publications. Price 2*d.*
(2) Adv. *LC* 30.12.81–1.1.82, p. 7, as to be had of EN. Price 2*d.*
(3) An edition of 1783. Pr f EN. Price 2*d.* S&W Cat.

THE | HISTORY | OF | LITTLE KING PIPPIN; | WITH AN | ACCOUNT OF THE MELANCHOLY DEATH | OF FOUR NAUGHTY BOYS, WHO WERE | DEVOURED BY WILD BEASTS. | AND THE | WONDERFUL DELIVERY OF MASTER | HARRY HARMLESS, BY A LITTLE | WHITE HORSE. | [d.p.rule] |

LONDON: | PR F E. NEWBERY, AT THE COR- | NER OF SPCY. 1783. | [PRICE TWO-PENCE.]

Pp. 62[63]. Wct FP and wcts in text. Bk-list on last page. D.f.b. (Communicated.)

[Ball.

(4) An edition of 1786. EN. Mentioned by Opie, *Oxford Dict. of Nursery Rhymes*, 352; but at pp. 84 and 432 they date '*ca.* 1786'.

(5) An edition of 1793. EN.

[CtHi.

(6) ENC, 5 lists as the *History of Little King Pippin, to which is added the Story of the Children in the Wood*, price 2*d*. So also Hugo, II, 309. And listed in *Menagerie*, 1800, as pr f EN, price 2*d*.

HISTORY OF LUCY WELLERS. See Smythies, Miss.

J169. HISTORY OF NORTH AMERICA, THE, 1789. First edition. Pr f EN. Price 1*s* 6*d*. Welsh 192; Sabin 16583; Weedon 35. Richard Johnson's Day-book records: *1789. Mr Badcock——To writing The Hist. of North America 30 Lines of MS. made a Page of Print.——£10. 10s.* The bk is not a rarity, but I have found no later ed. in this country. America, on the other hand, produced not less than 12 edd. in the period 1793–1818 (see Weedon). There is nothing to show if these were pirated.

THE | HISTORY | OF | NORTH AMERICA. | CONTAINING, | A REVIEW OF THE CUSTOMS AND MANNERS | OF THE | ORIGINAL INHABITANTS; | THE FIRST SETTLEMENT OF THE | BRITISH COLONIES, | THEIR | RISE AND PROGRESS, | [3 lines] | [p.rule] | BY THE REV. MR. COOPER. | [p.rule] | EMBELLISHED WITH COPPER-PLATE CUTS. | [d.p.rule] | LONDON: | PR F E. NEWBERY, THE CORNER OF S | PC-Y. 1789.

In 6's. 90 leaves+6 insets. Pp. [13]–184. Engvd FP and 5 engvd leaves in text. Marbled bds, green vell. spine with label.

[BM, 13·9×8·7 cm; Weedon; Bell; Opie; UCLA; Osborne, Cat. p. 167; Maxwell Hunley, Cat. 48 [winter 1969] item 169.

J170. HISTORY OF PRINCE LEE BOO, THE. The dated ed., no. (1), was probably (though not certainly) the first. The undated edd. are all too numerous; they indicate the great popularity of the book, as do the worn and reworked states of the engvd FP.

Dr d'Alté Welch reported that copies of two different undated edd., one in his colln, one in CLU, list Berquin's *Looking-Glass for the Mind*, without mention of wcts, at 2*s* 6*d*. This gives a date not after 1792, the date of the first ed. of the *Looking-Glass* recorded as pubd with wcts, at 3*s*.

(1) An edition of 1789 (probably the 1st). Pr f EN. Welsh 251; *CBEL*, II, 563.

THE INTERESTING AND AFFECTING | HISTORY | OF | PRINCE LEE BOO, | A NATIVE OF THE | PELEW ISLANDS, | BROUGHT TO ENGLAND BY CAPT.

WILSON. | TO WHICH IS PREFIXED, | A SHORT ACCOUNT OF THOSE ISLANDS, | [2 lines] | [p.s.rule] | LONDON: | PR F E. NEWBERY, THE CORNER OF | SPCY. | MDCCLXXXIX.

In 6's. 96 leaves+engvd FP portrait of the prince. Pp. viii+178[184]. Drab bds, green vell. spine. List of bks pr f EN on last 6 pages. There are variant states of the engvd FP, especially to be found in the background – see the 2 copies in Oup.

[BM, 13·4×8·3 cm; CUL; Oup; Bath; BmPL; Hannas; Opie; Traylen; Pollard; Osborne, Cat. p. 166; UCLA; MiDW; Welch; Gardner; Schiller, Cat. 26, item 1877.

(2) A 'new edition', undated. Pr f EN. ? Gum 4629. A 'new ed.' was adv. *LC* 17–19.1.93 as a 'new publication', price 1*s* 6*d.*

Engraved title: THE | HISTORY | OF | PRINCE LEE BOO | A NATIVE OF THE | PELEW ISLANDS. | BROUGHT TO ENGLAND | BY CAPT^N WILSON. | A NEW EDITION. | [engvd vignette of a ship in a storm] | LONDON. | PR F E. NEWBERY THE CORNER OF | SPCY.

In this ed. the long 'f' is used; text of the 'Advertisement' begins on A2^r (p. iii) (9 lines) and ends on p. viii (4 lines). Last word in line 11, p. 157, is 'prove'; last word in line 16, p. 134, is 'enlivened'. In the TP vignette the waves have white crests, 4 rather indistinct figures on the ship.

In 6's. 96 leaves+7 insets. Pp. viii+178[184]. Engvd FP portrait of the prince, engvd TP, 5 other engvd leaves. List of bks pr f EN on last 6 pages. Marbled bds, green vell. spine with label.

[BM (imperf.), 12·8×7·6 cm.

(3) Another 'new edition', undated. Not later than 1795 (ms date '1795 Jany 10th' in BM copy). Pr f EN. Price 1*s* 6*d.* ? Gum 4629.

Engvd FP and *title* and *imprint* as for no. (2). Type re-set, long 'f' used. Text of 'Advertisement' begins on A1^r, p. iii (15 lines), ends on p. vi (17 lines). Last word in line 11 on p. 157 is 'might'; last word in line 16 on p. 134 is 'enliven-'. The engvd leaves are so worn as to give mere ghosts of impressions. I place this ed. later than no. (2).

In 6's. 94 leaves+7 insets. Pp. vi (? should be iv) +178[184]. Engvd FP and TP and 5 other engvd leaves. Bk-list on last 6 pages. Drab bds, green vell. spine.

[BM, 12·9×8·3 cm; MH; copy once with Seven Gables Bookshop, N.Y.

(3A) Another 'new edition', undated. Pr f EN.

Engvd *title* and *imprint* as for no. (2), but type re-set, long 'f' used. Text of 'Advertisement' begins on A2^r (15 lines), ends on p. vi (17 lines); last word in line 11, p. 157, is 'prove'; last word in line 16 on p. 134 is 'enlivened'.

In 6's. Pp. vi+178[184]. 5 engvd leaves in text. Vignette on TP as in no. (2). Marbled bds, green vell. spine. List of bks pr f EN on last 6 pages.

[Bell, 13·0×8·5 cm; Sotheby, 5.2.68, lot 55.

(4) Another 'new edition', undated. Pr f EN. Has ms date 1800.

Engvd FP and *title* and *imprint* as for no. (2). Type re-set. Short 's' used. Imprint of 'Hodson, Printer, Cross-Street, Hatton-Garden.' at foot of pp. [iii]+ 178 and [184]. 'Advertisement' as in no. (3). Last word in line 11, p. 157, is 'might'; last word in line 16 on p. 134 is 'enliven-'. Engvd vignette on TP heavily reworked, white crests to waves hatched over, 5 distinct figures on the ship.

Specification as for no. (3). Marbled bds, green vell. spine.

[V&A(GL); Grey, 13·3 × 8·5 cm.

(5) There are copies of undated editions in Oup, RePL, DES, Melbourne, Welch, MiDW, UCLA, Shiers, NLA.

J171. HISTORY OF SINBAD THE SAILOR, THE.

(1) An edition of 1794. EN.

[Ball.

(2) An edition of 1798. Pr f EN. Price 6d.

THE | HISTORY | OF | SINBAD | THE | SAILOR; | CONTAINING | AN ACCOUNT | OF HIS SEVERAL | SURPRISING VOYAGES | AND | MIRACULOUS ESCAPES. | [d.p.rule] | LONDON: | PR F E. NEWBERY, THE CORNER OF SP | CY. 1798.

Pp. 128. Engvd FP and other illustrations. D.f.b. (Communicated.)

[Welch; Ball; MB; UCLA.

J172. HISTORY OF SOUTH AMERICA, THE, 1789. First edition.

Pr f EN. Price 1s 6d. Welsh 193; Sabin 16584; Weedon 37. Richard Johnson's Day-book records: *1789. Mr Badcock——To writing The Hist. of South America ——£10. 10s.* This work seems to have been less of a success than its companion the *History of North America*: only one English ed. (not a scarce bk), and 3 American.

THE | HISTORY | OF | SOUTH AMERICA. | CONTAINING THE | DISCOVERIES OF COLUMBUS, | THE | CONQUEST OF MEXICO AND PERU, | AND THE | OTHER TRANSACTIONS OF THE SPANIARDS | IN THE | NEW WORLD. | [p.rule] | BY THE REV. MR. COOPER. | [p.rule] | EMBELLISHED WITH COPPER-PLATE CUTS. | [d.p.rule] | LONDON, | PR F E. NEWBERY, THE CORNER OF | SPC-Y, 1789.

In 6's. 90 leaves+6 insets. Pp. 168. Engvd FP and 5 engvd leaves in text. Marbled bds, green vell. spine with label.

[BM, 13·5 × 8·7 cm; Bodley; RePL; Bell; Traylen; Opie; UCLA; Ries; McKell; Osborne*; Maxwell Hunley, Cat. 48 [winter 1969] item 170.

HISTORY OF THE BIBLE. See A34(7).

J173. HISTORY OF THE CREATION. Perhaps = THE MOSAIC CREATION.

(1) Listed as 'sold at Mr Newbery's' in *Goody Two-Shoes*, 3rd ed., 1766, price 6d.

(2) Listed as s b 'F. Newbery, Jun. & Co' in undated ed. of *Pretty Play-thing* (J309(4)).

HISTORY OF THE ENCHANTED CASTLE, THE = J48.

HISTORY OF THE DAVENPORT FAMILY. See S., H.

HISTORY OF THE FAMILY AT SMILEDALE, THE. See M., A.

HISTORY OF THE GRECIAN STATES. See J261.

J174. HISTORY OF THE LIFE OF OUR LORD AND SAVIOUR JESUS CHRIST. Forms vol. II in the *Young Christian's Library* (no. J392A). Has been attributed to Goldsmith: see R. W. Seitz, in *Modern Philology*, vol. 26, pp. 296–9; *CBEL*, II, 645; IAW 166–7. An advert. in *MC&LA* also ascribes to Goldsmith (1.7.74).

(1) Listed as 'just pubd' by JN in no. J175, 1763. ? = no. (2).

(2) An edition of 1764. Pr f JN. Price 1*s*.

AN | HISTORY | OF THE | LIFE | OF OUR | LORD AND SAVIOUR | JESUS CHRIST. | TO WHICH IS ADDED, | THE LIFE OF THE BLESSED | VIRGIN MARY. | [3 lines] | LONDON: | PR F J. NEWBERY, AT THE BIBLE AND | SUN IN SPC-Y. 1764.

In 8's. 100 leaves+8 insets. Pp. 192. A1 a blank. Engvd FP and 7 engvd leaves. D.f.b.

[St Bride, 9·7×6·2 cm.

(3) Listed frequently in 1769–70 as pr f N & C. Probably only stock in hand taken over from JN. Welsh 183.

(4) An edition of 1774, by C & N. Price 1*s*. This ed. is recorded by Prior in his *Life of Goldsmith*, 1837 (vol. I, p. 488) as having been published under Goldsmith's name by C & N. Prior refers to the advert. of this ed. in *MC&LA* for 1 July 1774 in a footnote, and it seems probable that he had seen no copy of the ed. but, as IAW suggests (at pp. 166–7), was relying on the advert. If so, the ed. must be regarded as no more than a possibility. That Goldsmith's name appeared in the TP is more than unlikely.

(4A) An edition of 1777. Pr f C & N.

Title as for no. (2). *Imprint:* PR F T. CARNAN, AND F. NEWBERY, | JUN. AT NO. 65, IN SPC-Y. | MDCCLXXVII.

In 8's. 100 leaves+7 insets; first leaf a blank. Pp. viii+192. Engvd FP as in no. (2), 6 (? should be 7) engvd leaves in text. White or buff bds impressed with illustrative designs in black.

[Traylen, 9·5×6·3 cm.

(5) Listed as pr f TC in *Newtonian System*, 1787. Price 1*s*.

J175. HISTORY OF THE LIVES...OF THE APOSTLES AND EVANGELISTS. Forms vol. III in the *Young Christian's Library* (no. J392A).

(1) An edition of 1763. Pr f JN. Price 1*s*.

AN | HISTORY | OF THE | LIVES, ACTIONS, TRAVELS, | SUFFERINGS

AND DEATHS | OF THE | APOSTLES | AND | EVANGELISTS, | VIZ. | [2 parallel columns of 9 and 8 lines] | ADORNED WITH VARIETY OF COPPER-PLATE CUTS. | LONDON: | PR F J. NEWBERY, AT THE BIBLE AND SUN, IN SPC-Y. 1763. | [PRICE ONE SHILLING BOUND.]

In 8's. 128 leaves+8 insets. Pp. 246[252]. Engvd FP and 7 other engvd leaves. List of bks 'just pubd' by JN on last 5 pages. D.f.b.

[St Bride, 9·9×6·5 cm; Preston, Cat. p. 71; McKell.

(2) Frequently listed in 1769–70 as pr f N & C. Probably stock in hand inherited from JN. Welsh 170.

(3) Listed as pr f TC in *Newtonian System*, 1787. Price 1s.

HISTORY OF THE LIVES...OF THE FATHERS OF THE CHRISTIAN CHURCH... Goldsmith's *History of the Lives...of the... Martyrs, and Primitive Fathers* (J148) is often so listed.

HISTORY OF THE LIVES OF THE MARTYRS... See Goldsmith, Oliver, J148.

HISTORY OF THE WHITE CAT. See RENOWNED HISTORY...

HISTORY OF THE WORLD. See COMPENDIOUS HISTORY...

J176. HISTORY OF TOMMY CARELESS, THE. Welsh 318; Weedon 38 (records no English ed. before 1809). Richard Johnson's Day-book records:
1787 July. Mr Badcock———To writing The Misfortunes of a Week }
——— ——— Rural Felicity——— } £2. 2s.

(1) An edition of 1788. Pr f EN. Price 1d.

THE | HISTORY | OF | TOMMY CARELESS; | OR, THE | MISFORTUNES | OF | A WEEK. | [p.s.rule] | ADORNED WITH CUTS. | [p.s.rule] | LONDON: | PR F E. NEWBERY, THE CORNER OF | SPC-Y. 1788. | [PRICE ONE PENNY.]

16mo. 16 leaves. Pp. 31. Wct FP and 7 wcts in the text, perhaps by Lee. Floral bds. (Communicated.)

[MWA; Roscoe (photocopied selected leaves).

(2) Listed in *The Menagerie*, 1800, as pr f EN, price 1d.

HISTORY OF TOMMY PLAYLOVE AND JACKY LOVEBOOK. See J., S.

J177. HISTORY OF TOMMY TITMOUSE, THE.

(1) Adv. *LC* 26–8.12.86, p. 620, as one of 'Newbery's New Publications for the Christmas Holidays...just pubd by EN'. Price 2d. Welsh 318. Perhaps = no. (1A).

(1A) An undated edition. Pr f EN. Price 2d.

THE | HISTORY | OF | TOMMY TITMOUSE, | A LITTLE BOY, | WHO
BECAME A GREAT MAN BY MINDING | HIS LEARNING, DOING AS HE WAS
BID, | AND BEING GOOD-NATURED AND OBLIG- | ING TO EVERY BODY. |
TOGETHER WITH | THE ADVENTURES OF THE OLD MAN | OF THE WOODS,
AND OTHER STORIES | EQUALLY PLEASING AND INSTRUCTIVE. | [p.rule] |
EMBELLISHED WITH CUTS. | [d.p.rule] | LONDON: | PR F E. NEWBERY, THE
CORNER OF | S P C Y. | [PRICE TWO-PENCE.]

In 8's. 32 leaves. Pp. 56[61]. Wct FP, 15 wcts in text. List of 'New Bks just
pub^d by E.N.' on pp. [57–61].

[CUL, 9·5 × 5·9 cm.

(2) An edition of 1799. Pr f EN. Price 2d.

Title approx. as for no. (1A). *Imprint:* LONDON: | PR F E. NEWBERY, THE
CORNER OF | SPC-Y. | 1799. | [PRICE TWO-PENCE.] | PR B S. GOSNELL,
LITTLE QUEEN STREET, | HOLBORN.

Pp. 56[61]. Wct FP and wcts in text. Bk-list on pp. [57–61]. (Communicated.)
[Ball.

J178. HISTORY OF YOUNG EDWIN AND LITTLE JESSY, THE.
(1) An edition by FN(N). Price 1s. Welsh 335.
(2) An edition of 1797. Pr f EN. Price 1s.

THE | HISTORY | OF | YOUNG EDWIN AND LITTLE JESSY: | TOGETHER
WITH | AN ACCOUNT OF THE PLEASANT WALK | WHICH | WILLIAM AND
WINIFRED | TOOK WITH | MARGERY, WHO LIVES AT THE FOOT OF |
PARNASSUS. | [p.s.rule] | WRITTEN BY | THE AFORESAID MARGERY, | FOR
THE PURPOSE OF MAKING EVERY LITTLE GIRL AND | BOY GOOD AND
HAPPY. | [d.p.rule] | LONDON: | PR F E. NEWBERY, CORNER OF S | PC-Y. |
[p.rule] | 1797.

In 6's. 60 leaves+engvd FP by J. Saunders. B1 a blank. Pp. 120. Pink bds.

[BM, 13·7 × 8·0 cm; Melbourne.

(3) An edition of 1798, pubd by EN. Price 1s. Adv. *LC* 23–6.12.97, p. 614;
CBEL, II, 564; ENC 8. I have not traced the hypothetical *Young Edwin and his
Sister Jessy* referred to by *CBEL*.

(4) An edition of 1802 by J. Harris has a FP dated 6.7.97 pubd by EN, presumably
the FP to no. (2). (Communicated.)

[Gardner.

HOBBY HORSE, THE; OR, THE CHRISTMAS COMPANION.
See 'Ticklepitcher, Toby'.

J179. HOLIDAY ANECDOTES. Weedon 39. Richard Johnson's Day-
book records: *1780 Sept. 26. Delivered to Mrs Newbery the Copy of Holiday
Anecdotes——£1. 1s.* Weedon considers that *Holiday Anecdotes* probably = *The
Holiday Spy* (no. J181).

J180. HOLIDAY ENTERTAINMENT.
(1) An edition listed in J88(3), vol. I, 1786, as pr f EN. Price 1*d*.
(2) Entry deleted.
(3) An edition of 1793. Pr f EN.

HOLIDAY ENTERTAINMENT; | OR THE | GOOD CHILD'S FAIRING: | CONTAINING | THE PLAYS AND SPORTS | OF | CHARLEY AND BILLY WELLDON, | AND OTHER | LITTLE BOYS AND GIRLS WHO WENT | WITH THEM TO THE FAIR. | WITH THE | FANCIES | OF THE | OLD MAN THAT LIVED UNDER | THE HILL. | LONDON: | PR F E. NEWBERY, AT THE | CORNER OF SPC-Y. | MDCCXCIII.

Pp. 31. Wct FP and wcts in text. (Communicated.)
[Ball.
(4) An edition of 1796. Pr f EN.

Title and *imprint*, with date 1796, approx. as for no. (3). Pp. 31. Last leaf a paste-down. Wct FP and 12 wcts in text. Green embossed wrappers. (Communicated.)
[UCLA, 10·2×6·5 cm.
(5) An edition of 1801, by EN. Recorded by Lyon.

J181. HOLIDAY SPY, THE. See Weedon 39 (sub *Holiday Anecdotes*).
(1A) Adv. *LC* 19–21.12.80, p. 589, as one of EN's new Publications in the Christmas holidays. Price 1*d*.
(1B) An undated edition (1786 or before). Pr f EN. Price 1*d*, bd and gilt. The CLU copy has a ms inscription 'Sarah Gorton her book 1786'. Welsh 237.

THE | HOLIDAY SPY; | BEING THE | OBSERVATIONS | OF | LITTLE TOMMY THOUGHTFUL, | ON THE | DIFFERENT TEMPERS, GENIUS, | AND MANNERS, | OF THE | YOUNG MASTERS AND MISSES | IN THE | SEVERAL FAMILIES WHICH HE VISITED, DU- | RING HIS LAST BREAKING-UP. | TO BE | CONTINUED OCCASIONALLY FOR THE ENTER- | TAINMENT OF HIS SCHOOL FELLOWS. | [d.p.rule] | LONDON: | PR F E. NEWBERY, AT THE CORNER | OF SPCY. | [PRICE ONE PENNY, BOUND AND GILT.]

Pp. 31. First and last leaves pastedowns. Wct FP and 8 wcts in text. D.f.b. (Communicated.)
[UCLA.
(2) Listed in *The Menagerie*, 1800, as pr f EN, price 1*d*.

J182. Entry deleted.

J183. HURRY, Mrs Ives (*née* Mitchell, Margaret). MITCHELL'S MORAL AND INSTRUCTIVE TALES. 2 vols, price 6*s*. Listed in Trimmer's *Silver Thimble*, 1799 and 1801, as pr f EN. ENC 11. Probably = no. J184.

J184. HURRY, Mrs Ives (*née* Mitchell, Margaret). TALES OF INSTRUCTION AND AMUSEMENT, 1795. Pr f EN. 2 vols, price 6*s*. Welsh 271.

Vol. I. TALES | OF | INSTRUCTION | AND | AMUSEMENT. | WRITTEN FOR THE USE | OF | YOUNG PERSONS. | [d.p.rule] | BY MISS MITCHELL. | [p.s.rule] | IN TWO VOLUMES. | VOL. I. | LONDON: | PR F E. NEWBERY, CORNER OF S | PCY. | 1795. | [ENTERED AT STATIONERS' HALL.]

12mo. 113 leaves+engvd FP sgd 'Cook sculp'. Pp. x+215.

Vol. II. *Title* and *imprint* approx. as for vol. I, omitting 'In two Volumes'.

12mo. 116 leaves+engvd FP sgd 'Cook sc'. Pp. 230.

[BM, 17·3×9·6 cm; Roscoe; Renier (vol. I); UCLA; Bondy, Cat. 73 [1967] item 551.

HYMNS FOR THE AMUSEMENT OF CHILDREN. See Smart, Chris.

ILLUSTRATIONS OF THE SCHOOL-VIRGIL. See Thornton, Robt. J.

J185. IMPORTANT POCKET BOOK, THE.

(1) An undated edition, pr f JN (see Plate 6). Not before 1765, the bk-list including *Goody Two-Shoes*. Listed in *Goody Two-Shoes*, 1768. Welsh 285.

THE IMPORTANT | POCKET BOOK, | OR THE | VALENTINE'S LEDGER. | FOR THE | USE OF THOSE WHO WOULD LIVE HAPPILY IN | THIS WORLD, AND IN THE NEXT. | [p.rule] | [7 lines quotes] | [d.p.rule] | LONDON: | PR F J. NEWBERY, AT THE BIBLE AND SUN IN | SPC-Y.

In 6's. 80 leaves+6 insets; pp. xxxii+20[22]; no pagination from C3^v to M2^r. Engvd FP and 5 engvd leaves in text; wcts at N4^r and N5^r. From C5^v to M1^r the book consists of an account book for each day, the left page of the opening providing for cash entries, the right headed 'The Moral Account' with columns headed 'Good' and 'Bad'. List of bks pubd by JN on N5^v and N6^{r,v}. List of medicines sold by JN on N6^v. D.f.b.

[BM, 12·1×7·5 cm; V&A; Melbourne; Lapides.

(2) Listed as pr f C & N in *Mother's Gift*, 1770, price 1s. Probably stock in hand inherited from JN.

(3) Listed as pr f TC, price 1s, in 'Abraham Aesop', 1783 and *Newtonian System*, 1787.

J186. INFANT TUTOR, THE. One of the 'Introductory' works for the *Circle of the Sciences* series; see General Note J60.

(1) First and second edition not traced.

(2) Third edition adv. *PA* 9.1.53 as pr f JN, price 6d neatly bd and gilt. Still listed as for sale in 1767. Welsh 190; Alston, IV, 595.

(3) Fourth edition, 1756. Pr f JN. Price 6d bd and gilt.

Title and *imprint* approx. as for no. (5), with THE FOURTH EDITION and date MDCCLVI. 96 leaves. Pp. vi+[7]–193[194]. Bk-list on last page. (Communicated.)

[Ball; Welch (imperf.).

(4) Fifth edition, 1760. Pr f JN. Pressler, p. 8.

Title and *imprint* approx. as for no. (5), with THE FIFTH EDITION and date 1760. Pp. vi+7–192. Illustrations.

[ICU-Judd Lib. (imperf.).

(5) Sixth edition, 1763. Pr f JN. Alston, IV, 596 and plate LVI.

THE INFANT TUTOR; | OR, AN EASY | SPELLING-BOOK, | FOR | LITTLE MASTERS AND MISSES. | DESIGNED AS AN | INTRODUCTORY PART | TO THE | CIRCLE OF THE SCIENCES. | [p.rule] | PUBLISHED BY THE KING'S AUTHORITY. | [p.rule] | THE SIXTH EDITION. | [p.rule] | LONDON: | PR F J. NEWBERY, AT THE BIBLE | AND SUN, IN SPC-Y. | MDCCLXIII.

In 8's. 96 leaves. Pp. vi+[7]–193[194] (error for 189[190]). 12 wct headpieces within ornam. frames. List of bks just pubd by JN on last page. D.f.b.

[BM, 9·7×6·3 cm.

(6) An edition of 1769. Pr f N & C. Price 6*d* bd and gilt. Alston, IV, 597.

Title approx. as for no. (5). *Imprint:* PR F F. NEWBERY, AND CARNAN, AT NO. 65. THE NORTH-SIDE OF SP | C-Y, 1769. | (PRICE 6*d*.)

In 8's. 96 leaves. Pp. 188[192]. Wcts as for no. (5). D.f.b.

[V&A, 9·7×6·5 cm; Ball.

(7) An edition of 1776. Pr f C & N. Price 6*d* bd and gilt. Welsh 190; Alston, IV, 598.

Title approx. as for no. (5). *Imprint:* PR F T. CARNAN AND F. NEWBERY, | JUNIOR, AT NO. 65, IN SPC-Y, | BUT NOT FOR F. NEWBERY, AT THE CORNER OF | LUDGATE-STREET, WHO HAS NO SHARE IN THE LATE | MR. JOHN NEWBERY'S BOOKS FOR CHILDREN. | MDCCLXXVI. | (PRICE SIXPENCE, BOUND AND GILT.)

In 8's. 96 leaves. Pp. viii+9–188[192]. Wcts as in no. (5). List of bks pr f C & N on last 4 pages. Drab or white bds with wct ornam. designs in black.

[BM, 9·8×6·4 cm; UCLA.

(8) An edition of 1783. Pr f TC. Price 6*d*. Not in Alston.

Title approx. as for no. (5). *Imprint:* PR F T. CARNAN, SUCCESSOR TO MR. J. | NEWBERY, AT NO. 65, IN SPC- | Y. (PRICE SIX-PENCE, BOUND.) | MDCCLXXXIII.

In 8's. 96 leaves. Pp. viii+188[192]. 12 wcts in text. List of bks pr f TC on pp. [189–92]. Bds with impressed floral design; also drab bds, overprinted in red. Details taken from the BmPL copy.

[BmPL (imperf.); UCLA.

INFANT'S DELIGHT, THE. See Fenn, Lady E.

INFANT'S FRIEND, THE. PTS I, II AND III. See Fenn, Lady E.

INFANT'S PATH STREWED WITH FLOWERS. See Fenn, Lady E.

J187. INSTRUCTIVE FRAGMENTS. Pr f EN. Price 6*d*. Weedon 57, x. Listed in *Anecdotes of Mary*, 1795. One of the 10 vols forming the *Lilliputian Library* (no. J218). It is to be questioned whether the work is in fact Lilliputius Gulliver's *Instructive Lessons* as stated by Weedon. See J152.

INSTRUCTIVE LESSONS CONVEYED. See 'Gulliver, Lilliputius'.

INSTRUCTIVE RAMBLES. See Helme, Eliz.

INSTRUCTIVE RAMBLES EXTENDED. See Helme, Eliz.

J188. INTRODUCTION TO THE STUDY OF HISTORY, AN, 1772. Pr f TC. Price 3*s* in the vell. manner. Welsh 237; Weedon 40.

The only recorded bk having Richard Johnson's name in the TP. But his Daybook did not claim that he was the author; it reads: *1771 May 1. Delivered to Mr Carnan the copy of an Introduction to the Study of History.——Value Twenty Guineas.*

In the Preface to the bk Johnson says: 'If the following pages should meet with a favourable reception...I shall with pleasure resign the credit of them to the late M. L'Abbe de Saint Real, from whom I have collected the greater part of the sentiments they contain. Indeed, almost the whole of them may be considered as little more than a *very free* translation of part of the historical writings of that author.'

Also Johnson makes it clear that the work was intended for the perusal of youth: 'Let us then endeavour to encourage youth in the pursuit of wisdom and truth; let us try, if we cannot persuade them from the perusal of such books [i.e. novels and romances] as tend rather to increase than conquer their passions; and let us repeat the experiment how far the Study of History will answer that end.'

AN | INTRODUCTION | TO THE | STUDY OF HISTORY: | WHEREIN IS CONSIDERED THE | PROPER METHOD OF READING | HISTORICAL WORKS, | IN ORDER TO ACQUIRE A | PERFECT KNOWLEDGE OF MANKIND; | [7 lines] | [p.rule] | BY R. JOHNSON. | [d.p.rule] | LONDON, | PR F T. CARNAN, AT NUMBER 65, IN S | PC-Y. MDCCLXXII.

12mo. 144 leaves. Pp. viii+269[279].

[BM, 16·7 × 10·0 cm.

J., S. See Jones, Stephen.

J189. J., S. (? Stephen Jones). HISTORY OF TOMMY PLAYLOVE AND JACKY LOVEBOOK, THE.

(1) An edition of 1783. EN.

[MiDW.

(2) An edition of 1788. EN. Probably the ed. adv. *LC* 27–9.12.87, p. 619, as to be pubd in the Christmas Holidays, price 6*d*. D.f.b. S&W Cat.

[Ball.
(3) An edition of 1789. EN. Welsh 318.
(4) An edition of 1793. Pr f EN. Price 6*d*.

THE | HISTORY | OF | TOMMY PLAYLOVE | AND | JACKY LOVEBOOK. | WHEREIN IS SHEWN | THE SUPERIORITY OF VIRTUE OVER VICE, | HOWEVER DIGNIFIED BY | BIRTH OR FORTUNE. | [d.p.rule] | WRITTEN BY A FRIEND. | [p.rule] | ADORNED WITH CUTS. | [d.p.rule] | LONDON: | PR F E. NEWBERY, THE CORNER OF | SPC-Y. | [p.rule] | MDCCXCIII.

In 8's. 64 leaves. Pp. xiii+[15]–125[127][?128]. Wct FP sgd 'Lee'. 14 wcts in text, 2 sgd 'L' (i.e. Lee). Bk-list on last 2 (?3) pages.

[BM, 10·9×7·6 cm (lacks last leaf); Harding; Welch.
(5) An edition of 1800. EN.
[Ball.
(6) An undated edition. EN.
[Ball.

J190. J., S. (? Stephen Jones). LIFE AND ADVENTURES OF A FLY, THE, n.d. [1787–9]. Pr f EN. Price 6*d*. Not before 1787, the bk-list including *The Foundling*, of which the 1st ed. appeared in that year; and listed in *Prince Lee Boo*, 1789. Welsh 255; Hugo, II, 4109; Gum 3787; *CBEL*, II, 563; NBL 703; S&W Cat.

THE | LIFE AND ADVENTURES | OF A | FLY. | SUPPOSED TO HAVE BEEN WRITTEN BY | HIMSELF. | [p.s.rule] | ILLUSTRATED WITH CUTS. | [d.p.rule] | LONDON: | PR F E. NEWBERY, | AT THE CORNER OF SPC-Y. | [PRICE 6*d*.] (*or* (PRICE 6*d*.))

Four gatherings of 16 leaves each, sgd [A]–[H8]. 64 leaves. Pp. [19]–121[128]. Wct FP sgd 'Bwk' (i.e. John Bewick) and 12 wcts by him in text, unsgd. List of bks pr f EN on pp. [122–8]. D.f.b.

The following variant editions or issues have come to light; there may well be others:

(1) LONDON in TP in roman caps, 2·3 cm long; d.p.rule above imprint 5·4 cm long; price 6*d* in brackets []; A6ʳ: plain rule below 'Preface' 2·7 cm long; B2ʳ: tapering rule below caption 4·1 cm long; p. 121: THE END in roman caps 1·5 cm long.

[BM, 10·4×7·2 cm.

(2) LONDON in TP in large italic caps, 1·3 cm long; price 6*d* in brackets (); A6ʳ: tapering rule below 'Preface' 2·7 cm long; B2ʳ: a wavy rule below caption, 3·5 cm long; p. 121: The END in roman caps and lower-case, 1·7 cm long. (Communicated.)

[MWA; Ball; Roscoe (photocopied selected leaves).

(3) LONDON in TP in roman caps, 2·5 cm long; A6ʳ: no rule below 'Preface'; B2ʳ: a line below caption; p. 121: The END in roman caps and lower-case, 2·1 cm long. (Communicated.)

[Copy seen by Welch; Roscoe (photocopied selected leaves).

(4) LONDON in TP in roman caps, 2·3 cm long; d.p.rule above imprint 5·7 cm, long; price 6d in brackets []; A6^r tapering rule below 'Preface' 3·2 cm long; B2^r: tapering rule below caption 3·1 cm long; THE END in roman caps 1·5 cm long. D.f.b. (Communicated.)

⌈Ries; Roscoe (photocopied selected leaves).

(5) Unchecked copies in ReU; Hannas; NNC-T (Darton Coll.).

J190A. JACKSON, Richard. LITERATURA GRÆCA, 1769. Pr f FN(N) et al. Price 2s 6d. Welsh 241.

LITERATURA GRÆCA. | CONTAINING, | [2 columns of 10 and 12 lines] | TO WHICH IS PREFIXED, | AN ESSAY ON THE STUDY OF THE | GREEK LANGUAGE; | [4 lines] | [p.rule] | DESIGNED FOR THE USE OF SCHOOLS. | [p.rule] | BY RICHARD JACKSON, M.A. | [d.p.rule] | LONDON: | PR F F. NEWBERY, AT THE CORNER OF | SPCY; AND B. COLLINS, IN | SALISBURY. MDCCLXIX.

12mo. 122 leaves. Pp. xxxix[xlvii]+196.
⌈BM, 17·0×9·9 cm; Bodley; Temperley.

JAMES MANNERS. See J157.

JESUS CHRIST, LIFE OF. See J174(2).

JEU DES FAUTES. See Gaultier, A. E. C.

JOE THOMPSON, LIFE AND ADVENTURES OF. See Kimber, Edwd.

J190B. 'JOHN-THE-GIANT-KILLER'. FOOD FOR THE MIND.
(1) An edition listed in *GM* Jan. 1757, p. 47, as by JN. Price 6d bd and gilt.
(2) Second edition, ?1758. Pr f a s b JN. Price 6d bd and gilt. Welsh 221; *CBEL*, II, 561; Opie, *Dict. Nursery Rhymes*, 403.
(3) Third edition, 1759. Pr f the Booksellers of Europe...[JN].

FOOD FOR THE MIND, | OR A | NEW RIDDLE BOOK; | COMPILED FOR THE USE OF | THE GREAT AND THE LITTLE | GOOD BOYS AND GIRLS | IN | ENGLAND, SCOTLAND, AND IRELAND. | [p.rule] | BY JOHN-THE-GIANT-KILLER, ESQ; | [p.rule] | [6 lines quote] | [p.rule] | THE THIRD EDITION. | [p.rule] | LONDON: | PR F THE BOOKSELLERS OF EUROPE, | ASIA, AFRICA AND AMERICA, AND SOLD AT | THE BIBLE AND SUN IN SPC- | Y. 1759.

In 8's. 64 leaves. Pp. viii+112[120]. Many wcts in text. List of bks pr f JN on last 8 pages. (Communicated.)
⌈McKell (imperf.), 9·6×6·3 cm; MH; NRU.
(4) Adv. *LC* 6–8.1.63, p. 28, as to be had of JN, price 6d. And frequently thereafter up to 1767.

(5) An edition of 1771. Pr f the Booksellers of Europe... *English Children's Books, 1563–1900*, no. 11. The attribution of the wcts to Thomas Bewick – or even to John – cannot be accepted.

(6) An edition of 1778. Pr f the Booksellers of Europe...S b C & N. *CBEL*, II, 561. Facsimile by the Leadenhall Press, *ca.* 1900.

Title approx. as for no. (3) (no ed. stated). *Imprint:* PR F THE BOOKSELLERS OF EUROPE, ASIA, | AFRICA, AND AMERICA; A S B T. CARNAN | AND E. NEWBERY, JUN. AT NUMBER 65, S | PCY. 1778.

In 8's. 60 leaves. Pp. viii+112. 68 wcts (one to each fable). On A1^v is the diatribe against FN(N) and his 'paltry compilations'.

⌈Bath; Ball.

(7) Listed as pr f TC in 'Abraham Aesop', 1783, price 6*d*.

(8) An edition of 1787. Pr f TC. Price 6*d*. D.f.b.

⌈Opie.

J191. JOHNSON, Richard.

Richard Johnson's work as hack-writer and compiler for the Newberys and Carnan (and other publishers) in the years 1770–93, as revealed by his Day-books (in the possession of the Company of Stationers), has been fully dealt with by Miss M. J. P. Weedon in her *Richard Johnson and the Successors to John Newbery* (see p. xxx).

An examination of the Day-book entries, and of the bks there referred to, does not reveal a single instance in which one can feel certain, beyond all doubt, that Johnson was the real author. The frequent entry 'To writing...' (28 cases in all, marked with an asterisk (*) in the list of Johnson's work set out below) proves to be no reliable evidence whatever of his authorship (I do not suggest he intended it should be so read): as witness, for instance, *Juvenile Rambles* recorded in the Day-book as 'written' by Johnson and with a Dedication sgd 'R.J.'; but which Miss Weedon (her no. 42) shows to have been 'borrowed', though a 'harsher expression would apply' from a work by Mrs Trimmer; as witness, even more forcibly, the entries 'To writing' Day's *Sandford and Merton* and Kimber's *Life of Joe Thompson*. Even the *Introduction to the Study of History*, 1772, described in the TP as 'By R. Johnson' is, as, to give him his due, Johnson frankly admits, no more than 'a very free translation' from the Abbé de Saint Réal.

In view of such a record I have listed no work under his name, although Miss Weedon would incline to give him the benefit of the doubt as regards the *Drawing School*, the *Picture Exhibition* and *Juvenile Sports* (see p. 33 of her paper).

Johnson is recorded as having had a hand (of what sort is often not clear) in the following works (all in the 'J' section): J2*, 3*, 7(3), 15, 16, 25, 26*, 39*, 49, 55*, 83*, 89, 92*, 104, 105, 111*, 113(2), 136*, 140*, 142*, 151, 161*, 162, 163*, 166*, 169*, 172*, 176*, 179, 181, 187, 188, 198, 200*, 211*, 214, 216, 217, 218, 222, 224*, 228*, 229, 245, 247*, 261, 263, 264, 265, 272, 276*, 280, 297, 300, 313, 327*, 347, 351, 357*, 370*, 372*, 395*.

I have done no original work on Johnson; at most I have added an edition here and there to Miss Weedon's lists, and made a few corrections arising from later researches (e.g. Berquin as author of the *Mountain Piper*). I record again my gratitude to her – and also to the Stationers' Company – for permission to quote from her writings and from the Day-books.

JOHNSON, Richard. INTRODUCTION TO THE STUDY OF HISTORY. See J188.

J191A. JOHNSON, Samuel, LL.D. LIVES OF THE ENGLISH POETS, ABRIDGED, 1797. Pr f EN. Price 3s 6d [?4s]. Welsh 242; Courtney 143.

JOHNSON'S LIVES | OF THE | ENGLISH POETS, | ABRIDGED: | WITH | NOTES AND ILLUSTRATIONS | BY THE EDITOR. | DESIGNED FOR | THE IMPROVEMENT OF YOUTH | IN THE KNOWLEDGE OF | POLITE LITERATURE, | AND AS | A USEFUL AND PLEASING COMPENDIUM FOR | PERSONS OF RIPER YEARS. | [p.s.rule] | TO WHICH IS PREFIXED, | SOME ACCOUNT | OF THE | LIFE OF DR. JOHNSON. | [d.p.rule] | LONDON: | PR F E. NEWBERY, AT THE CORNER OF | SPC-Y. | 1797.

12mo. 132 leaves+mezzotint FP sgd 'H. Richter del et sc'. Pp. xxi[xxiv]+239. [BM, 17·6×9·3 cm; Pollard.

J192. JONES, Stephen (attributed to). NATURAL HISTORY OF BEASTS, THE. S.J., who signs the 'Advertisement' to the *Natural History of Fishes* (J194) says that that work is a companion to his *Natural History of Birds* and this *Beasts*.

(1) A one-volume edition of 1793. Pr f EN. Price 2s 6d. Welsh 240.

Title and *imprint* approx. as for no. (2), vol. I, with date '1793'.

In 6's. 108 leaves+*ca*. 40 insets. Pp. xii+204. *Ca*. 40 engvd leaves of figures of animals etc. Marbled bds, green vell. spine with label.

[Opie; BmPL; Osborne*, 13·5×8·4 cm; CtNSCSC; Grant.

(2) A two-volume edition of 1798. Pr f EN. Price 4s.

Title to vol. I. THE | NATURAL HISTORY | OF | BEASTS, | COMPILED FROM THE BEST AUTHORITIES, | AND | ILLUSTRATED BY A GREAT VARIETY OF | COPPER PLATES, | COMPRISING NEAR | ONE HUNDRED AND TWENTY FIGURES, | ACCURATELY DRAWN FROM NATURE, AND BEAUTIFULLY ENGRAVED. | VOL. I. | [d.p.rule] | LONDON: | PR F E. NEWBERY, AT THE CORNER OF SP | C-Y. 1798.

The *title* to vol. II is wanting in the BM copy.

Vol. I. In 6's. 90 leaves+4 engvd leaves of figures of animals, three figures to a leaf. Pp. xv+17–180.

Vol. II. In 6's. 90 leaves+22 engvd leaves of figures of animals, three figures to a leaf. Pp. 180.

[BM, 12·9×8·1 cm.

J193. JONES, Stephen (attributed to). NATURAL HISTORY OF BIRDS, THE. The preface to the 1793 ed. is sgd 'S.J.'; and the work is a companion to the *Beasts* (J192) and the *Fishes* (J194).

(1) A one-volume edition of 1793. Pr f EN. Price 2s 6d. Welsh 240; NBL 258.

THE | NATURAL HISTORY | OF | BIRDS, | COMPILED FROM THE BEST AUTHORITIES, | AND | ILLUSTRATED BY A GREAT VARIETY OF | COPPER PLATES, | COMPRISING NEAR | ONE HUNDRED FIGURES, | ACCURATELY DRAWN FROM NATURE, AND BEAUTIFULLY ENGRAVED. | [p.s.rule] | LONDON: | PR F E. NEWBERY, AT THE CORNER OF SP | CY. 1793.

In 6's. 108 leaves+38 engvd leaves of figures of birds. Pp. xii+204. Marbled bds, green vell. spine, white label.

⌈Weedon, 13·7×8·5 cm; Roscoe; Grey; Opie; Welch; Shiers; Osborne*; UCLA.

(2) A two-volume edition, ?1798. Pubd by EN. Price 4s. Listed in Fenn's *Parsing Lessons for elder Pupils*, 1798.

J194. JONES, Stephen (attributed to), NATURAL HISTORY OF FISHES, A. The 'Advertisement' to the 1795 ed. is sgd 'S.J.' who says it is a companion to his *History of Beasts* and *History of Birds*.

(1) An edition of 1793. EN. The only record of this I have traced is in the Sale Catalogue of Edwin Pearson's Bewick Collection, 1868, lot 342, of which included 'Insects, Fishes, Butterflies, &c. E. Newbery, 1793'.

(2) An edition of 1795. Pr f EN. Price 2s 6d. Welsh 240.

A | NATURAL HISTORY | OF | FISHES, | AND OF | REPTILES, INSECTS, WATERS, | EARTHS, FOSSILS, MINERALS, | AND VEGETABLES, | COMPILED FROM THE BEST AUTHORITIES, | AND | ILLUSTRATED BY A GREAT VARIETY OF | COPPER PLATES, | COMPRISING NEAR | ONE HUNDRED FIGURES, | [1 line] | [p.s.rule] | LONDON: | PR F E. NEWBERY, AT THE CORNER OF SP | CY. 1795.

In 6's. 108 leaves+40 engvd leaves of fishes etc. Pp. 208.

⌈BM, 13·0×8·1 cm; CUL; Bodley; Hannas; Grey; Osborne, 13·3×8·6 cm, Cat. pp. 204–5; NNC-T (Darton Coll.); UCLA; Gardner; Maxwell Hunley, Cat. 48 [winter 1969] item 232.

J194A. ? JONES, Stephen. ORACLES, THE. The initials 'S.J.' are appended at the end of the text. Welsh 280; Rothschild 611.

(1) An undated edition, 1792 or before; the NUTP copy is sgd 'Robert Elliot Bewick's book, 1792'. Pr f EN. Price 6d. NUTP Cat. no. 56.

THE | ORACLES: | CONTAINING | SOME PARTICULARS OF THE | HISTORY | OF | BILLY AND KITTY WILSON; | INCLUDING | ANECDOTES | OF | THEIR PLAYFELLOWS, &c. | INTENDED FOR THE ENTERTAINMENT OF | THE LITTLE WORLD. | AND ILLUSTRATED BY ENGRAVINGS. | LONDON: | PR F E. NEWBERY, AT THE CORNER OF | SPC-Y. | [PRICE SIX-PENCE.]

In 8's. 63 leaves [? a final blank]. Pp. 118[126]. Wct FP (perhaps by Lee) and

13 wct roundels, some very probably by John Bewick. Adverts on last 8 pages. D.f.b.

[NUTP.

(2) Another undated edition. Pr f EN. Price 6*d*.

Title and *imprint* approx. as for no. (1).

In 8's. 66 leaves. Pp. 16 (error for 116), [124]. Wct FP (in a frame of single p.rules) and 13 wcts in text, probably as in no. (1). List of bks pr f EN on pp. [117–24]. D.f.b. 'And illustrated by Engravings' on TP is 5·6 cm long. 'Printed for... Corner of' on TP is 5·7 cm long. P.s.rule above imprint 4·6 cm long.

[Bell, 10·7×7·8 cm.

(3) Another undated edition. Pr f EN. Price 6*d*. Hugo, II, 5391, has ms date 15 Feb. 1803, and is presumably now the Ball copy.

The *imprint* reads: PR F E. NEWBERY, AT THE CORNER OF SPC-Y, BY E. RIDER, NO. 36, LITTLE-BRITAIN. [PRICE SIXPENCE.]

Pp. 124. D.f.b. 13 wct roundels, probably as for no. (1).

[Ball, has the ms date as in the Hugo copy.

(4) Another undated edition. Pr f EN. Price 6*d*.

Title and *imprint* approx. as for no. (1).

In 8's. 64 leaves. Pp. 124[128]. Wct FP (in a frame of single rules) and 13 wcts in text. List of bks pr f EN on last 4 pages. D.f.b. The p.s.rule preceding the imprint in TP is 2·1 cm long. (Communicated.)

[McKell, 11·0×7·8 cm; Ball.

(5) Another undated edition. Pr f EN. Price 6*d*.

Title and *imprint* approx. as for no. (1).

Pp. 118[126]. List of bks on pp. [119–26]. D.f.b. Wct FP (within a frame of printers' ornaments), wcts in text. 'And illustrated by Engravings' in TP is 6·3 cm long; 'Printed for... Corner of' in TP is 6·3 cm long. (Communicated.)

[UCLA, 11·5 cm; Roscoe (photocopied selected leaves).

(6) A copy in the Ball colln is stated to have a p.s.rule preceding the TP imprint 3·2 cm long.

J195. JONES, Stephen (attributed to). RUDIMENTS OF REASON, 1793. Pr f EN. 3 vols, price 4*s* 6*d*. The preface to vol. 1 is sgd 'S.J.'. Welsh 302–3; Gum 5004.

RUDIMENTS OF REASON; | OR, THE | YOUNG EXPERIMENTAL | PHILOSOPHER: | BEING A SERIES OF | FAMILY CONFERENCES; | IN WHICH THE CAUSES AND EFFECTS | OF THE VARIOUS | PHENOMENA | THAT NATURE DAILY EXHIBITS, ARE | RATIONALLY AND FAMILIARLY | EXPLAINED. | [p.s.rule] | IN THREE VOLUMES. | VOL. I. [II. III.] | [p.s.rule] | LONDON: | PR F E. NEWBERY, AT THE CORNER OF SP | CY. 1793. | [ENTERED AT STATIONERS HALL.]

In vols II and III 'In three Volumes' is omitted.

Vol. I. In 6's. 90 leaves. Pp. xvi+163.

Vol. II. In 6's. 94 leaves. Pp. 186.

Vol. III. In 6's. 113 leaves. Pp. 204[224]. The last 10 leaves of vol. III are un-numbered and have independent sigs, A–[B4]. They comprise a list of 'Definitions ...occurring in these Volumes', and may well have been issued separately.

[BM, 14·2×8·2 cm; CUL; Traylen (vol. I); UCLA; Sotheby, 5.2.68, lot 36 (vol. I); Osborne, Cat. p. 205.

J196. JOSSE, Augustin Louis. JUVENILE BIOGRAPHY, 1801. S b 'Newbury' et al. 2 vols, price ?3s.

JUVENILE BIOGRAPHY; | OR, | LIVES | OF | CELEBRATED CHILDREN. | INCULCATING VIRTUE BY EMINENT EXAMPLES | FROM REAL LIFE. | TO WHICH ARE ADDED | MORAL REFLECTIONS, | ADDRESSED TO THE YOUTH OF BOTH SEXES. | [d.p.rule] | BY MR. JOSSE, | PROFESSOR OF SPANISH AND FRENCH LANGUAGES. | [d.p.rule] | [5 lines] | [d.p.rule] | TRANSLATED BY MRS. CUMMYNG, | TRANSLATRESS OF ESTELLE. | [p.s.rule] | LONDON: | S B A. DULAU AND CO., SOHO SQUARE; | NEW- | BURY, SPCY; T. N. LONGMAN | AND O. REES, PN R; H. D. SYMONDS, | PN R; BOOSEY, OLD BROAD STREET, ROYAL | EXCHANGE; HOTMAN, OXFORD ROAD; GEISWEILER, | PARLIA-MENT STREET; TABARD, OLD BROAD STREET; | HOPKINS, BROOK STREET, HOLBORN; AND KAY, STRAND. | [d.p.rule] | PRICE [?] 3s. 1801.

Title and *imprint* for Part (i.e. vol.) II approx. as above, with PART II added above the imprint, and price and date omitted at foot.

Part I. In 6's. 120 leaves. Pp. x[xii]+228. Advert. of bks on A6^r,v.
Part II. In 6's. 109 leaves. Pp. 229–443.

[BM, 16·6×10·2 cm.

JOURNEY TO THE ISLAND OF WISDOM. See ENTERTAINING TRAVELLER, THE.

JULIANA; OR, THE AFFECTIONATE SISTERS. See Sandham, Eliz.

J197. JULIUS, OR THE DEAF AND DUMB ORPHAN, 1801. Pr f EN. Price 1s.

JULIUS, | OR THE | DEAF AND DUMB ORPHAN; | A TALE | FOR | YOUTH OF BOTH SEXES: | FOUNDED ON THE | POPULAR PLAY | OF | DEAF AND DUMB. | [d.p.rule] | LONDON: | PR F E. NEWBERY, CORNER | OF SPC-Y. | [p.rule] | 1801.

In 6's. 54 leaves+engvd FP. Pp. 106[108]. Half-title. List of bks 'just pubd' by EN on pp. [107–8]. Pink paper bds, with label. 'The popular Play' referred to was no doubt *Deaf and Dumb or the Orphan protected...taken from the French of M. Bouilly*, 1801 (*CBEL*, II, 469).

[CUL, 12·6×8·0 cm; Schiller.

J198. JUVENILE BIOGRAPHER, THE. Richard Johnson recorded in his Day-book the delivery of this to 'Mrs Newbery' on 16 Oct. 1780, the charge being £3. 3s. Advertised *LC* 19–21.12.80, p. 589, as one of Newbery's new publications for the Christmas holidays. Welsh 244; Weedon 41; S&W Cat.

(1) An undated edition. Pr f EN. Price 3*d* bd and gilt.

THE | JUVENILE BIOGRAPHER; | CONTAINING THE | LIVES | OF | LITTLE MASTERS AND MISSES; | INCLUDING A | VARIETY OF GOOD AND BAD | CHARACTERS. | [p.rule] | BY A LITTLE BIOGRAPHER. | [d.p.rule] | LONDON: | PR F E. NEWBERY, THE CORNER OF S | PCY. | [PRICE THREE PENCE BOUND AND GILT.]

Pp. 91[95]. Wct FP and wcts in text. List of 25 bks pr f EN on pp. [92–5]. The heading on p. [5] is THE | JUVENILE BIOGRAPHER. [4·1 cm long] | [d.p.rule, thin and thick] | INTRODUCTION. [2·2 cm long]. (Communicated.)

[Ball; MWA; Roscoe (photocopied selected leaves).

(2) Another undated edition. Pr f EN. Price 3*d* bd and gilt.

Title approx. as for no. (1). *Imprint:* LONDON: | PR F E. NEWBERY, THE CORNER | OF SPCY. | [PRICE THREE PENCE BOUND AND GILT.]

In 8's. 48 leaves, first and last pastedowns. Pp. 91[95]. Wct FP and 18 wcts in text. List of 27 bks pr f EN on pp. [92–5]. Green floral design on buff paper wrappers.

[Bell, 10·0×6·3 cm.

(3) Another undated edition. Pr f EN. Price 3*d* bd and gilt.

Title, *imprint* and *specification* approx. as for no. (1). On p. [5] the heading is: THE | JUVENILE BIOGRAPHER. [4·6 cm long] | [d.p.rule, thick and thin] | INTRODUCTION. [3·2 cm long]. (Communicated.)

[Ball, 10·0 cm.

(4) Listed ENC, p. 6. Price 3*d*.

JUVENILE BIOGRAPHY. No. J198 is sometimes listed under this title.

JUVENILE BIOGRAPHY. See Josse, A. L.

J199. Entry deleted.

JUVENILE OLIO, THE. See Mavor, W. F.

J199A. JUVENILE PRECEPTOR, THE, 1800. Vol. i. Pr f E. Newbury (*sic*) et al.

THE JUVENILE | PRECEPTOR, | OR A | COURSE | OF | MORAL AND SCIENTIFIC | INSTRUCTIONS. | FOR THE USE OF | BOTH SEXES. | [wavy rule] | VOL. i. | CONTAINING | SPELLING AND READING LESSONS, | NOT EXCEEDING ONE SYLLABLE. | [wavy rule] | PR A S B GEORGE NICHOLSON, POUGHNILL, NEAR | LUDLOW: | AND ALSO IN LONDON BY | CHAMPANTE AND WHITROW, JEWRY-STREET, ALDGATE; E. NEWBURY, CORNER OF | SPCY; R. BICKERSTAFF, 210 STRAND; | AND ALL OTHER BOOKSELLERS. | 1800.

In 6's. 124 leaves+engvd FP sgd 'W. M. Craig delt J. Chapman sculpt'. Pp. xiii[xiv]+234. Many small wct head- and tailpieces.

[Parkinson, 14·4×8·3 cm.

J200. JUVENILE RAMBLES THROUGH THE PATHS OF NATURE. Weedon 42, and p. 35 n. 6.

The dedication is sgd 'R.J.'. Richard Johnson recorded in his Day-book: *1786 May 29. M⁰ Badcock——To writing Juvenile Rambles, 5 Half Sheets. 32°.—— £5. 5s.* An edition of 1830 (copy in V&A(GL)) states in the TP that the bk was by the author of the *Toy Shop*.

(1) An edition of 1786. Pr f EN. Price 6*d*. Welsh 240; *CBEL*, II, 563.

JUVENILE RAMBLES | THROUGH THE | PATHS OF NATURE; | IN WHICH MANY PARTS OF THE | WONDERFUL WORKS OF THE CREATION | ARE BROUGHT FORWARD, | AND MADE | FAMILIAR TO THE CAPACITY OF EVERY | LITTLE MISS AND MASTER, | WHO WISHES TO BECOME | WISE AND GOOD. | [p.rule] | EMBELLISHED WITH CUTS. | [d.p.rule] | LONDON: | PR F E. NEWBERY, THE CORNER OF | SPC-Y. | [PRICE SIX-PENCE.] | MDCCLXXXVI.

16mo in 8's. 64 leaves. Pp. 128. Wct FP and 12 wcts in text. D.f.b.

[Bodley, 10·5×7·1 cm; Osborne*.

(2) An undated edition. Pr f EN. Price 6*d*.

TP and specification approx. as for no. (1), the date omitted. In this ed. on the TP 'Embellished with Cuts' is 5·1 cm long and 'Price six-pence' is within square brackets []; on p. [6] 'Paths of Nature' is 5·9 cm long and is followed by a p.s.rule 3·5 cm long; the last line of text on p. 128 reads 'So God bless you both, and good bye'. D.f.b.

[BM, 10·6×7·4 cm; Roscoe (photocopied selected leaves).

(3) Another undated edition. Pr f EN. Price 6*d*.

TP and specification approx. as for no. (1), the date omitted. In this ed. on the TP 'Embellished with Cuts' is 3·4 cm long and 'Price six-pence' is within round brackets (); on p. [6] 'Paths of Nature' is 4·8 cm long and is followed by a p.rule 3·4 cm long; the last line of text on p. 128 is 'and good bye'. D.f.b.

[Welch, 11·5 cm; Roscoe (photocopied selected leaves).

(4) Another undated edition. Pr f EN. Price 6*d*.

TP and specification approx. as for no. (1), the date omitted. In this ed. on the TP 'Embellished with Cuts' is 4·2 cm long and 'Price Six-pence' is within round brackets (); on p. [6] 'Paths of Nature' is 4·3 cm long and is followed by a d.s.rule 2·7 cm long; the last line of text on p. 128 is 'and good bye'. Blue bds.

[Bodley (lacks FP), 11·0×7·3 cm; Roscoe (photocopied selected leaves).

(5) Unidentified copies in NBL 127; Gum 3477; BCE; Ball; Sotheby, 16.3.70, lot 234.

JUVENILE REDUPLICATIONS. See Bisset, Jas.

J201. JUVENILE SPEAKER, THE. Listed in Trimmer's *Silver Thimble*, 1799, as pr f EN. Price 2*s*. Also in ENC p. 9. There is another work of the same name, 1787, not by EN.

JUVENILE SPORTS AND PASTIMES. See 'Angelo, Master Michel'.

J201A. JUVENILE STORIES. ENC p. 9, price 1*s* 6*d*. Probably = J202(1).

J202. JUVENILE STORIES AND DIALOGUES.
(1) A probable edition prior to no. (2) is J201A. But not mentioned in the very full bk-list in Trimmer's *Silver Thimble*, 1799.
(2) An edition of 1801. Pr f EN et al.

JUVENILE | STORIES AND DIALOGUES, | COMPOSED CHIEFLY IN | WORDS OF TWO SYLLABLES, | FOR THE | USE OF SCHOOLS, | AND | YOUNG READERS. | [d.p.rule] | [wct ornament] | [d.p.rule] | LONDON: | PR F VERNOR AND HOOD, | NO. 31, POULTRY; | AND E. NEWBERY, SPCY; | BY J. BONSOR, SALISBURY SQUARE. | [p.rule] | 1801.

In 6's. 90 leaves+engvd FP sgd 'P. Thompson sculp'. Pp. 176. Marbled bds, green vell. spine with label.

⌈Oup, 13·6×8·5 cm; LEI; LWaPL.

JUVENILE TRIALS FOR ROBBING ORCHARDS. See 'Littleton, Master Tommy'.

KEEPER'S TRAVELS. See Kendall, E. A.

J203. KENDALL, Edward Augustus. ADVENTURES OF MUSUL, 1800. Pr f EN et al. Price 1*s* 6*d*.

ADVENTURES | OF | MUSUL: | OR | THE THREE GIFTS: | WITH | OTHER TALES. | [d.p.rule] | LONDON: | [d.p.rule] | PR B J. BONSOR, SALISBURY SQUARE; | FOR VERNOR AND HOOD, POULTRY; | AND E. NEWBERY, SPCY. | [d.p.rule] | 1800.

In 6's. 90 leaves+engvd FP. Pp. 175[176]. Bk-list on last page. Green or marbled bds, green vell. spine. (Communicated.)

⌈Renier; Quayle; Osborne, Cat. p. 229, 13·5×8·8 cm; Sotheby, 13.3.72, lot 122.

J204. KENDALL, Edward Augustus. CANARY BIRD, THE, 1799. Pr f EN. Price 1*s* 6*d*. *CBEL*, II, 559; NBL 554; Gum 3491.

THE | CANARY BIRD: | A MORAL FICTION. | INTERSPERSED WITH | POETRY. | [d.p.rule] | BY THE AUTHOR OF THE SPARROW, KEEPER'S TRAVELS, | THE CRESTED WREN, &c | [d.p.rule] | [1 line quote] | [d.p.rule] | LONDON: | PR F E. NEWBERY, | CORNER OF SPC-Y; | BY J. CUNDEE, IVY LANE. | [d.s.rule] | 1799.

THE

CRESTED WREN.

BY **k**

EDWARD AUGUSTUS KENDALL.

O ! guard from harm his golden head,
And listen to his lore!

BEATTIE.

LONDON:
PRINTED FOR E. NEWBERY,
AT THE CORNER OF ST. PAUL'S CHURCH-YARD.

1799.

Fig. 17. Title-page of J205.

In 6's. 81 leaves+engvd FP sgd 'I. Scott sculp'. Pp. xi+148[150]. Half-title.
A number of small wct tailpieces, many found in other bks with cuts by the
Bewick workshop or school. Marbled bds, red roan spine.

[BM, 17·3×8·4 cm; SomCL; BmPL; ReU; LKePL; Osborne, Cat. p. 271;
UCLA; OOxM; Maxwell Hunley, Cat. 48 [winter 1969] item 177.

J205. KENDALL, Edward Augustus. CRESTED WREN, THE, 1799.
Pr f EN. Price 1s 6d. Welsh 246; Hugo no. 129; Gum 3492; *CBEL*, II, 559.
See Fig. 17.
In 6's. 81 leaves+engvd FP sgd 'Taylor sculp'. Pp. vi+156. Half-title. The wct
of the Wren on the title most probably by T. Bewick. A few small wct tailpieces.
List of bks 'which may be had of' EN on last 4 pages. Marbled bds, green vell.
spine.

158

[BM, 13·3×8·2 cm; V&A(GL); Opie; SomCL; Traylen; Osborne, Cat. p. 271; UCLA; INC; CtNSCSC; Bondy, Cat. 77 [1969] item 158 (*ex* Sotheby, 24.2.69, lot 12).

J206. KENDALL, Edward Augustus. KEEPER'S TRAVELS. Welsh 246; *CBEL*, II, 559.

(1) First edition, 1798. Pr f EN. Price 1s 6d.

KEEPER'S TRAVELS | IN SEARCH OF | HIS MASTER. | [d.p.rule] | [3 lines quote] | [d.p.rule] | LONDON: | PR F E. NEWBERY, AT THE CORNER | OF SPC-Y. | [p.rule] | 1798.

In 6's. 99 leaves+engvd FP by Dadley after John Thurston. Pp. viii+190. Marbled bds, green vell. spine, label.

[BM, 13·0×8·3 cm (lacks FP); CUL; Bell; Renier; BmPL; Osborne, Cat. pp. 271–2; McKell; MiDW; Melbourne; Sotheby, 5.2.1945 (the Bussell sale), lot 146; Fletcher, Cat. 116 [1961] item 652.

(2) Second edition, 1799. Pr f EN. Price 1s 6d.

Title and *imprint* (with SECOND EDITION and date 1799) and specification approx. as for no. (1).

[BM, 12·6×7·8 cm; DES; BmPL; Renier; Shiers; NNC-T (Darton Coll.).

J207. KENDALL, Edward Augustus. LESSONS OF VIRTUE, 1801. Pr f EN. Price 2s. Welsh 246; *CBEL*, II, 559.

LESSONS OF VIRTUE; | OR, THE | BOOK OF HAPPINESS. | INTENDED FOR YOUTH. | [d.s.rule] | BY THE AUTHOR OF KEEPER'S TRAVELS, THE | CRESTED-WREN, THE SPARROW, &c | [d.s.rule] | [3 lines quote] | [d.p.rule] | LONDON: | PR B J. CROWDER, WARWICK-SQUARE, | FOR E. NEWBERY, THE CORNER OF SPC-Y | [d.p.rule] | 1801.

In 6's. 90 leaves+engvd FP. Pp. 174 (error for 176) [178]. List of Kendall's bks s b EN on last 2 pages. Marbled bds, red roan spine, gilt.

[BM, 13·6×8·3 cm; LUL; Shiers.

J208. KENDALL, Edward Augustus. SPARROW, THE. Listed in ENC p. 10, as *Memoirs of a Sparrow*.

(1) An edition of 1798. Pr f EN. Price 2s; also listed at 1s 6d.

THE | SPARROW. | [d.p.rule] | [3 lines quote] | [d.p.rule] | [wct vignette] | LONDON: | PR F | E. NEWBERY, AT THE CORNER OF | SPC-Y. | [orn. rule]. | 1798.

In 6's. 108 leaves. ? a FP. Pp. xv+200. Marbled bds, green vell. spine. The wct on the TP is of the Bewick school.

[BM, 13·6×8·7 cm; BmPL; UCLA.

(2) An edition of 1800. EN. Welch 665.

J209. KENDALL, Edward Augustus. STORIES OF SENEX, THE, 1800. Pr f EN. Price 1s 6d. Welsh 246; *CBEL*, II, 559.

THE | STORIES OF SENEX; | OR, | LITTLE HISTORIES | OF | LITTLE
PEOPLE. | [p.rule] | BY E. A. KENDALL, | AUTHOR OF KEEPER'S TRAVELS,
THE SPARROW, THE | WREN, THE SWALLOW, THE CANARY BIRD, &c. &c. |
[p.rule] | LONDON: | PR F E. NEWBERY, THE CORNER OF S | PC-Y. | BY G.
WOODFALL, PN-R, LONDON. | [p.s.rule] | 1800.
 In 6's. 90 leaves+engvd FP. Pp. 176. Marbled bds, green vell. spine.
 [BM, 13·2×8·1 cm; Opie; Osborne, Cat. p. 272.

J210. KENDALL, Edward Augustus. SWALLOW, THE, 1800. Pr f EN.
Price 1s 6d. Welsh 247; *CBEL*, II, 559; Gum 3499.
 THE | SWALLOW: | A FICTION. | INTERSPERSED WITH | POETRY. | [d.p.
rule] | BY E. A. KENDAL (*sic*). | [d.p.rule] | [5 lines quote] | [d.p.rule] | LONDON:
| PR F E. NEWBERY, | AT THE CORNER OF SPC-Y; | BY T. BAYLIS, GREVILLE-
STREET, HATTON-GARDEN. | [p.rule] | 1800.
 In 6's. 90 leaves+engvd FP. Pp. xviii[xix]+157[159]. A number of small wct
ornam. tailpieces. Marbled bds, green vell. spine; also marbled bds, roan gilt.
 [BM, 13·5×8·8 cm; Bodley; LUL; Oup; Opie; Osborne, Cat. p. 272; Grant.

KEY TO POLITE LITERATURE. See GENTLEMAN AND
LADY'S KEY...

J211. KIMBER, Edward. LIFE AND ADVENTURES OF JOE
THOMPSON. ABRIDGED... Richard Johnson recorded in his Day-book:
1787 Aug. Mr Badcock——To writing the Life of Joe Thompson——£10. 10s.
Weedon 50. See F. G. Black, *Edward Kimber*, 1935, p. 28; Welsh 242 and 317.
(1) An edition of 1788. Pr f EN. Price 1s. Not in Black.
 THE | LIFE | AND | ADVENTURES | OF | JOE THOMPSON. | ABRIDGED
FROM THE | ORIGINAL WORK, | WRITTEN BY HIMSELF. | [p.rule] |
EMBELLISHED WITH COPPER-PLATES. | [d.p.rule] | LONDON: | PR F E.
NEWBERY, AT THE CORNER OF | SPCY. | [p.rule] | MDCCLXXXVIII.
 In 6's. 90 leaves+6 insets. Pp. 178[180]. Engvd FP and 5 other engvd leaves.
List of bks 'just pubd by EN' on last 2 pages. Dutch paper bds, with diamond
stencils in variegated colours, pr over a green leaf design. (Communicated.)
 [Preston, Cat. p. 129; Osborne*, 11·4×7·0 cm; Ball.
(2) Black mentions an ed. adv. in 1789, by Newbery. Welsh quotes a listing of
that year. Probably reference is to no. (1).
(3) Listed in Fielding's *Joseph Andrews*, 1799, as pr f EN. Price 1s.

LADDER TO LEARNING. See J359–361, ? Trimmer, S.

LECTURE UPON GAMES AND TOYS. See 'Comical, Christopher'.

LECTURE UPON TOYS. Comical's *Lectures upon Games*...is sometimes
so listed.

LECTURES GRADUÉES POUR LES ENFANS. See Gaultier, A. E. C.

LEE BOO. See HISTORY OF PRINCE LEE BOO.

J212. LENGLET DU FRESNOY, Nicolas. GEOGRAPHY FOR CHILDREN. Welsh 224; *CBEL*, II, 788.

(1) Fourteenth edition. Adv. *LC* 10–12.3.85, p. 244, as pr f J. Johnson and E. Newbery; but pubd under the imprint of Johnson alone. (Copy in LOU.)

(2) Fifteenth edition, 1787. Pr f EN et al. Price 1s 6d.

GEOGRAPHY | FOR | CHILDREN: | OR, | A SHORT AND EASY METHOD OF TEACHING AND LEARNING | GEOGRAPHY. | DESIGNED PRINCIPALLY FOR THE USE OF SCHOOLS. | [7 lines] | DIVIDED INTO LESSONS, BY WAY OF | QUESTION AND ANSWER: | [2 lines] | TRANSLATED FROM THE FRENCH OF ABBOT LENGLET DU FRESNOY, | AND NOW GREATLY AUGMENTED AND IMPROVED THROUGHOUT THE WHOLE. | THE FIFTEENTH EDITION. | [3 lines] | AND | A TABLE OF THE LATITUDE... | [1 line] | [p.s.rule] | LONDON: | PR F J. JOHNSON, NO. 72, SPC-Y, AND | E. NEWBERY, AT THE CORNER OF LUDGATE-STREET. —— 1787. | [PRICE, BOUND, 1s 6d.]

12mo. 84 leaves+2 insets. Pp. x[xii]+151[156]. Folding engvd FP showing 'The three different positions of the Sphere'; folding leaf of engvd circular maps of the world. List of bks pr f J. Johnson on last 5 pages. Brown canvas 'school' binding.

⌈BM, 16·1×10·1 cm; BCE (imperf.); Platt.

(2A) Another fifteenth edition, n.d. Pr f EN et al. Price bd in sheep 1s 6d, in calf 2s.

GEOGRAPHY | [as for no. (2) down to 'greatly augmented', then read:] AND IMPROVED THROUGHOUT THE | WHOLE, AND CORRECTED TO THE TREATY OF PEACE IN 1783. | THE FIFTEENTH EDITION. | [4 lines] | AND TO THIS EDITION IS NOW ADDED, | A TABLE... | [2 lines] | [p.s.rule] | LONDON: | PR F J. JOHNSON, NO. 72, SPC- | Y, AND E. NEWBERY, THE CORNER OF LUDGATE- | STREET. | [PRICE BOUND IN SHEEP 1s 6d IN CALF 2s.]

Folding engvd FP as in no. (2).

⌈Grant.

(3) Sixteenth edition, 1791. Pr f EN et al. Price 1s 6d.

Title and *imprint* approx. as for no. (2), with THE SIXTEENTH EDITION and date 1791.

12mo. 84 leaves+3 insets. Pp. xii+154[156]. 3 engvd folding leaves, 2 sgd 'T. Conder sculpt'. List of bks pr f J. Johnson on H6ʳ·ᵛ.

⌈BM, 17·2×9·0 cm.

(4) Seventeenth edition, 1793. Pr f EN et al. Price 1s 6d bd.

Title approx. as for no. (2), with THE SEVENTEENTH EDITION. *Imprint:* LONDON: | PR F J. JOHNSON, NO. 72, SPC-Y, AND | E. NEWBERY, AT THE CORNER OF LUDGATE-STREET. 1793. | [PRICE, BOUND, 1s 6d.]

In 12's. 84 leaves+4 insets. Pp. xii+155[156]. Engvd folding map, and engvd folding leaf showing 'the three different Positions of the Sphere', sgd 'T. Conder sculp', 2 other engvd leaves sgd by Conder. Brown canvas 'school' binding.

⌈LEI, 16·4×9·9 cm.

(4A) Eighteenth edition, 1794. Pr f 'L. Newbury' (*sic*) et al. (presumably a misprint for EN who pubd other edd.). Price 1*s* 6*d* bd.

Title approx. as for no. (2), with THE EIGHTEENTH EDITION. *Imprint:* PR F T. JOHNSTON, AND L. NEWBURY, 1794. | [PRICE, BOUND, 1*s* 6*d*.]

Collates [A]–[G12]. 84 leaves+3 insets. Pp. xii+154. Last leaf a blank. Plates I and II, geographical terms and figures exemplified; plate III, 3 different parts of a sphere. (Communicated.)

⌈NoU.

(4B) Another eighteenth edition, 1795. Pr f EN et al. Price bound 1*s* 6*d*.

Title and *imprint* approx. as for no. (2), with THE EIGHTEENTH EDITION and date 1795.

In 12's. 78 leaves. Pp. xii+143[144]. Folding engvd maps and other engvgs. Bk-list on pp. 143–4. Sheep, also canvas 'school' binding.

⌈UCLA; Sotheby, 16.3.70, lot 257, 16·9×10·4 cm; M. Reissman, Victoria Book Shop, N.Y., Cat. 9, item 382.

(5) Nineteenth edition, 1797. Pr f EN et al. Price 1*s* 6*d*.

Title and *imprint* approx. as for no. (2), with THE NINETEENTH EDITION and date 1797.

12mo. 72 leaves+4 insets. Pp. 143. Two folding leaves of engvd diagrams and map, one sgd 'T. Conder sculpt'; two leaves of engvd maps explaining geographical terms, sgd by Conder.

⌈Marchmont Bookshop, Cat. 18 [1963] item 77, 17·0×10·2 cm; Preston, Cat. pp. 84–5; UCLA.

(5A) Twentieth edition, 1797. Pr f T. Newbury (*sic*) et al. Price 1*s* 6*d*.

The 20th ed. of 1799 (no. 6) was, like earlier edd., pubd by J. Johnson and E. Newbery. The present ed., 1797, looks suspiciously like an attempt by rivals to forestall J.J. and EN's 20th ed. The book was obviously a successful work. The folding map and chart and other engvgs have been redrawn; the title-page omits two lines of text following 'The Twentieth Edition'. The *imprint* reads: LONDON: | PRINTED FOR S. JOHNSTON, AND T. NEWBURY, | 1797. | [p.rule] | [PRICE, BOUND, 1*s* 6*d*] but in other respects is similar to 1799. Absence of addresses is to be noted. There is no bk-list at the end.

In 12's [A]–[G12], the last a blank. 84 leaves. Pp. xii+154.

A T. Newbury appears in the imprint to the 10th ed. of *The Rambler*, 1784 (no. A273(6)). S. Johnston I have not met elsewhere.

⌈J. Foreman, Highgate Rd, London, 16·5×10·2 cm.

(6) Another twentieth edition, 1799. Pr f EN et al. Price 1*s* 6*d*. Welsh 224.

Title and *imprint* approx. as for no. (2) with THE TWENTIETH EDITION and date 1799.

12mo. 76 leaves+4 insets, as in no. (5). Pp. 144[152]. Bk-list on pp. 144ff. Sets of maps (see no. J236) were issued to go with this work, to be had of J. Johnson and EN, price 4s done up in bds; see footnote at p. v of this ed., and advert. on G4ᵛ. Brown canvas 'school' binding; also sheep.

[Roscoe, 16·7×10·0 cm; NoU; Quayle; Sotheby, 13.3.72, lot 87.

J213. LE SAGE, Alain René. GIL BLAS...ABRIDGED.
(1) Adv. as pr f FN(N) in *GM* May 1774. Price 1s.
(1A) An edition listed as pr f FN(N) in Chesterfield's *Maxims*, 1777, price 1s.
(2) An edition of 1782. Pr f EN. Price 1s.

THE | ADVENTURES | OF | GIL BLAS | OF | SANTILLANE, | ABRIDGED. | ADORNED WITH COPPER PLATES. | [wct device] | LONDON: | PR F E. NEWBERY, AT THE CORNER OF | SPC-Y, 1782. | [PRICE ONE SHILLING.]

In 6's. 108 leaves+6 insets. Pp. 216. Engvd FP and 5 engvd leaves in text.
[BM, 11·6×7·5 cm; Ball.
(3) An edition of 1788. Pr f EN. Price 1s. ? Welsh 251; NBL 659.
Title and *imprint* approx. as for no. (2), with date 1788.
In 6's. 108 leaves+5 or 6 insets. Pp. 216. Engvd FP and 4 or 5 other engvd leaves. D.f.b. Details taken from the CLU copy.
[CLU, 11·2×7·8 cm; Ball.
(4) An edition of 1798. Pr f EN. Price 1s.
Title and *imprint* approx. as for no. (2), with date 1798.
In 6's. 78 leaves+engvd FP. Pp. 156. Blue bds, label on upper.
[BM, 13·5×8·5 cm. Welch.

LESSONS OF VIRTUE. See Kendall, E. A.

J214. LETTERS BETWEEN MASTER TOMMY AND MISS NANCY GOODWILL. Weedon 47. Richard Johnson recorded in his Daybook that before 1770 he had received £5. 5s for these Letters, and under date 1775 Aug. he entered £1. 11s 6d for correcting them. Whether the 1776 ed. was corrected I do not know, but the 1786 ed. certainly was heavily revised. Miss Weedon has recorded that the work was 'partly borrowed' from Sarah Fielding's *Governess*.
(1) An edition of 1770. Pr f C & N. Price 6d bd and gilt. Welsh 253.

LETTERS | BETWEEN | MASTER TOMMY | AND | MISS NANCY GOODWILL; | CONTAINING THE | HISTORY | OF THEIR | HOLIDAY AMUSEMENTS. | [p.rule] | EMBELLISHED WITH CUTS. | [p.rule] | [2 lines quote] | [d.p.rule] | PR F T. CARNAN AND F. NEWBERY, JUNIOR, AT | NO. 65, IN SPC-Y. 1770. | [PRICE SIX-PENCE.]

In 6's. 60 leaves. Pp. iv+116. 19 wcts in the text, mostly in the manner of the cuts in *Goody Two-Shoes*. D.f.b.
[BM, 11·6×7·6 cm; NorBM; Gardner; MH (lacks many leaves).
(1A) Another issue or edition of no. (1), 1770. The TP imprint reads PR F CARNAN AND NEWBERY, AT NO. 65, | IN SPC-Y. 1770. | [PRICE SIX-PENCE.] D.f.b.

[BCE, 11·1×8·0 cm.

(2) Third edition, 1776. Pr f C & N. Price 6d.

Title and *imprint* approx. as for no. (1), omitting the quote and adding THE THIRD EDITION, CORRECTED, and date 1776.

12mo. 48 leaves. Pp. iv+92. 15 wcts. D.f.b. (Communicated.)

[McKell, 11·2×7·5 cm; Maggs Cat. 446, item 404.

(3) An edition of 1779. TC. D.f.b. S&W Cat.

[Ball.

(4) An edition of 1786. Pr f TC. Price 6d.

Title as for no. (1), the quote omitted. *Imprint:* PR F T. CARNAN IN SPCY. | MDCCLXXXVI. | [PRICE SIX-PENCE]

12mo in 6's. 48 leaves. Pp. 92. 14 wcts in the text, used previously in no. (1). D.f.b.; also green bds with embossed floral pattern. This ed. is substantially revised and shortened: 14 wcts, as against 19 in no. (1) – the five omitted (at pp. 18, 29, 49, 70 and 96 in the 1770 ed.) all have some element which parents of that age would not have considered 'altogether properly adapted to the Improvement and Entertainment of little Masters and Misses' (see the 'Advertisement'); the text has been largely revised and shortened, there are 14, as against 18, letters, and no contents list.

[BM, 11·4×7·8 cm; Roscoe; Welch.

LETTERS ON SEVERAL SUBJECTS. See Palmer, Charlotte.

J215. LETTERS ON THE HISTORY OF ENGLAND. In various bk-lists 1769–70. Price 6s. Probably = Goldsmith's *History of England in a Series of Letters...*

LETTERS ON THE MOST COMMON...OCCASIONS IN LIFE. See Newbery, John.

LIFE AND ADVENTURES OF A FLY. See J., S.

LIFE AND ADVENTURES OF JOE THOMPSON. See Kimber, Edward.

LIFE AND ADVENTURES OF PETER WILKINS, ABRIDGED. See Paltock, R.

LIFE OF OUR LORD AND SAVIOUR. See J174.

LIFE OF ROLLA. See Brewer, Geo.

LILLIPUTIAN AUCTION, THE. See 'Chatter, Charley'.

J216. LILLIPUTIAN BIOGRAPHER, THE. Listed in *Anecdotes of Mary*, 1795, as pr f EN. Price 6*d*. See Weedon 57, VIII. One of the 10 vols forming the *Lilliputian Library* 'compiled' by Richard Johnson (no. J218), and first pubd by W. Domville et al.

J217. LILLIPUTIAN LETTER-WRITER, THE, n.d. Pr f EN. Price 6*d*. One of the 10 vols forming the *Lilliputian Library* (Weedon 57, and no. J218), 'compiled' by Richard Johnson and first pubd by Domville et al. It is described at the end as 'the fifth volume' (i.e. of the *Lilliputian Library*). Adv. *Anecdotes of Mary*, 1795.

EN's ed. of this bk is no more than the sheets of the Domville ed. with a new title-leaf, leaf A3 and the wct FP omitted.

See Plate 7. In 12's. 59 leaves. Cancel title-leaf. Pp. viii+[9]–120. Details taken from the Bell copy.

[Bell.

J218. LILLIPUTIAN LIBRARY, THE. Weedon 57.

The 10 vols forming this 'Library' were 'compiled' by Richard Johnson for Henry Baldwin and pr f W. Domville and others. Johnson's Day-book records: *1779. Compiling The Lilliputian Library, 10 Vol^s for Mr H. Baldwin Began in Novr last.——£21 May 12. Received of Mr Henry Baldwin 20^s deduct from thence 20^s laid out for Books——£19.* In 1795 they were listed in *Anecdotes of Mary* (but separately and not as forming a 'library'), as pr f EN.

Miss Weedon's article was based on a 10-vol. ed. pubd in Berlin in 1782, she at the time of writing having no information, apart from newspaper adverts., as to the Domville ed. adv. in *LC* 9–11.12.79, 10 vols, price 5*s*. (of which vols I–III, V, VI, VIII and X are in CUL, vols VI and VIII in BCE, vols II and IV in NorBM and 2 vols in Oup; a complete set was on the market in 1962). Of the Newbery ed. Miss Weedon was able to record as having survived into the present century only a copy of the *White Cat* and possibly a copy of *Instructive Fragments*. She could also record an 1803 copy of the *White Cat* by Harris.

Copies of 5 of the Newbery edd. have now come to light: the *Curious Collection of Voyages*, the *Poetical Flower-Basket*, the *White Cat*, the *Entertaining Medley* and the *Lilliputian Letter-Writer*. None is dated. The Newbery copies of the *Voyages* and the *Letter-Writer* consist of the sheets of the Domville edd. with one or two leaves of prelims omitted and cancel title-leaves inserted. One may assume this would be the case with the others. It seems fairly clear that EN bought up the whole stock of Domville's 10 vols and issued them with her own title-leaf.

The small number of survivors of the series, of both Domville and Newbery edd., is to be noted. It may well be that the total number printed was only small; and it would seem not to have been a very successful venture. None is mentioned in ENC.

The vols forming the *Library* are specified below. I give the titles appearing in *Anecdotes of Mary* preceded by the vol. numbers quoted by Miss Weedon and followed by the numbers in this bibliography.

master *Hiron*, a folid and lasting peace was concluded ; which left king *Miram* at full liberty to reform some vices in the state ; and to encourage virtue, learning and commerce.

Now liberty sprung up and displayed itself, like the tree of life in paradise ; the dews of heaven came upon it, and the earth offered all her nourishment ; its trunk was reared in strength and beauty, its branches spread over the land, its root was deep in virtue, on its leaves were the sciences written, the people were happy who dwelled under its shade, and the fruit of glory dropped upon them. King *Miram* took no step without the advice of master *Hiron*; and as he studied the interest and peace both of the prince and the people, the whole community was exceedingly happy.

How master Hiron *improved the arts and sciences in* Lilliput, *and taught even little children to become polite gentlemen and ladies, will be shewn in the future part of this work ; which all our society are defired to learn, for by learning of that account perfectly, they will also learn the arts and sciences.*

A

35

A
L E T T E R
FROM
Master *L O W T H E R,*
TO THE
SPEAKER of the SOCIETY,

In Behalf of honest *Robin,* Mr. *Littlewit's* Dunghill Cock, dated from BARNET, *Feb.* 16, 1750.

Mr. SPEAKER,

I Have often addressed your honour in favour of my own species, and have hitherto

Fig. 18(*a*). A page opening from J219(2).

J219. LILLIPUTIAN MAGAZINE, THE. Welsh 255–6; *CBEL,* II, 564, 645; J. E. Grey, *The Lilliputian Magazine*; O. M. Brack, Jr. 'William Strahan', in *Book Collector* (spring 1971), p. 105.

Authorship not determined. Has been attributed to JN, to Goldsmith (BM, Gen. Cat.), and to Chris. Smart in an article in *The European Magazine* for April 1819, p. 306, by John Jones, the Editor, who says: 'The ingenious Christopher

[44]

THE
HAPPY NIGHTINGALE,
A SONG.

By POLLY NEWBERY.

I.

THE Nightingale, in dead of night,
  On fome green hawthorn, hid from
fight,
      Her wond'rous art difplays;
While all the feather'd choir's at reft,
Nor fowler's fnares her joys moleft.
      She fings melodious lays.
             The

[45]

II.

The groves her warbling notes repeat,
The filence makes her mufic fweet,
      And heightens every note.
Benighted travellers admire
To hear her thus exert her fire,
      And fwell her little throat.

III.

No fear of phantoms, frightful noife,
Nor hideous form her blifs deftroys;
      Darknefs no terror brings;
But each returning fhade of night
Affords the fongfter new delight;
      Unaw'd fhe fits and fings.

IV.

So children who are good and wife,
Hobgoblin ftories will defpife,
      And all fuch idle tales;
Virtue can fortitude inftil,
And ward off-all impending ill,
      Which over vice prevails.
             A Re-

Fig. 18(*b*). A page opening from J219(2).

Smart was the first man of genius that thought the minds and morals of children deserved literary attention. In his Lilliputian Magazine, he inculcated the best of principles...'

Mrs Grey's article establishes beyond reasonable doubt that this work was originally designed by JN to be pubd as a periodical, at 3*d* a time. That it was of JN's designing, not of Carnan's (the ostensible publisher) there can be no doubt; he launched it and paid for it. Carnan at this time was somewhere between 14 and 19 years old, working in JN's business and under his control.

GEP for 9–12 Feb. 1751 adv. the work as about to be pubd and on 2–5 March announced the issue of 'Number I' price 3*d*. I have not traced an advertisement of 'Number II', but doubtless there was one. 'Number III' was adv. in *GA* for 17 Aug. 1752. These advertisements certainly indicated a periodical publication, but it was for Mrs Grey to bring to light the conclusive evidence of the ledgers of William Strahan, the printer. These, under date 'Janny' [1751], record the printing for JN of 4000 copies of 'Lilliputian Magazine No 1' with 'Cover for D°' together with 8000 'Proposals for D°', and 4000 of 'No 2' with its 'Cover', at a total

[64]

for he believed them not, and when they
told him the words of *Joseph*, and he saw
the waggons that were sent to carry him
down, the spirit of *Jacob* revived, and he
said, it is enough, *Joseph* my son is yet a-
live; I will go and see him before I die.
So *Jacob* made ready to go down into
Egypt, and *Joseph* prepared his chariot to
meet him, and presented himself to his father; and he fell on his neck, and wept
greatly; and *Israel* said unto *Joseph*, now
let me die; since I have seen thy face, and
thou art yet alive, O my son.

A Nar-

[65]

A

Narrative of a VOYAGE to the Island
of ANGELICA:

By Master JEMMY GADABOUT.

MASTER *Jemmy Gadabout*, the
only son of an eminent merchant
in the city, was an extraordinary fine boy,

.G 3   and

Fig. 18(c). A page opening from J219(2).

cost of £15 5s. Number 3 was not entered by Strahan until Aug. 1752 (cf. the date
of advertisement), 3500 copies at a cost of £5 (no 'Covers' mentioned). There
were no further advertisements of parts, or references in the ledger to the *Magazine*. What happened, then? No copies of any of the three parts have as yet turned
up, and it remains a matter for conjecture.

Mrs Grey questions whether 'No. III' was in fact ever published as a separate
number, but inclines to the view that it was. She concludes: 'The long interval
between the first two issues and the third, and especially the lack of printed covers
and the reduction by 500 copies in the printing order for "No. 3", certainly seems
to indicate that Newbery could not have been receiving the response that he had
anticipated when embarking on his magazine for children. It would appear that,
in spite of his various advertising methods, Newbery did not obtain sufficient
subscribers for his attempt at publishing a children's periodical to be a financial
success. He therefore must have abandoned his original plan to publish further
separate issues...in favour of combining copies of the three issues already printed
...into a single volume...' The British Museum copy [no. (2) below] is probably
of this reprinted edition.

The PEACOCK.

THE Peacock, of his gaudy train
And tread majestic idly vain,
Each simple gazer views with joy,
And dotes upon the feather'd toy;
But when he screams with hideous cry,
The ear is plagu'd to please the eye.

MORAL.

By this allusion justly stung,
Each tinsel'd fop should hold his tongue.
AN

AN

HISTORY

OF THE

RISE and PROGRESS

OF

LEARNING

IN

LILLIPUT.

MASTER HIRON, the young gentleman of whom we gave you some account in page 29, observing, that the language of the *Lilliputians* was irregular, and difficult to be understood, established the following alphabet of letters, and regulated their sounds, when blended and intermixed with each other, in this manner,
'The

Fig. 18(*d*). A page opening from J219(2).

(1) The part issues, I, II and III. 1751–2. No copies traced.

(2) An edition of 1752 or later. Pubd by TC. (See Figs. 18(*a–d*).) This may well be the ed. adv. in *PA* for 20.12.52 and later, price 1*s* neatly bd and gilt. The 'Last Ænigma answered' at p. 129 is dated 19.7.51, the 'Will and Testament' at pp. 131–4 is dated 3.7.52.

Engraved title: See Plate 8.

In 6's. 73 leaves+13 insets. Pp. ii+[3]–144. Engvd FP and 12 engvd leaves in the text. Four wcts, those of birds being very similar to those in *Tommy Trip*. The wct at p. 65 is sgd 'J. (or I.) Bell'.

[BM, 10·8×6·8 cm; Opie, exhibited Festival of Britain Book Exhibition, 1951 (Cat. no. 46).

(3) The S&W Cat. has a copy which may be identical with no. (2), except that it is described as having '10 curious copper-plates and many wood cuts'.

(4) An edition of 1765. JN.

Pp. ii+[3]–142. Engvd FP and 11 other engvd leaves. (Communicated.)
[UCLA.

(5) An edition of 1768. N & C.
⌈Ball.

(6) An edition of 1772 (the 7th). Pr f C & N. Price 1s. Adv. as the 7th ed. in *LC* 13–16.6.72, p. 575.

THE | LILLIPUTIAN MAGAZINE: | OR, THE | YOUNG GENTLEMAN'S AND LADY'S | GOLDEN LIBRARY. | [13 lines] | [d.p.rule] | LONDON: | PR F T. CARNAN AND F. NEWBERY, JUN. NO. 65, | IN SPC-Y: BUT NOT FOR F. NEWBERY, | AT THE CORNER OF LUDGATE-STREET, WHO HAS NO SHARE IN | THE LATE MR. JOHN NEWBERY'S BOOKS FOR CHILDREN. | MDCCLXXII. | [PRICE ONE SHILLING.]

In 6's. 72 leaves+11 engvd plates. Pp. iv+5–144. 4 wcts as in no. (2). D.f.b.
⌈Moon, 11·4×7·8 cm; Opie.

(7) An edition of 1777. C & N.
⌈Ball.

(8) An edition of 1783. Pr f TC. Price 1s. Hugo 22; NBL 877.
⌈Ball.

(9) An undated edition. TC. Bears holograph sig. '1787 Moore'.
⌈Ball.

J220. LILLIPUTIAN MASQUERADE, THE. In spite of the disparity between the description of no. (1) and the title of no. (2) below, I think these are in fact the same work, if only because of the extreme unlikelihood of TC running two *Lilliputian Masquerades*, both children's books, concurrently. The description of no. (1), quoted from *LC*, is clearly no more than advertising 'blurb'.

(1) Adv. *LC* 1–4.1.74, p. 11, as pr f TC, price 2d, under the following description: 'The Lilliputian Masquerade, recommended to the perusal of those sons and daughters of Folly, the frequenters of the Pantheon, Almack's, and Cornelly's. Embellished with cuts. For the instruction and amusement of the rising generation. Price of a subscription ticket, not two guineas, but two pence.'

(2) An edition of 1783. S b TC. Price 2d. S&W Cat.

THE | LILLIPUTIAN | MASQUERADE. | OCCASIONED | BY THE CONCLU-SION OF PEACE | BETWEEN THOSE POTENT NATIONS, | THE LILLIPUTIANS | AND | TOMMYTHUMBIANS. | [wct of a mask] | BEHIND OUR MASK YOU'LL SOMETHING FIND | TO PLEASE AND TO IMPROVE THE MIND. | [p.s.rule] | LONDON: | S B T. CARNAN, | IN SPC-Y. | PRICE OF A SUBSCRIPTION TICKET NOT TWO GUINEAS, | BUT TWO-PENCE. | MDCCLXXXIII.

A single gathering of 32 leaves. Pp. 63. First and last leaves pastedowns. Wct FP and 18 wcts in text. D.f. paper wrappers.
⌈CUL, 9·6×6·3 cm; Ball.

(3) Welsh, p. 256, records the bk in a TC list of 1787, price 2d, under a description indentical with that of no. (1).

LITERATURA GRÆCA. See J190A.

J221. LITTLE BOOK OF LETTERS AND CARDS, A, TO TEACH YOUNG LADIES AND GENTLEMEN HOW TO WRITE TO THEIR FRIENDS IN A POLITE, EASY AND ELEGANT MANNER. Listed in *Goody Two-Shoes*, 1766, as 'sold at Mr. Newbery's, at the Bible and Sun...', price 1*s*. Perhaps an ed. of J266.

LITTLE EMIGRANT, THE. See Peacock, Lucy.

J222. LITTLE FEMALE ORATORS, THE. Welsh 256; Weedon 58. Richard Johnson recorded in his Day-book: *1770 Jan. 8. Deliverd to Mr Carnan, The Little Female Orators. Forty Pages, Quarto. Value Five Guineas. 1772 Nov. 7. Corrected for Mr Carnan The Little Female Orators, for the Second Edition.——— Value One Guinea———*

(1) First edition, 1770. Pr f TC. Price 6*d*; *CBEL*, ii, 562.

THE | LITTLE FEMALE ORATORS; | OR, | NINE EVENINGS ENTERTAIN-MENT: | WITH OBSERVATIONS. | EMBELLISHED WITH CUTS. | [4 lines quote] | LONDON: | PR F T. CARNAN, AT NO. 65, IN | SPC-Y. 1770. | [PRICE SIX-PENCE.]

In 6's. 54 leaves. Pp. 104. 12 wcts in text. D.f.b.; also D.f.b. with red overtone.

[BM, 10·9×7·3 cm; Oup; NorBM; McKell; Gardner.

(2) Second edition, 1773. TC. Price 6*d*. NBL 501. For Richard Johnson's Day-book entry relating to this ed. see the general note, above.

(3) Third edition, 1778. Pr f TC. Price 6*d*.

Title approx. as for no. (1), with THE THIRD EDITION. *Imprint:* PR F T. CARNAN, IN SP | C-Y. PRICE SIX-PENCE. | [p.s.rule] | MDCCLXXVIII.

In 6's. 54 leaves. Pp. 106[108]. 12 wcts in text. List of bks pr f TC on pp. [167–8]. D.f.b. gilt.

[CUL, 11·7×7·4 cm; MH.

(4) An edition of 1783. Pr f TC. Price 6*d*.

Title approx. as for no. (1). *Imprint:* PR F T. CARNAN, IN SP | CY. PRICE SIXPENCE. | MDCCLXXXIII.

In 6's. 54 leaves. Pp. 106[108]. 12 wcts in text. List of Children's bks pr f TC on last 2 pages. D.f.b.; also a red wct design on paper bds. (Communicated.)

[Osborne, Cat. p. 271, 11·2×7·4 cm; NNC-T (Darton Coll.).

(5) An edition of 1788. Pr f TC. Price 6*d*.

Title and *imprint* (with date MDCCLXXXVIII) and specification approx. as for no. (4). D.f.b.

[BM, 11·2×7·3 cm; Ball.

LITTLE KING PIPPIN. See HISTORY OF...

J223. LITTLE LOTTERY-BOOK FOR CHILDREN, A. Welsh 256–7.

(1) Listed in *GM* Nov. 1756, and frequently up to 1765, price 3*d* bd and gilt, as

'Pr f all the Booksellers, and sold at the Bible and Sun in s p c-y'. Adv. *PL* 12.2.60 as pubd by JN.

(2) See Plate 9.

Four gatherings of 8, only A2 and A3 sgd. 32 leaves. Only pp. 3–7 numbered. 52 wcts for a picture alphabet. List of bks 'pubd for. . .children a s b J. Newbery' on last 5 pages. D.f.b.

[Bodley, 9·7×6·5 cm.

(3) An edition of 1768. Pr f all the Booksellers. . . Price 3*d* bd and gilt.

Title and *imprint* (with date 1768) and specification approx. as for no. (2). D.f.b.

[BM; St Bride, 9·4×6·4 cm.

(4) An edition of 1769. Pr f N & C. Price 3*d* bd and gilt.

Title approx. as for no. (2). *Imprint:* PR F NEWBERY AND CARNAN, NO. 65, THE NORTH SIDE OF SP | C-Y. 1769. | [PRICE 3*d* BOUND AND GILT.] 34 unsgd leaves. Pp. 7 (remainder unnumbered). Last leaf a blank. Alphabet with wcts as for no. (2). Bk-list on last 5 pages.

[Traylen, 9·7×6·4 cm.

(5) Listed as pr f TC in *Newtonian System*, 1787, price 2*d*.

J224. LITTLE MORALISTS, THE. Welsh 257; Weedon 59, and p. 35, note 6. The 'Dedication' is sgd R.J. (= Richard Johnson); his Day-book records: *1786 July. Mr Badcock——To writing The Little Moralists——3 Half Sheets ——32°.——£3. 3s.*

(1) First edition, 1786. Pr f EN. Price 3*d*. *CBEL*, II, 563.

THE | LITTLE MORALISTS; | OR, | THE HISTORY | OF | AMINTOR AND FLORELLA, | THE PRETTY LITTLE | SHEPHERD AND SHEPHERDESS | OF THE | VALE OF EVESHAM. | [p.rule] | EMBELLISHED WITH CUTS. | [d.p.rule] | LONDON: | PR F E. NEWBERY, THE CORNER OF | SPC-Y. | 1786. | [PRICE. 3*d*.]

In 8's. 48 leaves. Pp. 96. Wct FP and 12 wcts (circular within square frames) in text, those at pp. 16 and 33 sgd 'Jackson', others in the manner of Lee. The attribution of the cuts to John Bewick is surely misconceived. D.f.b.

[Bodley, 10·2×6·1 cm; Ball.

(2) An edition of 1792. EN.

[Knaster; MSaE.

(3) An edition of 1795. Pr f E. Newbury (*sic*). Price 6*d*.

Title and *imprint* approx. as for no. (1), with NEWBURY and date 1795. Pp. 96. FP [? wct] and 12 wcts in text, those at pp. 9, 12, 16, 21, 25, 33 sgd 'Jackson'. D.f.b. (Communicated.)

[Ries; Ball.

(4) An edition of 1799. EN. Price 3*d*.

[PPiU.

LITTLE MOUNTAINEERS OF AUVERGNE. See Ducray-Dumenil, F. G.

J225. LITTLE PRETTY POCKET-BOOK, A.

CBEL tentatively credits JN with the authorship. Probably the first of his bks deliberately intended to 'entertain' children. No copy prior to that of the 10th ed. (1760) has come to light so far. Writers generally have confidently assigned 1744 as the year of publicn of the 1st ed.; this is solely (it seems) because it was adv. as 'this day is publish'd' in the *Penny London Morning Advertiser* for 18.6.44, also in the *Daily Post* for 18.5.44. In my note on Newspaper adverts. I have stressed that these adverts. are not, in themselves, sufficient evidence for date of publishing. Very likely the *Pocket-Book* was pubd in 1744; but it could have been 1743 or 1745. See Mrs M. F. Thwaite's Essay 'John Newbery and his first Book for Children' in the facsimile ed. of the 1767 ed. of the *Pocket-Book* (Oxford, 1966). Since I wrote this note on the *Little Pretty Pocket-Book* Mrs J. E. I. Grey has drawn my attention to a newspaper cutting (date not shown) in Daniel Lysons' *Collectiana* (BM, 1881.b.6, vol. 2, pp. 51–2) which prints a letter 'To the Author of the Little Pretty Pocket Book', praising the work in exaggerated and unctuous terms, including thirty-three lines of verse, and concluding 'Pray send me a Dozen neatly bound in Calf and gilt'. The letter is dated 14 June 1744, and is signed by 'Your unknown humble Servant A.Z.'. Though undoubtedly a piece of Newbery 'puff' this does go a good way to confirm that the book was for sale by June 1744.

(1) An edition of *ca.* 1744 (discussed in the general note above). Probably the first. Pr f JN, at the Bible and Crown, without Temple Bar. 'Price of the Book 6*d* alone, with a Ball or Pincushion 8*d*'. *CBEL*, II, 561; Welsh 293–4; Darton, p. 2.

(2) Second edition. Pr f JN, R. Baldwin and W. Owen. Price 6*d* bd and gilt. Adv. *GA* for 21.10.47.

(3) Sixth edition. Pr f JN. Price 6*d*. Adv. *GA* 4.1.52.

(4) Eighth edition. Pr f JN. Price 6*d* bd and gilt. Adv. *PA* 22.4.56.

(5) Ninth edition, 1760. Adv. *PL* 12.2.60 as pubd by JN. Price 6*d* bd and gilt. *CBEL*, II, 561 (but was CB relying on the advert.?).

(6) See Plate 10. BMECBs, no. 2.

In 8's. 48 leaves+engvd FP printed in sanguine. Pp. 95. 58 small wcts in text. List of bks pr f a s b JN on pp. 91–5.

[BM, 9·6×6·3 cm (imperf.).

(7) Eleventh edition, 1763. JN.

[Ball (imperf.).

(8) An edition of 1767. Pr f JN. Price 6*d*. *Festival of Britain, Exhibition of Books, 1951, Cat.*, no. 45.

Title and *imprint* approx. as for no. (6), with date 1767.

In 8's. 48 leaves+engvd FP printed in sanguine. Pp. 90[96]. 58 small wcts as in no. (6). List of bks pr f a s b JN on pp. [91–6]. D.f.b.

[BM, 9·9×6·6 cm.

(9) An edition of 1770. Pr f N & C. Price 6*d*. Welsh 293–4; *Pierpont Morgan Cat.*, item 148.

Title approx. as for no. (6). *Imprint:* PR F NEWBERY AND CARNAN, NO. 65, | THE NORTH SIDE OF SPC-Y. 1770. | [PRICE SIX-PENCE BOUND].

In 8's. 48 leaves+engvd FP printed in pale sepia. Pp. 90[96]. 57 wcts in text, used in previous edd. List of bks pr f N & C on pp. [91–6]. D.f.b.

[BM, 9·8×6·0 cm; Welch.

(10) An edition of 1783. Pr f TC. Price 3*d*. Welsh 294.

Title approx. as for no. (6). *Imprint:* PR F T. CARNAN, | SUCCESSOR TO MR. J. NEWBERY, | IN SPC-Y, 1783. | [PRICE THREE-PENCE.]

A single gathering of 48 leaves, sgd [A]–[F8]. Pp. 92[94]. F8 a blank. First and last leaves pastedowns. Wct FP and 57 wcts in text. List of bks pr f TC on last 2 pages. Gilt floral paper wrappers.

[Bodley, 9·8×5·9 cm.

J226. LITTLE ROBIN RED BREAST, A COLLECTION OF PRETTY SONGS. Welsh 257.

(1) An edition of 1782. Pr f EN. Price 6*d*.

LITTLE | ROBIN RED BREAST; | A | COLLECTION | OF PRETTY | SONGS, | FOR | CHILDREN, | ENTIRELY NEW. | LONDON: | PR F E. NEWBERY, AT THE CORNER | OF SPC-Y. 1782. | PRICE SIX-PENCE.

In 8's. 63 leaves. Pp. 120[124]. Wct FP and 32 wcts in text. Bk-list on pp. [121–4]. D.f.b.

[Bell, 9·6×6·6 cm.

(2) Listed as pr f EN in *Anecdotes of Mary*, 1795. Price 6*d*.

J227. LITTLE TALES FOR LITTLE PEOPLE. Pr f EN. Price 2*d*.
Listed in *The Menagerie*, 1800, and ENC, p. 6.

J228. LITTLE WANDERERS, THE. Welsh 257; Weedon 60. Recorded by Richard Johnson in his Day-book: *1786 July. Mr Badcock——To writing The Little Wanderers. 3 Half Sheets, 32°. £3. 3s.* The dedication to the 1806 (J. Harris) ed. is sgd R.J. So also, presumably, in any earlier edd.

(1) Adv. *LC* 26–8.12.86, as pr f EN, price 3*d*, 'just published'. Perhaps = no. (2).

(2) An undated edition. Pr f EN. Price 3*d*.

THE | LITTLE WANDERERS; | OR THE | SURPRISING HISTORY | AND MIRACULOUS ADVENTURES | OF | TWO PRETTY ORPHANS. | [p.rule] | EMBELLISHED WITH CUTS. | [d.p.rule] | LONDON: | PR F E. NEWBERY, THE CORNER OF | SPC-Y. | [PRICE THREE-PENCE.]

Wct FP. (Communicated.)

[Ball; MBSPNEA.

(3) An edition of 1792. EN.

[Knaster.

(4) Listed in ENC, p. 6. Price 3*d*.

J229. 'LITTLETON, Master Tommy'. JUVENILE TRIALS FOR ROBBING ORCHARDS. Welsh 257–8; *CBEL*, II, 562; Weedon 44; F. V. Barry, *A Century of Children's Books*, 1922, pp. 77–8. Richard Johnson's Day-book records: *1770 Aug. 20. Delivered to M*^r *Carnan, Juvenile Trials. Value Five Guineas.*
(1) First edition, 1772. Pr f TC. Price 6*d*.

JUVENILE TRIALS | FOR | ROBBING ORCHARDS, | TELLING FIBS, | AND OTHER | HIGH MISDEMEANOURS. | EMBELLISHED WITH CUTS. | [p.rule] | BY MASTER TOMMY LITTLETON, | SECRETARY TO THE COURT. | [p.rule] | [2 lines quote] | [p.s.rule] | LONDON: | PR F T. CARNAN, | AT NUMBER 65, SPC-Y. | MDCCLXXII. | [PRICE SIX-PENCE.]

In 6's. 60 leaves. Pp. xviii+19–120. Wct FP and 16 wcts in text. D.f.b. (Communicated.)
[Opie.
(2) Second edition, 1774. Pr f TC. Price 6*d*.

Title and *imprint* approx. as for no. (1), substituting HEINOUS OFFENCES for HIGH MISDEMEANOURS, with date MDCCLXXIV.

In 6's. 62 leaves. Pp. xxii+23–124. Wcts. D.f.b. Details taken from the Traylen copy.
[Traylen; BCE, 11·1×7·8 cm; Ball.
(3) Third edition, 1776. Pr f TC. Price 6*d*. NBL 504.

Title and *imprint* approx. as for no. (2), with THE THIRD EDITION and date MDCCLXXVI.

In 6's. 62 leaves. Pp. xxii+23–124. Wct FP and 16 wcts in text. White or buff bds impressed with wct scenes of children playing, within decorative frames, in black.
[CUL, 11·3×7·5 cm; Sotheby, 5–6.2.45, lot 145.
(4) An edition of 1781. Pr f TC. Price 6*d*.

In 6's. Pp. xxii+23–124. Wct FP and wcts in text. Details from the Renier copy.
[Renier.
(5) An edition of 1786. Pr f TC. Price 6*d*.

Title approx. as for no. (2). *Imprint:* PR F T. CARNAN, | IN SPC-Y. | MDCCLXXXVI. | [PRICE SIX-PENCE.]

In 6's. 62 leaves. Pp. xxii+23–124. Wct FP and 15 wcts in text, in the manner of the *Goody Two-Shoes* cuts. D.f.b.
[BM, 10·9×7·3 cm; Roscoe; Osborne, Cat. p. 270; Ball; UCLA.

LIVES OF THE ADMIRALS, THE. No. J230 is sometimes so listed.

J230. LIVES OF THE BRITISH ADMIRALS, THE.
(1) An edition of 1776, 1777. 2 Parts. Pr f FN(N). Price 1*s* each part.

THE LIVES OF THE | BRITISH ADMIRALS. | DISPLAYING, | IN THE MOST STRIKING COLOURS, | THE | CONDUCT AND HEROISM | OF THE | NAVAL COMMANDERS OF GREAT | BRITAIN & IRELAND. | [10 lines] | [p.rule] |

PART I. [II.] | [d.p.rule] | LONDON: | PR F. NEWBERY, AT THE CORNER OF |
SPCY. | [p.rule] | MDCCLXXVI. [MDCCLXXVII.]

Part I, 1776. Engvd FP and engvd leaves in text. D.f.b. (Communicated.)

Part II, 1777. Pp. 175[180]. Engvd FP. Bk-list at end. (Communicated.)

[Opie (Pt I); Preston (Pt I; Cat. p. 80); BCE (Pt I), 11·3×7·3 cm; Ball (Pts I and II); Welch (Pts I and II).

(2) An edition of 1783. Pr f EN. 2 vols. D.f.b. (Communicated.)

[T. Crowe's Bookshop, Norwich, 1964.

(3) An edition of 1787, 1788. Pr f EN. 2 Parts, price 1s each. NBL 139.

Titles approx. as for no. (1). *Imprints:* PR F E. NEWBERY, AT THE CORNER OF | SPCY. | [p.rule] | MDCCLXXXVII. [MDCCLXXXVIII].

Part I, 1787. In 6's. 90 leaves+6 insets. Pp. 179[180]. 6 leaves of engvd portraits.

Part II, 1788. In 6's. 90 leaves+6 insets. Pp. 175[180]. List of new bks pubd by EN on pp. [178–80]. 6 leaves of engvd portraits.

[Bodley, 11·6×7·1 cm; BM; SomCL; CLU-C.

(4) Listed in Trimmer's *Silver Thimble*, 1799, as pr f EN. Price 1s each part, and 'two volumes in one' 2s.

LIVES OF THE FATHERS OF THE CHRISTIAN CHURCH.
Goldsmith's HISTORY OF THE LIVES...OF THE FATHERS... is sometimes so listed.

J231. LOCKMAN, John. NEW HISTORY OF ENGLAND, A, BY QUESTION AND ANSWER.

(1) Eleventh edition. *CBEL*, II, 645 dates [1761?]. IAW, 125–6, dates 1762, the authority relied on being apparently Prior's *Life of Goldsmith* which records that the 'Proprietors' were Hawes, Woodfall, Newbery, Baldwin and others. R. M. Wardle, *Oliver Goldsmith*, 1957, p. 308, note 41, says 'the *History of England in Questions and Answers* [*sic*]...appeared in its eleventh edition on September 11, 1759'. As to Goldsmith's hand in this work, see *CBEL*.

(2) Listed in T.G's *Description of the Isle of Thanet*, 1765 (A172(2)), as pr f a s b JN. Price 3s.

(3) Fourteenth edition. Adv. *LC* 29–31.12.68, p. 631, as pr f H. Woodfall, J. Rivington, Newbery and Carnan, R. Baldwin, W. Johnston, W. Strahan, B. Law, T. Caslon, Hawes & Co, G. Kearsly, R. Horsfield, S. Crowder, S. Bladon, and Robinson and Roberts. Price 3s without cuts, 4s with copper-plates.

(4) Fifteenth edition. Listed in the bk-list bound up with the BM copy (3902.cc.11) of Voltaire's *Genuine Letters*, 1770, as either pr f or 'to be had of' FN(N). Price as for no. (3).

(5) Sixteenth edition. Adv. *LC* 10–12.9.72, p. 251, as pr f J. Rivington, W. Johnston, Hawes, Clarke and Collins, R. Horsfield, T. Caslon, Carnan and Newbery, W. Nicoll, B. Law, S. Bladon, G. Robinson, and R. Baldwin. Price as for no. (3).

(6) Seventeenth edition. Adv. *LC* 12–14.4.74, p. 356, as pr f J. Rivington, Hawes,

Clarke and Collins, R. Horsfield, B. Law, T. Caslon, Carnan & Co, F. Newbery, G. Robinson, R. Baldwin, E. Johnston, W. Strahan, and W. Woodfall. Price as for no. (3). What is the significance of this appellation 'Carnan & Co'? One cannot believe that Francis the son would have submitted to being the humble '& Co'. Probably he is the 'F. Newbery' named separately in the imprint; his name appears in edd. of the bk after 1780. (But so does the name of EN, the widow of Francis the nephew.) This may perhaps be an occasion on which the partnership (TC and Francis the son) had temporarily broken down and TC was stressing his independence by this '& Co'. There is other evidence that the partnership was not always of the happiest (see the Introduction at pp. 20ff.).

(7) Eighteenth edition, 1777. Pr f TC & Co, FN [?S] et al. Price as for no. (3). As to 'Carnan & Co' etc see no. (6).

A NEW | HISTORY | OF | ENGLAND, | BY | QUESTION AND ANSWER, | EXTRACTED FROM THE | MOST CELEBRATED ENGLISH HISTORIANS, | PARTICULARLY | M. RAPIN DE THOYRAS, | [2 lines] | [p.rule] | BY THE AUTHOR OF THE ROMAN HISTORY | BY QUESTION AND ANSWER. | [p.rule] | THE EIGHTEENTH EDITION... | [5 lines] | [d.p.rule] | LONDON: | PR F J. BUCKLAND; J. RIVINGTON AND SONS; | W. STRAHAN; T. LONGMAN; T. CASLON; B. LAW; | E. AND C. DILLY; T. CADELL; T. CARNAN AND CO. | G. ROBINSON; F. NEWBERY; W. STUART; AND R. BALDWIN. | 1777. | (PRICE BOUND 3s WITHOUT CUTS, OR 4s WITH CUTS.)

12mo. 198 leaves+insets in the 4s copies. Pp. 390. The TP speaks of 32 engvd plates. Bk-list on A1r.

[Bodley, 17·0×9·9 cm (no plates); Opie.

(8) Nineteenth edition not traced.

(9) Twentieth edition. Adv. LC 24–6.8.84, p. 198, as pr f J. Buckland, J. Rivington & Sons, W. Strahan, T. Longman, B. Law, C. Dilly, T. Cadell, T. Carnan, G. Robinson, F. Newbery, W. Goldsmith, R. Baldwin, Scatcherd and Whitaker, and George Wilkie. Price as for no. (3).

(10) Twenty-first edition. Adv. LC 20–23.12.88, p. 607, as pr f J. Buckland et al., as in no. (9) but omitting TC, and G. G. J. and J. Robinson in place of J. Robinson. Price as for no. (3).

(11) Twenty-second edition, 1790. Pr f EN, F. Power et al. Price as for no. (3).

Title approx. as for no. (7), with THE TWENTY-SECOND EDITION. *Imprint:* PR F J. RIVINGTON AND SONS; T. LONGMAN; B. LAW; | T. CADELL; G. ROBINSON AND CO. C. DILLY; A. STRAHAN; | W. GOLDSMITH; SCATCHERD AND WHITAKER; E. NEW- | BERY; G. AND T. WILKIE; F. POWER; R. BALDWIN; AND | W. LOWNDES. 1790.

12mo. 252 leaves. Pp. viii+486[487]. Half-title.

[BmPL (no plates), 16·9×10·2 cm.

(12) Twenty-third edition, 1794. Pr f EN et al. Price as for no. (3). Higson, B.661.

Title approx. as for no. (7), with THE TWENTY-THIRD EDITION COR-RECTED, AND BROUGHT | DOWN TO THE PRESENT TIME. *Imprint:* PR F T. LONGMAN; B. LAW AND SON; C. DILLY; G. G. | AND J. ROBINSON; T. CADELL;

W. RICHARDSON; R. BALD- | WIN; W. GOLDSMITH; F. AND C. RIVINGTON; W. LOWNDES; | W. BENT; G. AND T. WILKIE; I. SCATCHERD; AND E. NEW- | BERY. | [p.rule] | 1794.

 12mo. 240 leaves. Pp. xi+462[468]. Half-title. Bk-list on pp. [463–8]. [LEI (no plates), 17·2×10·2 cm.

(13) Twenty-third edition [? a re-issue of no. (12) – or identical]. Adv. *LC* 10–12.12.99, p. 564, as pr f Rivington & Co, W. Richardson, W. Bent, T. Longman, C. Dilly, T. Cadell, G. G. and J. Robinson, E. Newbery, R. Baldwin, Scatcherd and Whitaker, and G. Wilkie. Price as for no. (3).

(14) Twenty-fourth edition, 1801. Pr f EN et al. Price 5*s* with plates, 3*s* without.

 Title approx. as for no. (7). *Imprint:* PR F G. G. AND J. ROBINSON, W. RICHARDSON, | R. BALDWIN, F. AND C. RIVINGTON, W. LOWNDES, | G. WILKIE, J. SCATCHERD, E. NEWBERY, J. WALKER, | CADELL AND DAVIES, LONGMAN AND REES, | C. LAW, J. MAWMAN, AND J. KAY. | [p.rule] | 1801.

 12mo. 228 leaves+32 insets. Pp. xi+443. Engvd FP and 31 other engvd leaves. Half-title.

 [Bodley, 16·9×10·1 cm (with plates).

J232. LOCKMAN, John. NEW ROMAN HISTORY, A, BY QUESTION AND ANSWER.

(1) Sixth edition, 1762. Pr f JN et al.

 A NEW | ROMAN HISTORY, | BY | QUESTION AND ANSWER; | IN | A METHOD MUCH MORE COMPREHENSIVE | THAN ANY OF THE KIND EXTANT: | EXTRACTED FROM | ANCIENT AUTHORS, | AND THE | MOST CELEBRATED AMONG THE MODERNS; | [3 lines] | [p.rule] | [1 line] | [p.rule] | [1 line] | [p.rule] | BY THE AUTHOR OF THE HISTORY OF ENGLAND BY | QUESTION AND ANSWER. | [p.rule] | THE SIXTH EDITION CORRECTED, | AND ADORNED WITH SIXTEEN COPPER-PLATES... | [1 line] | [d.p.rule] | LONDON: | PR F C. HITCH AND L. HAWES, H. WOODFALL, J. RIVING- | TON, J. NEWBERY, R. BALDWIN, W. JOHNSTON, J. RI | CHARDSON, S. CROWDER AND CO. B. LAW AND CO. T. CASLON, | R. WITHY, AND M. COOPER. MDCCLXII.

 12mo. 186 leaves+16 insets. Pp. xii+342[360]. Engvd FP and 15 other engvd leaves sgd 'S. Wale invt' and 'N. Parr sculpt' or 'G. Child sculp'. Advertisement on Q12ᵛ.

 [BM, 16·9×9·7 cm; Bodley; Opie.

(2) Seventh edition. Adv. *LC* 29–31.12.68, p. 631, as pr f H. Woodfall, J. Riving-ton, Newbery and Carnan, R. Baldwin, W. Johnston, W. Strahan, B. Law, T. Caslon, Hawes & Co, G. Kearsly, R. Horsfield, S. Crowder, S. Bladon, and Robinson and Roberts. Price 3*s* 6*d* with cuts, 3*s* without.

(3) Eighth edition. Adv. *LC* 31.7.73–3.8.73, p. 117, as pr f J. Rivington, W. Johnston, Hawes, Clarke and Collins, R. Horsfield, T. Caslon, W. Nicoll, B. Law, S. Crowder, Carnan and Newbery, S. Bladon, G. Robinson, W. Wood-fall, and R. Baldwin. Price as for no. (2).

(4) Ninth edition, 1778. Pr f Carnan & Co et al. The title-leaf for this ed. is in

Bodley vol. 2582.b.2 at p. 223. Pr f J. Rivington, T. Longman, C. Bathurst, J. Wilkie, B. Law, T. Caslon, Carnan & Co, G. Robinson, W. Woodfall, S. Bladon, W. Nicoll, R. Baldwin, and Fielding and Walker. Price as for no. (2).

(5) Tenth edition. Adv. *LC* 27–9.12.85, p. 621, as pr f J. Rivington, T. Longman, C. Bathurst, T. Carnan, B. Law, J. Johnson, S. Bladon, G. Robinson, G. and T. Wilkie, W. Woodfall and R. Baldwin. Price as for no. (2).

(6) Eleventh edition, 1791. Pr f TC et al. Price as for no. (2). An advert. of this ed. in *LC* for 5–7.7.92 mentions EN (but not TC) as one of the conger. As to TC's name in an imprint 3 years after his death, see the Introduction, at p. 25.

Title approx. as for no. (1) with THE ELEVENTH EDITION, CORRECTED. *Imprint:* PR F J. RIVINGTON, T. LONGMAN, C. BATHURST, | B. LAW, J. JOHNSON, T. CARNAN, G. ROBINSON, | W. WOODFALL, S. BLADON, R. BALDWIN, AND G. AND | T. WILKIE. | MDCCXCI.

Specification approx. as for no. (1). Some engvgs sgd 'S. Wale del', 'J. June scul'. Advert. of 21st ed. of Lockman's *New History of England* on vso of last leaf. (Communicated.)

⌈NoU.

LOGIC MADE FAMILIAR. See CIRCLE OF THE SCIENCES, J66.

LOGIC, ONTOLOGY AND THE ART OF POETRY. See CIRCLE OF THE SCIENCES, J67.

J233. LONDON CRIES, THE. Price 1*d.* Not to be confused with the *Cries of London* (J86), which cost 6*d.* Welsh 259.

(1) An edition of 1770. Pr f TC. Price 1*d.*

THE | LONDON CRIES, | FOR THE | AMUSEMENT | OF ALL THE | GOOD CHILDREN | THROUGHOUT THE WORLD. | TAKEN FROM LIFE. | [d.p.rule] | LONDON: | PR F T. CARNAN, AT NO. 65, IN | SPC-Y. 1770. | [PRICE ONE PENNY.]

A single gathering of 16 leaves. Pp. 29[31]. First and last leaves pastedowns. 26 wcts. List of bks pr f C & N on last 2 pages. D.f. paper wrappers.

⌈Bodley, 9·1×6·6 cm.

(2) Listed as pr f TC in the *Picture Exhibition*, 1783, price 1*d.*

(3) An edition of 1788. Pr f TC. Price 1*d.*

Title as for no. (1). *Imprint:* PR F. T. CARNAN, | IN SPC- | Y. 1788. | [PRICE ONE PENNY.]

Pp. 29[31]. FP and 25 wcts. The FP is as in no. (1). Book-list at end. Flowered wrappers. (Communicated.)

⌈Ball, 9·6×6·4 cm.

LOOKING-GLASS FOR THE MIND. See Berquin, Arnaud.

'LOVECHILD, Mrs'. See Fenn, Lady E., J114 etc.

J234. LOWE, Solomon. THE CRITICAL SPELLING = BOOK. Welsh 309.

(1) Adv. *LC* 10–13.2.70, p. 148, as pr f FN(N). Price 2*s*. Probably = no. (2).

(2) Second edition, 1770. Pr f FN(N). Price 2*s*. Adv. *LC* 10–13.3.70, p. 243 (and later) as t.d.w.p. Alston, IV, 623.

THE | CRITICAL | SPELLING= BOOK | [p.rule] | AN INTRODUCTION TO | READING AND WRITING | READILY AND CORRECTLY. | [p.rule] | IN A MANNER | MORE COMMODIOUS THAN ANY, | AND MORE COMPREHENSIVE THAN ALL | THE SPELLING-BOOKS THAT EVER WERE PUBLISHT. | [p.rule] | [2 lines] | [p.rule] | [5 lines] | [p.rule] | BY MR. LOWE, | [2 lines] | [p.rule] | THE SECOND EDITION. | [p.rule] | [6 lines quote] | LONDON, | PR F F. NEWBERY, AT THE CORNER OF SP | CY. 1770.

In 6's. 105 leaves. Pp. 1–22, 1–185[186]. Wct tailpiece at p. 34. Bk-list on R3ᵛ.

[BM, 16·0×9·8 cm.

(3) Adv. *GM*, Supplement 1774 as to be had of FN(N), price 2*s*.

LUCINDA; OR, VIRTUE TRIUMPHANT. See Smith, Rev Thos.

J235. M., A. THE HISTORY OF THE FAMILY AT SMILEDALE, n.d. (1797 or before – listed in J88(7) 1797). Pr f EN. Price 6*d*. Welsh 216; Hugo, II, 4105; *CBEL*, II, 563; Gum 2471; ENC, p. 6.

Hugo specifies 10 wcts, Gum a wct FP and 12 in text; the latter is correct for the copy specified below and for an undated ed. by Harris.

THE HISTORY | OF THE | FAMILY AT SMILEDALE, | PRESENTED | TO ALL LITTLE BOYS AND GIRLS | WHO WISH TO BE GOOD, | AND MAKE THEIR FRIENDS HAPPY. | [d.p.rule] | LONDON: | PR F E. NEWBERY, AT THE CORNER | OF SPCY. | [PRICE SIX-PENCE.]

In 8's. 64 leaves. Pp. 128. Wct FP and 12 whole-page wcts in text. The converse of each leaf with a wct is blank. The wcts are by, or in close imitation of, John Bewick. The Letter of Dedication to 'Mrs Teachwell' (i.e. Lady Fenn) is signed A.M. The Osborne copy is in an original bookseller's binding of shell marbled bds and red leather turkey spine; it may have crossed the Atlantic in sheets and been bound up there. (Communicated.)

[Osborne*, 10·5×7·0 cm.

J236. MAPS TO THE GEOGRAPHY FOR CHILDREN. A series of 11 maps under this description, comprising the World, Europe, England, Scotland, Ireland, Asia, India, Africa, North America, West Indies, South America. The series is mentioned at p. v of Lenglet du Fresnoy's *Geography for Children*, 20th ed. 1799. The above maps, each of which has its several parts divided by colours, 'may be had of J. Johnson...and E. Newbery... Price Four Shillings done up in boards, by giving orders for "Maps to the Geography for Children"'.

The entry in Welsh at p. 224 is obscure: the description he gives fits the 20th ed. of *The Geography* (except that he gives the price as 2*s*, the bk cost 1*s* 6*d*) rather than a set of maps.

J237. MASSON, Charles Francois Philbert. ELMINA; OR, THE FLOWER THAT NEVER FADES. Welsh 208; Welch 757.2. A review of this work in the *European Magazine* for July 1791 says 'The following Tale was written for the Princess Wilhelmina...by Mr Masson, of Blamont, whose sister is governess to the young Princess'.

(1) An edition of 1791. Pr f EN. Price 2*d*.

ELMINA; | OR, THE | FLOWER THAT NEVER FADES. | A TALE FOR | YOUNG PEOPLE. | [p.s.rule] | LONDON: | PR F E. NEWBERY, AT THE CORNER OF S | PCY. 1791. | [PRICE TWO PENCE.]

In 8's. 32 leaves. Pp. 60[63]. First and last leaves pastedowns. Ornam. wct inside front cover; 8 whole-page wcts in the manner of John Bewick, perhaps by Lee. List of bks pr f EN on pp. [61–3]. Orange-red wrappers with ornam. wct designs impressed in brown.

[BM; Bodley, 10·1×6·2 cm.

(2) An edition of 1794. Pr f EN. Price 2*d*.

Title and *imprint* (with date 1794) and specification approx. as for no. (1). D.f. paper wrappers.

[Bell, 10·1×5·9 cm; Adomeit.

(3) An edition of 1800. Pr f EN. Price 2*d*. Hugo, II, 4108.

Title and *imprint* approx. as for no. (1), with date 1800. Pp. 60. Wcts as in no. (1). (Communicated.)

[Welch.

J238. MAVOR, William Fordyce. HISTOIRE NATURELLE, 1801. Se vend chez EN et al. Price 5*s*. Welsh 236; Higson D905.

HISTOIRE NATURELLE, | À | L'USAGE DES ÉCOLES; | CALQUÉE | SUR LA CLASSIFICATION DES ANIMAUX DE LINNAEUS, | [2 lines] | ORNÉE DE VINGT-SIX PLANCHES EN TAILLE-DOUCE, REPRÉ- | SENTANT LES OBJECTS LES PLUS CURIEUX. | [d.p.rule] | TRADUIT DE L'ANGLAIS DE | GUILLAUME MAVOR, DOCTEUR EN DROIT, | [2 lines] | [d.p.rule] | [11 lines quotes] | [d.p.rule] | À LONDRES: | DE L'IMPRIMERIE DE T. BAYLIS, | GREVILLE-STREET, HATTON-GARDEN; | ET SE VEND CHEZ E. NEWBERY, SPC-Y; | VERNOR ET HOOD, POULTRY; BOOSEY, BROAD-STREET, PRÈS | DE LA BOURSE ROYALE; ET CHEZ LACKINGTON, ALLEN ET CO. | FINSBURY-SQUARE. | [p.rule] | 1801.

12mo. 216 leaves+13 insets. Pp. xii+420. 26 engvd plates of animals etc on 13 leaves. Text in French.

[LEI, 17·1×9·9 cm.

J239. M A V O R, William Fordyce. J U V E N I L E   O L I O,   T H E,   1796. Pr f
EN. Price 3s 6d. Welsh 266; *CBEL*, II, 559.

THE | JUVENILE OLIO; | OR | MENTAL MEDLEY: | CONSISTING OF |
ORIGINAL ESSAYS, | MORAL AND LITERARY; | TALES, FABLES, REFLEC-
TIONS, &c | [4 lines] | [wavy rule] | [3 lines quotes] | [wavy rule] | WRITTEN
BY A FATHER, | CHIEFLY FOR THE USE OF HIS CHILDREN. | [d.p.rule] |
LONDON: | PR F E. NEWBERY, THE CORNER OF SP | CY. | 1796. | ENTERED
AT STATIONER'S HALL.

12mo. 138 leaves+engvd FP sgd 'Courbould del', 'Cook sculp'. Pp. viii+
266[268]. List of bks pr f EN on last 2 pages.

[BM, 17·5×10·3 cm; CUL; V&A(GL) (imperf.); LUL; EdUL; Renier;
Shiers; Grant; Schiller.

J240. M A V O R, William Fordyce. Y O U T H ' S   M I S C E L L A N Y,   1798. Pr f
EN. Price 4s. Welsh 267; Gum 6243; *CBEL*, II, 559.

YOUTH'S MISCELLANY; | OR, A | FATHER'S GIFT | TO HIS | CHILDREN: |
CONSISTING OF | ORIGINAL ESSAYS, | MORAL AND LITERARY; | TALES,
FABLES, REFLECTIONS, &c. | [5 lines] | [wavy rule] | [3 lines] | [d.p.rule] |
BY THE AUTHOR OF THE JUVENILE OLIO, | &c. &c. | [d.p.rule] | LONDON:
PR F E. NEWBERY, THE CORNER OF | SPC-Y. | 1798.

12mo. 150 leaves+engvd FP by Saunders after Kirk. Pp. xi+286, 288. List of
new publications for young minds sold by EN on last leaf.

[BM, 17·2×10·1 cm; CUL; LUL; MPL; BI; Osborne*; UCLA; Bondy, Cat.
59 [1962] item 77.

MAXIMS. See Chesterfield, Lord.

MEMOIRS OF A SPARROW. Kendall's *The Sparrow*, 1798, is sometimes
so listed.

J241. MEMOIRS OF DICK, THE LITTLE PONEY.
(1) *CBEL*, II, 564 lists an ed. 'before 1800'. This would seem to refer to the ed.
with the Dedication dated 14 Dec. 1799, pubd by Whittingham and Arliss (copy
in V&A(GL)), but which will be found to have the date 'September 1816' at A2ᵛ.
The bk was adv. *LC* 21–4.12.99, p. 604, as one of EN's publicns for the Christmas
holidays, price 2s. This must refer to the 1800 ed. (no. (2)), on the FP to which
the publicn date is also 14 Dec. 1799.
(2) An edition of 1800. S b EN. Price 2s.

MEMOIRS | OF | DICK, | THE LITTLE PONEY, | SUPPOSED TO BE WRITTEN
BY HIMSELF; | AND PUBLISHED FOR THE | INSTRUCTION AND AMUSEMENT
OF GOOD | BOYS AND GIRLS. | [wct] | [d.s.rule] | LONDON: | PR F J. WALKER,
| NO. 44 PATERNOSTER-ROW; | A S B | E. NEWBERY, CORNER OF SPC-Y. |
[p.rule] | J. CUNDEE, PRINTER, IVY-LANE. | [d.p.rule] | 1800.

In 6's. 98 leaves+engvd FP sgd 'Howitt delt', 'J. Scott sculpt'. Pp. xii+184. Half-title. Decorated or marbled bds, green vell. spine with label.

[BM, 13·4×8·5 cm; V&A(GL) (imperf.); SomCL; BCE; NUCC-IAU; Gardner.

J242. MEMOIRS OF THE DANBY FAMILY, 1799. Pr f EN. Price 4s. Welsh 197.

MEMOIRS | OF THE | DANBY FAMILY: | DESIGNED CHIEFLY | FOR THE | ENTERTAINMENT AND IMPROVEMENT | OF | YOUNG PERSONS. | [d.p.rule] | BY A LADY. | [d.p.rule] | LONDON: | PR F E. NEWBERY, CORNER OF | SPC-Y. | [d.p.rule] | 1799.

12mo. 138 leaves+engvd FP sgd 'Thurston del', 'Dadley sculpt'. Pp. xii+ 258[264]. Half-title.

[BM, 16·7×10·0 cm; CUL; Renier; Osborne*; UCLA; Ball.

J243. MENAGERIE, THE; OR, A PEEP AT THE QUADRUPED RACE, 1800. Pr f EN. Price 1s 6d, and 'a few copies coloured' 2s 6d. Welsh 267.

THE | MENAGERIE; | OR, | A PEEP AT THE QUADRUPED RACE. BEING | AN EXHIBITION | OF | ONE HUNDRED AND TEN ANIMALS, | NEATLY ENGRAVED ON COPPER-PLATES, | WITH THEIR CHARACTERS. | INTENDED AS A PRESENT FOR EVERY CURIOUS MISS AND MASTER. | [d.p.rule] | [2 lines quote] | [d.p.rule] | LONDON: | PR F E. NEWBERY, | CORNER OF SPC-Y, | BY J. CUNDEE, IVY-LANE. | [p.rule] | 1800.

In 6's. 18 leaves of text, followed by 20 leaves of engvd figures of animals etc. Pp. 34[36]. Engvd leaves unnumbered, but each lettered 'to face p. ....'. List of bks pr f EN, on pp. [35–6]. Half-title. Marbled stiff paper wrappers, with oval pink label.

[DES, 14·1×8·2 cm.

J243A. MERRICK, James. ANNOTATIONS...ON ST. JOHN, CHAP. I, 1–14. Welsh 268.

(1) An edition of 1764. S b JN et al. Price 6d. Legg 42.

ANNOTATIONS, | CRITICAL AND GRAMMATICAL, | ON | CHAP. I. V. 1–14. | OF THE | GOSPEL ACCORDING TO ST. JOHN. | BEING | PART OF A WORK, | PARTICULARLY DESIGNED | FOR THE USE OF YOUNG PERSONS, AS AN INTRODUCTION | TO THE STUDY OF THE GREEK TESTAMENT. | [4 lines] | [p.rule] | BY JAMES MERRICK, M.A. | [1 line] | [d.p.rule] | READING: | PR A S B J. CARNAN AND CO. | SOLD ALSO BY MR. NEWBERY, IN SPC-Y, | LONDON; AND BY MR. FLETCHER AND MR. PRINCE, | IN OXFORD. 1764. [PRICE SIXPENCE.]

In 4's. 18 leaves. Pp. 8, 26. Details taken from the BM copy.

[BM; Bodley; CUL; Lambeth; RePL; EdUL (this or no. (2)); Traylen, 19·6 ×12·4 cm.

(2) Another edition of 1764. S b JN et al. Price 6d. Not in Legg.

Title and *imprint* as for no. (1).

In 4's. 68 leaves. Pp. 8, 126. Advert. on last page.

[BM, 20·4×12·2 cm; Bodley; CUL; EdUL (this or no. (1)); UCL.

J243B. MERRICK, James. SECOND PART, A, OF ANNOTATIONS
...ON ST. JOHN'S GOSPEL, 1767. S b 'Mr Newbery' et al. Price 2*s* sewed.
Legg 47.

A | SECOND PART | OF | ANNOTATIONS, | CRITICAL AND GRAMMATICAL,
| ON | ST. JOHN'S GOSPEL, | REACHING TO THE | END OF THE THIRD
CHAPTER. | [d.p.rule] | BY JAMES MERRICK, M.A. | [1 line] | [d.p.rule] |
READING: PR A S B J. CARNAN AND CO. | SOLD ALSO BY MR. NEWBERY, IN
SPC-Y, | LONDON; AND BY MR. FLETCHER AND MR. PRINCE, | IN OXFORD. |
1767. [PRICE TWO SHILLINGS.]

In 4's. 52 leaves. Pp. [23–4]25–126. Advert. on last page.

[Bodley, 19·1×11·8 cm; CUL; Sion; EdUL; UCL; RePL.

J244. MERRICK, John. FESTIVAL HYMNS, 1742. 3rd Edition. Pr b JN
et al. Price 6*d*. Legg 18; Coates, *Supplement to Hist. and Antiquities of Reading,*
1810.

FESTIVAL | HYMNS | FOR THE USE OF | CHARITY-SCHOOLS. | ORIGI-
NALLY COMPOSED FOR THE | FRATERNITY | OF THE | BLUE AND GREEN
COAT BOYS | IN THE | CORPORATION | OF | READING. | [rule] | THE THIRD
EDITION. | [rule] | READING, | PR B J. NEWBERY AND C. MICKLEWRIGHT, |
AT THE BIBLE AND CROWN IN THE MARKET-PLACE. | MDCCXLII. | (PRICE
SIX-PENCE.)

12mo. 16 leaves. Pp. vii[viii]+22[24]. Details taken from Legg.

[Loveday, 18·5×11·6 cm.

J245. MERRY COMPANION, THE, OR ORACLE OF MIRTH
AND WISDOM. Pr f EN. Price 6*d*. Listed in *Anecdotes of Mary*, 1795. See
Weedon 57, VII. One of the 10 vols of the *Lilliputian Library* 'compiled' by
Richard Johnson (no. J218).

MIRROR FOR THE FEMALE SEX. See Pilkington, M. (H.), J284.

MITCHELL, Margaret. See Hurry, Mrs Ives.

MITCHELL'S MORAL AND INSTRUCTIVE TALES. See J183.

J246. MORAL AMUSEMENT; OR, A SELECTION OF TALES...
(1) An edition of 1798. Pr f EN et al. Price 1*s* 6*d*.

MORAL AMUSEMENT; | OR, | A SELECTION OF TALES, | HISTORIES, |
AND | INTERESTING ANECDOTES; | INTENDED TO | AMUSE AND INSTRUCT
| YOUNG MINDS. | [d.p.rule] | BATH: | PR B S. HAZARD, | FOR VERNOR AND

HOOD, NO. 31, POULTRY, | AND E. NEWBERY, SPC-Y. | [ornam. rule] | 1798.

18mo. 90 leaves+engvd FP sgd 'J. Thurston del', 'G. Rivers sculp'. Pp. iv+ 175[176]. Bk-list on last page. Marbled bds, green vell. spine.

[BM, 13·6×8·7 cm.

(2) An edition of 1799. Pr f EN et al. Price 1s 6d.

Title and *imprint* (with date 1799, but omitting the name of S. Hazard) and specification approx. as for no. (1). Marbled bds, green vell. spine.

[BM, 13·5×8·3 cm; Ball; UCLA.

MORAL LECTURES. See 'Winlove, Solomon'.

J247. MORAL SKETCHES FOR YOUNG MINDS. Weedon 65. Richard Johnson's Day-book records: *1790 April. Mr Badcock——To writing Moral Sketches——£8. 8s.*

(1) An edition of 1790. Pr f EN. Price 1s. Welsh 271.

MORAL SKETCHES | FOR | YOUNG MINDS. | [p.s.rule] | [6 lines quote] | [p.s.rule] | LONDON, | PR F E. NEWBERY, THE CORNER | OF SPCY, 1790. | (PRICE ONE SHILLING.)

In 6's. 90 leaves+6 insets. Pp. iv+176. Engvd FP and 5 other engvd leaves. D.f.b.; also pink bds, white label on upper.

[BM, 11·4×7·5 cm; V&A (imperf.); Weedon; Osborne*; MSaE; Melbourne; Grant; Oppenheimer.

(2) An edition of 1797. Pr f EN. Price 1s. Gum 4178.

Title and *imprint* approx. as for no. (1), with date 1797.

In 6's. 90 leaves+6 insets. Pp. iv+[5]–180. Engvd FP and 5 other engvd leaves. D.f.b.

[V&A(GL); Bell, 11·3×7·7 cm; Welch; Ball.

MORAL TALES: DESIGNED TO AMUSE... See Butcher, Rev. Edmund.

J248. MOSAIC CREATION, THE: OR, DIVINE WISDOM DISPLAY'D... Welsh 271.

(1) An edition of 1749 was adv. in *GA* for 25.12.49 as the *Mosaic Creation; or, Divine Wisdom display'd in the Works of the first six Days...to which is added The Philosophy of Children extracted from the universally admired Belles Lettres of Mr. Rollin. Embellished with a great variety of Copper-plates*...pr a s b J. Jefferies, J. Newbery and J. Fuller. Price 1s, or the two works could be had separately at 6d each. But the copy of this 1749 ed. in Elkin Mathews' Cat. 163 [1965], item 276 was by J. Jefferies and J. Fuller alone; so also the Welch copy. See no. J321.

(2) An undated edition. Pr f JN. Price 6d. This does not include Rollin's *Philosophy of Children*.

THE | MOSAIC CREATION: | OR, | DIVINE WISDOM | DISPLAYED | IN

THE WORKS OF THE | FIRST SIX DAYS. | [4 lines] | IN | PROSE AND VERSE, | WITH | OCCASIONAL REMARKS. | [p.rule] | EMBELLISHED WITH VARIETY OF COPPER-PLATES, | NEATLY ENGRAVED. | [p.rule] | [4 lines quote] | [p.rule] | LONDON, | PR F J. NEWBERY, AT THE BIBLE AND SUN, | IN SPC-Y. PRICE 6d BOUND.

In 8's. 48 leaves+6 or 7 insets. Pp. iv+[5]–96. Engvd FP and engvd plates for the 2nd to 6th days [? should be one for 1st day]. D.f.b.

[BM, 10·1×6·2 cm; UCLA.

(3) Another undated edition. Pr f JN. Price 6d. Ms date 1766.

THE | MOSAIC CREATION: | OR, | DIVINE WISDOM DISPLAYED | IN THE | WORKS OF THE FIRST SIX DAYS. | [4 lines] | IN PROSE AND VERSE, | WITH | OCCASIONAL REMARKS. | [p.rule] | EMBELLISHED WITH VARIETY OF COPPER-PLATES, | NEATLY ENGRAVED. | [p.rule] | [4 lines quote] | [p.rule] | LONDON: PR F J. NEWBERY, AT THE BIBLE AND SUN | IN SPC-Y. PRICE 6d.

In 8's. 48 leaves. Pp. iv+85[96]. Engvd FP and 6 engvd plates in text. List of bks pubd a s b JN on last 11 pages. D.f.b. (Communicated.)

[McKell, 10·2×6·4 cm.

(3A) Listed as pubd by JN, price 6d, in *Newtonian System*, 1761 and 1766, and *New Testament...abridged and harmonized*, 1764, no. J31.

(3B) A copy in the Ball Colln has ms date 1769.

(4) For other possible listings see no. J173.

MOTHER BUNCH'S FAIRY TALES. See Aulnoy, Marie C. de la M.

J249. Entry deleted.

J250. MOTHER GOOSE'S MELODY. The literature and bibliographical references are numerous; see in particular: Welsh 272; W. H. Whitmore, *The original Mother Goose's Melody...*, Boston, 1892, pp. 5ff; *CBEL*, II, 251, 554; Opie, *Oxford Dict. of Nursery Rhymes*, pp. 33ff; Muir, *English Children's Books*, p. 76; Darton, pp. 103–5; *Pierpont Morgan Cat.* item 154; J. Barchilon and H. Pettit, *The authentic Mother Goose*, Denver, USA, 1960; Welch, Introduction, p. 146. The suggested date of publicn – 1765 or 1766 – mentioned, but not advocated, by the Opies is most unlikely: JN was most assiduous and methodical in his advertising practices, and I know of no mention of this work prior to no. (1) below.

(1) An edition adv. *LC* 30.12.80–2.1.81, p. 5, as s b TC. Price 3d. Welsh records its entry at Stationers' Hall on 28.12.80.

(2) An edition of 1791. Pr f Francis Power & Co. Price 3d. Facsimile of this ed., with Introduction by Col. F. W. Prideaux, A. H. Bullen, 1904.

MOTHER GOOSE'S | MELODY: | OR, | SONNETS FOR THE CRADLE. | IN TWO PARTS. | [10 lines] | [p.s.rule] | LONDON: | PR F FRANCIS POWER, (GRANDSON TO | THE LATE MR. J. NEWBERY,) AND CO. | NO. 65. SPCY, 1791. | [PRICE THREE PENCE.]

In 8's. 48 leaves. Pp. x+11–92[95].

Wct FP and 51 small wcts in text. Pp. 92. List of bks s b Power on last 3 pages. (Communicated.)

⌐Ball.

MOTHER GOOSE'S TALES. See Perrault, Chas, HISTORY OR TALES OF PAST TIMES.

J250A. MOTHER SHIPTON, 1800. Pr a pubd b EN et al. Price *6d*, or *1s* coloured.

Imprint: PR & PUBLISHED SEPT^R 10th 1800. | BY I. STRUTT, LITTLE QUEEN STREET, LINCOLN'S FIELDS, | E. BURNS, N^O 54, TOTTENHAM COURT ROAD AND | E. NEWBERY, CORNER OF SPCY, | LONDON. | [p.s.rule] | PRICE SIX PENCE. COLOURED 1 SHILLING.

A Harlequinade of 4 folding leaves, each with flap-overs at head and tail. Engvd text and 8 engvd illustrations, hand coloured. Measures 18·2×7·8 cm when folded. The engvg on the lower flap of the 1st leaf is sgd 'Tringham Jun invent et sculpt', as also is the Harlequinade *Sister Witches*, J334A.

⌐Osborne*.

J251. MOTHER'S GIFT, THE. Welsh 272.

(1) First edition, 1769. Pr f C & N. Price *4d*.

THE | MOTHER'S GIFT: | OR, A | PRESENT | FOR ALL LITTLE | CHILDREN | WHO ARE GOOD. | [p.rule] | EMBELLISHED WITH CUTS. | [d.p.rule] | LONDON: | PR F CARNAN AND NEWBERY, AT | NO. 65, IN SPC-Y, 1769. | [PRICE FOUR-PENCE.]

In 8's. 40 leaves. Pp. iv+5–71[80]. 14 wcts, most of them by the hand that did the *Goody Two-Shoes* cuts. List of bks pr f N & C on pp. [72–80]. D.f.b.

⌐Bodley, 9·3×6·2 cm; NorBM.

(2) Second edition, 1770. Pr f C & N. Price *4d*.

Title and *imprint*, with THE SECOND EDITION and date 1770, and specification approx. as for no. (1). D.f.b.

⌐BM, 9·3×6·2 cm; V&A(GL).

(2A) An edition of 1773, described as THE SECOND PART. Pr f C & N. Price *4d*.

THE | MOTHER'S GIFT: | OR, A | PRESENT | FOR ALL LITTLE | CHILDREN | WHO ARE GOOD. | [p.rule] | EMBELLISHED WITH CUTS. | [p.rule] | THE SECOND PART. | [p.rule] | LONDON: | PR F CARNAN AND NEWBERY, AT | NO. 65, IN SPC-Y. 1773. [PRICE FOUR-PENCE.]

In 8's. 40 leaves. Pp. iv+5–68[80]. Wct FP and 20 wcts in text, many as for no. (1). List of bks pr f C & N on pp. [69–80]. D.f.b.

⌐V&A(GL), 9·2×6·3 cm.

(3) An edition of 1775, described as THE THIRD PART. Pr f C & N. Price *4d*.

Title and *imprint* approx. as for no. (2A) with THE THIRD PART and date 1775.

In 8's. 34 leaves. Pp. iv+64. Wct FP and 9 wcts in text. D.f.b.

[Bodley, 9·6×6·4 cm; V&A.

(4) An edition of 1783. Pr f TC. 2 vols. Price 3*d* each. S&W Cat.

THE | MOTHER'S GIFT: | OR, A | PRESENT | FOR ALL | LITTLE CHILDREN, | WHO WISH TO BE GOOD. | [p.rule] | IN TWO VOLUMES. | [p.rule] | VOL. I. [II.] | [p.rule] | LONDON: | PR F T. CARNAN, IN SP | CY. MDCCLXXXIII. | [PRICE THREEPENCE.] ([PRICE THREE-PENCE] in Vol. II.)

Vol. I. A single gathering of 48 leaves, first and last pastedowns. Pp. 95. Wct FP and 27 wcts in text.

Vol. II. A single gathering as in vol. I. Pp. 85[95]. Wct FP and wcts in text. List of bks pr f TC on last 10 pages. The FP is the same as in vol. I.

D.f.b. Also buff paper wrappers with illustrative designs in red impress, that on the lower cover being also the FP.

[Bell, 10·1×6·3 cm; UCLA (vol. II, imperf.); NNC-T (Darton Coll. vol. I).

(5) Listed in *Newtonian System*, 1787, as pr f TC. Price 3*d*. Apparently a 1 vol. ed.

MOTHER'S GRAMMAR, THE. See Fenn, Lady E.

MOUNTAIN PIPER, THE. See Berquin, Arnaud.

MRS LOVECHILD'S GOLDEN PRESENT. See Fenn, Lady E.

J252. Entry deleted.

J253. MUSEUM FOR YOUNG GENTLEMEN AND LADIES, A. Adv. *GEP* 26.7.50. Welsh 273–5; *CBEL*, II, 561.

(1) An undated edition. Pr f JN et al. Price 1*s*. NBL 250.

A MUSEUM | FOR | YOUNG GENTLEMEN AND LADIES: | OR, A | PRIVATE TUTOR FOR LITTLE MASTERS AND MISSES. | CONTAINING A VARIETY OF USEFUL SUBJECTS, AND IN PARTICULAR, | [2 parallel columns of 19 lines each] | INTERSPERSED WITH LETTERS, TALES, AND FABLES FOR | AMUSEMENT AND INSTRUCTION, AND ILLUSTRATED WITH CUTTS. | (BEING A SECOND VOLUME TO THE PRETTY BOOK FOR CHILDREN.) | LONDON: | PR F J. HODGES, ON THE BRIDGE; J. NEWBERY, IN | SP-CY; AND B. COLLINS, IN SALISBURY. | [PRICE ONE SHILLING, NEATLY BOUND.]

In 8's. 116 leaves. Pp. vi+226. 2 diagrams and *ca.* 23 wcts. The *Pretty Book for Children* referred to is no. J307, which is described as 'vol. 1'.

[DES; McKell; UCLA (imperf.); Osborne*.

(1A) Another undated edition. Pr f JN et al. Price 1*s*.

Title as for no. (1). *Imprint:* PR F J. HODGES, ON THE BRIDGE; J. NEWBERY, IN | SPCY; R. BALDWIN, IN PATER- | NOSTER-ROW; AND B. COLLINS, IN SALISBURY. | [PRICE ONE SHILLING, NEATLY BOUND.]

Pp. vi+204. Wcts. (Communicated.)

A
MUSEUM.
FOR
Young Gentlemen and Ladies:
OR,
A Private TUTOR
For Little Masters and Misses.
CONTAINING.
A Variety of useful Subjects, and in particular,

I. Directions for Reading with Elegance and Propriety.

II. The antient and present State of Great-Britain; with a compendious History of England.

III. An Account of the Solar System.

IV. Historical and Geographical Description of the several Countries in the World; with the Manners, Customs, and Habits of the People.

V. An Account of the Arts and Sciences.

VI. Rules for Behaviour.

VII. Advice to young Persons on their entering up-

on the World; with short Rules of Religion and Morality.

VIII. Tables of Weights and Measures.

IX. Explanation of Abbreviations used in Words and Dates.

X. The seven Wonders of the World.

XI. Prospect and Description of the burning Mountain.

XII. Dying Words and Behaviour of Great Men, when just quitting the Stage of Life; with many other useful Particulars, all in a plain familiar Way for Youth of both Sexes.

WITH
Letters, Tales, and Fables, for Amusement and Instruction; illustrated with Cuts.

The FOURTH EDITION.

LONDON:
Printed for J. Newbery, in St. Paul's Church-Yard; and B. Collins, in Salisbury. 1763. [Price 1s.]

Fig. 19. Title-page of J253(5).

[Bishop Lonsdale, 11·5 × 9·0 cm.

(2) A 'new edition' adv. in *PA* for 1.1.53 as t.d.i.p. Price 1s. Pr f JN, J. Hodges and B. Collins.

(3) Second edition, 1758. Pr f JN and B. Collins. Price 1s.
    In 6's. Pp. vi+206[+ ?]. Wcts. Details taken from the Renier copy.
    [Renier (imperf.); Welch.

(4) Third edition, 1760. JN.
    [Ball.

(5) See Fig. 19. *CBEL*, II, 222.
    In 6's. 108 leaves. Pp. vi+209[210]. 27 wcts and diagrams. Adverts. of bks pr f Baldwin and Collins on A1ᵛ and S6ᵛ. D.f.b.
    [BM; Roscoe, 12·8 × 8·3 cm; NorBM; NNC-T (Darton Coll.); Oppenheimer; Sotheby, 16.3.70, lot 36.

(6) Fifth edition not traced.

(7) Sixth edition, 1770. Pr f N & C et al. Price 1s.

Title approx. as for no. (5), with THE SIXTH EDITION. *Imprint:* PR F
MESSRS. NEWBERY AND CARNAN, AT THE BIBLE AND SUN, NO. 65, IN
SPC-Y; AND B. COLLINS, IN SALISBURY, 1770. [PRICE 1*s*.]

Pp. vi+222. *Ca.* 28 wcts and diagrams. D.f.b. (Communicated.)

[Opie; Lapides; R. C. Pearson, Cat. 21 [1958] item 309.

(8) Seventh edition, 1773. Pr f C & N. Price 1*s*.

Title and *imprint* approx. as for no. (7), with THE SEVENTH EDITION and
date 1773.

In 6's. 114 leaves. Pp. vi+222. 27 wcts etc as in no. (5). D.f.b.

[BM, 12·6×8·6 cm; Ball.

(9) Eighth edition, 1776. Pr f Newbury (*sic*) & Carnan. Price 1*s*.

Title and *imprint* approx. as for no. (7), with THE EIGHTH EDITION,
NEWBURY in place of NEWBERY, and date 1776.

In 6's. 96 leaves. Pp. vi+186. 27 wcts etc as before. D.f.b.

[BM, 12·4×8·3 cm; V&A(GL); Bell; Renier; Welch; ICU-J.

(10) An edition of 1777. See *N&Q* (1886), VIII, I, p. 503. A copy in D.f.b. was in
the possession of Col. W. F. Prideaux, the writer of the article.

(11) Ninth edition, 1778. Pr f N & C, and B. Collins. Price 1*s*. Welsh 273–4.

Title approx. as for no. (5), with THE NINTH EDITION, except that there are
only 15 lines in each of the 2 columns of 'Subjects' in place of 20 as in earlier edd.
Imprint: PR F MESSRS NEWBERY AND CARNAN, AT THE BIBLE | AND SUN,
NO. 65, IN SPC-Y; AND | B. COLLINS, IN SALISBURY. 1778. [PRICE 1*s*.]

In 6's. 96 leaves. Pp. vi+186. Wcts. Buff or white bds, impressed with pictorial
designs in black.

[Ball; MH; Grant; Sotheby, 16.3.70, lot 37, 13·0×8·3 cm; Bondy, Cat. 79
[1970] item 203.

(12) Tenth edition, 1782. Pr f TC et al. Price 1*s*.

Title approx. as for no. (11), with THE TENTH EDITION. *Imprint:* PR F T.
CARNAN, AT THE BIBLE AND SUN, NO. 65, | IN SPC-Y; AND B. C. COLLINS,
IN | SALISBURY. 1782. [PRICE 1*s*.]

In 6's. 96 leaves. Pp. vi+186. 28 wcts. (Communicated.)

[MPL; UCLA.

(13) Eleventh edition, 1784. Pr f TC et al. Price 1*s*.

Title and *imprint* approx. as for no. (12), with THE ELEVENTH EDITION and
date 1784.

In 6's. 97 leaves, the last a blank. Pp. iv (error for vi)+186. 25 wcts and 2
diagrams. Drab bds, with a large wct in maroon within an ornam. frame on
each cover (see Plate 11). CUL copy examined.

[BM (very imperf.), *ca.* 14·1×8·8 cm in uncut state; CUL; MiDW.

(14) Another eleventh edition, n.d. (? a variant issue). TC.

[Ball.

(15) Twelfth edition, 1790. Pr f Power & Co and B. C. Collins. Price 1*s*. Gum
2767; Rothschild 610.

Title approx. as for no. (12), with THE TWELFTH EDITION. *Imprint:* PR F

F. POWER AND CO. (SUCCESSORS TO THE LATE T. CARNAN) NO. 65, IN SPC-Y; AND B. C. COLLINS, IN SALISBURY. 1790. (PRICE 1s.)

12° in 6's. 96 leaves. 28 wcts and diagrams. D.f.b. (Communicated.)

[Opie; Welch; Sotheby, 5.2.1945 (the Bussell sale), lot 183; Marchmont Bookshop, Cat. 23 [1966] item 78; G. Sexton (Books) Brighton, Cat. 55 (supplement) item 880.

(16) Another twelfth edition, 1793 (? a variant issue). F. Power.

[Ball.

(17) Thirteenth edition, n.d. S. Crowder and B. C. Collins only.

[V&A(GL); HU; McKell.

(18) Fourteenth edition not traced.

(19) Fifteenth edition, n.d. (1799–1800). Pr f Darton & Harvey, Crosby & Letterman, EN and B. C. Collins.

In 6's. 96 leaves. Pp. vi+186. 28 wcts. D.f.b.

[NoU; BCE, approx. 13·1×8·0 cm (imperf.); Ries; Welch; MWA (lacks titleleaf); Elkin Mathews, Cat. 163 [1965] item 279.

MUSEUM FOR YOUTH. Listed in *Goody Two-Shoes*, 1766 and 1767. Presumably = no. J253.

J253A. NATURAL HISTORY OF BEASTS. Listed in *Joseph Andrews*, 1799, as pr f EN, price 4s, 'with copper plates, 2 vols'. Probably an ed. or issue of extracts from Ward's *Modern System of Nat. Hist.*

J253B. NATURAL HISTORY OF BIRDS. Listed in *Joseph Andrews*, 1799, as pr f EN, price 4s, 'with copper plates, 2 vols'. Probably an ed. or issue of extracts from Ward's *Modern System of Nat. Hist.* (J376).

NATURAL HISTORY OF BEASTS ⎫
NATURAL HISTORY OF BIRDS ⎬ See JONES, Stephen
NATURAL HISTORY OF FISHES ⎭ (attributed to).

NATURAL HISTORY OF BIRDS, FISHES, QUADRUPEDS, INSECTS, WATERS, VEGETABLES. See Brookes, Richard, *New and accurate System...*

NATURAL HISTORY OF BIRDS ⎫ See
NATURAL HISTORY OF FOUR-FOOTED ⎬ 'TELLTRUTH,
  BEASTS ⎭ Mr'.

NATURAL HISTORY OF BIRDS ⎫
NATURAL HISTORY OF FISHES ⎬ See WARD, Samuel.
NATURAL HISTORY OF FOUR-FOOTED ⎪
  BEASTS ⎭

J254. NEW AND NOBLE HISTORY OF ENGLAND. Listed as pr f or to be had of JN in the period 1763–6. Price 6*d*. Listed as s b FN(S) in J309(4), n.d. Not identified; perhaps Goldsmith's *History of England in a Series of Letters from a Nobleman.* The 1st ed. of that work was dated 1764.

NEW BOOK FOR THE IMPROVEMENT OF YOUNG
GENTLEMEN = FILIAL DUTY, J134.

J254A. NEW BOOK OF EMBLEMS, A, 1800. Pr and pubd by EN et al. Price 6*d*, coloured 1*s*.

A NEW BOOK OF | EMBLEMS | OF THE DIFFERENT DIVERSIONS FROM | INFANCY TO MANHOOD. | THE CRADLED INFANT FIRST YOU VIEW | IN INOFENSIVE STATE | HE WITH THE RATTLE IS CONTENT | NOR THINKS OF FUTURE FATE, | TURN UP | [engvg: the infant in its cradle, with rattle] | TURN DOWN | MORAL | GENTLY OUR INFANT MOVEMENTS FLOW | UNKNOWN TO CARE, UNKNOWN TO WOE. | PRINTED & PUBLISH'D | JUNE 27th 1800, BY I. STRUTT, LITTLE QUEEN STREET, LINCOLN'S INN FIELDS; | E. BURNS, NO 54, TOTTENHAM COURT ROAD, & | E. NEWBERY, CORNER OF SPCY, LONDON. | PRICE 6*d*. COLOUR'D 1*s*.

A Harlequinade. Four pages, each with a tipped-on flap at head and foot, making 8 pages of text, each with an engvg illustrating the text of that page. All text engvd. The UCLA copy has no wrappers, is uncoloured; Mr Wilbur J. Smith, of UCLA, is uncertain if it is complete, as 'there is no sign of finality in the last verse and the words "The End" do not appear'. (Details from the photocopy.)

⌈UCLA; Roscoe (photocopy of UCLA copy).

J255. NEW CHILDREN'S FRIEND, THE. Welsh 183; *CBEL*, II, 566.
(1) An edition of 1797. Pr f EN et al. Price 1*s* 6*d*.

THE | NEW CHILDREN'S FRIEND: | OR, | PLEASING INCITEMENTS | TO | WISDOM AND VIRTUE; | CONVEYED | THROUGH THE MEDIUM | OF | ANECDOTE, TALE, AND ADVENTURE. | [3 lines] | [d.p.rule] | TRANSLATED CHIEFLY FROM THE GERMAN. | [d.p.rule] | LONDON: | PR F VERNOR AND HOOD, IN THE | POULTRY; AND E. NEWBERY, AT THE CORNER OF SPC-Y. | [p.rule] | 1797.

In 6's. 90 leaves+engvd FP sgd 'Kirk del', 'Scott sc'. Pp. viii+171.
⌈BM, 13·7×8·1 cm.
(2) Second edition, 1798, was pr f Vernor & Hood, and Darton & Harvey.
⌈Renier; NNC-Pl; UCLA.

J256. NEW FRENCH PRIMER, A. Welsh 295; Muir, p. 75, dates 1750. Apparently = *Alphabet Royal*, no. J9. Welsh's record is quite obscure.

J257. NEW HISTORY OF ENGLAND, A, BY AN ENGLISHMAN, 1757. Pr f JN et al. 4 vols, price 12s. Welsh 212. The bk was still being listed as pr f a s b N & C in 1768. There is no record of a 2nd ed.

A NEW | HISTORY | OF | ENGLAND, | FROM THE TIME OF ITS | FIRST INVASION BY THE ROMANS, | FIFTY-FOUR YEARS BEFORE THE BIRTH OF CHRIST, | TO THE PRESENT TIME. | [7 lines] | BY AN ENGLISHMAN. | IN FOUR VOLUMES. | VOL. I. [&c] | LONDON: | PR F J. NEWBERY, IN SPC-Y; | AND W. OWEN, AT TEMPLE-BAR. | MDCCLVII.

Vol. I. 12mo. 207 leaves+3 insets. Pp. 401[408]. Engvd FP sgd 'Ant. Walker del et sculp'; 2 folding engvd maps. A number of ornam. wct tailpieces. List of bks pr f a s b JN on T2$^{r, v}$ and T3^r; list of bks pr f Owen on last 3 pages.

Vol. II. 12mo. 211 leaves+engvd FP sgd as in vol. I. Pp. 420. A few ornam. wct tailpieces.

Vol. III. 12mo. 193 leaves+FP as before. Pp. 382[384]. List of bks pr f Owen on R12$^{r, v}$.

Vol. IV. 12mo. 260 leaves+FP as before. Pp. 495[514]. Last leaf a blank. A copy in the Opie Coll. has folding plates in this volume.

[BM, 16·5×9·6 cm; Opie.

NEW HISTORY OF ENGLAND, BY QUESTION AND ANSWER. See Lockman, John.

NEW HISTORY OF ENGLAND, FROM THE EARLIEST PERIOD...ON A PLAN RECOMMENDED BY THE EARL OF CHESTERFIELD. See 'Cooper, Rev. Samuel'.

J258. NEW HISTORY OF ENGLAND, A, FROM THE INVASION BY [OF] JULIUS CAESAR...
(1A) An edition of 1759. Pr f JN. Price 6d bd and gilt.

A NEW | HISTORY | OF | ENGLAND, | FROM | THE INVASION BY JULIUS CAESAR | TO THE PRESENT TIME. | ADORNED WITH CUTS OF ALL THE KINGS | AND QUEENS WHO HAVE REIGNED SINCE | THE NORMAN CONQUEST. | [p.rule] | [4 lines quote] | [d.p.rule] | LONDON: | PR F J. NEWBERY, AT THE BIBLE | AND SUN IN SPC-Y. | [p.rule] | MDCCLIX. | [PRICE SIX-PENCE BOUND AND GILT.]

In 8's. 96 leaves. Pp. [iv]+188. Wcts. D.f.b.

[Welch, 10·5 cm; Sotheby, 16.3.70, lot 166, 10·1×6·4 cm.
(1B) See Fig. 20. Welsh 212.

Title and *imprint* approx. as for no. (1A), with INVASION OF JULIUS CAESAR in place of INVASION BY JULIUS CAESAR, and date MDCCLXI.

In 8's. 96 leaves+engvd FP. Pp. 188. 31 whole-length wct figures of sovereigns, the majority sgd JB and used also in *Compendious History of England*, 1758. D.f.b.

[BM, 9·6×6·2 cm; Opie; Sotheby, 5.2.68, lot 29.
(2) An edition of 1763. Pr f JN. Price 6d.

A NEW
HISTORY
OF
ENGLAND;
FROM
The Invaſion of JULIUS CÆSAR
to the preſent TIME.

Adorned with CUTS of all the KINGS
and QUEENS who have reigned ſince
the NORMAN Conqueſt.

---

*The Memory of Things paſt ought not to be ex-
tinguiſhed by Length of Time, nor great and
admirable Actions remain deſtitute of Glory.*
HERODOTUS.

LONDON:
Printed for J. NEWBERY, at the *Bible and
Sun* in St. *Paul's Church-yard.*
MDCCLXI.
[Price Six-pence Bound and Gilt.]

Fig. 20. Title-page of J258(1B).

Title and *imprint* (with date MDCCLXIII) and specification approx. as for no. (1B). Engvd FP as for no. (1B) but without letters. 32 wcts in text.

[BM, 9·8×6·2 cm; NoU; UCLA; Ball.

(3) An edition of [?1765]. Pr f JN.

[BM, 9504.aa.14 (missing).

(4) An edition of 1766. Pr f JN. Price 6*d*.

Title and *imprint* approx. as for no. (1B) with date MDCCLXVI.

In 8's. 96 leaves+engvd FP (with letters, reworked). Pp. 188. *ca.* 32 wcts in text.

[BM, 10·0×6·3 cm (imperf.); Preston; Gardner (imperf.).

(5) An edition of 1768. Pr f FN, Jun. & Co (= FN(S)). Price 6*d*.

Title approx. as for no. (1B). *Imprint:* PR F F. NEWBERY, JUN. AND CO. AT THE | BIBLE AND SUN, NO. 65, IN SPC- | Y. 1768. [PRICE SIX-PENCE.]

In 8's. 96 leaves+engvd FP. Pp. 188. *ca.* 32 wcts in text. D.f.b.

[BM (imperf.), 10·0×6·4 cm; Opie; Ball.

(6) An edition of 1770. Pr f C & N. NBL 136; Pressler, p. 1.

Title approx. as for no. (1B). *Imprint:* PR F CARNAN AND NEWBERY, AT THE BIBLE AND SUN, NO. 65, IN SPCY, 1770.

Pp. 3, 188. FP. Illustrations.

[ICU-J.

(7) An edition of 1772. Pr f C & N. Welsh 83; Pressler, p. 2.

The *title* reads TO THE END OF GEORGE II in place of TO THE PRESENT TIME. *Imprint* approx. as for no. (8), with date 1772.

In 8's. 96 leaves. Pp. 188. ?FP. Wcts. D.f.b.

⌈Bell, 9·9×6·4 cm; Osborne*; ICU-J; Elkin Mathews, Cat. 163 [1965] item 201.

(8) An edition of 1777. Pr f C & N. Price 6d.

Title approx. as for no. (7). *Imprint:* PR F T. CARNAN AND F. NEWBERY, JUNIOR, | AT NO. 65, IN SPCY, (BUT NOT | FOR F. NEWBERY, AT THE CORNER OF LUDGATE STREET, | WHO HAS NO SHARE IN THE LATE MR. JOHN NEWBERY'S | BOOKS FOR CHILDREN.) PRICE SIXPENCE. | MDCCLXXVII.

32mo in 8's. 96 leaves. Pp. 188. Diatribe against FN(N) and his 'paltry compilations' on vso of title-leaf. 32 full-length wct figures of sovereigns. Buff or white bds with pictorial designs in black on both covers.

⌈Bodley, 9·6×6·4 cm; Renier.

(9) An edition of 1781. Pr f TC.

⌈Ball.

(10) An edition of 1785. Pr f TC. Price 6d.

Title approx. as for no. (7). *Imprint:* PR F T. CARNAN, IN SPCY. | (PRICE SIXPENCE.) | MDCCLXXXV.

Pp. 188. Wcts. Illustrated paper over bds, pr in red. (Communicated.)

⌈Welch, 10·5 cm; MWA; CtNSCSC.

(11) An edition of 1790. Pr f Power & Co. Price 6d. Welsh 212.

The *title* now reads FROM THE | INVASION OF JULIUS CAESAR | TO THE | BEGINNING OF THE YEAR MDCCXC. *Imprint:* PR F F. POWER (GRANDSON TO THE LATE | MR. J. NEWBERY) AND CO. NO. 65, IN S | PCY. | (PRICE SIXPENCE.) | MDCCXC.

Pp. 126. 32 wcts of sovereigns. D.f.b. (Communicated.)

⌈UCLA.

(12) In 1797 Darton and Harvey issued an ed. bringing the *History* down to 1794.

J259. NEW HISTORY OF FRANCE. Pr f EN. Price 1s 6d. Listed in J170(1), 1789 and J391(1), 1794. Probably an ed. or edd. of Cooper's *History of France, from the earliest Period* (J83).

J260. NEW HISTORY OF GREECE, BY QUESTION AND ANSWER. Whether the following refer to later edd. of the *History of Greece, by way of Question and Answer*, no. J165B, cannot be determined on present evidence; there is no accord between the dates.

(1) An edition, price 2s 6d, adv. *LC* 29–31.12.68, as pr f H. Woodfall, J. Rivington, Newbery and Carnan, R. Baldwin, W. Johnston, W. Strahan, B. Law, T. Caslon, Hawes & Co, G. Kearsly, R. Horsfield, S. Crowder, S. Bladon, and Robinson and Roberts.

(2) Second edition, price 2s 6d, adv. *LC* 10–12.9.72, p. 251, as pr f J. Rivington, W. Johnston, Hawes, Clarke and Collins, R. Horsfield, T. Caslon, Carnan and Newbery, W. Nicoll, B. Law, S. Bladon, G. Robinson, and R. Baldwin.

J261. NEW HISTORY OF THE GRECIAN STATES, A. Weedon 68. Richard Johnson's Day-book records: *1785 Nov. Compiling The History of the Grecian States. 4 Sheets 18ᵐ for Mʳˢ Newbery——£8. 8s.*

(1) First edition, 1786. Pr f EN. Price 1s 6d. Welsh 194.

A NEW | HISTORY | OF THE | GRECIAN STATES, | FROM | THEIR EARLIEST PERIOD TO THEIR EXTINCTION | BY THE OTTOMANS. | [9 lines] | [p.s.rule] | [2 lines] | [p.s.rule] | DESIGNED FOR THE USE OF | YOUNG LADIES AND GENTLEMEN. | [d.p.rule] | LONDON: | PR F E. NEWBERY, THE CORNER OF S | PC-Y. | MDCCLXXXVI.

In 6's. 72 leaves+6 insets. Pp. 132[136]. Engvd FP and 5 engvd leaves in the text. Marbled bds, green vell. spine with label.

[BM, 13·4×8·3 cm; Weedon; Opie; Quayle; Grant.

(2) An edition listed in Wynne's *Tales for Youth*, 1794, as pr f EN, price 1s 6d.

(3) An edition of 1795. Pr f EN. Price 1s 6d.

Title and *imprint* approx. as for no. (1) with date MDCCXCV.

In 6's. 72 leaves+6 insets. Pp. 132[136]. Engvd FP and 5 other engvd leaves. Marbled bds, green vell. spine.

[Roscoe, 13·6×8·5 cm; LEI; Welch; Shiers; Ries.

J262. Entry deleted.

NEW POCKET-BOOK FOR YOUNG GENTLEMEN... See Buchanan, Jas.

NEW RIDDLE BOOK. See 'John-the-Giant-Killer'.

NEW ROBINSON CRUSOE. See Campe, J. H.

NEW ROMAN HISTORY, BY QUESTION AND ANSWER. See Lockman, John.

J263. NEW ROMAN HISTORY, A, FROM THE FOUNDATION OF ROME TO THE END OF THE COMMON-WEALTH. Weedon 71. Richard Johnson's Day-book records: *1770 July 26. Delivered to Mʳ F. Newbery, Roman History.——Value Eight Guineas.*

(1) First edition, 1770. Pr f FN(N). Price 1s 6d.

A NEW | ROMAN HISTORY, | FROM THE | FOUNDATION OF ROME | TO THE END OF THE | COMMON-WEALTH. | [p.rule] | EMBELLISHED WITH COPPER-PLATE CUTS. | [p.rule] | DESIGNED FOR THE USE OF | YOUNG LADIES AND GENTLEMEN. | [p.rule] | [device] | [d.p.rule] | LONDON: | PR F F. NEWBERY, AT NO. 20, THE | CORNER OF SPC-Y. | MDCCLXX.

In 6's. 72 leaves+5 insets. Pp. iv, ii+136. Engvd FP and 4 other engvd leaves. Blue bds, green vell. spine with label.

[BM, 13·5×8·3 cm; CUL; V&A(GL); Osborne, Cat. p. 167; UCLA; ICU-J.

(2) An edition of 1784. Pr f EN. Price 1s 6d. NBL 137.

Title approx. as for no. (1). *Imprint:* PR F E. NEWBERY, THE CORNER OF | SPC-Y. | MDCCLXXXIV.

In 6's. 72 leaves+6 insets. Pp. vi+136. Engvd FP and 5 other engvd leaves. Marbled bds, green vell. spine with label.

⌈Weedon, 13·6×8·0 cm; Opie; Quayle; Welch; UCLA.

(3) An edition of 1793. Pr f EN.

Title approx. as for no. (1). *Imprint* approx. as for no. (2), with date 1793.

Pp. iv[vi]+136. Engvd FP and 4 other engvd leaves. Marbled bds, green vell. spine with label. (Communicated.)

⌈Opie; CLU.

(4) An edition of 1800. Pr f EN. Price 1s 6d. Welsh 302.

Title approx. as for no. (1). *Imprint:* PR F E. NEWBERY, | THE CORNER OF SPC-Y; | BY TEGG AND DEWICK, | WESTMORELAND-BUILDINGS, | ALDERSGATE-STREET. | [printer's ornament] | 1800.

In 6's. 72 leaves+6 insets. Pp. vi[viii]+136. Engvd FP and 5 other engvd leaves. Marbled bds, green vell. spine.

⌈BM, 13·7×8·5 cm; UCLA; DLC; KU.

J263A. NEW SPELLING DICTIONARY OF THE ENGLISH LANGUAGE, A. See Weedon 74.

(1) An undated edition, probably not later than 1780. Pr f FN(?N). Price 1s. Welsh 200. Alston, IV, 576.

A NEW | SPELLING DICTIONARY | OF THE | ENGLISH LANGUAGE, | ON A | CONCISE, BUT COMPREHENSIVE PLAN, | FOR THE | INSTRUCTION OF YOUTH OF BOTH SEXES. | AND TO WHICH IS PREFIXED, | A SHORT ENGLISH GRAMMAR, | [4 lines] | IN WHICH | EVERY WORD IS ACCENTED, TO RENDER THE PRO- | NUNCIATION PERFECTLY EASY. | [p.rule] | LONDON: | PR F F. NEWBERY, SP | C-Y. | [PRICE ONE SHILLING BOUND.]

In 8's. 168 leaves. Pp. 32, 7. The 17th to 165th leaves unnumbered.

⌈BM, 9·8×6·0 cm.

(2) Perhaps listed as 'A new Spelling Dictionary', pr f EN in *Prince Lee Boo*, 1789, *Anecdotes of Mary*, 1795 and *Joseph Andrews*, 1799. Price 1s. But these adverts. may refer to no. J265.

NEW TALES OF THE CASTLE. See Pilkington, M. (H.).

NEW TESTAMENT. See under BIBLE, J31ff.

J264. NEWBERY'S FAMILIAR LETTER WRITER. Weedon 73.

Richard Johnson's Day-book records: *1787. M*^r^ *Badcock——To compiling Newbery's Letter Writer——£10. 10s.*

(1) An edition of 1788. Pr f EN. Price 1s 6d bd in red. Also listed at 2s. Welsh 254.

NEWBERY'S | FAMILIAR LETTER WRITER: | CONTAINING A VARIETY

OF | USEFUL LETTERS, | CALCULATED FOR THE | MOST COMMON OCCUR-
RENCES, | AND ADAPTED TO THE | CAPACITIES OF YOUNG PEOPLE, | [3 lines]
| [p.s.rule] | LONDON: | PR F E. NEWBERY, THE CORNER OF | SPC-Y, | 1788.
  18mo. 108 leaves+engvd FP. Pp. iv[xii]+204.
  [Bodley (lacks FP), 13·4×8·4 cm; Oup; BCE.
(2) A 'new edition', 1801. Pr f EN et al. Price 1s 6d.
  Title approx. as for no. (1). *Imprint:* PR F E. NEWBERY, THE CORNER OF
SPC | Y; AND CROSBY AND LETTERMAN, STATIONERS COURT, | PATER-
NOSTER ROW. | [PRICE 1s 6d BOUND.] | [p.s.rule]
  18mo. 108 leaves. ? a FP. Pp. iv[xii]+204. Bk-list on a1ᵛ.
  [BM, 13·9×8·5 cm.

NEWBERY'S NEW HISTORY OF ENGLAND. See J258.

J265. NEWBERY'S NEW SPELLING DICTIONARY OF THE
ENGLISH LANGUAGE. Welsh 200; Weedon 74. Richard Johnson's Day-
book records: *1787. Mʳ Badcock——To compiling Newbery's Spelling Dictʸ——
£10. 10s.* Welsh refers to an ed. of 1786 by TC; clearly this is the *Spelling Dictionary* of that date (J268(14)), not the *New Spelling Dictionary*.
(1) First edition, 1788. Pr f EN. Price 1s. Alston, IV, 578.
  NEWBERY'S | NEW SPELLING DICTIONARY | OF THE | ENGLISH
LANGUAGE. | WHEREIN | ALL THE WORDS ARE PROPERLY ACCENTED, |
SHEWING | HOW TO WRITE AND PRONOUNCE THEM WITH | EASE AND
PROPRIETY. | [4 lines] | [d.p.rule] | LONDON: | PR F E. NEWBERY, THE
CORNER OF S | PC-Y. | 1788.
  In 8's. 156 leaves. Pp. vi+[7]-24. B–U4 unnumbered.
  [BM, 10·3×6·4 cm; UCLA; ICU-J; Muirhead, Cat. 23 [1959] item 136.
(2) A 'new edition', 1792. Pr f EN. Price 1s. Johnson's Day-book records: *1792.
Mʳ Badcock——To reading the Spelling Dictionary——£1. 11s. 6d.*
  Title and *imprint* approx. as for no. (1) with date 1792.
  In 8's. 160 leaves. Pp. 24; no numbering after b4ᵛ.
  [BM, 9·9×6·8 cm.

J266. NEWBERY, John (attributed to). LETTERS ON THE MOST
COMMON, AS WELL AS IMPORTANT, OCCASIONS IN LIFE.
The attribution is, it seems, based on the Dedication, 'To the Parents, Guardians
and Governesses in Great Britain' by 'their most obedient servant, John Newbery'.
A brisk run of seven or more edd. in the period 1756–67, then, apparently, nothing
for some 19 years, is remarkable. See also J268. For an apparent imitation by
FN(N) of the title to this work, see J365(2). Welsh 253–4.
(1) First edition, 1756. Pr f JN. Price 1s.
  LETTERS | ON THE MOST COMMON, AS WELL AS IMPORTANT, |
OCCASIONS IN LIFE, | BY | 2 parallel columns, *left* CICERO, [5 names], LD
LANSDOWNE, *right*, TEMPLE, [5 names], ROWE | AND | OTHER WRITERS

OF DISTINGUISHED MERIT; | WITH MANY | ORIGINAL LETTERS AND CARDS, | BY THE EDITOR. | WHO HAS ALSO PREFIX'D, | A DISSERTATION ON THE | EPISTOLARY STYLE; | WITH PROPER DIRECTIONS FOR ADDRESSING | PERSONS OF RANK AND EMINENCE. | FOR THE USE OF YOUNG GENTLEMEN AND | LADIES. | [p.rule] | LONDON: PR F J. NEWBERY, IN | SPC-Y. 1756.

In 8's. 192 leaves. Pp. xxvi[xxxii]+352.

[BM, 10·2×6·4 cm; NNC-T (Darton Coll.).

(1A) An edition of 1757. Pr f JN.

Title and *imprint* approx. as for no. (1), with date 1757. Pp. xxiv+373[374]. The copy in the Osborne Coll. appears to be a revised and perhaps enlarged ed., though not described as 'the second'; it was probably the ed. referred to as the 'small Edition...Price 1s bound in red' in the advert. of the 2nd ed. in *LC* for 21–3.4.57 (see no. (2) below).

[Osborne, Cat. p. 133, 10·0×6·4 cm.

(2) Second edition, n.d. [?1757]. Pr f JN.

LETTERS | ON THE MOST COMMON, AS WELL AS IMPORTANT, | OCCASIONS IN LIFE. | BY | 2 parallel columns, *left*, CICERO, [9 names], Sir WILLIAM TEMPLE, *right*, Sir W. TRUMBULL, [9 names], ROWE | AND | [10 lines as in no. (1)] | [p.rule] | THE SECOND EDITION. | [p.rule] | LONDON: | PR F J. NEWBERY, AT THE BIBLE AND SUN, | IN SPC-Y.

Pp. xii, xiv+[15]–204. (Communicated.) *LC* for 21–3.4.57 advertised the 2nd ed. at 2s bd, also 'a small Edition...Price 1s bd in red'. The UCLA copy would appear to be of the ed. sold at 2s.

[UCLA, 16·6 cm.

(3) Third edition not traced.

(4) Fourth edition, 1758. Pr f JN. A 'small ed. for those who are very young' was issued at 1s; an ed. 'in a new Elzevir letter', bd, at 1s 6d; and an ed. 'in twelves, on a larger letter, bd in gilt' at 2s. *CBEL*, II, 25.

Title and *imprint* approx. as for no. (2) with THE FOURTH EDITION and date 1758.

In 6's. 126 leaves. Pp. xii, xviii+[19]–240. This ed. was still being listed as pr f JN in 1776 (in no. J67).

[BM (probably the 1s ed.), 13·5×8·3 cm; SomCL.

(5) Fifth edition, 1760. Pr f JN. Prices as for no. (4). *CBEL*, II, 25.

Title and *imprint* approx. as for no. (2) with THE FIFTH EDITION and date 1760. 'Occasions' in line 3 is mis-spelt 'Oocasions' and the last names in the right-hand column are ROWE, SEVIGNE.

In 8's. 184 leaves. Pp. v[xiii], xxvi+[27]–352. D.f.b.

[BM, 9·8×6·5 cm; Weedon; Opie; UCLA; Marchmont Bookshop, Cat. 23 [1966] item 98.

(6) Sixth edition, 1764. Pr f JN. Welsh 254.

Title and *imprint* approx. as for no. (2), with THE SIXTH EDITION and date 1764. Last names in right-hand column ROWE, SEVIGNE.

In 8's. 198 leaves, 1st a blank. Pp. xiv+370.

[BCE, 10·0×8·4 cm; Sotheby, 13.3.72, lot 95.

(7) Seventh edition, 1767. Pr f JN. A 'small size for the Pocket' 1*s*, an 18mo 1*s* 6*d*, a 12mo 2*s*.

LETTERS | ON THE MOST COMMON, AS WELL AS IMPORTANT | OCCASIONS IN LIFE. | 2 parallel columns, *left* BY CICERO, [9 names], Sir WILLIAM TEMPLE, *right* Sir W. TRUMBULL, [9 names], ROWE, SEVIGNE, | AND OTHER WRITERS... | [5 lines] | ...RANK AND EMINENCE. | THE SEVENTH EDITION. | [p.rule] | LONDON: | PR F J. NEWBERY, AT THE BIBLE AND SUN, | IN SPC-Y. 1767.

8° or in 8's. 192 leaves. Pp. 370. (Communicated.)

[Renier.

(8) An edition of 1786. Pr f TC. Price 1*s* and 1*s* 6*d*.

Title approx. as for no. (7). *Imprint:* PR F T. CARNAN, IN SP | C-Y. | 1786.

In 8's. 160 leaves. Pp. 303. Half-title. List of bks pr f TC on last page.

[Bodley, 9·9×6·2 cm; CUL; M. G. Atkins, List CHI/11 (1964) item 121.

(9) An edition of 1787. Pr f TC. Price 2*s* bd.

Title approx. as for no. (7) with the words FOR THE USE OF YOUNG GENTLEMEN AND LADIES restored. *Imprint:* PR F T. CARNAN, SPC-Y. | MDCCLXXXVII. | [PRICE TWO SHILLINGS BOUND.]

In 6's. 126 leaves. Pp. xii, xvii+[18]–238[240]. List of bks pr f TC on last 2 pages.

[BM, 13·6×8·4 cm.

J267. NEWBERY, John (attributed to). RENOWNED HISTORY OF GILES GINGERBREAD, THE. The attribution is speculative at best. Algar attributed to Giles Jones. Darton, p. 129, backs JN. Goldsmith and Griffith Jones have been suggested. *CBEL*, 11, 561; see NBL 107; Welsh 225.

(1) An edition of 1761 recorded by Lyon. This seems doubtful, as *LC* for 27–9.12.64 recorded, at p. 619, that 'Mr Newbery intends to publish' this work, along with *The Fairing*, the *Easter Gift*, the *Whitsuntide Gift* and the *Valentine's Gift*, 'on 1st January next'. This sounds like an announcement of quite new books, not new edd.; and of the four others named in the advert. I know of no earlier edd.

(1A) An edition of 1764. Pr f JN. Price 1*d*.

Title and *imprint*, with date 1764, as for no. (3).

In 4's. 16 leaves. Pagination not visible. Wct FP 'Old Gaffer Gingerbread', with 7 lines of verse. 15 wcts in text, probably as for no. (3). D.f. paper wrappers.

[NorBM, 9·5×6·0 cm.

(2) An edition of 1765, recorded by Algar. Pr f JN. Price 1*d*. Listed in *Valentine's Gift*, 1765. But ? = no. (1A) or (3).

(3) An edition of 1766. Pr f JN. Price 1*d*.

THE RENOWNED | HISTORY | OF | GILES GINGERBREAD: | A | LITTLE BOY WHO LIVED UPON LEARNING. | [d.p.rule] | LONDON: | PR F J. NEWBERY, IN SP | C-Y, 1766. | [PRICE ONE PENNY.]

In 4's. 16 leaves. Pp. 31. Wct FP with verses, 15 wcts in text, all by the *Goody Two-Shoes* woodcutter.

⌈BM (mutilated), *ca.* 9·6×6·4 cm.

(4) An edition of 1769. Pr f N & C. Price 1*d* bd and gilt.

Title approx. as for no. (3). *Imprint:* PR F NEWBERY AND CARNAN, | NO. 65, THE NORTH SIDE OF SP | C-Y, 1769. | [PRICE ONE PENNY.] (see Plate 12). A single gathering of 16 leaves. Pp. 29[31]. First and last leaves pastedowns. 16 wcts, some as in no. (3). List of bks s b N & C on pp. 29–30. D.f. paper wrappers.

⌈Bodley, 9·3×6·3 cm.

(5) An edition of 1777. Pr f C & N. Price 1*d*. Recorded by Wallis, who gives the following details:

Title approx. as before. *Imprint:* PR F T. CARNAN, AND F. NEWBERY, JUN. | AT NUMBER 65, IN SPC-Y; (BUT | NOT FOR F. NEWBERY, AT THE CORNER OF LUD- | GATE STREET, WHO HAS NO SHARE IN THE LATE MR. | JOHN NEWBERY'S BOOKS FOR CHILDREN.) 1777. | [PRICE ONE PENNY.]

16mo in 8's. Pp. 32. 14 cuts.

(6) An edition of 1782. Pr f TC. Price 1*d*. NBL 510.

J268. NEWBERY, John (attributed to). SPELLING-DICTIONARY, A, OF THE ENGLISH LANGUAGE, ON A NEW PLAN. The attribution seems to be no more than guess-work. If the 'Jack Whirler' portrait is anything like a fair one (even with some exaggeration of the lights and shadows) it is difficult to imagine JN settling down to the laborious plodding details of such a work as this.

Not to be confused with *Newbery's New Spelling Dictionary of the English Language* (J265) or the *New Spelling Dictionary* (J263A).

In JN's lifetime some 11 edd. of the present work appeared – an average of one every other year; yet between 1770 and 1786 there were only three or four. The competition of other similar works may account for this. But it was much the same with JN's *Letters* (J266) where there were 7 edd. between 1756 and 1767 and then no more (so far as I know) until 1786. And in that case I have found no rival work.

(1) First edition, 1745. This is no. J71, which formed vol. III in the 1st ed. of the *Circle of the Sciences*. The 2nd and later edd. were removed from that series and treated as independent publicns, but forming 'an Introductory Part of the *Circle*'; see note at J60.

(2) Second edition, 1748. Pr f JN. Price 1*s*.

A | SPELLING-DICTIONARY | OF THE | ENGLISH LANGUAGE, | ON A NEW PLAN. | FOR THE USE OF | YOUNG GENTLEMEN, LADIES, | AND FOREIGNERS. | BEING AN | INTRODUCTORY PART | OF THE | CIRCLE OF THE SCIENCES, &c. | [p.rule] | PUBLISHED BY THE KING'S AUTHORITY. | [p.rule] | THE SECOND EDITION. | [p.rule] | LONDON PR F J. NEWBERY, AT THE BIBLE | AND SUN, IN SPC-Y. | 1748.

In 8's. 138 leaves. No pagination.

[BCE, 9·3×6·0 cm, cropped.

(3) Third edition, 1752. Pr f JN. Price 1s. A copy recorded by Wallis. Adv. *GA* 4.1.52. Alston, IV, 562.

[Exhibited Victoria Art Gallery, Bath, Nov. 1944, Cat. item 117.

(4) Fourth edition. Pr f JN. Price 1s. Adv. *PA* 4.5.53. Alston, IV, 564.

(5) Fifth edition, 1755. Pr f JN. Price 1s. Welsh 338; Alston, IV, 565.

Title and *imprint* approx. as for no. (6) with THE FIFTH EDITION and date 1755. 32mo in 8's. 160 leaves. Pp. 48 (no subsequent pagination).

[BM (imperf.), 9·8×5·8 cm; DES; NoU; Wellcome; Grant.

(6) Sixth edition, 1757. Pr f JN. Price 1s neatly bd in red. Alston, IV, 566.

A | SPELLING-DICTIONARY | OF THE | ENGLISH LANGUAGE, | ON A NEW PLAN. | FOR THE USE OF | YOUNG GENTLEMEN, LADIES, AND | FOREIGNERS. | BEING AN | INTRODUCTORY PART | OF THE | CIRCLE OF THE SCIENCES. | [p.rule] | [1 line] | [p.rule] | THE SIXTH EDITION. | TO WHICH IS PREFIXED | A COMPENDIOUS ENGLISH GRAMMAR; | WITH A CONCISE HISTORICAL ACCOUNT | OF THE LANGUAGE. | [p.rule] | LONDON: | PR F J. NEWBERY, AT THE BIBLE AND | SUN, IN SPC-Y. 1757. | [PRICE ONE SHILLING BOUND.]

32mo in 8's. 160 leaves. Pp. 50 (no subsequent pagination). Advert. of JN's *Letters* on vso of last leaf.

[BM, 9·6×6·1 cm; Bodley; CUL; Bath; NLWa; Osborne*; DLC; NPV; SUT; Pv.

(7) Seventh edition, 1760. Pr f JN. Price 1s. Alston, IV, 567.

Title and *imprint* (with THE SEVENTH EDITION and date 1760) and specification approx. as for no. (6).

[BM, approx. 9·8×5·9 cm; Bell; Welch; UCLA; NNC; PPL; Sotheby, 16.3.70, lot 56; A. R. Heath, Cat. 22 [1972] item 160.

(8) Eighth edition, 1762. Pr f JN. Price 1s. Alston, IV, 568.

Title and *imprint* (with THE EIGHTH EDITION and date 1762) and specification approx. as for no. (6). (Communicated.)

[NLSc; Welch.

(9) Ninth edition, 1763. Pr f JN. Price 1s. Alston, IV, 569.

Title and *imprint* (with THE NINTH EDITION and date 1763) and specification as for no. (6).

[BM (not seen); Marchmont Bookshop, 1969, 10·2×6·6 cm; Gabrielson; Bondy, Cat. 79 [1970] item 205; Sotheby, 19.4.71, lot 210.

(10) Tenth edition, 1764. Pr f JN. Price 1s. Welsh 191; Alston, IV, 570.

A | SPELLING DICTIONARY | OF THE | ENGLISH LANGUAGE, | ON A | NEW PLAN. | FOR THE USE OF YOUNG GENTLEMEN, | LADIES, AND FOREIGNERS. | [p.rule] | PUBLISHED BY THE KING'S AUTHORITY. | [p.rule] | THE TENTH EDITION. | TO WHICH IS PREFIXED, | A COMPENDIOUS ENGLISH GRAMMAR; | WITH A CONCISE | HISTORICAL ACCOUNT OF THE LANGUAGE. | [p.rule] | LONDON: | PR F J. NEWBERY, AT THE BIBLE AND | SUN, IN SPC-Y. 1764. | [PRICE ONE SHILLING BOUND.]

Specification as for no. (6).

[BM, 9·7×5·7 cm; V&A(GL); UCLA; Welch.

(11) Eleventh edition, 1766. Pr f JN. Price 1s. Alston, IV, 571.

Title and *imprint* (with THE ELEVENTH EDITION and date 1766) approx. as for no. (10).

32mo in 8's. 168 leaves. Pp. 8+320–36 (intermediate pages unnumbered). The instructions on letter-writing etc appear in this ed. for the first time.

[BM, approx. 9·6×5·3 cm; Welch; UCLA; BGu; Bondy, Cat. 75 [1968] item 236.

(12) Twelfth edition, 1770. Pr f C & N. Price 1s in the vell. manner. Alston, IV, 574.

Title and *imprint* (with THE TWELFTH EDITION and date 1770) approx. as for no. (13).

32mo in 8's. 168 leaves. Pp. 50, 320–36 (intermediate pages unnumbered). Blue bds, green vell. spine with white label.

[Weedon, 9·5×6·2 cm; NLWa; BCE; Pollard; CtY; MH.

(13) Thirteenth edition, 1774. Pr f C & N. Price 1s. Alston, IV, 575.

A | SPELLING DICTIONARY | OF THE | ENGLISH LANGUAGE, | ON A | NEW PLAN. | FOR THE USE OF YOUNG GENTLEMEN, | LADIES AND FOREIGNERS. | [p.rule] | [1 line] | [p.rule] | THE THIRTEENTH EDITION. | TO WHICH IS PREFIXED, | A COMPENDIOUS ENGLISH GRAMMAR; | WITH A CONCISE | HISTORICAL ACCOUNT OF THE LANGUAGE. | AND AT THE END ARE ADDED, | RULES FOR SPEAKING AND WRITING ENG- | LISH, AND DIRECTIONS FOR ADDRESSING PER- | SONS OF DISTINCTION. | [p.rule] | LONDON: | PR F T. CARNAN AND F. NEWBERY, | JUN. AT NO. 65. IN SPCY. | 1774. [PRICE ONE SHILLING BOUND.]

Specification as for no. (12).

[BM, 10·2×5·9 cm; Grey.

(13A) An undated edition, [?1780]. FN(?S). Alston, IV, 576.

[BM.

(14) An edition of 1786. Pr f TC. Price 1s. Welsh 191. Alston, IV, 577.

Title approx. as for no. (13), no ed. stated. *Imprint:* PR F T. CARNAN, IN SP | C-Y. 1786. | [PRICE ONE SHILLING BOUND.] Specification approx. as for no. (12). Blue vell. spine, marbled bds.

[BM, 9·9×6·6 cm; NLWa; BCE.

(15) Welsh p. 191, lists an ed. of 1788 by EN. This is almost certainly J265(1).

J268A. NEWCOMBE, Mr., of Hackney. A SHORT INTRODUC-TION TO GEOGRAPHY, CONTAINING A DESCRIPTION OF THE SEVERAL PARTS OF THE KNOWN WORLD, THEIR SITUATION AND CHIEF TOWNS. A bk-list at the end of the *County Album*, 1829, says of this bk that 'It was originally compiled by Mr Newcombe of Hackney, for the use of his seminary, and has been adopted by his successors....'. Welsh, at p. 218, quotes an undated list by Harris as authority for the authorship of Lady Fenn (writing *sub nom*: 'Mrs Lovechild'); it may be that Lady Fenn edited or re-wrote the book.

(1) An edition adv. *MC&LA*, 10.6.72 and listed in Chesterfield's *Maxims*, 1777, as pr f FN(N). Price 6*d*. Welsh 224.

(2) Listed as pr f EN in *Cries of London*, 1784. Price 6*d*.

(3) Listed as pr f EN in *Anecdotes of Mary*, 1795, and listed in ENC, p. 6. Price 6*d*.

NEWLY-INVENTED COPY-BOOK. See Palmer, Charlotte.

NEWTON, Sir Isaac. See J348.

NEWTONIAN SYSTEM OF PHILOSOPHY. See 'Telescope, Tom.'.

NOUVELLE HISTOIRE D'ANGLETERRE, 1788. See J85.

J269. NURSE TRUELOVE'S CHRISTMAS-BOX. Welsh 279. *CBEL*, II, 561.

(1) Adv. *GA* 9.1.50 and *GEP* 20–22.12.50 as given gratis at the Bible and Sun in SPCY, '(only paying one penny for the binding)'. Mrs J. E. Grey, in her articles on 'The Strahan Archives' and 'The Lilliputian Magazine', has demonstrated that what was presumably the 1st ed. of this work was printed for J. Newbery by William Strahan in or before 1750, the entry in Strahan's ledger recording a printing of 14,000 copies at a cost of £5. 15*s* 6*d*. One is inclined to suspect that this huge printing lasted Newbery for the remaining 17 years of his life and that the records (2), (3) and (4) below were mere reminders to the book-buying public, not advertisements of new edd.

(2) The '45th edition' adv. *PA* 18.12.53 as: 'Pr f the Author, who has ordered these books to be given to all little good Boys and Girls, at The Bible and Sun... they paying for the binding, which is only One Penny each Book.'

(3) Adv. *PL* 12.2.60 as 'just published' by JN. Price 1*d*.

(4) 'A new edition this day published' adv. *LC* 6–8.1.63, p. 28, the advert. being dated 21.12.1762. Also listed in *Goody Two-Shoes*, 1766, as 'sold at Mr Newbery's', price 1*d*.

(5) An undated edition. S b C & N. Price 1*d*.
  See Plate 13. A single gathering of 16 leaves, the 9th to 12th sgd B, B2, B3, C4. Pp. 27[31]. First and last leaves pastedowns. Pictorial alphabet of 24 wcts and 6 other wcts. List of bks pr f C & N on pp. [28–30]. D.f. paper wrappers.
  [Bodley, 7·7×5·8 cm.

(6) An edition of 1776. TC.
  [Ball.

(7) An edition of 1787. TC. *CBEL*, II, 561.

J270. NURSE TRUELOVE'S NEW-YEAR'S-GIFT. Welsh 278; *CBEL*, II, 561.

(1) Adv. *PA* 18.12.53, the price being 'Two pence for the Binding'. JN. Mrs J. E. Grey, in her articles 'The Strahan Archives' and 'The Lilliputian Magazine' has demonstrated that what was presumably the 1st ed. of this work was printed for J. Newbery by William Strahan in or before 1750, the entry in the printer's ledger recording 6000 copies at a cost of £5. 14s. But unlike the *Christmas Box* (J269 above) entered in the ledger along with the present book, I have found no advert. or other mention of the *New Year's Gift* before 1753. It is hard to believe that the sale of this book was deferred for three years after printing, unless perhaps owing to some mischance such as a fire. I suspect I have failed to notice an advert. somewhere.

(2) Entry deleted.

(3) Adv. *PL* 12.2.60 as 'just published' by JN. Price 2d.

(4) 'A new edition this day published' adv. *LC* 6–8.1.63, p. 28, the advert. being dated 21.12.62. Also listed in *Goody Two-Shoes*, 1766, as 'sold at Mr Newbery's', price 2d.

(5) An undated edition. N & C. Price 2d. Not later than Feb. 1770 (MS date 5.2.1770 on p. 62 of Bodley copy).

NURSE TRUELOVE'S | NEW-YEAR'S-GIFT: | OR, THE | BOOK OF BOOKS FOR CHILDREN. | [p.rule] | ADORNED WITH CUTS. | [p.rule] | [7 lines] | [p.rule] | N.B. YOU MAY HAVE THIS BOOK AT NEW- | BERY'S AND CARNAN'S, | AT NO. 65, THE | BIBLE AND SUN, IN SPC- | Y, OVER AGAINST THE NORTH- DOOR OF | THE CHURCH, PAYING ONLY TWO-PENCE FOR | THE BINDING; BUT NOT UNLESS YOU ARE | GOOD. | NURSE TRUELOVE.

Erratic format and irregular sigs. 32 leaves. Pp. 62[63]. 35 wcts. List of bks pr f N & C on pp. 57–9. List of patent medicines s b Newbery on pp. 60–1, the text of the book continuing on p. [63]. D.f. paper wrappers.

[Bodley, 8·5 × 6·0 cm; NB.

(6) An undated edition. To be had of TC.

Title approx. as for no. (5). *Imprint:* N.B. YOU MAY HAVE THIS LITTLE BOOK OF | T. CARNAN, (SUCCESSOR TO MR. J. NEW- | BERY) AT NO. 65, IN SPC- | Y, ONLY PAYING TWO-PENCE FOR THE | BINDING; BUT NOT UNLESS YOU ARE GOOD. | NURSE TRUELOVE.

Pp. 54[55–63]. Bk-list on pp. [55–62]. 'A virtuous Woman is a Crown to her Husband' (wct and text) on p. [63].

[Ball; Roscoe (photocopied selected leaves).

(7) An edition in S&W Cat., given unreliable date '(1785)', and stated to be bd in white bds with 'four curious wcts, printed in red'.

(8) An edition of 1787. TC. Price 2d. Welsh 278; *CBEL*, II, 561.

OBEDIENCE REWARDED. See Pilkington, M. (H.).

ORACLES, THE. See J194A.

J271. Entry deleted.

J272. ORIENTAL MORALIST, THE. Weedon 75; Welsh 195 (as by 'Rev. S. Cooper'). Richard Johnson's Day-book records: *1791. Mr Badcock——To abridging The Oriental Moralist——£16. 16s.*

The following notes may all refer to the same ed.

(1) An undated edition. Pr f EN (?1791/2). Price 3s 6d.

Engraved title-page: THE | ORIENTAL MORALIST | OR | THE BEAUTIES | OF THE | ARABIAN NIGHTS ENTERTAINMENTS | TRANSLATED FROM THE ORIGINAL & | ACCOMPANIED WITH SUITABLE REFLECTIONS ADAPTED | TO EACH STORY. | BY THE REVD. MR. COOPER, | AUTHOR OF THE HISTORY OF ENGLAND &c. &c. &c. | [engvd vignette] | LONDON. | PR F E. NEWBERY THE CORNER OF | SPCY

12mo. 138 leaves+7 insets. Pp. 263[264]. Engvd FP and TP and 5 other engvd leaves. List of bks 'by Rev. Mr Cooper, sold by E. Newbery' on last page.

[BM, 17·4×10·2 cm; Weedon; Grey; UCLA.

(2) An undated edition. EN. NBL 484, there described as 'first edition' and dated '[ca. 1790]'.

(3) Listed in Pinchard's *Blind Child*, 1791, and in *Joseph Andrews*, 1799, as pr f EN, price 3s 6d.

(4) An undated edition (?1800). EN.

[DLC.

(5) An undated edition. Pr f EN. Pp. 262. Engvd FP and 5 other engvd leaves. (Communicated.)

[Osborne*.

(6) An undated edition. EN. Elkin Mathews, Cat. 163 [1965] item 98. Described as 'first edition', and dated '[ca. 1796]'.

ORPHAN BOY, THE. See Bisset, Jas.

J273. PALMER, Charlotte. LETTERS ON SEVERAL SUBJECTS, 1797. Pr f EN. Price 2s 6d. Welsh 281.

LETTERS | ON | SEVERAL SUBJECTS, | FROM A | PRECEPTRESS | TO HER | PUPILS WHO HAVE LEFT SCHOOL. | ADDRESSED CHIEFLY TO | REAL CHARACTERS, | [3 lines] | [p.s.rule] | [8 lines quote] | [p.s.rule] | LONDON: | PR F E. NEWBERY, AT THE CORNER OF SPC- | Y. | [p.rule] | MDCCXCVII.

8°. 76 leaves. Pp. viii+138[142]. The 4th leaf in quire A an inset. Half-title. Advert. of Palmer's *Copy Book* on p. [139]; list of bks pr f EN on pp. [140–2].

[BM, 15·5×9·7 cm; Renier; Roscoe.

J274. PALMER, Charlotte. A NEWLY-INVENTED COPY-BOOK. Welsh 281.

(1) See Fig. 21. Price 1s 3d; for a subscription of 3s three copies could be had.

Eighteen unsgd leaves, the 3rd and 4th numbered –, 2, 3, 4; no subsequent pagination. First leaf blank. Printed text on title (2nd) leaf and on 3rd–5th leaves.

A

NEWLY-INVENTED

COPY-BOOK,

BY

CHARLOTTE PALMER.

—————————————

LONDON:

PRINTED, FOR THE AUTHOR, BY H. L. GALABIN, INGRAM-COURT,
FENCHURCH-STREET,
AND SOLD BY E. NEWBERY, AT THE CORNER OF
ST. PAUL'S CHURCH-YARD, LONDON.

———

M.DCC.XCVII.

[Price One Shilling and Three-Pence.]

[Entered at Stationers' Hall.]

Fig. 21. Title-page of J274(1). (Slightly reduced.)

Each subsequent leaf has engvd text on the recto, written large at the head of the page for copying below; small engvd text (notes etc) at the foot of seven of these pages. On the 14th leaf the text is engvd vertically.

⌈BM, 23·1 × 18·6 cm.

(2) The advert. of this work in Palmer's *Letters on several Subjects*, 1797, mentions that a second ed. was then in preparation; not traced.

J275. PALMER, Charlotte. THREE INSTRUCTIVE TALES. Welsh 313. No dated ed. recorded, but the work was in existence by 1800 (listed in ENC, p. 6).

(1) An edition pr f EN. Price 3*d*.

THREE | INSTRUCTIVE TALES | FOR | LITTLE FOLK: | [p.s.rule] | SIMPLE AND CAREFUL, | INDUSTRY AND SLOTH, | AND | THE COUSINS. | [d.p.rule] | BY C.P———. | [d.p.rule] | LONDON: | PR F E. NEWBERY, AT THE COR- | NER OF SPC-Y. | [PRICE THREE-PENCE.]

In 8's. 48 leaves. Pp. 94. Last leaf a blank pastedown. Wct FP and 8 wcts in text, unsgd but probably by Lee, certainly not by Bewick (*pace* Welsh). List of bks, comprising 82 numbered titles, pr f EN, on pp. 85–94. D.f. paper wrappers; also orange wrappers impressed with floral design.

No rule above the price in the TP imprint. P. [29] has p.s.rules above and below 'Industry and Sloth', 2·5 cm long. On p. [48] last line reads 'and Sloth.'. P. [57] has p.s.rules above and below 'The Cousins', 2·5 cm long. P. [85], 'Newbery' spelt correctly.

⌈BM, 9·9 × 6·0 cm.

(2) Another edition [pr f EN. Price 3*d*].

Title-leaf wanting. P. [29] had ornam. rules above and below 'Industry and Sloth.'. On p. [48] last line reads 'Sloth.'. P. [57] has ornam. rules above and below 'The Cousins'. P. [85], 'Newbery' spelt 'Newberry'. (Communicated.)

⌈Welch (imperf.).

(3) Another undated edition pr f EN. Price 3*d*.

Title and *imprint* approx. as for no. (1). Pp. 94. List of bks, comprising 88 numbered titles, on pp. 85–94.

There is a p.rule 0·4 cm long above the price in the TP imprint. P. [29] has p.s.rules 5·1 cm long above and below 'Industry and Sloth'. On p. [48] last line reads 'and Sloth.'. P. [57] has p.s.rules 5·1 cm long above and below 'The Cousins'. P. [85], 'Newbery' spelt correctly. (Communicated.)

⌈Ball.

(4) A copy in CUL not checked.

J276. PALTOCK, Robert. LIFE AND ADVENTURES OF PETER WILKINS, THE. The following items are abbreviated edd., a fact nowhere mentioned in the TPs. Weedon 51. Richard Johnson's Day-book records: *1787 Sept. Mr Badcock———To writing the Life of Peter Wilkins———£5. 5s.* Johnson's record of the receipt of his fee says 'abridging'.

(1) An edition of 1788. Pr f EN. Price 6*d*. Welsh 331.

THE | LIFE AND ADVENTURES | OF | PETER WILKINS, | A CORNISH MAN. | TAKEN FROM HIS OWN MOUTH, IN HIS | PASSAGE TO ENGLAND, | FROM OFF | CAPE HORN IN AMERICA, | IN THE | SHIP HECTOR. | [p.rule] | BY A PASSENGER IN THE SHIP. | [p.rule] | EMBELLISHED WITH CUTS. | [d.p.rule] | LONDON: | PR F E. NEWBERY, AT THE CORNER OF | SPC-Y. 1788. | [PRICE SIX-PENCE.]

64 leaves. Pp. 128. Wct FP and 12 wcts in text. D.f.b. (Communicated.) [Melbourne, 10·0×5·0 cm.

(2) An edition of 1793. Pr f EN. Price 6*d*.
Title and *imprint* approx. as for no. (1), with date 1793.
In 8's. 64 leaves. Pp. 128. Wct FP and 12 wcts in text. D.f.b.
[BmPL, 11·0×7·3 cm; McKell.

(3) An edition of 1797. Pr f EN. Price 6*d*.
Title and *imprint* approx. as for no. (1), with date 1797.
In 8's. 64 leaves. Pp. 128. Wct FP and wcts in text. D.f.b.
[Renier, 10·5×7·3 cm; Welch; UCLA.

(4) An edition of 1800. EN. Recorded by Lyon.

PARSING LESSONS FOR ELDER PUPILS. See Fenn, Lady E.

PARSING LESSONS FOR YOUNG CHILDREN. See Fenn, Lady E.

PATHS OF VIRTUE DELINEATED. See Richardson, Saml.

J277. PATHS OF VIRTUE, EXEMPLIFIED IN THE LIVES OF EMINENT MEN AND WOMEN.
(1) An edition of 1777. Pr f FN(N). Price 1*s* 6*d*.
[Ball.
(2) An edition pr f EN listed in Chesterfield's *Maxims*, 1786, price 1*s* 6*d*. Perhaps stock in hand of no. (1).
(3) An edition of 1789. EN. Price 1*s* 6*d*. Welsh 282.
(4) Listed as pr f EN in *Joseph Andrews*, 1799, and listed in ENC, p. 9. Price 1*s* 6*d*.

PAUL ET VIRGINIE. See Bernardin de Saint-Pierre.

J278. PEACOCK, Lucy. THE LITTLE EMIGRANT.
(1) First edition, 1799. S b EN et al. Price 3*s*. *H&L*, iii, 378.

THE | LITTLE EMIGRANT, | A TALE. | INTERSPERSED WITH | MORAL ANECDOTES AND INSTRUCTIVE | CONVERSATIONS. | [orn. rule] | DESIGNED FOR THE PERUSAL OF YOUTH. | [orn. rule] | BY THE AUTHOR OF | THE ADVENTURES OF THE SIX PRINCESSES OF BABY-|LON... | &c &c | [d.p.rule] | [2 lines] | [d.p.rule] | LONDON: | PR B S. LOW, BERWICK STREET, SOHO; | FOR THE AUTHOR, | AT THE JUVENILE LIBRARY, NO. 259, OXFORD

| STREET; | A S B MESSRS CARPENTER, OLD BOND STREET; C. LAW, | AVE-MARIA LANE; AND E. NEWBERY, THE CORNER OF | SPCY. | [p.rule] | 1799.

12mo. 104 leaves+2 insets. Pp. ii+203. Engvd FP sgd 'T. Stothard del', 'P. Audinet sculp'; engvd leaf in text.

[BM, 18·1×10·5 cm; Oup; BCE; Osborne*; UCLA; NNC-T (Darton Coll.); Sotheby, 19.4.71, lot 198.

(2) Second edition, 1802. S b EN et al. Welsh 256; *CBEL*, II, 558.

THE | LITTLE EMIGRANT, | A TALE: | INTERSPERSED WITH | MORAL ANECDOTES AND INSTRUCTIVE | CONVERSATIONS. | DESIGNED FOR THE PERUSAL OF YOUTH. | [d.p.rule] | BY LUCY PEACOCK. | [d.p.rule] | THE SECOND EDITION. | [d.p.rule] | [2 lines quote] | [d.p.rule] | LONDON: | PR B J. BARFIELD, WARDOUR-STREET, SOHO, | PRINTER TO HIS ROYAL HIGHNESS THE PRINCE OF WALES, | FOR R. AND L. PEACOCK, | THE JUVENILE LIBRARY, NO. 259, OXFORD-STREET; | A S B | MESSRS. CARPENTER, OLD BOND-STREET; C. LAW, AVE-MARIA-LANE; | AND E. NEWBERY, THE CORNER OF SPC-Y. | [p.rule] | 1802.

12mo. 102 leaves+engvd FP. Pp. iv+196[200]. Bk-list on last 4 pages.

[BM, 17·2×10·1 cm.

J279. PERRAULT, Charles. HISTORIES OR TALES OF PAST TIMES, TOLD BY MOTHER GOOSE. *CBEL*, II, 565; Muir, pp. 51, 76; Opie, *Dictionary*, p. 40; Welch 894.1 (pp. 61–2).

The 4th ed., pr f James Hodges, was adv. *GA* 2.1.52 as t.d.i.p. Apart from this, and no. (1) below, the records are strangely silent as to edd. prior to the 6th, of 1772, of what was, prima facie, a successful publication.

(1) Listed as 'sold at Newbery and Carnan's' in *Tom Thumb's Folio*, 1768. Price 9*d*.

(2) See Figure 22. Pp. 156. Wct FP and wcts in text. (Communicated.)
[Ball.

(3) Seventh edition, 1777. Pr a s b C & N et al. Price 9*d* neatly bd. Welsh 272.

Title and *imprint* approx. as for no. (2), with THE SEVENTH EDITION CORRECTED and date MDCCLXXVII. Pp. 156. Wct FP and wcts in text. D.f.b. with blind impress. (Communicated.)
[Opie.

(4) Eighth edition, 1780. ? TC. Welsh 272.

(5) An edition of '1719' (i.e. 1799). B. C. Collins. Price 9*d*. Muir, pp. 49 and 51; ENC, p. 7. The bk-list at the end is in the joint names of Collins, EN et al., and is dated 1799. (Communicated.)
[Knaster.

PETER WILKINS, LIFE AND ADVENTURES OF. See Paltock, Robt.

HISTORIES
OR
TALES
OF
PAST TIMES,
TOLD BY
MOTHER GOOSE.
WITH
MORALS.

Written in French by M. PERRAULT,
And Englifhed by G. M. Gent.

The SIXTH EDITION, corrected.

SALISBURY:
Printed and fold by B. COLLINS; alfo by
CARNAN and NEWBERY, in St. Paul's
Church-Yard; and S. CROWDER, in Pater-
nofter-Row, London, M,DCC,LXXII.
(Price 9d. neatly bound.)

Fig. 22. Frontispiece and title-page of J279(2).

PHILOSOPHY FOR CHILDREN. See Rollin, Chas.

J279A. PHILOSOPHY OF TOPS AND BALLS. Welsh 282 and 313–14. The *Monthly Review* for April 1761, at p. 277, reviews Tom Telescope's *Newtonian System*, and notes that 'this is the book advertised under the title of *The Philosophy of Tops and Balls*'. This latter title was frequently used in adverts. and bk-lists.

J280. PICTURE EXHIBITION, THE. *CBEL*, II, 562; Weedon 76. Richard Johnson's Day-book records: *1772 Jan. 6. Delivered to Mr Carnan The Picture Gallery.——Value Five Guineas.*
(1) An edition of 1774. Pr f TC. Price 6*d* bd and gilt. Gum 2769.
　[Ball.
(2) An edition of 1783. Pr f TC. Price 6*d*. Welsh 283.
　THE | PICTURE | EXHIBITION; | CONTAINING THE | ORIGINAL
DRAWINGS | OF EIGHTEEN | DISCIPLES. | TO WHICH ARE ADDED, |
MORAL AND HISTORICAL | EXPLANATIONS, | PUBLISHED UNDER THE

INSPECTION OF | MASTER PETER PAUL RUBENS, | PROFESSOR OF POLITE ARTS. | [d.p.rule] | LONDON: | PR F T. CARNAN, IN SP | C-Y. [PRICE 6d.] | [p.s.rule] | MDCCLXXXIII.

In 6's. 45 leaves. Pp. 77[82]. 18 wcts in text. White bds impressed with wct pictures in red, those on the lower cover sgd 'J. Bell sc', used also on the lower cover to J348(6). List of bks pr f TC on last 5 pages.

[BM, 11·3×7·5 cm; Ball.

J281. PILKINGTON, Mary (Hopkins). ASIATIC PRINCESS, THE, 1800. Pr f EN et al. 2 vols, 'vellum backs', price 1s 6d each. Welsh 283; NBL 490.

THE | ASIATIC PRINCESS. | DEDICATED, BY PERMISSION, | TO | HER ROYAL HIGHNESS | PRINCESS CHARLOTTE OF WALES. | [d.p.rule] | [royal coat of arms] | [d.p.rule] | BY MRS. PILKINGTON. | [d.p.rule] | LONDON: | PR F VERNOR AND HOOD, IN THE | POULTRY; | AND E. NEWBERY, CORNER OF SP | C-Y; | BY J. CUNDEE, IVY-LANE. [p.rule] | 1800.

In the second volume VOL. II. appears below BY MRS. PILKINGTON.

Vol. I. In 6's. 90 leaves+engvd FP. Pp. ix+167. Bk-list on first leaf. Half-title. Marbled bds, green vell. spine.

Vol. II. In 6's. 78 leaves, the last a blank. Pp. vi+141[146]. Half-title. Bk-list on last 2 leaves. Marbled bds, green vell. spine.

[BM, 13·6×8·3 cm; Bodley; HeCL; Renier; UCLA.

J282. PILKINGTON, Mary (Hopkins). BIOGRAPHY FOR GIRLS. (1) See Fig. 23. Welsh 284; *CBEL*, II, 559.

In 6's. 108 leaves+engvd FP. Pp. 207[211]. Bk-list on last 3 pages. Marbled bds, sheep or calf back-strip; also marbled bds, green vell. spine with label.

[BM, 14·0×8·9 cm; Weedon; Opie; BCE; UCLA; Osborne, Cat. p. 288.

(2) Second edition not traced.

(3) Third edition, 1800. Pr f [E]N et al. Price 2s 'vellum back'.

BIOGRAPHY FOR GIRLS; | OR, | MORAL AND INSTRUCTIVE | EXAMPLES | FOR | THE FEMALE SEX. | [d.p.rule] | THIRD EDITION. | [p.s.rule] | BY | MRS. PILKINGTON. | [p.s.rule] | LONDON: | PR F VERNOR AND HOOD, POULTRY; | AND NEWBERY, SPCY; | BY J. CUNDEE, IVY-LANE. | [p.rule] | 1800.

Specification as for no. (1). Marbled bds, green vell. spine.

[BM, 13·3×8·8 cm; CUL; ReU; Renier; McKell; Adomeit.

J283. PILKINGTON, Mary (Hopkins). EDWARD BARNARD, 1797. Pr f EN. Price 2s. Welsh 284; *CBEL*, II, 559.

EDWARD BARNARD; | OR, | MERIT EXALTED; | CONTAINING | THE HISTORY | OF THE | EDGERTON FAMILY. | [p.s.rule] | BY M. S. PILKINGTON. | [p.s.rule] | LONDON: | PR F E. NEWBERY, AT THE CORNER OF | SPC-Y. | [p.rule] | 1797.

BIOGRAPHY FOR GIRLS;

OR,

MORAL AND INSTRUCTIVE

EXAMPLES,

FOR

YOUNG LADIES.

By Mrs PILKINGTON.

LONDON:

PRINTED FOR VERNOR AND HOOD, POULTRY;
AND NEWBERY, ST. PAUL'S CHURCH YARD.
—
1799.

Fig. 23. Frontispiece and title-page of J282(1). (Slightly reduced.)

12mo. 84 leaves+engvd FP sgd 'Cook sc'. Pp. 167. 'M. S. Pilkington' is perhaps a misprint for 'Mrs Pilkington'.

[BM, 17·8×10·0 cm; Bodley; CUL; Oup; EdUL; Hannas; UCLA; Shiers; NNC-T (Darton Coll.).

J284. PILKINGTON, Mary (Hopkins). HISTORICAL BEAUTIES FOR YOUNG LADIES. (A MIRROR FOR THE FEMALE SEX.) *CBEL*, II, 559.

(1) First edition, 1798. S b EN. Price 3s 6d. Hugo 123; Gum 4560.

A MIRROR FOR THE FEMALE SEX. | [p.s.rule] | HISTORICAL BEAUTIES | FOR | YOUNG LADIES. | INTENDED TO LEAD THE | FEMALE MIND | TO THE LOVE AND PRACTICE OF | MORAL GOODNESS. | DESIGNED PRINCI- PALLY FOR THE USE OF LADIES' SCHOOLS. | BY MRS. PILKINGTON. | [p.s.rule] | [2 lines] | [d.p.rule] | [2 lines quote] | [d.p.rule] | LONDON: | PR F VERNOR AND HOOD IN THE POULTRY. | AND S B E. NEWBERY, THE CORNER OF | SPC-Y. | [p.rule]. | 1798.

12mo. 126 leaves+engvd FP sgd 'Thurston Delt', 'Hawkins Sculpt'. Pp.

213

xxiv+226[228]. 17 wct vignette headpieces, 18 wct vignette tailpieces; some may be John Bewick's work; but Hugo's statement that they are the work of Thomas Bewick cannot be supported. Bk-list on last 2 pages. Blue bds.

[BM; V&A; NUTP; MPL; Roscoe, 18·9×10·6 cm, untrimmed; LEI. (2) Second edition, 1799. S b EN. Price 3s 6d. Welsh 284.

Title approx. as for no. (1), with THE SECOND EDITION following 'By Mrs. Pilkington' and a wct vignette (in the Bewick manner) following the quote. *Imprint:* LONDON: | PR B T. MAIDEN, SHERBOURNE-LANE, | FOR VERNOR AND HOOD, IN THE POULTRY; | AND S B E. NEWBERY, THE CORNER OF | SPC-Y. | [p.rule] | 1799.

12mo. 132 leaves+engvd FP as in no. (1). Pp. xxiv+240. 18 wct vignette headpieces, 17 wct vignette tailpieces (see no. (1)). Pink bds, white back-strip with red label.

[BM; CUL; V&A(GL); LUL; NUTP; HU; LEE; Roscoe, 19·2×11·1 cm ntrimmed; Osborne, Cat. p. 289; UCLA; A. R. Heath, Cat. 22 [1972] item 173.

PILKINGTON, Mary (Hopkins). MIRROR FOR THE FEMALE SEX. See J284.

J284A. PILKINGTON, Mary (Hopkins). NEW TALES OF THE CASTLE, 1800. S b E. Newberry (*sic*). *CBEL*, II, 559; Welsh 284.

NEW TALES | OF THE | CASTLE; | OR, | THE NOBLE EMIGRANTS, | A STORY | OF | MODERN TIMES. | [rule] | BY MRS. PILKINGTON. | [rule] | PR F VERNOR AND HOOD, | POULTRY, BY H. FRY, FINSBURY-PLACE, | A S B | E. NEWBERRY, SPC-Y. | [rule] | 1800.

Engvd FP sgd 'Satchwell delt, J. Scott sculpt'. Pp. 215. (Communicated.) [UCLA.

J285. PILKINGTON, Mary (Hopkins). OBEDIENCE REWARDED, 1797. Pr f EN et al. Price 3s 6d (in 1798), 3s (in 1799). Welsh 284; *CBEL*, II, 559.

OBEDIENCE REWARDED, | AND | PREJUDICE CONQUERED; | OR, THE | HISTORY | OF | MORTIMER LASCELLS. | [d.p.rule] | WRITTEN FOR THE INSTRUCTION AND AMUSE- | MENT OF YOUNG PEOPLE. | [d.p.rule] | BY MRS. PILKINGTON. | [d.p.rule] | LONDON: | PR F VERNOR & HOOD, NO. 31, POULTRY; | AND E. NEWBERY, CORNER OF SP | C-Y. | [p.rule] | 1797.

12mo. 108 leaves+engvd FP sgd 'Kirk delin', 'Taylor sculp'. Pp. 206[212]. List of bks pr f a s b EN and Vernor and Hood on last 6 pages. Half-title.

[BM, 17·1×10·1 cm; Bodley.

J286. PILKINGTON, Mary (Hopkins). SCRIPTURE HISTORIES, 1798. Pr f EN et al. Price 2s 6d. Welsh 284.

SCRIPTURE HISTORIES; | OR, | INTERESTING NARRATIVES | EXTRACTED FROM THE | OLD TESTAMENT, | FOR THE | INSTRUCTION AND AMUSEMENT | OF | YOUTH. | [p.s.rule] | BY MRS. PILKINGTON. | [p.s.rule] | LONDON: |

PR F E. NEWBERY, SPCY; | AND VERNOR AND HOOD, NO. 31, POULTRY. | [p.s.rule] | 1798.

12mo. 84 leaves+engvd FP sgd 'Thurston delt', 'Ridley sculpt'. Pp. v+162. [BM, 16·6×9·9 cm; Ball.

J287. PILKINGTON, Mary (Hopkins). TALES OF THE COTTAGE. (1) An edition of 1798. S b EN. Price 2s.

TALES | OF | THE COTTAGE; | OR | STORIES, | MORAL AND AMUSING, | FOR | YOUNG PERSONS. | WRITTEN ON THE PLAN OF THE CELEBRATED WORK | LES VEILLÉES DU CHATEAU, | BY MADAME LA COMPTESSE DE GENLIS. | [d.p.rule] | LONDON: | PR F VERNOR AND HOOD, IN THE POULTRY; AND | S B E. NEWBERY, CORNER OF SP | C-Y. | [p.rule] | 1798.

In 6's. 114 leaves+engvd FP sgd 'Thurston Invt', 'Dadley Sculp'. Pp. viii+ 218[220]. 9 wct tailpieces, those at pp. 15 and 30 in the Bewick manner. List of bks on last leaf. Marbled bds, green vell. spine with white label.

[BM; Weedon, 13·7×8·4 cm; ReU; UCLA.

(2) An edition of 1799. S b EN. Price 2s. *CBEL*, II, 559.

Title and *imprint* approx. as for no. (1), BY MRS PILKINGTON added following BY MADAME... GENLIS, and date 1799.

In 6's. 114 leaves+FP as in no. (1). Pp. viii+218[220]. Bk-list on last leaf. Marbled bds, green vell. spine with label. No head- or tailpieces.

[BM, 13·5×8·8 cm; LI; Opie; Welch; PPiU.

(3) An edition of 1800. S b EN. Price 2s, 'vellum back'. Welsh 285; *CBEL*, II, 559.

Title approx. as for no. (2). *Imprint:* PR B J. BONSOR, SALISBURY SQUARE: | FOR VERNOR AND HOOD, IN THE POULTRY; A S | B E. NEWBERY, CORNER OF SPC | Y. | [d.p.rule] | 1800.

Specification and binding as for no. (2).

[BM, 13·2×8·6 cm; V&A(GL); UCLA.

J288. PILKINGTON, Mary (Hopkins). TALES OF THE HERMITAGE. *CBEL*, II, 559. (1) An edition of 1798. S b EN. Price 2s.

TALES | OF | THE HERMITAGE: | WRITTEN FOR THE | INSTRUCTION AND AMUSEMENT | OF THE | RISING GENERATION. | [d.p.rule] | LONDON: | PR F VERNOR AND HOOD, POULTRY; | A S B E. NEWBERY, THE CORNER OF | SPC-Y. | [p.rule] | 1798.

In 6's. 117 leaves+engvd FP. Pp. 228[230]. Bk-list on last leaf. Marbled bds, green vell. spine.

[BM, 13·4×8·3 cm; V&A(GL); LI; Renier; Opie; MiDW.

(2) An edition of 1799. S b EN. Price 2s, 'vellum backs'.

Title and *imprint* approx. as for no. (1), with date 1799.

In 6's. 114 leaves+engvd FP as in no. (1). Pp. 221[224]. Bk-list on last leaf. Marbled bds, green vell. spine.

[BM, 13·5×8·7 cm; Bodley; CUL; NPV.

(3) An edition of 1800. S b EN.

Title approx. as for no. (1). *Imprint:* PR B J. DEWICK, ALDERSGATE STREET, | FOR VERNOR AND HOOD 31, POULTRY; AND | S B E. NEWBERY, THE CORNER OF | SPCY. | [p.rule] | 1800.

In 6's. 109 leaves+engvd FP. Pp. 209[212]. List of bks pr f Vernor and Hood on pp. [211–12]. Marbled bds, green vell. spine with label.

[CUL, 13·4×8·5 cm; V&A(GL); Quayle; UCLA; Maxwell Hunley, Cat. 48 [winter 1969] item 263.

J289. PINCHARD, Mrs Elizabeth, of Taunton. BLIND CHILD, THE. Welsh 174–5; *CBEL*, II, 558.

(1) First edition, 1791. Pr f EN. Gum 4568; NBL 490a.

THE | BLIND CHILD, | OR | ANECDOTES | OF THE | WYNDHAM FAMILY. | WRITTEN FOR THE USE OF | YOUNG PEOPLE, | BY A LADY. | [p.s.rule] | LONDON: | PR F E. NEWBERY, AT THE CORNER OF SP | C-Y. | 1791. | [ENTERED AT STATIONERS' HALL.]

12mo. 90 leaves+engvd FP. Pp. vii+[9]–178[180]. List of bks pr f EN on last leaf.

[BM, 16·9×9·4 cm; CUL; EdUL; Renier; Opie; Osborne*; UCLA; Welch; Ries; Gardner; KU; Grant.

(2) Second edition, 1793. Pr f EN. Price 2s.

Title and *imprint*, with THE SECOND EDITION and date 1793, approx. as for no. (1).

12mo. 90 leaves+engvd FP. Pp. vii+[9]–138 (error for 178) [180]. Bk-list as in no. (1).

[BM, 17·0×9·9 cm; Bodley; CUL; V&A(GL); Renier; Hannas; LI; Osborne, Cat. p. 289; Welch; McKell; NNC-T (Darton Coll.).

(3) Wallis claimed the (or a) 3rd ed. was dated 1793, price 2s. He is too dogmatic to be altogether reliable.

(4) An edition of 1794. ? EN. Price 2s.

[Wallis.

(5) Third edition, 1795. Pr f EN. Price 2s.

Title and *imprint*, with THE THIRD EDITION and date 1795, and specification approx. as for no. (1).

[BM, 16·8×10·1 cm; CUL; Grey; Renier; Melbourne; UCLA; NNC-T (Darton Coll.); Muirhead, Cat. 31 [1967] item 115; Sotheby, 5.2.68, lot 321.

(6) Fourth edition, not traced. Is this in fact the 1796 ed. mentioned by H&L, I, 210?

(7) Fifth edition, 1798. Pr f EN. Price 2s.

Title and *imprint*, with THE FIFTH EDITION and date 1798, and specification approx. as for no. (1).

[BM, 16·9×10·1 cm; CUL; ReU; OOxM.

J290. PINCHARD, Mrs Elizabeth, of Taunton. DRAMATIC DIALOGUES.

(1) An edition (probably the 1st) of 1792. Pr f EN. 2 vols, price *2s 6d* each. Welsh 206; *CBEL*, II, 558; Gum 4569.

DRAMATIC DIALOGUES, | FOR THE | USE | OF | YOUNG PERSONS. | [p.s.rule] | BY THE AUTHOR OF | THE BLIND CHILD. | [d.p.rule] | [4 lines quote] | LONDON: | PR F E. NEWBERY, THE CORNER OF S | PC-Y. | [p.rule] | MDCCXCII. | [p.rule] | [ENTERED AT STATIONER'S HALL.]

In the TP to vol. II there are minor variations and VOL. II. takes the place of the 4-line quote.

Vol. I. 12mo. 102 leaves+3 insets. Pp. vii+196. Engvd FP and 2 engvd leaves in text.

Vol. II. 12mo. 84 leaves+3 insets. Pp. 163. Engvd FP and 2 engvd leaves in text. Half-title.

[BM, 17·5×10·5 cm; Bodley; CUL; V&A(GL) (vol. II); Preston, vol. I (Cat. p. 122); Exeter; Traylen; NoU; Osborne, Cat. p. 289, vol. I; Osborne*, vol. II; UCLA; NNC-T (Darton Coll.); Welch; Grant, vol. I.

(2) A 'new edition' was adv. *LC* 19–21.12.93, p. 596, as pr f EN, 2 vols, price *5s*.

J291. PINCHARD, Mrs Elizabeth, of Taunton. TWO COUSINS, THE. Welsh 285; Gum 4570–1; *CBEL*, II, 559.

(1) An edition (? the 1st) of 1794. Pr f EN. Price *2s*.

THE | TWO COUSINS, | A | MORAL STORY, | FOR THE USE OF YOUNG PERSONS. | IN WHICH IS EXEMPLIFIED | THE NECESSITY OF MODERATION AND JUSTICE | TO THE ATTAINMENT OF HAPPINESS. | BY THE AUTHOR OF THE BLIND CHILD | AND | DRAMATIC DIALOGUES. | [p.rule] | [11 lines quote] | [p.rule] | LONDON: | PR F E. NEWBERY, AT THE CORNER OF S | PC-Y. | MDCCXCIV. | [ENTERED AT STATIONERS-HALL.]

12mo. 76(78) leaves+engvd FP. Pp. vii+144, 4. Half-title. The last 4 pages comprise a bk-list, noted in the CLU copy, not elsewhere.

[BM, 17·2×10·0 cm; CUL; ReU; LI; Knaster; Pollard; Osborne, Cat. p. 289; UCLA; McKell; NNC-T (Darton Coll.); MiDW.

(2) An edition of 1798. Pr f EN. Price *2s*. NBL 491 (describes as '1st ed.').

Title, imprint (with date MDCCXCVIII) and specification approx. as for no. (1); no bk-list at end.

[BM, 17·3×10·3 cm; UCLA; ReU; Maxwell Hunley, Cat. 48 [winter 1969] item 265.

PITY'S GIFT. See Pratt, Saml Jackson.

PLAIN AND CONCISE EXPOSITION OF THE BOOK OF COMMON PRAYER. See J40.

PLEASANT AND USEFUL COMPANION TO THE CHURCH OF ENGLAND. See J40.

J292. PLEASANT TALES, TO IMPROVE THE MIND, 1801. Pr f EN. Price 1s 6d.

PLEASANT TALES, | TO | IMPROVE THE MIND, | AND | CORRECT THE MORALS | OF | YOUTH. | [wct device] | LONDON: | PR F E. NEWBERY, AT THE CORNER OF S | PC-Y. | BY H. BRYER, BRIDEWELL-HOSPITAL. | [p.rule] | 1801.

In 6's. 76 leaves+engvd FP. Pp. 147. Marbled bds, green vell. spine with label. [BM, 13·6×8·4 cm; Osborne, Cat. p. 289; UCLA.

J293. PLEASING REFLECTIONS ON LIFE AND MANNERS. Pr f EN. Price 3s. Listed in Pinchard's *Blind Child*, 1791. *CBEL*, II, 242 lists an ed. of 1788; Welsh 285; ENC, p. 18.

J294. PLUTARCH. PLUTARCH'S LIVES, ABRIDGED (Goldsmith and Collyer's ed.). Welsh 229–30; *CBEL*, II, 641; IAW 124–5; Scott 83ff. The work ran to 7 vols, *pace* BM, Gen. Cat. and *CBEL*, which record 5 only. Designed by JN as the first part of his *Compendium of Biography* – no. J77A.

Advtd to appear, in 1762, at 1s 6d the vol., monthly, the complete set going at 10s 6d. In later years the set cost 14s in calf, 12s 6d in the vell. manner, labelled, and 10s 6d sewed.

(1) An edition of 1762. Pr f JN.

PLUTARCH'S LIVES, | ABRIDGED FROM THE | ORIGINAL GREEK, | ILLUSTRATED WITH | NOTES AND REFLECTIONS, | AND EMBELLISHED WITH | COPPER-PLATE PRINTS. | VOLUME THE FIRST [&c] | CONTAINING THE LIVES OF | [names in 2 columns, 3 to 5 lines] | [d.p.rule] | LONDON: | PR F J. NEWBERY, AT THE BIBLE AND | SUN, IN SPC-Y. | [p.rule] | MDCCLXII.

Vol. I. In 6's. 126 leaves+9 insets. Pp. xviii[xxiv]+222[228]. Engvd FP and 8 engvd leaves in text. List of bks pubd by JN on last 3 leaves.

Vol. II. In 6's. 119 leaves+9 inset engvd leaves in text. Pp. 226.

Vol. III. In 6's. 114 leaves+9 inset engvd leaves in text. Pp. 216.

Vol. IV. In 6's. 120 leaves+9 inset engvd leaves in text. Pp. 227.

Vol. V. In 6's. 113 leaves+9 inset engvd leaves in text. Pp. 218.

Vol. VI. In 6's. 120 leaves+9 inset engvd leaves in text. Pp. 236[240]. List of bks pubd by JN on last 2 leaves.

Vol. VII. In 6's. 126 leaves+9 inset engvd leaves in text. Pp. 244.

[BM (vols I–V); Weedon (vols I–VII), *ca.* 13·0×7·6 cm; Quayle (*ex* 1 vol.); Welch (*ex* vol. V).

(2) Frequently adv. and listed as by N & C in the years following 1767. 7 vols. Prices as above. And listed as s b TC in J147(9), vol. II, 1786.

(3) An edition of 1790. Pr f F. Power & Co. The title-leaf to vol. IV of this ed. is in the Bodley vol. 2582.b.2, otherwise not traced.

(4) An edition listed in J285, 1797, as pr f a s b EN and Vernor and Hood. Price 14s bd in red.

J295. POCKET DICTIONARY, A, OR COMPLETE ENGLISH EXPOSITOR. Welsh 198–9.
(1) First edition, 1753. Pr f JN. Price 3s.

A | POCKET DICTIONARY | OR COMPLETE | ENGLISH EXPOSITOR: | SHEWING READILY | THE PART OF SPEECH TO WHICH EACH WORD BELONGS; ... | [15 lines] | A WORK ENTIRELY NEW, AND DESIGN'D FOR THE YOUTH OF BOTH SEXES, | THE LADIES AND PERSONS IN BUSINESS. | TO WHICH IS PREFIX'D | AN INTRODUCTION, | [2 lines] | AND A RECOMMENDATION OF THE MANUSCRIPT COPY, | IN A LETTER FROM DR. BEVIS TO THE PUBLISHER. | [p.rule] | [1 line Greek] | [p.rule] | LONDON: | PR F J. NEWBERY, AT THE BIBLE AND SUN, IN | SPC-Y, 1753.

In 8's. 200 leaves. No pagination after p. 11. List of bks pr f a s b JN on last leaf.

[BM, 17·2×11·1 cm; Bodley; HuPL; Roscoe; BAS; CtY; STF; MTLs; Gardner.

(2) Second edition, 1758. Pr f JN. Price 3s. Alston, v, 166.

Title and *imprint* approx. as for no. (1), with THE SECOND EDITION and date MDCCLVIII.

In 8's. 224 leaves. No pagination after p. xvi. List of bks pr f a s b JN on last leaf.

[BM, 17·9×11·0 cm; Bodley; Gabrielson; MB.

(3) Third edition, 1765. Pr f JN. Price 3s. Alston, v, 167.

Title and *imprint* approx. as for no. (1), with THE THIRD EDITION and date 1765.

In 8's. 224 leaves. No pagination after p. xiv. Bk-list on last 2 pages.

[BM, 17·1×11·7 cm; Bodley; BmPL; BmU; ICU-J.

(4) Fourth edition, 1779. Pr f C & N. Price 3s. Alston, v, 168.

Title approx. as for no. (1), with THE FOURTH EDITION. *Imprint:* PR F T. CARNAN AND F. NEWBERY, JUN. NO. 65, | IN SPC-Y. | MDCCLXXIX.

In 8's. 224 leaves. Pp. xvi, no subsequent pagination. (Communicated.)

[PPL, 18·4×11·2 cm; IU.

J296. POCKET GULLIVER, THE. Adv. *MC&LA* 30.12.72, price 6d, as by FN(N). Perhaps = *Adventures of Captain Gulliver* which had been adv. in the same paper on 10.6.72.

J297. POETICAL BLOSSOMS, 1793. Pr f EN. Price 1s 6d. Welsh 195; *CBEL*, II, 248; Weedon 77 and p. 37. Richard Johnson's Day-book records: *1792. Mʳ Badcock——To compiling The Poetical Blossoms——£10. 10s.*

POETICAL BLOSSOMS. | BEING A | SELECTION | OF | SHORT POEMS, | INTENDED FOR | YOUNG PEOPLE | TO REPEAT FROM MEMORY. | [p.rule] |

BY THE REV. MR. COOPER. | [d.p.rule] | LONDON: | PR F E. NEWBERY, CORNER OF S | PC-Y. | [p.rule] | 1793.

In 6's. 90 leaves+engvd FP sgd 'Cook sc'. Pp. iv+176.

[BM, 11·4×7·5 cm; CUL; Exeter; MH; Welch; McKell; UCLA.

J298. POETICAL DESCRIPTION OF BEASTS, A.

(1) An edition of 1773 (probably the 1st). Pr f TC. Price 6*d*. Welch 173; NBL 582. Title etc apparently approx. as for no. (2).

[Hodgson's 8.5.53, in lot 561.

(2) An edition of 1777. Pr f TC. Price 6*d*.

Engraved title: A | POETICAL DESCRIPTION | OF | BEASTS, | WITH | MORAL REFLECTIONS | FOR THE | AMUSEMENT OF CHILDREN. | [10 lines of verse] | LONDON: | PR F T. CARNAN, AT NUMBER 65 IN | SPCY. | MDCCLXXVII. PR. 6*d*.

Pp. 72. Engvd FP. Wcts. On p. 70 semi-colon at end of line 2 is below space between 'him' and 'spread' in line above; full-stop at end of last line below 'ir' in 'admire' in line above.

[Welch (imperf.); Roscoe (photocopied selected leaves).

(3) Another edition of 1777. Pr f TC. Price 6*d*.

TP as for no. (2).

Pp. 72. Wcts. A variant setting of type: on p. 70 semi-colon at end of line 2 is below 'r' in 'spread' in line above; full-stop at end of last line below comma at end of line above. D.f.b.

[Welch (imperf.); Roscoe (photocopied selected leaves); Ball.

(4) An edition of 1777 (? = nos. (2) or (3)). Pr f TC. Price 6*d*.

TP as for no. (2).

In 6's. Wcts. Pp. 72. White or buff bds with designs in black showing animals, within ornam. frames.

[Sotheby, 9.11.64, lot 120.

(5) An edition of 1777. Pr f TC. May = one of the above.

[Ball.

J299. POETICAL DESCRIPTION OF SONG BIRDS, A.

(1) An edition of 1773 (probably the 1st). Pr f TC. Price 6*d*. Adv. *LC* 15–18.5.73, p. 471.

(2) An edition of 1779. Pr f TC. Price 6*d*.

Engraved title: A | POETICAL DESCRIPTION | OF | SONG BIRDS: | INTERSPERSED WITH | ENTERTAINING SONGS, FABLES, AND TALES, | ADAPTED TO EACH SUBJECT. | FOR THE | AMUSEMENT OF CHILDREN. | [p.rule] | [2 lines quote] | [p.s.rule] | LONDON: | PR F T. CARNAN, AT NUMBER 65, | IN SPC-Y. PR. 6*d*. | MDCCLXXIX.

Pp. vii[viii]+80. Wcts. Buff paper bds with wcts surrounded by floral designs. (Communicated.)

[SomCL, 11·3×7·3 cm; Welch.

(3) An edition of 1787. TC.
⌈Opie.

J300. POETICAL FLOWER BASKET, THE. An undated edition. Pr f
EN. Price 6*d*. Weedon 57, VI. One of the 10 vols forming the *Lilliputian Library*
'compiled' by Richard Johnson, no. J218, and originally published by Domville
and others. The EN ed. consists of the sheets of the Domville ed. from which the
title-leaf (A2) and A3 have been removed, a cancel title-leaf substituted. It was
no. VI in the *Lilliputian Library*; hence the statement at p. 120: 'end of the sixth
volume'.

> THE | POETICAL FLOWER BASKET | BEING A | SELECTION OF APPROVED
> | AND | ENTERTAINING PIECES | OF | POETRY, | CALCULATED FOR YOUNG
> MINDS. | [p.s.rule] | EMBELLISHED WITH CUTS, | [p.s.rule] | LONDON: | PR
> F E. NEWBERY, AT THE CORNER OF SP | CY. | [PRICE SIX-PENCE.]

In 12's. 59 leaves. Pp. viii (i.e. [i–iv], vii, viii)+[9]–120. Wct FP and 12 wcts
in text; a number of large ornam. wct tailpieces. D.f.b.
⌈Hannas, 9·5×8·6 cm.

POETICAL FLOWER GARDEN. See Waters, [   ].

J300A. POETICAL TALES, AMUSING AND INSTRUCTIVE,
WITH CUTS BY BEWICK. Pr f EN. So listed in Smythies' *History of a
Pin*, 1801. Price 2*s*. Not identified.

POETRY MADE FAMILIAR. See CIRCLE OF THE SCIENCES,
J68.

J301. POLITE ACADEMY, THE; OR, INSTRUCTIONS FOR A
GENTEEL BEHAVIOUR AND POLITE ADDRESS IN MASTERS
AND MISSES...
(1) In the *Pretty Book of Pictures*, 1765 (JN, S. Crowder and B. Collins – no.
J308(8)) and the 1778 ed. of the same work (C & N, S. Crowder and B. Collins –
no. J308(13)) there was listed as 'lately published' (by whom is not stated) *The
Polite Academy;...* (as above), price 1*s*. A work of somewhat similar title: *The
Polite Academy; or, School of Behaviour*, was pubd by Baldwin and Collins in
1762, 1765 and 1771.
⌈1762 UCLA; 1765 BM; 1771 Bodley and Gardner.
(2) Listed as pr f EN in Trimmer's *Silver Thimble*, 1779 and 1801. Price 1*s*.

POLITE LADY, THE. See Allen, Chas.

J302. POLITE TALES AND FABLES.
(1) Adv. *MC&LA* 10.6.72 as to be had of FN(N). Price 6*d*.
(2) Listed as pr f a s b EN in *Clarissa...abridged*, n.d. (no. J315(2)).

J303. PORTIA. Allen's *Polite Lady* is sometimes listed under this title. 'Portia' was the writer of the letters forming the bk.

J304. POTTER, John. WORDS OF THE WISE, THE.
(1) An edition of [1768]. Price 1*s*. Pr f FN(N); but the bk was adv. *LC* 17–19.3.68 ('t.d.w.p.') as pr f N & C. JN had died on the previous 22 Dec., and the 'Dedication' is dated Jan. 1768. It looks as though N & C were able, presumably by reason of the terms of JN's will (see Introduction, pp. 16–17), to get the bk of out FN(N)'s hands and to publish it themselves. They did not trouble to change the TP imprint. This indicates that FN(N) had only acted as nominee for JN, and had no proprietory interest.

THE | WORDS OF THE WISE. | DESIGNED FOR THE | ENTERTAINMENT AND INSTRUCTION | OF | YOUNG MINDS. | [ornamental rule] | [3 lines quote] | [orn. rule] | LONDON: | PR F F. NEWBERY, IN P-N- | R. [PRICE ONE SHILLING.]

8°. 44 leaves. Pp. vii[viii]+9–87. Half-title.

⌈BM, 14·2×8·8 cm.

(2) Listed as pr f TC in *Newtonian System*, 1787. Price 1*s*. Welsh 332.

J305. PRATT, Samuel Jackson. PITY'S GIFT. *CBEL*, II, 377.
(1) First edition, 1798. Pr f EN et al. Price 1*s* (*per LC* 7–9.6.98, p. 551; but cf. the price for no. (2)). Hugo 122; Gum 4614.

PITY'S GIFT: | A | COLLECTION | OF | INTERESTING TALES, | TO EXCITE THE | COMPASSION OF YOUTH | FOR | THE ANIMAL CREATION. | [1 line] | FROM THE WRITINGS OF MR. PRATT. | [d.p.rule] | SELECTED BY A LADY. | [d.p.rule] | LONDON: | PR F T. N. LONGMAN, PATERNOSTER-ROW; | AND E. NEWBERY, SPC-Y. | [p.s.rule] | 1798.

12mo. 78 leaves. Pp. viii+147[148]. List of bks pr f Longman on last page. 15 wcts, possibly the work of Isaac Nicholson, but nothing to do with the Bewicks (*pace* Hugo). Mrs Pilkington has been suggested as the 'Lady' who made the selection.

⌈BM, 16·5×10·0 cm; Bodley; NUTP; LWaPL; Traylen; Hannas; Renier; Roscoe; Shiers; NRU; OOxM; Grant.

(2) Second edition, 1798. Pr f EN et al. Price 2*s* in bds, also given as 2*s* 6*d*. Welsh 289.

Title and *imprint*, with THE SECOND EDITION, and specification approx. as for no. (1).

⌈BM, 16·9×9·7 cm; NUTP; LUL; Traylen; Osborne, Cat. p. 211; UCLA; Welch; Grant.

(3) Third edition, 1801. Pr f EN et al.

Title approx. as for no. (1), with THE THIRD EDITION. *Imprint:* PR B C. WHITTINGHAM, | DEAN-STREET, FETTER-LANE; | FOR T. N. LONGMAN AND O. REES, PN-R; | AND E. NEWBERY, SPC-Y. | [p.s.rule] | 1801. Specification approx. as for no. (1). (Grey copy examined.)

⌈BM; Grey; Preston, Cat. p. 94; Renier; Sotheby, 9.10.71, lot 443.

PRESENT FOR AN APPRENTICE, A. See Barnard, Sir John.

J306. Entry deleted.

PRETTIEST BOOK FOR CHILDREN. See 'Bunyano, Don Stephano'.

J307. PRETTY BOOK FOR CHILDREN, A; OR, AN EASY
GUIDE TO THE ENGLISH TONGUE. Welsh 290–1.
(1) The 1st (*ca.* 1743 or 1744) and 2nd (1746) edd. were pubd by B. Collins of
Salisbury.
(2) Third edition. Adv. *GA* 23.2.48 as pr f JN, R. Baldwin and B. Collins. Price
6*d* bd and gilt.
(2A) Fourth edition not traced.
(3) Fifth edition, 1751. Pr f JN et al. Price 6*d*. Welsh 290; S&W Cat.
    A | PRETTY BOOK FOR CHILDREN: | OR, AN | EASY GUIDE | TO THE |
ENGLISH TONGUE. | PERFECTLY WELL ADAPTED TO THEIR TENDER
CAPACITIES, AND | ANSWERS THE END OF A CHILD'S GUIDE, SPEL- |
LING-BOOK, AND HISTORY-BOOK ALL IN ONE, ... | [3 lines] | AND
CONSISTS OF | [12 & 11 lines in two columns] | [p.rule] | VOL. I. THE FIFTH
EDITION. | [p.rule] | LONDON: PR F J. NEWBERY, AT THE BIBLE AND | SUN,
IN SPC-Y; J. HODGES, OVER- | AGAINST ST. MAGNUS-CHURCH, AND B.
COLLINS, ON | THE NEW CANAL IN SALISBURY. MDCCLI. [PR. 6*d*.]
    Wcts. D.f.b. (Communicated.) The 'Vol. II' to balance the 'Vol. I' referred
to in the TP was the *Museum for young Gentlemen and Ladies*, no. J253.
    [Ball.
(4) A 'new edition' adv. *PA* 1.1.53, as t.d.i.p. by JN, J. Hodges and B.
Collins.
(4A) Seventh edition, 1756. Pr f JN. NBL Cat. of 'The English at School', 1949,
item 260.
    [Birchenough.
(4B) Ninth edition, 1760. Pr f JN et al. Price 6*d*.
    Title as for no. (5A), with THE NINTH EDITION. *Imprint* as for no. (5A), with
date 1760 and Crowder's address 'over-against St. Magnus-Church'. TP within
a frame of printer's ornaments.
    In 6's. Copy seen imperfect, lacks all after K6. 60 leaves. Pp. 120. Pictorial
alphabet with 24 wcts, *ca.* 12 other wcts in text. D.f.b.
    [NorBM, 10·8×7·5 cm.
(5) Frequently listed between 1761 and 1767 as by JN, price 6*d* bd and gilt.
(5A) Tenth edition, 1761. Pr f JN et al. Price 6*d*.
    A | PRETTY BOOK FOR CHILDREN: | OR, AN EASY GUIDE TO THE |
ENGLISH TONGUE. | PERFECTLY WELL ADAPTED TO THEIR TENDER CA- |
PACITIES, AND IS DESIGN'D AS WELL FOR THE MORE | EASY INSTRUCTION
OF THOSE THAT CAN BUT JUST READ, | AS FOR THE ENTERTAINMENT OF

OTHERS THAT ARE A | LITTLE ADVANCED. | AND CONSISTS OF | [13 lines in 2 parallel columns] | [p.rule] | VOL. I. THE TENTH EDITION. | [p.rule] | LONDON: PR F J. NEWBERY, AT THE BIBLE | AND SUN, IN SPC-Y; S. CROW- | DER, IN P-N R; AND B. COLLINS, | ON THE NEW CANAL, IN SALIS-BURY. 1761. | (PRICE SIX-PENCE.) (the whole within a frame of printer's ornaments).

In 6's. 72 leaves. Pp. 144. 36 wcts in text. D.f.b. (Communicated.)
[Osborne*, 10·8×7·4 cm.

(6) Listed between 1768 and 1778 as by N & C (sometimes with Crowder and Collins), price 6*d*.

(7) Listed in *Newtonian System*, 1787, as pr f TC, price 6*d*. Welsh 290.

(8) An edition of 1789. Pr f the Executors of the late TC et al. Price 6*d*.

Title approx. as for no. (5A). *Imprint:* PR F THE EXECUTORS OF THE | LATE T. CARNAN, IN SPC-Y; | S. CROWDER, IN P-N-R, AND B. C. | COLLINS, IN SALISBURY. 1789. | [PRICE SIX-PENCE.]

In 6's. 71[+?] leaves. Pp. 142[+?]. Wcts. Details taken from the Renier copy.
[Renier (imperf.).

(9) Listed in *Anecdotes of Mary*, 1795, as pr f EN. Price 6*d*.

J308. PRETTY BOOK OF PICTURES, A, FOR LITTLE MASTERS AND MISSES: OR, TOMMY TRIP'S HISTORY OF BEASTS AND BIRDS. Welsh 291–2; *CBEL*, II, 561. Edwin Pearson's (very unreliable) Introduction to the 15th ed., 1867. As to Goldsmith's authorship see *Century Mag.*, Sept. 1882. *CBEL* lists as a bk which might have been written by JN.

(1) An edition of 1752. Pr f JN. Price 6*d*, bd and gilt. Rothschild 604; Scott 359; *TLS* 18 Dec. 1919, at p. 772, under 'Notes on Sales', mentions a copy in the coll. of H. W. Bruton.

Title approx. as for no. (8). *Imprint:* PR F J. NEWBERY, IN SPC-Y, OPPOSITE THE NORTH DOOR, AND BENJ. COLLINS, BOOKSELLER, ON THE NEW CANAL, IN SALISBURY. MDCCLII.

16mo in 8's. Advert. on last leaf. D.f.b. (The Rothschild Cat. makes no mention of wcts, and gives no note of pagination.)

(2) Second edition adv. *PA* 12.1.54 as pr f JN, J. Hodges and B. Collins. Price 6*d* bd and gilt.

(3) An edition of 1755 was recorded by Lyon. Possibly = the ed. adv. *PA* 17.5.56 as pr f JN, Hodges and Collins, price 6*d* neatly bd and gilt.

(4) Listed in *Little Pretty Pocket-Book*, 10th ed., 1760, and *Newtonian System*, 1761, as pr f or pubd by JN. Price 6*d* bd and gilt.

(5) Entry deleted.

(6) Fifth edition, undated (before 1765). Pr f JN, S. Crowder and B. Collins. Scott, pp. 359–60; Edwin Pearson, *op. cit.* pp. v–vi.

Title, with THE FIFTH EDITION, *imprint* and specification approx. as for no. (8). Wct FP sgd 'I.B.', and cuts in text; see no. (8) of this book. (Communicated.)

⌈PP.

(7) Sixth and seventh editions not traced.

(8) Eighth edition, 1765. Pr f JN et al.

A | PRETTY BOOK | OF | PICTURES | FOR LITTLE MASTERS AND MISSES: | OR, | TOMMY TRIP'S | HISTORY OF BEASTS AND BIRDS. | WITH A FULL DESCRIPTION OF | EACH IN VERSE AND PROSE. | TO WHICH IS PREFIX'D, | THE HISTORY OF LITTLE TOM TRIP HIMSELF, OF | HIS DOG JOULER, AND OF WOGLOG THE | GREAT GIANT. | [p.rule] | THE EIGHTH EDITION. | [p.rule] | LONDON: | PR F J. NEWBERY, IN SPC-Y, | OPPOSITE THE NORTH DOOR; S. CROWDER IN P-N- | R; AND B. COLLINS, BOOKSELLER, ON THE NEW- | CANAL, IN SALISBURY. MDCCLXV. [The whole within a frame of printer's ornaments.]

12mo. 66 leaves. Pp. viii+124. Wct FP and 59 wcts in text. The FP is sgd 'I.B.' – very probably the J. Bell who did cuts for the *Lilliputian Magazine*, the wct designs on the lower cover for the *Newtonian System*, 1784 etc. The cuts of the llama, the bison and the rhinoceros derive from Topsel's *Beasts*. It is very noticeable that the cuts of the birds are, both as to drawing and cutting, by a much more expert hand than those of the animals.

Lists of bks 'lately published' on recto of first and vso of last leaves. D.f.b.

⌈Roscoe, 9·7×8·1 cm.

(9) Ninth edition, 1767. Pr f JN et al.

Title, with THE NINTH EDITION, approx. as for no. (8). *Imprint*, with date MDCCLXVII, and specification approx. as for no. (8). D.f.b.

⌈BM, 9·9×8·0 cm; Bell.

(10) See Fig. 24.

In 12's. Specification approx. as for no. (8). D.f.b.

⌈Oup, 9·7×8·3 cm.

(11) Eleventh edition not traced.

(12) A twelfth edition, n.d. Rothschild 605; NBL 583, where it is described as 'Pr f the Booksellers...[ca. 1785]. With frontispiece and numerous cuts in the text by Bewick'. Seemingly a pirated ed., perhaps copied from the 1779 ed. Pubd by Saint of Newcastle (Hugo 16). Bewick was too young to have done the cuts in the Newbery edd. (born 1753).

(13) Thirteenth edition, 1778. Pr f C & N et al.

Title as for no. (8) with THE THIRTEENTH EDITION. *Imprint:* PR F CARNAN AND NEWBERY, IN SP | C-Y; S. CROWDER, IN P-N- | R; AND B. COLLINS, ON THE NEW CANAL, IN | SALISBURY. MDCCLXXVIII.

Specification as for no. (8).

⌈Schiller (imperf.), 9·9×7·9 cm; UCLA.

(14) Fourteenth edition, 1787. Pr f TC, Crowder and Collins. Price 6d.

Title as for no. (8), with THE FOURTEENTH EDITION. *Imprint:* PR F T. CARNAN, IN SPC-Y; | S. CROWDER, IN P-N-R; AND B. C. | COLLINS, BOOKSELLER, ON THE NEW-CANAL, IN | SALISBURY. MDCCLXXXVII.

A
PRETTY BOOK
OF
PICTURES
For Little MASTERS and MISSES:
OR,
TOMMY TRIP's
HISTORY of BEASTS and BIRDS.
With a familiar DESCRIPTION of
Each in VERSE and PROSE.
To which is prefix'd,
The History of little TOM TRIP himself, of
his Dog JOULER, and of WOGLOG the
great Giant.
THE TENTH EDITION.
LONDON:
Printed for NEWBERY and CARNAN, in St. Paul's
Church-Yard; S. CROWDER. in Pater-Noster-
Row; and B. COLLINS, Bookseller, on the New-
Canal, in Salisbury. M DCC LXIX.

Fig. 24. Frontispiece and title-page of J308(10). (Reduced.)

In 12's. 66 leaves. Pp. viii+124. Wcts (? as for no. (8)). Advert. of *Royal Psalter* on p. 124. White or buff bds impressed with red pictorial designs.

[NorBM, 9·9 × 8·4 cm.

J309. PRETTY PLAY-THING, A, FOR CHILDREN OF ALL DENOMINATIONS. Welsh 292–3; Welch 960.2 (p. 100).

(1) Listed as pr f JN in no. J190B(3), 1759; and adv. *PL* 12.2.60 as pubd by JN, price 3*d* bd and gilt.

(2) An undated edition. [Pr f JN.] Price 3*d*.

A | PRETTY PLAY-THING | FOR | CHILDREN OF ALL DENOMINATIONS: | CONTAINING | I. THE ALPHABET IN VERSE, FOR THE USE | OF LITTLE CHILDREN. | II. AN ALPHABET IN PROSE, INTERSPERSED | WITH PROPER LESSONS IN LIFE, FOR THE | USE OF GREAT CHILDREN. | III. THE SOUND OF THE LETTERS EX- | PLAINED BY VISIBLE OBJECTS, DELINEATED | ON COPPER PLATES. | IV. THE CUZ'S CHORUS, SET TO MUSIC. | TO BE SUNG BY CHILDREN, IN ORDER TO | TEACH THEM TO JOIN THEIR LETTERS INTO | SYLLABLES, AND PRONOUNCE THEM PROPERLY. | V. AN EXACT REPRESENTATION OF A GOOD FAT | CUZ ARRAYED IN THE ROBES OF HIS ORDER. | THE WHOLE EMBELLISHED WITH VARIETY OF | CUTS, AFTER THE MANNER OF PTOLOMY. | (*Imprint* approx. as for no. (4).)

Pp. iv, [v–vii, Alphabet in verse, 12 plates for 'The Alphabet displayed by

A

PRETTY PLAY-THING

FOR

Children of all Denominations:

CONTAINING

I. The Alphabet in Verſe, for the Uſe **of**
Little Children.

II. *Tom Noddy* and his Siſter *Sue*, a Lilliputian Story.

III. The Sound of the Letters explained
by viſible Objeᶜts.

IV. An Alphabet in Proſe, interſperſed
with proper Leſſons in Life, for the Uſe
of Great Children.

V. The Cuz's Chorus ſet to Muſic; to
be ſung by Children, in order to teach
them to join their Letters into Syllables,
and pronounce them properly.

VI. An exaᶜt Repreſentation of a good Fat
Cuz arrayed in the Robes of his Order.

The Whole embelliſhed with Variety of
Cuts, after the Manner of Ptolomy.

A NEW EDITION.

ALEXANDRIA:
Printed for the Bookſellers of *Egypt* and *Pal-
myra*, and ſold at the *Bible and Sun* in *St. Paul's
Church-Yard, London.*
[Price bound half a Shaſs, or 3d. Engliſh.]

Fig. 25. Title-page of J309(4).

---

sensible Objects']+[17]–59[60–4 list of bks s b JN]. D.f.b. Letter G of 'Good' at p. iii has an ornam. surround. No tailpiece at p. 60. (Communicated.)

[Welch, 8·5 cm; Roscoe (photocopied selected leaves).

(2A) Another undated edition. [Pr f JN.] Price 3d. Inscription in the Welch copy 'Thos Barrett his Book. He was born March 29th 1759'.

Title, imprint and specification approx. as for no. (2), except pp. iv[v–xvii]+ 17–60[61–4] and bk-list on last 4 pages. D.f.b. Letter 'G' in 'Good' at p. iii has no surround. Square ornam. tailpiece at p. 60. (Communicated.)

[Welch, 8·5 cm (imperf.).

(3) An edition of 1762. JN. Price 3d. Welsh 292; *CBEL*, II, 562.

(4) A 'new edition', n.d. Probably 1770 or after, as the bk-list includes the *London Cries*, the 1st recorded ed. of which is dated in that year. [FN(S) and/or N & C.] Price 3d.

See Fig. 25.

In 8's. 32 leaves. Pp. 62[64]. 24 small wcts to illustrate each of the 2 alphabets. Whole-page wct of 'a good fat Cuz' opposite p. 52 sgd 'J. Bell'. Music at p. 56. List of bks at end s b FN Jun. & Co. D.f.b.

[St Bride (imperf.), 9·5×6·5 cm.

(4A) A 'new edition' in the Ball colln may be identical with no. (4). D.f.b.

(5) Another undated edition. [TC.] Not before *ca.* 1780 (bk-list includes *Mother Goose's Melody* – see J250(1)). Price 2d.

Title approx. as for no. (4). *Imprint:* ALEXANDRIA: | PR F THE BOOK-
SELLERS OF EGYPT AND | PALMYRA, AND SOLD AT NO. 65, IN S | PC-Y,
LONDON. | [PRICE TWO-PENCE.]

In 8's. 32 leaves. Pp. 62[63]. First and last leaves pastedowns. 49 wcts, that at
p. 53, 'a good fat Cuz', sgd 'J. Bell' (so also no. (4)). D.f.b. List of bks pr f TC
on last page.

[Bodley, 9·6×6·2 cm.

(6) Listed as pr f TC in *Newtonian System*, 1787, price 2*d*. ? = no. (5).

(7) For certain other variant issues see Welch, *op. cit.*

PRETTY POEMS. See J74 and J346.

PRIMROSE PRETTYFACE. See RENOWNED HISTORY OF...

PRINCE LEE BOO. See HISTORY OF...

J310. 'PUZZLEBRAINS, Peregrine'. CHRISTMAS AMUSEMENT,
1799. Pr f EN. Price 1*s* 6*d*. Welsh 297; *CBEL*, II, 564; Gum 4659.

CHRISTMAS AMUSEMENT; | OR, THE | HAPPY ASSOCIATION | OF |
MIRTH AND INGENUITY: | BEING AN | ELEGANT COLLECTION | OF |
ORIGINAL RIDDLES, CHARADES, &c. | CULLED FROM THE | VASE OF
FANCY, | AT | CONUNDRUM CASTLE. | [d.p.rule] | BY PEREGRINE PUZZLE-
BRAINS. | [d.p.rule] | LONDON: | PR F E. NEWBERY, CORNER OF SP | CY. |
[p.s.rule] | 1799.

In 6's. 72 leaves+engvd FP sgd 'J. Scott sculpt'. Pp. v+134[138]. Advert. on
last page. Yellow bds, oval label on upper.

[BM, 13·6×8·6 cm; Preston, Cat. p. 100; Platt.

J311. 'PUZZLEWELL, Peter'. CHOICE COLLECTION OF
RIDDLES, A. Welsh 297; *CBEL*, II, 564.

(1) An edition of 1792. Pr f EN. Price 1*s*.

A | CHOICE COLLECTION | OF | RIDDLES, | CHARADES, REBUSSES, | &c.
| CHIEFLY ORIGINAL. | BY | PETER PUZZLEWELL, ESQ. | [d.p.rule] |
LONDON: | PR F E. NEWBERY, CORNER OF S | PC-Y. | 1792.

In 6's. 54 leaves+engvd FP. Pp. iv+104.

[BM, 13·2×8·2 cm; CUL; Bondy, Cat. 77 [1969] item 173 (*ex* Sotheby, 24.2.69;
lot 12); Brimmell, Cat. 67 [1970] item 18.

(2) An edition of 1794. Pr f EN. Price 1*s*. NBL 924.

Title and *imprint*, with date 1794, approx. as for no. (1).

In 6's. 54 leaves+engvd FP. Pp. iv+108. Rose bds, vell. spine.

[V&A(GL); BmPL; Traylen, 13·4×8·6 cm (imperf.); Welch; Ries; UCLA.

(2A) An edition of PART SECOND, 1795. Pr f EN.

Title and *imprint*, with date 1795, as for no. (3). Pp. 108. FP. Light green bds,
label on upper. (Communicated.)

[UCLA, *ex* Welch.

(3) An edition of PART SECOND, 1796. Pr f EN. Price 1s.

A | CHOICE COLLECTION | OF | RIDDLES, | CHARADES, REBUSSES, | &c | PART SECOND. | [p.s.rule] | BY PETER PUZZLEWELL, ESQ. | [d.p.rule] | LONDON: | PR F E. NEWBERY, CORNER OF S | PC-Y. | 1796.

54 leaves+engvd FP. Pp. 108. Marbled bds, green vell. spine; also pink bds with label; green bds.

[Traylen, 13·4×8·6 cm; Pollard; Welch; Shiers; McKell.

(4) An edition of PART THIRD, 1796. Pr f EN. Price 1s.

Title and *imprint* approx. as for no. (3), but reading PART THIRD.

In 6's. 54 leaves+engvd FP. Pp. 108. Pink bds, label on upper.

[Bodley, 13·6×8·2 cm; Opie; Osborne*; Welch; MH; Elkin Mathews, Cat. 163 [1965] item 90.

(5) An edition of 1800. Pr f EN.

[BM (destroyed).

J312. PUZZLING CAP, THE (also PUZZLING-CAP).

(1) Listed as pr f FN(N) in the *Sugar Plumb*, 1771 and in the *Brother's Gift*, 1777, price 3d.

(2) An edition of 1786. Pr f EN. Price 3d. S&W Cat.

THE | PUZZLING CAP: | A CHOICE | COLLECTION OF RIDDLES, | IN FAMILIAR VERSE; | WITH A CURIOUS CUT TO EACH. | [p.s.rule] | LONDON: | PR F E. NEWBERY, AT THE CORNER | OF SPC-Y, 1786. | [PRICE THREE PENCE.]

Pp. 95. Wcts. Bk-list at end. Half-title. D.f.b. (Communicated.)

[Ball.

(3) An edition of 1789. Pr f EN. Price 3d. Welsh 297. Listed in *Prince Lee Boo*, 1789.

(4) An edition of 1795. Pr f EN. Price 3d.

Title (with THE PUZZLING-CAP), and *imprint* (with date 1795) approx. as for no. (2).

Pp. 32. Wcts. (Communicated.)

[Ball.

(5) Another edition of 1795. Pr f EN. Price 6d.

The TP is that used for no. (4).

Pp. 95. 42 wcts. List of bks pr f EN on pp. 91–5. D.f.b. (Communicated.)

[PP.

RATIONAL DAME, THE. See J124.

RENOWNED HISTORY OF GILES GINGERBREAD. See J267.

J312A. RENOWNED HISTORY OF PRIMROSE PRETTYFACE, THE. Recorded in Trimmer's *Guardian of Education*, vol. I, p. 436, as a Newbery publication and 'originally one of Newbery's Lilliputian Library'. Similarly recorded by Lyon. The only copies seen were by John Marshall of Aldermary Church-Yard.

J313. RENOWNED HISTORY OF THE WHITE CAT, THE, n.d. Pr f EN. Price 6*d.* Weedon 57, IV; Gum 4725 and plate 80. Listed in *Anecdotes of Mary*, 1795. One of the 10 vols forming the *Lilliputian Library* 'compiled' by Richard Johnson in 1779 (no. J218).

THE | RENOWNED HISTORY | OF THE | WHITE CAT, | AND | OTHER INTERESTING STORIES. | [p.s.rule] | ADORNED WITH CUTS. | [p.s.rule] | LONDON: | PR F E. NEWBERY, AT THE CORNER OF S | PC-Y. | [p.rule] | [PRICE SIX-PENCE.]

Wct FP and 10 wcts in text. Flowered paper bds. (Communicated.) This will probably be found to consist of the Domville ed. with a cancel title-leaf and some leaves of prelims removed (cf. nos. J89 and J217). The title of the Domville ed. was *Gulliver's Travels, containing the Renowned History of the White Cat, and other interesting Stories.*

⌈Ball.

RHETORICK MADE FAMILIAR. See CIRCLE OF THE SCIENCES, J69.

J314. RICHARDSON, Samuel. AESOP'S FABLES, with Life by Richardson. Muir, p. 71. For earlier edd. see *CBEL*, II, 515.
(1) Listed in Paterson's *Travelling Dictionary*, 1777, as pr f TC. Price 2*s* 6*d.*
(2) Adv. as pr f Power & Co et al. in *LC* 25–8.10.88, p. 412, under the description: *Aesop's Fables, with instructive Morals and Reflections... And Life of Aesop prefixed. By Mr. Richardson.* Pr f J. F. and C. Rivington, T. Longman, B. Law, J. Johnson, G. G. J. and J. Robinson, T. Cadell, R. Baldwin, W. Goldsmith, W. Lowndes, and Power & Co. Price 2*s* 6*d.*

J315. RICHARDSON, Samuel. CLARISSA...ABRIDGED. Welsh 299–300; Welch 993.1, p. 166 and his Introduction, p. 147.
(1) An edition by FN(N) adv. *LC* 27–9.12.68, p. 619, as to be pubd 'in a few days', price 1*s*; and listed in Winlove's *Moral Lectures*, 1769, as s b FN(N).
(1A) Listed in Chesterfield's *Maxims*, 1777, as pr f FN(N), price 1*s.*
(2) A 'new edition', n.d. Pr f EN. Price 1*s.*

CLARISSA; | OR, THE | HISTORY | OF A | YOUNG LADY. | COMPREHENDING | THE MOST IMPORTANT CONCERNS OF | PRIVATE LIFE. | ABRIDGED FROM THE WORKS OF | SAMUEL RICHARDSON, ESQ. | AUTHOR OF | PAMELA, AND SIR CHARLES GRANDISON. | [p.rule] | A NEW EDITION. | [d.p.rule] | LONDON: | PR F E. NEWBERY, AT THE CORNER OF S | PCY. | (PRICE ONE SHILLING.)

In 6's. 90 leaves+6 insets. Pp. 176. Engvd FP and 5 other engvd leaves. Catchword at p. [3] 'dispo-'. 'Young Lady' in line 5 of TP in italic caps. Last line of

bk-list on p. [177] 'Stories, embellished with cuts. Price *6d*'. List of bks pr f a s b
EN on last 4 leaves. Floral designs in black on brown bds. Also D.f.b.

[Oup, 11·1×7·7 cm; Ball; Sotheby, 16.3.70, lot 7; Roscoe (selected leaves Ball copy).

(3) Entry deleted.

(4) Another undated edition by EN. Catchword at p. [3] 'disposition'. 'Young Lady' in line 5 of TP in roman caps. Last line of bk-list on p. [177] 'ment for Leisure Hours. Being an en-' (plus catchword 'tertaining').

[Ball; Roscoe (selected leaves Ball copy).

(5) Listed in *Prince Lee Boo*, 1789 and *Anecdotes of Mary*, 1795, price 1*s*.

(6) Another undated edition by EN. May be one of the above. Not seen.

[Bondy, Cat. 79 [1970] item 216.

J316. RICHARDSON, Samuel. HISTORY OF PAMELA...
ABRIDGED. Welsh 300; Welch 994.1, p. 168 and his Introduction, p. 147.

(1) An edition of 1769. Pr f FN(N). Price 1*s*.

THE | HISTORY | OF | PAMELA, | OR, | VIRTUE REWARDED. | ABRIDGED
FROM THE WORKS OF | SAMUEL RICHARDSON, ESQ; | ADORNED WITH
COPPER PLATES. | [d.p.rule] | LONDON: | PR F F. NEWBERY, AT THE CORNER
OF | SPCY. | [p.rule] | MDCCLXIX.

Pp. 132. Engvd FP sgd 'J. Lodge delin et sculp', and other illustrations. Bk-list on pp. [iv–vi]. Advert. of pills etc on pp. [vi, vii]. D.f.b. (Communicated.)

[Welch.

(2) An undated edition. Pr f FN(N). Price 1*s*. Gum 4749.

Title and *imprint* approx. as for no. (1).

In 6's. 90 leaves+7 insets. Pp. 168. Engvd FP and 6 engvd leaves in text, all sgd 'J. (? I or T) Lodge delin et sculp'. List of bks pr f a s b FN(N) on a2ᵛ–a5ʳ. D.f.b.

In this ed. in line 9 of TP read 'Copper-Plates.' followed by d.p.rule of thin and thick rules; S of 'St' in last line is under 'te' of 'Printed' in preceding line. Five lines of text on p. 168 beginning 'will be habituated' and ending 'at the hazard of their lives'.

[BM, 11·1×7·6 cm; Ball; OOxM (Welch and Roscoe have photocopied selected leaves).

(2A) Listed in Chesterfield's *Maxims*, 1777, as pr f FN(N). Price 1*s*. Perhaps = no. 2 or (2B).

(2B) Another undated edition. Pr f FN(N). Price 1*s*.

Title and *imprint* approx. as for no. (1). Pp. 168. Engvd FP as in no. (2) and 5 engvd leaves in text. Bk-list as in no. (2). A different setting of type: in line 9 of TP read 'Copper Plates.' followed by d.p.rule of thick and thin rules; S of 'St' in last line under the 'd' of 'Printed' in preceding line. Nine lines of text on p. 168 beginning 'taught to rejoice in...', ending 'their lives.'. (Communicated.)

[Welch, 11·0 cm; Roscoe (photocopied selected leaves).

(3) An undated edition. Pr f EN. Price 1s. Bodley dates *ca.* 1790. Gum 4748 (*not* 4751) and pl. 79.

Title approx. as for no. (1). *Imprint:* PR F E. NEWBERY, AT THE CORNER OF S | PC-Y. | [p.rule] | [PRICE 1s.]

In 6's. 90 leaves+6 insets. Pp. 161[172]. Engvd FP and 5 engvd leaves in text, sgd as for no. (2). List of bks pr f a s b EN on pp. [163–72]. Orange floral bds. The word 'Esq.' on TP in italics; there are no type-ornaments at foot of p. [172]; last line on p. 161 'lives'.

[Bodley, 11·2×7·8 cm; Welch; Ball; Roscoe (photocopied selected leaves Welch copy).

(4) Another undated edition. Pr f EN. The word 'Esq.' on TP in Roman type; three type-ornaments at foot of p. [172]; last line on p. 161 'at the hazard of their lives.'. Gum 4751. (Communicated.)

[Ball.

(5) A variant issue of no. (4). No type-ornaments on p. [172]. (Communicated.)

[McKell.

J317. RICHARDSON, Samuel. HISTORY OF SIR CHARLES GRANDISON...ABRIDGED. Welsh 300.

(1) Adv. *LC* 27–9.12.68, p. 619, as to be pubd 'in a few days' by FN(N), price 1s; and listed in Winlove's *Moral Lectures*, 1769.

(1A) An undated edition. Pr f FN(N). The chronological position of this ed. is not established.

THE | HISTORY | OF | SIR CHARLES GRANDISON, | ABRIDGED FROM THE WORKS OF | SAMUEL RICHARDSON, ESQ; | [p.rule] | AUTHOR OF PAMELA AND CLARISSA. | [p.rule] | [device] | [p.rule] | LONDON: | PR F F. NEWBERY, AT THE CORNER OF | SPC-Y.

Pp. iii[viii]+178. Engvd FP sgd 'J. Lodge delin et sculp' and 5 other engvd leaves. (Communicated.)

[RP.

(1B) An undated edition, pp. 178. Very possibly identical with no. (1A).

[UCLA.

(2) Second edition, n.d. FN(N).

[NNC-T (Darton Coll. Cat. no. 27).

(3) Third edition, n.d. Pr f FN(N). Price 1s. *N&Q*, vii, 1 (June 1886), p. 504.

Title, with THE THIRD EDITION, approx. as for no. (4). *Imprint:* PR F F. NEWBERY, AT THE CORNER OF SPC-Y. [PRICE ONE SHILLING.]

Pp. 180. 6 engvd leaves (*per N&Q*).

[Ball; Col. W. F. Prideaux (in 1886).

(3A) Listed in Chesterfield's *Maxims,* 1777, as pr f FN(N). Price 1s.

(4) A 'new edition', 1783. Pr f EN. Price 1s. Gum 4752 and pl. 78.

THE | HISTORY | OF | SIR CHARLES GRANDISON, | ABRIDGED FROM THE WORKS OF | SAMUEL RICHARDSON, ESQ; | AUTHOR OF PAMELA AND CLARISSA. | [p.rule] | A NEW EDITION, ADORNED WITH COPPER PLATES. |

[p.rule] | LONDON: | PR F E. NEWBERY, AT THE CORNER | OF SPC-Y. |
MDCCLXXXIII. | [PRICE ONE SHILLING.]
　　Pp. 182. Engvd leaves. (Communicated.)
　　[Opie; Welch; UCLA; Ball; McKell.
(5) A 'new edition', 1789. Pr f EN. Price 1s. NBL 663.
　　Title and *imprint* approx. as for no. (4), with date 1789.
　　In 6's. 90 leaves+5 insets. Pp. 180. 5 engvd leaves sgd 'J. Lodge delin et sculp'.
　　[BM, 11·3×7·3 cm; Welch; UCLA; Ball.
(6) Listed as pr f EN in *Joseph Andrews*, 1799, price 1s.

J318. RICHARDSON, Samuel. PATHS OF VIRTUE
DELINEATED, THE; OR, THE HISTORY IN MINIATURE OF
THE CELEBRATED PAMELA, CLARISSA HARLOWE, AND
SIR CHARLES GRANDISON. *CBEL*, II, 515. Welsh records (p. 300) that
Newbery sold Collins a half share in this for £6. 8s 6d. The 1756 ed. was by R.
Baldwin (copy in BM) and I have traced no ed. under the imprint of JN or others
of the family.
　　See Muir, p. 71; Welch 993.1; W. M. Sale, *Samuel Richardson, A bibliographical
Record* (New Haven, 1936), p. 134.

RILEY'S EMBLEMS. See J389.

J319. RIVAL PUPILS, THE. Nos. (2), (3) and (4) may be identical.
(1) An undated edition described by Welsh, p. 300, as 'printed for J. Newbery,
at the corner of SPCY'. JN never was at that address. And at p. 340 Welsh lists
the bk as 'N.D. 1766'.
(2) Adv. *LC* 3–5.1.75, p. 11, as pr f FN(N), price 1s.
(3) An undated edition by FN(N), with ms date 5 July 1779. The TP is identical
with that for no. (4).
　　[MH (very imperf.).
(4) An undated edition pr f FN(N). Ball copy has ms date 20 Oct. 1781.
　　THE | RIVAL PUPILS; | OR, A | NEW HOLIDAY GIFT | FOR A | BOARDING-
SCHOOL. | [device] | LONDON; | PR F F. NEWBERY, AT THE CORNER OF |
SPC-Y.
　　12mo. 90 leaves+engvd FP and 4 other engvd leaves. Half-title. Pp. xi[xii]+
151[152], 81–91[92]. D.f.b. (Communicated.)
　　[McKell, 11·3×7·2 cm; Ball; RP.
(5) Listed as pr f EN in J134(3), n.d. (pr f EN). Price 1s.

J320. ROBIN GOODFELLOW; A FAIRY TALE. Welsh 301.
(1) Adv. *LC* 19–21.12.69, and listed in Winlove's *Moral Lectures*, 1769, as s b
FN(N), price 2d bd and gilt. Probably = no. (2).
(2) An edition of 1770. Pr f FN(N). Price 2d.
　　ROBIN GOODFELLOW; | A | FAIRY TALE. | WRITTEN BY A FAIRY. | FOR

233

THE AMUSEMENT OF | ALL THE PRETTY LITTLE FAIES AND FAIRIES IN | GREAT BRITAIN AND IRELAND. | LONDON, | PR F F. NEWBERY, AT THE CORNER OF | SPC-Y, 1770. | [PRICE TWO-PENCE.]

In 8's. Pp. 58[63]. Wct FP and 23 wcts in text. List of bks pubd by FN(N) on pp. [59–63]. Advert. of medicines on p. [63]. D.f.b.

[BM, 9·1×6·1 cm; MH.

(3) Listed in *Brother's Gift*, 1777, as pr f FN(N). Price 2*d*.

(4) An edition of 1785. Pr f EN. Price 2*d*.

Title approx. as for no. (2). *Imprint:* PR F E. NEWBERY, AT THE CORNER | OF SPC-Y. 1785. | [PRICE TWO-PENCE.]

Pp. 62[63]. Wct FP and wcts in text. Advert. on p. [63]. (Communicated.)
[Ball.

(5) Listed in *The Menagerie*, 1800, as pr f EN. Price 2*d*.

ROBIN HOOD. See ENTERTAINING AND REMARKABLE HISTORY OF...

ROLLA, LIFE OF. See Brewer, Geo.

J321. ROLLIN, Charles. PHILOSOPHY FOR CHILDREN.
(1) The *GA* for 25.12.49 advtd the *Mosaic Creation; or, Divine Wisdom display'd ...to which is added The Philosophy of* (sic) *Children extracted from the universally admired Belles Lettres of Mr. Rollin. Embellished with a great variety of Copper plates...* Pr a s b J. Jefferies, J. Newbery and J. Fuller. Price 1*s*; or the two works could be had separately at 6*d* each. But the copy of the 1749 ed. in Elkin Mathews' Cat. 163 [1965] item 276 was by Jefferies and Fuller alone; so also the Welch copy. See J248(1).
(2) Adv. as by JN between 1759 and 1764. Price 6*d*. Welsh 301.
(3) See Fig. 26.

In 8's. 39 leaves+8 insets. Pp. 78. Engvd FP and 7 other engvd leaves, each showing the figures of 3 beasts, birds, reptiles, insects etc. These figures derive from, or from a common prototype for, corresponding figures in Boreman's *Three Hundred Animals*, no. J41, most, if not all, of which followed 16th- or 17th-century originals.

[Roscoe, 10·3×6·6 cm.

J321A. ROMAN HISTORY BY QUESTION AND ANSWER.
Listed in J69(4), 1769 and A222(9), 1767. Presumably = Lockman's *New Roman History by Question and Answer*.

J322. ROYAL ALPHABET, THE; OR, CHILD'S BEST INSTRUCTOR. [TO WHICH IS ADDED, THE HISTORY OF A LITTLE BOY FOUND UNDER A HAYCOCK.] Richard Johnson 'wrote' the *History of a little Boy found under a Haycock* (see the note to J163)

PHILOSOPHY for CHILDREN:
Extracted from the universally admired
BELLES LETTRES of M. *ROLLIN.*
In which is introduced,
An accurate, though compendious DE-
SCRIPTION of several select ANIMALS.

VIZ.

BIRDS,   } { FISHES, *and*
BEASTS, } { INSECTS.

Compiled from the
WRITINGS of the most approved NA-
TURALISTS, both Ancient and Modern.

Embellished with a great Variety of curious Copper-Plates, neatly engraved, expressive of each
Animal.

*O Lord, how manifold are thy Works! in Wisdom
hast thou made them all.* Pf. civ. ver. 24.

LONDON:
Printed for J. NEWBERY, at the *Bible and Sun,*
in *St.* Paul's Church-Yard. 1766.
[Price *Six-pence.*]

*Each fish the footsteps of Gods Wisdom bears,
And ev'ry Bird & Beast his Pow'r declares.*

Fig. 26. Frontispiece and title-page of J321(3).

which appears to be a continuation of the present *History of a little Boy.* It is not apparent whether Johnson's Day-book entry comprised no. J163 alone or that and the present *History.* He makes no mention in the Day-book of the *Royal Alphabet.* Johnson's entry for the *Little Boy* is dated July 1786, so no. (3) below can be dated 1780 or after (because pubd by EN) if Johnson did not 'write' the *Little Boy,* part of it, 1786, or after if he did; and in the latter event nos. (1) and (2) below would comprise the *Royal Alphabet* alone.

(1) Adv. *LC* 31.12.78–2.1.79 as pubd by FN(N). Price 1*d.*
(2) Listed in *Cries of London,* 1784, as pr f EN. Price 1*d.* Welsh 169.
(3) An undated edition. Pr f EN. Price 1*d* bd and gilt.

THE | ROYAL ALPHABET; | OR, | CHILD'S BEST INSTRUCTOR. | TO WHICH IS ADDED, | THE HISTORY OF A LITTLE BOY, | FOUND UNDER A HAYCOCK. | [rule] | LONDON: | PR F E. NEWBERY, THE CORNER OF | SPC-Y. | (PRICE ONE PENNY, BOUND AND GILT.)

In 8's. Pp. 31. Wct FP and 26 other wcts. First and last leaves pastedowns. D.f.b. (Communicated.)

⌐MB.

(4) Listed in *Flights of a Lady-Bird*, 1794 and *The Menagerie*, 1800 as pr f EN. Price 1*d*.

ROYAL BATTLEDORE. See *sub* BATTLEDORE.

J323. ROYAL GUIDE, THE; OR, AN EASY INTRODUCTION TO READING ENGLISH. Welsh 302; Alston, IV, 711–12. Of the 7 copies here recorded 5 are imperfect. Was there deliberate mutilation, perhaps by careful parents? I cannot say whether the imperfections in these copies correspond.

(1) Adv. *LC* 30.5.69–1.6.69, p. 515, as pr f FN(N). Price 6*d* bd and gilt. ? = nos. (2) or (3).

(2) An undated edition pr f FN(N). Price 6*d*. Last line on p. 118 reads: 'the glory, for ever and ever, Amen.'

Title-page engvd and printed in brown ink: THE | ROYAL GUIDE; | OR, AN | EASY INTRODUCTION | TO | READING ENGLISH. | EMBELLISHED | WITH A GREAT VARIETY OF COPPER PLATES, | AND OTHER CUTS. | [p.rule] | MOST HUMBLY INSCRIBED TO | HIS ROYAL HIGHNESS PRINCE | EDWARD. | [ornam. rule] | LONDON: | PR F F. NEWBERY, AT THE CORNER | OF SPCY. | PRICE SIX PENCE.

16mo. Pp. 128. Engvd FP and title-leaf; 26 engvd leaves of illustrations for alphabet and text, pr in pairs using alternately brown and black ink; many whole p. engvgs; 24 very small wcts for an alphabet at pp. 81–91. D.f.b.

[V&A (imperf.), 10·3×6·4 cm; Bath (imperf.); Welch (imperf.).

(3) Another issue of no. (2), undated. Pr f FN(N). Price 6*d*. Last line on p. 118 reads: 'ever Amen.'. (Communicated.)

[Ball (imperf.).

(3A) Listed in Chesterfield's *Maxims*, 1777, as pr f FN(N). Price 6*d*. Perhaps = nos (2) or (3).

(4) An undated edition by EN. Perhaps = nos (5) or (6).

[Harding.

(5) An undated edition by EN. P. 128, line 1 reads: 'monstrated against treating his fair friends in'. (Communicated.)

[Ball (imperf.).

(6) Another undated edition. Pr f EN. Price 6*d*. P. 128, line 1 reads: 'to secure his future happiness; and the'.

THE | ROYAL GUIDE; | OR, AN | EASY INTRODUCTION | TO | READING ENGLISH. | EMBELLISHED WITH A GREAT VARIETY OF CUTS. | MOST HUMBLY INSCRIBED | TO | HIS ROYAL HIGHNESS | PRINCE EDWARD. | [p.s.rule] | LONDON: | PR F E. NEWBERY, THE CORNER OF SP | C-Y. | [PRICE SIXPENCE.]

In 8's. 63 leaves+engvd FP and 26 engvd leaves of Alphabet and text. Pp. [3–28], 31–128. Wcts in text. D.f.b. (Communicated.)

[McKell, 10·9×7·1 cm.

(7) Listed as pr f EN in J88(3), vol. I, 1786, and up to 1800 (ENC, p. 6). Price 6*d* bd and gilt.

J324. ROYAL PRIMER, THE; OR, AN EASY...GUIDE TO THE ART OF READING. Welsh 302.

(1) Adv. *GEP* 26–9.10.51 as pr f JN, J. Hodges, R. Baldwin and B. Collins. Price 3*d* neatly bd and gilt. A copy described as 'The only recorded copy of the second and first surviving edition', from the Oppenheimer colln, was exhibited at the Pierpont Morgan Lib. in 1954–5, under the description THE ROYAL PRIMER; OR, AN EASY AND PLEASANT GUIDE TO THE ART OF READING ...LONDON: PR F J. NEWBERY...AND B. COLLINS AT SALISBURY, [1751]. (Cat. item 8.) It is not apparent whether the date '[1751]' is established or conjectural. This would seem to be the copy which formed lot 326 in the Bussell sale at Sotheby's on 6 Feb. 1945.

(2) A 'new edition' adv. *PA* 1.1.53 as pr a s b JN, J. Hodges, and B. Collins. Price 3*d*.

(3) An edition of 1755. JN and B. Collins. Recorded by Lyon. Presumably the ed. adv. *PA* 14.5.55, price 3*d* neatly bd and gilt. Or was Lyon relying on the advert.?

(4) Listed up to 1767 as pr f JN (in J225(8)). Price as before.

(5) An undated edition. Pr f JN et al. Price 3*d*. A difficulty arises in respect of this ed. which, for the present, cannot be resolved satisfactorily: The advert. on the recto of the 1st leaf (p. [1]) is of the 3rd ed. of the *Royal Psalter* which is there stated to be pr f a s b JN et al. But the 2nd ed. of the *Psalter* was by R. Baldwin in 1767 (copy in BM) and Welsh gives the date of the 3rd as 1776, a date confirmed by the copy of Collins' Ledger Account set out at p. 364 in Welsh. In the note on the 3rd ed. of the *Psalter* (J326(5)) I have suggested that that Account refers to a reprinting of that ed.

[The Royal Arms] | THE | ROYAL PRIMER; | OR, AN EASY AND PLEASANT | GUIDE TO THE ART OF READING. | AUTHORIZ'D BY | HIS MAJESTY KING GEORGE II. | TO BE USED THROUGHOUT | HIS MAJESTY'S DOMINIONS. | ADORN'D WITH CUTS. | [p.rule] | LONDON: PR F J. NEWBERY, AT THE BIBLE | AND SUN, IN SPC-Y, AND | B. COLLINS AT SALISBURY. (PRICE BOUND 3*d*.) [The whole within an ornam. frame of rosettes.]

In 12's. 36 leaves. Pp. 72. Wct FP with verses above and below. Advert. of *Royal Psalter* (see above). Alphabet with 24 wct illustrations; 25 wcts in text, many used elsewhere in Newbery bks of this period. D.f.b.

The advert. of the *Psalter* states: PR FOR AND SOLD BY R. BALDWIN, AT THE | ROSE IN PATER-NOSTER-ROW; J. NEWBERY, IN SP | C-Y, OPPOSITE THE NORTH DOOR; AND B. COLLINS, | ...

In the 1st line of verse on p. [2] the letter A is immediately beneath 'ir' in 'their' in the line above. (Details from photocopies.)

[Copy once owned by Seven Gables Bookshop, N.Y. Welch and Roscoe have photocopies of selected leaves.

(5A) Another edition or issue of no. (5), undated. Stated in TP to be pr f JN and B. Collins. Price 3*d*. *Title, imprint* and specification as for no. (5). But the advert. of the 3rd ed. of the *Royal Psalter* on p. [1] states: PR FOR AND SOLD BY R. BALDWIN, AT THE | ROSE IN PATER-NOSTER-ROW; NEWBERY AND CARNAN, IN | SPC-Y, OPPOSITE THE NORTH DOOR; AND | B. COLLINS, ...

Apparently sheets of no. (5) re-issued by N & C unaltered except as to the advert. of the *Psalter*.

[BM, 8·3 × 7·5 cm.

(5B) Another edition or issue of no. (5), undated. Pr f JN and B. Collins. The text of the TP is surrounded by an ornam. frame of oval lozenges. The letter A in the 1st line of verse on p. [2] is immediately below B in 'Books' in the line above. (Communicated.)

[Osborne*.

(5C) An undated edition or issue pr f JN and B. Collins. No details given.

[McKell.

(5D) Another undated edition. Pr f TC. Price 3*d*.

[The Royal Arms] | THE | ROYAL PRIMER; | OR, | AN EASY AND PLEASANT GUIDE | TO THE | ART OF READING. | ADORN'D WITH CUTS. | [p.rule] | LONDON: PR F T. CARNAN AT NO. 65, | SPC-Y, AND B. C. COLLINS | AT SALISBURY. | (PRICE 3*d*.) [The whole within an ornam. frame of oval lozenges.]

Pp. 71. Alphabet with wcts. Advert. of 3rd ed. of the *Royal Psalter* (stated to be pr f a s b R. Baldwin, T. Carnan and B. C. Collins) on p. [1]. D.f.b. (Details from photocopies.)

[Private colln U.S.A.; Welch and Roscoe have photocopies of selected leaves.

(5E) A copy dated [1776] by JN (*sic*) was lot 327 in the Bussell sale at Sotheby's on 6.2.1945.

(6) Listed as pr f TC in *Newtonian System*, 1787. Price 3*d*.

(7) Listed in ENC, p. 6. Price 3*d*.

J325. ROYAL PRIMER, THE; OR, SECOND BOOK FOR CHILDREN. Mentioned in the imprint to the *Royal Battledore* (J21(4)), which was pr b N & C, and B. Collins. Price 3*d*, bd and adorned with cuts. It is not impossible that this is an ed. of no. J324.

J326. ROYAL PSALTER, THE; OR, KING DAVID'S MEDITATIONS. Welsh 296. The confusion in the following records is obvious. It looks as if there were two rival productions, with very similar titles: Baldwin's (nos. (3) and (4)), and that of other publishers (nos. (1) and (2)). Then the two groups combined to produce no. (5). Whether the Baldwin edd. were pirated from the earlier ones it is impossible, on present evidence, to say; or to what extent the rival edd. corresponded in contents.

(1) One or more edd. prior to 1753 not traced.

(2) A 'new edition' adv. *PA* 1.1.53 as pr a s b JN, J. Hodges, and B. Collins price 10*d*, and there described as the *Royal Psalter, curiously printed (with the Life of King David prefixed) and the useful Proverbs and wise Sayings of King Solomon; and at the bottom of each page rational Meditations on moral and divine Subjects; and at the Beginning of each Psalm an Explanation thereof and its Beauties.*
(3) An edition 'lately published' by R. Baldwin, adv. in *Tommy Trip*, 1765 (no. J308(8)). Price 10*d*.
(4) 'Second edition', 1767. Pr f a s b Baldwin alone. (BM, 3089.aaa.24.)
(5) 'Third edition'. Recorded as pr f a s b R. Baldwin, JN (later N & C), and B. Collins in the advert. in J324(5 and 5A). Price 10*d*. See Welsh, p. 364, for a transcript of Collins' Ledger Account for this ed. But this Account is dated May 1776, whereas the ed. had been advtd in J324(5), which ostensibly was pubd by JN (i.e. not later than 1767 or early 1768). The account must refer to a new printing of the ed.
(6) Listed in *Newtonian System*, 1787, as pr f TC. Price 9*d*.

RUDIMENTS OF REASON. See Jones, Stephen (attrib. to).

J327. RURAL FELICITY; OR, THE HISTORY OF TOMMY AND SALLY. Weedon 80. Richard Johnson's Day-book records:
1787 July. Mr Badcock———To writing The Misfortunes of a Week.———$\Big\}$£. 2. 2*s*.
——— Rural Felicity ———
(1) An edition of 1788. Pr f EN. Price 1*d*. Welsh 344. Adv. *LC* 27–9.12.87, p. 619, as to be pubd in the Christmas holidays.
(2) An undated edition. Pr f EN. Price 1*d*. Welsh 303.
RURAL FELICITY; | OR, THE | HISTORY | OF | TOMMY AND SALLY. | [p.rule] | EMBELLISHED WITH CUTS. | [d.p.rule] | LONDON: | PR F E. NEWBERY, THE CORNER | OF SPCY. | [PRICE ONE PENNY.]
Pp. 31. Wct FP and wcts in text. (Communicated.)
[Ball; UCLA; NRU.
(3) Listed in Masson's *Elmina*, 1800, as by EN.

J328. S., H. ANECDOTES OF MARY, 1795. Pr f EN. Price 2*s*. Welsh 169; *CBEL*, II, 564.
ANECDOTES | OF | MARY; | OR, | THE GOOD GOVERNESS. | [p.s.rule] | BY THE AUTHOR OF THE HISTORY OF THE | DAVENPORT FAMILY. | [d.p.rule] | [4 lines quote] | [d.p.rule] | LONDON: | PR F E. NEWBERY, CORNER OF SP | C-Y, | [p.rule] | MDCCXCV.
12mo. 84 leaves. Pp. 159, 4. Half-title. In some copies is an engvd FP 'The Pleasures of Benevolence', ascribed to Blake (Keynes, *Biblio. of Blake*, no. 289); this seems open to doubt. List of bks pr f EN on last 4 pages.
[BM; Roscoe, 17·1×10·2 cm; HammPL; SomCL; Renier; Grey; NoU; Hannas; Osborne*; UCLA; Adomeit; Gardner; D. Low, Cat. 135 [1960] item 302.

J329. S., H. HISTORY OF THE DAVENPORT FAMILY, THE. Welsh 304; Gum 3008; *CBEL*, II, 564 (dates [1791]). I have not determined with any certainty the priority as between nos. (1) and (2). Both refer, at p. 120, to the intended vol. II, but no. (1) does not describe itself as 'vol. I', whereas no. (2) does. It seems likely that on issuing no. (2) the opportunity was taken to correct the TP of the (earlier) no. (1) in this respect. The two vols were listed in *Anecdotes of Mary*, 1795.

(1) An undated edition. Pr f EN. Price 1s.

THE | HISTORY | OF THE | DAVENPORT FAMILY: | IN WHICH IS DISPLAYED | A STRIKING CONTRAST | BETWEEN | HAUGHTY INDOLENCE AND HEALTHFUL ACTIVITY, | IN THE CHARACTERS OF THE | YOUNG DAVENPORTS, | AND THEIR COUSINS | SOPHIA AND AMELIA EASY. | [1 line] | BY H.S. | [p.s.rule] | EMBELLISHED WITH CUTS. | [p.s.rule] | LONDON: | PR F E. NEWBERY, THE CORNER OF | SPC-Y. | [p.rule] | [PRICE ONE SHILLING BOUND.]

In 6's. 60 leaves+6 insets. Pp. 120. Engvd FP and 5 other engvd leaves. D.f.b.

[BM, 11·6×8·1 cm; Bell; Maxwell Hunley, Cat. 48 [winter 1969] item 148.

(1A) An undated edition of VOL. I. Pr f EN. Price 1s.

Title approx. as for no. (1), VOL. I. added preceding 'Embellished with cuts'.

60 leaves. Pp. 120. Engvd FP and 2 engvd leaves in text (? should be 5). Type reset. D.f.b. (Communicated.)

[NoU, 11·6×7·7 cm.

(1B) Copies in Osborne*; DES; Ball may be either nos. (1) or (1A).

(2) An undated edition of VOL. II. Pr f EN. Price 1s.

THE | HISTORY | OF THE | DAVENPORT FAMILY: | EXHIBITING THE | CHARACTERS | OF THE | YOUNG DAVENANTS, | AND THEIR COUSINS | SOPHIA AND AMELIA EASY. | INTERSPERSED WITH MORAL REFLECTIONS. | BY H.S. | [p.s.rule] | VOL. II. | [p.s.rule] | EMBELLISHED WITH CUTS. | [p.s.rule] | LONDON: | PR F E. NEWBERY, THE CORNER OF SP | C-Y. | [PRICE ONE SHILLING BOUND.]

In 6's. 72 leaves+6 insets. Pp. 134, 8. Engvd FP and 5 other engvd leaves. 8-page list of bks pr f EN following p. 134, numbered 1–8 but sgd in sequence with the preceding leaves. D.f.b.

[DES, 11·4×7·6 cm; Bell (lacks bk-list).

(3) An edition of 1798. Pr f EN. Price 1s 6d.

Title approx. as for no. (1). *Imprint:* PR F E. NEWBERY, AT THE CORNER OF SPC-Y. 1798.

In 6's. 90 leaves. Pp. 173[180]. Engvd FP and 6 other engvd leaves. Bk-list on pp. [175–80]. Bds, green vell. spine. (Communicated.)

[Opie; UCLA.

ST PAUL'S CATHEDRAL. ACCURATE AND HISTORICAL ACCOUNT OF... This is vol. III of J88.

J330. SANDHAM, Elizabeth. HAPPY FAMILY AT EASON HOUSE, THE. *CBEL*, II, 560. Listed *GM* Dec. 1799, and adv. *LC* 21–4.12.99, p. 604, as one of EN's publications for the Christmas holidays, price 1*s* 6*d*. But the 1799 ed. (copy in Osborne*) was by T. Hurst alone. It was very unusual for one of EN's Christmas publications to appear under another imprint; for another instance see J342A.

J330A. SANDHAM, Elizabeth. JULIANA; OR, THE AFFECTIONATE SISTERS. The 1800 ed. was pubd by T. Hurst alone (copy in BM). But the bk was listed as pr f EN in Smythies' *History of a Pin*, 1801, price 2*s*.

J331. SANDHAM, Elizabeth. TRIFLES; OR, FRIENDLY MITES, 1800. Adv. *LC* 6–9.12.1800, p. 559, as pr f T. Hurst, s b EN; and an ed. listed in Smythies' *History of a Pin*, 1801, as pr f EN, price 2*s* in the vell. manner. But the 1800 ed. was pubd under the imprint of Hurst alone (copy in BM).

J332. Entry deleted.

SCRIPTURE HISTORIES. See Pilkington, M. (H).

SECOND COPY BOOK FOR YOUTH. See Webb, Benjn, jr.

SELECT FABLES OF AESOP AND OTHERS. See J7(2).

J333. SELECTOR, THE, 1797. Pr f EN. Price 3*s*. Welsh 304; *CBEL*, II, 253.
THE | SELECTOR: | BEING A | NEW AND CHASTE COLLECTION | OF | VISIONS, TALES, AND ALLEGORIES, | CALCULATED FOR THE | AMUSE-MENT AND INSTRUCTION | OF | THE RISING GENERATION. | [d.p.rule] | LONDON: | PR F E. NEWBERY, AT THE CORNER OF | SPC-Y. | [rule of dots] | 1797.
    12mo. 114 leaves+engvd FP sgd 'Corbould del' 'Taylor sc'. Pp. iv+223.
    [BM, 17·1×10·4 cm; Osborne, Cat. p. 298; Opie; Renier; Oppenheimer; A. R. Heath, Cat. 22 [1972] item 190.

SHEPHERD'S SON, THE. See Smith, Rev. Thos.

SHORT AND EASY INTRODUCTION TO ENGLISH GRAMMAR. See Davis, Mr.

J333A. SHORT ACCOUNT OF THE APOSTLES, A. Adv. *GM* May 1774 as pr f FN(N), price 6*d*. Not identified. Cannot = J175, which cost 1*s* and was pubd by N & C or TC alone.

J334. SHORT HISTORIES FOR THE IMPROVEMENT OF THE MIND.

(1) An edition of 1760. Pr f JN. Price 1s bd and gilt.

SHORT HISTORIES | FOR THE | IMPROVEMENT OF THE MIND. | EXTRACTED | CHIEFLY FROM THE WORKS OF THE CELE- | BRATED JOSEPH ADDISON, ESQ; | SIR RICHARD STEELE, AND | OTHER EMINENT WRITERS. | WITH SUITABLE | REFLECTIONS | BY THE EDITOR. | [d.p.rule] | LONDON: | PR F J. NEWBERY, AT THE BIBLE | AND SUN, IN SPC-Y. | [p.rule] | MDCCLX.

In 6's. 92 leaves+10 insets. Pp. [iv]+176[178]. Last leaf a blank or bk-list. Engvd FP and 9 engvd leaves in text. D.f.b.

⌈Weedon, 11·1×7·0 cm; NorBM, 11·0×7·4 cm; Opie.

(2) An edition of 1769. Pr f N & C. Price 1s bd and gilt. Welsh 306.

Title approx. as for no. (1). *Imprint:* PR F NEWBERY AND CARNAN, NO. 65 | THE NORTH SIDE OF SPC-Y. | [p.rule] | MDCCLXIX. | [PRICE ONE SHILLING.]

In 6's. 90 leaves+9 insets. Pp. 176. Engvd FP and 8 other engvd leaves. D.f.b.

⌈V&A(GL), 11·5×7·1 cm; Opie; MH.

(3) An edition of 1775. Pr f C & N. Price 1s.

Title approx. as for no. (1). *Imprint:* PR F T. CARNAN AND F. NEWBERY, JUN. | AT NUMBER 65, IN SPC-Y. | [PRICE ONE SHILLING.] | [p.rule] | MDCCLXXV.

Pp. 176. 7 engvd leaves (? should be a FP). D.f.b. (Communicated.)

⌈Ball; Col. W. F. Prideaux (in 1886); UCLA.

(4) An edition of 1782. Pr f TC. Price 1s. D.f.b. S&W Cat.

⌈Ball.

SHORT HISTORY OF BEES. See J21A.

SHORT HISTORY OF INSECTS. See Fenn, Lady E.

SHORT HISTORY OF QUADRUPEDS. See ? Fenn, Lady E.

SHORT INTRODUCTION TO GEOGRAPHY. See Newcombe, Mr, of Hackney.

SIAMESE TALES. See Brewer, Geo.

SILVER THIMBLE, THE. See ? Trimmer, Sarah.

SINBAD THE SAILOR. See HISTORY OF...

J334A. SISTER WITCHES, THE, OR MIRTH AND MAGIC, 1782. Pubd by EN et al. Price 6d, or 1s coloured.

See Plate 14.

A Harlequinade measuring approx. 17·9×7·6 cm when folded; consists of 4 strips each showing a hand-coloured etched scene with 6 lines of verse (etched) above the scene and 6 below; flap-overs at head and tail show other scenes, 3 of them with 6 lines of verse at head only, the 4th being the title-leaf (see the Plate). In a dark blue paper wrapper. The etching on the TP is sgd 'Jane Tringham delin' (see J250A).

A (? later) undated issue appeared under the imprint of G. Marlin, 6 Gt St Thomas Apostle, price 1s coloured, using the same plates. Details taken from the Bell copy.

⸢Bodley; Bell.

J335. SISTER'S GIFT, THE. Welsh 306.
(1) Listed in Winlove's *Moral Lectures*, 1769, as s b FN(N), price 1d. And adv. *LC* 29–31.5.70 as 'on Monday next w.b.p.' and on 2–5 June as 't.d.w.p.'.
(2) Listed in *Brother's Gift*, 1777, as pr f FN(N), price 1d.
(3) Listed in J88(3), vol. I, 1786, as pr f EN. Price 1d.
(4) An edition of 1793. Pr f EN. Price 1d.

Title and *imprint* approx. as for no. (5), with date 1793.

32mo in 16's. 16 leaves. Pp. 32. Wct FP and 7 wcts in text. Red and black floral wrappers. (Communicated.)

⸢McKell, 10·3×6·3 cm.
(5) An edition of 1799. Pr f EN. Price 1d.

THE | SISTER'S GIFT, | OR THE | NAUGHTY BOY REFORMED | PUBLISHED FOR | THE ADVANTAGE OF THE RISING | GENERATION. | [p.rule] | [4 lines quote] | [p.rule] | LONDON. | PR F E. NEWBERY, AT THE CORNER | OF SPC-Y. 1799. | [PRICE ONE PENNY.]

16mo. 16 leaves. Pp. 31. Wct FP and 7 wcts in text. First and last leaves pastedowns. Dutch printed green floral paper wrappers. (Communicated.)

⸢Osborne, Cat. p. 305, 9·9×6·4 cm.

J336. SIX-PENNYWORTH OF WIT.
(1) An undated edition. Pr f JN (see Plate 15). Can be dated 1767 or early 1768 at latest, as the date 8 Jan. 1767 is mentioned in the Introduction. *CBEL*, II, 562 wrongly dates [ca. 1675]; no advert. or listing traced before 1767. Price 6d bd and gilt. Welsh 306–7.

In 8's. 64 leaves+inset engvd FP. Pp. 5+vi–xxi+22–126[128]. 15 small wcts in text. List of bks sold at Mr Newbery's on last 2 pages. D.f.b. As to *Twelve Pennyworth of Wisdom* see no. J367.

⸢St Bride, 9·7×6·5 cm; UCLA.
(2) Listed in *Newtonian System*, 1770, and adv. *LC* 11–14.4.72 as pr f C & N. Price 6d. Perhaps=(2A).
(2A) An undated edition. Pr f C & N.

Title as for no. (1). *Imprint:* PR F CARNAN AND NEWBERY, AT | NO. 65,

IN SPCY: A S B | ALL THE BOOKSELLERS IN THE WORLD. | [PRICE SIX-PENCE BOUND AND GILT.]

In 8's. 64 leaves+inset engvd FP. 15 small very poor wcts in text. Pp. 5+vi-xi+22–126[128]. List of bks pr f C & N on pp. [127–8]. D.f.b.

[Hannas, 9·9×6·2 cm.

(3) An undated edition. Pr f TC. Price 6*d* bd and gilt.

Title approx. as for no. (1). *Imprint:* PR F T. CARNAN, IN SP | C-Y; A S B ALL THE BOOK- | SELLERS IN THE WORLD. | [PRICE SIXPENCE BOUND AND GILT.]

In 8's. 64 leaves. Pp. xx+21–128. 15 wcts in text. D.f.b.

[BM, 9·6×6·4 cm.

(4) Undated ed. by TC in CUL, Ball and Opie collns, perhaps = no. (3).

(5) Listed in *Newtonian System*, 1787, as pr f TC. Price 6*d*.

J337. SKETCHES FROM NATURE, 1801. Pr f EN. Price 1*s* 6*d*.

SKETCHES FROM NATURE, | INTENDED | FOR THE USE | OF | YOUNG PERSONS. | [wct orn. vignette] | LONDON: | PR F E. NEWBERY, AT THE CORNER OF SP | C-Y, | BY H. BRYER, BRIDEWELL-HOSPITAL. | [p.rule] | 1801.

In 6's. 67 leaves+inset engvd FP (illegible sig.). Pp. iv(v)+130. Marbled bds, green vell. spine.

[BM, 13·7×8·4 cm; Opie; Welch; DLC; UCLA; Sexton, Cat. 57 [1961] item 355.

J338. SMART, Christopher. HYMNS FOR THE AMUSEMENT OF CHILDREN. For bibliographical references see A546. Gray (p. 299) records that he knows of no ed. earlier than no. (3). Welsh 239.

(1) The first edition is generally considered to be the one which, as mentioned below, was advtd at the end of Dec. 1770. So it is assumed that it bore the date 1770. It is also supposed that no copy of that ed. is now extant, the earliest known being that dated 1771, which is written down as the second.

The Introduction to the Luttrell Society's facsimile ed. of no. (3) states: '"Hymns for the Amusement of Children" duly "embellished with Cuts" was entered at Stationers' Hall on 24 Dec. 1770, by Thomas Carnan...On 27 Dec. 1770, an announcement of Smart's "Hymns" appeared in the Public Advertizer ...Issued then at the end of 1770...the "Hymns" cannot have stirred much critical notice...'. The book was also advtd in *LC* for 25–7.12.70 at p. 615, printed for TC, price 6*d*.

It seems probable that the ed. so advtd was, as supposed, the first. But the assumption that it was dated 1770 is not justified. I have pointed out, in the article on 'Newspaper Advertisements as evidence for the dating of Books', at p. 391, that it was common enough practice in that period for a book advtd towards the end of December to bear date the year following, and I quote Nichols' very definite statement on the subject (repeated here for clarity's sake): 'The Rule in general observed among Printers is, that when a Book happens not to be ready for Publication before November, the date of the ensuing year is used.' So it may be that the ed. of 1771, of which two copies are recorded, is in fact the first – I will go so far as to say that it most probably is. This of course leaves the second edition unrecorded, but that is a common enough state of affairs. The third edition was so designated in its TP; one might suppose the same could have applied to the second. I have seen no advert. of an ed. described as 'the Second'; but the book was listed in Weston's *Gardener's Calendar*, 1773, and that might refer to such an ed.

(2) An edition of 1771. Pr f TC. Price 6*d*. Very probably the first (see no. (1) above). Unknown to Gray. A copy in the Oppenheimer colln, dated 1771, might be nos. (1) or (2).

Engraved title: HYMNS, | FOR THE | AMUSEMENT | OF | CHILDREN. | [p.rule] | EMBELLISHED WITH CUTS. | [d.p.rule] | LONDON. | PR F T. CARNAN, | IN SPCY. | MDCCLXXI. | PRICE SIX-PENCE.

Pp. iii+2–84. Engvd FP sgd 'W. Walker sct'; wcts in text. Bk-list. D.f.b. (Communicated.)

[Ball, 11·5 cm; Hodgson's 8.5.53, lot 561; Opie.

(3) Third edition, 1775 (see Plate 16). Pr f TC. Price 6*d*. Welsh 308; Gray LIII; *CBEL*, II, 339; Facsim. ed. by Luttrell Soc., 1947.

In 6's. 46 leaves. Pp. ii+83[84]. Wct FP and 36 oval wcts in text, by the hand which did those in early edd. of Wynne's *Choice Emblems*. List of bks pr f TC on last page. White or buff bds, impressed with wcts in black, the upper cover lettered HYMNS | FOR | CHILDREN.

[Bodley, 11·2×7·5 cm.

(4) An edition of 1786. Pr f TC. Price 6*d*. Unknown to Gray.

HYMNS | FOR THE | AMUSEMENT | OF | CHILDREN. | BY CHRISTOPHER SMART, M,A, | [p.s.rule] | LONDON: | PR F T. CARNAN, IN SP | C-Y. PRICE SIXPENCE. | MDCCLXXXVI.

Pp. 88. Wct FP and 36 wcts in text. D.f.b. (Communicated.)

[UCLA.

J339. SMITH, Rev Thomas. LUCINDA; OR, VIRTUE TRIUMPHANT, 1801. Pr f EN. Price 2*s*.

LUCINDA; | OR, | VIRTUE TRIUMPHANT: | A MORAL TALE. | [p.s.rule] | DESIGNED FOR THE INSTRUCTION OF YOUTH. | [p.s.rule] | BY THE REV. THOMAS SMITH. | [d.p.rule] | [6 lines quote] | [d.p.rule] | LONDON: | PR B G. AULD, GREVILLE STREET, | FOR E. NEWBERY, | CORNER OF SPC-Y. | [p.rule] | 1801.

In 6's. 96 leaves+inset engvd FP. Pp. 187. Marbled bds, red or green roan back-strip, or green vell. back-strip with label.

[BM, 13·7×8·5 cm; BCE; Muir; Osborne, Cat. p. 306; UCLA; McKell; Ball; PPiU.

J340. SMITH, Rev. Thomas. SHEPHERD'S SON, THE, 1800. Pr f EN. Price 1s 6d. Welsh 309.

THE | SHEPHERD'S SON; | OR, | THE WISH ACCOMPLISHED. | A MORAL TALE. | INTERSPERSED WITH | POETICAL EFFUSIONS, | DESIGNED FOR | THE IMPROVEMENT OF YOUTH. | [d.p.rule] | BY THE REV. THOMAS SMITH. | [d.p.rule] | [4 lines quote] | [d.p.rule] | LONDON: | PR F E. NEWBERY, THE CORNER OF | SPC-Y. | BY G. WOODFALL, PN-R, LONDON. | [p.s.rule] | 1800.

In 6's. 90 leaves+inset engvd FP. Pp. iv+[5]–179[180]. List of bks to be had of EN on last page. Marbled bds, green vell. spine with label.

[BM, 13·5×8·8 cm; Grey; Muir; Osborne*; UCLA; McKell.

J341. SMYTHIES, Miss (   ) of Colchester. HISTORY OF A PIN, THE. Attributed by Algar to a Miss Eliza Andrews. The attribution of this and no. J342 to Miss Smythies follows the BM Gen. Cat. I have been unable to identify the lady in R. H. R. Smythies' *Records of the Smythies Family*, 1912, which gives pedigrees of this family, of Colchester and elsewhere, covering this period. Welsh 237.

(1) An edition of 1798. Pr f EN. Price 1s. NBL 516; *CBEL*, II, 564.

THE | HISTORY | OF | A PIN, | AS RELATED BY ITSELF. | INTERSPERSED WITH | A VARIETY OF ANECDOTES, | [3 lines] | [wavy rule] | BY THE AUTHOR OF THE BROTHERS, A TALE FOR | CHILDREN, &c. | [d.p.rule] | LONDON: | PR F E. NEWBERY, AT THE CORNER | OF SPC-Y. | [p.rule] | 1798.

In 6's. 56 leaves (? +engraved FP). Pp. 109[110]. List of new publns to be had of EN on last page.

[BM, 13·8×8·5 cm; Welch.

(2) An edition of 1801. Pr f EN.

Title approx. as for no. (1). *Imprint:* PR F E. NEWBERY, AT THE COR- | NER OF SPC-Y. | J. SWAN AND CO. PRINTERS, GRACECHURCH-STREET. | [p.rule] | 1801.

In 6's. 53 leaves+inset engvd FP sgd 'Ecstein del', 'Scott sculp'. Pp. 101[106]. List of bks pr f EN on pp. [103–5]. List of bks to be had of EN on pp. [105–6]. Blue bds, label on upper.

[LWaPL, 13·6×8·1 cm; BCE.

J342. SMYTHIES, Miss (   ) of Colchester. HISTORY OF LUCY WELLERS, THE. Adv. *PA* 29.10.53 as to be pubd on 27 Nov. The BM copy is dated 1754, under the imprint of R. Baldwin. From its frequent listing and advertising by the Newberys and Carnan over a period of many years, the bk would seem to have been in demand; yet I have been unable to trace a copy of any ed. under a Newbery or Carnan imprint. As to the authorship of this bk, see no. J341.

(1) Listed in T.G.'s *Isle of Thanet*, 1765, as pr f a s b JN. 2 vols, price 6s.

(2) Listed and adv. as by N & C in 1768, 1769, 1773, 1774. 2 vols, price 6s; or 2 vols in one, in the vell. manner 5s, in calf 6s.

(3) Listed in *Telemachus abridged*, 1781, as pr f TC. Welsh, p. 260, quotes 'Carnan's List about 1789'.

J342A. SOMERVILLE, Elizabeth (*alias* Elizabeth HELME, Junr). FLORA; OR, THE DESERTED CHILD, 1800.

Adv. *LC* 23–5.12.1800, p. 611, as one of 'Newbery's New Publications for the Christmas Holidays'. Price 1*s*. Listed in Trimmer's *Silver Thimble*, 1801, as 'just published by EN'.

But the 1800 ed. of *Flora* was pr b A. Strahan for Longman and Rees. It is a remarkable thing that one of EN's Christmas publicns should appear under the imprint of another publishing house; for another instance see J330. But it is also very noticeable that the engvd FP to *Flora* bears the statement 'Published July 10, 1800, by E. Newbery, Corner of St. Paul's'. Clearly there must have been some arrangement between EN and Longman; but what, I am unable to say.

As to the authorship – Helme junior or Eliz. Somerville – there seems little doubt but that they were one and the same person. For the 1799 ed. of *James Manners* (no. J157) was stated in the TP to be by Elizabeth Helme, junior, while the 1800 and 1806 edd. of *Flora* and the *Village Maid*, 1801 state that *James Manners* was by Somerville. See also the note to no. J157.

J343. SOMERVILLE, Elizabeth. VILLAGE MAID, THE, 1801. S b EN. Gum 5404 and 5405; *CBEL*, II, 570.

THE | VILLAGE MAID; | OR, | DAME BURTON'S | MORAL STORIES | FOR THE | INSTRUCTION AND AMUSEMENT OF YOUTH. | [d.p.rule] | BY ELIZABETH SOMERVILLE, | AUTHOR OF JAMES MANNERS, LITTLE JOHN, | AND THEIR DOG BLUFF; | FLORA, OR THE DESERTED CHILD, &c. &c. | [d.p.rule] | LONDON: | PR B J. BONSOR, SALISBURY SQUARE, | FOR VERNOR AND HOOD, POULTRY; | AND S B | E. NEWBERY, SPCY. | [d.p.rule] | 1801.

In 6's. 78 leaves+inset engvd FP, dated April 1802. Pp. viii+148. A number of wct vignette tailpieces. Half-title. Marbled bds, red roan back-strip; also marbled bds, green vell. spine.

[BM, 13·6×8·6 cm; V&A(GL) (imperf.); Osborne, Cat. pp. 306–7; Ball; CtNSCSC.

SPARROW, THE. See Kendall, E. A.

SPELLING BOOK. See Lowe, Solomon.

SPELLING DICTIONARY. See J263A and J265.

SPELLING-DICTIONARY OF THE ENGLISH LANGUAGE, ON A NEW PLAN. See J268.

Fig. 27. Title-page of J344(1).

J344. SPIRITUAL LESSONS, FOR CHILDREN TO READ AND LEARN TO BE WISE. Pafford, *Isaac Watts Divine Songs* (London, 1971), no. B70 (p. 298).

(1) An undated edition. Pr f FN(N). Adv. *LC* 31.12.78–2.1.79, p. 4, as t.d.w.p. Price 6*d*. Welsh 309.

See Figure 27. Pr throughout from engvd plates. 27 leaves, unnumbered and unsgd, each pr on one side only, usually alternate recto and vso. There are 26 'Prints', one for each letter of the alphabet, of very crude workmanship, none sgd. Pafford says about half of the poems are from Watts' *Divine Songs*.

[BM, approx. 12·0×7·8 cm, 3436.ee.31; MWA.

(2) Listed as pr f EN in *Anecdotes of Mary*, 1795; listed in ENC, p. 7. Price 6*d*.

STORIES OF SENEX. See Kendall, E. A.

J345. SUGAR PLUMB, THE.

(1) An edition of 1771. Pr f FN(N). Price 6*d* neatly bd and gilt.

THE | SUGAR PLUMB; | OR | SWEET AMUSEMENT | FOR LEISURE HOURS: | BEING AN | ENTERTAINING AND INSTRUCTIVE | COLLECTION OF STORIES. | EMBELLISHED WITH CURIOUS CUTS. | LONDON: | PR F F. NEWBERY, AT THE CORNER | OF SPC-Y. 1771. PRICE SIX-PENCE.

In 6's. 54 leaves+inset engvd FP sgd 'Lodge del et sculp'. Pp. 99[104]. 12 wcts in text. List of bks pr f EN on last 5 pages. D.f.b.

⌈BM, 11·4×7·6 cm; Fox; UCLA (imperf.).

(1A) An edition of 1775. FN(N). D.f.b.

⌈Sotheby, 5.2.1945 (the Bussell sale), lot 133.

(2) An edition of 1781. EN. Listed in S&W Cat. as 16mo, with cuts. D.f.b. Adv. *LC*, 30.12.81–1.1.82, p. 7, price 6*d*.

(3) An edition of 1788. Pr f EN. Price 6*d*. Welsh 312.

Title as for no. (1). *Imprint:* PR F E. NEWBERY, AT THE CORNER | OF SPC-Y. 1788. | PRICE SIX-PENCE.

In 8's. 64 leaves+inset engvd FP sgd 'Lodge del et sculp'. Pp. 122[124]. 12 or more wcts in text. List of bks 'just published' by EN on last 2 pages. D.f.b.

⌈Bodley (imperf.), 10·4×6·9 cm; Ball; MSaE; MWA.

(4) Listed in *Anecdotes of Mary*, 1795, as pr f EN. Price 6*d*.

SUNDAY MISCELLANY, THE. See Fenn, Lady E.

SWALLOW, THE. See Kendall, E. A.

SWIFT, Jonathan. ADVENTURES OF CAPTAIN GULLIVER. See J5.

J346. 'TAGG, Tommy'. A COLLECTION OF PRETTY POEMS FOR THE AMUSEMENT OF CHILDREN THREE FOOT HIGH. Welsh 294; *CBEL*, II, 561.

(1) The 'fifty fourth edition', 1756. Pr f the Booksellers of Europe, Asia, Africa, and America, and sold at the Bible and Sun, in SPC-Y, [i.e. pr f JN]. Price 6*d* bd and gilt. Wcts. NBL 333; Pierpont Morgan Cat. item 146.

An unspecified ed., very probably this one, was adv. in *PA* 20.1.56, price 6*d* bd and gilt. No earlier record of the bk traced, and this may well be, in fact, the 1st ed.

⌈Oppenheimer.

(2) The 'fifty-fifth edition', 1756. [JN.]

⌈PPiU.

(3) The 'fifty-sixth edition', 1758. [JN.] Price 6*d* bd and gilt.

Title and *imprint* approx. as for no. (5), with THE FIFTY SIXTH EDITION and date MDCCLVIII. 54 leaves. Pp. 104. Wcts. D.f.b. (Communicated.)

⌈Gardner, formerly Tighe, 11·0 cm.

(4) The 'fifty-seventh edition', 1760. [JN.]

⌈Ball.

(5) The 'fifty-eighth edition', 1763. [JN.] Price *6d* bd and gilt.

A | COLLECTION | OF | PRETTY POEMS | FOR THE AMUSEMENT OF | CHILDREN THREE FOOT HIGH. | BY TOMMY TAGG, ESQ; | [p.rule] | THE FIFTY EIGHTH EDITION, | ADORNED WITH ABOVE SIXTY CUTS. | [p.rule] | LONDON: | PR F THE BOOKSELLERS OF EUROPE, ASIA, | AFRICA AND AMERICA, AND SOLD AT THE BIBLE AND | SUN IN SPC-Y. | [p.rule] | MDCCLXIII. | PRICE SIX-PENCE BOUND AND GILT.

In 6's. 54 leaves. Pp. 104. *ca.* 62 wct headpieces and a number of orn. wct tailpieces. D.f.b.

⌈Oup, 10·5×7·2 cm.

(6) The 'fifty-ninth edition' not traced; but unspecified edd. were listed in nos. J31, 1764, J167(3), 1766 and J225(8), 1767.

(7) The 'sixtieth edition', 1768. [FN(S) and/or TC.] Price *6d* bd and gilt.

Title and *imprint* approx. as for no. (5), with THE SIXTIETH EDITION and date MDCCLXVIII.

In 6's. 54 leaves. Pp. 108. 62 wcts. D.f.b.

⌈St Bride, 11·1×7·6 cm; Welch.

(8) An edition of 1770. S b C & N. Price *6d* bd and gilt.

Title approx. as for no. (5), no ed. stated. *Imprint:* PR F THE BOOKSELLERS OF EUROPE, ASIA, | AFRICA AND AMERICA, AND S B T. CARNAN | AND F. NEWBERY, JUNIOR, NO. 65, IN S | PC-Y. | [p.rule] | MDCCLXX. | [PRICE SIX-PENCE BOUND AND GILT.]

In 6's. 54 leaves. Pp. 108. 60 wcts, 31 tailpieces of printers' ornaments, one headpiece. D.f.b. (Communicated.)

⌈Opie; Kent; Osborne (imperf., Cat. p. 73); RP.

(9) An edition of 1777. S b C & N. Price *6d. CBEL*, II, 232, 561.

Title and *imprint* approx. as for no. (8), with date MDCCLXXVII.

In 6's. 54 leaves. Pp. 108 (also pp. 106 – CLU copy). 62 half-page wcts. D.f.b.

⌈Bodley, 11·4×7·7 cm; UCLA.

(9A) A sixteenth edition, 'London: Pr f the Booksellers in Town and Country.' and dated MDCCLXXXI, omits the words 'three Foot High' in the title. Probably a piracy. (Communicated.)

⌈McKell.

(10) An edition of 1783. S b TC. Price *6d.*

Title approx. as for no. (8). *Imprint:* PR F THE BOOKSELLERS OF EUROPE ...AND S B T. CARNAN, SUC- | CESSOR TO MR. NEWBERY, IN SPC- | Y. PRICE SIX-PENCE. | [p.rule] | MDCCLXXXIII.

In 6's. 54 leaves. Pp. 108. 62 half-page wcts. D.f.b.

⌈Roscoe, 10·8×7·2 cm (cropped); Opie; Ball.

TALES FOR YOUTH. See J391(1).

TALES OF INSTRUCTION AND AMUSEMENT. See Hurry, Mrs Ives.

TALES OF THE COTTAGE. See Pilkington, M. (H).

TALES OF THE HERMITAGE. See Pilkington, M. (H).

TASTE OF ANCIENT TIMES, A. J77 was frequently adv. under this title.

J347. TEA-TABLE DIALOGUES. Welsh 313; Weedon 82. Richard Johnson's Day-book records: *1770 May 15. Delivered to Mr Carnan, Tea-Table Dialogues.——Value——Five Guineas. 1776 June. Tea-Table Dialogues, for Mr Carnan.——£5. 5s. [Paid 1777 Feb. 12.]* The 2 payments recorded in the Day-book would be accounted for by the revisions appearing in the 1779 ed.
(1) An edition of 1771. Pr f TC. Price 6d bd and gilt. Recorded by Lyon. Adv. LC 28–30.5.71, p. 519, as 'On Thursday, June 20 w.b.p.'. But was Lyon following the advert.?
(2) An edition of 1772. Pr f TC. Price 6d. Gum 5562; *CBEL*, II, 562.

TEA-TABLE | DIALOGUES; | BETWEEN |

MISS THOUGHTFUL	MAST. THOUGHTFUL
MISS STERLING	MASTER GOODWILL
MISS PRATTLE	MASTER POPLIN.

WHEREIN IS DELINEATED THE | CHARMS OF INNOCENCE AND VIRTUE, | AND THE | PLEASURES OF RURAL AMUSEMENTS. | EMBELLISHED WITH CUTS. | [p.rule] | [2 lines quote] | [d.p.rule] | LONDON: | PR F T. CARNAN, AT NO. 65, S | PC-Y. | MDCCLXXII.
    In 6's. 54 leaves. Pp. ii+104. 12 wcts in the text. (Communicated.)
    [Osborne*; Ball.
(3) An edition of 1779. Pr f TC. Price 6d. NBL 505.

TEA-TABLE | DIALOGUES, | BETWEEN A | GOVERNESS | AND |

MISS SENSIBLE,	MISS STERLING,
MISS THOUGHTFUL,	MISS LIVELY,
MISS BLOOM,	AND
MISS HOPEFUL,	MISS TEMPEST.

[d.p.rule] | LONDON: | PR F T. CARNAN, AT NUMBER 65, | SPC-Y. PRICE SIXPENCE. | MDCCLXXIX.
    In 6's. 54 leaves. Pp. iv+5–105[108]. 12 wcts in text. List of bks pr f TC on pp. [106–8]. D.f.b.
    [V&A(GL), 11·4×7·5 cm.
(4) An edition of 1784. TC.
    [Knaster; Ball.

J348. 'TELESCOPE, TOM'. THE NEWTONIAN SYSTEM OF PHILOSOPHY. Frequently listed and adv. as the *Philosophy of Tops and Balls* (see J279A). Welsh 313–15; *CBEL*, II, 561, which lists as possibly written by JN. (1) First edition, 1761. Pr f JN. Price 1s bd and gilt, or bd in embossed paper; 1s 6d in calf gilt. *CBEL*, II, 645; Babson 115.

THE | NEWTONIAN SYSTEM OF | PHILOSOPHY | ADAPTED TO THE CAPACITIES OF YOUNG | GENTLEMEN AND LADIES,... | [3 lines] | BEING | THE SUBSTANCE OF SIX LECTURES READ TO THE | LILLIPUTIAN SOCIETY, | BY TOM TELESCOPE, A.M. | AND COLLECTED AND METHODIZED FOR THE BENEFIT | OF THE YOUTH OF THESE KINGDOMS, | BY THEIR OLD FRIEND MR. NEWBERY, IN S | PCY; | [2 lines] | [p.rule] | [5 lines quote] | [d.p.rule] | LONDON, | PR F J. NEWBERY, AT THE BIBLE AND SUN, | IN SPCY. 1761.

In 6's. 72 leaves+9 insets. Pp. iv, 140. Engvd FP and 8 engvd leaves in text; 5 small wcts in text. List of JN's bks on pp. 126–40. D.f.b.

[BM, 11·6×7·4 cm; CUL; Oup; Roscoe; Weedon; Welch; Ball; McKell; Reichner; Babson; ICU-J; Sotheby, 4.6.71, lot 474.

(2) Second edition, 1762. Pr f JN. Price 1s. Babson 116.

Title and *imprint*, with THE SECOND EDITION and date 1762, and specification approx. as for no. (1).

[BM, 11·3×7·2 cm; Bodley (imperf.); McKell; Babson; M. G. Atkins' List CHI/26 [1967] item 2.

(3) Third edition, 1766. Pr f JN. Price 1s bd and gilt, 1s 6d 'in calves leather gilt'.

Title and *imprint* approx. as for no. (1), with THE THIRD EDITION and date 1766.

In 6's. 72 leaves+9 insets. Pp. [iv]+139. Engvd FP and 8 other engvd leaves. 5 small wcts in text. List of bks pr f JN on pp. 127–39. D.f.b., also calf (see above).

[NorBM, 11·5×7·5 cm; Bell; CLU; McKell, 11·5×7·5 cm; OClW-LS; Welch; Sotheby, 13.3.72, lot 9.

(4) Fourth edition, 1770. Pr f C & N. Price 1s.

Title approx. as for no. (1), with THE FOURTH EDITION. *Imprint:* PR F T. CARNAN AND F. NEWBERY, JUN, | AT NO. 65, IN SPC-Y. 1770. | [PRICE ONE SHILLING.]

In 6's. 72 leaves+6 or 9 insets. Pp. 125[140]. Engvd FP and 5 (sometimes 8) engvd leaves in text. List of bks pr f C & N on pp. [126–40]. D.f.b.

[Roscoe, 11·5×7·0 cm; Bell; Opie; Osborne (Cat. p. 209); Ball; ICU.

(5) Fifth edition, 1779. Pr f C & N. Price 1s. NBL 654.

Title approx. as for no. (1), with THE FIFTH EDITION. *Imprint:* PR F T. CARNAN AND F. NEWBERY, JUN. | AT NO. 65, IN SPC-Y. 1779. | [PRICE ONE SHILLING.]

In 6's. 72 leaves+9 insets. Pp. 125[140]. Engvd FP and 8 other engvd leaves. 5 small wcts in text. List of bks pr f C & N on pp. [126–40]. Drab paper wrappers with pictorial designs in black.

[BM, 11·1×7·1 cm; LEI (imperf.); UCLA.

(6) Sixth edition, 1784. Pr f TC.

Title approx. as for no. (1), with THE SIXTH EDITION. *Imprint:* PR F T. CARNAN, (SUCCESSOR TO | MR. J. NEWBERY) SPC-Y. | MDCCLXXXIV.

In 6's. 72 leaves+8 insets. Pp. 140. Engvd FP and 7 other engvd leaves. 4 small wcts in text. List of bks pr f TC on pp. 127–40. Bds impressed with crude wcts in red sgd 'J. Bell Sc' (see Plate 17 and J280(2)).

[BM, 11·7×7·5 cm; Oup; Ball; McKell.

(7) Seventh edition, 1787. Pr f TC. Price 1s 6d.

Title and *imprint* approx. as for no. (6), with THE SEVENTH EDITION, date MDCCLXXXVII and price at foot. 72 leaves +9 insets. Pp. 140. Engvd FP and 8 engvd leaves in text. 5 small wcts in text. List of bks pr f TC on pp. 127–40. Marbled bds, green vell. spine.

[BM, 11·6×7·7 cm; V&A(GL) (imperf.); Roscoe, 12·6×11·7 cm trimmed; Welch; Ball; UCLA; McKell; Grant; Osborne*.

(8) Listed as pr f EN in *Joseph Andrews*, 1799, price 1s 6d. There were edd. in 1794 by Ogilvy and Speare, and 1798 by Ogilvy & Son et al.

J349. 'TELTRUTH, T.', 'TELLTRUTH, T.', 'TELLTRUTH, Mr'. NATURAL HISTORY OF BIRDS.

(1A) Adv. as by FN(N) in no. J316(1), 1769. ? = no. (1B).

(1B) An edition of 1770. Pr f FN(N). Price 6d.

THE | NATURAL HISTORY | OF | BIRDS. | BY T. TELTRUTH. | EMBEL-LISHED WITH CURIOUS CUTS. | LONDON: | PR F F. NEWBERY, AT THE COR- | NER OF SPC-Y. 1770. | PRICE SIX-PENCE.

Pp. 106. Engvd FP sgd 'J. Lodge sculpt' and other illustrations. (Communicated.)

[Ball.

(2) An edition of 1778. Pr f FN(N). Price 6d.

THE | NATURAL HISTORY | OF | BIRDS. | BY | T. TELLTRUTH. | EMBEL-LISHED WITH CURIOUS CUTS. | LONDON: | PR F F. NEWBERY, AT THE CORNER | OF SPC-Y. 1778. | [PRICE SIX-PENCE.]

In 8's. 64 leaves+engvd FP. Pp. 123[128]. 32 wcts in the text. List of bks s b FN(N) at end.

[BM, 10·1×6·2 cm; Ball.

(3) Listed as pr f EN in *History of Prince Lee Boo*, 1789. Price 6d. Welsh 315.

J350. 'TELLTRUTH, Mr.', 'TELTRUTH, T.'. NATURAL HISTORY OF FOUR-FOOTED BEASTS.

(1) Listed in Winlove's *Moral Lectures*, 1769, as s b FN(N). Price 6d.

(2) An edition of 1778. Pr f FN(N).

[Ball.

(3) An edition of 1781. Pr f EN. Price 6d.

THE | NATURAL HISTORY | OF | FOUR-FOOTED BEASTS. | BY | T. TELTRUTH. | EMBELLISHED WITH CURIOUS CUTS. | LONDON: | PR F E.

NEWBERY, AT THE CORNER | OF SPC-Y. | MDCCLXXXI. | [PRICE SIX-PENCE.]

   ? An engvd FP. Wcts in text. (Communicated.)

   [Welch.

(4) Listed as pr f EN in *History of Prince Lee Boo*, 1789. Price 6*d*. Welsh 315.

J351. TEN DIALOGUES ON THE CONDUCT OF HUMAN LIFE TO WHICH IS ADDED ZARA A MORAL TALE. Weedon 83. Richard Johnson's Day-book records: *1770 Nov. 8. M*^r *Carnan agreed to print the delivered Copy of Dialogues on the Oeconomy of Human Life. To be paid for about the End of January.——Value Ten Guineas.* The charge was paid, the title being given as *Ten Dialogues on the Conduct of Human Life.* Johnson never mentions *Zara.*

(1) Noticed in the *Critical Review*, April 1771, pp. 322–3; and adv. *LC* 13–16.7.71, p. 55, as to be had of TC, price 2*s*.

(2) Listed in no. J68(4), 1776, as s b C & N. Price 2*s*.

(3) Listed in no. J113(4), 1781, as pr f TC. Price 2*s*.

J352. THORNTON, Robert John. ILLUSTRATIONS OF THE SCHOOL-VIRGIL, 1814. Pubd by 'Newberry' et al. Price 4*s*. The 'Newberry' named in the imprint could be either Francis(S) or Elizabeth, though the address 'SPCY' makes Francis the more likely. See *Blake's Illustrations of Thornton's Virgil*, ed. G. L. Keynes, 1938. One of the last books to appear (so far as I know) with a Newbery imprint.

   ILLUSTRATIONS | OF THE | SCHOOL-VIRGIL, | IN | COPPER-PLATES, | AND | WOOD-CUTS; | [5 lines] | [p.s.rule] | BY | ROBERT JOHN THORNTON, M.D. | [2 lines] | [d.p.rule] | [3 lines quote] | [d.p.rule] | LONDON: | PUBLISHED BY F. C. AND J. RIVINGTON; J. JOHNSON; AND NEWBERRY, ST. | PC-Y; R. BALDWIN; J. WALKER; SCATCHERD AND LETTERMAN; | ROBINSONS; WILKIE AND ROBINSONS; LONGMAN, HURST, REES, ORME, AND | BROWNE; SHERWOOD, NEELY, AND JONES; GALE AND CURTIS, PATERNOSTER-ROW; | J. AND F. RICHARDSON, CORNHILL; COX, ST. THOMAS'S-STREET, BOROUGH; | LACKINGTON, ALLEN, AND CO. FINSBURY-SQUARE; J. MAWMAN, LUDGATE-HILL; | DARTON AND HARVEY, GRACE-CHURCH-STREET; LUNN, SOHO-SQUARE; POTE AND | WILLIAMS, ETON; J. HEARNE, 218, TOTTENHAM-COURT-ROAD; AND MAY BE HAD | OF ALL BOOKSELLERS IN TOWN AND COUNTRY. | 1814. | [p.rule] | [PRICE ONLY FOUR SHILLINGS.]

   12mo. 64 leaves. Pp. iv (remainder unnumbered). 2 leaves of letterpress+62 unnumbered leaves comprising 150 wcts. Drab bds.

   [BM, 18·8×11·0 cm approx. uncut; V&A(GL); Grant.

THREE INSTRUCTIVE TALES. See Palmer, Charlotte.

J353. 'THUMB, Thomas'. A BAG OF NUTS READY CRACKED. Welsh 317.

(1) Adv. in *GM* May 1774 as pr f FN(N). Price 3*d* bd.

(2) Second edition, 1776. Pr f FN(N).

⌈Formerly Seven Gables Bookshop, N.Y.

(3) Third edition not traced.

(4) Fourth edition, 1781. EN.

⌈NN-C.

(5) An undated edition. Pr f EN. Hugo, II, 325, no. 38. Described as 24mo. Pp. xv+94.

(6–7) Fifth and sixth editions not traced.

(8) Seventh edition, n.d. EN.

⌈CtHi.

(9) Eighth edition, n.d. EN.

⌈OOxM; MWA.

(10) Ninth edition, n.d. Pr f EN.

A | BAG OF NUTS | READY CRACKED, | OR, | INSTRUCTIVE FABLES, INGENIOUS RID- | DLES, AND MERRY CONUNDRUMS. | BY THE CELEBRATED AND FACETIOUS | THOMAS THUMB, ESQ. | PUBLISHED FOR THE BENEFIT OF ALL | LITTLE MASTERS AND MISSES WHO | LOVE READING AS WELL | AS PLAYING. | THE NINTH EDITION. | [d.p.rule] | PR F E. NEWBERY, THE CORNER OF | SPC-Y; BY J. CROW- | DER, WARWICK-SQUARE.

Pp. xv+16–95. Illustrations in text and wct FP. D.f.b. (Communicated.)

⌈Welch.

J354. 'TICKLEPITCHER, Toby'. THE HOBBY-HORSE, OR CHRISTMAS COMPANION. Welsh 237.

(1) Adv. *LC* 8–10.1.71, p. 39, as to be had of FN(N). Price 2*d* bd and gilt.

(2) Listed in *Brother's Gift*, 1777, as pr f a s b FN(N). Price 2*d*.

(3) An edition of 1784. Pr f EN. Price 2*d*. S&W Cat. D.f.b.

⌈Ball.

(4) An edition of 1788. Pr f EN. Price 2*d*. Recorded by Lyon.

(5) An edition of 1790. Pr f EN. Price 2*d*.

THE | HOBBY-HORSE, | OR | CHRISTMAS COMPANION: | CONTAINING | AMONG OTHER INTERESTING PARTICULARS, | THE SONG OF A COCK AND A BULL, | A | CANTERBURY STORY, | AND | A TALE OF A TUB. | FAITHFULLY COPIED FROM THE ORIGINAL MANU- | SCRIPT, IN THE VATICAN LIBRARY. | BY TOBY TICKLEPITCHER. | EMBELLISHED WITH ELEGANT CUTS. | LONDON: | PR F E. NEWBERY, AT THE CORNER | OF SPC-Y. 1790. | PRICE TWO PENCE.

Sgd in 8's, but gathered in 2 quires of 16 each. 32 leaves. Pp. 63. First leaf a blank; first and last leaves pastedowns. 40 wcts. List of bks pr f EN on last 2 pages. D.f. paper wrappers, gilt.

⌈Hannas, approx. 10·0×6·5 cm.

(6) An edition of 1796. EN.
⌈MSaE.

TOILES D'ARAIGNÉES. See Fenn, Lady E.

J355. TOM THUMB'S EXHIBITION. Welsh 317.
(1) Adv. in *GM* Supplement, 1774, as to be had of FN(N). Price 3*d*.
(1A) Listed in *Cries of London*, 1775, as pr f FN(N).
(2) Adv. *LC* 31.12.81–1.1.82, p. 7, as to be had of EN. Perhaps stock in hand of
the previous ed.
(3) An undated edition. Pr f EN. Price 2*d*.

TOM THUMB'S | EXHIBITION, | BEING | AN ACCOUNT | OF MANY
VALUABLE AND SURPRIZING | CURIOSITIES | WHICH HE HAS COLLECTED
| IN THE COURSE OF HIS TRAVELS, | FOR THE | INSTRUCTION AND
AMUSEMENT | OF THE | BRITISH YOUTH. | LONDON: | PR F E. NEWBERY,
AT THE COR- | NER OF SPC-Y.

Pp. 62[63]. Last leaf a pastedown. 19 or more wcts. List of bks pr f EN on p.
[63]. D.f. wrappers. All TP in roman type. On p. 63 line-endings of first 6 lines
are: Newbery, | Church- | En- | little | Great-Bri- | America. The bks listed are:
1. *Mrs Lovechild's Golden Present*, ... 7. *The Hobby Horse*. (Communicated.)
⌈OOxM (imperf.), 10·5 cm; Welch and Roscoe have selected photocopied
leaves.
(4) Another undated edition. Pr f EN. Price 2*d*.
TP and specification as for no. (3). A variant setting of type: on p. 63 the line-
endings for the first 6 lines are: Newbery, | Church- | Instruc- | the | of | the | .
The bks listed are: 1. *The Holiday Spy*, ... 7. *The Sister's Gift*. (Communicated.)
⌈MWA; Welch and Roscoe have photocopied selected leaves.
(5) Another undated edition. Pr f EN.
Title approx. as for no. (3), with first, sixth and ninth lines in italic type.
Imprint: PR F E. NEWBERY, THE CORNER OF S | PC-Y. | BY J. CROWDER,
WARWICK-SQUARE.
⌈MH (lacks all after p. 32).
(6) Listed in ENC, p. 6. Price 2*d*.

J356. TOM THUMB'S FOLIO. Welsh 317.
(1) Listed in *Goody Two-Shoes*, 1767, as 'sold at Mr Newbery's'. Price 1*d*.
(2) An edition of 1768. 'Pr f The People of all Nations; a s at Newbery &
Carnan's'. Price 1*d*. *CBEL*, II, 562; NBL 49. Pierpont Morgan Cat. item 80.
Title as for no. (3). *Imprint:* PR F THE PEOPLE OF ALL NATIONS; AND |
SOLD AT NEWBERY AND CARNAN'S, NO. | 65, THE NORTH SIDE OF SPC- |
Y. 1768. | [PRICE ONE PENNY.]
In 8's. 16 leaves. Pp. 31. First and last leaves pastedowns. 9 wcts. List of bks
sold at N & C's on pp. 29–30. D.f. paper wrappers.
⌈Bodley, 8·8 × 6·1 cm; Oppenheimer.

(2A) An edition of 1779. S b C & N. Price 1*d.*

Title approx. as for no. (3). *Imprint:* PR F THE PEOPLE OF ALL NATIONS; AND | S B T. CARNAN AND F. NEWBERY, | JUNIOR, NO. 65, IN SPC- | Y. 1779. | [PRICE ONE PENNY.]

16 leaves. Pp. 31. Wct FP and other wcts in text. Illustrated paper over bds. (Communicated.)

[Welch, 9·5 cm.

(3) An edition of 1786. S b TC (see Plate 18). Price 1*d.* S&W Cat.; *CBEL*, II, 562.

In 8's. 16 leaves. Pp. 29[31]. First and last leaves pastedowns. 9 wcts. List of bks pr f a s b TC on pp. [30–1]. D.f. paper wrappers.

[Bodley, 9·8×5·8 cm; CUL; Ball.

TOMMY CARELESS. See HISTORY OF...

TOMMY LOVEBOOK. See J372 and J373.

TOMMY TITMOUSE. See HISTORY OF...

TOMMY TRIP. See PRETTY BOOK OF PICTURES.

TOWER OF LONDON, DESCRIPTION OF THE, THE WILD BEASTS AND BIRDS... This is J88, vol. I.

J357. TOY-SHOP, THE. Welsh 319; Weedon 85. Pierpont Morgan Cat. item 295. Richard Johnson's Day-book records: *1781 May. Mr Badcock——To writing the Toy-Shop——£5. 5s.* The work was by the anonymous author of *Juvenile Rambles*, no. J200.

(1) An edition of 1787 recorded by Lyon. Adv. *LC* 27–9.12.87, p. 619, as pr f EN, price 6*d*; and listed in Kimber's *Joe Thompson*, 1788.

(2) See Fig. 28.

In 8's. 64 leaves. Pp. 127. Last leaf a pastedown. Wct FP and 13 wcts in text. Bk-list on pp. 121–7. D.f.b.

[BM, 10·8×7·4 cm.

(3) Another undated edition (? a variant issue of no. (2)). Pr f EN. Price 6*d.* The words 'Sentimental Preceptor' in the TP are in italic caps, the word 'London' in BL. Gum 5611 and pl. 75.

Title approx. as for no. (2). *Imprint:* PR F E. NEWBERY, THE CORNER OF | SPC-Y. | BY E. RIDER, LITTLE-BRITAIN. | [PRICE SIX-PENCE.]

Gum records a FP and 15 wcts and 'flowered-paper bds'.

[Sotheby, 6.2.1945 (the Bussell sale) lot 254.

(4) Another undated edition. Pr f EN. Price 6*d.*

The words on the TP 'Sentimental Preceptor' and 'London' in roman caps; the words 'Embellished with Cuts' are preceded by a p.rule *ca.* 6·3 cm. The TP

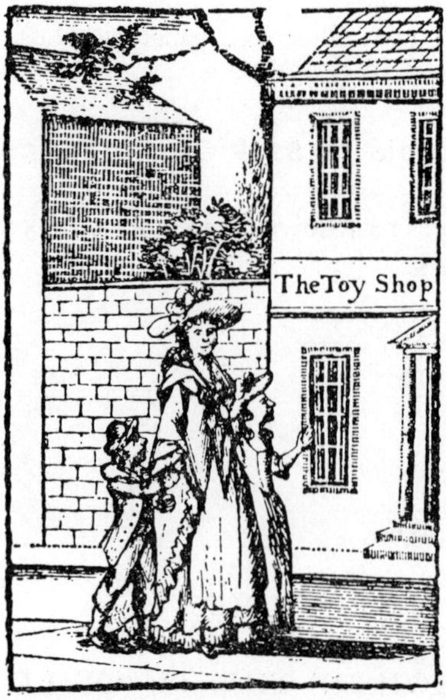

THE

TOY-SHOP;

OR,

SENTIMENTAL PRECEPTOR.

CONTAINING

SOME CHOICE TRIFLES,

FOR THE

INSTRUCTION AND AMUSEMENT

OF EVERY

LITTLE MISS AND MASTER.

Emb llished with CUTS.

LONDON:

Printed for E. NEWBERY, the Corner of St. Paul's Church-Yard.

[Price SIX-PENCE.]

Fig. 28. Frontispiece and title-page of J357(2).

imprint reads PR F E. NEWBERY, THE CORNER OF ST. | PC-Y. | [PRICE SIX-PENCE.] A1^{r} is headed by a d.p.rule *ca.* 6·3 cm. On p. 121 the bk-list runs to 12 lines, the last being *Robin Goodfellow*; on p. 127 the list runs to 26 lines, the last line reading 'the Pack.'.

[Bell; UCLA; Welch and Roscoe (have photocopied selected leaves); McKell.

(5) Another undated edition. Pr f EN. Price *6d.*

Title and *imprint* approx. as for no. (4). A1^{r} is headed by a rectangular block of printer's ornaments, *ca.* 0·7×6·0 cm. On p. 121 the bk-list runs to 17 lines, the last being *Tom Thumb's Exhibition*; on p. 127 the list runs to 22 lines, the last line reading '*2s. 6d.* the Pack.'.

[Welch; Roscoe (has photocopied selected leaves).

(6) Unspecified copies, pr f EN, in Opie; Osborne*; Oppenheimer; Elkin Mathews, Cat. 163 [1965] item 389; Maxwell Hunley, Cat. 48 [winter 1969] item 324a.

(7) Listed as pr f EN in *Anecdotes of Mary*, 1795, and in ENC, 1800, price *6d.*

J358. 'TRAPWIT, Tommy'. BE MERRY AND WISE. Welsh 319; *CBEL*, II, 561.

(1) Listed as by JN in *GM* for Feb. 1753, price *6d.* Also listed in *LM* for Feb. 1753 under the title *Collection of Jests and Maxims.*

(2) Second edition, 1756. Pr f the Author, a s at The Bible and Sun in SPC-Y. Price 6d. Welsh 319; *CBEL*, II, 561.

BE MERRY AND WISE: | OR, THE | CREAM OF THE JESTS, | AND THE | MARROW OF MAXIMS, | FOR THE CONDUCT OF LIFE. | PUBLISH'D FOR THE USE OF ALL GOOD LITTLE | BOYS AND GIRLS, | BY TOMMY TRAPWIT, ESQ; | [p.rule] | THE SECOND EDITION. | [p.rule] | ADORN'D WITH CUTS. | [p.rule] | [5 lines quote] | LONDON: | PR F THE AUTHOR, A S AT | THE BIBLE AND SUN IN SPC- | Y. MDCCLVI. | (PRICE SIX-PENCE.)

Pp. iv+5–128. Engvd FP sgd 'A. Walker in. del. et sculp.' 12 wcts in text. D.f.b. (Communicated.)

⌜UCLA.

(3) Third edition, by JN, listed in J31, 1764 and J40(1), 1764. But the 5th ed. was dated 1761 (see no. (5)).

(4) Fourth edition not traced.

(5) Fifth edition, 1761. Pr f The Author, sold at The Bible & Sun... Price 6d.

Title and *imprint* approx. as for no. (2), with THE FIFTH EDITION and date 1761.

In 8's. 64 leaves+engvd FP. Pp. iv+[5]–67 (error for 128). 12 wcts in text. D.f.b.

⌜Bodley, 9·7×6·3 cm.

(6) Listed in J7A(6), 1768 as pr f a s b N & C. Price 6d.

(7) An edition of 1770. Pr f the Author, s b C & N. Price 6d bd and gilt.

Title approx. as for no. (2). *Imprint:* PR F THE AUTHOR, A S B CARNAN | AND NEWBERY AT NO. 65, IN SP | C-Y, 1770. | (PRICE SIX-PENCE.)

In 8's. 64 leaves+engvd FP. Pp. iv+[5]–127. 12 wcts in text. D.f.b.

⌜V&A; Roscoe, 9·8×6·7 cm.

(8) An edition of 1774. C & N.

⌜Ball.

(9) An edition of 1781. Pr f the Author, s b TC. Price 6d. Hugo 4041.

Title approx. as for no. (2). *Imprint:* PR F THE AUTHOR, AND S B T. CARNAN, | IN SPC-Y, 1781. | (PRICE SIX PENCE.)

Pp. vi+7–128. Wct FP and 12 wcts in text, used in no. (2). Drab bds, illustrated with black impress; also D.f.b. (Communicated.)

⌜UCLA; Ball; Phillips, Son & Neale, 20.6.67, lot 280.

(10) An edition of 1787. S b TC. Price 6d.

Title and imprint approx. as for no. (9), with date 1787.

Pp. vi+7–128. Wcts. D.f.b. (Communicated.)

⌜Welch, 9·5 cm (imperf.); Sotheby, 24.2.69, lot 1 (imperf.).

TRIFLES; OR, FRIENDLY MITES. See Sandham, Eliz.

J358A. TRIMMER, Sarah. FACILE INTRODUCTION A LA CONNOISSANCE DE LA NATURE, 1788.

See Fig. 29.

I N T R O D U C T I O N

A L A

CONNOISSANCE de la NATURE

E T A L A L E C T U R E D E S

SAINTES ECRITURES.

Mife à la portée des

JEUNES GENS des DEUX SEXES.

———————————

Traduit de l'Anglois de Mrs. TRIMMER,
par M. LE BAS de St. AMAND.

———————————

Prix 2 Shel. rélié.

━━━━━━━━━━━━━━━━

L O N D R E S:
Se vend chez le Traducteur, à Iflington;
et chez E. Newbery, Libraire, au Coin du
Cimetière de St. Paul.
M.DCC.LXXXVIII.

Fig. 29. Title-page of J358A.

In 6's. [A]–[O6]. 84 leaves. Pp. xi+156. Bd sheep.
[Roscoe; Renier, *ca.* 16·0×8·8 cm untrimmed (imperf.).

J359. ? TRIMMER, Sarah. LADDER TO LEARNING, THE, STEP THE FIRST. Welsh 249. Mr Peter Opie is of opinion that the *Ladder* was not by Mrs Trimmer. He points out that she herself said that her first bk was *An easy Introduction to the Knowledge of Nature*, pubd in 1780.
(1) Adv. *MC&LA*, 30.12.72. FN(N).
(2) An undated edition, not later than 1778 or 1779, pr f FN(N). Price *6d.* MS dates 20 March 1778 and 20 March 1779 in Opie copy.
    THE | LADDER TO LEARNING, | STEP THE FIRST: | BEING A COLLECTION OF | SELECT FABLES, | WITH | ORIGINAL MORALS, ON A NEW PLAN, | [4 lines] | LONDON: | PR F F. NEWBERY, AT THE CORNER OF | SPC-Y. | (PRICE SIX PENCE.)

D.f.b. Perhaps identical with no. (3). (Communicated.)

⌜Opie.

(3) An undated edition. Pr f FN(N). Perhaps identical with no. (2).

Title and *imprint* may be as for no. (2). Pp. iv+[5]–110[112]. Illustrations. Bk-list at end. (Communicated.)

⌜Ball.

(4) An undated edition. Pr f EN. Price 6*d*. ? NBL 50, dates [1789].

THE | LADDER | TO | LEARNING, | STEP THE FIRST: | BEING A COLLECTION OF | SELECT FABLES, | CONSISTING OF WORDS OF | ONLY ONE SYLLABLE, | INTENDED AS AN EASY INTRODUCTION | TO | THE USEFUL ART OF READING. | LONDON: | PR F E. NEWBERY, AT THE CORNER | OF SPC-Y. | (PRICE SIX-PENCE.)

In 8's. 56 leaves. Pp. vi+[7]–111[112]. Many wcts in text. On the TP 'Select Fables' is in roman caps; there are no rules. On A2ʳ there is no rule above 'Preface' and the text is 17 lines plus catch-word 'quently'. The Preface ends on p. vi, 11 lines. Fable xxxiv, 'The Crow & the Jug', begins on p. 108.

⌜Pollard (imperf.); Welch; Roscoe (photocopied selected leaves).

(4A) Another undated edition. Pr f EN. Price 6*d*. ? NBL 50.

Title and *imprint* approx. as for no. (4).

Pp. vii+128. Wcts. On the TP 'Select Fables' in italic caps; p.s.rule above the imprint, p.rule below. On A2ʳ there is a d.p.rule 5·8 cm above 'Preface' and the text is 11 lines plus catch-word 'Words'. Preface ends on p. vii, 5 lines. Fable xxxiv is on pp. 127–8.

⌜Grant.

(5) Listed as pr f EN in J88(3), vol. I, 1786, and thereafter up to 1800.

(6) An edition of 1799. Pr f EN. Price 6*d*.

Title approx. as for no. (4). *Imprint:* PR F E. NEWBERY, AT THE CORNER OF | SPC-Y; | BY J. CROWDER, WARWICK-SQUARE. | 1799. | (PRICE SIX PENCE.)

Collates [A]–H8. Pp. 128. (Communicated.)

⌜Schiller (1970).

J360. ? TRIMMER, Sarah. LADDER TO LEARNING, THE, STEP THE SECOND. Welsh 249. As to Trimmer's authorship, see J359.

(1) Adv. *MC&LA* 30.12.72, and listed in Chesterfield's *Maxims*, 1777, as pr f FN(N). Price 6*d*.

(2) An undated edition. Pr f EN. Price 6*d*. MS dates 1792 and 1793 in Welch copy. ? Rothschild 609.

THE | LADDER | TO | LEARNING, | STEP THE SECOND: | BEING A COLLECTION OF | SELECT FABLES, | WITH | ORIGINAL MORALS, UPON A NEW PLAN. | CONSISTING OF WORDS NOT EXCEEDING | TWO SYLLABLES. | [p.s.rule] | PR F E. NEWBERY, AT THE CORNER | OF SPC-Y. | (PRICE SIX-PENCE.)

Pp. 110. Wct headpiece to each of the 33 'Fables'. D.f.b. (Communicated.)

⌈Welch.

(3) An undated edition. EN. Price *6d*. NBL 50, dates [1789]. ? = no. (2).

(3A) An undated edition by EN. Elkin Mathews, Cat. 163 [1965] item 15; described as 'first edition' and dated '[*ca.* 1789]'. In view of item (1) above almost certainly not the 1st ed. 29 wcts. D.f.b. ? = no. (2).

(4) Listed as pr f EN in *Prince Lee Boo*, 1789, and frequently thereafter up to 1800.

(5) A copy, wanting title-leaf, has pp. 127. Ms date 17 July 1797 inside front cover. Wct to each Fable. D.f.b.

⌈V&A(GL), 60.z.110., 10·7×7·3 cm.

(6) An undated edition. Pr f EN. Price *6d*.

Title and *imprint* approx. as for no. (2). Collates [A]–H8. Pp. 127. (Communicated.)

⌈Schiller (1970).

J361. ? TRIMMER, Sarah. LADDER TO LEARNING, THE, STEP THE THIRD. Welsh 249. As to Trimmer's authorship, see J359.

(1) Adv. in *GM* Supplement, 1774, as to be had of FN(N), price *6d*.

(1A) Adv. *LC* 30.12.81–1.1.82, p. 7, as to be had of EN, price *6d*.

(2) An undated edition. Pr f EN. Price *6d*.

THE | LADDER | TO | LEARNING, | STEP THE THIRD: | BEING A COLLECTION OF | SELECT FABLES, | INTENDED AS AN EASY INTRODUCTION | TO | THE USEFUL ART OF READING. | ADORNED WITH CUTS. | [p.s.rule] | LONDON: | PR F E. NEWBERY, AT THE CORNER | OF SPC-Y. | [p.rule] | [PRICE SIX-PENCE.]

Pp. 135. Illustrations. D.f.b. (Communicated.)

⌈Ries.

(2A) An undated edition. Pr f EN. Price *6d*. A copy in the Schiller collection is probably no. (2). Collates [A]–H8, I4. Pp. 135. (Communicated.)

(3) An undated edition by EN. NBL 50, dates [1789]. ? = no. (2).

(4) Listed in *Prince Lee Boo*, 1789, as pr f EN. Price *6d*, and thereafter frequently up to 1800.

J362. ? TRIMMER, Sarah. SILVER THIMBLE, THE. Mr Peter Opie doubts Mrs Trimmer's authorship. He says 'Mrs Trimmer had no compunction about having her name attached to her work; and her name was much too big in 1799 for a publisher not to blazon it forth. And I do not really think the style is Mrs Trimmer's either.' This is presumably the work listed in ENC, p. 8, as 'The History of a Silver Thimble', price *1s*.

(1) An edition of 1799. Pr f EN. Price *1s*. NBL 518.

THE | SILVER THIMBLE. | [d.s.rule] | BY THE AUTHOR OF | INSTRUCTIVE TALES, &c. | [d.p.rule] | [wct device] | [d.p.rule] | LONDON: | PR F E. NEWBERY, AT THE CORNER OF SP | C-Y. 1799.

In 6's. 60 leaves+engvd FP sgd 'Scott, sculpt'. Pp. 113[120]. List of bks pr f EN on last 6 pages. Green or yellow bds, label on upper.

[BM, 13·5×8·3 cm; BCE, 13·8×8·4 cm (imperf.); Opie; Osborne, Cat. p. 304.

(2) An edition of 1801. Pr f EN.

Title approx. as for no. (1). *Imprint:* PR F E. NEWBERY, AT THE CORNER OF SP | C-Y, | BY H. BRYER, BRIDEWELL-HOSPITAL. | [p.rule] | 1801.

In 6's. 60 leaves+engvd FP as for no. (1). Pp. 113[120]. List of bks pr f EN on last 6 pages and list of bks 'just published by EN' on K3ᵛ. Pink bds, label on upper.

[BM, 12·8×8·1 cm; CUL; Welch.

'TRIP, Tom'. TOM TRIP'S HISTORY OF BEASTS AND BIRDS. The *Pretty Book of Pictures for little Masters and Misses* (J308) was frequently advtd under this title.

J363. TRIUMPH OF GOODNATURE, THE.

(1) An undated edition. Pr f EN. Pp. 110. 12 wcts. Price 6*d*. Hugo II, 4106.

(2) An undated edition. Pr f EN. NBL 509, which describes it as 'first edition' and dates [*ca*. 1780]. May be identical with some other here listed.

(2A) An undated edition. Pr f EN. Price 6*d*.

Title approx. as for no. (3), with a p.s.rule 3·2 cm long following 'Ornamented with Cuts'. *Imprint:* PR F E. NEWBERY, THE CORNER | OF SPC-Y. | [p.rule 2·3 cm] | PRICE SIX PENCE.

Pp. 112. Wct FP as in no. (3). List of bks pr f EN on pp. 111–12. Probably not later than 1792, the bk-list including Berquin's *Looking-Glass for the Mind* without mention of the wcts, which first appeared in the ed. of that year. (Communicated.) [MB.

(3) Another undated edition. Pr f EN. Price 6*d*. Not later than 1801 (MS on front fly-leaf of Welch copy 'Sanders Bennett Book, 1801').

THE | TRIUMPH OF GOODNATURE, | EXHIBITED IN THE | HISTORY | OF | MASTER HARRY FAIRBORN | AND | MASTER TRUEWORTH. | INTER-SPERSED WITH | TALES AND FABLES, | AND | ORNAMENTED WITH CUTS. | [d.p.rule 5·2 cm long] | LONDON: | PR F E. NEWBERY, THE CORNER OF | SPC-Y. | [p.rule] | PRICE SIXPENCE.

Pp. 110[111–27]. Wct FP sgd 'Bwk' [= John Bewick] and other wcts in text. Bk-list at pp. [111–24]; list of games at pp. [125–7]. At A3ʳ there is a d.p.rule 4·9 cm long above the title, a p.s.rule 1·7 cm long below. At p. [111] the 1st bk listed is *Holiday Entertainments*, the last *Rural Felicity*. D.f.b. (Communicated.) [Welch; Roscoe (photocopied selected leaves).

(4) Another undated edition. Pr f EN. Price 6*d*. Not later than 1799 (see below), but probably 1792 or before, as for no. (2A).

Title and *imprint* as for no. (3) except p.s.rule 2·0 cm long below 'Ornamented with cuts', and 3rd line of imprint reads: ...E. NEWBERY, THE CORNER | OF...

Pp. 123. ? a FP as in no. (3). At A3ʳ d.p.rule 5·6 cm long above title, p.rule 3·2 cm below. At p. 111 the 1st bk listed is *Pleasing Reflections*, the last *Prince Lee*

Boo. MS inscription 'Harry S. Austin his Book bought in the year 1799'. D.f.b. (Communicated.)

⌈Gardner, 11·4×6·3 cm (imperf.); Roscoe (photocopied selected leaves).

J364. 'TRUELOVE, Mr.' ADVENTURES OF A SILVER THREE-PENCE, THE, n.d. Pr f EN. Price 6*d*. ENC, p. 7; Hugo, II, p. 326, no. 39.

THE | ADVENTURES | OF A | SILVER THREE-PENCE. | CONTAINING | MUCH AMUSEMENT AND MANY CHARACTERS | WITH WHICH | YOUNG GENTLEMEN AND LADIES | OUGHT TO BE ACQUAINTED. | ADORNED WITH CUTS. | [d.p.rule] | WRITTEN BY MR. TRUELOVE. | FOR THE BENEFIT OF ALL GOOD CHILDREN WHO LOVE TO BE | MERRY AND WISE. | [d.p.rule] | LONDON: | PR B J. CUNDEE, IVY LANE, NEWGATE STREET; | FOR E. NEWBERY, | CORNER OF SPC-Y. | [PRICE SIX-PENCE.]

In 8's. 60 leaves. Pp. 119. Wct FP and 16 wcts in text. Green floral impress design on [? drab] bds, gilt.

⌈BM, 10·8×7·5 cm.

J365. TUTOR, THE; OR, EPISTOLARY GUIDE. See note to no. (2) below.

(1) An edition of 1772. Pr f FN(N). Price 2*s*. Welsh 320; Alston, IV, 727 and plate LXXVIII; Pressler, p. 7.

THE | TUTOR; | OR | EPISTOLARY GUIDE. | BEING A COLLECTION OF | FAMILIAR LETTERS | ON THE | COMMON OCCURRENCES OF LIFE; | SELECTED FROM | THE MOST CELEBRATED ENGLISH WRITERS. | [1 line] | TO WHICH ARE PREFIXED, | A NEW INTRODUCTION TO | ENGLISH GRAMMAR, | AND A | COMPLETE SPELLING DICTIONARY, | [5 lines] | LONDON: | PR F F. NEWBERY, THE CORNER OF S | PC-Y. MDCCLXXII. | [PRICE TWO-SHILLINGS.]

Pp. xxiv+240.

⌈ICU-Judd Lib.; MH; NN; Oppenheimer.

(2) Listed as pr f FN(N), price 2*s* bd, in Chesterfield's *Maxims*, 1777, under the following description: THE TUTOR; OR, EPISTOLARY GUIDE, BEING A COLLECTION OF FAMILIAR LETTERS ON THE COMMON OCCURRENCES OF LIFE, WITH PROPER FORMS OF ADDRESS, TO WHICH ARE PREFIXED, A NEW INTRODUCTION TO ENGLISH GRAMMAR, AND A COMPLETE SPELLING DICTIONARY. This may in fact be identical with no. (1).

Whatever the contents of this book, pubd by FN(N), may have been its title certainly (and one may suspect deliberately) reflects the *Letters on the most common...occasions in Life...With proper Directions for addressing Persons of Rank*...(no. J266), pubd b JN and afterwards by TC. In the general note to J266 I have pointed out the 19-year period during which no ed. of the *Letters* appears to have been pubd. It may well be no mere coincidence that the first 2 records of *The Tutor* fall in that period.

(3) Listed in *Prince Lee Boo*, 1789 as pr f EN. Price 1*s* 6*d*. Welsh 320.

J366. TWELFTH-DAY GIFT, THE. Welsh 320–1; *CBEL*, II, 561 (lists as a bk which might have been written by JN).

(1) Listed in no. J40(1), 1764, and *Goody Two-Shoes*, 1766. Apparently only advance publicity; see Introduction at p. 11.

(2) An edition of 1767. Pr f JN. Price 1s bd and gilt. Gum 2773; NBL 648.

THE | TWELFTH-DAY GIFT: | OR, THE | GRAND EXHIBITION. | CONTAINING | A CURIOUS COLLECTION OF PIECES IN PROSE | AND VERSE (MANY OF THEM ORIGINALS) WHICH | WERE DELIVERED TO A NUMEROUS AND POLITE | AUDIENCE, ON THE IMPORTANT SUBJECTS OF | RELIGION,... | [10 lines] | [p.rule] | [2 lines quote] | [p.rule] | LONDON: | PR F J. NEWBERY, AT THE BIBLE AND | SUN IN SPCY. 1767.

In 6's. 107 leaves+9 insets. Pp. 208. Engvd FP and 8 other engvd leaves. D.f.b.
[BM, 11·5×6·7 cm; Fox; NorBM; McKell; NNC-T (Darton Coll.); NWebyC.

(3) Second edition, 1770. Pr f C & N. Price 1s.

Title approx. as for no. (2), with THE SECOND EDITION. *Imprint:* PR F CARNAN AND NEWBERY, AT NO. 65. | IN SPCY. 1770.

In 6's. 108 leaves+9 insets as in no. (2). Pp. 209.
[BM, 12·0×7·7 cm; Opie; UCLA.

(4) Third edition, 1774. Pr f C & N.

Title and *imprint* approx. as for no. (3), with THE THIRD EDITION and date MDCCLXXIV.

In 6's. 108 leaves+9 insets as before. Pp. 209. D.f.b.
[BM, 11·4×7·6 cm.

(5) Fourth edition, 1777. Pr f C & N. *CBEL* dates 1783 in error.

Pp. 209. TP, FP and 7 wcts. Contemporary sheep. (Communicated.)
[Ball; Welch.

(6) An edition of 1783. Pr f TC. Price 1s.

Title approx. as before. *Imprint:* PR F T. CARNAN, SUCCESSOR TO MR J. NEWBERY, | IN SPC-Y. PRICE ONE SHILLING. | [p.rule] | MDCCLXXXIII.

In 6's. 112 leaves. Pp. 212[216]. Wct FP and 7 wcts in text. White or buff bds, with crude wcts in red.
[BM, 11·7×7·8 cm; MH; MB; Sotheby, 16.3.70, lot 43.

(7) An edition of 1788. Pr f TC. Price 1s. Gum 2774.

Title approx. as before. *Imprint* as for no. (6), with date MDCCLXXXVIII.
Pp. 158[160]. Wct FP and 8 wcts in text. D.f.b. (Communicated.)
[Opie; Ball; Welch; UCLA.

J367. TWELVE PENNYWORTH OF WISDOM. The TP to JN's undated ed. of *Six-Pennyworth of Wit* (no. J336(1)) states 'when you have read this six-pennyworth of Wit, you would do well to buy Twelve-Pennyworth of Wisdom, which is much better, and may be had at the Place where this is sold'. The nearest approach is Trapwit's *Be Merry and Wise*. Probably not a book at all, but an advice, in the true Newbery manner, to buy a shilling's worth of his books.

TWO COUSINS, THE. See Pinchard, Mrs E.

J368. VALENTINE'S GIFT, THE. Welsh 323.
(1) Listed in no. J40(1), 1764. Probably advance publicity.
(2) An edition of 1765. Pr f JN. Price 6*d* bd and gilt.

THE | VALENTINE'S GIFT: | OR, | A PLAN | TO ENABLE CHILDREN OF ALL SIZES AND | DENOMINATIONS TO BEHAVE WITH HO- | NOUR, INTEGRITY AND HUMANITY. | [1 line] | TO WHICH IS ADDED, | SOME ACCOUNT OF OLD ZIGZAG, AND OF | THE HORN WHICH HE USED TO UNDERSTAND THE | LANGUAGE OF BIRDS, BEASTS, FISHES, AND | INSECTS. | [p.rule] | [4 lines quote] | [p.rule] | LONDON: | PR F J. NEWBERY, AT THE BIBLE AND | SUN IN SPC-Y. 1765. | PRICE SIX-PENCE BOUND AND GILT.

64 leaves+engvd FP. Pp. 118[128]. Wcts in text. Bk-list on pp. [121–8]. D.f.b. (Communicated.)
[Welch.

(2A) An edition of 1767. Pr f JN. Price 6*d* bd and gilt.
Title and *imprint* as for no. (2), with date 1767.
In 8's. 64 leaves+engvd FP. Pp. iv+5–122[128]. 25 small wcts in the text, some by the *Goody Two-Shoes* cutter. List of bks pubd for children on pp. [125–8]. D.f.b.
[NorBM, 9·5×6·6 cm.

(3) An edition of 1774. Pr f C & N. Price 6*d* bd.
Title approx. as for no. (2). *Imprint:* PR F T. CARNAN AND F. NEW- | BERY JUNIOR, AT NO. 65, IN SP | C-Y. MDCCLXXIV. | PRICE SIX-PENCE BOUND.
In 8's. 64 leaves, ?+engvd FP. Pp. 122[128]. *Ca.* 21 wcts in text. List of bks pr f C & N on pp. [123–8]. D.f.b.
[Exeter (imperf.), 9·7×6·3 cm; Ball.

(4) An edition of 1777. Pr f C & N. Price 6*d* bd.
Title approx. as for no. (2). *Imprint* approx. as for no. (3), with date MDCCLXXVII (see Plate 19).
In 8's. 64 leaves+engvd FP. Pp. iv+5–122[128]. 25 wcts in text. List of bks pr f C & N on pp. [123–8]. Drab paper wrappers, each with an engvd design in black.
[BM, approx. 9·6×5·9 cm; V&A(GL); NRU; Ball.

(4A) An undated edition. Pr f C & N.
[Ball.

(5) An edition of 1782. Pr f TC. Price 6*d*. S&W Cat.
Title approx. as for no. (2). *Imprint:* PR F T. CARNAN, | (SUCCESSOR TO MR. J. NEWBERY,) | IN SPC-Y. 1782. | [PRICE SIX-PENCE BOUND.]
In 8's. 64 leaves. Pp. 122[128]. Engvd FP. 24 wcts in text. List of bks pr f TC on pp. [123–8]. 'Red pictorial boards' (*per* S&W Cat.).
[Bath (imperf.), 9·2×5·8 cm; Welch; UCLA.

(6) An edition of 1790. Pr f Francis Power & Co. Price 6*d* bd.

Title approx. as for no. (2). *Imprint:* PR F FRANCIS POWER, (GRANDSON TO | THE LATE MR. J. NEWBERY,) AND CO. | NO. 65. SPCY, 1790. | [PRICE SIX-PENCE BOUND.]

In 6's. 54 leaves. Pp. iv+105[108]. Wcts. List of bks s b Francis Power on pp. [106–8].

[BM (imperf.), 11·3×7·1 cm.

J369. VICE IN ITS PROPER SHAPE. Welsh 325.
(1) Adv. in *GM* May 1774 as pr f FN(N). Price 6*d*.
(1A) An undated edition. S b FN(N).

VICE | IN ITS | PROPER SHAPE; | OR, THE | WONDERFUL AND MELANCHOLY | TRANSFORMATION | OF SEVERAL NAUGHTY MASTERS AND MISSES | INTO THOSE | CONTEMPTIBLE ANIMALS WHICH THEY MOST | RESEMBLE IN DISPOSITION. | PRINTED FOR THE BENEFIT OF ALL GOOD BOYS | AND GIRLS. | SOLD BY F. NEWBERY, AT THE CORNER OF S | PCY.

In 8's. 68 leaves. Pp. xi (error for ix)+10–130[136]. Wcts. List of bks pr f FN(N) at pp. [131–6]. D.f.b.

[Sotheby, 9.6.69, lot 251, 10·1×6·4 cm.
(2) Adv. *LC* 30.12.81–1.1.82, p. 7, as to be had of EN. Price 6*d*.
(2A) An undated edition. EN.
[Ball.
(3) Listed in *Anecdotes of Mary*, 1795, as pr f EN, price 6*d*.
(4) A copy in the Welch Coll. lacks all leaves except the FP prior to p. 19, has MS date and signature 1789.

VILLAGE MAID, THE. See Somerville, Eliz.

VILLAGE MATRON. See ? Fenn, Lady E.

J370. VILLAGE TATLERS, THE. Welsh 326; Weedon 87. Richard Johnson's Day-book records: *1786 July. Mr Badcock——To writing The Village Tattlers* (sic), *2 Half Sheets. 32°.——£2. 2s.*
(1) Adv. *LC* 26–8.12.86, p. 620, as one of EN's 'New Publications for the Christmas Holidays—just published', price 2*d*.
(2) An edition of 1788. EN. Welsh 344.
(2A) Listed in *Flights of a Lady-Bird*, 1794, as pubd by EN.
(3) An edition of 1797. Pr f EN. Price 2*d*.

THE | VILLAGE TATLERS; | OR, | ANECDOTES | OF THE | RURAL ASSEMBLY. | [p.s.rule] | EMBELLISHED WITH CUTS. | [p.s.rule] | LONDON: | PR F E. NEWBERY, AT THE CORNER OF | SPC-Y. | [p.rule] | MDCCXCVII. | (PRICE TWO PENCE.)

Pp. 64. Wcts. (Communicated.)
[Welch (imperf.).

VIRGIL. See J352.

J371. VIRTUE AND VICE. Welsh 326. How far the following entries refer to different editions it is not possible to say.

(1) Adv. *LC* 19–21.12.80, p. 589, as one of EN's New Publications for the Christmas Holidays. Price 2*d*. D.f.b.

(2) Listed in J88(3), vol. 1, 1786, as pr f EN. Price 2*d*.

(3) An undated edition (MS date 1800). Pr f EN. Price 2*d* bd and gilt.

VIRTUE AND VICE: | OR THE | HISTORY | OF | CHARLES CAREFUL, | AND | HARRY HEEDLESS; | SHEWING | THE GOOD EFFECTS OF CAUTION AND PRU- | DENCE,... | [4 lines] | [d.p.rule] | LONDON: | PR F E. NEWBERY, THE CORNER OF | SPC-Y. | (PRICE TWO-PENCE BOUND AND GILT.)

Wct FP and wcts in text. D.f.b. (Communicated.)

⌜OOxM.

(4) Listed in ENC, p. 5. Price 2*d*.

J372. VISITS OF TOMMY LOVEBOOK, THE, TO HIS NEIGHBOURING LITTLE MISSES AND MASTERS, 1792.
Pr f EN. Price 2*d*. Richard Johnson records in his Day-book: *1791 Oct. M*^r *Badcock——To writing The Visits of Tommy Lovebook——£2. 2s.* Weedon 88 (this ed. unrecorded). ? Welsh 318.

THE | VISITS | OF | TOMMY LOVEBOOK | TO HIS NEIGHBOURING | LITTLE MISSES AND MASTERS. | [d.p.rule] | EMBELLISHED WITH CUTS. | [d.p.rule] | LONDON: | PR F E. NEWBERY, THE CORNER | OF SPCY, 1792. | [p.rule] | [PRICE TWO-PENCE.]

In 8's. 32 leaves. Pp. 64. 1st leaf a pastedown. Wct FP and 12 wcts in text. D.f. paper.

⌜Bell, 10·0×6·3 cm.

J373. VISITS OF TOMMY LOVEBOOK TO HIS YOUNG FRIENDS. ENC p. 5. Price 2*d*. ? Welsh 318. Probably identical with no. J372.

J374. VISITS TO THE AVIARY, 1800. S b EN. Price 2*s*, 'vellum back'.

VISITS | TO | THE AVIARY. | [p.s.rule] | FOR THE | INSTRUCTION OF YOUTH. | [d.p.rule] | LONDON: | PR F VERNOR AND HOOD, POULTRY, | BY J. WRIGHT, DENMARK-COURT, | A S B | E. NEWBERY, SPC-Y. | [p.rule] | 1800.

In 6's. 72 leaves+engvd FP sgd 'Crutchwell delt, Cooke sculp'. Pp. 136[140]. Half-title. List of bks pubd by Vernor and Hood on last 2 leaves. Marbled bds, green vell. spine with label.

⌜BM, 13·9×8·5 cm; CUL; V&A(GL); Osborne, Cat. p. 215; UCLA.

VOYAGES. See J89.

J375. WAKEFIELD, Priscilla. AN INTRODUCTION TO BOTANY. *CBEL*, II, 559.

(1) First edition, 1796 (*CBEL* dates 1795 in error). Pr f E. Newberry (*sic*) et al. Price 3*s* 'neat in boards'.

AN | INTRODUCTION | TO | BOTANY, | IN | A SERIES OF | FAMILIAR LETTERS, | WITH ILLUSTRATIVE ENGRAVINGS. | [d.p.rule] | BY PRISCILLA WAKEFIELD, | [2 lines] | [d.p.rule] | LONDON: | PR F E. NEWBERRY, SPC- | Y; DARTON AND HARVEY, GRACECHURCH- | STREET; AND VERNOR AND HOOD, | BIRCHIN-LANE. | [p.s.rule] | MDCCXCVI.

12mo. 100 leaves+13 insets. Pp. xiii+184. 12 leaves of engvd plates, numbered I–XI (no. IV being 2 conjugate leaves), one folding leaf. Half-title.

[BM, 17·7×10·1 cm; CUL; EdUL; UCL; Renier; Osborne, Cat. p. 215.

(2) Second edition, 1798. Pr f EN et al. Price 3*s* in bds. Welsh 329.

Title and *imprint* approx. as for no. (1), with THE SECOND EDITION and date 1798.

100 leaves+13 insets. Pp. xv+[17]–200. Insets as for no. (1). Half-title.

[BM, 17·8×10·4 cm; Bodley; UCLA; Brimmell, Cat. 61 [1968] item 160; Sotheby, 14.3.72, lot 305; A. R. Heath, Cat. 22 [1972] item 253.

J376. WARD, Rev. Samuel. MODERN SYSTEM OF NATURAL HISTORY, A. Perhaps this work could equally well have been included in the 'A' section of this Bibliography.

Adv. *LC* 24–7.6.75, p. 603, as 'to be completed in twelve pocket volumes' at 1*s* 6*d* each. The complete set was to be had at 18*s* sewed, 1 gn in the vell. manner, £1 4*s* calf.

(1) The edition of 1775–6. Pr f FN(N). 12 vols. For price see note above and nos. (2) and (5). Welsh 329–30.

A | MODERN SYSTEM | OF | NATURAL HISTORY. | CONTAINING | ACCURATE DESCRIPTIONS, AND FAITHFUL HISTORIES, | OF | ANIMALS, VEGETABLES, AND MINERALS. | [3 lines] | ILLUSTRATED | WITH A GREAT VARIETY OF COPPER-PLATES, ACCURATELY | DRAWN FROM NATURE, AND BEAUTIFULLY ENGRAVED. | [p.rule] | BY THE REV. SAMUEL WARD, | VICAR OF COTTESTOCK, CUM GLAPTHORNE, NORTHAMP- | TONSHIRE; AND OTHERS. | [p.rule] | [4 lines quote] | [d.p.rule] | LONDON: | PR F F. NEWBERY, THE CORNER OF SP | C-Y, LUDGATE-STREET. 1775.

In vols. II–XII, the vol. number is printed immediately preceding the 4-line quote. All vols are in 6's, collating either [A]–[P6] or [B]–[Q6], 90 leaves. Some vols seen in blue bds, green vell. spine.

Vol. I. 1775. Pp. xv+[17]–180. 4 leaves of engvd figures.

Vol. II. 1775. Pp. 180. 21 leaves of engvd figures.

Vol. III. 1775. Pp. 178[180]. 11 leaves of engvd figures. List of bks pr f FN(N) on Q6$^{r, v}$.

Vol. IV. 1775. Pp. 124+xlviii[lvi]. 4 leaves of engvd figures. List of bks pr f FN(N) on Q5^r–Q6^v.

Vol. V. 1775. Pp. 180. 7 leaves of engvd figures. Individual TP: NATURAL HISTORY OF BIRDS VOL. I.

Vol. VI. 1775. Pp. 180. 7 leaves of engvd figures. Individual TP: NATURAL HISTORY OF BIRDS VOL. II.

Vol. VII. 1775. Pp. 179. 16 leaves of engvd figures. Individual TP: NATURAL HISTORY OF BIRDS VOL. III.

Vol. VIII. 1776. Pp. 120+li[lx]. 7 leaves of engvd figures. Individual TP: NATURAL HISTORY OF BIRDS VOL. IV.

Vol. IX. 1776. Pp. 180. 13 leaves of engvd figures. Individual TP: NATURAL HISTORY OF FISHES VOL. I.

Vol. X. 1776. Pp. 164+xv[xvi]. 7 leaves of engvd figures. Individual TP: NATURAL HISTORY OF FISHES VOL. II.

Vol. XI. 1776. Pp. 178[180]. 10 leaves of engvd figures. Individual TP: NATURAL HISTORY OF REPTILES AND INSECTS VOL. I.

Vol. XII. 1776. Pp. 171[178]. Last leaf a blank. 10 leaves of engvd figures. Individual TP: NATURAL HISTORY OF WATERS, EARTHS, FOSSILS...

[BM, 13·8×8·1 cm; CUL (vols XI and XII); Opie (4 vols); Wellcome; Pollard (vols IX and X); NNC-T (Darton Coll. vols V and VI); Sotheby, 6.2.1945 (the Bussell sale), lot 272.

(2) The 1st 4 vols were adv. by themselves in *LC* 28–30.11.75, p. 527, as *Natural History of four-footed Beasts*, price 6s sewed.

(3) Vols IX and X were adv. by themselves as *Natural History of Fishes*, vol. I and vol. II. See no. (6).

(4) NATURAL HISTORY OF BIRDS, 1775–6. Pr f FN(N). 4 vols. This is vols V–VIII of the MODERN SYSTEM.

(5) The whole work was listed as pr f EN in Pinchard's *Blind Child*, 1791, in 6 vols, price £1 4s 'elegantly bound', £1 1s in the vell. manner.

(6) NATURAL HISTORY OF FISHES, 1795. EN.

[NNC-T (Darton Coll., Cat. item 25).

J377. WATERS, [ ]. THE POETICAL FLOWER GARDEN.

(1) Adv. *LC* 10–12.1.75, p. 39, as pr f TC, and to be pubd in a few days. Price 6d bd and gilt.

(2) An edition of 1778. Pr f TC. Price 6d. H&L, IX, p. 259.

THE | POETICAL | FLOWER GARDEN: | WITH | MORAL REFLECTIONS, | FOR THE | AMUSEMENT OF CHILDREN. | EMBELLISHED WITH CUTS. | [p.rule] | [3 lines quote] | [p.rule] | LONDON: | PR F T. CARNAN, AT NUMBER 65, | IN SPC-Y. | MDCCLXXVIII.

In 6's. 47 leaves. Pp. ii, iv+[5]–88. 40 wcts in text. White or buff bds, impressed with floral design in black; also D.f.b.

[BM, 11·3×7·6 cm; UCLA; McKell; Ball.

(3) Listed in no. J5(4) (not before 1790), as pr f EN. Price 1s.

WATTS, Isaac. See *Spiritual Lessons.*

J378. WEBB, Benjamin, jr. COPY BOOK FOR YOUTH, A. Sometimes listed as A FIRST COPY BOOK FOR YOUTH. Welsh 195. Unknown to Heal.

(1) Adv. *LC* 14–16.1.72, p. 51, as to be pubd on 1st Feb. S b C & N. Price 1*s*. The advert. describes the book as A COPY BOOK FOR YOUTH. BY WHICH THEY MAY LEARN TO WRITE WITHOUT THE ASSISTANCE OF A MASTER, AND PROPERLY ADAPTED FOR SCHOOLS, AS IT WILL SAVE THE TEACHER MUCH TIME AND LABOUR. FORMED ON THE PLAN OF MR. LOCKE.

(2) Listed in no. J266(8), 1786, as pr f TC. Price 1*s*. Welsh 195.

J379. WEBB, Benjamin, jr. SECOND COPY BOOK FOR YOUTH, A. Unknown to Heal.

Adv. *LC* 31.12.72–2.1.73, p. 7, as s b C & N. Price 1*s*. The bk is described as 'formed on the Plan of Mr. Locke'.

WESTMINSTER ABBEY, DESCRIPTION OF, WITH A PARTICULAR ACCOUNT OF THE MONUMENTS. This is J88, vol. IV.

WHITE CAT, THE. See RENOWNED HISTORY OF THE...

J380. WHITSUNTIDE-GIFT, THE. Welsh 331.

(1) An edition of 1764 (most probably the 1st). Pr f JN. Price 2*d* bd. Adv. *LC* 27–9.12.64, p. 619, 'On 1st January Mr Newbery intends to publish....'.

Title and *imprint* as for no. (2), with date 1764. Specification as for no. (2), except that on p. [62] is a wct 'A little wise Woman' and 10 lines of text, in place of the list of medicines. D.f. paper wrappers.

[NorBM, 9·9×6·4 cm.

(2) An edition of 1767. Pr f JN. Price 2*d* (see Plate 20).

In 8's. 32 leaves. Pp. 58[63]. 1st and last leaves pastedowns. Wct FP (with text), 16 other wcts, some by the hand that did the cuts in *Goody Two-Shoes*. List of bks 'sold at Mr Newbery's' on pp. [59–61]; list of medicines s b JN on p. [62]. Floral paper wrappers.

[Bodley, 9·6×6·4 cm.

(3) An edition of 1781. Pr f TC. Price 2*d*.

Title approx. as for no. (2). *Imprint:* PR F T. CARNAN, | IN SPC-Y. | MDCCLXXXI. | PRICE TWO-PENCE.

Pp. 59 [64]. Wcts. Bk-list at end. D.f.b. (Communicated.)

[MWA, 10·0 cm; MSaE; UCLA.

(4) Listed in *Newtonian System*, 1787, as pr f TC. Price 2*d*.

J381. 'WINLOVE, Solomon'. COLLECTION OF THE MOST APPROVED ENTERTAINING STORIES, A. Welsh 210 and 331; *CBEL*, II, 562; Welch 1263.I.

(1) First edition, 1770. Pr f FN(N). Price 6*d* bd and gilt.

Title approx. as for no. (3). *Imprint:* PR F F. NEWBERY, AT THE CORNER OF | SPCY. 1770. | [PRICE SIXPENCE.]

24mo in 6's. 54 leaves+engvd FP and 5 other [? engvd] leaves. Pp. 99[104]. List of bks pubd by FN(N) on last 2 leaves. (Communicated.)

[McKell, 11·0×7·2 cm.

(2) Second edition, 1770. Pr f FN(N). Price *6d*. NBL 646.

(2A) An undated edition. Pr f FN(N). Price *6d*.

Title approx. as for no. (3). *Imprint:* PR F F. NEWBERY, AT THE CORNER | OF SPCY. | [PRICE SIX-PENCE.]

Collates [a2]B–[H8][I6]. 64 leaves+6 insets. Pp. 3–121[124]. Engvd FP and 5 other engvd leaves. List of bks pubd by FN(N) on last 3 pages. (Communicated.)

Perhaps to be dated not before 1775, as the bk-list includes *A Bag of Nuts ready cracked*, of which the first record is in a bk-list of that year (see J353(1)).

[Osborne* (imperf.).

Note: Except for no. (9) no chronological ordering of the following entries is possible. Several of them very probably refer to the same ed. The work was frequently listed and adv.

(3) An undated 'new edition'. Pr f EN. Price *6d*.

A | COLLECTION | OF THE MOST APPROVED | ENTERTAINING STORIES, | CALCULATED FOR THE | INSTRUCTION AND AMUSEMENT OF ALL THE LITTLE | MASTERS AND MISSES IN THIS VAST EMPIRE. | [p.s.rule] | BY SOLOMON WINLOVE, ESQ. | [d.p.rule] | A NEW EDITION. | [d.p.rule] | LONDON: | PR F E. NEWBERY, THE CORNER OF SP | CY. | [p.rule] | [PRICE SIX-PENCE.]

In 8's. 64 leaves+6 insets. Pp. 121[124]. Engvd FP and 5 other engvd leaves. List of bks pubd by EN on last 3 pages. D.f.b.

On the TP there are a p.s.rule above BY SOLOMON WINLOVE and d.p.rules above and below A NEW EDITION. *Imprint* reads: PR F...SP | C-Y. | [p.rule] | ... On A2^r above CONTENTS a d.p.rule 5·5–5·6 cm, and below a p.rule 2·5 cm; last item on this page is 'The Milk Maid'. On p. 124 1st item is 22 'History of the enchanted Castle', last item 32 'Sir Charles Grandison'.

[Bodley, 10·9×7·4 cm.

(4) An undated 'new edition'. EN. NBL 647.

(5) Adv. *LC* 30.12.81–1.1.82, p. 7, as to be had of EN. Price *6d*.

(6) An undated 'new edition'. Pr f EN. Price *6d*.

This differs from no. (3) in the following points (et al): On the TP no rule above BY SOLOMON WINLOVE; p.rules above and below A NEW EDITION. *Imprint* reads: PR F...THE CORNER | OF SPC-Y. | ... On A2^r above CONTENTS a line of printer's ornaments, no rule below; last item on this page is 'Good Nature abused...'. On p. 124 1st item is 22 'A new Edition of Aesop's Fables'; last item is 33 'Sir Charles Grandison, abridged'.

Pp. 121[124]. Engvd FP and other engvd leaves. List of bks pubd by EN on last 3 pages.

[Welch (imperf.); Roscoe (photocopied selected leaves).

(7) An undated edition. EN. Said to differ from no. (6). Pp. 121[124]. D.f.b. (Communicated.)

⌠UCLA.

(8) Listed as pr f EN in *Prince Lee Boo*, 1789, and *Anecdotes of Mary*, 1795, price 6d.

(9) A 'new edition', undated. Pr f EN. Price 6d. ? Hugo, II, p. 325, no. 35.

Title approx. as for no. (3). *Imprint:* PR F E. NEWBERY, | CORNER OF SPC-Y; | BY J. CUNDEE, IVY-LANE. | [p.rule] | [PRICE SIX-PENCE.]

In 8's. 64 leaves. Pp. 121[124]. 6 wcts in text. List of bks pubd b EN on last 3 pages. Pr on coarse, grey paper. Yellow bds, with texts, marbled paper spine.

Text on upper cover: MR. WINLOVE'S COLLECTION | OF | ENTERTAINING STORIES. | PRICE SIX-PENCE. | FROM | HARRIS'S | JUVENILE LIBRARY, | AT | THE CORNER | OF | SPC-Y, | LONDON.

Text on lower cover: THIS, | AND EVERY USEFUL | AND | ENTERTAINING PUBLICATION | FOR | YOUNG MINDS. | PR F J. HARRIS, | MAY BE HAD | AT | THE PRINCIPAL BOOKSELLERS | AND | TOY-WAREHOUSES | IN THE | WORLD.

These texts on the covers indicate a very late publication date – probably 1802 – when Harris was in the final stages of taking over from EN.

⌠BM, 10·7×7·7 cm.

J382. 'WINLOVE, Solomon'.

MORAL LECTURES. Welsh 331; *CBEL*, II, 562.

(1) An edition of 1769 (probably the 1st). See Fig. 30. Gum 2765.

In 6's. 54 leaves. Pp. iv[vi]+95[99]. 28 small wcts. List of bks s b FN(N) on last 4 pages. 'Flowered bds' (per Gum).

⌠Roscoe, 10·6×6·8 cm; Opie.

(2) Listed in Chesterfield's *Maxims*, 1777, as pr f FN(N). Price 6d.

(3) An edition of 1780. ?FN(N). *CBEL*, II, 562.

(4) An edition of 1781. Pr f EN. Price 6d. NBL 702.

Title approx. as for no. (1). *Imprint:* PR F E. NEWBERY, AT THE COR- | NER OF SPCY, 1781. | PRICE SIX-PENCE.

32mo in 8's. 64 leaves. Pp. vi+120. 28 wcts in text. NBL Cat. says the cuts are 'by Bewick'; if they are those used in no. (1) they have nothing to do with either Thomas Bewick (born 1753) or John (b. 1760). D.f.b. (Communicated.)

MORAL LECTURES,

ON THE

FOLLOWING SUBJECTS.

Pride,	Induſtry,
Envy,	Wiſdom,
Avarice,	Indolence,
Anger,	Application,
Hypocriſy,	Beauty,
Charity,	Advice,
Generoſity,	Company,
Compaſſion,	Splendor,
Ill-Humour,	Happineſs,
Good-Humour,	Friendſhip,
Affectation,	Mankind,
Truth,	Credulity,
Falſhood,	Contempt,
Education,	Modeſty.

By SOLOMON WINLOVE, Eſq;

Embelliſhed with twenty-eight curious CUTS.

LONDON:

Printed for F. NEWBERY, at the Cor- ner of St Paul's Church Yard, 1769. Price Six-pence.

Fig. 30. Title-page of J382(1).

[McKell, 9·9 × 6·4 cm.

(4A) An edition of 1787. Pr f EN.

[Oppenheimer; *ex* Stone.

(5) Listed in *Anecdotes of Mary*, 1795, as pr f EN, price 6*d*.

J383. WISEMAN, Charles. A COMPLETE ENGLISH GRAMMAR ON A NEW PLAN. The ed. of 1764 (*CBEL*, II, 641; Scott 118; Alston I, no. 257 – copy in BM) was by W. Nicol, but JN had a hand in the book: the Preface was written by Goldsmith, and the 'Newbery-Goldsmith Papers' in PP have two statements of account by Goldsmith (dated 7.6.66 and 11.10.66) charging Newbery 2 gns for the 'Preface to Wiseman's Grammar'.

(1) Listed in A61(2), vol. II, 1771, as s b C & N, and in A640(3), vol. X, 1773, as pr f C & N. Price 3*s* 6*d*.

(2) Listed in Paterson's *Roads*, 5th ed., 1781, as pr f TC. Price 3*s* 6*d*.

J384. WIZARD, THE, WHICH CONTAINS A COMPLETE COLLECTION OF RIDDLES, CALCULATED ENTIRELY FOR THE AMUSEMENT AND IMPROVEMENT OF YOUTH. ADORNED WITH CUTS. PRINTED, BY ASSIGNMENT OF T. CARNAN, SPC-Y, BY P. NORBURY, BRENTFORD. PRICE ONE PENNY. [n.d.]

No copy of an ed. other than Norbury's has been traced, but the possibility of TC having put out an ed. before assigning his rights to Norbury seems likely. See also the *Entertaining...History of Robin Hood* (no. J102A). (Communicated.)

[Ball.

J385. WONDERS OF NATURE AND ART, A637. This is frequently classed as a 'Juvenile'; in point of fact this may well be so. But there is nothing to indicate that JN so regarded it.

WORDS OF THE WISE. See Potter, John.

J386. WORLD DISPLAYED, THE, A640. Perhaps this should have been classed as a 'Juvenile', as JN several times included it in lists of bks pr f him 'For the Instruction and Amusement of Young Gentlemen and Ladies'; e.g. in the *Newtonian System*, 1766, under the title *A Curious Collection of Voyages and Travels*. Apart from this the bk would seem to be addressed to adult readers. But no doubt it was used – as JN knew it would be – by young people, and this was a way of bringing it to their attention.

J387. WREN, THE. Listed as pr f JN in *Joseph Andrews*, 1799. Price 1*s* 6*d*. Probably Kendall's *Crested Wren*, 1799. *The Wren; or, the Fairy of the Green-house* had been pubd b John Marshall at 7*d* bd.

J388. Entry deleted.

WYNNE, John Huddlestone. AMUSING AND INSTRUCTIVE TALES. See J391.

WYNNE, John Huddlestone. CHOICE EMBLEMS. See J389.

J389. WYNNE, John Huddlestone. EMBLEMS. Titled CHOICE EMBLEMS in 1st (1772), 2nd (1775), 5th (1784) and subsequent edd., and RILEY'S EMBLEMS in 3rd (1779) and 4th (1781) edd. Welsh 209; *CBEL*, II, 562. The 1st and 2nd edd. were pr f George Riley.
(1) Third edition, 1779. Pr f FN(N) et al. Gum 4776.

RILEY'S EMBLEMS, | NATURAL, HISTORICAL, FABULOUS, | MORAL AND DIVINE; | FOR THE IMPROVEMENT AND PASTIME OF | YOUTH: | SERVING TO DISPLAY THE BEAUTIES AND MORALS | OF THE | ANCIENT FABULISTS: | [3 lines] | [p.rule] | WRITTEN FOR THE AMUSEMENT OF A YOUNG NOBLE-MAN. | [p.rule] | THE THIRD EDITION. | [p.rule] | [4 lines quote] | [d.p.rule] | LONDON: | PR F F. NEWBERY, THE CORNER OF SP | C-Y; AND G. RILEY, CURZON-STREET, MAY- | FAIR. | MDCCLXXIX.

12mo. 108 leaves+engvd FP. Pp. xxiv+192. 64 wct headpieces as to which see Hugo 13; John Bewick may have had a hand in some of the headpieces to Emblems XLVIIff, but they are poor things. Half-title.

[Roscoe, 15·0×8·6 cm; Lapides.
(2) Third edition, another issue, 1779. Hugo 13.

The *imprint* reads: PR F G. RILEY, CURZON-STREET, MAY-FAIR; | A S B | J. WALTER, CHARING-CROSS; AND F. NEWBERY, THE | CORNER OF SPC-Y. | MDCCLXXIX. Otherwise as for no. (1).

[BM, 15·4×8·5 cm; UCLA.
(3) Fourth edition, 1781. Pr f EN et al. Price 2s. Gum 4777.

Title approx. as for no. (1), with THE FOURTH EDITION. *Imprint:* PR F E. NEWBERY, CORNER OF SPC-Y; | G. RILEY, (NO. 73) SPC-Y; | AND R. TULLOH, STERNE'S HEAD, CURZON-STREET, MAY-FAIR; | MDCCLXXXI. | BY J. CHAPMAN, JOHNSON'S COURT, FLEET-STREET.

12mo. 108 leaves. Pp. xxiv+192. ? engvd FP. 64 wct headpieces. Half-title. Details taken from the Traylen copy.

[Traylen; A. R. Heath, Cat. 22 [1972] item 265; Shiers, 15·5×9·0 cm; NNC-T (Darton Coll.); Osborne*.
(4) Fifth edition, 1784. Pr f EN.

CHOICE EMBLEMS, | [continue approx. as for no. (1) with THE FIFTH EDITION.] PR B J. CHAPMAN, ST. JAMES'S-WALK, | CLERKENWELL, | FOR | E. NEWBERY, CORNER OF SP-C-Y. | MDCCLXXXIV.

12mo. 108 leaves+engvd FP. Pp. xxiv+192. 64 wct headpieces, all (except those for Emblems 11–14, 38, 41, 47) as in no. (1). Half-title.

[BM, 14·4×8·8 cm; Bodley; V&A(GL); Weedon; Renier; Welch; UCLA; Sotheby, 27.2.1967, lot 253.
(5) Sixth edition, 1788. Pr f EN. NBL 735.

Title and *imprint* approx. as for no. (4), with THE SIXTH EDITION and date MDCCLXXXVIII.

12mo. 108 leaves+engvd FP. Pp. xxiv+192. 64 wct headpieces, see no. (4). Half-title.

[CUL; Roscoe, 15·1×8·8 cm; Welch.

(6) Seventh edition, 1793. Pr f EN.

Title and *imprint* approx. as for no. (4), with THE SEVENTH EDITION and date MDCCXCIII.

12mo. 108 leaves+engvd FP. Pp. xxiv+192. 64 wct headpieces, see no. (4). Half-title.

[BM, 15·7×8·8 cm; Bodley; CUL; V&A(GL); LUL; Grey; Roscoe; Traylen; McKell; UCLA; NNC-T (Darton Coll.); Welch.

(7) Eighth edition not traced. Perhaps the ed. listed in *Anecdotes of Mary*, 1795.

(8) Ninth edition, 1799. Pr f EN. Price 2s.

Title approx. as for no. (4), with THE NINTH EDITION. *Imprint:* PR F E. NEWBERY, CORNER OF SP | C-Y; | BY J. CUNDEE, IVY LANE, NEWGATE STREET. | 1799.

In 6's. 108 leaves+engvd FP. Pp. xxii+192. 64 wct headpieces as before. Last leaf a blank. Half-title. Marbled bds, green vell. spine.

[BM (imperf.), 13·5×8·7 cm; NUTP, Cat. no. 363; Ries; Adomeit.

J390. WYNNE, John Huddlestone. FABLES OF FLOWERS, 1781. Pr f EN et al. Price 2s. Welsh 216; Gum 2455. There was an ed. of 1773 by Geo. Riley and John Wilkie. The bk was dedicated to 'Charlotte, Princess Royal of England' (born 1766); and the Preface recommended it to 'Parents, Guardians, and the Teachers of Schools. . .'.

FABLES | OF | FLOWERS, | FOR | THE FEMALE SEX. | WITH | ZEPHYRUS AND FLORA, | A VISION. | [p.rule] | BY THE AUTHOR OF CHOICE EMBLEMS | FOR YOUTH. | [d.p.rule] | LONDON: | PR F E. NEWBERY, THE CORNER | OF SPC-Y; | AND | G. RILEY, NO. 73, IN SPC-Y. | [p.rule] | MDCCLXXXI.

12mo. 87 leaves+5 insets. Pp. viii, iv+2–162. 5 inset engvd leaves and 1 integral engvd leaf (A12), each with 5 roundels illustrating the Fables, no. 5 sgd (in reverse) 'W. Grainger In. Sc.' the others sgd (in reverse) 'W.G. In. Sc.'. The Dedication Leaf [a2] is sometimes bd in at the end.

[BM, 15·4×8·9 cm; Bodley; Oup; Renier; SomCL; UCLA; MiDW.

WYNNE, John Huddlestone. RILEY'S EMBLEMS. See J389(1–3).

J391. WYNNE, John Huddlestone. TALES FOR YOUTH (no. (1) below). AMUSING AND INSTRUCTIVE TALES FOR YOUTH (no. (2) below).

(1) An edition of 1794. Pr f EN. Price 2s. Welsh 329; Hugo 72 and 4072; *CBEL*, II, 562.

TALES FOR YOUTH; | IN | THIRTY POEMS: | TO WHICH ARE ANNEXED, | HISTORICAL REMARKS | AND | MORAL APPLICATIONS | IN PROSE. |

T A L E XVIII.

AVARICE PUNISHED.

A MISER happy only in his gold,

Who kept it, not for *use*, but *to behold*;

With age and trouble, pain and weakneſs

ſpent,

Fearing no med'cine could his death prevent,

His

Fig. 31. A page from J391(1), showing a woodcut which is undoubtedly the work of John Bewick.

[d.p.rule] | BY THE AUTHOR OF 'CHOICE EMBLEMS | FOR THE IMPROVEMENT OF YOUTH,' &c. | [d.p.rule] | ORNAMENTED WITH CUTS, NEATLY DESIGNED AND | ENGRAVED ON WOOD, | BY BEWICK. | [p.s.rule] | [8 lines quote] | [p.s.rule] | LONDON: | PR B J. CROWDER, | FOR E. NEWBERY, THE CORNER OF SP | C-Y. | [p.rule] | 1794. | [p.rule] | [ENTERED AT STATIONERS HALL.]

In 6's. 84 leaves+engvd FP sgd 'Cook sculp'. Pp. x (error for viii)+158[160].

30 wct headpieces by John Bewick (see Fig. 31). List of books pr f EN on last 2 pages.

[BM, 17·5×10·0 cm; CUL; V&A(GL); NUTP (not in printed Cat.); BCE; Roscoe; Bell; Osborne, Cat. p. 88; Welch; UCLA; INC; Gardner; Schiller.

(2) An edition of 1800. Pr f EN. Price 2s.

AMUSING AND INSTRUCTIVE | TALES FOR YOUTH: | IN | THIRTY POEMS. | WITH | MORAL APPLICATIONS | IN PROSE. | [d.p.rule] | BY THE AUTHOR OF | 'CHOICE EMBLEMS FOR THE IMPROVEMENT OF YOUTH,' &c. | [d.p.rule] | ORNAMENTED WITH CUTS, NEATLY DESIGNED AND | ENGRAVED ON WOOD | BY | I. BEWICK [in a wct vignette] | LONDON: | PR B J. CROWDER, | FOR E. NEWBERY, THE CORNER OF SP | C-Y. | [p.rule] | 1800.

In 6's. 90 leaves+engvd FP. Pp. viii+9–179. About 47 wcts in text by John Bewick and the Bewick school or workshop. Marbled bds, green vell. spine with label.

[V&A(GL), 13·8×8·6 cm; V&A; Ball; Ries; UCLA.

J392. YOUNG ALGEBRAIST'S COMPANION, 1750. JN. Muir, p. 75. Daniel Fenning's work of this title and date (copy in BM) was pr f the Author, s b the Booksellers...

J392A. YOUNG CHRISTIAN'S LIBRARY, THE. *Modern Philology*, vol. 26 (1928–9), at p. 296.

The only references I have found to this series, as such, are adverts. in *Lloyd's Evening Post* for 24–6.12.64 and *LC* for 27–9.12.64, at p. 623, announcing the publication.

The series consisted of:

Vol. I. NEW TESTAMENT OF OUR LORD...ABRIDGED AND HARMO-NISED IN THE WORDS OF THE EVANGELISTS. (no. J31.)

Vol. II. HISTORY OF THE LIFE OF OUR LORD... (no. J174.)

Vol. III. HISTORY OF THE LIVES...OF THE APOSTLES AND EVANGE-LISTS. (no. J175.)

Vol. IV. HISTORY OF THE LIVES...OF THE...MARTYRS... (no. J148.)

Vol. V. PLEASANT AND USEFUL COMPANION TO THE CHURCH OF ENGLAND...OR SHORT...EXPOSITION OF THE BOOK OF COMMON PRAYER. (no. J40.)

The books were to be had separately, in 'embossed paper' (i.e. D.f.b.) at 1s each, or bound up as one in red leather, gilt, price 5s 6d.

YOUNG EDWIN AND LITTLE JESSY. See HISTORY OF...

J393. YOUNG GENTLEMAN'S AND LADY'S MAGAZINE, THE, [1799–1800]. S b EN et al. Issued in monthly parts at 1s each, 'tastefully done up in patent paper', the 2 vols to be had for 13s in bds, 14s half-bound, 15s calf gilt.

The prospectus for the work (copies in BM and Oup) said that the first Part was to be issued on 1 Feb. 1799, and to continue monthly; on this basis the last (12th) Part would have appeared in Jan. 1800. No Part is dated, but the publication date on the FP to vol. 1 is 1 Feb. 1799.

There is an engraved TP to each volume, in which EN's name does not appear; that name is to be found in the imprint to the TP to each Part.

Welsh 335; *CBEL*, II, 683; *BUCOP*, IV, 589.

The engraved title: THE | YOUNG GENTLEMAN'S & LADY'S | MAGAZINE, | OR | UNIVERSAL REPOSITORY | OF | KNOWLEDGE, INSTRUCTION | AND | AMUSEMENT, | INTENDED TO OPEN THE TENDER MIND | TO AN ACQUAINTANCE WITH | LIFE, MORALS, & SCIENCE, | [6 lines] | [d.s.rule] | VOL. I. | [d.s.rule] | LONDON. | PR F J. WALKER, 44 P-N R. (In vol. II the reading is still 'vol. I', but altered in MS to 'vol. II'.)

The *imprint* to the TP to each Part reads: LONDON: - PR F THE EDITORS, AND S B J. WALKER, | NO. 44, PN R; E. NEWBERY, THE CORNER OF S | PC-Y; AND ALL OTHER BOOKSELLERS AND STATIONERS | IN GREAT BRITAIN, IRELAND, AND AMERICA.

In each Part of vol. I there is a conjugate pair of identical engravings of flowers etc., one coloured, the other plain. The engvd FP and TP are conjugate. All numbers in 6's.

Vol. I, no. I. 42 leaves+2 insets. Pp. 84. 2 engvd leaves.

Vol. I, no. II. 42 leaves+3 insets. Pp. [85]–268 (error for 168). 2 engvd leaves and 1 map.

Vol. I, no. III. 42 leaves+3 insets. Pp. [169]–252. 2 engvd leaves and 1 map.

Vol. I, no. IV. 36 leaves+5 insets. Pp. [253]–324. 2 engvd leaves, 2 folding leaves (one on pink paper), 1 map.

Vol. I, no. V. 36 leaves+4 insets. Pp. [325]–396. 3 engvd leaves (2 coloured), 1 map.

Vol. I, no. VI. 38 leaves+2 insets. Pp. [397]–468[472]. 2 engvd leaves (one coloured).

Vol. II, no. VII. 38 leaves+2 insets. Pp. iv+72. 1 engvd leaf, 1 map.

Vol. II, no. VIII. 36 leaves+2 insets. Pp. [73]–144. 1 engvd leaf, 1 map.

Vol. II, no. IX. 36 leaves+2 insets. Pp. [145]–216. 1 engvd leaf, 1 map.

Vol. II, no. X. 36 leaves+2 insets. Pp. [217]–288. 1 engvd leaf (coloured), one engvd leaf of shorthand symbols.

Vol. II, no. XI. 36 leaves+2 insets. Pp. [289]–360. 1 engvd leaf (coloured), 1 map.

Vol. II, no. XII. 38 leaves. Pp. [361]–432[436].

[BM, 17·2×10·2 cm; LUL; LEI (vol. II); Grey (vol. I); Opie; Osborne, Cat. p. 407.

J394. YOUNG MAN'S COMPANION. Welsh 335. Perhaps Gordon's *Every Young Man's Companion*. But not identified with any certainty. The title, in various forms, was common enough in the second half of the eighteenth century.

J395. YOUTHFUL JESTER, THE. Weedon 91. Richard Johnson's Day-book records: *1789 Nov. 25. Mr Badcock——To writing The Youthful Jester——£5. 5s.* One of the bks which Mrs. Trimmer desired to be committed to the flames.

(1) An undated edition, ? *ca.* 1790. Pr f EN. Price *6d.* NBL 922.

Title and *imprint* approx. as for no. (3). Pp. 118. D.f.b.

⌈Osborne, 11·2×7·2 cm, Cat. p. 271; Ball.

(2) An edition of 1793. EN.

⌈Ball.

(3) An edition of 1797. Pr f EN. Price *6d.*

THE | YOUTHFUL JESTER; | OR, | REPOSITORY OF WIT | AND | INNOCENT AMUSEMENT. | CONTAINING | MORAL AND HUMOROUS TALES; | MERRY JESTS, | LAUGHABLE ANECDOTES, | AND SMART REPARTEES. | THE WHOLE BEING AS INNOCENT AS IT IS ENTERTAINING. | [p.rule] | EMBELLISHED WITH CUTS. | [d.p.rule] | LONDON: | PR F E. NEWBERY, THE CORNER OF S | PC-Y. 1797. | [PRICE SIX-PENCE.]

In 8's. 64 leaves. Pp. 120. Wct FP and 12 wcts in the text, in the manner of John Bewick. D.f.b.

⌈BM, 10·7×7·2 cm.

(4) An edition of 1800. Pr f EN. Price *6d.* NBL 925.

⌈CtHi.

J396. YOUTHFUL PORTRAITS, 1796. Pr f EN. Price *1s 6d.* Welsh 335; Hugo 89; ENC, p. 9.

YOUTHFUL PORTRAITS; | OR, | SKETCHES OF THE PASSIONS: | EXEMPLIFYING THE | DIGNITY, | AND INCULCATING THE | ADVANTAGES | OF | VIRTUE. | [d.p.rule] | EMBELLISHED WITH ENGRAVINGS. | [d.p.rule] | [wct device] | [d.p.rule] | LONDON: | PR F E. NEWBERY, THE CORNER OF | SPC-Y. | [p.rule] | MDCCXCVI.

In 12's. 60 leaves. Pp. 115. 7 wct headpieces to the 'Tales' by a follower of the Bewicks; 7 wct tailpieces. Green vell. spine, marbled bds.

⌈BM, 16·6×10·6 cm; V&A(GL); Osborne, Cat. p. 319; DLC; UCLA.

J397. YOUTHFUL RECREATIONS.

(1) An edition of 1789. Pr f EN. Price *6d.* Welsh 335.

YOUTHFUL | RECREATIONS, | CONTAINING | AMUSEMENTS OF A DAY, | AS SPENT | BY MASTER FREELOVE AND HIS COMPANIONS. | INTER-SPERSED | WITH STORIES, SUITABLE OBSERVATIONS, VERSES, | AND OTHER MATTERS OF INSTRUCTION AND | ENTERTAINMENT. | [d.p.rule] | LONDON: | PR F E. NEWBERY, AT THE CORNER | OF SPCY, 1789. | [PRICE SIX-PENCE.]

In 8's. 64 leaves. Pp. 128. Wct FP by Lee (sgd 'L'), 14 wcts in the text, that at p. 78 sgd by Lee. D.f.b.

⌈BM, 10·6×7·2 cm; Ball.

(2) An edition of 1796. Pr f EN. Price *6d.*

Title and *imprint*, with date 1796, and specification approx. as for no. (1). D.f.b.

⌈Schiller, 10·9×7·4 cm.

(3) An edition of 1799. Pr f EN. Price 6*d*.

Title approx. as for no. (1). *Imprint:* PR F E. NEWBERY, AT THE CORNER OF | SPC-Y, | BY J. CROWDER, WARWICK-SQUARE. | [p.rule] | 1799. | (PRICE SIX PENCE.)

Pp. 128. Wcts. D.f. paper wrappers. (Communicated.)

⌈MPlyA, 12·0 cm; W. T. Spencer's Bkshop, 1953.

(4) An undated edition. Pr f EN. Price 6*d*. Hugo, II, 4107.

Pp. 128. 12 wcts.

YOUTH'S MISCELLANY. See Mavor, W. F.

ZARA. A MORAL TALE. See J351.

PART II

BOOKS OTHER THAN THOSE IN PART I, LETTERED 'A'

===

A SHORT TITLE CATALOGUE
WITH SOME NOTES

A1. ACCOMPLISH'D HOUSEWIFE, THE.
(1) An ed. of 1745. Pr f JN. Price 3s. Welsh 237–8; A. W. Oxford, p. 75. [Wellcome; DLC (imperf.); MH; ICU-J.
(2) Listed as pr f a s b N & C in no. A640(3), vol. IV, 1768. Probably stock in hand of no. (1). Price 3s.

A2. ADDRESS TO THE PEOPLE OF ENGLAND, AN, ON THE MANNERS OF THE TIMES. Listed *LM* May 1767, p. 262. Pr f the Author, s b JN. Price 9d. Welsh 261.

A3. ADVENTURER, THE (ed. by John Hawkesworth). *BUCOP*, I, 52; *CBEL*, II, 467.
(1) An ed. of 1778. 'A new edition', pr f FN(? N) et al. 4 vols. [BM; Bodley; CUL.
(2) An ed. of 1788. Pr f EN et al. Price 12s. 4 vols. [BM; Bodley.
(3) A new ed. in 3 vols, price 18s in bds, pr f EN et al. Adv. *LC* 17–19 Feb. 1795, p. 172.

A4. AGREEABLE COMPANION FOR A FEW HOURS, AN, 1773. Pr f FN(N) et al. Price 2s. ? Welsh 168. [Bodley.

A5. AGREEABLE COMPANION, THE; OR, AN UNIVERSAL MEDLEY OF WIT AND GOOD HUMOUR. Listed as pr f C & N in A640(3), vol. XVIII, 1778, price 3s. A bk with this title was pubd by W. Bickerton in 1745. ? Welsh 168.

A6. ALGAROTTI, Francesco. THE LADY'S PHILOSOPHY: OR SIR ISAAC NEWTON'S THEORY OF LIGHT AND COLOURS …, 1772. A 'new ed.'. Pr f FN(N). Adv. price 5s, subsequently 6s. Nat. Union Cat. NA0166296. [ITH, not seen.

A7. (1) ALMANACKS (including CALENDARS, DAILY JOURNALS, DIARIES, POCKET BOOKS).

No class of bks, small bks for children not excluded, is scarcer than the Almanacks and their kind. Of those here recorded (and I include with them the Sheet Almanacks) I have traced copies of only about one in every six. I know of no bibliography of them apart from the following list.

I have dealt briefly with Carnan's legal battle with the Stationers' Co. in my Introduction (pp. 22–4). See Plate 2 for a page of *LC* for 21–3 Nov. 1775, advertising, in adjacent columns, the rival products of Carnan and the Company, several of the rivals bearing exactly similar titles.

Items marked ** are only recorded in adverts. as 'to be had of' Carnan. It is, however, legitimate to assume that his name will be found in their imprints. It is better to allow a few trespassers than to exclude any having the right to be present.

Dating. Many Almanacks have no publication date on the TP. When dated the year is that for which the book is to be used. The newspapers were, as a rule, advertising these productions at the latest by the middle of November of the preceding year; and it is clear that, with the intense competition between publishers, especially in the seventies and eighties, any such work not advertised by then would have the slimmest chance of selling well. So the real date of publication may be taken to be the year in which the work was advertised. The dates shown in each case are those of advertising in *LC*, usually the first occasion.

An Almanack may be advertised under more than one name. There is a *Small London Sheet* and a *New London Sheet*; they are very probably identical; Moore's *Vox Stellarum* may be the same as the contemporary *Moore's Almanack. Parker's Ephemeris* and *Parker and White's Ephemeris* are both advertised in 1775. This gives ample occasion for duplication in the following list. Many of the titles given in the list are in fact only the descriptions given in the newspaper advertisements, e.g. nos. (335) and (336).

Issues with no publisher's or printer's imprint were presumably by TC alone. But he had frequent collaborators (as seller or otherwise), e.g. George Robinson, with whom he was afterwards to quarrel. A number of issues were published by TC and bear also the imprints of Stockdale and Sprag. C & N co-operated from 1767 to 1779 (nos. 125–35), and Power (with others) put out a few issues after 1789.

Except where otherwise stated, the item was printed and/or published by Carnan. FN* indicates that it is not apparent which Francis was the one involved.

(1A) ALMANACK FOR THE YEAR…ON THE SAME PLAN AS THAT FORMERLY PUBLISHED BY VINCENT WING. See nos. (19–31).

(2) ALMANACK JOURNAL, AN, FOR THE YEAR 1780. Price 2*s*. 30.11.79–2.12.79.

(3) **ALMANACK JOURNAL RULED FOR 1780. 4–6.11.79. ? identical with no. (2).

(3A) **ALMANACK JOURNAL PRINTED IN RED AND RULED FOR 1781. 21–3.11.80.

(4) ALMANACK MEMORANDUM BOOK RULED FOR EVERY DAY IN THE YEAR, FOR 1780. Price 1*s* 6*d*. 4–6.11.79.

(5) ANDREWS, Henry. ROYAL ALMANACK FOR 1777. Price 1*s*. 2–5.11.76.

(6) *idem* for 1778. Price 1*s*. 13–16.12.77. 8 leaves. [BM.

(7) *idem* for 1779. Price 9*d*. 12–14.11.78. A single sheet. [Stationers.

(8) BALDWIN'S DAILY JOURNAL FOR 1777. 2–5.11.76.

(9) **idem* for 1778. 29.11.77–2.12.77.

(10) *idem* for 1779. Price 1*s* 8*d*. 10–12.11.78.

(11) **idem* for 1780. Price 1*s* 8*d*. 4–5.11.79.

(12) **idem* for 1781. 21–3.11.80.

(13) *idem* for 1782. 22–4.11.81.

(14) *idem* for 1783. 19–21.11.82.

(15) *idem* for 1784. 4–6.11.83. Price 1*s* 8*d*.

(16) *idem* for 1785. 11–13.11.84. Price 1*s* 8*d*.

(17) *idem* for 1786. 27–9.10.85. Price 1*s* 8*d*.

(18) *idem* for 1787. 28–31.10.86. Price 1*s* 8*d*.

(19) *idem* for 1788. 13–15.11.87. Price 1*s* 8*d*.

(20) BURROW, Reuben. DIARY FOR THE YEAR 1774. 9–11.73; also 24–6.3.74. Prices 5*d* to 7*d*.

(21) *idem* for 1775 not traced.

(22) BURROW, R. DIARY OR SHEET ALMANACK FOR 1776. Pr f TC and George Robinson. 16–18.11.75. Price 6*d*. Also described as BURROW'S DIARY ON A SHEET.

(23) BURROW, R. *idem* for 1777. 2–5.11.76.

(24) BURROW, R. DIARY FOR THE YEAR 1778. 8–11.11.77. A single sheet. ⌈Oup.

(24A) BURROW'S LADY'S & GENTLEMAN'S DIARY. *BUCOP*, III, 8. For Burrow see *DNB* which says he was editor of this publicn.

(25) BURROW, Reuben. LADY'S AND GENTLEMAN'S DIARY ...FOR...1776. Pr f TC and George Robinson. Price 9*d*. 2–4.11.75. ⌈BM.

(26) *idem* (see Plate 21). 7–10.12.76. ⌈BM; Stationers.

(27) *idem* for 1778. 29.11.77–2.12.77. ⌈BM; Stationers.

(28) *idem* for 1779. 12–14.11.78. ⌈BM.

(29) BURROW, Reuben. A COMPANION TO THE LADIES AND GENTLEMENS DIARY FOR 1779. ⌈BM.

(30) BURROW, Reuben. SHEET DIARY FOR 1778. 29.11.78–2.12.78. Probably = no. (24).

(31) CAMBRIDGE SHEET ALMANACK FOR 1776. Pr f TC and George Robinson. 2–4.11.75. Price 6*d*.

(32) *idem* for 1777. 2–5.11.76.

(33) **idem* for 1778. 29.11.77–2.12.77.

(34) **idem* for 1779. 12–14.11.78.

(35) **idem* for 1780. 4–6.11.79.

(36) **idem* for 1781. 21–3.11.80.

(37) *idem* for 1782. 22–4.11.81.

(38) *idem* for 1783. 19–21.11.82.

(39) *idem* for 1784. Pr f T C; s b Stockdale and M. Sprag. Price 7*d*. 4–6.11.83.

(40) *idem* for 1785. Price 7*d*. 11–13.11.84.

(41) *idem* for 1786. Price 7*d*. 27–9.10.85.

(42) *idem* for 1787. Price 7*d*. 28–31.10.86.

(43) *idem* for 1788. Price 7*d*. 13–15.11.87.

(43A) COMPANION TO THE ROYAL KALENDAR. See no. (353).

(44) **CORNWALL ALMANACK FOR 1778. 29.11.77–2.12.77.

(45) *idem* for 1779. 12–14.11.78. A single sheet. ⌈Stationers.

(46) **idem* for 1780. 4–6.11.79.

(47) **idem* for 1781. 21–3.11.80.

(48) CORNWALL AND DEVONSHIRE ALMANACK FOR 1782.
22–4.11.81.

(49) *idem* for 1783. 19–21.11.82.

(50) *idem* for 1784. Pr f TC; s b Stockdale and M. Sprag. Price 8*d*. 4–6.11.83.

(51) *idem* for 1785. Price 8*d*. 11–13.11.84.

(52) *idem* for 1786. Price 8*d*. 27–9.10.85.

(53) *idem* for 1787. Price 8*d*. 28–31.10.86.

(54) *idem* for 1788. Price 8*d*. 13–15.11.87.

(54A) COURT AND CITY REGISTER FOR 1779. A new ed.,
corrected to 9 May 1779. Pr f 'Newbery' et al. Price 2*s* 6*d* with Ryder's Sheet
Almanack, 2*s* without. 25–7.5.79.

(54B) *idem* for 1780. A new ed. corrected to the end of January last. Pr f 'Newbery'
al. Prices as for no. (54A). 10–12.2.80.

(54C) *idem* for 1780. A new ed. corrected to 20.4.1780. Pr f FN* et al. Prices as
for no. (54A). 25–7.4.80.

(54D) DAILY JOURNAL; OR GENTLEMAN AND
TRADESMAN'S ANNUAL ACCOMPT BOOK FOR THE
POCKET. [?1768 or before.] Welsh 285 and 356. N & C.

(54E) DAILY JOURNAL, THE, OR THE COMPLETE ANNUAL
ACCOMPT BOOK FOR...1787. Price 1*s* 8*d* neatly bd in red. 21–3.11.86.

(55) DAILY JOURNAL; OR, GENTLEMAN'S, MERCHANT'S
AND TRADESMAN'S COMPLETE ANNUAL ACCOMPT
BOOK FOR 1788. Price 1*s* 8*d* neatly bd in red. 29.11.87–1.12.87.

(56) *idem* for 1789 not traced.

(57) *idem* for 1790. Pr a s b F. Power et al. Price 1*s* 8*d* neatly bd in red. 31.10.89–
3.11.89.

(58) **DEVONSHIRE ALMANACK FOR 1778. 29.11.77–2.12.77.

(59) *idem* for 1779. 12–14.11.78. A single sheet. [Stationers.

(60) **idem* for 1780. 4–6.11.79.

(61) **idem* for 1781. 21–3.11.80.

(61A) Devonshire for 1782 etc. was combined with Cornwall, *q.v.*

(62) **DORSETSHIRE ALMANACK FOR 1778. 29.11.77–2.12.77.

(63) *idem* for 1779. 12–14.11.78. A single sheet. [Stationers.

(64) **idem* for 1780. 4–6.11.79.

(65) **idem* for 1781. 21–3.11.80.

(65A) Dorset for 1782 etc was combined with Somerset, *q.v.*

(66) **ESSEX, HERTFORDSHIRE, AND CAMBRIDGESHIRE
ALMANACK FOR 1778. 29.11.77–2.12.77.

(67) *idem* for 1779. 12–14.11.78. A single sheet. [Stationers.

(68) **idem* for 1780. 4–6.11.79.

(69) **idem* for 1781. 21–3.11.80.

(69A) Essex for 1782 etc was combined with Middlesex, *q.v.*

(70) FRENCH SHEET ALMANACK, A, FOR THE YEAR 1773,
PARTICULARLY CALCULATED FOR THE USE OF

THE
LADIES and GENTLEMENS
DIARY,
OR,
ROYAL ALMANACK;

For the Year of our LORD, 1777 :
Being the First after Bissextile, or Leap Year.

CONTAINING,

Besides the CALENDAR, a great Variety of Ænigmas,
Rebusses, Mathematical Solutions, &c. &c.

By REUBEN BURROW,

Late Assistant Astronomer at the Royal Observatory,
and Teacher of the Mathematics.

LONDON:

Printed for T. CARNAN, in St. Paul's Church Yard, who dispossessed the Stationers Company of the exclusive Privilege of Printing Almanacks, which they had monopolized 170 Years, to the discouragement of Genius and the great Prejudice of the Booksellers
throughout the kingdom, in Consequence of a Patent obtained from
King James I. which his most Sacred Majesty had no Right to Grant.

Pl. 21. Title-page of A7(26). (See also Introduction p. 23.)

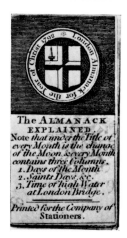

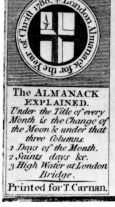

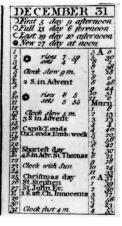

Pl. 22. (*a*) Example of a title-page of an *Almanack* published for the company of Stationers (1972); (*b*) Title-page and portrait from Carnan's *Almanack* for 1788 A7(191); (*c*) and (*d*) Page openings from A7(191).

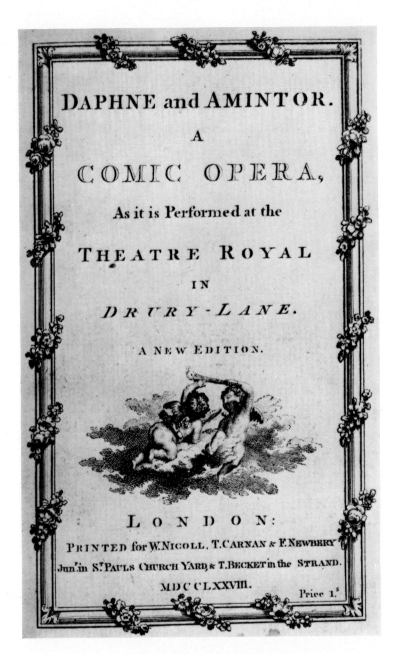

Pl. 23. Title-page of A35(5).

THE

FRUGAL HOUSEWIFE,

OR

Complete Woman Cook.

WHEREIN

The Art of dreffing all Sorts of VIANDS,
with Cleanlinefs, Decency, and Elegance,

Is explained in

Five Hundred approved R E C E I P T S, in

Gravies,		Pafties,
Sauces,		Pies,
Roafting,		Tarts,
Boiling,		Cakes,
Frying,		Puddings,
Broiling,		Syllabubs,
Stews,		Creams,
Haffies,		Flummery,
Soups,		Jellies,
Fricaffees,		Grams, and
Ragoos,		Cuftards.

Together with the B E S T M E T H O D S of

Potting,		Dr;ing,
Collaring,		Candying,
Preferving,		Pickling,

And Making of E N G L I S H . W I N E S.

To which are added,

T W E L V E N E W P R I N T S,

Exhibiting a proper Arrangement of Dinners, Two
Courfes, for every Month in the Year.

With various B I L L S O F F A R E.

By S U S A N N A H C A R T E R,

Of CLERKENWELL.

L O N D O N:

Printed for E. NEWBERY, at the Corner of St. Paul's
Church-Yard. Price One Shilling.

Pl. 24. Title-page of A76(5).

THE

Christians Magazine

Or a Treasury

OF

Divine Knowledge.

Vol. VII.

LONDON.

Printed Pursuant to his Majestys Royal Licence,

for J. NEWBERY in St. Pauls Church Yard and J. COOTE in

Pater Noster Row.

Pl. 25. Title-page of vol. VII of A82.

Pl. 26. Frontispiece of A316(2), 1775. A slightly reworked version of the engraving used as a frontispiece to A172(2), the title-page of which is shown opposite.

A Description OF THE Isle of Thanet,

and particularly of the

TOWN of MARGATE;

WITH

An Account of the Accommodations *provided* *there for Strangers; their manner of* Bathing *in the* Sea, *and* Machines *for that purpose; their* Assemblies, Amusements *and* Diversions, *public and private; the* Antiquities *and remarkable Places to be seen on the* Island, *as well as on some Short but pleasant Tours along the Coasts of* Kent; *with a Description of* Sandwich, Deal, Dover, Canterbury, Rochester, Chatham, *and other Places eminent for their Situation, and celebrated in Antient History.*

The whole illustrated with a correct Map *of the* Island, *a* Plan *of* Ramsgate-Pier, *and a* Representation *of the* Machines *for Bathing.*

LONDON.

Printed for J. Newbery *and* W. Bristow *in* S.t *Paul's Church Yard.* 1765.

Price One Shilling.

THE
DEATH of ABEL

IN FIVE BOOKS.

Attempted from the
GERMAN
OF
MR GESSNER.

THE TENTH EDITION.

LONDON.

Printed for J. Collyer, in Plough Court Fetter Lane, and
Sold by J. Dodsley, in Pall-mall, T. Caston in Stationers Court,
and F. Newbery, the corner of Ludgate Street.
MDCCLXXI.

Pl. 27. Title-page of A183(4).

THE
DESERTED VILLAGE,
A
POEM.

By Dr. GOLDSMITH.

THE NINTH EDITION.

The sad historian of the pensive plain.

LONDON:

Printed for J. RIVINGTON and SONS, and T. CARNAN, St. Paul's Church-
Yard; and T. CADELL, Strand.

M DCC LXXIX.

Pl. 28. Title-page of A191(2). (Reduced.)

THE
TRAVELLER,
A
POEM.

BY

OLIVER GOLDSMITH, M.B.

S. Wale delin.
C. Grignion sculp.

LONDON:
Printed for T. CARNAN and F. NEWBERY jun.
in St. Pauls Church Yard.
MDCCLXXIV.

Pl. 29. Title-page of A199(12). (Reduced.)

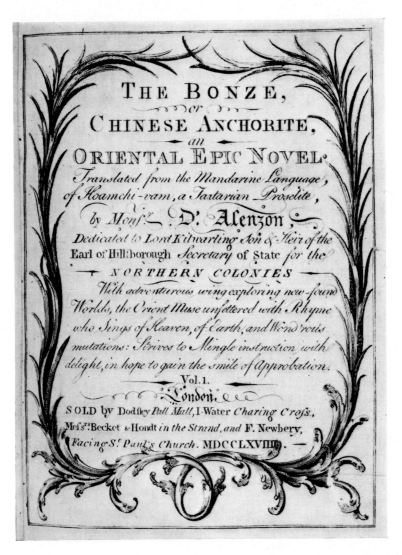

THE BONZE,
or
CHINESE ANCHORITE,
an
ORIENTAL EPIC NOVEL:

*Translated from the Mandarine Language,
of Hoamchi-vam, a Tartarian Proselite,*

by Monsr. Dr. Alenzon;

Dedicated to Lord Kilwarling Son & Heir of the
Earl of Hillsborough *Secretary* of State *for the*
— *NORTHERN COLONIES* —

*With adventurous wing exploring new-found
Worlds, the Orient Muse unfettered with Rhyme
who Sings of Heaven, of Earth, and Wond'rous
mutations: Strives to Mingle instruction with
delight, in hope to gain the smile of Approbation.*

Vol. 1.

London.

SOLD by Dodsley *Pall Mall,* 1·Water *Charing Cross,*
Messrs Becket & Hondt *in the Strand, and* F. Newbery,
Facing St *Paul's Church.* MDCCLXVIII.

Pl. 30. Title-page of A235. The name 'Hoamchi-vam' is fictitious.

Frontispeice.

EXPLANATION.

The grand Figure represents a human Creature. The Dart in his right Hand intimates Cruelty: the black Spot on the left denotes Artifice and Disguise: the yellow in his Raiment is a Sign of Jealousy, and the red of Anger; the Flower at his Feet betokens Vivacity of Genius and the Feather in his Cap bespeaks Promotion.

THE

CARD

VOL. I.

Quicquid agunt Homines, Votum, Timor, Ira,
Voluptas,
Gaudia, Discursus, nostri Farrago Libelli.

JUV.

LONDON:

Printed for the MAKER,

AND

Sold by J. NEWBERY, at the Bible and Sun,
in St. Paul's Church-Yard.

MDCCLV.

Pl. 31. Frontispiece and title-page of A282(1). (Reduced.)

A SETT of New

Pſalm-Tunes and Anthems,

In FOUR PARTS:

On Various Occasions, Viz.

For CHRISTMAS-DAY, the Martyrdom of the Bleſſed KING
CHARLES I. EASTER-DAY, ASCENSION-DAY, or the
Sunday after, WHITSUNDAY, the Happy Reſtoration of
King CHARLES II. GUN-POWDER-TREASON; for
the Uſe of the People of *Blandford*, on the Fourth of *June*,
being the Day that the Town was deſtroy'd by Fire, on a
King or Queen's Acceſſion to the Throne; for the HOLY
SACRAMENT, WEDDINGS, FUNERALS, &c.

By WILLIAM KNAPP.

The Second Edition Corrected,

With an Additional Number of ſeveral New *ANTHEMS* and
PSALM-TUNES by the Author, never Printed before, together with an excellent *ANTHEM* in Six Parts, by a very
eminent Maſter; and an Introduction to *PSALMODY*, after
a Plain and Familiar Manner.

To bleſs thy Name and ſing thy Praiſes:
Almighty God, my Voice inſpire. O!
liſ-ten gracious to my Lays, And
let me joyn the Heav'nly Choir

LONDON:

Printed by J. LEAKE, for the AUTHOR; and Sold by Meſſers. WARD and CHANDLER
at the *Ship* juſt without *Temple-Bar*, *London*; MR. WILLIAM NORRIS in
TAUNTON; Mr. BEN. COLLINS in *Saliſbury*, Mr. JOSHUA COOK in *Sherborne*,
Mr. JOHN NEWBURY in *Reading*, Mr. EDWARD LEE in *Exeter*, by moſt Bookſellers
in the Country; and by the AUTHOR in POOLE. Price Bound 2s. 6d. MDCCXLI.

Pl. 32. Title-page of A286(1).

THE
London Companion:
OR,
AN ACCOUNT OF THE FARES OF
HACKNEY COACHMEN, CHAIRMEN,
And WATERMEN;
With the RATES of CARMEN and PORTERS,
Plying in
LONDON, WESTMINSTER, or SOUTHWARK.

CONTAINING,

I. The Fares of HACKNEY COACHES, from One to Five Shillings, from all their different Stands, to the principal Streets, Squares, Places of public Entertainment, and neighbouring Villages; comprehending upwards of 30,000 different Fares.

II. The Fares of HACKNEY CHAIRS, to and from all the Squares and Places of public Resort, in or about London.

III. The Fares of WATERMEN, from all the Stairs, Wharfs, and Docks, between Vauxhall and Limehouse; and to all the Towns and Villages up to Windsor, or down to Gravesend.

IV. The New Rates of CARMEN, as settled by the Lord Mayor and Court of Aldermen, on the 7th of September last.

V. The Rates taken by PORTERS for Shipping, Landing, Loading, Housing, and Weighing of Goods.

Interspersed with

ABSTRACTS of the Acts of Parliament relating to each.

The Whole on a PLAN entirely New, and far more Extensive than any Work of the Kind ever yet attempted.

LONDON:
Printed for T. CARNAN, at Number 65, in St. Paul's Church Yard. MDCCLXXIII.

Pl. 33. Title-page of A308(1).

Die Martis, ad fenatum fuperiorem acceffit majeftas regia, more folito ftipata &, poft duodecim articulos affenfu regio ftabilitos, hujufmodi orationem benevolam habuit.

Barones mei & Generofi.

HUIC fectioni Senatoræ haud licet finem prius ftatuere, quam mea in veftram confiliorum prudentiam benevolentia exprimatur. Illa pietas & fortitudo, quarum, in imperii falutem, finguli ad unum fpecimina edidiftis, ut rueret nechanda nuperrimè conjurantium exercitus, & noxii juftitiæ tela non effugerent, quæ inter agenda, fubditorum jurata fides tantum attulit auxilii, non folum ex opinione de veftro fenatu efformatà evenère, verum etiam ejufmodi funt, ut mihi fuadeam, res præclarè adeo geftas pace optimà domi ftabilità, Pfeudo-principia & fociorum fpem futuram amovente, vobis effe perficiendi confilium.

Illa agendi autoritas, quam mihi in re tam ardua minimè negandam cenfuiftis, non fruftrà nec inaccuratè adhibita, illa fola fpectavit, quæ potiffimum vobis in votis fuerant ; & noftris confiliis quam evidentiffimè clementia divina favit: non ignoro ì u'ta adhuc ftabilienda fupereffe, quo falus noftra magis diuturna fiat, & fceleri futuro locus nullus pateat : quoniam verò res illæ fapientur agitatæ funt, quæ in fenatu poftero fufiùs funt evolvendæ, vos e veftris comitatibus diutius non detinendos cenfui, dum intempeftivum adeù anni tempus volvitur. Non fine lætitià vos certiores factos, rerum exterarum fortunam fecundiorem videri, quam cum antehac ad vos orationem habui. Simul ac per triplicis imperii falutem licuit, manum pro viribus numerofam ad Belgas expedii, quæ exercitui fœ lera'o cum provi.ciis fœderatis fubfidio foret, & Gallos audaciora meditantes repelleret. Hæc, aliæque fubfidia a vobis conceffa, vires multo ampliores illis copiis addidère, quam inorunte animo vel fpes potuiffet pingere. Hic rerum exitus, cum felicieri utriufque exercitus Auftriaci & Sardonici fortunà, aliifque cafibus caufæ publicæ pergratis, evidentiùs innuere videtur, hoftes noftros tandem rationis normam neceffario fecuturos, & fines Britannicos pacem tutam & illuftrem exornaturam. Hæc mihi potiffimum in votis habeo.

Generofi e fenatu inferiori,

Veftra inter in annum infequentem fubfidia concedenda alacritas, gratiaque a me benigniores poftulat. Non me latet anxia illa difficultas, quam temporis ordo & huic officio fubfidiario & etiam fidei publicæ mifcuit, quamque fola veftra fapientia evincere potuit. Subfidia conceffa ex votis veftris eroganda curabo ; nec vos fugere poteft meus impenfias publicas minuendi animus, juffo dato, ne legiones fubditorum nobiliorum pietate confcriptæ, ftipendia merere pergerent.

Barones mei & generofi,

Tot in me meofque fidei veftræ inconcuffæ amoris & obfervantiæ fpecimina ob oculos habeo, ut de veftrà in pofterum pietate minimè dubitandum cenfeam, perfuafum omnino habeo, fingulos, pro varià veftrà autoritate, &c. omnes vias perfecuturos, quibus, & pacem genti reddatis, & redditam confervetis ; conjurationis iniquiffimæ vulnera fugetis ; apud animos fubditorum in imperium pietatem a nuperrimà haud alienam colendam curetis. Nunquam illa animo excidet ; noftra follicitudo regia femper imperii faluti & fubditorum (quantum in me erit) felicitati invigilatura, memorem animum probabit.

Dein, Ornatiffimus Cancellarius, Rege . imperante, in hunc modum loquutus eft.

Barones mei & Generofi,

Volunt Regia monita & mandata, Senatum

---

hunc Parliamentarium, ad Martis diem, feptembris inftantis trigefimum prorogandum. Unde Senatus hic Parliamentarius, ufque ad Martis diem, Septembris inftantis trigefimum, prorogatur.

Ducem Somerfetienfem mortuum effe falfo rumor afferebat.

Nobilis admodum Baro Hobart, Magnæ Britanniæ comes, fub titulo comitis Buckinghamienfis (fertur) brevi conftituetur ; necnon

Nobilis aomodum Baro Fitzwilliams, Vicecomes, & Comes, fub titulo vice Comitis Milton, in agro Northamptonienfi, & Comitis Fitz-Williams, de Norborough, in eodem.

Die Mercurii, nob. admodum Senatus inferioris prolocutor, Majeftatem regiam invifit, ab eadem quàm humaniffimè acceptus.

Die Saturni, Jacobus Stewart, Baronettus, in novum carcerem Sudovicenfem traditus eft.

Literæ e Munimento Auguftenfi datæ afferunt, Dominum de Moor, cum feptingentis aliis rebellibus, nuper in cuftodiam effe traditum.

In rebellium numero, non ita pridem mari ad Londinenfes advecto, eft Glenbucketius, junior.

Die Saturni, Comes de Traquair in turrem Londinenfem tradebatur.

Eodem die, Comitiffe Cromartie, cum filio Barone Mac Leod, apud turrem captivo, & filiabus ternis, Comitem invifendi & una cum eodem prædendi veniam obtinuit.

Die hefterna, horà ferà tertià, Baro Lovat, cujus fama, ne dicam infamia in fingulorum ore verfatur, turrem Londinenfem attigit ; ftipante militum coronà. Ipfe inter cæteros Londinum ingredientem utroque oculo luftrabam ; vultum mirabar Fallaciis natum, pro varià occafione et fceleris et pietatis larvà indutum. O prudentiam fenilem ! Clamans, ad calamum Latinum redii.

CONNUBIO JUNCTI.

Baro Peterfham, comitis de Harrington filius natu maximus, cum Dominà Carolinà Fitzroy, Clementiæ fuæ, Ducis Graftonenfis, filià natu maximà.

Georgius Goatly, Arm. de Alsford, apud Cantianos, cum Dominà Mills, Cantuarienfi, et auro et Pulchritudine dotatà.

Dom. Michael Batt, apud collem Margaretatem Sudovicenfem, Mercator ferrarius, cum Dominà Wicks, viduà benè locupletatà.

Neomagi, apud furrienfes, Joannes Fuller, Arm. cum Dominà Dorrel,—Dorrel apud cantabrigienfes Armigeri filià, virgine formofà et dotem honeftam numerante.

MORTUI.

In vico Piccadilly, Thomas Smith, Arm. aleatorum cohorti benè notus.

Nob. Joannes Brudenell, Arm. morbo apoplectico fublatus.

N. B. Uni et alteri epiftolæ a viris eruditis de linguà Gallicà, &c. acceptæ fufius brevi refponfum dabitur. Interea probo utriufque confilia.

N B. In Mercurio 22. in col 2. pro fatebat, lege fatebatur : non fine horrore illum errorem infpexi : non autem in fingulos irrefperat, fed in ultimis lineis literæ fæpius manu incautà inter excudendum e loco fuo deturbantur. Interea vix fibi in animum inducet lector nofter affiduus, in re tam apertà ipfum Agricolam peccaffe. In eodem Mercurio, in col. 1. pro manum, lege manuum. Hos & hujufmodi errores facile legenti calamu fugare poterit & juventutis captui accommodare.

GEORGE R.

GEORGE the Second, by the Grace of God, King of Great Britain, &c. to all to whom thefe prefents fhall come, Greeting. Whereas our Trufty and Well-beloved John Newbery, of London, Bookfeller, hath, with great Expence and much Labour, compiled a Work, intitled, The Circle of the Sciences ; or, The compendious Library ; digefted in a Method entirely new, whereby each Branch of Polite Literature is render'd extremely eafy and inftructive. We being willing to encourage all Works of public Benefit, are gracioufly pleafed to grant him our Royal Privilege and Licence, for the fole Printing, Publifhing, and Vending the fame.

Given at St. James's the 8th of December 1744.
By his Majefty's Command,
HOLLES NEWCASTLE.

To the PUBLIC.

THIS Work, which is principally intended to lead CHILDREN from the very Cradle thro' the moft polite and ufeful of the Literary Arts and Sciences, is render'd as inftructive and entertaining as poffible.

In the firft Place, a proper Method is taken to open their tender Minds, and give them a Tafte for Letters after which their Ideas are enlarg'd by familiar, eafy, and progreffive Steps, till they arrive at a tolerable Knowledge of Books and Men.

Nor will this Work (as the Author humbly conceives) be lefs ufeful to thofe who are advanced in Years ; there being as much faid on each Science as is neceffary for any Gentleman to lay up in his Memory, who does not intend to make that Science his particular Employment. And as the whole is made entertaining, the fair Sex ('tis prefum'd) will find fomething to engage their Attention, efpecially under the Heads, Rhetoric, Poetry, Criticifm, Geography, Chronology, Hiftory, Philofophy, &c. as well as in the Preface or Introduction to each Book, which contains a fhort Hiftorical Account of the Science.

Of this novel and ufeful Undertaking feven Volumes are now publifh'd, viz.

VOL. I. An eafy and entertaining Spelling Book. Price bound 6d.

VOL. II. A Compendious Grammar of the Englifh Tongue Price 6d.

VOL. III. A Spelling Dictionary, on a new Plan. Price 1s.

VOL. IV. The Art of Writing illuftrated with Copper Plates ; to which is added a Collection of ufeful Letters, and Directions for addreffing Perfons of Diftinction either in Writing or Difcourfe. pr 1s.

VOL. V. The Art of Arithmetick made familiar and eafy. Price 1s.

VOL. VI. The Art of Rhetorick laid down in an eafy entertaining Manner and illuftrated with feveral beautiful Orations from Demofthenes, Cicero, Salluft, Homer, Shakfpear, &c. &c. &c. Humbly infcribed to his Royal Highnefs Prince George. Price 1s.

VOL. VII. The Art of Poetry made eafy, and embellifh'd with a Variety of the moft fhining Epigrams, Epitaphs, Songs, Odes, Paftorals, &c. &c. &c. from the beft Authors. Humbly infcrib'd to her Royal Highnefs the Princefs Augufta. Price 1s.

N. B. The Arts of Logick, Criticifm, Geography, Chronology, Hiftory, and Philofophy, are in the Prefs, and will be publifh'd with all Expedition.

Alfo may be had,

MATHURINI Corderii Colloquia Selecta : or, Select Colloquies of Mathurin Cordier : Better adapted to the Capacities of Youth, and fitter for Beginners in the Latin Tongue, than any Edition of thofe Colloquies, or any other Book yet publifh'd. Containing. Part I. The Colloquies in Latin, from a correct Edition publifh'd at the Hague: but for the Eafe of Beginners, the Words are placed in the Order of Conftruction. Part II. An Englifh Literal Tranflation, in a New Method : By the Help of which the young Scholar may with Eafe, attain to the rendering of the Latin Colloquies into Englifh ; and cannot miftake what Englifh Words which anfwer to the Latin Part III. An Analyfis, or Grammatical Refolution of the Latin Words in the Colloquies, By Samuel Loggin, M. A. For the ufe of Schools. The fecond Edition, with Improvements. Price 1s.

LONDINI : Typis GULIELMI FADEN, in viculo Sarifberienfi, vulgò Salifbury-Court, in vico de Fleet-ftreet, ubi venalis proftat & epiftolæ ad Autorem accipiuntur. Proftat pariter apud Joannem Newbery, ad infigne Bibliorum & Solis, in cœmiterio Sancti Pauli ; necnon apud G. Jones, ad infigne Flabelli & Syderis, in vico vulgo dicto Compton-ftreet, Soho, J. Fletcher, bibliopolam Oxonienfem, & circumforaneos Mercuriopolas.

N. B. Advertifements in any Language are taken in by the Printer of this Paper, at Three Shillings each. Care is likewife taken to difperfe this Paper, throughout Scotland, Ireland, Germany, and Holland.

Pl. 34. A page from *Mercurius Latinus* for 16 August 1746 (A345), announcing the publication of the *Circle of the Sciences*. (Reduced.)

Frontispiece.

A. Walker del. et sculp.

Millenium Hall.

A DESCRIPTION of

MILLENIUM HALL,

AND THE

COUNTRY ADJACENT:

Together with the

CHARACTERS of the INHABITANTS,

And such Historical

ANECDOTES and REFLECTIONS,

A S

May excite in the READER proper Sentiments of Humanity, and lead the Mind to the Love of VIRTUE.

BY

A GENTLEMAN on his Travels.

LONDON:

Printed for J. NEWBERY, at the Bible and Sun, in St. Paul's Church-yard.

MDCCLXII.

Pl. 35. Frontispiece and title-page of A365(1). (Reduced.)

SCHOOLS AND FAMILIES. S b George Robinson and TC. Price 6*d.*
12–15.12.72.

(70A) **FRENCH SHEET ALMANACK FIT FOR A POCKET.
George Robinson and TC. Price 8*d.* 12–15.12.72.

(71) GENTLEMAN'S DIARY CALENDAR ONLY, WITHOUT
AENIGMAS, FOR 1781. 21–3.11.80.

(72) GENTLEMAN'S POCKET BOOK FOR 1779. Price 1*s.*
17–19.11.78.

(73) *idem* for 1780. Price 1*s.* 28–30.12.79.

(74) **idem* for 1781. 21–3.11.80.

(75) **GENTLEMEN'S POCKET BOOKS FOR 1779. 12–14.11.78.

(76) GOLDSMITH, John. GOLDSMITH'S ALMANACK FOR
1776. Pr f TC and George Robinson. Price 6*d.* 2–4.11.75.

(76A) *idem.* COMPANION TO GOLDSMITH'S ALMANACK FOR
1776. Pr f TC and George Robinson. Price 3*d,* or bd with the Almanack 1*s.*
5–7.12.75.

(77) *idem.* ALMANACK FOR 1777. 2–5.11.76.

(78) *idem.* COMPANION TO GOLDSMITH'S ALMANACK FOR
1777. Price 3*d.* 2–5.11.76.

(79) **idem.* ALMANACK FOR 1778. 29.11.77–2.12.77.

(80) **idem.* ALMANACK FOR 1779. 12–14.11.78.

(81) **idem.* ALMANACK FOR 1780. 4–6.11.79.

(82) **idem.* ALMANACK FOR 1781. 21–3.11.80.

(83) *idem.* BOOK ALMANACK FOR 1782. 22–4.11.81.

(84) *idem.* ALMANACK FOR 1783. 19–21.11.82.

(85) *idem.* ALMANACK FOR 1784. Pr f TC, s b Stockdale and M. Sprag.
Price 8*d.* 4–6.11.83.

(86) *idem.* ALMANACK FOR 1785. Price 8*d.* 11–13.11.84.

(87) *idem.* ALMANACK FOR 1786. Price 8*d.* 27–9.10.85.

(88) *idem.* ALMANACK FOR 1787. Price 8*d.* 28–31.10.86.

(89) *idem.* ALMANACK FOR 1788. Price 8*d.* 13–15.11.87.

(90) HAMPSHIRE ALMANACK FOR 1778. A single sheet. 29.11.77–
2.12.77. [Oup.

(91) *idem* for 1779. A single sheet. 12–14.11.78. [Stationers.

(92) **idem* for 1780. 4–6.11.79.

(93) **idem* for 1781. 21–3.11.80.

(94) HAMPSHIRE, SURREY AND BERKSHIRE ALMANACK
FOR 1782. 22–4.11.81.

(94A) Hampshire for 1783 was combined with Middlesex, and for 1784 etc with
Kent, *qq.v.*

(94B) HOUSEKEEPER'S ACCOMPT BOOK. See A242.

(95) JONES, Cain. WELSH ALMANACK FOR 1776. Pr b J. Eddowes,
Shrewsbury; s b TC. Price 8*d.* 23–6.12.75.

(96) KENT ALMANACK FOR 1778. A single sheet. 29.11.77–2.12.77. [Oup.

(97) *idem* for 1779. A single sheet. 12–14.11.78. [Stationers.

(98) *idem* for 1780. 4–6.11.79.

(99) *idem* for 1781. 21–3.11.80.

(99A) Kent for 1782–3 was combined with Sussex, *q.v.*

(100) KENT, SUSSEX, SURREY AND HAMPSHIRE ALMANACK FOR 1784. Pr f TC, s b Stockdale and M. Sprag. Price 8*d*. 4–6.11.83.

(101) *idem* for 1785. 11–13.11.84. Price 8*d*.

(102) *idem* for 1786. Price 8*d*. 27–9.10.85.

(103) *idem* for 1787. Price 8*d*. 28–31.10.86. Welsh 169.

(104) *idem* for 1788. Price 8*d*. 13–15.11.87.

(105) LADIES COMPLETE POCKET BOOK. Ran from 1750 until 1789, undoubtedly one of the most successful of all the Newbery/Carnan productions, bearing up against the fierce rivalry of many similar annuals by other publishers, the Stationers' Company above all. Welsh 249–51 and 285–6.

Blagden (at p. 26) records the publicn in about Nov. 1749 of the issue of this *Pocket Book* for 1750; and a note by TC in *LC* for 2–4.11.86, p. 436, says that the work had then been published for 37 years. Assuming this to include the 1786 issue, the first would have been that for 1750. Of the issue for 1751 I have traced no record, but from that year onwards the record of annual publicn is unbroken, the last issue, that for 1789, appearing under the imprint of the Administrators of the late TC. I have found no evidence of the publicn being taken over by anyone else.

Welsh, at pp. 249 and 286, says the 'third edition' was advtd in *PL* for 11 Feb. 1761, and concludes from this that the publicn began in 1759. Actually reference in that advert. is to the 3rd ed. of the issue for 1761 (see nos. (112)–(114)).

During JN's lifetime the adverts. of the *Pocket Book* always announced that it was pubd 'at the request of several Ladies, eminent for their Oeconomy'. A pleasant and picturesque puff, worthy of the seller of James's Fever Powders. But after 17 years it must have worn rather thin, and the slogan was dropped by Carnan and Francis the son.

The total printed of all copies of all issues must have been immense. Yet of all those only three are known to me, nos. (125), (126) and (127), of which two are in the BM and the third came to me from the U.S.A. The 'Explanation' in the *Pocket Book* recommends (p. ii) 'the careful preserving of these Books, as they may be of Use, even Years after, to have Recourse to on many Occasions'. Would that that advice had been heeded. Except where otherwise stated the price in all cases was 1*s*.

(106) LADIES COMPLETE POCKET-BOOK FOR 1750. Blagden, p. 26. One of the earliest bks to bear TC's imprint. Price not recorded.

(106A) *idem* for 1751 not traced.

(106B) *idem* for 1752. Pr f JN. Adv. *GEP* 21–4.12.51.

(106C) *idem* for 1753. Pr f JN. Adv. *London Daily Advertiser*, 6.12.52.

(106D) *idem* for 1754. Pr f JN. Adv. *PA*, 19.11.53.

(106E) *idem* for 1755. Pr f JN. Adv. *PA*, 20.11.54.

(106F) *idem* for 1755, SECOND EDITION, not traced.

(106G) *idem* for 1755, THIRD EDITION. Pr f JN. 'A new edition, being the third printed this Season.' Adv. *PA* 9.1.55.

(107) *idem* for 1756. Pr f JN. Adv. *PA* 14.11.55.

(108) *idem* for 1757. Pr f JN. Adv. *PA* 18.11.56.

(109) *idem* for 1758. Pr f JN. 19–22.11.57.

(110) *idem* for 1759. Pr f JN. 28–30.11.58.

(111) *idem* for 1760. Pr f JN. 20–22.11.59.

(112) *idem* for 1761. Pr f JN. 29.11.60–2.12.60.

(113) *idem* for 1761, SECOND EDITION. Pr f JN. 24–6.2.61.

(114) *idem* for 1761, THIRD EDITION. Pr f JN. Adv. *PL* 11.2.61. On this issue see the general note no. (105).

(115) *idem* for 1762. Pr f JN. 24–6.11.61. Welsh 250.

(116) *idem* for 1763. Pr f JN. 18–20.11.62.

(117) *idem* for 1764. Pr f JN. 19–21.11.63.

(118) *idem* for 1764, SECOND EDITION, not traced.

(119) *idem* for 1764, THIRD EDITION. Pr f JN. 21–3.2.64.

(120) *idem* for 1765. Pr f JN. 17–20.11.64.

(121) *idem* for 1765. NEW EDITION. Pr f JN. 14–16.2.65.

(122) *idem* for 1766. Pr f JN. 14–16.11.65.

(123) *idem* for 1767. Pr f JN. 13–15.11.66.

(124) *idem* for 1768. Pr f JN. 14–17.11.67. Price 2s, ? a misprint in the advert.

(125) *idem* for 1769. Pr f N & C. 8–10.11.68. Imprint date 1769. *BUCOP*, III, 6. [BM.

(126) *idem* for 1770. Pr f N & C. 7–9.11.69. Imprint date 1770. [BM.

(127) *idem* for 1771. Pr f C & N. 6–8.11.70. Imprint date 1771. [Roscoe (imperf.).

(128) *idem* for 1772. Pr f C & N. 14–16.11.71.

(129) *idem* for 1773. Pr f C & N. 14–17.11.72.

(130) *idem* for 1774. Pr f C & N. 23–5.11.73.

(131) *idem* for 1775. Pr f C & N et al. 12–15.11.74.

(132) *idem* for 1776. Pr f C & N. 21–3.11.75.

(133) *idem* for 1777. Pr f C & N et al. 9–12.11.76.

(134) *idem* for 1778. Pr f C & N. 29.11.77–2.12.77. Welsh 285–6.

(135) *idem* for 1779. Pr f C & N et al. 3–5.12.78.

(136) *idem* for 1780. Pr f TC & Co et al. 2–4.11.79.

(137) ****idem* for 1781. Pr f TC. 21–3.11.80.

(138) *idem* for 1782. Pr f TC. 22–4.11.81.

(139) *idem* for 1783. Pr f TC. 26–9.10.82.

(140) *idem* for 1784. Pr f TC, s b Stockdale and M. Sprag. 4–6.11.83.

(141) *idem* for 1785. Pr f TC. 11–13.11.84.

(142) *idem* for 1786. Pr f TC. 10–12.11.85.

(143) *idem* for 1787. Pr f TC. 2–4.11.86. Price 3s, ? a misprint. The advert. noted that the Pocket-Book had then been pubd for 37 years; see general note, above.

(144) *idem* for 1788. Pr f TC. 22–4.11.87.

(145) *idem* for 1789. Pr f the Administrators of the late TC. 1–4.11.88.

(145A) LADIES DIARY. According to *DNB* article on Reuben Burrow this *Diary* was edited by him, and was the continuation of a *Lady's and Gentleman's Diary* pubd by him.

(146) **LADIES DIARY CALENDAR ONLY WITHOUT AENIGMAS &c FOR 1780. Price 1*s*. 4–6.11.79.

(147) **LADIES DIARY WITH AENIGMAS FOR 1780. 4–6.11.79.

(148) **COMPANION TO THE LADIES DIARY FOR 1780. 4–6.11.79.

(149) **LADIES DIARY CALENDAR ONLY WITHOUT AENIGMAS FOR 1781. 21–3.11.80.

(150) **LADIES DIARY WITH AENIGMAS FOR 1781. 21–3.11.80.

(151) **COMPANION TO THE LADIES DIARY FOR 1781. 21–3.11.80.

(152) LADIES DIARY WITH AENIGMAS &c FOR 1782. 22–4.11.81.

(153) *idem* for 1783. 19–21.11.82.

(154) *idem* for 1784. Pr f TC, s b Stockdale and M. Sprag. 4–6.11.83. Price 9*d*.

(155) *idem* for 1785. 11–13.11.84. Price 9*d*. [Hannas, Cat. 17 [1965] item 337, not seen.

(156) *idem* for 1786. 27–9.10.85. Price 9*d*. [Hannas, Cat. as for no. (155), not seen.

(157) *idem* for 1787. 28–31.10.86. Price 9*d*.

(158) *idem* for 1788. 13–15.11.87. Price 9*d*.

(158A) LADIES MOST ELEGANT AND CONVENIENT POCKET BOOK. A deliberate attempt to rival TC's well-established *Ladies Complete Pocket Book* (nos. 106–45); see the Introduction, at p. 21. It was preceded by Newbery's *Ladies Pocket Book*, 1772–3 (nos. 273–4).

(159) LADIES MOST ELEGANT AND CONVENIENT POCKET BOOK FOR 1774. Pr f FN(N) and John Wheble. 16–18.11.73. Price 1*s* neatly bd in red.

(160) *idem* for 1775. Pubd by J. Bew (*per* advert.).

(160A) *idem* for 1776–82 not traced. Probably for 1778–81 the gap was filled by nos. (409–12).

(161) *idem* for 1783. 26–8.11.82. Price 1*s* neatly bd in red.

(162) *idem* for 1784. 13–15.11.83. Price as before.

(163) *idem* for 1785–8 not traced.

(163A) *idem* for 1789. F. Cass, Cat. no. 8, item 247.

(164) *idem* for 1790. [Oup (imperf.).

(164A) *idem* for 1791–1803 not traced.

(164B) *idem* for 1804. Price 1*s* 4*d*. (See Fig. 32.) One of the cases in which EN's name appeared in an imprint after she had sold out to John Harris. See also A395. [Roscoe.

(165) **LADIES NEW MEMORANDUM BOOK FOR 1780. 4–6.11.79. Price 1*s*.

(166) ***idem* for 1781. 21–3.11.80.

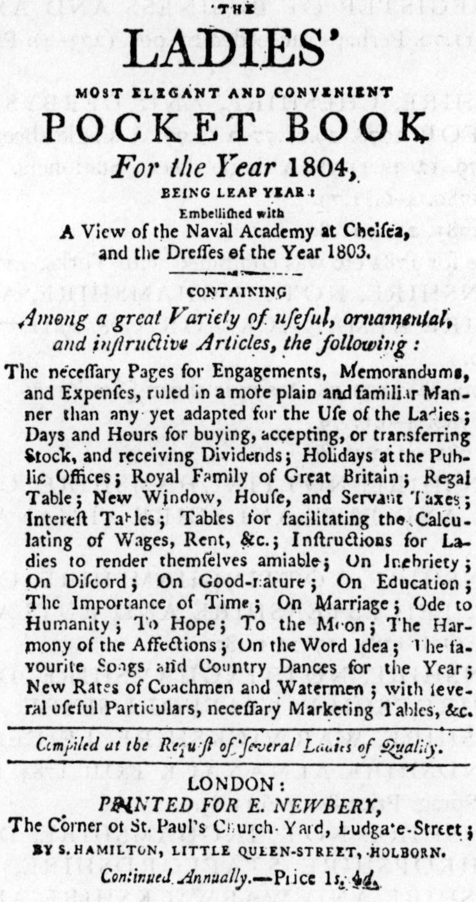

THE

LADIES'

MOST ELEGANT AND CONVENIENT

POCKET BOOK

For the Year 1804,

BEING LEAP YEAR:

Embellished with

A View of the Naval Academy at Chelsea, and the Dresses of the Year 1803.

CONTAINING

Among a great Variety of useful, ornamental, and instructive Articles, the following:

The necessary Pages for Engagements, Memorandums, and Expenses, ruled in a more plain and familiar Manner than any yet adapted for the Use of the Ladies; Days and Hours for buying, accepting, or transferring Stock, and receiving Dividends; Holidays at the Public Offices; Royal Family of Great Britain; Regal Table; New Window, House, and Servant Taxes; Interest Tables; Tables for facilitating the Calculating of Wages, Rent, &c.; Instructions for Ladies to render themselves amiable; On Inebriety; On Discord; On Good-nature; On Education; The Importance of Time; On Marriage; Ode to Humanity; To Hope; To the Moon; The Harmony of the Affections; On the Word Idea; The favourite Songs and Country Dances for the Year; New Rates of Coachmen and Watermen; with several useful Particulars, necessary Marketing Tables, &c.

Compiled at the Request of several Ladies of Quality.

LONDON:

PRINTED FOR E. NEWBERY,

The Corner of St. Paul's Church-Yard, Ludgate-Street;

BY S. HAMILTON, LITTLE QUEEN-STREET, HOLBORN.

Continued Annually.—Price 1s. 4d.

Fig. 32. Title-page of A7(164B).

(167) *idem* for 1782. 22–4.11.81.
(168) *idem* for 1783. 19–21.11.82.
(169) *idem* for 1784. Pr f TC, s b Stockdale and M. Sprag. 4–6.11.83. Price 1*s*.
(170) *idem* for 1785. 11–13.11.84. Price 1*s*.
(171) *idem* for 1786. 27–9.10.85. Price 1*s*.
(172) *idem* for 1787. 28–31.10.86. Price 1*s*.
(173) *idem* for 1788. 13–15.11.87. Price 1*s*.
(174) LADIES POCKET BOOK; OR, DAILY REGISTER OF BUSINESS AND AMUSEMENT. See no. (175).
(174A) LADIES TOWN AND COUNTRY POCKET JOURNAL, OR, SELECT MEMORANDUM BOOK FOR 1777. Pr f Alexander Ross, s b FN(N). 15–17.10.76. Price 1*s* neatly bd in red.
(175) LADY OF HONOUR, A. LADIES POCKET BOOK, THE;

OR, DAILY REGISTER OF BUSINESS AND AMUSEMENT
FOR 1771. 8–10.11.70. Perhaps succeeded by nos. (273–4). Price 1s neatly bd in
red. FN(N).

(176) LANCASHIRE, CHESHIRE, AND DERBYSHIRE
ALMANACK FOR 1778. 29.11.77–2.12.77. A single sheet. [Oup.

(177) *idem* for 1779. 12–14.11.78. A single sheet. [Stationers.

(178) **idem* for 1780. 4–6.11.79.

(179) **idem* for 1781. 21–3.11.80.

(179A) Lancashire for 1782 etc was combined with Yorks, *q.v.*

(180) LINCOLNSHIRE, NOTTINGHAMSHIRE, AND
RUTLANDSHIRE ALMANACK FOR 1778. 29.11.77–2.12.77. A
single sheet. [Oup.

(181) *idem* for 1779. 12–14.11.78. A single sheet. [Stationers.

(182) **idem* for 1780. 4–6.11.79.

(183) **idem* for 1781. 21–3.11.80.

(184) LINCOLNSHIRE, NOTTINGHAMSHIRE, CHESHIRE,
DERBYSHIRE AND RUTLANDSHIRE ALMANACK FOR 1782.
22–4.11.81.

(185) LINCOLNSHIRE, NOTTINGHAMSHIRE, CHESHIRE,
DERBYSHIRE, LEICESTERSHIRE AND RUTLANDSHIRE
ALMANACK FOR 1783. 19–21.11.82.

(186) LINCOLNSHIRE, NOTTINGHAMSHIRE, DERBYSHIRE,
CHESHIRE, SHROPSHIRE, STAFFORDSHIRE,
WORCESTERSHIRE, WARWICKSHIRE, LEICESTERSHIRE
AND RUTLANDSHIRE ALMANACK FOR 1784. Pr f TC, s b
Stockdale and M. Sprag. Price 8d. 4–6.11.83.

(187) LINCOLNSHIRE, NOTTINGHAMSHIRE, DERBYSHIRE,
CHESHIRE, SHROPSHIRE, STAFFORDSHIRE,
WORCESTERSHIRE AND WARWICKSHIRE ALMANACK
FOR 1785. 11–13.11.84. Price 8d.

(188) *idem* for 1786. 27–9.10.85. Price 8d.

(189) *idem* for 1787. 28–31.10.86. Price 8d.

(190) *idem* for 1788. 13–15.11.87. Price 8d.

(190A) LONDON ALMANACK FOR 1783. Not seen. Bondy, Cat. 79
[1970] item 528.

(190B) LONDON ALMANACK FOR 1787. A miniature bk. [Bondy, Cat.
66 [1965] item 556, not seen.

(191) *idem* for 1788. A miniature bk (see Plate 22). [Bodley; Roscoe.

(192) LONDON COPPER-PLATE SHEET ALMANACK FOR
1784. Pr f TC, s b Stockdale and M. Sprag. 4–6.11.83. Price 8d. This series (nos.
192–6) was probably in continuation of nos. (210–13).

(193) *idem* for 1785. 11–13.11.84. Price 8d.

(194) *idem* for 1786. 27–9.10.85. Price 8d.

(195) *idem* for 1787. 28–31.10.86. Price 8d.

(196) *idem* for 1788. 13–15.11.87. Price 8*d*.

(197) LONDON KALENDAR AND CORRECT ANNUAL
REGISTER FOR 1784. Pr f TC, s b Stockdale and M. Sprag. 4–6.11.83.
Price 1*s* 6*d* sewed.

(198) *idem* for 1785. 11–13.11.84. Price 1*s* 6*d* sewed.

(199) *idem* for 1786. 27–9.10.85. Price 1*s* 6*d* sewed.

(200) *idem* for 1787. 28–31.10.86. Price 1*s* 6*d*.

(201) *idem* for 1788. 13–15.11.87. Price 1*s* 6*d*.

(202) LONDON KALENDAR, OR, COURT AND CITY
REGISTER FOR 1783. Pr f TC et al. 19–21.11.82. [BM.

(203) COMPANION TO THE LONDON KALENDAR FOR 1783.
19–21.11.82.

(203A) LONDON KALENDAR, OR COURT AND CITY
REGISTER FOR 1783. A NEW EDITION CORRECTED TO
THE PRESENT TIME. Pr f TC et al. 31.5.83–3.6.83. Price 1*s* 6*d* sewed, 2*s*
bd.

(204) *idem* for 1784. [BM.

(205) COMPANION TO THE LONDON CALENDAR FOR 1784.
Pr f TC, s b Stockdale and M. Sprag. 4–6.11.83. Price 1*s*.

(206) LONDON CALENDAR, OR, COURT AND CITY
REGISTER FOR 1785. 14–16.12.84. Price 1*s* 6*d* sewed, 2*s* bd in red, 2*s* 9*d* bd
with an almanack. [BM.

(207) *idem* for 1786. Pr f TC et al. 6–8.12.85. Price 2*s*.

(208) *idem* for 1787. Pr f TC et al. [BM.

(208A) *idem* for 1787, CORRECTED TO THE END OF APRIL. Pr f
TC et al. 10–12.5.87. Price 1*s* 6*d* sewed, 2*s* bd.

(209) *idem* for 1788. Pr f TC et al. 20–2.11.87. Price 1*s* 6*d* sewed, 2*s* bd, 2*s* 9*d*
with an almanack. [BM.

(209A) *idem* for 1789 not traced.

(209B) *idem* for 1790, first issue not traced.

(209C) *idem* for 1790, CORRECTED TO FEB. 20. Pr f Power & Co et al.
20–3.2.90. Price 1*s* 6*d* sewed, 2*s* bd.

(209D) *idem* for 1791, 1st issue, not traced.

(209E) *idem* for 1791, CORRECTED TO 6 MAY, 1791. Pr f F. Power & Co
et al. 17–19.5.91. Price 1*s* 6*d* sewed, 2*s* bd.

(210) **LONDON SHEET ALMANACK FOR 1780. 4–6.11.79.

(211) ***idem* for 1781. 21–3.11.80.

(212) *idem* for 1782. 22–4.11.81.

(213) *idem* for 1783. 19–21.11.82.

(214) LONDON SHEET ALMANACK, WITH COURT AND
CITY KALENDAR FOR 1781. 21–3.11.80.

(215) NEW LONDON ALMANACK, i.e. NEW LONDON SHEET
ALMANACK. The *New London Almanack* is, it seems, always advtd with the
word SHEET, though it seems from no. (220) that this is omitted in the title.

A rival *New London Almanack* was put out in Oct. 1776 by W. Cavell, claimed to be by Wm Wing.

(216) NEW LONDON SHEET ALMANACK FOR 1776. 18–21.11.75. Price 6*d*.

(217) NEW [SMALL] LONDON SHEET, PRINTED ON A PEARL LETTER, FOR 1776. Pr f TC and George Robinson. 21–3.11.75. Price 6*d*.

(218) NEW LONDON SHEET ALMANACK FOR 1777. 2–5.11.76.

(219) *idem* for 1778. 29.11.77–2.12.77.

(220) *idem* for 1779. 12–14.11.78. Price 6*d*. [Stationers.

(221) *idem* for 1780 not traced.

(222) *idem* for 1781 not traced.

(223) *idem* for 1782. 22–4.11.81.

(224) *idem* for 1783. Pr f TC. 19–21.11.82.

(225) *idem* for 1784. Pr f TC, s b Stockdale and M. Sprag. 4–6.11.83. Price 9*d*.

(226) *idem* for 1785. 11–13.11.84. Price 9*d*.

(227) *idem* for 1786. 27–9.10.85. Price 9*d*.

(228) *idem* for 1787. 28–31.10.86. Price 9*d*.

(229) *idem* for 1788. 13–15.11.87. Price 9*d*.

(230) Entry deleted.

(231) MIDDLESEX AND SURREY ALMANACK FOR 1778. 8–11.11.77. Price 6*d*. 'May be had folded up for the pocket'.

(232) *idem* for 1779. 12–14.11.78. A single sheet. [Stationers.

(233) *idem* for 1780. 4–6.11.79.

(234) *idem* for 1781. 21–3.11.80.

(235) MIDDLESEX, ESSEX, AND HERTFORDSHIRE ALMANACK FOR 1782. 6–8.12.81.

(236) MIDDLESEX, SURREY, AND HAMPSHIRE ALMANACK FOR 1783. 19–21.11.82. A single sheet. [Oup.

(237) MIDDLESEX, HERTFORDSHIRE, BEDFORDSHIRE, BUCKINGHAMSHIRE, BERKSHIRE, OXFORDSHIRE, HUNTINGDONSHIRE, AND NORTHAMPTONSHIRE ALMANACK FOR 1784. Pr f TC, s b Stockdale and M. Sprag. 4–6.11.83. Price 8*d*.

(238) MIDDLESEX, HERTFORDSHIRE, BEDFORDSHIRE, BUCKINGHAMSHIRE, BERKSHIRE, OXFORDSHIRE, HUNTINGDONSHIRE, NORTHAMPTONSHIRE, LEICESTERSHIRE, AND RUTLANDSHIRE ALMANACK FOR 1785. 11–13.11.84. Price 8*d*.

(239) *idem* for 1786. 27–9.10.85. Price 8*d*.

(240) *idem* for 1787. 28–31.10.86. Price 8*d*.

(241) *idem* for 1788. 13–15.11.87. Price 8*d*.

(242) MOORE'S ALMANACK, 1776–88. The contemporaneous numbers of this series may be identical with nos. (265–8). Without seeing issues of both it is impossible to be certain.

(243) MOORE, Francis. MOORE'S ALMANACK FOR 1776. Pr f TC and George Robinson. 2–4.11.75.

(244) *idem* for 1777 not traced.

(245) *idem* for 1778 not traced.

(246) *idem.* COMPANION TO MOORE'S ALMANACK FOR 1778. 29.11.77–2.12.77. Imprint date 1777 altered to 1778. Price 6*d*. [Stationers.

(247) *idem.* ALMANACK FOR 1779 not traced.

(248) *idem.* COMPANION TO THE ALMANACK FOR 1779. 12–14.11.78.

(249) **idem.* ALMANACK FOR 1780. 4–6.11.79.

(249A) *idem.* COMPANION TO THE ALMANACK FOR 1780 not traced.

(250) **idem.* ALMANACK FOR 1781. 21–3.11.80.

(250A) *idem.* COMPANION TO THE ALMANACK FOR 1781 not traced.

(251) *idem.* ALMANACK FOR 1782. 22–4.11.81.

(252) *idem.* COMPANION TO THE ALMANACK FOR 1782. 22–4.11.81.

(253) *idem.* ALMANACK FOR 1783. 19–21.11.82.

(254) *idem.* COMPANION TO THE ALMANACK FOR 1783. 19–21.11.82.

(255) *idem.* ALMANACK FOR 1784. Pr f TC, s b Stockdale and M. Sprag. 4–6.11.83. Price 9*d*.

(256) *idem.* COMPANION TO THE ALMANACK FOR 1784. Pr f TC, s b Stockdale and M. Sprag. 4–6.11.83. Price 6*d*.

(257) *idem.* ALMANACK FOR 1785. 11–13.11.84. Price 9*d*.

(258) *idem.* COMPANION TO THE ALMANACK FOR 1785. 11–13.11.84. Price 6*d*.

(259) *idem.* ALMANACK FOR 1786. 27–9.10.85. Price 9*d*.

(260) *idem.* COMPANION TO THE ALMANACK FOR 1786 not traced.

(261) *idem.* ALMANACK FOR 1787. 28–31.10.86. Price 9*d*.

(262) *idem.* COMPANION TO THE ALMANACK FOR 1787. 28–31.10.86. Price 6*d*.

(263) *idem.* ALMANACK FOR 1788. 13–15.11.87. Price 9*d*.

(264) *idem.* COMPANION TO THE ALMANACK FOR 1788. 13–15.11.87. Price 6*d*.

(265) MOORE, Francis. VOX STELLARUM: OR, A LOYAL ALMANACK FOR 1776. Pr f TC and George Robinson. 16–18.11.75. Price 9*d*.

(266) *idem* for 1777. 2–5.11.76. [Stationers.

(267) *idem* for 1778. 29.11.77–2.12.77. [Stationers.

(268) *idem* for 1779. 12–14.11.78. [Stationers.

(269) *idem* for 1780–3 not traced.

(269A) *idem* for 1784. Price 9*d*. [Sotheby, 1.8.68, lot 108, vol. XI.

(269B) *idem* for 1785. Price 9*d*. Welsh 271. [Sotheby, 1.8.68, lot 108, vol. XI.

(270) NEW LONDON SHEET ALMANACK. See nos. (216–29).

(271) NEW ROYAL KALENDAR AND COURT AND CITY REGISTER FOR 1783. Pr f TC et al. Price 2*s*. [BM.

(272) NEWBERY'S LADIES POCKET BOOK FOR 1763. Listed *LM* Nov. 1762. Price 1*s*. Probably = no. (116).

(273) NEWBERY'S LADIES POCKET BOOK FOR 1772. Pr f FN(N). 12–14.11.71. Price 1*s* neatly bd in red. This and the next were succeeded by nos. (158A)ff and were no doubt deliberate rivals to the *Ladies Complete Pocket Book*, nos. 104–45. See Introduction, p. 21.

(274) *idem* for 1773. Pr f FN(N). 19–21.11.72. Price 1*s*.

(275) NORFOLK ALMANACK FOR 1778. 29.11.77–2.12.77.

(276) *idem* for 1779. 12–14.11.78. A single sheet. [Stationers.

(277) **idem* for 1780. 4–6.11.79.

(278) **idem* for 1781. 21–3.11.80.

(279) NORFOLK, SUFFOLK AND CAMBRIDGE ALMANACK FOR 1782. 22–4.11.81.

(280) NORFOLK, SUFFOLK, ESSEX AND CAMBRIDGE ALMANACK FOR 1783. 19–21.11.82.

(281) *idem* for 1784. Pr f TC, s b Stockdale and M. Sprag. 4–6.11.83. Price 8*d*.

(282) *idem* for 1785. 11–13.11.84. Price 8*d*.

(283) *idem* for 1786. 27–9.10.85. Price 8*d*.

(284) *idem* for 1787. 28–31.10.86. Price 8*d*.

(285) NORFOLK, SUFFOLK, ESSEX, CAMBRIDGE AND ISLE OF ELY ALMANACK FOR 1788. 13–15.11.87. Price 8*d*.

(286) NORTHAMPTONSHIRE, HUNTINGDONSHIRE, AND LEICESTERSHIRE ALMANACK FOR 1778. 29.11.77–2.12.77.

(287) *idem* for 1779. 12–14.11.78. A single sheet. [Stationers.

(288) **idem* for 1780. 4–6.11.79.

(289) **idem* for 1781. 21–3.11.80.

(290) NORTHAMPTONSHIRE, HUNTINGDONSHIRE, LEICESTERSHIRE, OXFORDSHIRE, BUCKINGHAMSHIRE AND BEDFORDSHIRE ALMANACK FOR 1782. 22–4.11.81.

(291) NORTHAMPTONSHIRE, HUNTINGDONSHIRE, HERTFORDSHIRE, OXFORDSHIRE, BUCKINGHAMSHIRE, BEDFORDSHIRE AND BERKSHIRE ALMANACK FOR 1783. 19–21.11.82.

(291A) Northamptonshire etc for 1784–8 are combined with Middlesex, *q.v.*

(292) NORTHUMBERLAND, CUMBERLAND, WESTMORELAND AND DURHAM ALMANACK FOR 1778. 29.11.77–2.12.77.

(293) *idem* for 1779. 12–14.11.78. A single sheet. [Stationers.

(294) *idem* for 1780. 4–6.11.79.

(295) *idem* for 1781. 21–3.11.80.

(296) *idem* for 1782. 22–4.11.81.

(297) *idem* for 1783. 19–21.11.82.

(297A) Northumberland etc for 1784–8 are combined with Yorks, *q.v.*

(298) OXFORDSHIRE, BUCKINGHAMSHIRE, AND BEDFORDSHIRE ALMANACK FOR 1778. 29.11.77–2.12.77.

(299) *idem* for 1779. 12–14.11.78. A single sheet. ⌈Stationers.

(300) **idem* for 1780. 4–6.11.79.

(301) **idem* for 1781. 21–3.11.80.

(301A) Oxford, Bucks and Beds for 1782–3 are combined with Northamptonshire, and for 1784–8 with Middlesex, *qq.v.*

(302) PARKER'S EPHEMERIS, IMPROVED BY CHARLES VYSE, FOR 1776. Pr f TC and George Robinson. 18–21.11.75. Price 9*d.*

(303) PARKER AND WHITE'S EPHEMERIS, IMPROVED BY CHARLES VYSE, FOR 1776. 2–4.11.75. ? = no. (302).

(304) PARTRIDGE, John. JOHN PARTRIDGE'S ALMANACK FOR 1782. 22–4.11.81.

(305) 'PHILOMATH, B. R.' AN ALMANACK FOR 1779. Price 6*d.* A single sheet. ⌈Stationers.

(306) POOR ROBIN'S ALMANACK FOR 1776. BY REUBEN ROBIN. Pr f TC and George Robinson. 2–4.11.75. Price 9*d.*

(307) *idem* for 1777. 2–5.11.76. ⌈Stationers.

(308) *idem* for 1778. 29.11.77–2.12.77. ⌈Stationers.

(309) *idem* for 1779. 12–14.11.78.

(310) *idem* for 1780 not traced.

(311) *idem* for 1781 not traced.

(312) *idem* for 1782. 22–4.11.81.

(313) *idem* for 1783. Pr f TC. 19–21.11.82.

(314) *idem* for 1784. Pr f TC, s b Stockdale and M. Sprag. 4–6.11.83. Price 9*d.*

(315) *idem* for 1785. 11–13.11.84. Price 9*d.*

(316) *idem* for 1786. 27–9.10.85. Price 9*d.*

(317) *idem* for 1787. 28–31.10.86. Price 9*d.*

(318) *idem* for 1788. 13–15.11.87. Price 9*d.*

(319) RIDER'S ALMANACK FOR 1776. Pr f TC and George Robinson. 2–4.11.75. Price 6*d.* This, and nos. (320–34), are in book form.

(320) *idem.* COMPANION FOR 1776. Pr f TC and George Robinson. 5–7.12.75, where it is stated: 'A Companion is printed for Rider and Goldsmith's Almanacks. Price 3*d* or bd together 1*s.*'

(321) *idem.* ALMANACK FOR 1777. 2–5.11.76.

(322) **idem* for 1778. 29.11.77–2.12.77.

(323) **idem* for 1779. 12–14.11.78.

(324) **idem* for 1780. 4–6.11.79.

(325) **idem.* COMPANION FOR 1780. 4–6.11.79.

(326) **idem.* ALMANACK FOR 1781. 21–3.11.80.

(327) **idem.* COMPANION FOR 1781. 21–3.11.80.

(328) *idem*. ALMANACK FOR 1782. 22–4.11.81.

(329) *idem* for 1783. 19–21.11.82.

(330) *idem* for 1784. Pr f TC, s b Stockdale and M. Sprag. 4–6.11.83. Price 9*d*.

(331) *idem* for 1785. 11–13.11.84. Price 9*d*. ⌈BM.

(332) *idem* for 1786. 27–9.10.85. Price 9*d*.

(333) *idem* for 1787. 28–31.10.86. Price 9*d*.

(334) *idem* for 1788. 13–15.11.87. Price 9*d*.

(334A) RIDER'S BRITISH MERLIN. See no. (342).

(334B) RIDER'S SHEET ALMANACK. Always advertd in the Press under this title, though the true title is simply RIDER'S ALMANACK: FOR THE YEAR OF OUR LORD... To be sharply distinguished from the *Rider's Almanack* in bk form, nos. (319–34).

(335) RIDER'S [SHEET] ALMANACK [for 1776] ON A SIZE BETWEEN WING AND THE LONDON SHEET. Pr f TC and George Robinson. 5–7.12.75. Price 6*d*.

(336) RIDER'S [SHEET] ALMANACK TO BIND UP WITH THE LISTS (for 1777). 2–5.11.76.

(337) RIDER'S [SHEET] ALMANACK FOR 1778 not traced.

(338) *idem* for 1779. 12–14.11.78. Price 6*d*. A single sheet. ⌈Stationers.

(339) **idem* for 1780. 4–6.11.79.

(340) **idem* for 1781. 21–3.11.80.

(341) 'ROBIN, Reuben'. See no. (306).

(342) ROYAL KALENDAR, THE. *BUCOP*, III, 753. Pubd both with and without an Almanack. So far as I can see this Almanack was *Rider's British Merlin*. BM has copies with and without the Almanack.

(343) ROYAL KALENDAR FOR 1769. Pr f FN(N) et al. 19–21.11.68. Price 2*s* 9*d* with 'Rider's Almanack', 2*s* without. ⌈BM; Oup.

(344) *idem* for 1769, NEW EDITION. Pr f FN(N) et al. 2–4.2.69. Price as for no. (343).

(345) *idem* for 1770. Pr f FN(N) et al. Price as for no. (343). ⌈BM.

(346) *idem* for 1770, NEW EDITION. Pr f FN(N) et al. 3–5.4.70. Price as for no. (343). ⌈BM.

(347) *idem* for 1771. Pr f FN(N) et al. Price as for no. (343). ⌈BM.

(348) *idem* for 1772. Pr f FN(N) et al. Price as for no. (343). ⌈BM; Oup.

(349) *idem* for 1772, NEW EDITION. Pr f FN(N) et al. Price as for no. (343). ⌈BM.

(350) *idem* for 1773. Pr f FN(N) et al. Price as for no. (343). ⌈BM.

(351) *idem* for 1773, NEW EDITION. Pr f FN(N) et al. Price as for no. (343). ⌈BM.

(352) *idem* for 1774. Pr f FN(N) et al. Price as for no. (343). ⌈BM.

(353) *idem*. COMPANION TO THE... Began *ca.* 1774; was by Almon alone.

(354) *idem* for 1775. Pr f FN(N) et al. Price as for no. (343). ⌈BM.

(355) *idem* for 1775, NEW EDITION. Pr f FN(N) et al. Price as for no. (343). ⌈BM.

(356) *idem* for 1776. Pr f FN(N) et al. 28–30.11.75. Price 2*s* 6*d* with Ryder's Sheet Almanack, 2*s* without. [BM.

(357) *idem* for 1776, NEW EDITION. Pr f FN(N) et al. Price 2*s* 6*d* with Almanack, 2*s* without. [BM.

(358) *idem* for 1777. Pr f FN(N) et al. Price as for no. (357). [BM.

(359) *idem* for 1777, NEW EDITION. Pr f FN(N) et al. 4–6.2.77. Price as for no. (357).

(360) FN's name does not appear in subsequent issues.

(361) ST JAMES'S REGISTER; OR, ROYAL ANNUAL KALENDAR, [1764]. Pr f JN et al. 15–17.11.64.

(362) *idem*. SECOND EDITION, CORRECTED TO DEC. 15, 1764. Pr f JN et al. 20–2.11.64. Price 1*s* 6*d* sewed, 2*s* bd, 2*s* 9*d* with an Almanack. [BM.

(363) *idem*. THIRD EDITION, CORRECTED TO 10th JAN. 1765. Pr f JN et al. 8–10.1.65. Price as for no. (362).

(364) *idem*. FOURTH EDITION, CORRECTED TO 27th FEB. 1765. Pr f JN et al. 2–5.3.65. Price as for no. (362).

(365) *idem* for 1766. Pr f JN and FN(N) et al. 14–16.11.65. Welsh 304. Price 2*s* bd, or 2*s* 9*d* with Almanack. [BM.

(366) *idem*. SECOND EDITION not traced.

(367) *idem*. THIRD EDITION CORRECTED TO 3rd MARCH. Pr f JN and FN(N) et al. 6–8.3.66. Price as for no. (365).

(368) *idem* for 1767. Pr f JN and FN(N) et al. 4–6.11.66. Price as for no. (365).

(369) SAUNDERS'S ENGLISH APOLLO FOR 1782. 22–4.11.81.

(370) SEASON ON SEASONS FOR 1782. 22–4.11.81.

(371) SHROPSHIRE, HEREFORDSHIRE AND MONMOUTHSHIRE ALMANACK FOR 1778. 29.11.77–2.12.77. A single sheet. [Oup.

(372) *idem* for 1779. 12–14.11.78. [Stationers.

(373) **idem* for 1780. 4–6.11.79.

(374) **idem* for 1781. 21–3.11.80.

(375) Shropshire, Herefordshire and Monmouthshire for 1782–3 are combined with Staffordshire. For 1784–8 Shropshire is combined with Lincolnshire; Herefordshire and Monmouth with Somerset, *qq.v.*

(376) SMALL LONDON SHEET ALMANACK. See no. (217).

(377) **SOMERSETSHIRE AND GLOUCESTERSHIRE ALMANACK FOR 1778. 29.11.77–2.12.77.

(378) *idem* for 1779. 12–14.11.78. A single sheet. [Stationers.

(379) **idem* for 1780. 4–6.11.79.

(380) **idem* for 1781. 21–3.11.80.

(381) SOMERSETSHIRE, GLOUCESTERSHIRE, WILTSHIRE AND DORSETSHIRE ALMANACK FOR 1782. 22–4.11.81.

(382) *idem* for 1783. 19–21.11.82.

(383) SOMERSETSHIRE, DORSETSHIRE, WILTSHIRE, GLOUCESTERSHIRE, HEREFORDSHIRE AND

MONMOUTHSHIRE ALMANACK FOR 1784. Pr f TC, s b Stockdale and M. Sprag. 4–6.11.83. Price 8*d*.

(384) *idem* for 1785. 11–13.11.84. Price 8*d*.

(385) *idem* for 1786. 27–9.10.85. Price 8*d*.

(386) *idem* for 1787. 28–31.10.86. Price 8*d*.

(387) *idem* for 1788. 13–15.11.87. Price 8*d*.

(388) **STAFFORDSHIRE, WARWICKSHIRE, AND WORCESTERSHIRE ALMANACK FOR 1778. 29.11.77–2.12.77.

(389) *idem* for 1779. 12–14.11.78. A single sheet. [Stationers.

(390) **idem* for 1780. 4–6.11.79.

(391) **idem* for 1781. 21–3.11.80.

(392) STAFFORDSHIRE, WARWICKSHIRE, WORCESTERSHIRE, SHROPSHIRE, HEREFORDSHIRE AND MONMOUTHSHIRE ALMANACK FOR 1782. 22–4.11.81.

(393) *idem* for 1783. 19–21.11.82.

(394) Stafford, Warwick, Worcester and Shropshire were combined with Lincolnshire, and Hereford and Monmouth with Somerset for 1784–8, *qq.v.*

(395) **SUFFOLK ALMANACK FOR 1778. 29.11.77–2.12.77.

(396) *idem* for 1779. 12–14.11.78. A single sheet. [Stationers.

(397) **idem* for 1780. 4–6.11.79.

(398) **idem* for 1781. 21–3.11.80.

(399) Suffolk for 1782–8 was combined with Norfolk, *q.v.*

(400) **SUSSEX ALMANACK FOR 1778. 29.11.77–2.12.77.

(401) *idem* for 1779. 12–14.11.78. [Stationers.

(402) **idem* for 1780. 4–6.11.79.

(403) **idem* for 1781. 21–3.11.80.

(404) SUSSEX AND KENT ALMANACK FOR 1782. 22–4.11.81.

(405) *idem* for 1783. 19–21.11.82.

(406) Sussex for 1784–8 was combined with Kent, *q.v.*

(407) VOX STELLARUM. See nos. (265–9B).

(408) WELSH ALMANACK. See no. (95).

(409) WHEBLE'S LADIES MOST ELEGANT AND CONVENIENT POCKET BOOK FOR 1778. Pr f FN(N) and J. Wheble in Fleet St. 20–2.11.77. Price 1*s* neatly bd in red with pockets for letters. See no. (160A).

(410) *idem* for 1779. Pr f FN(N). 10–12.11.78. Price 1*s* neatly bd in red.

(411) *idem* for 1780. Pr f FN(N). 13–16.11.79. Price 1*s* neatly bd in red leather.

(412) *idem* for 1781. Pr f FN(N). 11–14.11.80. Price as for no. (411).

(413) **WILTSHIRE AND BERKSHIRE ALMANACK FOR 1778. 29.11.77–2.12.77.

(414) *idem* for 1779. 12–14.11.78. A single sheet. [Stationers.

(415) **idem* for 1780. 4–6.11.79.

(416) **idem* for 1781. 21–3.11.80.

(417) Wiltshire was combined with Somerset for 1782–8. Berkshire was combined with Hampshire for 1782, with Northants for 1783 and with Middlesex for 1784–8.

(418) WING, Tycho. TYCHO WING'S ALMANACK FOR 1782. 22–4.11.81.

(419) WING, Vincent. SHEET ALMANACK FOR 1776. Pr f TC and George Robinson. 18–21.11.75. 'A Sheet Almanack on the same plan as that formerly published by Vincent Wing'. Price 6*d*.

(420) *idem* for 1777. 2–5.11.76. Price 1*s*. A single sheet. [Bodley.

(421) **idem* for 1778. 29.11.77–2.12.77.

(422) *idem* for 1779. 12–14.11.78. Price 6*d*. A single sheet. [Stationers.

(423) **idem* for 1780. 4–6.11.79.

(424) **idem* for 1781. 21–3.11.80.

(425) *idem* for 1782. 22–4.11.81.

(426) *idem* for 1783. 19–21.11.82.

(427) *idem* for 1784. Pr f TC, s b Stockdale and M. Sprag. 4–6.11.83. Price 7*d*.

(428) *idem* for 1785. 11–13.11.84. Price 7*d*.

(429) *idem* for 1786. 27–9.10.85. Price 7*d*.

(430) *idem* for 1787. 28–31.10.86. Price 7*d*.

(431) *idem* for 1788. 13–15.11.87. Price 7*d*.

(432) **YORKSHIRE ALMANACK FOR 1778. 29.11.77–2.12.77.

(433) *idem* for 1779. 12–14.11.78. A single sheet. [Stationers.

(434) **idem* for 1780. 4–6.11.79.

(435) **idem* for 1781. 21–3.11.80.

(436) YORKSHIRE AND LANCASHIRE ALMANACK FOR 1782. 22–4.11.81.

(437) *idem* for 1783. 19–21.11.82.

(438) YORKSHIRE, LANCASHIRE, DURHAM, WESTMORE-LAND, CUMBERLAND AND NORTHUMBERLAND ALMANACK FOR 1784. Pr f TC, s b Stockdale and M. Sprag. 4–6.11.83. Price 8*d*.

(439) *idem* for 1785. 11–13.11.84. Price 8*d*.

(440) *idem* for 1786. 27–9.10.85. Price 8*d*.

(441) *idem* for 1787. 28–31.10.86. Price 8*d*.

(442) *idem* for 1788. 13–15.11.87. Price 8*d*.

A8. ANACREON, SAPPHO, BION, MOSCHUS AND MUSAEUS, Trans. Francis Fawkes.

(1) An ed. of 1760. Pr f JN et al. Price 3*s*. Welsh 217 (1750 in error). *CBEL*, II, 361 and 759. Title reads the *Works of Anacreon...translated into English. By a Gentleman of Cambridge*. [BM; LUL.

(2) Another issue, 1760. Price 3*s*. As for no. (1) except title reads the *Works... Translated from the original Greek. By Francis Fawkes, M.A.* [Roscoe; Bodley; AdE; LUL; UCL; DNS.

(3) Listed in A640(3), vol. IV, 1768, as pr f a s b N & C. Price 3*s*.

A9. ANNALS OF EUROPE, THE; OR, REGAL REGISTER. Pr f EN et al. Price 6s bd, 5s in bds. Adv. *LC* 21–3.11.80. Another bk of the same title was pubd in 1739–45.

A10. ANNUAL ABSTRACT OF THE SINKING FUND, 1764. Pr f JN et al. Price 5s in bds. [BM; LUL; NLA.

A11. ANNUAL ABSTRACT OF THE SINKING FUND, ?1765. Pr f JN et al. Price 1s. Adv. *LC* 9–12.2.65. Perhaps a supplement to no. A10.

A12. ANNUAL ABSTRACT OF THE SINKING FUND, ?1765. Pr f JN et al. Price 5s in bds. Adv. *LC* 23–5.5.65.

A13. ANNUAL ABSTRACT OF THE SINKING FUND. Listed in 1768 as pubd b JN in A637(2), vol. II. Price 5s.

A14. ANSTEY, Chris. NEW BATH GUIDE, 1794. S b EN et al. Recorded by Algar. There was an ed. of this year by Wenman and Hodgson of London (copy in CUL).

A15. ARNOLD, Stuart Amos. MERCHANTS AND OWNERS FRIEND, THE, 1778. Pr f TC. Price 1s 6d. Welsh 170. [BM; EdUL.

A16. ARNOLD, Stuart Amos. MERCHANT AND SEAMAN'S GUARDIAN, THE, 1778. Pr f TC. Price 1s 6d. [BM; EdUL; AdE.

A17. ASCHAM, Roger. ENGLISH WORKS, by Bennet, 1761. Pr f JN et al. Price 10s 6d sewed. Welsh 119 and 244; *CBEL*, II, 622 and 671; Courtney 100. [BM; Bodley; EdUL; Rylands; LGL; AdE; DNS.

A18. BACON, Matthew. NEW ABRIDGMENT OF THE LAW, 5th ed., 1798. Pr f EN et al. 7 vols. Price 5 gns in bds. Maxwell, 1, 16. [BM; LGL; AdE.

A19. BACON, Matthew. TREATISE, A, ON LEASES AND TERMS FOR YEARS, 1798. Pr f EN et al. Price 9s in bds. [BM; AdE.

A20. BAILEY, Nathan. UNIVERSAL ETYMOLOGICAL ENGLISH DICTIONARY.
(1) 24th ed. 1782. Pr f EN et al. Price 7s. Alston, v, 121. [BM; LUL; EdUL; AdE; CUL; NLSc; GlaUL; Bristol; BrUL; MB; NN.
(2) 25th ed. Pr f EN et al. Price 7s. Adv. *LC* 22–5.5.90.

A21. BALTIMORE, Frederick Calvert, Baron. TOUR TO THE EAST, 1767. Adv. *LC* 15–17.9.67 as to be had of JN et al. Price 3s sewed in marbled paper, 4s bd gilt and lettered. JN not named in the imprint. Welsh 172.

A22. BARETTI, Giuseppe Marc' Antonio (Joseph). DICTIONARY OF THE ENGLISH AND ITALIAN LANGUAGES.
(1) Ed. of 1778. Pr f FN(N) et al. 2 vols. Price 2 gns. [BM; Bodley.
(2) Ed. of 1790. Pr f EN et al. 2 vols. Price £1 10s. [BM; CUL.
(3) A 'new ed.' adv. *LC* 8–10.1.99 as pr f EN et al. Price £1 10s.

A23. BARROW, John. TABLES CALCULATED FOR THE USE OF ALL WHO ARE IN TRADE.
(1) An ed. of 1753. S b JN. Forms the concluding part of A178. [BM.
(2) Adv. *LC* 29–31.8.69 as pubd b C & N. Price 9d sewed.
(3) Listed in A91 (1781) as pr f TC. Price 9d.

A24. BATH, Robert. TREATISE ON...DISEASES OF THE LIVER, 1777. Pr f FN(N). Price 2s. [RCP; CUL; RCS.

A25. BEARDÉ DE L'ABBAYE. ESSAYS IN AGRICULTURE, 1776. Pr f TC. Price 4s 6d. Welsh 169. [BM; EdUL; AdE; CUL.

A26. BEAUTIES OF ANCIENT POETRY, 1794. Pr f EN et al. Price 2s sewed in marbled paper, 2s 6d bd. Welsh 288; *CBEL*, II, 249. [Weedon; BM; Bodley; CUL; LUL; Renier; DNS.

A27. BEAUTIES OF ENGLISH POETRY. SELECTED BY THOMAS TOMKINS. 6th ed. Adv. *LC* 21–4.12.93 as to be had of EN and J. Wallis. Price 2s sewed, 2s 6d bd. *CBEL*, II, 236, 248, 256, edd. 1782, 1793, 1800.

A28. BEAUTIES OF THE POETS, THE. 6th ed. 1799. Pr b a f EN et al. Price 3s in bds. *CBEL*, II, 254. [BM.

A29. BECCARIA, Cesare Bonesana. ESSAY ON CRIMES AND PUNISHMENTS. *CBEL*, II, 808; H. B. Evans, no. 146 etc.
(1) 1st ed. by J. Almon alone.
(2) 2nd ed. 1769. Pr f FN(N). Price 4s sewed, 5s bd. [BM; LUL; LL; Weedon; Wellcome.
(3) 3rd ed. 1770. Pr f FN(N). Price 4s sewed, 5s bd. [BM; UCL.
(4) 4th ed. 1775. Pr f FN(N). Price 5s. [BM; EdUL; LUL; Bodley.
(5) An ed. of 1777. ? FN(N). This, or no. (4), listed in Johnson's *Life of Savage*, 1777. [BM (destroyed).
(6) Another 4th ed. 1785. Pr f EN. Welsh 327. [CUL.

BENT, Chas. INTEREST IMPROVED. See Brent, Chas.

A30. BENTICK, Rev. John. SPELLING AND EXPLANATORY DICTIONARY OF THE ENGLISH LANGUAGE, 1786. Pr f TC. Price 2s. Alston, v, 335. [BM.

A31. BENTWELL, (   ). SPELLING DICTIONARY. Welsh 173.
Stated to have been entered by TC at Stationers Hall in 1785.

A32. BERKSHIRE. COPY OF THE POLL FOR THE KNIGHTS
OF THE SHIRE FOR THE COUNTY OF BERKS, TAKEN...
1768. S b N & C et al. Price 1*s* 6*d*. Legg, no. 52. [RePL.

A33. BEST METHOD OF PRESERVING HEALTH.
BEST AND EASIEST METHOD OF PRESERVING
UNINTERRUPTED HEALTH TO EXTREME OLD AGE. (These 2
titles apparently the same work.)
(1) Under 1st title, Welsh 236. 1752 or before.
(2) Under 2nd title, edd. by R. Baldwin in 1748 and 1752.
(3) Under 2nd title a 2nd ed. listed as pubd by JN in A370(2), 1753. Price 2*s*.
(4) Under 2nd title listed as s b TC in A222(17), 1788. Price 2*s*.

A34. BIBLE.
(1) HOLY BIBLE, WITH A COMMENTARY...BY WM DODD,
1765, 1767, 1770. Pr f JN, N & C et al. Pubd monthly at 2*s*, also in weekly pts at
6*d*. 3 vols. Welsh 204–6. [BM; Bodley.
(2) An ed. of 1768. S b JN et al. D&M 882; Herbert 1768. [BM; BFBS.
(3) COMMENTARY, A, ON THE BOOKS OF THE OLD AND
NEW TESTAMENT, 1770. By Wm Dodd. Pr f C & N et al. 3 vols. *CBEL*,
II, 360. [BM; CUL; Rylands; EdUL.
(4) HOLY BIBLE, ILLUSTRATED WITH A COMMENTARY...
BY WM DODD. *LC* for 19–21.1.73 announced that no. 1 of the work would
be pubd on 30 Jan., price 6*d*. Pr f C & N et al.
(5) HOLY BIBLE...WITH NOTES BY...ANSELM BAYLY, 1773.
Pr f FN* et al. To be pubd in 36 pts at 6*d*. 2 vols. Herbert 1234 (dates 1774). [BM.
(6) HISTORY OF A BIBLE, BY A CLERGYMAN. Listed in J289(1),
1791, as pr f EN. ? = A34(11).
(7) HISTORY OF THE BIBLE. With cuts. Price 3*s*. Adv. *GM* May 1774
as pr f FN(N). Apparently an ed. of the next following items. And see A34(12).
(8) NEW HISTORY OF THE HOLY BIBLE, A. BY A CLERGY-
MAN OF THE CHURCH OF ENGLAND. 1st and 2nd edd. not traced.
(9) *idem*, 3rd ed. Pr f FN(N). Price 3*s*. Adv. *LC* 5–7.1.75.
(10) *idem*, 4th ed. not traced.
(11) *idem*, 5th ed. 1785. Pr f EN. [BM.
(12) *idem*, 6th ed. ? listed in J328, 1795, as pr f EN, price 3*s*, under the title *History
of the Bible*.
(13) *idem*, 7th ed. 1796. Pr f EN. Price 3*s* 6*d*. Welsh 174. [BM; DES; Traylen.

A35. BICKERSTAFFE, Isaac. DAPHNE AND AMINTOR. *CBEL*,
II, 459; Nicoll, p. 237; Welsh 197.

(1) Ed. 1765. Pr f JN et al. Price 1s. [BM.

(2) *CBEL* records 5 edd. in 1765.

(3) Ed. 1766. Pr f JN et al. Price 1s. [BM; Bodley; Rylands.

(4) Listed in A401(3), 1777, as pr f TC. Price 1s.

(5) Ed. 1778. Pr f C & N et al. Price 1s (see Plate 23). [LL.

A36. BICKERSTAFFE, Isaac. LOVE IN A VILLAGE. *CBEL*, II, 459; Nicoll, p. 237.

(1) 1st ed. 1763. Pr f JN et al. Price 1s 6d. [Bodley; CUL.

(2) 2nd ed. 1763. Pr f JN et al. Price 1s 6d. [BM; UCL.

(3) 3rd ed. 1763. Adv. *LC* 30.12.62–1.1.63 as pr f JN et al. Price 1s 6d.

(4) 4th ed. 1763. Not by JN.

(5) 5th ed. 1763. Adv. *LC* 25–7.1.63 as pr f JN et al. Price 1s 6d.

(6) 6th ed. 1763. Pr f JN et al. Price 1s 6d. [BM; Bodley.

(7) 7th ed. 1763. Pr f JN et al. Price 1s 6d. [BM.

(8) 8th ed. 1763. Pr f JN et al. Price 1s 6d. [CUL.

(9) 9th ed. 1763 or 1764, not traced.

(10) 10th ed. 1764. Pr f JN et al. Price 1s 6d. Welsh 260. This ed. has 42 leaves, pp. ii+73[75]. [BM.

(11) Another 10th ed. 1764. As for no. (10) except this ed. has 40 leaves, pp. ii+72. [Bodley.

(12) Another 10th ed. 1765. Pr f JN et al. 33 or 34 leaves, pp. 64[66]. [BM; Bodley.

(13) 11th ed. 1765. Pr f JN et al. Price 1s 6d. [Bodley.

(14) New ed. 1767. Pr f JN et al. Price 1s 6d. [BM.

(15) New ed. 1771. Pr f C & N et al. Price 1s 6d. [Bodley; Rylands.

(16) An ed. of 1776. Pr f C & N et al. Price 1s 6d. [LUL.

(17) An ed. adv. *LC* 7–10.9.82, p. 247, price 6d, under the description *Love in a Village, marked with the Variations, and graced with the figures of Mr. Dubellamy and Mrs. Cargill, drawn by Mr. Dodd, and engraved by Mr. Collyer*. Pr f TC et al.

A37. BICKERSTAFFE, Isaac. THE MAID OF THE MILL. *CBEL*, II, 459; Nicoll, p. 237.

(1) *CBEL* lists 6 edd. in 1765.

(2) An ed. of 1765. Pr f JN et al. Price 1s 6d. Welsh 261. [BM.

(3) 4th ed. 1765. Pr f JN et al. Price 1s 6d. [Bodley.

(4) 5th ed. 1765. Pr f JN et al. Price 1s 6d. [BM.

(5) 6th ed. 1765. Pr f JN et al. [BM.

(6) A new ed. 1767 (see Fig. 33). Pr f JN et al. Welsh 261. [BM; CUL; Rylands.

(7) Adv. *LC* 15–17.6.73 as 'to be had of' C & N. Price 1s 6d.

(8) Listed in A35(5), 1778, as pr f TC & Co et al. Price 1s 6d.

(9) An ed. adv. *LC* 7–10.9.82, p. 247, price 6d, under the description the *Maid of the Mill, marked as played. The representations of Mr. Mattocks and Miss Harmer drawn by Mr. Dodd, and engraved by Mr. Collyer*. Pr f TC et al.

THE
MAID of the MILL.
A
𝒦 COMIC OPERA.

As it is Performed at the

THEATRE ROYAL

IN

COVENT GARDEN.

By the Author of

LOVE in a VILLAGE.

A NEW EDITION.

LONDON:
Printed for J. NEWBERY; R. BALDWIN;
T. CASLON; W. GRIFFIN; W. NICOLL;
T. LOWNDS; & BECKET & DE HONDT.
MDCCLXVII.

P. 1ˢ 6ᵈ

Fig. 33. Title-page of A37(6).

A38. BIOGRAPHICAL DICTIONARY. Listed in J239, 1796, as pr f EN, price '5s common, and elegantly bd 6s'. Probably A279, 1794 or 1796.

A39. BIOGRAPHICAL MAGAZINE, THE, OR, COMPLETE HISTORICAL LIBRARY, 1776–7. Pr f FN(N). *BUCOP*, I, 351. Pubd monthly, the first 8 numbers forming vol. I. Price 1s 6d each number, with a framed and glazed copper-plate engvg given free with each. A MS note in BM Gen. Cat. says there were no issues after vol. I; but no. xv was advertd in *LC* 1–3.7.77, p. 12. Nos. ix–xiv not traced, and it is not impossible they never existed, and that this later number was an attempt to revive a corpse; it was sold with the usual framed and glazed engvg, given free, and another unframed. [BM; Bodley.

A40. BITTERZWIGG, Pendavid (pseud.). THREE ORIGINAL POEMS; BEING THE POSTHUMOUS WORK OF PENDAVID BITTERZWIGG, n.d. Attributed to the Rev. Francis Fawkes. Adv. *GEP* 28.2.51–2.3.51. Pr f TC. Price 1s. [BM.

A41. BLACKRIE, Alexander. DISQUISITION ON MEDICINES THAT DISSOLVE THE STONE, 1771. Pr f FN(N) et al. Price 5s in bds; the 2nd pt price 2s 6d. [RCP; RCS; EdUL.

A42. BLAIR, Hugh. SENTIMENTAL BEAUTIES AND MORAL DELINEATIONS, FROM THE WRITINGS OF THE CELEBRATED DR. BLAIR, AND OTHER MUCH ADMIRED AUTHORS. A NEW EDITION. So listed in J273, 1797, as pr f EN. Price 2s 6d.

A43. BODMER, Johann Jacob. NOAH (trans. Joseph Collyer). *CBEL*, II, 56 and 805.
(1) Ed. 1767. Pr f FN(N) et al. 2 vols. Price 5s sewed, 6s calf. [BM; CUL; EdUL; UCL; AdE.
(2) Ed. 1770. S b FN(N) et al. Price 5s sewed, 6s bd. 2 vols. This is the 1767 ed. with a new engvd TP and engvd FP; the printed TP dated 1767 is retained. [BM; Bodley.
(3) Adv. *LC* 6–9.3.73, p. 231, as s b FN(N) et al. at 2s 6d sewed, 3s bd.

A44. BOOK OF COMMON PRAYER, THE. AN EXPOSITION OF...SHORT, PLAIN, AND PRACTICAL EXPOSITION OF THE PRAYERS...AUTHORISED AND PRESCRIBED..., 1742. Pr a s b JN et al. Price 8d or 6s 6d a dozen 'to those who are piously disposed to give them away'. Legg, no. 19. [RePL.

A45. BOOK OF NATURE, THE. A POEM, 1771. Pr f TC. Price 1s. [BM; Bodley.

A46. BOSCAWEN, SHIP. JOURNAL...OF BOSCAWEN'S VOYAGE TO BOMBAY...ANNO 1749.
(1) 1st ed. 1750. Pr f the Author, s b TC. Price 1s 6d. [BM (imperf.); CUL.
(2) 2nd ed. 1751. Pr f the Author, s b TC. Price 1s 6d. [BM.

A47. BOSSUET, Jacques Benigne. UNIVERSAL HISTORY.
(1) Listed in A553(1), 1757, as pr f JN, 2 vols, price 6s.
(2) Undated ed. [ca. 1768], pr f C & N. Price 6s, 2 vols. [LL.

A48. BOYCE, Samuel. AN ODE TO THE...MARQUIS OF
HARTINGTON, 1755. Pr f JN et al. Price 1s. CBEL, II, 354. [BM.

A49. BOYCE, Samuel. POEMS ON SEVERAL OCCASIONS, 1757.
Pr f JN et al. Welsh 176. CBEL, II, 355; Rothschild 486. [Bodley (thick paper
copy).

A50. BOYER, Abel. LE DICTIONNAIRE ROYAL, FRANCOIS-
ANGLOIS. THE ROYAL DICTIONARY, FRENCH AND
ENGLISH. Nouvelle edition. 1796. Se trouve chez EN et al. Price £1 16s, 2 vols.
[BM; NLA; GOB.

A51. BOYSE, Samuel. NEW PANTHEON, A (THE). In all edd. after the
1st the title is THE NEW... Welsh 176–7. CBEL, II, 311.
(1) 1st ed. 1753. Pr f JN et al. Price 3s 6d. [CUL; Roscoe; Gardner.
(2) 2nd ed. n.d. Pr f JN et al. Price 3s 6d. Adv. LC 15–18.3.60, p. 267. [BM;
Renier.
(3) 3rd ed. 1764. Pr f JN et al. Price 3s 6d. [Bodley.
(4) 4th ed. 1771. Pr f C & N et al. [LUL, not seen.
(5) 5th ed. 1777. Pr f C & N et al. [BM; Temperley.
(6) 6th ed. ?1787. Pr f F. Power & Co (Successors to the late T. Carnan) et al.
Price 4s. Adv. LC 1–4.5.90. Not seen. [T. D. Webster, list 156 [1963] item 105;
but the date is questionable: Carnan died in 1788.

A52. BRAMBLE, Benjamin (pseud.). THE FARMER CONVINCED,
1788. S b E. Newberry (sic) et al. Price 1s 6d. Welsh 177. At p. 31 is a near-
facsimile of the TP to George Winter's *New and Compendious System of Husbandry*,
1787 (no. A634(1)). [BM; LL.

A53. BRENT, Charles. INTEREST IMPROVED.
(1) An ed. of 1751. Pr f J. Newberry (sic). Price 2s. Pressler, p. 2. The author's
name is sometimes listed as BENT. [Bodley; CUL; ICU-J.
(2) Listed as by C & N, in A326(4), vol. I, 1771.

A54. BRITISH MAGAZINE, THE; OR MONTHLY
REPOSITORY FOR GENTLEMEN AND LADIES, by Smollett and
others. Jan. 1760–Dec. 1767. Welsh 39–40, 177, 309; CBEL, II, 525, 678; BUCOP,
I, 419. There is no reason to doubt the story of the inception of this periodical by
JN as given by Chalmers (quoted by Welsh, pp. 39–40). [BM (vol. I); Bodley.

A55. BROOKES, Richard, M.D. EXPLANATION OF THE TERMS OF ART IN...MEDICINE, 1769. Pr f N & C. Price 1s. The text forms pp. 497–556 of no. A59(1), 1754. [BM; Wellcome.

A56. BROOKES, Richard, M.D. GENERAL DISPENSATORY, THE.
(1) 1st ed. 1753. Pr f JN et al. Price 3s 6d. [BM; Wellcome; RCP; RCS; CUL.
(2) 2nd ed. 1765. Pr f JN et al. Price 3s 6d. Welsh 177. [Wellcome; RCP; EdUL.
(3) 3rd ed. ?1776. Pr f C & N et al. Price 3s 6d. Adv. *LC* 9–11.7.76, p. 37.

A57. BROOKES, Richard, M.D. GENERAL GAZETEER, THE. Welsh 177–8.
(1) 1st ed. 1762. Pr f JN. Price 6s. [BM; Bodley.
(2) 2nd ed. 1766. Pr f JN et al. Price 7s calf. Communicated. [NLA.
(3) 3rd ed. ?1773. Pr f C & N et al. Pubd in pts at 6d each, the whole at 7s calf. Adv. *LC* 16–18.9.73.
(4) 4th ed. 1778. Pr f TC et al. Price 7s calf. [EdUL, not seen.
(5) 5th ed. 1782. Pr f TC et al. Price 7s. [BM; Bodley; CUL.
(6) 6th ed. 1786. Pr f TC et al. Price 7s. [BM; Bodley; EdUL; CUL; AdE.
(7) 7th ed. 1791. Pr f F. Power & Co et al. Price 7s. [Bodley; NLA; Sotherby, 19.11.70, lot 63.

A58. BROOKES, Richard, M.D. GENERAL PRACTICE OF PHYSIC, THE. Welsh 179.
(1) 1st ed. 1751. Pr f JN. Price 6s, 2 vols. [RCP; Bodley (vol. II); Wellcome (vol. II); EdUL.
(2) 2nd ed. 1754. Pr f JN. Price 8s, 2 vols. [BM; EdUL; CUL.
(3) 3rd ed. 1758. Pr f JN. Price 8s, 2 vols. Still being advtd at the pubd price in 1776. Sotheby, 12.12.67, lot 278. [Wellcome (vol. II); Marchmont Bkshop Cat. 17 [1963] item 301.
(4) 4th ed. 1763. Pr f JN. Price 8s, 2 vols. [RCVS; Wellcome.
(5) 5th ed. 1765. Pr f JN. Price 9s, 2 vols. [Wellcome; RCP.
(6) APPENDIX to the 5th ed. 1766. Pr f JN. Price 1s. [Bodley; Wellcome.
(7) 6th ed. 1771. Pr f C & N. Price 9s in the vell. manner, labelled on the back, 10s calf. [Wellcome.
(8) 7th ed. 1777 or 1778. Pr f C & N. Price as for no. (7). Adv. *LC* 14–16.4.78, p. 365.

A59. BROOKES, Richard, M.D. INTRODUCTION TO PHYSIC AND SURGERY, AN.
(1) 1st ed. 1754. Pr f JN. Price 6s. [Wellcome; RCS; EdUL.
(2) 2nd ed. 1763. Pr f JN. Price 5s. Welsh 179. [BM; EdUL.
(3) Listed as pr f a s b C & N in J67, 1776. Price 6s.

A60. BROOKES, Richard, M.D. NATURAL HISTORY OF BIRDS, 1763. Pr f JN. Price 3s. This is no. A61(1) with a TP from which 'vol. II' has been omitted. [RCVS.

A61. BROOKES, Richard, M.D. NEW AND ACCURATE SYSTEM OF NATURAL HISTORY. For a full bibliography see Lisney 250 etc. Many of the figures are copied from Topsell's *Beasts*.

(1) 1st ed. 1763. Pr f JN. 6 vols. Price 3s each vol., 1 gn for the set of six. Welsh 178; *CBEL*, II, 641; IAW 128; Scott 103–4. [BM(NH); BM (vols I–IV); EdUL; Lisney; Wellcome; LL (vol. III); ZSL.

(1A) Another ed. of vol. I, 1766. Pr f JN. Lisney 251. Has general TP and TP for vol. I. [ZSL.

(2) 2nd ed. vols I, III–VI 1772; vol. II 1771. Pr f C & N. Price 3s sewed each vol.; the 6 vols 18s sewed, £1 in the vell. manner, £1 4s calf, lettered. Lisney 252 etc. [BM(NH); BM (vols V, VI); Wellcome (vols I, IV, V); ZSL (vols II–VI); Lisney; Weedon (vol. III); Roscoe.

(3) 3rd ed. 1782–91. Price 1 gn sewed, £1 3s in the vell. manner, £1 6s calf lettered. Only vol. II of this ed. seen.

(a) Vol. I (1st issue), 1790. Pr f Power & Co. Lisney 253. Sheets of the 1766 ed. with new TPs. [Lisney; RMO.

(b) Vol. I (2nd issue), 1790. Pr f Power & Co. Lisney 254. Type reset. Collates as for vol. I of 2nd ed. [MB.

(c) Vol. II, 1782. Pr f TC. Lisney 257. [BM(NH); MB.

(d) Vols III, IV and V, 1790. Pr f Power & Co. Lisney 260 etc. [MB; RMO.

(e) Vol. VI, 1791. Pr f Power & Co. Lisney 269. [RMO.

A62. BROOKES, Richard, M.D. and Joseph COLLYER. DICTIONARY OF THE WORLD; OR, GEOGRAPHICAL DESCRIPTION OF THE EARTH. The geographical pt by Brookes, the historical and biographical by Collyer.

(1) An ed. of 1772. Pr f C & N. 2 vols. Originally issued in pts, 3 sheets demy for 6d or 12 for 2s. In 1775 the price for the complete work was 2 vols, calf, 3 gns or in the vell. manner £2. 17s; or 2 vols in one, calf £2. 18s, in the vell. manner.

(2) Listed in A401(5), 1787, as pr f TC. Prices as for no. (1) for the complete work.

A63. BROWN, John, D.D. (of Newcastle-upon-Tyne). POLITICAL LOGIC DISPLAYED; OR, A KEY TO THE THOUGHTS ON CIVIL LIBERTY, LICENTIOUSNESS, AND FACTION. FN(N), The Crown, in PNR. Adv. *LC* 16–18.7.65, p. 62 as t.d.w.p. Price 1s 6d. See H&L, quoting *Bib. Lind.* III, col. 7194. Not located.

A64. Entry deleted.

A65. BROWNE, Thomas. UNION DICTIONARY, THE, 1800. Pr f EN et al. Price 8s. Alston, V, 349. [BM; NLWa; GOB.

A66. BRUCKSHAW, Samuel. ONE MORE PROOF OF THE... ABUSE OF A PRIVATE MADHOUSE. Adv. *LC* 8–10.2.74, p. 139, as pr f a s b 'Mr. Newberry, the Corner of Ludgate Street' et al. The imprint in the BM copy is 'Pr f the Author and s b him'.

A67. Entry deleted.

A68. BUILDER'S MAGAZINE, THE.
(1) 1st ed. 1774–[1778]. S b FN(N). Price 1s each monthly pt (15 pts). The 185 engvd plates are bd in at the end and have publicn dates up to 1 Oct. 1778. *BUCOP*, I, 441; *CBEL*, II, 679. [BM; Bodley; LUL; EdUL.
(2) 2nd ed. 1779. Pr f FN(N). Price 1s each pt. Plates bd in as in no. (1). [RIBA.
(3) A 'new ed.', 1788. EN. No. 1 adv. *LC* 26–8.8.88, p. 205, price 1s. [Sotheby, 21.10.68, lot 4173.
(4) A 'new ed.', 1800. Pr f EN et al. Price £2 5s half bd and lettered. (Communicated.) [ViU; Sotheby, 28.3.66, lot 1568.

A69. BURTON, John. ATTEMPT TOWARDS THE EULOGIUM OF CONYERS MIDDLETON, [1750]. Pr f TC. Price 6d. Listed *LM* Aug. 1750. [Bodley.

A70. BYNG, Hon. John, Admiral. TRIAL OF…TAKEN BY CHARLES FEARNE.
(1) An ed. of 1757. Pr f JN et al. Price 6s. The concluding leaves numbered 1–10, 9–19 form the Appendix and may have been issued separately. [BM; NMM; CUL; LGL.
(2) Adv. *LC* 11–13.2.79, p. 151, as to be had of C & N. Price 5s. Probably an attempt to sell off stock of no. (1).

A71. BYRON, Hon. John, Vice-Admiral. VOYAGE ROUND THE WORLD, IN H.M.'s SHIP THE DOLPHIN.
(1) 1st ed. 1767. Pr f JN and FN(N). Price 3s 6d sewed. Welsh 180–1; *CBEL*, II, 741; Sabin 9732. [Bodley; NMM; AdE; Roscoe; NLA.
(2) 2nd ed. 1767. Pr f JN and FN(N). Price 3s 6d for the 8vo size, 1s 6d for the 18mo. This ed. still listed in 1788, in A222(17), 20 years after the 3rd ed. The work was also reprinted in Hawkesworth's *Voyages*, 1773. [Bodley; LL; NLA.
(3) 3rd ed. Adv. *LC* 9–11.6.68, p. 555, as pr f N & C at the price of no. (2). In view of no. (2) being adv. in 1788 this 3rd ed. is suspect.

A72. CAMPBELL, John. LIVES OF THE ADMIRALS, 3rd ed. 1761. Pr f JN et al. Price 6d each monthly pt; 1 gn in bds (also £1 4s) for the complete work. 4 vols. Welsh 182; *CBEL*, II, 879. [BM.

A73. CANDID REMARKS ON SOME PARTICULAR PARTS OF MR. WHITFIELD'S SERMONS. JN. Price 1s. Listed *LM* July 1752.

A74. CANDIDUS, Agricola (pseud.). THE HIGH MASS. A POEM. Adv. as by JN in 6th issue of *Mercurius Latinus*, 19.4.76. Price 6*d*. Only name of J. Hart in imprint. Welsh 169. [BM, in Burney 416B.

A75. CARNAN, Thomas. MEMORIAL to the House of Commons, 1781. The memorial protesting against the increase in stamp duty on sheet almanacks, which had been engineered by the Stationers' Co. See Introduction, pp. 23–4. [BM.

A76. CARTER, Susannah. THE FRUGAL HOUSEWIFE.
(1) An ed. pr f FN(N) adv. *LC* 10–13.11.70, p. 461. Price 1*s*. ? Welsh 182.
(2) 2nd ed. adv. *LC* 14–17.9.71, p. 271, as pr f FN(N). Price 1*s*.
(3) A 'new ed.' adv. *LC* 31.12.78–2.1.79, p. 4, as pr f FN(N). Price 1*s*.
(3A) An ed. adv. *LC* 2–5.10.84, p. 333, as pr f EN. Price 1*s*.
(4) An ed. of 1795. Pr f EN. A. W. Oxford, p. 122. [Wellcome; BM (destroyed).
(5) An undated ed. pr f EN. Price 1*s* (see Plate 24). ? = ed. adv. *LC* 23–5.12.1800, p. 615. [BM.

A77. CAVILLER DETECTED, THE. JN. Price 6*d*. Listed *LM* June 1750. Welsh 298 misreads *The Cavalier detected*.

A78. Entry deleted.

A79. CERTAIN ANCIENT TRACTS CONCERNING THE MANAGEMENT OF LANDED PROPERTY. Comprises *Surveyinge*, attrib. to Sir Anthony Fitzherbert, Xenophon's *Treatise of Householde* and the *Boke of Husbandry*, attributed to Fitzherbert. The order of the pts varies in different copies. See *CBEL*, I, 809 and 845.
(1) Ed. 1767. Pr f JN et al. Price 4*s* 6*d* calf. Welsh 296. [BM; Bodley; CUL; LUL; UCL; LL; Wellcome; AdE.
(2) Listed as pubd b N & C in A640(3), vol. XVIII, 1778.
(3) Listed as pr f TC in A401(5), 1787.

A80. CERVANTES. DON QUIXOTE (Smollett's trans.). 5th ed. 1782. Pr f EN et al. Price 12*s*, 4 vols. [BM; Bodley.

A80A. CHAPPELL, Richard. THE UNIVERSAL ARITHMETIC, 1798. S b EN et al. Price 2*s* 6*d*. [BM.

A81. CHRISTIAN PILGRIM, THE. PART FIRST. Pr f FN(N). Price 6*d*. CHRISTIAN PILGRIM, THE. PART SECOND. Pr f FN(N). Price 6*d*. Both adv. *LC* 31.12.78–2.1.79, p. 4.

A82. CHRISTIAN'S MAGAZINE, THE, 1760–7 (ed. by Dr Dodd). Pr f JN and J. Coote. Welsh 201–4 and 351–5; *CBEL*, II, 678; *BUCOP*, I, 563.

Issued monthly at 6*d*. The BM set consists of vols I–VII (May 1760–Dec. 1766; Jan. 1767). Issues for March, April, May 1767 and a *Supplement* to 'the eighth volume' adv. *LC* 3.1.68–2.2.68. (See Plate 25.) [BM; DWL (incomplete).

CHRISTIAN'S NEW-YEAR'S GIFT. See J56, but probably not a Juvenile.

A83. CLAPARÈDE, David. CONSIDERATIONS UPON THE MIRACLES OF THE GOSPEL, 1767. Pr f JN and FN(N). Price 2*s* 6*d*. [BM.

A84. CLERMONT, B. THE PROFESSED COOK, 3rd ed. 1776. Pr f FN(N) et al. Price 6*s*. A. W. Oxford, p. 101.

A85. COAL-HEAVERS, THE, 1774. Pr a s b C & N. Price 1*s*. [BM.

A86. COBDEN, Edward. THE PARABLE OF THE TALENTS. A SERMON, [1748]. Pr a s b J. Newberry [*sic*] et al. Price 6*d*. [BM; CUL.

A87. COLMAN, George (the elder). JEALOUS WIFE, THE. Welsh 192; *CBEL*, II, 451; Nicoll 245.
(1) 1st ed. 1761. Pr f JN et al. Price 1*s* 6*d*. [BM; Bodley; CUL; DNS.
(2) 2nd ed. 1761. Pr f JN et al. Price 1*s* 6*d*. [BM; CUL; Bodley.
(3) 3rd ed. 1763. Pr f JN et al. [BM; Bodley.
(4) 4th ed. n.d. ([1764] *per CBEL*). Pr f JN et al. [BM; Bodley; Rylands; DNS.

A87A. COLMAN, George (the elder), and Bonnell THORNTON. THE CONNOISSEUR, 6th ed. 1774. Pr f FN(S) et al. Price 10*s* sewed, 4 vols. *CBEL*, II, 452. [BM; Bodley; CUL.

A88. COLSON, Gilles (pseud. Abbé Bellecourt). THE ACADEMY OF PLAY, n.d. Pr f FN(N). Adv. *LC* 3–5.3.68 as t.d.w.p. Price 3*s*. Welsh 173. [BM; Bodley.

A89. Entry deleted.

A90. COMPLETE ENGLISH FARMER, THE, 1771. Pr f FN(N). Price 5*s* 6*d* in bds, also 6*s*. G. E. Fussell, pp. 95–6. Frequently attrib. to David Henry. [CUL; Roscoe.

A91. COMPLETE LIST, A, OF ALL THE FAIRS IN ENGLAND AND WALES, 1781. Pr f TC. Price 6*d*. Also sold bd up with an ed. of Paterson's *Roads*. Welsh 216; Fordham I, 337. [BM; Weedon.

A92. COMPLEAT SPORTING TABLE, A. Price 1*s*. Pr f JN et al. Adv. *Country Journal: or, The Craftsman*, 2 June 1744. Welsh's note, p. 313, is incorrect.

A93. COMPLEAT TITHING TABLE, A, WHEREIN ALL THINGS TITHABLE ARE SHEWN AT ONE VIEW. Adv. *Country Journal: or, The Craftsman*, 2 June 1744, as pr f JN at Reading et al. Price 1*s*. Welsh 313, 318.

A94. CONDUCT OF A RT. HON. GENTLEMAN IN RESIGNING THE SEALS OF OFFICE...
(1) 1st ed. 1761. Pr f JN. Price 1*s* 6*d*. Welsh 270; Rothschild 155. [BM; Bodley; CUL.
(2) 2nd ed. 1761. Pr f JN. Price 1*s* 6*d*. [BM; Bodley; LUL; LL.

A95. CONSIDERATIONS ON THE USE AND PROPERTIES OF MR. TIDD'S AEOLUS, [1754]. Adv. *PA* 12.12.54 as to be pubd on Saturday next, price 4*d*, pr a s b 'Mr Newbery' et al. Later listed as 'Mr Tid's Eolus'. This was a 'portable machine for exchanging and refreshing the air of rooms, and bringing the same to any degree of temperature that shall be most agreeable'.

A96. COOPER, Rev Edward, of Droitwich. THE ELBOW-CHAIR, 1765. Pr f FN(N). Price 1*s* 6*d*. [BM.

A97. COPPER-PLATE MUSEUM, THE, 1775. Pr f A. Hamilton, nr St John's Gate, s b FN(N). Price 1*s* 6*d* each pt. Apparently unrecorded. Pt I adv. *LC* 31.1.75–2.2.75, pt II 4–7.3.75, pt III 1–4.4.75, pt IV 29.4.75–2.5.75. Only these 4 issues recorded.

A97A. CORRESPONDANCE HISTORIQUE, OU DÉVELOPMENT ABRÉGÉ DE L'HISTOIRE UNIVERSELLE. EN FORME DE LETTRES, 1797. Chez 'Newbery' et al. The dedication is sgd 'Le Pointe'. Cameron & Carroll, no. 343. [NLA.

A98. COSTARD, George. HISTORY OF ASTRONOMY.
(1) An ed. of 1767. S b JN. Price 10*s* 6*d* half-bd. Welsh 195–6. [BM; Bodley; CUL; LUL; UCL; EdUL; CSJC; CKC; Bristol; NLSc; RS; RAS; DNS.
(2) Adv. *LC* 6–8.12.70, p. 551, as pr f C & N. Price 10*s* 6*d* in the vell. manner.
(3) Adv. as pr f TC in *Universal Magazine*, Jan. 1775, price 10*s* 6*d* in the vell. manner.
(4) Adv. as pr f TC in J147(9), 1786, price as for no. (3).

A99. COUNTRY VICAR, A. THE HARD CASE OF A COUNTRY VICAR, IN RESPECT OF SMALL TYTHES. Pr f W. Crutwell in Sherborne; s b FN(N). Price 1*s*. Adv. *LC* 31.5.77–3.6.77, p. 527.

A100. COWLEY, Hannah. THE RUNAWAY. A COMEDY. Welsh 303; *CBEL*, II, 463; Nicoll 248.
(1) 1st ed. 1776. S b C & N et al. [BM; Bodley; CUL; LUL; Rylands; EdUL; AdE.
(2) 2nd ed. 1776. S b C & N et al. Price 1s 6d. The sheets of no. (1) with a new title-leaf. [BM; Bodley.

A101. COWLEY, Hannah. WHO'S THE DUPE? A FARCE. *CBEL*, II, 463; Nicoll 248.
(1) 1st ed. 1779. Pr f C & N et al. [BM; Bodley; CUL.
(2) 2nd ed. 1779. Pr f C & N et al. Price 1s. [BM; Bodley.

A102. CUNNINGHAM, Timothy. LAW OF BILLS OF EXCHANGE, 6th ed. 1778. Adv. *LC* 6–9.6.78, p. 547, price 7s, as pr f FN* et al., but his name not in the imprint.

A103. CURIOSITIES OF LONDON AND WESTMINSTER DESCRIBED, THE. Listed at 2s 6d in A172(2), 1765, and in J69(4), 1769. This seems to be David Henry's *Historical Account of the Curiosities...* (A219) which sold at 2s 6d, not the 4-vol. work (J88) which sold at 2s, and was probably first pubd in 1770.

A104. CURIOUS COLLECTION OF VOYAGES AND TRAVELS, SELECTED FROM THE WRITERS OF ALL NATIONS. This is the sub-title to A640, often used in bk-lists.

A105. CURSORY OBSERVATIONS UPON DR PRICE'S ESSAY ON CIVIL LIBERTY, 1776. Pr f TC. Price 6d. Welsh 255. [BM; EdUL.

A106. DAWSON, Benjamin. ANSWER TO A BOOK, ENTITULED LETTERS..., 1768. Pr f FN(N). Price 1s. Forms pt 1 of A107. [BM.

A107. DAWSON, Benjamin. ANSWER, AN, TO LETTERS CONCERNING ESTABLISHED CONFESSIONS OF FAITH, 1769. Pr f FN(N) et al. Consists of A106, A108 and A109 bd as one, with a general TP and half-title. [BM; AdE.

A108. DAWSON, Benjamin. SCRIPTURAL RIGHT, THE, OF ESTABLISHING...CONFESSIONS OF FAITH, 1769. Pr f F. Newberry (*sic*) (N). Forms pt II of A107. [BM.

A109. DAWSON, Benjamin. UTILITY OF ESTABLISHING... CONFESSIONS OF FAITH, 1769. Pr f FN(N). Price 1s 6d. Forms pt III of A107. [BM.

A110. DAWSON, Thomas, D.D. MEMOIRS OF ST GEORGE, THE ENGLISH PATRON. Welsh 197, who quotes 'F. Newbery's List, about 1769', price 3s. The only ed. I have traced is that of 1714.

A111. DEFENCE OF THE AUTHOR OF THE WHOLE DUTY OF MAN, 1740. Pr b JN et al. Price 6d. K. G. Burton, *Early Newspaper Press in Berkshire, 1723–1855*, p. 105 (Reading, 1954, thesis). Legg, no. 12. [Bodley.

A112. DESCRIPTION OF ENGLAND AND WALES, A.
(1) 1st ed. 1769–70. Pr f N & C. 10 vols. Prices 6d each weekly pt, 3s 6d each vol. sewed, £2 and £1 15s for the set. Welsh 210; Higgs 4794. Vols I–VIII dated 1769, vols IX, X 1770. [BM; Bodley; LUL (*ex* vol. I); Wellcome; Weedon (*ex* vol. I); Roscoe (*ex* vol. I).
(2) *LC* for 10–12.1.71, p. 43, announced that the work was being repubd by N & C in weekly pts at 6d, the vols of 6 pts at 3s 3d sewed.
(3) 2nd ed. 1775. Pr f C & N. Apparently confined to vol. I. [Roscoe; LUL; Weedon.
(4) Listed in A399(5), 1781, and (7), 1786, as pr f TC, and in A399(8), 1789, as pr f F. Power & Co. Prices for the set as before. Probably old stock.

A113. DESTRUCTION OF TRADE, THE, AND THE RUIN OF THE METROPOLIS PROGNOSTICATED FROM A TOTAL INATTENTION TO THE CONSERVANCY OF THE RIVER THAMES, 1770. FN*. Price 1s. Listed in *LM* May 1770, p. 267. [LGL (destroyed).

A114. DICEY, Thomas. HISTORICAL ACCOUNT OF GUERNSEY, 1751. S b JN. Price 3s. Welsh 197.
(1) An issue with 130 leaves, the last a blank. Pp. xxiv+1–12, [19]–220. [BM (large paper); Bodley; LUL (large and ordinary paper); LL (ordinary); ? Rylands.
(2) An issue with 2 additional leaves, numbered 1–4, following the TP, comprising an Address to the King. Thick paper. [BM; LGL; ? Rylands; ? AdE.

A115. DICTIONARY EXPLAINING THE MOST DIFFICULT TERMS...IN FORTIFICATION, 1745. JN. Price 1s. Adv. *Mercurius Latinus* 12.4.45. Also forms pp. 275–310 of A157. Welsh 222.

A116. DICTIONARY OF THE BIBLE. See (1) Alexander Macbean's *Dictionary of the Bible, historical and geographical*, 1779 (no. A312), price 6s; and (2) no. A117, various edd. at 2s 6d. Welsh, p. 174.

A117. DICTIONARY OF THE BIBLE, A; OR, AN EXPLANATION OF THE PROPER NAMES AND DIFFICULT WORDS USED IN THE OLD AND NEW TESTAMENT.

(1) An ed. of 1766. Pr f the Author, s b JN. Price 2*s* 6*d*. Welsh 174.
(2) An ed. of 1777. C & N. Welsh 174. Probably the 2nd ed. which was adv. *LC*
28–31.3.78, p. 309, price 2*s* 6*d*. Not seen. ⌈EdUL.

A118. DIMSDALE, Thomas, Baron. DESCRIPTION, A, OF THE
METHOD FOR...INOCULATION. Adv. *LC* 21–3.5.76 as pr f C & N
et al. It also forms pp. 1–18 of A121.

A119. DIMSDALE, Thomas, Baron. OBSERVATIONS ON THE
INTRODUCTION TO THE PLAN OF THE DISPENSARY
FOR GENERAL INOCULATION, 1778. Pr f C & N et al. Price 2*s*.
Welsh 201. ⌈BM; Bodley; RCP; EdUL.

A120. DIMSDALE, Thomas, Baron. PRESENT METHOD OF
INOCULATION, THE, 7th ed. 1779. S b C & N et al. Price 2*s* 6*d*. ⌈Well-
come; RCS.

A121. DIMSDALE, Thomas, Baron. THOUGHTS ON GENERAL
AND IMPARTIAL INOCULATIONS, 1776. Pr f C & N et al. Price 1*s*
6*d*. Welsh 201. ⌈BM; Bodley; RCS; RCP; EdUL; AdE.

A122. DIMSDALE, Thomas, Baron. TRACTS, ON INOCULATION,
1781. Pr f C & N et al. Price 3*s* in bds. ⌈BM; Wellcome; RCS; RCP; EdUL.

A123. DIONYSIUS HALICARNASSENSIS. ROMAN
ANTIQUITIES, 1758. No names in TP imprint, but adv. *LC* 11–13.3.60 as s
b JN et al. 4 vols. Price £3 12*s* 6*d* bd. ⌈BM; Bodley; LUL; Rylands; UCL;
EdUL; AdE.

A124. DISSERTATION ON THE KING'S EVIL, A.
(1) 1st ed. 1763. Pr f JN. Price 6*d*. ⌈BM; Schuman.
(2) 2nd ed. Pr f JN. Adv. *LC* 8–10.11.64. Price 6*d*. Welsh 248.

A125. DODD, William. ACCOUNT OF THE...MAGDALEN
CHARITY.
(1) 1st ed. 1761. S b JN et al. Price 3*s* sewed in blue paper. *CBEL*, II, 359. ⌈BM;
Bodley; LUL; LL; UCL.
(2) 2nd ed. 1763. S b JN et al. Price 3*s* sewed. ⌈Bodley.
(3) 3rd ed. 1766. S b JN et al. ⌈Bodley; LUL.

A126. DODD, Wm. POEMS, 1767. Adv. *LC* 6–8.10.67, p. 340, as pr f JN and
FN(N) et al. Price 4*s* 3*d* sewed, 5*s* bd. The only copy seen (Bodley) was by
Dryden Leach. Welsh 204.

A127. DODD, Wm. REFLECTIONS ON DEATH.
(1) 1st ed. 1763. Pr f J. Newberry (*sic*). Price 3*s* bd calf. Welsh 206. [Bodley; CUL.
(2) An ed. adv. *LC* 1–3.1.65, p. 15, as pr f JN, price 1*s*. ? error in the price.
(3) 2nd ed. 1765. Pr f JN. Price 2*s* 6*d*. Welsh 206. [BM.
(4) 3rd ed. 1769. Pr f C & N. Price 2*s*. 'Those who buy six will have a seventh gratis'. [BM.
(5) 4th ed. 1772. Pr f C & N. Price 2*s*. [BM; Bodley.
(6) An ed. of 1777. Pr f C & N. Price 2*s* in the vell. manner. Welsh 206. [BM; EdUL; AdE.
(7) An ed. of 1787. Pr f TC. [BM; Bodley.

A128. DODD, Wm. SERMON ON JOB, CHAP. XXIX, VER. 11–13, [1762]. S b JN et al. [BM; Bodley; CUL.

A129. DODD, Wm. SERMON. S b JN. Adv. *LC* 2–4.8.63, p. 115, as *The Rev. Mr Dodd's first Sermon before the President and Governors of the Magdalen House.* Price 6*d*, or 'a quarter of an hundred' for 10*s* 6*d*. Probably a reprint of a sermon preached on 26 April 1759 (BM, 1388.k.1(3)).

A130. DODD, Wm. SERMON ON ZECHARIAH, iv, 7, [1769]. S b FN(N). [Bodley.

A131. DODD, Wm. TRUTH OF THE CHRISTIAN RELIGION VINDICATED, THE.
(1) An ed. of 1765. Pr f JN. Price 5*s* calf; monthly numbers 6*d* each. Welsh 185. [Lambeth.
(2) Adv. as to be had of C & N in *LC* 18–20.1.74, p. 67. Price 5*s*.

DODD, Wm. See also A82, A360, A34(1–4), J94.

A132. DRELINCOURT, Charles. THE CHRISTIAN'S DEFENCE.
(1) 21st ed. 1776. Pr f FN* et al. [BM.
(2) A new ed. adv. *LC* 10–12.12.99, p. 564, as pr f EN et al. Price 6*s*.

A133. Entry deleted.

DU FRESNOY. See LENGLET DU FRESNOY.

A134. DU HALDE, Jean Baptiste. DESCRIPTION OF THE EMPIRE OF CHINA AND CHINESE-TARTARY. English trans. 1738–41. Adv. *LC* 27–9.4.69 as pr f FN(N), 2 vols, fo. 3 gns bd. ? a remainder lot bought up by FN.

A135. DU MARTRE, Antoine Pyron (pseud. Marc Antoine Porny).
ELEMENTS OF HERALDRY. Welsh 288–9.

(1) 1st ed. 1765. Pr f JN. Price 6s. [BM; Bodley; CUL; EdUL.
(2) 2nd ed. 1771. Pr f C & N. Price 6s. Moule no. DCXXVI. [BM; Bodley; EdUL.
(3) 3rd ed. 1777. Pr f C & N. Price 6s. [BM; Bodley; CUL; EdUL; LL.
(4) 4th ed. 1787. Pr f TC. Price 6s. [BM; Bodley; LUL; EdUL.

A136. DUNCAN, John. THE CONDEMNATION PRONOUNCED
...A SERMON..., [1769 or 1770]. (Preached 14.9.69.) Adv. *LC* 22–4.2.70, p.
189. S b C & N et al. Price 6d. Legg, no. 53. [BM.

A137. DYCHE, Rev. Thomas. NEW GENERAL ENGLISH
DICTIONARY.
(1) 14th ed. 1771. Pr f FN* et al. Price 6s. Alston, v, 159. [BM; Bodley; CUL;
UCL; MB; Madison; HAN; NBuG; OB.
(2) 15th ed. not traced.
(3) 16th ed. 1777. Pr f FN* et al. Price 6s. Alston, v, 160. [BM; NUTU; WRPL;
DLC; MH; DTPL; ITH.
(4) 17th ed. 1794. Pr f EN et al. Price 7s. Alston, v, 162. [Bodley; NOUL; SPT;
MH; DLC; CLU; CVh; PPL; PU; CtY; CHH.

A138. Entry deleted.

A139. ELMER (or ELMORE), J. (of Farnham, Surrey). TABLES OF
WEIGHTS AND PRICES.
(1) An ed. of 1758. S b JN. Price 2s 6d. Welsh 208–9. [BM; Bodley.
(2) Frequently listed or adv. as s b or pr f C & N 1768–78. Price 2s 6d.
(3) Listed as pr f TC in no. A91, 1781, price 2s 6d.

A140. ELPHINSTON, James. ANALYSIS OF THE FRENCH AND
ENGLISH LANGUAGES, THE, 1756. S b JN et al. Price 6s, 2 vols. [BM.

A141. ELPHINSTON, James. EDUCATION, IN FOUR BOOKS.
Adv. *LC* 27–9.1.63, p. 103, as s b JN et al. JN's name not in the TP imprint.

A142. ENGLAND DISPLAYED. Welsh 210–11. The *PL* for 12.8.61 (p.
765) and *LC* for 27–9.8.61 (p. 207) contained proposals for *England Displayed, or
a Geographical, Historiographical...and Poetical Description of this Kingdom,* to
be pubd in pts by JN, to appear monthly, 18 pence each vol. The advert. says that
'The whole of the copy is prepared for the Press...but he [JN] is obliged to
postpone the publication for the present...', because a number of contributors
had failed to produce their copy. I suggest this may have taken shape as no. A112,
1769–70.

A143. EPIGRAMS FRESHLY GATHER'D FROM THE
CONVERSATION OF THE POLITE AND INGENIOUS; OR,

GLEAN'D FROM THE MOST SPRIGHTLY AUTHORS, 1751. JN. Welsh 213.

A144. EPISTLE, AN, TO THE BISHOP OF LONDON OCCASIONED BY HIS LORDSHIP'S LETTER...ON THE SUBJECT OF THE TWO LATE EARTHQUAKES..., 1750. JN. Listed *GM* May 1750, p. 240. Price 6*d*. The letter from the Bishop (Thos Sherlock) was dated 1750 (*CBEL*, II, 853).

A145. ESSAY, AN, CONCERNING THE NATURE, ORIGIN, AND PROGRESS OF THE HUMAN AFFECTIONS, TENDING TO SHOW THEY ARE NOT INNATE BUT ACQUIRED. Pr f C & N. Price 3*s* sewed. Listed in A61(2), vol. IV, 1772.

A146. ESSEX. NEW AND COMPLETE HISTORY OF ESSEX, A, 1769–72. S b FN(N) et al. 6 vols. Issued in fortnightly pts at 6*d*, 36 pts. Vols I and III 1770; vol. II 1769; vol. IV 1771; vols V and VI 1772. Preface to vol. I sgd b Peter Muilman, F.S.A. [BM; Bodley; CUL; LL.

A147. Entry deleted.

A148. FALCONER, William. OBSERVATIONS ON DR. CADOGAN'S DISSERTATION ON THE GOUT.
(1) 1st ed. 1771 or 1772. Pr f FN(N) et al. [Wellcome; Bodley; CUL; RCS; EdUL.
(2) 2nd ed. 1772. S b FN(N) et al. Price 1*s* 6*d*. [BM; RCS; RCP; EdUL; Wellcome; CUL; LUL.
(3) 3rd ed. 1772. S b FN(N) et al. Price 1*s* 6*d*. [BM; Bodley; EdUL; RCP.

A149. FARMER'S LAWYER, THE.
(1) 1st ed. 1774. S b F. Newbury (*sic*) (N) et al. Price 3*s* 6*d*. [BM; Bodley.
(2) 2nd ed. ('A new ed. greatly enlarged'). S b FN(N) et al. Adv. *LC* 2–5.7.74, p. 15. Price 3*s* 6*d*.
(3) 3rd ed. S b FN(N) et al. Adv. *LC* 24–6.2.78, p. 197. Price 3*s* 6*d*.

A150. FAVART, Charles Simon. THE REAPERS, 1770. Pr f TC. Price 1*s* 6*d*. Nicoll 121 and 341. *CBEL*, II, 780. [BM; LUL.

A151. FAWKES, Francis. DESCRIPTION OF WINTER, A, 1754. Pr f J. Newberry (*sic*) et al. Welsh 217; *CBEL*, II, 361 and 914. [BM; LUL; NLA.

A152. FAWKES, Francis. ORIGINAL POEMS AND TRANSLATIONS, 1761. S b JN et al. Price 5*s*. Welsh 217; *CBEL*, II, 361 and 762. Large and thick paper copies were issued. [BM (large and ordinary); Bodley; CUL; AdE; Roscoe (ordinary); LL; DNS.

A153. FENELON, Francois de Salignac de la Mothe. TELEMAQUE. For the abridged edd. see J113.

(1) AVANTURES DE TELEMAQUE...SOIGNEUSEMENT CORRIGEE PAR J. PERRIN. Adv. *LC* 7–9.6.87, p. 549, as 'Londres: Chez...E. Newbery'. Price 3*s* 6*d*.

(2) ADVENTURES OF TELEMACHUS (Hawkesworth's trans.). *LC* 19–21.5.68, p. 485, announced an ed. ready for delivery on 30th of that month by FN(N), N & C et al. Welsh 217.

(3) ADVENTURES OF TELEMACHUS (trans. b Mr Des Maizeaux), 7th ed. 1779. Pr f FN* et al. Price 3*s*. [BM.

(4) 'Boyer's Telemachus' listed as pr f EN in A378, 1781. Price 6*s*.

A154. FENN, Lady Ellenor. SOME HINTS TO YOUNG WOMEN ENGAGED IN REARING INFANTS, 1799. Pr f EN. Price 2*s*. (Communicated.) [Pollard.

A155. FENTON, Richard. ODE ADDRESSED TO THE SAVOIR VIVRE CLUB, 1773 or before. Pr f FN(N). Price 1*s*. Listed in *Town and Country Mag.* 1773, p. 266. [BM.

A156. FERIÆ POETICÆ...REDDITA A SAM. BISHOP, 1766. S b JN et al. Price 10*s* 6*d*. Welsh 174; *CBEL*, II, 224. [BM; Bodley.

A157. FLANDERS DELINEATED, 1745. Price 3*s* 6*d*; in 12 weekly pts of 2 sheets each at 3*d*. Welsh 220–1.

(1) The London Imprint. Pr f J. Robinson and JN. [BM; CUL; AdE.

(2) The Reading Imprint. Pr f JN and C. Micklewright. [BM; Bodley.

(3) Adv. *GA* 11.5.48 as pr f J. Robinson, price 2*s* 6*d*.

A158. FOOD FOR POETS, A POEM, 1775. S b FN(N). Price 1*s*. [Bodley.

A159. FOOTE, Samuel. THE BANKRUPT, 1776. Adv. *LC* 23–5.5.76 as pr f FN* et al. His name not in imprint. *CBEL*, II, 450.

A160. FOR EVER! A POEM, [1768]. Pr f FN(N). Price 1*s*. Noticed in *LM* June 1768, p. 334, as 'a piece of poetical infanity (*sic*) on the times'. 8 leaves. Pp. 3–13. Half-title. (Communicated.) [UCLA, 25·8 cm.

A161. FOREIGN ESSAYS ON AGRICULTURE AND THE ARTS. Listed in A640(3), vol. IV, 1768, as pr f a s b N & C, but their names not in the imprint of the only ed. seen, dated 1765.

A162. FORM OF PRAYER TO BE USED ON THE GENERAL FAST DAY, 1781 or before. ? TC. The *Annual Register* for 1781 (p. 177) reported an action by Eyre and Strahan in the Court of Exchequer against TC for printing a Form of Prayer for a General Fast Day. The Court found in favour of Eyre & Co as having the sole right to print such a Prayer. Bodley has a set of these (Gough Pamph. 1519) in which no. 23 has no printer or publisher's name, in very rough chap-book form. The other prayers are in the best official form. It is very unlikely that this no. 23 was the subject of the litigation, but not impossible.

A163. FORMEY, Jean Henri Samuel. CONCISE HISTORY OF PHILOSOPHY AND PHILOSOPHERS.
(1) 1st English ed. 1766. Pr f FN(N). Price 2s 6d and 3s. Welsh 222 and 228; IAW 138–9; *CBEL*, II, 642 and 781; Scott 195–6. [BM; Bodley; LUL; LL; Wellcome; AdE.
(2) Ed. 1769. FN (probably S). Welsh 228.
(3) Listed in A640(3), vol. x, 1773 as pr f C & N. Price 3s.
(4) Listed in J113(4), 1781, as pr f TC. Price 3s.

A164. FORMEY, Jean Henri Samuel. ECCLESIASTICAL HISTORY. Also listed as *New Eccles. Hist.*
(1) Ed. 1766. Pr f JN et al. Price 9s, 2 vols. Welsh 222; *CBEL*, II, 781. [BM; Bodley; CUL; EdUL; AdE.
(2) An ed. adv. *LC* 26–8.8.73, p. 203, as to be had of C & N, 2 vols in one, price 7s in the vell. manner. ? a sale of old stock at reduced price.

A165. FORMEY, Jean Henri Samuel. ELEMENTARY PRINCIPLES OF THE BELLES LETTRES.
(1) Ed. 1766. Pr f FN(N). Price 2s 6d sewed, 3s bd. *CBEL*, II, 781. [BM; Bodley.
(2) Listed in J113(4), 1781, as pr f TC. Price 3s.

A166. FOTHERGILL, Samuel. PRAYER OF AGUR, THE, [1768]. S b N & C et al. Price 1s. Joseph Smith, *Descriptive Cat. of Friends' Books*, 1867, I, 637. [BM; Bodley; Friends.

A167. FOTHERGILL, Samuel. TWO DISCOURSES AND A PRAYER. Joseph Smith, *Descriptive Cat. of Friends' Books*, 1867, I, 636–7.
(1) 5th ed. [1767 or 1768]. S b 'Newbery' [? FN(S)] et al. Price 1s. [Friends.
(2) 6th ed. [1768]. S b 'Newbery' [? FN(S)] et al. [BM; Friends.

A168. FRANCIS, John, M.A. LIFE OF DAVID. Listed in A241(3), 1770, vol. I, as pr f C & N. Price 2s 6d. ? = A169.

A169. FRANCIS, John, M.A. REFLECTIONS ON THE MORAL AND RELIGIOUS CHARACTER OF DAVID.
(1) Ed. 1764. Pr f JN. Price 2s 6d sewed. Welsh 222–3. [BM; Bodley; CUL; LUL.

(2) Adv. *LC* 18–20.1.74 as to be had of C & N. Price 2*s* 6*d*.

(3) 'In Carnan's List, 1789' (Welsh 223). Possible, but TC had died in July 1788.

A170. FRANKLIN, Benjamin. EXPERIMENTS AND OBSERVATIONS ON ELECTRICITY. P. L. Ford, *Franklin Bibliography*, Brooklyn, N.Y., 1889.

(1) Ed. 1769. S b FN(N). Price 10*s* 6*d*. Ford 307. [BM; Bodley; CUL; EdUL; LScM; UCL.

(2) 5th ed. 1774. Pr f FN(N). Price 10*s* 6*d* in bds. Welsh 223; Ford 318; Sabin 25506. [BM; CUL; AdE.

A171. FRUITLESS REPENTANCE, THE; OR, THE HISTORY OF KITTY LEFEVRE, 1769. Pr f FN(N). Price, 2 vols, 6*s*, 5*s* sewed, also 3*s*. Welsh 223; *CBEL*, II, 547.

A172. G., T. A DESCRIPTION OF THE ISLE OF THANET.

(1) 1st ed. 1763. Pr f JN et al. Price 1*s*. [Kent; Bodley; LUL.

(2) 2nd ed. 1765. Pr f JN et al. Price 1*s* (see Plate 26). Welsh 261–2 and 316. [BM; Roscoe.

A173. GARRICK, David. THE GUARDIAN. Welsh 234; Nicoll 262; *CBEL*, II, 445.

(1) 1st ed. 1759. Pr f JN. Price 1*s*. [BM; Bodley; CUL; AdE.

(2) 2nd ed. 1759. Pr f JN. Price 1*s*. [Bodley.

(3) 3rd ed. 1767. Pr f JN. Price 1*s*. [Bodley.

(4) 4th ed. 1773. Pr f C & N. Price 1*s*. Rothschild 900. [BM; Bodley; CUL; UCL.

(5) 5th ed. 1788. TC. [Colin Richardson, Cat. 115 [1960] item 1104, not seen.

A174. GAY, John. BEGGAR'S OPERA, THE. Pr f TC et al. Price 6*d*. Adv. *LC* 7–10.9.82, p. 247, under the description: *The Beggar's Opera…marked with the Variations at Drury-Lane House, and ornamented with the Portraits of Mr Mattocks and Mrs Cargill, drawn by Mr Dighton, and engraved by Mr Walker.*

A175. GAY, John. FABLES.

(1) An ed. 2 vols in one, price 3*s*, pr f TC, listed in A401(3), 1777.

(1A) Ed. 1778. Pr f TC, FN(? N) et al. Price 3*s* 6*d* bd, with copperplates to each Fable, 2*s* without. [Bodley.

(1B) Ed. 1783. Pr f TC, EN et al. (Communicated.) [Ries.

(2) Ed. 1785. Pr f TC, EN et al. Price 7*s*. [BM.

(3) An ed. adv. *LC* 18–21.8.87, p. 172, price 3*s*, 'with a new set of copper plates', pr f TC, EN et al. Welsh 224.

(4) Ed. 1788. Pr f TC, EN et al. Price 2*s*. Wcts by John Bewick. Welsh 224; Hugo 4056. [BM; V&A(GL); LGL; Roscoe.

(5) Ed. 1792. Pr f EN et al. Price 2s. Hugo 63. [NUTP; BM; Roscoe.
(6) Ed. 1793. Pr f EN et al. [BM (large and thick paper); Opie.
(7) Ed. 1796. Pr f EN et al. Price 2s 6d. Hugo 5386. [Weedon; Osborne.
(8) Ed. 1801. Pr f EN et al. Gum 2683. [NUTP; BM; CUL; UCL.

A176. GAYTON, Edmund. FESTIVIOUS NOTES ON...DON QUIXOTE, ed. John Potter. First pubd 1654.
(1) 1st ed. by Potter, 1768. Pr f FN(N) et al. [BM; Bodley; LUL.
(2) 2nd ed. by Potter, 1771. Pr f FN(N) et al. [BM; Bodley; CUL.

A177. GENIUS. A POETICAL EPISTLE. JN. Price 1s. Listed *LM* May 1767, p. 262.

A178. GENTLEMAN, TRADESMAN, AND TRAVELLER'S POCKET LIBRARY, THE.
(1) 1st ed. 1753. S b JN. Price 'neatly bd' 3s, or with maps coloured 3s 6d. Includes Barrow's *Tables*, also issued separately (A23). [BM; Weedon.
(2) 2nd ed. 1756. S b JN. Prices as for no. (1). Adv. *PA* 7.6.56. Welsh 224.

A179. GENTLEMAN'S MAGAZINE, THE, 1767 (vol. XXXVII)–1800 (vol. LXX). S b FN(N), 1767–79, EN 1780–1800. Price up to 1782 6d each monthly issue, thereafter 1s. Yearly Supplements, 6d or 1s. Welsh 84, 224 and 356; *CBEL*, II, 673, 676–7 and V, 479; *BUCOP*, 2, 266–7. As to FN(N)'s interest in *GM* see Introduction, p. 18. [BM; Bodley; CUL; and see *BUCOP*.

A180. GENUINE COLLECTION OF ALL THE NEW SONGS... NOW SINGING AT VAUXHALL GARDENS, 1766. Pr f FN(N). Price 1s. Adv. *LC* 5–7.8.66, p. 132. *CBEL*, II, 224. Not in *BUCM*.

A181. GENUINE COLLECTION OF NEW SONGS...SUNG AT VAUXHALL GARDENS THIS SEASON. Adv. *LC* 23–6.9.69 as to be had of FN(N). Price 6d. Not in *BUCM*.

A182. GENUINE DISTRESSES, THE, OF DAMON AND CELIA: IN A SERIES OF LETTERS BETWEEN THE LATE GENERAL CRAUFURD...AND TWO UNFORTUNATE LOVERS. Adv. *LC* 28–30.3.71, p. 308, as 'In the Press and w.b.p. some day in May', subscriptions being taken by (*inter alia*) FN(N). Price 6s, 2 vols. Perhaps = no. A438.

A183. GESSNER, Salomon. THE DEATH OF ABEL, trans. b Mary Collyer.
(1) Entry deleted.
(2) 7th ed. 1765. Pr f FN(N) et al. [BM.
(3) 9th ed. 1768. Pr f FN(N) et al. [UCL; CUL.
(4) 10th ed. 1771. Pr f FN(N) et al. (see Plate 27). [BM; UCL.

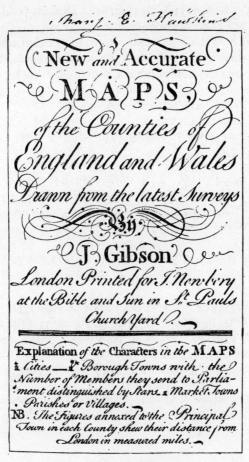

Fig. 34. Title-page of A185(1).

(5) 11th ed. Welsh 192 specifies an 11th ed. of 1773, 'F. Newbery' the last named of 3 publishers. The BM 11th ed. is dated 1776, Newbery's name not in the imprint.

A184. GIBSON, James. JOURNAL, A, OF THE LATE SIEGE BY THE TROOPS...AT CAPE BRETON, 1745. Pr f JN. Price 1s 6d. Welsh 225. [BM; Bodley; Rylands.

A185. GIBSON, John. NEW AND ACCURATE MAPS OF THE COUNTIES OF ENGLAND... See Chubb, *Printed Maps in the Atlases of G.B. and Ireland*, 1927.
(1) Undated ed. Pr f JN (see Fig. 34). Price 4s calf or 5s 6d with maps coloured. Adv. *Lloyd's Evening Post* 22–4.5.59. Welsh 210 and 225. Chubb, CCXIII. [Roscoe (plain); BM; Bodley (coloured).

(2) Listed as pr f C & N in J348(4), 1770, price 4s plain, 5s 6d coloured; and in J147(6), 1776, as pr f C & N, price 4s.
(3) An undated ed. by TC, Chubb ccxiv who dates 1770, but says 'it may possibly have been issued after the 1779 edition; the plates are considerably worn'.
(4) Ed. 1779. Recorded by Chubb, ccxiva, as in Bodley; but the copy is unknown there.
(5) Listed as s b TC in A222(17), 1788, price 4s.

GIBSON, John. POCKET MAPS OF THE WORLD = ATLAS MINIMUS, J146A.

A186. GILES, Joseph. MISCELLANEOUS POEMS: ON VARIOUS SUBJECTS..., REVISED...BY THE LATE WILLIAM SHENSTONE, 1771. Pr f FN(N) et al. IAW p. 63. *CBEL*, II, 308. [BM; Bodley; EdUL.

A187. GLASSE, Hannah. THE ART OF COOKERY. A. W. Oxford (no details). J. M. D. Passey, *Bibliography of the Works of Hannah Glasse*, 1955 (Diploma, London).
(1) A 'new ed.', 1778. Pr f FN(? N) et al. Price 5s. Passey 18. [BM; LEB.
(2) A 'new ed.', 1784. Pr f EN et al. Price 5s. Passey 19. [BM; CUL; LEB.
(2A) A 'new ed.', 1788. Pr f EN et al. Passey 20. [Bristol, not seen; Sotheby, 15.5.69, lot 251, and 5.11.71, lot 539.
(3) A 'new ed.', 1796. Pr f EN et al. Price 6s. Passey 22. [BM; CUL; Oup; LEB.

A188. GOBELIN, Marie Madeleine Marguerite, Marchioness de Brinvilliers. THE FEMALE PARRICIDE, 1752. S b JN. Price 1s. Legg no. 32. [Bodley; Rylands; RePL.

A189. Entry deleted.

A190. GOLDSMITH, Oliver. CITIZEN OF THE WORLD. Welsh 227.
(1) 1st ed. 1762. Pr f JN. Price 6s, 2 vols. IAW 124; *CBEL*, II, 641; Scott, 73–4; Isham 6; Rothschild 1021. [BM; CUL; PP; DNS.
(2) 1st ed. another issue, 1762. Pr f the Author; s b JN, W. Bristow et al. 2 vols. IAW 123–4; Welsh 227; Scott 70ff. [LUL; PP.
(3) 2nd ed. not traced and apparently not recorded.
(4) 3rd ed. 1774. Pr f C & N. 2 vols, price 6s calf, or 2 vols in one 5s in the vell. manner. *CBEL*, II, 641. [BM; Bodley.

A191. GOLDSMITH, Oliver. DESERTED VILLAGE, THE. *CBEL*, II, 643.
(1) 8th ed. 1775. Listed in A401(3), 1777, as pr f TC; but pubd under the imprint of Griffin alone. Price 2s.

(2) 9th ed. 1779. Pr f TC et al. Price 2s (see Plate 28). [BM; Bodley; CUL; LL; Quayle; PP; DNS.

(3) 10th ed. 1783. TC et al. Cameron and Carroll 4034. [NLA not seen.

(4) 11th ed. 1784. TC et al. Price 6d. Scott 250; Cameron and Carroll 4035. [PP; NLA not seen.

A192. GOLDSMITH, Oliver. ESSAYS. Adv. *LC* 11–13.6.65 as pr f JN et al. but the edd. of 1765 and 1766 were under the imprint of Griffin alone.

A193. GOLDSMITH, Oliver. HISTORY OF ENGLAND FROM THE EARLIEST TIMES TO THE DEATH OF GEORGE II.
(1) 3rd ed. Adv. *LC* 18–21.11.80 as pr f FN(? N) et al. 4 vols, price £1 4s.
(2) 4th ed. 1784. Pr f EN et al. 4 vols, price £1 4s. *CBEL*, II, 643. [Bodley; CUL.
(3) 5th ed. 1787. Pr f EN et al. 4 vols, price £1 4s. *CBEL*, II, 643. [BM.
(4) 6th ed. Adv. *LC* 29–31.7.90 as pr f EN et al. 3 vols, price £1 1s.
(5) 7th ed. Not traced, but ? = Hugo 81, EN, 1795. If the 'heads' mentioned by Hugo are as in earlier edd. they have nothing to do with Bewick.
(6) 8th ed. 1800. Pr f EN et al. 3 vols. *CBEL*, II, 643. [BM.

A194. GOLDSMITH, Oliver. LIFE OF RICHARD NASH, THE. Welsh 226; *CBEL*, II, 641; Scott 92ff.
(1) 1st ed. 1762. Pr f JN et al. Price 4s. IAW 126; Rothschild 1022. [BM; Bodley; CUL; LUL; LL; OEFL; EdUL; DNS.
(2) 2nd ed. 1762. Pr f JN et al. Price 4s. [BM; Bodley; CUL; LUL; UCL; DNS.
(3) Listed in A640(3), vol. IV, 1768 as pr f a s b N & C. Price 4s. Probably stock in hand of no. (2).

A195. GOLDSMITH, Oliver. MISCELLANEOUS WORKS, 1801. Pr f EN et al. 4 vols. *CBEL*, II, 637. [BM; Bodley; CUL; LL; LGL.

A196. GOLDSMITH, Oliver. POETICAL AND DRAMATIC WORKS. *CBEL*, II, 637.
(1) An ed. 1780. Pr f C & N et al. 2 vols. IAW 174. [BM; Bodley; CUL; DNS.
(2) A 'new ed.', 1786. Pr f TC, EN et al. 2 vols. [BM; Bodley; CUL; Weedon.
(3) A 'new ed.', 1791. Pr f F. Power & Co, EN et al. 2 vols. [Bodley; LUL; EdUL (vol. I); DNS.

A196A. GOLDSMITH, Oliver. RETALIATION, 8th ed. 1777. Welsh 226. Listed as pubd by C & N, in A199(14), 1778. Copies seen were by G. Kearsley alone.

A197. GOLDSMITH, Oliver. SHE STOOPS TO CONQUER. Welsh 226; *CBEL*, II, 643; IAW 153–61; Scott 292ff and 301ff; Nicoll 265. There are variant issues of the 1st ed. not mentioned here.

(1) 1st ed. 1773. Pr f FN(N). Price 1*s* 6*d*. TP imprint reads: *Pr f F. Newbery, in SPC-Y*. No price in imprint. Pp. 114 (error for 104). [OEFL.

(2) 1st ed. 1773, another issue. Pr f FN(N). Imprint as for no. (1) with *Price One Shilling and Six Pence* added. [BM (Ashley 800).

(3) 1st ed. 1773, another ed. Pr f FN(N). Price 1*s* 6*d*. Imprint as for no. (1). Pp. 106[107]. [BM; Bodley (imperf.); CUL.

(3A) 1st ed. 1773, another issue. Pr f FN(N). TP imprint reads: *Pr f F. Newbery, No. 20, Ludgate-Street, The Corner of S P C-Y*. Pp. 106. [Sotheby, 12.6.67, lot 310.

(4) 2nd ed. 1773. Pr f FN(N). Price 1*s* 6*d*. [BM; Bodley; DNS.

(5) 3rd ed. 1773. Pr f FN(N). [Bodley; LUL.

(6) 4th ed. 1773. Pr f FN(N). [Bodley; DNS.

(7) 5th ed. 1773. Pr f FN(N). [BM; Bodley; Rylands.

(8) A 'new ed.', 1785. Pr f EN. Price 1*s* 6*d*. [BM.

(9) A 'new ed.', 1786. Pr f EN. Price 1*s* 6*d*. [BM; Bodley.

A198. GOLDSMITH, Oliver. SURVEY OF EXPERIMENTAL PHILOSOPHY, A. Welsh 63 and 229; *CBEL*, II, 644; IAW 171–2; Scott 345–6; Isham 53.

(1) Ed. 1776. Pr f C & N. 2 vols. Price 10*s* 6*d*. [BM; Bodley; CUL; LUL; EdUL (this or no. (2)); AdE (this or no. (2)).

(2) Another issue, 1776, TC alone. Fr. Edwards Cat. 745 [1954] item 694. Not checked.

(3) Listed in A401(5), 1787, as pr f TC, price 12*s*, 2 vols.

A199. GOLDSMITH, Oliver. TRAVELLER, THE. Welsh 227; IAW 135; *CBEL*, II, 641–2; Scott 141ff.

(1) 1st ed. 1st issue, 1764. Pr f JN. Price 1*s* 6*d*. The title includes the words *Inscribed to the Rev. Henry Goldsmith. By Oliver Goldsmith, M.B.* See Scott.

(2) 1st ed. 1st issue, 1764, a Variant. Pr f JN. The words *Inscribed...* omitted from the title. See Scott.

(3) 1st ed. 2nd issue, 1765. Pr f JN. Price 1*s* 6*d*. Rothschild 1024. [BM; Bodley; CUL; LUL.

(4) 2nd ed. 1765. Pr f J. Newbury (*sic*). Price 1*s* 6*d*. [BM; Bodley; CUL; AdE; DNS.

(5) 3rd ed. 1765. Pr f J. Newbury (*sic*). Price 1*s* 6*d*. [BM; Bodley; CUL.

(6) 4th ed. 1765. Pr f JN. Price 1*s* 6*d*. [BM (imperf.); Bodley; CUL; LGL.

(7) 5th ed. 1768. Pr f FN, jun, & Co. Price 1*s* 6*d*. Rothschild 1025. [BM; Bodley; CUL; DNS.

(8) 6th ed. 1770. Pr f C & N. Price 1*s* 6*d*. Printed TP. Catchword at p. [i] 'where'. [Bodley (Firth d.4(6)); LUL.

(9) Another ed. 1770. Pr f C & N. Price 1*s* 6*d*. (? 7th ed.). Engvd TP. Catchword at p. [i] 'harvest'. [BM (79.i.10(2) and 11632.g.21); CUL (7700.b.98(4)).

(10) Another ed. 1770. Pr f C & N. Price 1*s* 6*d* (? 7th ed.). Engvd TP. Catchword at p. [i] 'where'. [Bodley (Vet. A5.d.696); CUL (S721.b.74.1(7)); LUL.

(11) 8th ed. adv. *LC* 11–13.2.72 as pr f C & N. Price 1s 6d.

(12) 9th ed. 1774. Pr f C & N. Price 1s 6d (see Plate 29). [BM; Bodley; DNS; Marchmont Bkshop (1962).

(13) Entry deleted.

(14) An ed. of 1778. Pr f C & N. Price 1s 6d. [Bodley (Vet. A5.d.480(1)).

(15) 10th ed. 1778. Pr f C & N. Price 1s 6d. [BM; CUL; Quayle; NLA.

(16) An ed. 1786. ? TC. *CBEL*, II, 641.

A200. GOLDSMITH, Oliver. VICAR OF WAKEFIELD, THE.
Traylen, Cat. 76 [1972] item 312A; Welsh 54–6 and 227–8; *CBEL*, II, 642; IAW 136–8; Scott 164ff.

(1) 1st ed. 1766. Pr f FN(N). 2 vols, price 6s bd, 5s sewed. [BM; LUL; Bodley.

(2) There are variant issues of the 1st ed. See Scott, Rothschild 1028, etc.

(3) 2nd ed. 1766. Pr f FN(N). 2 vols. [BM; CUL; LUL; Bodley.

(4) 3rd ed. 1766. Pr f FN(N). 2 vols. Price 6s bd, 5s sewed. [BM; Bodley; Oup.

(5) 4th ed. 1770. Pr f C & N. 2 vols, price 6s. [BM; Bodley; Roscoe.

(6) 5th ed. 1773. Pr f C & N. Price 5s for the 2 vols in one in the vell. manner, 6s in 2 vols calf. [BM; Bodley; CUL; Weedon.

(7) 6th ed. 1779. Pr f C & N. One vol. Price 1s 6d in the vell. manner. [BM; Bodley.

(8) 7th ed. 1781. Pr f TC. One vol. [BM; Bodley.

(9) 8th ed. 1787. Pr f TC et al. Price 1s 6d. [Weedon.

(10) 9th ed. 1791. Pr f F. Power & Co et al. Price 1s 6d. [Bodley.

A201. GOUGH, James. BRITANNIA: A POEM, 1767. S b JN et al. Price 1s 6d. Welsh 177; H&L, I, 250. [BM; CUL.

A202. GRENVILLE, Hon. George (1712–70). A CANDID REFUTATION OF THE CHARGES BROUGHT AGAINST THE PRESENT MINISTERS..., 1765. Pr f FN(N). Price 1s. [Bodley.

A203. GREY, Oliver. APOLOGY FOR THE SERVANTS, AN, 1760. Pr f JN. Price 6d. Has been attribd to Jas Townley, see Welsh 233 and 318–19. [BM; Bodley; LL.

A204. GRIFFIN, Robert. INTEREST TABLES, 1775. Pr f TC. Price 6s bd in the vell. manner. [BM; CUL; EdUL.

A205. GROVE'S COMPLAINT, THE, AND THE OWNER'S REPLY, A POEM. Adv. *GEP* 28–30.5.45, price 6d, s b JN et al. Welsh 233.

A206. GUTHRIE, William. COMPLETE HISTORY, A, OF ENGLISH PEERAGE, 1763. Pr f JN et al. Apparently issued in monthly pts at 5s. 2 vols of 6 pts each. Welsh 234–5; Moule, no. DXCVI; *CBEL*, II, 887. [BM; Bodley.

A207. GUTHRIE, William, JOHN GRAY et al. A GENERAL HISTORY OF THE WORLD. Welsh 235; *CBEL*, II, 641 and 887; IAW 132–3; Scott 118.

(1) An ed. 1764–7. Pr f JN et al. 12 vols, price 5s each, sewed in bds. The whole set listed in 1769 at £3 12s. [BM; EdUL.

(2) *LC* for 23–5.3.79, p. 282, adv. that on 1 April w.b.p. vol. 1, price 5s in bds; to comprise 13 vols 8vo, one each month. S b TC. The complete set in the vell. manner £3 10s.

(3) A COMPLETE INDEX TO THE GENERAL HISTORY, 1764. Pr f JN et al. The date is obviously false as the last vol. of the *History* did not appear until 1767. [BM; EdUL; Roscoe.

A208. GUTHRIE, William. MOTHER, THE; OR, THE HAPPY DISTRESS. A NOVEL. BY THE AUTHOR OF THE FRIENDS. H&L, IX, 213.

(1) First issued in 1759 under R. Baldwin's imprint and in 1761 under J. Wilkie's, it was listed in A172(2), 1765, as pr f a s b JN, 2 vols, 6s. Between 1768 and 1774 it was listed as by N & C, 6s in calf, 5s for the 2 vols in one in the vell. manner.

(2) Listed as pr f TC in J113(4), 1781, 2 vols calf 6s, 2 vols in one in the vell. manner 5s.

A209. HALLER, Baron Albrecht von. USONG. AN EASTERN NARRATIVE, 1772. S b FN(N). 2 vols, 5s sewed. *CBEL*, II, 63. [BM (thick paper); Bodley; UCL.

A210. HAMILTON, Antoine (Anthony). HISTORY OF MAYFLOWER, 2nd ed. 1796. Pr f EN. Welsh 236; *CBEL*, II, 782. [BM.

A211. HARDY, James. COMPLETE SYSTEM OF INTEREST AND ANNUITIES, A, 1753. To be had of JN et al. [Actuaries.

A212. HARDY, James. ELEMENTS OR THEORY OF ARITHMETIC, THE, 2nd ed. 1777. S b FN(N) et al. Price 4s 6d. [UCL.

A213. HART, Joseph. HYMNS, &c COMPOSED ON VARIOUS SUBJECTS.

(1) An ed. adv. *LC* 6–9.7.65, p. 28, as pr f the Author, s b JN. Price 2s.

(2) 6th ed. 1769. S b FN(N). Price 2s. [BM; Bodley.

(3) 7th ed. n.d. S b FN(N). Price 2s. [BM.

(4) 8th ed. 1774. S b FN(N). Price 2s. [BM; CUL.

(5) 9th ed. 1777. S b FN(N). Price 2s. [Bodley.

(6) 10th ed. 1784. S b EN. Price 2s. [BM.

(7) 11th ed. 1788. S b EN. Price 2s. [BM.

(8) 12th ed. not traced.

(9) 13th ed. 1793. S b 'Mrs Newberry' et al. Price 2s. [BM.

A214. HARVEST, George. THE REASONABLENESS...OF SUBSCRIPTION TO...ARTICLES OF FAITH, 1772. Pr f FN(N). Price 2s 6d. [BM.

A215. HAWKINS, Sir Thomas. LIFE OF SAMUEL JOHNSON, THE. *CBEL*, II, 898; Courtney 162.

(1) 1st ed. 1787. Pr f TC, EN et al. Price 7s. Another issue is vol. 1 of the 1787 ed. of Johnson's *Works*, A274. [BM; CUL; LUL; EdUL; AdE; UCL.

(2) 2nd ed. 1787. Pr f TC, EN et al. Price 7s in bds. [BM.

A216. HAWNEY, William. THE COMPLETE MEASURER.

(1) 16th ed. 1789. Pr f EN et al. Price 3s 6d. [Bodley; RICS; Sotheby, 24.10.66, lot 2462; NoU.

(2) A 'new ed.', 1798. Pr f EN et al. Price 3s 6d. [BM; Sotheby, 24.10.66, lot 2462.

HELIOCRENE. See Merrick, John.

A217. 'HELVETIUS, Claude Adrien' (pseud.). ESTIMATE OF THE MANNERS...OF THE MODERN FRENCH, 1767. Pr f FN(N). Price 2s. [BM.

A218. HENRY, David. HISTORICAL ACCOUNT OF ALL THE VOYAGES ROUND THE WORLD. *CBEL*, II, 741 (dates 1773–6). Sabin 54897; Spence, p. 25.

(1) Ed. 1774–3. Vols I–IV. Pr f FN(N). Vols I and II 1774, vols III and IV 1773. See the Introduction at p. 24. 48 weekly pts at 6d; £1 5s in bds. [BM; Bodley; LL; Wellcome; A. Hancox, Cat. 83 [1961] item 179; Sotheby, 6.4.70, lot 154 and 30.10.70, lot 471.

(2) Vol. v is no. A317, 1775. *LC* for 10–12.4.81 adv. the 5-vol. set as to be had of EN for £1 9s in bds.

(3) Vol. VI is no. A224, 1785.

A219. HENRY, David. HISTORICAL ACCOUNT OF THE CURIOSITIES OF LONDON AND WESTMINSTER. This is the General Title for nos. A222, A223 and A221 when issued together as one vol. The date on each TP usually bears no relation to the dates of the components. The make up of the composite vols seems to have been entirely haphazard, e.g. no. (10). Other composite vols than those mentioned below no doubt exist. All copies seen priced 2s 6d.

(1) Ed. 1753. Pr f JN. Comprises *Tower*, *Westm. Abbey*, *St Paul's*, all dated 1753. [LGL; UCL; Traylen.

(2) Ed. 1755. Pr f JN. *Tower* 1755, *Abbey* 1753, *Paul's* 1753. [LGL.

(3) Ed. 1763. Pr f JN. [A. Muirhead, Cat. 21 [1958] item 122 not seen.
(4) Ed. 1765. Pr f JN. *Tower* 1765, *Abbey* 1764, *Paul's* 1765. Welsh 258.
(5) Ed. 1767. Pr f JN. *Tower* 1767, *Abbey* 1767, *Paul's* 1765. [Bodley; LGL.
(6) Ed. 1767. Pr f JN. *Tower* 1768, *Abbey* 1767, *Paul's* 1765. Welsh 258.
(7) Ed. 1769. Pr f N & C. *Tower* 1771, *Abbey* 1767, *Paul's* 1770. [Bodley.
(8) Ed. 1769. Pr f N & C. *Tower* 1767, *Abbey* 1767, *Paul's* 1765. [Roscoe.
(9) Ed. 1769. Pr f N & C. *Tower* 1771, *Abbey* 1770, *Paul's* 1770. [LGL.
(10) Ed. 1776. Pr f C & N. *Tower* 1774, *Abbey* 1770, *Paul's* 1777. [LGL.
(11) Ed. 1785. Pr f TC. *Tower* 1784, *Abbey* 1783, *Paul's* 1784. [Bodley.
(12) Ed. 1785. Pr f TC. *Tower* 1788, *Abbey* 1788, *Paul's* 1784. Noted by Wallis.
(13) Ed. 1788. Pr f TC. *Tower* 1789, *Abbey* 1788, *Paul's* 1784. [LGL.

A220. HENRY, David. HISTORICAL DESCRIPTION OF ST PAUL'S CATHEDRAL. A221.
HISTORICAL DESCRIPTION OF THE TOWER OF LONDON. A222.
HISTORICAL DESCRIPTION OF WESTMINSTER ABBEY. A223.
GM for June 1792, p. 579, in the course of an obituary notice of Henry, observes: 'Those useful and popular publications which describe the curiosities in Westminster Abbey, St Paul's Church and the Tower of London were originally compiled by Mr Henry; and have been improved by him through many successive impressions.'

A221. HENRY, David. HISTORICAL DESCRIPTION OF ST PAUL'S CATHEDRAL. Welsh 258 and 310. All copies seen priced 6*d*.
(1) Ed. 1753. Pr f JN. [LGL.
(2) Ed. 1759. Pr f JN. [LGL.
(3) Ed. 1765. Pr f JN. [Bodley; LGL; Roscoe.
(4) Ed. 1770. Pr f C & N. [Bodley; LGL.
(5) Ed. 1777. Pr f C & N. [LGL.
(6) Ed. 1784. Pr f TC. [Bodley; LGL.

A222. HENRY, David. HISTORICAL DESCRIPTION OF THE TOWER OF LONDON. Welsh 258. An immensely successful guide-bk; started in 1753 it was still going strong at the turn of the century. There are probably other edd. not noted here. All copies seen (except no. (11)) priced 6*d*.
(1) Ed. 1753. Pr f JN. [BM (imperf.); LGL.
(2) Ed. 1754. Pr f JN. [BM; Weedon.
(3) Ed. 1755. Pr f JN. [BM; LGL.
(4) Ed. 1757. Pr f JN. [LGL.
(5) Ed. 1760. Pr f JN. [BM.
(6) Ed. 1762. Pr f JN. [BM; LGL.
(7) Ed. 1764. Pr f JN. [BM.

(8) Ed. 1765. Pr f JN. [Deighton Bell, Cat. 90 [1964] item 331, not seen.

(9) Ed. 1767. Pr f JN. [Oup; Bodley; LGL; Roscoe.

(10) Ed. 1768. Pr f N & C. [LGL.

(11) Ed. 1769. Pr f N & C. An ed. in French. Price 1s. In a Rouen bkseller's Cat. in 1910.

(12) Ed. 1771. Pr f C & N. [Bodley; LGL.

(13) Ed. 1774. Pr f C & N. [BM; LGL.

(14) Ed. 1778. Pr f C & N. [BM.

(15) Ed. 1784. Pr f TC. [Bodley.

(16) Ed. 1787. Pr f TC. [BM.

(17) Ed. 1788. Pr f TC. [Roscoe.

(18) Ed. 1789. Pr f F. Power & Co. [LGL.

(18A) Ed. 1792. No printer etc. A piracy. [Wellcome.

(19) Listed in J328, 1795, as pr f EN.

(20) Edd. of 1799 and later were pubd elsewhere.

A223. HENRY, David. HISTORICAL DESCRIPTION OF WESTMINSTER ABBEY. Welsh 258 and 330. All copies seen priced 1s.

(1) Ed. 1753. Pr f JN. [LGL; Weedon.

(2) Ed. 1754. Pr f JN. [BM.

(3) Ed. 1761. Pr f JN. [BM.

(4) Ed. 1764. Pr f JN. [BM.

(5) Ed. 1767. Pr f JN. [BM; Bodley; LGL; Roscoe.

(6) Ed. 1770. Pr f C & N. [LGL.

(7) Ed. 1783. Pr f TC. [BM; Bodley.

(8) Ed. 1788. Pr f TC. [BM; LGL.

A224. HENRY, David. JOURNAL OF CAPT. COOK'S LAST VOYAGE, a 'new ed.', 1785. Pr f EN. Price 6s in bds. Ed. b Henry and forms vol. VI of no. A218. M. Holmes, *Capt. James Cook – a Bibliographical Excursion*, 1952, no. 53. Spence, p. 20. [BM.

A225. HEY, John. NATURE OF OBSOLETE ORDINANCES, THE: A SERMON, 1773. S b C & N et al. Price 6d. [BM; CUL; LUL.

A226. HEY, John. SERMON PREACHED BEFORE THE UNIVERSITY OF CAMBRIDGE, NOV. 5, 1774. S b C & Newberry (*sic*) et al. Price 1s. [Bodley; CUL; LUL.

A227. HEY, John. SUBSTANCE, THE, OF A SERMON PREACHED AT...WHITEHALL...27th FEBRUARY, 1778. S b C & Newberry (*sic*) et al. Price 6d. [BM; CUL; LUL.

A228. HILL, 'Sir' John. ACTOR, THE, 1750. Listed in A370(1), 1751, as 'just pubd' b JN. Under imprint of R. Griffiths alone.

A229. HILL, 'Sir' John. BRITISH HERBAL, THE, 1756. Pr f JN et al. Price £1 11s 6d; also a 'royal impression with the Cuts coloured from Nature, after originals done by the Author' £10 10s. E. S. Rohde, *Old English Herbals*, 1922, p. 222. [BM (coloured); Bodley (coloured and plain); LUL; EdUL; CUL; LGL; Sotheby, 4.11.69, lot 240.

A230. HILL, 'Sir' John. POWER OF WATER-DOCK, THE, AGAINST SCURVY, 1777. 10th ed. Pr f FN(N) et al. Price 1s. [Bodley; Sotheby, 12.12.67, lot 356.

A231. Entry deleted.

A232. HISTORICAL ACCOUNT OF THE RISE...OF THE... QUAKERS, 1756. Pr f JN. Price 6d. [CUL.

A233. HISTORY AND ADVENTURES OF A DARK LANTERN. Adv. *PA* 19.1.71 as s b FN(N), 2 vols, price 5s sewed.

A234. HISTORY OF MISS SOMMERVILE. WRITTEN BY A LADY.
(1) An ed. 1769. Pr f N & C. 2 vols, price 6s. [BM; DLC.
(2) Listed in J113(4), 1781, as pr f TC; and recorded by Welsh, 270, as in a TC list *ca.* 1789.

A235. 'HOAMCHI-VAM' (pseud.). THE BONZE, OR CHINESE ANCHORITE, 1769 (see Plate 30). S b FN(N) et al. Price 6s sewed, 2 vols. Welsh 176; *CBEL*, II, 552. [Bodley; Sotheby, 8.3.71, lot 37.

A236. 'HODGE, Farmer, of Golders Green.' THE HAMPSTEAD CONTEST, A LAW CASE SUBMITTED TO COUNSEL, AND INSCRIBED TO MRS L——M. FN*. Listed *LM* Oct. 1775, p. 538. Price 6d. At p. 594 the lady is named as Mrs Lessingham.

A237. HOMER. HOMERI ILIAS, ed. Samuel Clarke.
(1) 11th ed. Adv. *LC* 10–13.7.90, p. 45, as pr f EN et al. Price 14s, 2 vols.
(2) 12th ed. 1794. Pr f EN et al. 2 vols, price 14s. [BM; Bodley.

A238. HOMER. Pope's trans. of *Iliad* and *Odyssey*. *LC* for 9–11.12.83, p. 568, adv. a new ed. without notes in 4 vols, 12mo, pr f EN et al. Perhaps a re-issue of vols 35–8 of Johnson's *Poets*, 1779, without the notes. Price 12s.

A239. HOPPUS, E[dward or Edmund]. PRACTICAL MEASURING.
(1) 11th ed. 1784. Pr f EN et al. [LUL; Sotheby, 24.10.66, lot 2534, and 14.10.69, lot 413.
(2) 12th ed. 1790. Pr f EN et al. [LUL; RICS; Bodley.
(3) 13th ed. 1795. Pr f EN et al. Price 3s bd. [Sotheby, 24.10.66, lot 2534.

A240. HORACE. SECOND EPISTLE OF THE FIRST BOOK OF HORACE, TO LOLLIUS, trans. F[rancis] N[ewbery], 1800. Pr b W. Bulmer & Co. [BM; Bodley.

A241. HORACE. WORKS, trans. Christopher Smart. Welsh 308; *CBEL*, II, 339, 766.
(1) 1st ed. 1756. Pr f JN. 2 vols, price 5s. Gray xxxv; Rothschild 1879. [BM; Sotheby, 8.4.68, lot 174 and 8.3.71, lot 382; Bodley.
(2) 2nd ed. 1762. Pr f JN. 2 vols, price 6s. Gray xxxv(2). [BM; Bodley.
(3) 3rd ed. 1770. Pr f C & N. 2 vols, price 6s, 7s and 5s. Gray xxxv(3). [BM.
(4) 4th ed. 1774. Pr f C & N. 2 vols, price 6s and 5s. Gray xxxv(4). [BM.
(5) 5th ed. 1780. Pr f TC. 2 vols, price 6s. Gray xxxv(5). [Bodley (vol. 1).
(6) 6th ed. adv. *LC* 15–17.12.91, p. 580, as to be had of F. Power & Co, 2 vols, price 6s. Not in Gray.

A242. HOUSEKEEPER'S ACCOMPT BOOK, THE, 1773–95. I have seen no copy of any issue. I assume it contained printed matter of some sort. All issues adv. at price 1s 6d, those up to and including 1783 'in blue covers'. Edd. for 1773–81 pr f or s b FN(N). Ed. for 1782 not traced. Edd. for 1783–95 pr f or s b EN et al.

A243. HOYLE, Edmond. MR. HOYLE'S GAMES OF WHIST. *CBEL*, II, 826. F. Jessel, *Biblio. of Works in English on Playing Cards and Gaming*, 1905.
(1) 15th ed. n.d. Pr f JN 'in Ludgate-Street' et al. Price 3s 'neatly bd' or 'in red leather'. Jessel, no. 808. [BM; Bodley; LGL.
(2) 16th ed. n.d. Pr f FN(N) et al. Adv. *LC* 10–13.6.75, p. 559. Jessel, no. 809. Price 3s 'neatly bd'. [BM; Bodley.
(3) A 'new ed.' adv. *LC* 6–8.1.84, p. 31, price 3s. Pr f 'Mrs Newbery' et al.

A244. HOYLE, Edmond. HOYLE'S GAMES IMPROVED... REVISED AND CORRECTED BY CHARLES JONES. *CBEL*, II, 826. None of the following in Jessel's *Biblio*.
(1) 15th ed. n.d. JN. Welsh 239, who dates *ca.* 1760.
(2) Ed. 1775. Pr f FN(N) et al. Price 3s neatly bd. [CUL.
(3) Ed. 1779. Pr f FN(N) et al. Price 3s. [BM; Bodley; LUL; AdE.
(4) A 'new ed.', 1786. Pr f EN et al. Price 3s. [BM; Bodley.
(5) A 'new ed.', 1790. Pr f EN et al. Price 3s bd in red leather. [BM; Bodley.
(6) A 'new ed.', pr f EN et al. Adv. *LC* 14–16.1.94, p. 51. Price as for no. (5).
(7) A 'new ed.', 1796. Pr f EN et al. Price 3s 6d in red leather. Welsh 239. [BM; Bodley.
(8) A 'new ed.', 1800. Pr f EN et al. Price 4s. [BM; Bodley; CUL.

A245. HUGHES, Charles. THE COMPLEAT HORSEMAN, [1772]. Pr f FN(N). Price 1s. *CBEL*, II, 817. [BM.

A246. IMPRISONMENT FOR DEBT CONSIDERED, 1772. Pr f FN(N). Price 1s. [BM.

A247. INDEX TO THE SERMONS PUBLISHED SINCE THE RESTORATION, 1751. Pr f JN et al. Price 2s 6d sewed, 4s 6d half bd and interleaved. Welsh 304–5. [BM.

A248. INGRAM, Dale. AN ESSAY ON THE CAUSE AND SEAT OF THE GOUT, 1743. Pr b JN et al. Price 1s 6d. Legg, no. 20. [BM; Bodley.

A249. INSPECTOR, THE: CONTAINING A CONCISE AND IMPARTIAL COLLECTION OF NEWS, &c. Forms sections B to D of vol. II of *The Student*, 1751 (A577). 3 undated pts issued by 'The Proprietors of The Student'. Monthly pts cost 6d. [BM.

A250. JACKSON, Henry. ESSAY ON BRITISH ISINGLASS, AN, 1765. Pr f JN. Price 1s 6d. Welsh 240–1. [BM; Bodley; CUL.

A251. JACKSON, J. L. THE ART OF RIDING; OR HORSEMANSHIP MADE EASY, 1765. Listed *LM Supplement*, 1765 and Aug. 1766, p. 440, as by FN(N), and adv. *LC* 20–2.5.66, p. 487, as by Cooke and FN(N). Only A. Cooke's name in imprint. *CBEL*, II, 817.

A252. JACOB, Giles. COMPLETE PARISH OFFICER, THE, 16th ed. 1772. Pr f FN* et al. Price 3s 6d. Maxwell, I, 234. [LUL (imperf.).

A253. JACOB, Giles. EVERY MAN HIS OWN LAWYER. Maxwell, I, 34.
(1) 8th ed. ?1778 (Maxwell dates 1787 in error). Pr f FN* et al. Price 6s. Adv. *LC* 27–9.4.79, p. 402.
(2) 9th ed. 1784. Pr f EN et al. Price 6s. Adv. *LC* 17–19.8.84, p. 175.
(3) 10th ed. 1788. Pr f EN et al. Price 7s. [BM.

A254. JACOB, Giles. LAW DICTIONARY...ENLARGED AND IMPROVED BY T. E. TOMLINS, 1797. Pr f EN et al. 2 vols, price 3 gns in bds, £3 10s bd. Maxwell, I, 9. [BM; Bodley; AdE.

A255. JACOB, Giles. NEW LAW-DICTIONARY...CORRECTED AND GREATLY ENLARGED BY J. MORGAN, 10th ed. 1782. Pr f F. Newberry* (*sic*) et al. Price 2 gns. [BM.

A256. JAMES, Robt, M.D. DISSERTATION ON FEVERS, A.
(1) 1st ed. 1748. Pr f JN. Price 6d. [BM; RCS.
(2) 2nd ed. 1749. Pr f JN. Price 6d. Welsh 241. [BM; Bodley; CUL; Wellcome.

(3) 3rd ed. 1755. Pr f JN. Price 6d. [BM; Bodley; RCS; Melbourne.
(4) 4th ed. 1758. Pr f JN. Price 6d. [BM; Wellcome.
(5) 5th ed. 1761. Pr f JN. Price 6d. [BM; Viner & Hart, Cat. 1 [1971] item 45.
(6) 6th ed. 1764. Pr f JN. Price 6d. [Wellcome; CUL; RCP; EdUL.
(7) 7th ed. 1770. Pr f FN(S). Price 6d. Welsh 241. [BM; RCP.
(8) 8th ed. 1778. Pr f FN(S). Welsh 242. The copy in RCS is a set of the sheets bd up and issued in 1849 by 'Messrs Newbery – the present owners of Dr James's Fever Powder'. [BM; Bodley; CUL; RCS; RCP; EdUL.

A257. JAMES, Robert, M.D. MEDICINAL DICTIONARY. The 1st ed. was pubd b T. Osborne in 1743–5. In 1750–3 *GEP* was advertising that 'the few remaining copies' of the work 'formerly sold for £8 11s in sheets, are now to be had at the moderate Price of Five Guineas in Sheets', of M. Cooper. The bk was listed in A256(6), 1764, as pr f a s b JN at £6 for the 3 vols, and in A401(5), 1787, as pr f TC at 7 gns. I have traced no copy under the Newbery or Carnan imprint. *LC* for 17–20.12.68 stated that N & C had purchased the remaining sets and would sell them at £7 until next midsummer, when the price would be increased. The same paper, for 16–18.1.70, stated that TC had purchased all the remaining sets and would sell at 7 gns. One is left wondering as to the true history of this bk. And from whom did C & N buy in 1768, and TC in 1770? I suggest that John Newbery had bought up the whole remaining stock; under his will his wife and daughter each took a quarter share in this; and it was these shares that C & N bought in 1768; in 1770 TC bought out Francis the son's augmented share. I make this only as a suggestion; I am not convinced.

A258. JAMES, Robert, M.D. TREATISE ON CANINE MADNESS, A, 1760. Pr f JN. Price 4s 6d neatly bd in calf. Welsh 241. [BM; Bodley; Wellcome; RCP; RCS; EdUL.

A259. JENKS, Benjamin. PRAYERS AND OFFICES OF DEVOTION FOR FAMILIES.
(1) 19th ed. Adv. *LC* 2–4.5.76, p. 428, as pr f FN* et al. Price 3s.
(2) 20th ed. 1780. Pr f FN(?N) et al. Price 3s. [BM.
(3) 21st ed. Adv. *LC* 11–14.11.86, p. 469, as pr f EN et al. Price 3s.

A260. JENNER, Charles. THE DESTRUCTION OF NINIVEH: A POEM, 1768. Pr f Newberry (*sic*) and TC. *CBEL*, II, 366. A Seaton Prize Poem for 1768. [BM; Bodley; CUL.

A261. JERVEY, William. PRACTICAL THOUGHT ON... SCURVY, 1769. Pr f FN(? S) et al. Price 2s. [MSL; UCL.

A262. JESTS OF BEAU NASH, THE. Adv. *LC* 10–13.1.67, p. 44, as pr f FN(N) a s b the bksellers of Bath. Price 1s.

A263. JOHNSON, Samuel, LL.D. DICTIONARY. Courtney 44ff; Chapman 137–8; *CBEL*, ii, 615; Alston lists some 40 locations (vol. v, 181ff).

(1) 5th ed. 1784. F°. Pr f M. Newberry (*sic*) (i.e. 'Mrs' EN) et al. 2 vols. Alston, v, 181. [BM; Bodley; GlaPL; BmPL; MB; P; PP (et al. – see Alston).

(2) 6th ed. 1785. 4°. Pr f M. Newbery (*sic*) et al. 2 vols, price 3 gns. Alston, v, 186. [BM; Bodley; CUL; LL; LUL; NLSc; P; PPL; MB; CtY; NLA (et al.).

(3) 7th ed. 1785. F°. Pr f EN et al. Alston, v, 182. [BM; NLWa; NOUL; OEFL; BmPL; MOWl (et al. – see Alston).

(4) 8th ed. 1799. 4°. Pr f EN et al. 2 vols. Price 3 gns, on fine wove paper 4 gns. Alston, v, 191. [BM; LGL; BmPL; HuPL; LEB; MB; NN; NLA (et al. – see Alston).

A264. JOHNSON, Samuel, LL.D. IDLER, THE. Welsh 243; Courtney 83–4; Chapman 142; *CBEL*, ii, 616; *BUCOP*, 4, 426.

(1) 1st coll. ed. 1761. Pr f JN. Price 6s bd, 5s sewed. Rothschild 1248. [BM; Bodley; LUL; OEFL.

(2) 2nd coll. ed. 1762. JN. Recorded by Lyon, not elsewhere. But *LC* adv. an ed. 12–15.3.63, price 6s.

(3) 3rd coll. ed. 1767. Pr f JN et al. 2 vols, price 6s. [Bodley; CUL.

(4) 4th coll. ed. 1783. Pr f TC et al. 2 vols, price 6s. Publishers' addresses in imprints. [Bodley.

(5) 4th coll. ed. 1783. Another issue of vol. ii, the publishers' addresses omitted in the imprint. [Bodley (Douce, 1, 142).

(6) 5th ed. 1790. Pr f F. Power et al. 2 vols, price 6s. [Bodley.

A265. JOHNSON, Samuel, LL.D. INDEX TO THE ENGLISH POETS, 1780. Pr f FN* et al. 2 vols. Courtney 141. [BM.

A266. JOHNSON, Samuel, LL.D. LIFE OF ADMIRAL BLAKE, 1769. A reprint from *GM* for 1740 (see Courtney 11), pubd as an addition to Johnson's *Life of Savage*, 1769.

A267. JOHNSON, Samuel, LL.D. LIFE OF MR. RICHARD SAVAGE. Welsh 244; Courtney 15–17; *CBEL*, ii, 615.

(1) 4th ed. 1769. Pr f FN(N). Price 2s 6d sewed, 3s bd. [BM; Bodley; CUL; DNS.

(2) Another 4th ed. 1777. Pr f FN(N). Price 3s. See Courtney 16. [BM; Bodley.

A268. JOHNSON, Samuel, LL.D. LIFE OF SIR FRANCIS DRAKE, 1769. As for A266.

A269. JOHNSON, Samuel, LL.D. LIVES OF THE MOST EMINENT ENGLISH POETS. Courtney 141–2; Chapman 159; *CBEL*, ii, 616.

(1) An ed. of 1781. Pr f EN et al. 4 vols, price 1 gn in bds. Rothschild 1265–7. [BM; Bodley; LUL; UCL.

(2) A 'new ed.', 1783. Pr f EN et al. 4 vols, price 1 gn in bds. [BM; Bodley; LUL; EdUL; UCL.

(3) A 'new ed. corrected', 1790–1. Pr f EN et al. 4 vols, price £1 4s. [BM; Bodley; CUL.

(4) A 'new ed. corrected', 1794. Pr f EN et al. 4 vols, price £1 4s. 'Drawback' at foot of TP (see *The Book Collector*, winter 1963, pp. 494–5). [BM; LUL.

(5) A 'new ed. corrected', 1801. Pr f EN et al. 3 vols. [BM.

JOHNSON, Samuel, LL.D. LIVES OF THE ENGLISH POETS, ABRIDGED, 1797. See J191A.

A270. JOHNSON, Samuel, LL.D. MEMOIRS OF THE KING OF PRUSSIA, 1786. Pr f TC. Price 6d. So adv. *LC* 10–12.10.86, p. 360. The recorded ed. of 1786 (Courtney 75; Chapman 139; *CBEL*, II, 616) was pr f Harrison & Co, was a work of viii+480 pp. and could not have sold at 6d. Probably a reprint of the original article in the *Literary Magazine* for 1756 (Courtney 75), without the other matter included in Harrison's ed.

A271. JOHNSON, Samuel, LL.D. MISCELLANEOUS AND FUGITIVE PIECES, 1774. Apparently the names of N & C appear only in vol. III of 1st ed. In 2nd ed. N & C are named in cancel title-leaves to vols I and II. No 2nd ed. of vol. III traced. *CBEL*, II, 230 and 614; Courtney 116–17; Chapman 150; Rothschild 1254.

(1) 1st ed. Vol. III, 1774. Pr f C & N et al. Prices 3s 6d, 10s 6d and 11s. [BM; Bodley; LUL; OEFL; DNS.

(2) 2nd ed. Vols I and II, 1774. Pr f C & N et al. Prices 7s and 10s 6d. [OEFL; Bodley.

A272. JOHNSON, Samuel, LL.D. PREFACES TO THE WORKS OF THE ENGLISH POETS, 1779–81. Pr f FN(N) et al. (vols I–IV), pr f EN et al. (vols V–X). Price ?2s 6d each vol. *CBEL*, II, 616; Courtney 140–1; Rothschild 1262–4. [BM; CUL; EdUL; AdE.

A273. JOHNSON, Samuel, LL.D. RAMBLER, THE. Courtney 33–5; Chapman 131–4; *CBEL*, II, 615; *BUCOP*, 3, 657.

(1) 5th ed. 1761. Pr f JN et al. 4 vols, price 12s. Welsh 243. [Bodley; Rylands.

(2) 6th ed. 1763. Pr f JN et al. 4 vols, price 12s. Welsh 243. [Bodley; A. R. Heath, Cat. 13 [1969] item 276; Weedon.

(3) 7th ed. 1767. Pr f JN et al. 4 vols, price 12s. Welsh 243. [Bodley.

(4) 8th ed. 1771. Pr f C & N et al. 4 vols in 2, in the vell. manner, 10s. Courtney 34, dates MDCCLXXII. [Bodley.

(5) 9th ed. 1779. Pr f TC, FN* et al. 4 vols, price ?12s. [Bodley; Sotheby, 3.11.69, lot 212.

(6) 10th ed. 1784. Pr f TC, T. Newbury (i.e. EN or FN(S)) et al. 4 vols, price 12s. [BM; Bodley; UCL.
(7) 11th ed. 1789. Pr f TC, EN et al. 4 vols, price 12s. [BM; Bodley; UCL.

A274. JOHNSON, Samuel, LL.D. WORKS OF SAMUEL JOHNSON. Courtney 161–2; Chapman 163–4; *CBEL*, II, 614.
(1) 1st ed. 1787. With *Life* by Hawkins. Pr f TC, EN et al. Price for the set of 11 vols £3 6s in bds, £3 17s calf. Vol. 1 (the *Life*) 7s in bds. The 2 supplementary vols (*Debates in Parliament*) were by Stockdale, and the 13-vol. set was to be had for £3 18s in bds, £4 17s 6d calf gilt. For another issue of vol. 1 see A215. [BM; Bodley; CUL; LUL; Rylands; AdE; Weedon; DNS.
(2) A 'new ed.', with Murphy's *Essay* (see A373), 1792. Pr f EN et al. 12 vols, price £3 12s in bds. [BM; Bodley; CUL; EdUL; LGL; DNS.
(3) A 'new ed.', 1796. Pr f EN et al. 12 vols, price £3 12s in bds. [BM; Bodley.
(4) A 'new ed.', 1801. Pr f EN et al. 12 vols, price £4 4s in bds. [BM; Bodley.

A275. JOHNSON, Samuel, LL.D. WORKS OF THE ENGLISH POETS. Courtney 141; *CBEL*, II, 259.
(1) Ed. 1779. Pr f FN(? N) et al. 56 vols+*Index* (A265) 2 vols, and *Prefaces* (A272) 10 vols. Price 2s 6d per vol., the set of 68 vols selling at £10 4s (Bent's *General Catalogue*, 1786). [BM; Bodley.
(2) Ed. 1790. Pr f EN et al. 75 vols, price £11 5s sewed or in bds. [BM; Bodley; Rylands; LGL.

A276. JOHNSON, Rev. Samuel, A.M. (Vicar of Gt Torrington, Devon). CHRIST'S PRESENCE IN THE EUCHARIST, 1742. S b 'Mr Newberry' et al. Recorded by Algar.

A277. JOHNSON, Rev. Samuel, A.M. EXPLANATION OF SCRIPTURE PROPHECIES, 1742. Pr a s b JN et al. 2 vols. Legg, no. 15. [BM; RePL.

A278. JOHNSTONE, Charles (attrib. to). BUTHRED; A TRAGEDY, 1779. Pr f FN(N). Price 1s 6d. Welsh 180; Nicoll 321. [BM; Bodley.

A279. JONES, Stephen. NEW BIOGRAPHICAL DICTIONARY, A. Welsh 244; *CBEL*, II, 922.
(1) 1st ed. 1794. Pr f EN et al. Price 5s in 'neat', 6s in 'elegant' bindings. [BM; Bodley.
(2) 2nd ed. 1796. Pr f EN et al. Price 'elegantly bd' 6s, 'common' 5s. [BM; Bodley; Weedon.
(3) 3rd ed. 1799. Pr f EN et al. Price 5s in 'neat', 6s in 'elegant' bindings. [BM.
(4) *CBEL*, II, 922 lists a *New Biographical Dictionary in Miniature*, 1794, 1796 etc. Not traced. Perhaps one of the preceding edd.

JONES, Stephen. POCKET BIOGRAPHICAL DICTIONARY.
A279 is often so described in the Press &c.

A280. 'JUNIUS'. THE POLITICAL CONTEST. *CBEL*, II, 630–2.
J. Edmands, *Junius Bibliography*, 1890. F. Cordasco, *Junius Bibliography*, 1949.
(1) 1st ed. [1769]. Pr f FN(N). Price 1*s*. Edmands 1; Cordasco 14. [BM.
(2) 2nd ed. [1769]. Pr f FN(N). Price 1*s*. Edmands 2; Cordasco 15. [BM; Bodley.
(3) ...*Being a Continuation of Junius's Letters*...*Part II* [1769]. Pr f FN(N).
Price 6*d*. Edmands 7; Cordasco 18. [BM; Bodley; Rylands.
(4) 3rd ed. [1769]. Pr f FN(N) et al. Price 1*s*. Edmands 3; Cordasco 16. (Communicated.) [Rylands. (No copy BM, *pace* Edmands.)

A281. KELLY, Hugh. THE BABLER.
(1) Ed. 1767. Pr f JN et al. 2 vols, price 5*s* sewed, 6*s* bd. Welsh 172. *CBEL*, II,
474 and 665. [BM; Bodley; CUL; RePL (vol. 1).
(2) Listed as pr f C & N in A640(3), vol. XIII, 1774, price 6*s*. Probably stock in
hand of the 1767 ed.

A281A. KENRICK, William. THE KAPÉLION, OR POETICAL
ORDINARY. BY ARCHIMAGIRUS METAPHORICUS, [1750].
A. Sherbo, *Christopher Smart, Scholar of the University*, 1967, p. 42, records that
this was s b JN; there is no evidence of this in the bk itself, where no publisher,
seller or place is named. [BM.

A282. KIDGELL, John. THE CARD.
(1) Ed. 1755. S b JN (see Plate 31). 2 vols. Welsh 247. *CBEL*, II, 545. [BM;
Bodley; CUL; CLU.
(2) Listed in A637(2), 1768, vol. v, as pr f a s b JN. Price 6*s*. Probably stock in
hand of the 1755 ed.

A283. KIMBER, Edward. LIFE AND ADVENTURES OF JAMES
RAMBLE, THE, 1770. 'A new [i.e. the 2nd] ed.'. Pr f FN(N). 2 vols, price 5*s*
(also 6*s*). *CBEL*, II, 545. F. G. Black, *Edward Kimber*, 1935, p. 29. The 1st ed. was
by R. Baldwin in 1755. [BM.

KING'S EVIL. See DISSERTATION ON THE...

A284. KLOPSTOCK, Friedrich Gottlieb. THE MESSIAH. *CBEL*, II, 56
806.
(1) 2nd ed. 1766. Pr f FN(N) et al. 2 vols, price 6*s*. [BM; UCL.
(2) 3rd ed. 1769. S b FN(N) et al. 2 vols, price 5*s* sewed, 6*s* bd. [BM.
(3) 4th ed. 1769–71. S b FN(N) et al. 3 vols, price 9*s*; vol. III could be had alone,
price 2*s* 6*d* sewed, 3*s* bd. Vols I and II 1769, vol. III 1771. [Roscoe; BM.

A285. KNAPP, William. ANTHEM FOR CHRISTMAS DAY, AN, IN FOUR PARTS, WITH VARIETY OF HYMNS AND CARROLS FOR THAT JOYFUL FESTIVAL, NEVER BEFORE PUBLISHED. Adv. *GEP* 26–9.11.43 under this description as s b Mr Newbury (*sic*) et al. Price 1s.

A286. KNAPP, William. SETT OF NEW PSALM-TUNES [PSALMS] AND ANTHEMS, A. Welsh 248; *BUCM*, 1, 573. The 1st ed. was in 1738.
(1) 2nd ed. 1741. S b J. Newbury (*sic*) et al. Price 3s 6d (see Plate 32). [BM; NLSc.
(2) 3rd ed. 1747. S b J. Newberry (*sic*) et al. Price 3s 6d. [BM; Wigan; MPL.
(3) 4th ed. 1750. S b J. Newberry (*sic*) et al. Price 3s 6d. [BM.
(4) 5th ed. 1752. S b JN et al. Price 3s. [BM.
(5) 6th ed. 1754. Pr f JN et al. Price 3s. [BM.
(6) 7th ed. 1762. Pr f JN et al. Price 3s bd in red. [BM.
(7) 8th ed. 1770. Pr f C & N et al. Price 3s 6d 'bd sheep rolled'. [BM.

A287. LA CONDAMINE, Charles Marie de. AN EXTRACT FROM THE OBSERVATIONS MADE IN A TOUR TO ITALY.
(1) Ed. 1768. Pr f N & C. Price 2s in the vell. manner. Adv. *LC* 15–17.11.68, p. 475. *CBEL*, 11, 784. [BM.
(2) Listed as s b TC in J147(9), 1786. Listed in 1789. Welsh 192. Price 2s.

LALLY, Count. MEMOIRS OF. See Tollendal, T. A. de.

A288. LAMBERT, Edward. THE ART OF CONFECTIONARY, n.d. FN(N). A. W. Oxford, p. 81, gives impossible date *ca.* 1750. [BM (copy destroyed).

A289. LAND OF CAKES AND ALE, THE. Adv. *GA* 3.12.46 as s b JN et al. Price 1s. The only copy traced (NLSc) was pr f R. Williams. Welsh 251; *BUCM*, 2, 593.

A290. LA ROCHE, Marie Sophie von. HISTORY OF LADY SOPHIA STERNHEIM, ATTEMPTED FROM THE GERMAN OF MR. WIELAND. Listed in A640(3), vol. 18, 1778 as pr f C & N. No copy with their imprint seen.

A291. LENGLET DU FRESNOY, Nicolas. CHRONOLOGICAL TABLES OF UNIVERSAL HISTORY, 1762. Pr f JN et al. 2 pts. Listed at 12s in 1762, 10s in 1764. Welsh 185–6; *CBEL*, 11, 622 and 788. [BM; EdUL; AdE.

A292. LENNOX, Charlotte. THE LADY'S MUSEUM, 1760–1. Pr f J. Newberry (*sic*) et al. 2 vols, price 1s each number, monthly. Welsh 252; *CBEL*, 11, 476. [OEFL; BM (destroyed).

A293. LE ROY, Julien. SUCCINCT ACCOUNT OF THE ATTEMPTS...FOR FINDING THE LONGITUDE AT SEA, 1768. Pr f FN(N). Price 2s 6d. [Bodley.

A294. LETTER TO THE EARL OF HALIFAX ON THE PEACE. Pr f JN. Price 1s. Adv. *LC* 19–22.2.63, p. 184, and *LM* Aug. 1763.

A295. LETTER TO THE PEOPLE OF GREAT BRITAIN, A, IN ANSWER TO THAT PUBLISHED BY THE AMERICAN CONGRESS. Newbery*. Price 1s. Listed *LM* March 1775, p. 148.

A296. LETTERS OF CONSOLATION TO A NOBLEMAN UNDER SENTENCE OF DEATH. JN et al. Price 1s. Listed *LM* July 1760. Welsh 253, whose date 1750 is apparently ten years too early.

A297. LETTERS ON THE MEDICAL SERVICE IN THE ROYAL NAVY. [E]N. Noticed in *The English Review*, July 1783, p. 67. The authorship of Wm Rowley seems indicated; cf. A465 and A466.

A298. LETTRES PORTUGUISES (*sic*). Newbery*. Price 1s. Listed *LM* 1767 Appendix, p. 693.

A299. LINDLEY, George. A PLAN OF AN ORCHARD. S b EN et al. Price 2s. Adv. *LC* 17–19.3.96, p. 269. Not traced. Unknown to the Royal Horticultural Society.

A300. LINDSAY, Rev. John. THE EVANGELICAL HISTORY OF OUR LORD JESUS CHRIST. Welsh 214 and 242; *CBEL*, II, 621; Courtney 78; Chapman 140–1.
(1) Welsh records that B. Collins of Salisbury valued his fourth share in this book, in 1746, at 15 gns.
(2) An ed. of 1757. Pr f JN et al. 2 vols, price 8s. [BM.
(3) Adv. *LC* 26–8.8.73, p. 203, as to be had of C & N, price 7s for the 2 vols in one, in the vell. manner.

A300A. LITERARY MAGAZINE, THE, OR UNIVERSAL REVIEW, 1756–8. *CBEL*, II, 673 and 678; Courtney 75ff; *BUCOP*, 3, 65. Welsh 35–6 says this was one of JN's ventures, though his name is not mentioned in the production.

A301. LLOYD, Robert. THE PROGRESS OF ENVY. A POEM.
(1) Ed. 1751. Pr f JN. Price 1s. Welsh 295. [BM.
(2) Adv. *LC* 3–5.3.72, p. 223, as to be had of C & N. Price 1s.

A301A. LOCKE, John. ESSAY, AN, CONCERNING HUMAN UNDERSTANDING, 1795. Pr f TC, FN et al. Alston, VII, 109. H. O. Christophersen, *Bibliographical Introduction to the Study of John Locke*, Oslo, 1930, p. 93. As to TC's name in an imprint 7 years after his death. 'FN' could indicate Francis the son or be a misprint for 'EN'. [BM; Bodley; GlaUL; MBAt; MH; NjP; OB; NN; PPiU; Vi.

A302. LOCKMAN, John. HISTORY, A, OF THE CRUEL SUFFERINGS OF THE PROTESTANTS. Sometimes referred to as *Lockman's Persecutions.*
(1) Ed. 1760. Pr f JN et al. Price 3s. [BM; Bodley.
(2) Adv. *LC* 29–31.12.68 as pr f N & C et al. Price 3s.

A303. LOCKMAN, John. MISCELLANIES. Proposals for the work, to be pr in 2 vols by subscription, were adv. in *PA* 1.4.56, the subs. being taken in by 'Mr Newbery' et al.

A304. LOCKMAN, John. POEMS ON VARIOUS OCCASIONS. Proposals for printing the *Poems* by subscription, 2 vols, price 1 gn in sheets, appeared in *LC* for 9–11.3.62; receipts would be delivered by 'Mr Newbery' et al.

A305. LOGGON, Samuel. THE HISTORY OF THE BROTHER-HOOD OR GUILD OF THE HOLY GHOST, 1742. Pr b JN et al. Legg, no. 16. [BM; Bodley; RePL; Rylands.

A306. LOMMIUS, Jodocus. THE MEDICAL OBSERVATIONS OF JODOCUS LOMMIUS...WITH A LETTER AND PREFACE BY J. WYNTER.
(1) Listed in A370(2), 1753, as 'just pubd' by JN. W. Owen had put out an ed. in 1747 and JN may quite possibly have bought the stock of sheets.
(2) Listed in A640(3), vol. xx, 1778, as pr f C & N. Price 3s.

A306A. LONDON CHRONICLE, THE; OR, UNIVERSAL EVENING POST, 1757–. Welsh 336; *CBEL*, II, 698 and 710; *BUCOP*, 3, 87. Stanley Morison, *The English Newspaper*, pp. 135–7. There is no conclusive evidence that JN was concerned in the founding or subsequent conduct of this paper, which appeared in its early years under the imprint of J. Wilkie, but it seems likely enough – see the Introduction at pp. 10, 14, 16, 18. [BM, and see *BUCOP*.

A307. LONDON, CITY OF. ALL THE ROYAL CHARTERS GRANTED BY THE SEVERAL KINGS AND QUEENS OF ENGLAND TO THE CITY OF LONDON, FROM WILLIAM I (COMMONLY CALLED THE CONQUEROR) WITH AN EXPLANATION OF THE SAXON AND OTHER TERMS.

Pr f R. Crockatt, s b JN. Listed *LM* Dec. 1749, p. 580 and adv. *GA* 20.12.49. Price 6*d*, a few copies on a superfine royal paper 1*s*. Described in *GA* as 'adapted for framing, that they may hang always in view'. Apparently a broadsheet.

A308. LONDON COMPANION, THE...OR AN ACCOUNT OF THE FARES OF HACKNEY COACHMEN, CHAIRMEN, AND WATERMEN...
(1) 1st ed. 1773. Pr f TC. Price 2*s* sewed (see Plate 33). Welsh 258. [BM; EdUL; Oup.
(2) 2nd ed. 1775. Pr f TC. Price 2*s*. [Bodley.
(3) Listed as pr f TC in A399(5), 1781 and A399(6), 1784. Price 2*s*.

A309. LOVAT, Simon Fraser, Lord. THE AUTHENTIC LIFE OF SIMON FRASER, LORD LOVAT. Adv. in A310 as 'preparing for the Press, and speedily w b p by J. Newbery'.

A310. LOVAT, Simon Fraser, Lord. A CANDID AND IMPARTIAL ACCOUNT OF THE BEHAVIOUR OF SIMON, LORD LOVAT, 1747. Welsh 259. One of the following is in AdE. A copy of nos. (1) or (3) in DNS. All dated 1747.
(1) Pr f JN, W. Faden and W. Owen. Price 6*d*. Collates [a][A]–[C4][D3]; pp. 29[30]. [BM; Bodley; Rylands; EdUL.
(2) Another issue. Pr f JN and W. Faden, otherwise as for no. (1). [BM; Bodley; CUL.
(3) Another ed. Pr f JN, W. Faden and W. Owen. Price 6*d*. Collates [A]–[D4]; pp. 13 (error for 31). [Bodley.

A311. LYLE, David. THE ART OF SHORTHAND IMPROVED. Adv. *LC* 20–2.4.69 as pr f FN(N) et al. Price 10*s* 6*d*. There was an ed. of 1762 by A. Millar. Welsh 260.

A312. MACBEAN, Alexander. A DICTIONARY OF THE BIBLE. Welsh 174. See A116.
(1) Adv. *LC* 24–7.10.78, p. 405, as to be pubd b C & N on 31 Oct. Price 6*s*. Probably = no. (2).
(2) Ed. 1779. Pr f C & N. Price probably 6*s*. [BM; Bodley; EdUL; CUL; AdE.
(3) Listed in A401(5), 1787, as pr f TC. Price 6*s*.

A313. MACQUER, Pierre Joseph. THE ELEMENTS OF THE THEORY AND PRACTICE OF CHEMISTRY, 1758. Adv. in *PA* 5.10.54 as speedily to be pubd b JN. His name not in this ed. or that of 1764.

A314. MALLET, Paul Henri. NORTHERN ANTIQUITIES.
(1) Ed. 1770. Pr f Carnan & Co. 2 vols, price 10*s* 6*d* in the vell. manner, 12*s* calf.

The significance of 'Carnan & Co' as against the usual 'T. Carnan' is not apparent; see note to J231(6). Welsh 261; *CBEL*, II, 70. [BM; Bodley; CUL; LUL; LL; EdUL; UCL; LGL; AdE; DNS.

(2) Listed in J147(9), 1786, as s b TC, price 10*s* 6*d* 'in the vellum manner, labelled on the back', 12*s* calf, 'lettered with registers'.

A315. MARAT, Jean Paul. A PHILOSOPHICAL ESSAY ON MAN, 1773. Pr f FN(N) et al. 2 vols, price 10*s* 6*d* sewed. Another issue is under the imprints of J. Ridley and T. Payne. [BM; Bodley; CUL; LUL; EdUL.

A316. MARGATE GUIDE, THE. This is a revision of A172, the plate of the bathing machine (Pl. 26) and the map of Thanet used in the earlier work are included.
(1) Ed. 1770. Pr f C & N. Price 1*s*. [BM; Bodley.
(2) A 'new ed., corrected', 1775. Pr f C & N et al. Price 1*s*. [Roscoe; BM; EdUL.
(3) Ed. 1780. Pr f TC et al. Price 1*s*. [BM.
(4) Ed. 1785. Pr f TC et al. Price 1*s*. [BM (imperf.); Bodley; EdUL.

A317. MARRA, John. JOURNAL OF THE RESOLUTION'S VOYAGE, IN 1772–5, 1775. Pr f FN(N). Price 5*s* in bds. Ed. by David Henry and forms vol. v of A218. *CBEL*, II, 742; Spence p. 14. [BM; Bodley; LL; NLA.

A318. MARTIAL REVIEW, THE, 1763. Pr f JN. Price 3*s*. IAW 129–30; *CBEL*, II, 645. [BM.

A319. MARTIN, Benjamin. COURSE OF LECTURES IN NATURAL AND EXPERIMENTAL PHILOSOPHY, 1743. Pr a s b JN et al. Price 5*s*. Welsh 263–4; Legg no. 21. [BM; Bodley; LUL; RePL; POL; ReU; NUTPL; OMHS; RMS; PPL.

A320. MARTIN, Benjamin. DICTIONARY – ENGLISH DICTIONARY – NEW UNIVERSAL DICTIONARY – UNIVERSAL ENGLISH DICTIONARY. Probably advert. titles for A323.

A321. MARTIN, Benjamin. ESSAY ON ELECTRICITY, 1746. Pr f 'Mr Newbury' et al. Price 6*d*. [BM; Bodley; POL; CUL; CQC; LGL; LEB; Bath; OMHS; PPL; DLC.

A322. MARTIN, Benjamin. INSTITUTIONS OF LANGUAGE.
(1) Ed. 1748. Pr f J. Newberry (*sic*) et al. Price 2*s*. Afterwards forms pt of A323. Alston, I, 103. [BM; GlaUL; MH; INC; Gabrielson; DNS; PU.
(2) Listed in A326(4), 1771, as pr f C & N. Price 2*s* sewed.

A323. MARTIN, Benjamin. LINGUA BRITANNICA REFORMATA. *CBEL*, II, 930; Alston, v, 163, does not distinguish between nos. (1) and (2). For other locations see Alston.

(1) 1st ed. 1749. Pr f JN et al. Price 6*s*. Welsh 265. The section [A]–[P4] is A322(1). Title to this section has imprint in names of S. Birt, J. Hodges, J. Newberry (*sic*), R. Raikes, J. Leake, W. Frederick and B. Collins. [BM; Bodley; MPL; NUTU.

(2) Another issue, the imprint to the section title being in names of S. Birt, J. Hodges, J. Newberry (*sic*), B. Collins, J. Leake, W. Frederick and R. Raikes. [OEFL.

(3) 2nd ed. 1754. Pr f JN et al. Price 6*s*. Alston, v, 164. [BM; Bodley; POL; NLWa; BmPL; LEB; Gabrielson; Madison; MB; MH; CtY; DCL (et al. – see Alston).

(4) Still adv. *Morning Chronicle* 10 Oct. 1772.

A324. MARTIN, Benjamin. MICROGRAPHIA NOVA, 1742. Pr a s b JN et al. Price 2*s* 6*d*. Welsh 263; Legg no. 17. [BM; Bodley; LUL; ScM; POL; RS; OMHS; RMS; PPL.

A325. MARTIN, Benjamin. NEW PRINCIPLES OF GEOGRAPHY AND NAVIGATION. Welsh 262–3.

(1) Ed. 1758. S b JN. Price 10*s* 6*d* half-bd; the charts could be had separately at 1*s* 6*d*. [BM; CUL; POL; Adm; RAS; PPL.

(2) Listed in A326(4), 1771, as pr f C & N. Price 10*s* 6*d* half-bd.

A326. MARTIN, Benjamin. PHILOSOPHIA BRITANNICA. Welsh 264.

(1) 1st ed. 1747, adv. *GA* 23.8.49 as pr f JN et al. His name not in the imprint.

(2) 2nd ed. 2 vols, 1752. Pr f JN et al. Price 12*s*. [PPL, not seen.

(3) 2nd ed. 3 vols, 1759. Pr f JN et al. Price 18*s*. [RI; Bodley; CUL; EdUL (vol. II).

(4) 3rd ed. 1771. Pr f C & N et al. Price 18*s*. Babson 90. [BM; EdUL (vols I and III); ScM; UCL; CQC; Babson.

(5) 4th ed. 1788. Pr f TC et al. 3 vols, price 1 gn. [CUL; BmU(Wigan); LEIU(Phys.).

A327. MARTIN, Benjamin. PHYSICO-GRAMMATICAL ESSAY ON THE PROPRIETY AND RATIONALE OF THE ENGLISH TONGUE. Welsh 265. This is A322.

A328. MARTIN, Benjamin. SUPPLEMENT, A: CONTAINING REMARKS ON A RHAPSODY OF ADVENTURES, 1746. Pr f 'Mr Newbury' et al. Price 6*d*. [BM; Bodley; CQC; MPL; DLC; PPL; Wheeler.

A329. MARTIN, Benjamin. SUPPLEMENT TO THE
PHILOSOPHIA BRITANNICA.
(1) Ed. 1759. Listed as pr f a s b JN in A640(1), vol. IX, 1760. No names in
imprint. [BM; RS.
(2) An ed. to accompany A326(4), 1771, was 'to be had alone' for 2s 6d. (LC
8–10.10.72, p. 348.)

A330. MARTIN, Benjamin. SYNOPSIS SCIENTIÆ CELESTIS, OR
THE KNOWLEDGE OF THE HEAVENS AND THE EARTH.
Adv. in A324, 1742, and in *GEP* 17–20.9.43 as s b JN et al. Price 3s. Welsh 265;
Legg 122.

A331. MASON, Charlotte. THE LADY'S ASSISTANT. 8th ed. 1801. Pr
f EN et al. Price 7s. Not in A. W. Oxford. [BM.

A332. MASON, Henry. LECTURES UPON THE HEART, n.d. S b
JN. Price 1s 6d. Adv. *LC* 5–7.4.63, p. 332, as 'Saturday next w b p'. [RCP; RCS.

A333. MASSILLON, Jean Baptiste. SERMONS 'ON THE DUTIES
OF THE GREAT', 1769. Pr f FN(N) et al. Price 4s sewed. *CBEL*, II, 790.
[Bodley.

A334. MAVOR, William Fordyce. BRITISH TOURISTS, THE. Welsh
266.
(1) 1st ed. 1798–1800. Pr f EN. 6 vols. I–V 1798, VI 1800. Various prices, from 3s
each vol. [BM; Bodley; EdUL (*ex* vol. VI); Weedon.
(2) 2nd ed. 1800. Pr f EN. 5 vols. Price 15s sewed or 17s 6d bd and lettered. No
2nd ed. of vol. VI. [LUL.

A335. MAVOR, William Fordyce. HISTORICAL ACCOUNT OF
THE MOST CELEBRATED VOYAGES. *CBEL*, II, 741.
(1) The 20-vol. ed. of 1796–7. Pr f EN. 2s 6d each vol., the set £2 10s–£3 10s.
Welsh 266–7. [BM; Quayle; NLA (vols 4, 6, 7, 8, 9, 15).
(2) The 25-vol. ed. of 1796–1801. Pr f (or s b) EN. Consists of vols II–XX of
no. (1), plus a new vol. I and vols XXI–XXV, these six being dated 1801. Sold at
3s each. [Bodley; CUL; LUL.

A336. MAVOR, William Fordyce. LADY'S AND GENTLEMAN'S
BOTANICAL POCKET BOOK. Adv. *LC* 25–7.2.1800, p. 196, as pr f
EN, and Vernor and Hood. Only the latter's names in imprint.

A337. MAVOR, William Fordyce. NEW DESCRIPTION OF
BLENHEIM. Welsh 265–6.
(1) A 'new and improved ed.', 1793. Pr f EN et al. Price 2s 6d plain, 3s coloured.
[BM; Sotheby, 3.6.69, lot 615.

(2) 4th ed. 1797. Pr f EN et al. Price 2s 6d or 3s with the plan coloured. [BM; Bodley.

(3) 5th ed. n.d. Pr f EN et al. [Bodley.

(4) Welsh 266 records a French ed. *Blenheim, nouvelle Description de.* Listed 1797 as by EN, 2s 6d plain, 3s coloured. Cadell put out a French ed. in 1791.

A338. MAVOR, William Fordyce. POEMS. Welsh 266 records *Poems, descriptive Elegies, Epistles, Odes, Sylva or Miscellanies, Songs and Sonnets.* Listed 1797 as by EN. There was an ed. of 1793 by G. G. J. and J. Robinson.

A339. MAVOR, William Fordyce. UNIVERSAL STENOGRAPHY. An ed., sometimes 'the third', was adv. between 1792 and 1796 as pr f or s b EN et al., price 10s 6d. Welsh 266. No copy with EN's name seen.

A340. MAWE, Thomas, and John ABERCROMBIE. EVERY MAN HIS OWN GARDENER. It is recorded that all edd. after the 6th (1773) were by Abercrombie alone.

(1) 9th ed. 1782. Pr f EN et al. Price 5s. [RHS.

(2) 10th ed. Adv. *LC* 17–19.8.84, p. 173, as pr f EN et al. Price 5s.

(3) 11th ed. Adv. *LC* 26–8.4.87, p. 404, as pr f EN et al. Price 5s.

(4) 12th ed. 1788. Pr f EN et al. Price 5s. [BM; CUL.

(5) 13th ed. 1791. Pr f EN et al. [BM; A. R. Heath, Cat. 16 [1970] item 299.

(6) 14th ed. 1794. Pr f EN et al. [Sotheby, 18.12.67, lot 159.

(7) 15th ed. 1797. Pr f EN et al. Price 6s. [BM; Quaritch, Cat. 901 [1970] item 664.

(8) 16th ed. 1800. Pr f EN et al. Price 7s 6d. [BM.

A341. MEDICAL MUSEUM, THE. *BUCOP*, 3, 166; *CBEL*, II, 678.

(1) Vols I–III of 1st ed. pubd by W. Bristow 1763. *LC* for 28–30.12.69 announced the publicn 'on Monday next' of 'No. 1 of *The Medical Museum.* Volume IV and last' in 4 numbers at 1s 6d. To be pubd b FN(? S). This vol. IV not in *BUCOP*.

(2) 2nd ed. 1781. S b 'Newberry' (= ? EN) et al. 4 vols. [Wellcome (vols I–III); BM (vols I–IV destroyed); Sotheby, 12.12.67, lot 426.

A342. MEIER, Georg Friedrich. THE MERRY PHILOSOPHER.

(1) Ed. 1764. Pr f JN et al. Price 2s 6d sewed, 3s bd. *CBEL*, II, 806 (records 2 vols). [BM; CUL.

(2) Ed. 1765. Pr f JN et al. Prices as for no. (1). This is no. (1) with a new TP. [BM; Bodley; EdUL; Weedon (imperf.).

(3) Listed and adv. as by C & N up to A640(3), vol. XIX, 1778, prices as for no. (1).

A343. MELVILL, John. OBSERVATIONS ON THE NATURE AND PROPERTIES OF FIXIBLE AIR.

(1) An undated ed. S b EN et al. (BM dates [1780]). [BM (7460.aaa.25); CUL.

(2) Another undated ed. S b EN et al. (BM dates [1789]). The differences between this and no. (1) are not apparent. [BM (546.d.26(6)).

A344. MERCHANT AND TRADESMAN'S DAILY REGISTER, THE. Adv. *LC* 29–31.12.63, p. 631, as s b JN. Price 5s.

A345. MERCURIUS LATINUS, 1746 (see Plate 34). JN's name as seller (*prostat...apud Joannem Newbery*) appears in nos. 5–31, when the paper closed down. It is likely that JN was concerned in the paper from the beginning. Price for nos. 5–6 2d, 25–31 3d. *BUCOP*, 3, 184; *CBEL*, II, 719. [BM; Bodley.

A346. Entry deleted.

A347. MERRICK, James. ANNOTATIONS ON THE PSALMS, 1768. S b N & C et al. Price 10s sewed. Legg no. 49. [BM; Bodley; EdUL.

A348. MERRICK, James. DISSERTATION ON PROVERBS, CHAP. IX, V. 1–6.
(1) Ed. 1744. S b JN et al. Price 1s. [BM; Bodley; CUL; Lambeth.
(2) Adv. *LC* 6–9.8.68, p. 135, as to be had of N & C et al. Price 1s.

A349. MERRICK, James. LETTER TO THE REV. MR. JOSEPH WARTON, 1764. S b 'Mr. Newbery' et al. Price 3d. Welsh 268; Legg no. 41. [BM; Bodley; CUL; LGL; Loveday; Traylen.

A350. MERRICK, James. POEMS ON SACRED SUBJECTS, 1763. Sometimes adv. as 'to be had of' or s b N & C et al. No copy seen under their imprint. Welsh 268; *CBEL*, II, 374.

A351. MERRICK, James. PSALMS, THE, TRANSLATED OR PARAPHRASED IN ENGLISH VERSE. Welsh 267–8; *CBEL*, II, 374; Legg nos 44, 45.
(1) 1st ed. 1765. S b 'Mr Newbery' (no doubt JN) et al. Price 10s 6d sewed. [BM; Bodley; CUL; Rylands; EdUL; LUL.
(2) 2nd ed. 1766. S b 'Mr Newbery' et al. Price 3s. [BM; Bodley; CUL; LL; AdE; NLA.

A352. Entry deleted.

A353. MERRICK, James. SHORT MANUAL OF PRAYERS, A.
(1) 2nd ed. 1768. S b 'Newbery & Co' et al. Price 1d or 7s 6d a hundred. Legg 50. [Bodley; Loveday.
(2) Another, 'enlarged' 2nd ed. 1768. S b 'Mess Newbery & Co'. Price 2d or 15s a hundred. Legg 51. [Loveday, not seen.

A354. MERRICK, John. HELIOCRENE. A POEM IN LATIN AND ENGLISH, 1744. JN et al. Price 6*d*. See Chas. Coates, *Supplement to the History and Antiquities of Reading*, 1810. Legg 22. [Loveday, not seen.

A355. METASTASIO, Pietro A. D. B. DIDON ABANDONÉE, EN TROIS ACTES, trans. b Mary Grignon. Adv. *LC* 17–20.10.1801, p. 383, as s b EN et al. Price 2*s* 6*d* sewed.

A356. MIDDLESEX JOURNAL, THE: OR, UNIVERSAL EVENING POST, 1772–3. Nos 547–86 pr f FN(N), nos 587–91 pr f EN. Price 2½*d*. *BUCOP*, 3, 206; *CBEL*, II, 710. [BM; Bodley, and see *BUCOP*.

A357. MIHLES, Samuel. MEDICAL ESSAYS AND OBSERVATIONS, 1745. Pr f JN et al. 2 vols, price 10*s* (later 12*s*). Welsh 269. [BM; RCP; EdUL.

A358. MILLER, Philip. ABRIDGEMENT OF THE GARDENERS DICTIONARY, THE. 6th ed. 1771. S b FN* et al. Price £1 5*s*. [BM.

A359. MILTON, John. POETICAL WORKS.
(1) A 'new ed.', with notes by Thomas Newton. Pr f FN* et al. 3 vols, price £3 15*s*. Adv. *LC* 18–21.3.78, p. 309.
(2) An ed. by Newton. Adv. *LC* 20–3.3.90, p. 276, as pr f EN et al. 4 vols, price £1 6*s*.
(3) An ed. with Newton's text and *Life* by Aikin, 1801. Pr f EN et al. 4 vols, price 1 gn in bds. [LUL.

A360. MILTON, John. FAMILIAR EXPLANATION, A, OF THE POETICAL WORKS OF MILTON. Preface by Wm Dodd.
(1) Ed. 1762. Pr f JN et al. Price 2*s* 6*d* bd calf. Welsh 270; *CBEL*, II, 360. [Bodley; BM; CUL; AdE.
(2) Adv. *LC* 18–20.1.74, p. 67, as pr f C & N, price 2*s* 6*d*.

A361. MILTON, John. PARADISE LOST.
(1) An 8th ed. 1775. Notes by Newton. Pr f FN* et al. 2 vols. [LUL; CUL.
(2) Another 8th ed. 1778. Notes by Newton. Pr f F. Newbury* (*sic*) et al. Price 12*s*. [BM; Bodley.
(3) Another ed. 1778, in 1 vol. Ed. b Newton. Pr f FN* et al. Price 3*s* 6*d*. [BM.
(4) An ed. 1788, in 1 vol. John Gillies' ed. Pr f EN et al. Price 3*s* 6*d*. [BM; CUL; AdE.
(5) 9th ed. 1790. Notes by Newton. Pr f EN et al. 2 vols. [BM; LUL; AdE.
(6) Another 9th ed. 1790, Tonson's text. 1 vol. Pr f EN et al. [BM.
(7) Ed. 1795, with Fenton's *Life* and Johnson's Criticism. 1 vol. Pr f EN et al. [BM (thick paper); Bodley; LUL; Rylands; UCL.

A362. MISCELLANEOUS WORKS, SERIOUS AND HUMEROUS: IN VERSE AND PROSE, 1740. S b JN et al. Bodley attributes to Saml Boyse. Welsh 270; Legg no. 11. [BM; Bodley; RePL.

A363. MODERN FAMILY PHYSICIAN, THE, 1775. Pr f FN(N). Price 3s. Welsh 283. [BM.

A364. MODERN PARISH OFFICER, THE. Pr f FN(N) et al. Adv. *LC* 7–10.5.74, p. 443, as 'a new ed.', price 3s 6d.

A365. MONTAGU, Lady Barbara and Sarah SCOTT. A DESCRIPTION OF MILLENIUM HALL. Welsh 269; IAW 127; *CBEL*, II, 556 and 644; Scott 90–1.
(1) 1st ed. 1762. Pr f JN. Price 3s (see Plate 35). [BM; CUL; Bodley; LUL; LL; Traylen; Grant; Sotheby, 6.2.1945 (the Bussell sale), lot 224.
(2) 2nd ed. 1764. Pr f JN. Price 3s. [BM; Bodley; CUL; Sotheby, 18.3.71, lot 323.
(3) 3rd ed. 1767. Pr f JN. Price 3s in the vell. manner. [BM; Bodley; CUL.
(4) 4th ed. 1778. Pr f C & N. Price 3s. [BM; CUL; Renier; Falkner Grierson Cat. 7 [1967] item 576.

A366. MONTHLY CHRONICLE, A: OR, HISTORICAL REGISTER, 1773. Price 6d monthly. Apparently unrecorded. Adv. *LC* in 1773: *January issue* adv. 2–4 Feb., p. 117, as pr f TC. *February issue* adv. 27 Feb.–2 Mar., p. 203, as pr f TC, s b J. Walter. *March issue* adv. 1–3 April, p. 319, as s b TC and Walter. *April issue* adv. 1–4 May, p. 419, as pr f TC and Walter.

A367. MOORE, Francis. TRAVELS INTO THE INLAND PARTS OF AFRICA, 2nd ed. Recorded by Welsh 271 as in an undated FN* bk-list. The 2nd ed. was by Henry and R. Cave. *CBEL*, II, 749.

A368. MORE, Hannah. INFLEXIBLE CAPTIVE, THE. *CBEL*, II, 844; Nicoll 288.
(1) 1st ed. 1774. S b C & N et al. Price 1s 6d. [BM; Bodley.
(2) 2nd ed. 1774. The same.
(3) 3rd ed. 1774. The same. [BM; LUL; Rylands.

A369. MORE, Hannah. SEARCH AFTER HAPPINESS, A (THE). *CBEL*, II, 844; Nicoll 288. In 2nd and later edd. the title is *The Search...*
(1) Undated ed. [1768–73] (BM date [1777] is too late). The title *A Search...* indicates 1st ed. S b C & N et al. Price 2s 6d. [BM (11631.g.20); Bodley; Hannas, Cat. 25 [1968] item 537.
(2) 2nd ed. 1773. S b C & N et al. Price 1s 6d. [BM; Bodley; CUL.
(3) 3rd ed. 1774. As for no. (2). [BM (imperf.).
(4) 4th ed. 1774. As for no. (2). [BM (imperf.); CUL (imperf.).

(5) 5th ed. 1774. As for no. (2). [BM.
(6) 6th ed. 1775. As for no. (2). [BM (imperf.); Rylands.

A370. MORE, St THOMAS. UTOPIA (Burnet's trans.). Welsh 271.
(1) Ed. 1751. Pr f JN. Tp reads *improv'd by Thomas Williamson*. [BM; Bodley; LUL; UCL; NLA.
(2) Another issue, 1753. Pr f TC. Price 2s 6d. This is no. (1) with a new TP, reading *improv'd by a Gentleman of Oxford*. [Roscoe; BM; Bodley.
(3) Frequently listed up to 1767, and in 1768 and 1773 as pubd b N & C. Price 2s 6d.
(4) Listed in J147(9), vol. II, 1786, as s b TC. Price 2s 6d.

A371. MOSHEIM, Johann Lorenz von. ECCLESIASTICAL HISTORY. Welsh 271 refers to proposals in May 1761 for a trans. to be pubd b JN et al.

A372. MOURY, Chevalier de. THE FORTUNATE COUNTRY MAID. Listed as 'just pubd a s b' JN, price 5s, 2 vols, in A1(1), 1745. Both bk and author apparently unrecorded.

A373. MURPHY, Arthur. ESSAY ON THE LIFE AND GENIUS OF SAMUEL JOHNSON.
(1) 1st ed. 1792. Pr f EN et al. Price 4s in bds. Also issued as vol. I of A274(2), 1792. *CBEL*, II, 479. [BM; Bodley; CUL; EdUL; AdE; DNS.
(2) 2nd ed. 1793. Pr f EN et al. Price 4s in bds. [BM; Bodley; LUL; DNS.
(3) 3rd ed. 1796. Pr f EN et al. This is vol. I of A274(3), 1796.

A373A. MUSES BANQUET, THE. Welsh 273.
(1) Ed. 1752. Pr f TC et al. 2 vols, price 2s 6d. *CBEL*, II, 215; Legg no. 33. [Bodley.
(2) Frequently listed as pr f JN up to 1767, and in 1769 as by N & C. Price 2s 6d. There were several collns of songs under this title in this period.

A374. MUSEUM RUSTICUM ET COMMERCIALE. G. E. Fussell 154–5 *et passim*; *CBEL*, II, 645 and 678; *BUCOP*, 3, 280.
(1) 1st ed. [1763]1764–6. Pr f JN et al. 6 vols. Prices, monthly pts 1s, vols 6s or 6s 6d, the set of vols I–IV £1 5s, the set of 6 vols £1 19s in 1769. [BM; Bodley; CUL (vols I–V); LUL (vols II–VI); LL (vols II–VI); EdUL (vols I–V).
(2) 2nd ed. 1764–6. Pr f JN et al. The only reference to 'second edition' is in the drop title to the Sept. 1763 number in vol. I. There are minor textual revisions throughout the 6 vols. [Bodley; LUL (vol. I); LL.
(3) 3rd ed. vol. I, 1766. Pr f JN et al. [BM; Deighton Bell, Cat. 91 [1964] item 137.
(4) *CBEL* records a date 1768. Not traced.

A375. MUSIC MADE EASY; OR A NEW MUSICAL VADE-
MECUM, 1798. S b EN et al. to be completed in 8 pts at 1s. *BUCM*, 2, 717 says
probably only the 1st 8 leaves were published. [BM.

A376. NEEDHAM, John. HYMNS DEVOTIONAL AND MORAL,
1768. S b N & C et al. Price 3s. [BM; Bodley; LL.

A377. NELSON, Robert. A COMPANION FOR THE FESTIVALS
...OF THE CHURCH OF ENGLAND.
(1) 24th ed. 1782. Pr f EN et al. Price 5s. [BM.
(2) 25th ed., not by EN.
(3) 26th ed. 1791. Pr f EN et al. Price 6s. [Bodley.
(4) 27th ed. adv. *LC* 20–3.12.94, p. 606, as pr f EN et al. Price 6s.
(5) 28th ed. adv. *LC* 30.12.1800–1.1.1801, p. 7, as pr f EN et al. Price 7s.

A378. NEW BRITISH DISPENSATORY, 1781. Pr f FN(N). Price 3s.
[RCP; EdUL.

A379. NEW ENGLISH THEATRE, THE. *CBEL*, II, 392. The 12-vol.
colln adv. in the Press in 1776–7 as pubd b FN* et al. The name does not appear
in any imprint. *LC* for 5–7.5.91, p. 439, adv. the 13th and 14th vols, price 7s, by
F. Power & Co et al. (no copies seen). *London Catalogue* for 1811 listed the 14
vols at 2 gns.

NEW OXFORD GUIDE. See OXFORD.

A380. NEWBERY'S CATALOGUE OF INSTRUCTIVE...
PUBLICATIONS FOR YOUNG MINDS, 1800. Pr b J. Cundee. See the
Introduction, at p. 31. [BM.

A381. NEWBERY, Francis S. DONUM AMICIS, 1815. Pr f the Author.
Welsh 276. [BM; Bodley; CUL; Weedon; Hannas.

NEWBERY, Francis S. HORACE – SECOND EPISTLE... See
HORACE, A240.

A382. NEWBERY, Francis S. OBSERVATIONS ON THE INCOME
TAX ACT, 1801. Pr f G. & W. Nicol. Price 2s. Welsh 276 (dates 1800); Kress,
B.4426. [BM; Bodley.

A383. NEWBERY, Francis S. THOUGHTS ON TAXATION,
1799. Pr a s b D. Holt et al. Kress, B.3942. [BM.

A384. NEWBERY, John. ESSAY ON PERFECTING THE FINE
ARTS IN GREAT BRITAIN AND IRELAND, 1767. *CBEL*, II, 30.
No copy traced.

A385. NEWS-READERS POCKET-BOOK, THE.
(1) Ed. 1759. Pr f JN. Price 2*s*. Welsh 277. The section with running title 'Military Dictionary' is an enlarged ed. of pp. 275–310 of A157. [Weedon.
(2) Frequently listed and adv. between 1768 and 1778 as pubd b C & N, price 2*s*.

A386. NOUVEAU MAGAZIN FRANCOIS, LE, 1750. Pr f a s b JN et al. Welsh 278. Not in *BUCOP*. Price 6*d* for the Jan. 1750 number; to be continued monthly, but no further edition traced.

A387. NOVELLAS ESPANOLAS. Recorded by Welsh, p. 278, as 'From F. Newbery's List, 1769. Price 2*s* 6*d*.'

A388. ODE, AN, TO THE RT HON. THE MARCHIONESS OF GRANBY, [?1759]. Pr f JN. Price 1*s*. Welsh 233. [CUL (mutilated).

ODE, AN,...TO THE SAVOIR VIVRE CLUB. See Fenton, Richd.

A389. OECONOMY OF HEALTH, THE. S b FN* et al. Price 2*s* 6*d*. A free trans. from the Italian by Wm Combe. Adv. *LC* 16–19.3.76, p. 269, as t.d.w.p. [BM.

A390. OFFICES, THE, ACCORDING TO THE USE OF THE CHURCH OF ENGLAND FOR THE SOLEMNIZATION OF MATRIMONY... Adv. *LC* 23–5.4.67, p. 396, as s b JN et al. Price 3*s* 6*d* neatly bd black calf.

A391. OGILBY, John and William MORGAN. THE BEAUTIES OF GREAT BRITAIN, 1782. Pr f EN et al. Price 1*s* sewed in marbled paper, 2*s* 6*d* 'neatly bd with the Book of Roads'. Not in Fordham. [BM.

A392. OGILBY, John and William MORGAN. THE TRAVELLER'S POCKET-BOOK. Fordham 2, pp. 12–14. All listed were pr f EN et al.
(1) 21st ed. 1782. Price 1*s* 6*d*. [BM; Bodley.
(2) 22nd ed. 1785. Price '1*s* 6*d* single, or 2*s* 6*d* with the Companion'. [CUL.
(3) 23rd ed. 1788. Price as for no. (2). [BM; Oup.
(4) 24th ed. 1794. Price 2*s* in the vell. manner. [BM.

A393. O'HARA, Kane. MIDAS, AN ENGLISH BURLETTA, 6th ed. 1771. Nicoll 291; *CBEL*, II, 479. Listed in A401(3), 1777, as pr f TC, but his name not in the imprint.

OLD WOMAN'S MAGAZINE, THE. Sub-title to Smart's *The Midwife* (A552), which is sometimes so advertised.

OLIVET, Abbé d'. See Thoulier d'Olivet, P. J.

A394. ORIGINAL PIECES, CONCERNING THE PRESENT STATE OF THE PROTESTANTS AND GREEKS IN POLAND, 1767. No publr's name, but adv. *LC* 15–17.12.67, p. 581, as pr f FN(N) et al. [BM; Bodley; LUL; EdUL.

A395. OXFORD. THE NEW OXFORD GUIDE. Accurate dating of the many undated edd. of this work is almost impossible. Of the 6 undated 'sixth' edd. recorded here 3 vary chiefly in the engvd leaves and plan of the university and city. At least one ed., that of 1810 – probably more – appeared under the imprint (with others) of EN (spelt 'Newbury') after she had sold out to John Harris in 1802; see nos (13) and (14).
(1) 6th ed. n.d. Pr f FN(N) et al. Collates [a–a4]B–[G12]. Pp. vii+142[144]. Imprint names: J. Fletcher, S. Parker, W. Jackson, G. Kearsley, FN. [BM (731.b.24(1)); OxPL.
(2) Another 6th ed. n.d. Pr f FN(N) et al. Collates [a–a4]B–[G12][H6]. Pp. vii+556 (error for 156). Imprint names as for no. (1). [BM (731.b.24(2)).
(3) Another 6th ed. n.d. Pr f FN(N) et al. Collates as for no. (2). Pp. vii+156. Imprint names: J. Fletcher, S. Parker, W. Jackson, FN, J. Bew. [Bodley (Douce o.90).
(4) Another issue of the 6th ed. n.d. Pr f FN(N) et al. Collates and pagination as for no. (3). Imprint names as for no. (3). Variant engvd leaves and plan. [BM (10360.bbb.64).
(5) Another 6th ed. n.d. Pr f FN(N) et al. Collates [a–a4]B–[G12][H7]. Pp. vii+158. Imprint names as for no. (3). Variant engvd leaves. [BM (577.b.41).
(6) Another issue of the 6th ed. n.d. As for no. (5), with variant engvd leaves. [OxPL.
(7) 7th ed. 1786. Pr f EN et al. [Bodley (Gough Adds Gen Top 307(2)).
(8) Another issue of the 7th ed. 1787. This is no. (7), with altered date in TP. [Bodley (Gough Adds Oxon 8° 225).
(9) 8th ed. n.d. Pr f EN et al. [BM; OxPL.
(10) 9th and 10th edd. not traced.
(11) 11th ed. n.d. S b E. Newbury (*sic*) et al. [BM.
(12) 12th and 13th edd. not traced.
(13) 14th ed. n.d. Pr f E. Newbury (*sic*) et al. [BM.
(14) 15th ed. 1810. S b E. Newbury (*sic*) et al. [Oup.

A396. PALMER, Charlotte. FEMALE STABILITY, 1780. Pr f FN(N). 5 vols. *CBEL*, II, 548. [BM; EdUL.

A397. PARKHURST, John. GREEK AND ENGLISH LEXICON TO THE NEW TESTAMENT, 1769. Pr f FN(N) et al. Price 1 gn in bds, £1 11s 6d on royal paper. [BM; CUL; EdUL.

PARRY, R. LIFE OF SCIPIO AFRICANUS. See Seran de la Tour, Abbé.

A398. PARTHENIA; OR THE LOST SHEPHERDESS. Nicoll 339.
(1) Ed. 1764. S b JN. Price 1s. [BM.
(2) Adv. *LC* 11–13.2.72 as to be had of C & N; and listed in A35(5), 1778, as pr
f TC & Co et al. No later ed. traced.

A399. PATERSON, Daniel. NEW AND ACCURATE
DESCRIPTION OF ALL THE DIRECT AND PRINCIPAL
CROSS ROADS IN GREAT BRITAIN [ENGLAND AND
WALES]. Fordham 1, pp. 335–7. Fordham 2, pp. 27–8; Welsh 281.
(1) 1st ed. 1771. Pr f TC. Price 1s 6d. Weedon 31–3. [BM; Bodley; EdUL; AdE.
(2) 2nd ed. 1772. Pr f TC. Price 1s 6d sewed. [BM; Bodley; Oup.
(3) 3rd ed. 1776. Pr f TC. Price 2s sewed. [BM; Bodley; EdUL; Roscoe; AdE.
(4) 4th ed. 1778. Pr f TC. Price 2s sewed. [BM; Bodley; EdUL; AdE.
(5) 5th ed. 1781. Pr f TC. Price 2s sewed. In this and subsequent edd. *Great
Britain* in the title is altered to *England and Wales*. [BM; Bodley; EdUL.
(6) 6th ed. 1784. As for no. (5). [BM; Bodley; EdUL.
(7) 7th ed. 1786. As for no. (5). [BM; Bodley; LUL; Oup; Rylands.
(8) 8th ed. 1789. Pr f F. Power. Price 2s 6d sewed, 3s in bds. [BM; Bodley;
Weedon.
(9) 9th ed. 1792. Pr f F. Power & Co. Price 3s sewed. [BM; Bodley.
(10) Another issue of the 9th ed. 1792 was under the imprint of T. N. Longman,
on a cancel TP. See Introduction, pp. 17, 27, 28.

A400. PATERSON, Daniel. NEW AND ACCURATE
DESCRIPTION OF ALL THE DIRECT AND PRINCIPAL
CROSS ROADS OF SCOTLAND. Fordham 1, p. 342; Fordham 2, p. 35.
'Fifth' ed. 1781. Pr f TC. Price 6d. In fact the 1st ed. Previously the roads of
Scotland had been incorporated in the *Roads in Gt Britain*, 1st to 4th edd. [BM;
EdUL.

A401. PATERSON, Daniel. TRAVELLING DICTIONARY, A.
Fordham 1, pp. 342–3; Fordham 2, p. 29. All pr f TC.
(1) 1st ed. 1772. Price 4s sewed, or 6s bd up with the *Roads*. [BM; Bodley; CUL;
EdUL; AdE; Roscoe.
(2) 2nd ed. 1773. Price 4s sewed. Welsh 282. [BM; Sotheby, 19.3.71, lot 594 and
595.
(3) 3rd ed. 1777. Price 4s sewed, or 6s 6d bd up with the 4th ed. of the *Roads*.
[Bodley; PPL; Sotheby, 9.12.71, lot 221.
(4) 4th ed. 1781. Price 4s sewed. [BM; CUL; EdUL.
(5) 5th ed. 1787. Price 4s sewed. Welsh 282. [BM; CUL; Weedon.

A402. PENNY, Anne. POEMS, WITH A DRAMATIC
ENTERTAINMENT, n.d. (the Dedication is dated 13 May 1771). S b FN*
et al. Welsh 286; *CBEL*, II, 375. [BM; Bodley; EdUL; LL; CUL; AdE.

A403. PENROSE, Thomas. THE PRACTICE OF RELIGION AND VIRTUE RECOMMENDED, 1759. Pr f JN. Price 6*d*. Welsh 282. [BM.

'PENTWEAZLE, Ebenezer' (i.e. Chris. Smart). See A548.

A404. PERRY, Sampson (pseud. Wm Adams). DISQUISITION OF THE STONE AND GRAVEL. Adv. *LC* 29.6.73–1.7.73, p. 4, as pr f FN(N) et al. His name not in the imprint.

A405. PHIPPS, Constantine John, and Capt. LUTWIDGE. JOURNAL OF A VOYAGE FOR MAKING DISCOVERIES TOWARDS THE NORTH POLE, 1774. Pr f FN(N). Price 1*s* 6*d*. Welsh 283; *CBEL*, II, 743; Sabin 62573. [BM; Rylands; EdUL.

A406. 'PILKINGTON, MRS'. MRS PILKINGTON'S JESTS. *CBEL*, II, 219 and 222 lists edd. 1759 and 1764. Under the title *The celebrated Mrs Pilkington's Jests: or, the Cabinet of Wit and Humour* the 2nd ed. was adv. *LC* 24–6.1.69, p. 83, as to be had of N & C et al. Price 1*s*, and in A592(10), 1775, as pr f C & N. JN was not named in the 1759 ed.

A407. PINCOT, Daniel. ESSAY ON THE ORIGIN...OF ARTIFICIAL STONE, 1770. S b FN(N) et al. Price 1*s* 6*d* (altered in MS on TP to 2*s* 6*d*). [BM; LUL.

A408. PLAISTED, Bartholomew. A JOURNAL FROM CALCUTTA.
(1) 1st ed. 1757. Pr f JN. Price 2*s* 6*d* neatly bd calf. *CBEL*, II, 750. [BM; Bodley; LL; AdE; Sotheby, 2.3.70, lot 94.
(2) 2nd ed. 1758. A greatly enlarged ed. of no. (1), all after p. 222 being new. Under imprint of T. Kinnersly alone, but listed in A71(1), 1767, as one of JN's publicns, and adv. *LC* 20–2.5.73 as to be had of C & N. Price 3*s*. [BM; Bodley; CUL; Rylands.

A409. POCKET HERALD, THE, 1769. Pr f FN* et al. 2 vols, price 7*s*. Moule no. DCXIX (who implies that J. Almon was the author). [LCA.

A410. POCOCKE, Dr Richard. THE HAPPINESS OF DOING GOOD. A SERMON, [1761]. S b JN et al. Price 1*s*. [BM.

A411. POEMS, MORAL, ELEGANT AND PATHETIC...AND ORIGINAL SONNETS, BY HELEN MARIA WILLIAMS.
(1) Ed. 1796. Pr f EN et al. Price 6*s*. *CBEL*, II, 252. [BM; Marchmont Bkshop, Cat. 29 [1969] item 321; Hannas, Cat. 31 [summer 1970] item 353.
(2) Ed. 1801. Recorded by Lyon. Pr f EN.

A412. POETICAL DICTIONARY, A; OR, THE BEAUTIES OF THE ENGLISH POETS, 1761. (Ed. S. Derrick.) Pr f JN et al. 4 vols, price 10s in bds, 12s neatly bd calf. Welsh 287; *CBEL*, II, 220; IAW 121. [BM; Bodley; LL; Weedon; Falkner Grierson, Cat. 7 [1967] item 252.

A413. POETICAL DICTIONARY, OR ENGLISH EXPOSITOR. Pr f N & C. Price 12s, 4 vols. Listed in J61(3), 1769 and in A200(6), 1773. Probably = A412.

A414. POETICAL EPISTLE, A, FROM SHAKESPEAR IN ELYSIUM, 1752. Pr f JN et al. Price 1s. Welsh 305; CUL Cat. gives to Richard Rolt. [BM; CUL; Falkner Grierson, Cat. 7 [1967] item 506.

A415. POETICAL TELL-TALE, THE. Welsh 286 records 'B. Collins bought half share of Newbery in 1757 for £2 2s'. *The Poetical Tell-Tale; or, Muses in Merry Story*, 1763, was by J. Fletcher.

A416. POLLNITZ, Carl Ludwig. THE AMUSEMENTS OF AIX LA CHAPELLE. Adv. *LC* 5–8.5.70 as to be had of FN(N), 2 vols, price 6s.

A417. POLYHYMNIA: OR, THE COMPLETE SONG BOOK.
(1) Ed. 1769. Pr f FN(N). Price 2s 6d. *CBEL*, II, 226. [Oup.
(2) 2nd ed. adv. *LC* 25–7.9.70, p. 300, as pr f FN(N). Price 2s 6d.

PORNY, Marc Antoine (pseud.). See Du Martre, A. P.

A418. POTTER, John. CURATE OF COVENTRY, THE, 1771. Pr f FN(N). 2 vols, price 5s sewed. [Bodley.

A419. POTTER, John. HOBBY HORSE, THE. A CHARACTERISTIC SATIRE ON THE TIMES. Adv. *LC* 18–20.12.66, p. 599, as pr f FN(N) et al. Price 1s. H&L, 3, p. 94.

A420. POWYS, Thomas. A SERMON PREACHED AT...FAWLEY ...10th AUGUST 1766. Listed in *LM*, 1766 (appendix), p. 690. S b JN. Price 6d. Welsh 289; Legg no. 46. [Bodley.

A421. PRACTICAL REMARKS ON WEST INDIA DISEASES, 1776. Pr f FN(N). Price 2s. [Wellcome.

A422. PRATT, Ellis. THE ART OF DRESSING THE HAIR. A POEM, 1770. S b C & N et al. Price 1s 6d. [BM; Bodley.

A423. PRESENT STATE OF ENGLAND, THE. Welsh 213 indicates an ed. in JN's lifetime. The 1777 ed. in Bodley which he mentions not traced. Perhaps = J1.

A424. PRESENT STATE OF THE NATION, THE; OR, LOVES LABOUR LOST. A POEM IN EIGHT BOOKS. TO WHICH IS ADDED, THE MAIDS OF READING. A TALE. Adv. *LC* 14–16.4.72, p. 367, as s b FN(N) et al. Price 3s 6d sewed.

A424A. PRESTWICH, John. DISPLAY OF HONOR AND NOBILITY, A. A prospectus dated 1780 (copy in Oup) was issued, the work to be pr f FN(N) et al. In 1787 Prestwich's *Respublica; or Display of the Honors* ...was pubd b J. Nichols alone.

A425. PRESTWICH, John. DISSERTATION ON MINERAL, ANIMAL, AND VEGETABLE, POISONS, 1775. Pr f FN(N). Price 6s in bds. Welsh 290. [BM; Bodley; Wellcome; EdUL; UCL.

A426. PREVOST D'EXILES, Antoine Francois. MEMOIRS OF A MAN OF QUALITY.
(1) Welsh 267 says 'From F. Newbery's List, 1769'. Gives price 6d for 2 vols – ? error for 6s. ? = no. (2).
(2) Ed. 1770. Pr f FN(N). 2 vols, price 5s sewed, 6s bd. *CBEL*, 11, 543 and 795. [BM.

A427. PRICE, John, B.D. CHRISTMAS DAY. A POEM. Adv. *GEP* 28–30.5.45 as to be had of JN et al. Price 3d. Welsh 295.

A428. PRINCE ARTHUR: AN ALLEGORICAL ROMANCE, 1779. S b FN(N). 2 vols, price 5s. [BM.

A429. PSALMANAZAR, George (pseud.). MEMOIRS OF * * * *
(1) 1st ed. 1764. S b JN et al. Price 5s bd, 4s sewed in blue paper. *CBEL*, 11, 135; Scott, pp. 120ff (dates 1762 in error). [BM; CUL; EdUL; LL; LGL; AdE; NLA.
(2) 2nd ed. 1765. Pr f JN et al. Price 5s, or 4s sewed. Welsh 296. [BM; Bodley; CUL; LL; UCL; DNS.

A430. PUBLIC LEDGER. Welsh 40–4, 336; *CBEL*, 11, 709; *BUCOP*, 3, 627. *Public Ledger Bicentenary Supplement*, 12 Jan. 1960. Stanley Morison, *The English Newspaper*, p. 151. It seems more than likely that JN was one of the founders and controlled (or shared the control) of the paper in its early years, though Welsh 43 quotes from one of Benjn Collins of Salisbury's account bks an entry claiming that Collins was the prime mover: 'my own scheme, in which I had one share and a half'.

The 1st issue of the paper was on 12.1.60 under imprint of W. Bristow; the royal license to print and publish, dated 17.12.59, was granted to Wm Faden. Neither JN nor Collins was named. So it continued till the end of 1765. The earliest extant issue for 1766 is no. 2005 (7 June), pr f FN(N) at the Crown in

PNR. Issues between 1767 and June 1771 are wanting, but after that month the imprint is of FN(N), and that continued till the end of 1773. Thereafter H. Randall took over.

Under JN's will FN(N) took a reversionary interest in one quarter of JN's newspaper interests (see the Introduction at p. 16). It may well be that JN realised the *PL* would do best if left in his nephew's hands, as he had been concerned with it since early in 1766, and to give him a financial interest in it as part proprietor would encourage him to make a good thing of it. Whether FN(N) sold out to Randall at the end of 1773, or for what other reason Randall's name took the place of FN's, is not apparent.

⌈BM, and see *BUCOP*.

A430A. ? QUIN, Matthew. EASY INTRODUCTION TO BOOK-KEEPING, AN, 1776. Pr f FN(N). Price 1s 6d. The attribution to Quin is questionable. ⌈CA; CA(Sc).

A431. RACINE, Louis. RELIGION, A POEM, 1754. (Trans. E. Elphinston.) S b JN et al. *CBEL*, ii, 796. ⌈BM; Bodley; DNS.

A432. RALEIGH, Sir Walter. THE INTEREST OF ENGLAND WITH REGARD TO FOREIGN ALLIANCES, 1750. S b JN. Price 1s. Welsh 299; *CBEL*, i, 828. T. N. Brushfield, *Biblio. of Sir Walter Raleigh, Knt* (2nd ed. 1908), no. 275. ⌈BM.

A433. RAWLINS, Thomas. FAMILIAR ARCHITECTURE, 1768. To be had of FN(N) et al. Price 1 gn in sheets. ⌈BM; RIBA.

A434. REEVES, John. THE ART OF FARRIERY. Welsh 299.
(1) 1st ed. 1758. Pr f JN et al. Price 6s neatly bd calf. *CBEL*, ii, 816 dates 1757; the bk was listed in *LM* for Nov. of that year. Sir Fredk Smith, *Early Hist. of Vet. Literature*, ii, 97. ⌈BM; Bodley.
(2) 2nd ed. 1763. Pr f JN et al. Price 5s. *CBEL*, ii, 816. ⌈BM; CUL.
(3) 3rd ed. 1771. Pr f C & N et al. Price 5s, later 6s. ⌈RCVS; Bodley; Wellcome.
(4) 4th ed. 1778. Pr f C & N et al. ⌈RVC; Wellcome.

A435. REFLECTIONS ON THE AFFAIRS OF THE DISSIDENTS IN POLAND, 1767. No publr or prtr. Adv. *LC* 1–3.9.67, p. 221, as pr f FN(N) et al. ⌈Bodley; Rylands.

A436. REFLECTIONS ON THE RUINS OF AN ANCIENT CATHEDRAL, 2nd ed. 1770. S b FN(N) et al. Price 1s. ⌈BM.

A437. REGISTER OF FOLLY, THE, 1773. S b FN(N) et al. Price 2s 6d. ⌈Roscoe; BM; CUL.

A438. RENWICK, William. THE GENUINE HISTORY OF TWO UNFORTUNATE LOVERS. Adv. *LC* 21–4.9.71, p. 295, as s b FN(N) et al. 2 vols, price 6*s*. See A182.

A439. REPLY TO A PAMPHLET ENTITLED THE CASE OF THE DUKE OF PORTLAND, 1768. Pr f FN(N) et al. Price 1*s*. [BM; Rylands; NLA.

A440. RICHARDSON, Samuel. CLARISSA.
(1) 6th ed. 1768–9. Pr f FN* et al. 8 vols, price 24*s*. Vol. VI 1769, all others 1768. *CBEL*, II, 515 (dates 1768). [BM; Bodley; EdUL (*ex* vol. 8).
(2) 7th ed. 1774. Pr f FN* et al. 8 vols, price 24*s*. *CBEL*, II, 515. [BM; Bodley; UCL (vols 3–8).
(3) A 'new ed.', 1785. Pr f EN et al. 8 vols, price 24*s*. [BM; Bodley; UCL (vol. 1).
(4) An 8-vol. ed. adv. *LC* 2–4.5.93, p. 428, price £1 8*s*, pr f EN et al.

A441. RICHER, Adrien. GREAT EVENTS FROM LITTLE CAUSES. Welsh (p. 45, quoting Nichols) indicates this may have been trans. by Griffith Jones; also Welsh 300.
(1) Ed. 1767. Pr f FN(N). Price 2*s* 6*d* bd, 3*s* calf. [BM; Bodley; CUL; Weedon.
(2) Frequently listed between 1772 and 1781 as by C & N. Price 3*s* or 3*s* 6*d*.
(3) Listed in J147(9), 1786, as s b TC. Price 3*s*.

A442. RICKMAN, John. JOURNAL OF CAPTAIN COOK'S LAST VOYAGE. *CBEL*, II, 742. Sir Maurice Holmes, *Capt. James Cook: a Biblio. Excursion*, 1952. Spence, p. 20. Reviewed in *The Monthly Review*, 1781, vol. 2, p. 236.
(1) 1st ed. 1781. Pr f EN. Price 6*s* in bds. Holmes no. 38. [BM; H. M. Fletcher, Cat. 118 [1963] item 39.
(2) 2nd ed. 1781. Pr f EN. Price 6*s*. Holmes p. 45. [Bodley; Sotheby, 30.7.70, lot 75.

A443. RIVAL BALL-ROOMS, THE. Listed *Universal Mag.*, Jan. 1775, price 1*s*. No publr named. Algar recorded the bk as by one of the Newberys, but the copy seen (Bodley) was by R. Cruttwell.

A444. ROBINSON, William. SUPPLEMENT TO DR BURN'S JUSTICE OF THE PEACE. Adv. *Morning Chronicle*, 1.7.74, as pr f FN(N) et al. Price 3*s* 6*d* sewed, 4*s* 6*d* bd.

A445. RODWELL, (   ). INTEREST TABLES ON A NEW PLAN. Pr f TC. Adv. *LC* 7–9.4.74, p. 343, as 'in the Press, and speedily w.b.p.'.

A446. ROLLIN, Charles. ANCIENT HISTORY OF THE EGYPTIANS. *CBEL*, II, 797.
(1) 5th ed. 1768. Pr f N & C et al. 7 vols, price £1 17s sewed in bds, 2 gns bd. [Bodley; LL (*ex* vol. I).
(2) 6th ed. 1774. Pr f C & N et al. 8 vols. Price 1 gn in the vell. manner, £1 4s calf. [Bodley (*ex* vol. IV).
(3) 7th ed. adv. *LC* 28–30.12.80, p. 620, as pr f TC et al. 7 vols, price 2 gns.
(4) 8th ed. 1788. Pr f TC et al. 10 vols, price £1 10s. [BM.

A447. ROLLIN, Charles. HISTORY OF THE ARTS AND SCIENCES, 2nd ed. 1768. Pr f N & C et al. 3 vols, price 16s sewed in bds, 18s bd. *CBEL*, II, 797. [BM; CUL; LL; AdE.

A448. ROLLIN, Charles. METHOD OF TEACHING AND STUDYING THE BELLES LETTRES. *CBEL*, II, 29.
(1) 6th ed. 1769. Pr f C & N et al. 3 vols, price 16s sewed in bds, 18s bd. [BM; Bodley; LUL; AdE; NoU; CLU.
(2) 7th ed. 1770. Pr f N & C et al. 4 vols. [BM.

A449. ROLLIN, Charles. ROMAN HISTORY, THE, 3rd ed. 1768. Pr f N & C et al. 10 vols, price £2 12s 6d sewed in bds, £3 bd. *CBEL*, II, 297. [BM; Bodley; AdE.

A450. ROLLIN, Charles. WHOLE WORKS, THE, OF MR. ROLLIN. Adv. *LC* 13–15.12.68, p. 571, as to be had in 23 vols. Pubd by N & C et al.

A451. ROLT, Richard. MEMOIRS OF THE LIFE OF THE LATE ...EARL OF CRAUFURD, 1753. S b JN. Price 13s sewed, 15s bd. [BM; Bodley; CUL; EdUL; AdE.

A452. ROLT, Richard. MONODY ON THE DEATH OF HIS ROYAL HIGHNESS, 1751. Pr f JN et al. Price 1s. Welsh 271 and 301. [BM; Bodley.

A453. ROLT, Richard. NEW DICTIONARY OF TRADE AND COMMERCE. Welsh 301.
(1) 1st ed. 1756. Pr f JN et al. Price £1 10s. Pubd in weekly pts at 6d. *CBEL*, II, 926. [BM; LUL; AdE.
(2) 2nd ed. 1761, not under imprint of JN, but listed up to 1768 (in A637(2), vol. v) as pr f a s b him. [Sotheby, 5.4.71, lot 230.

A454. ROLT, Richard. TWO HYMNS ON THE NATIVITY, 1751. Pr f JN. Price 6d. [BM; Bodley.

A455. ROUPPE, Ludovicus (Lewis). OBSERVATIONS ON DISEASES INCIDENTAL TO SEAMEN, 1772. Pr f C & N. Price 6s. Welsh 302. [BM; Bodley; CUL; EdUL; AdE.

A456. ROWLEY, William, M.D. In addition to nos A457–482 below the following titles by this most prolific medical scribbler are mentioned in the bk-list in A462, 1788, as to be reprinted as speedily as possible, 'the major part of which perished in the late unfortunate fire at E. Newbery's' (i.e. in or before Dec. 1786). It may be assumed that these, or some of them, bore the imprint of EN or her late husband.
The Gout alleviated, 2nd ed.
Causes of Death in Childbirth investigated.
Treatise on Diet adapted to different Constitutions.
Observations on the new and extensive use of metalic Alteratives in chronic Disorders.
A Treatise on the Gonorrhoea; or, the mildest method of treating the Venereal Disease. 3rd ed.
The State of Medical Practice of all the Hospitals in Europe.
   Some of these may be included below. The adverts. of Rowley's works were by no means precise in the titles or descriptions used.

A457. ROWLEY, William, M.D. CAUSES OF THE GREAT NUMBER OF DEATHS, [1793]. Pr f E. Newberry (*sic*). Price 1s. Dedication dated 20 June 1793. [BM; Bodley; Wellcome.

A458. ROWLEY, William, M.D. ESSAY ON THE CURE OF GONORHOEA, 1771. Pr f FN(N). Price 1s. [Wellcome; RCS.

A459. ROWLEY, William, M.D. ESSAY ON THE CURE OF ULCERATED LEGS.
(1) 1st ed. 1770. Pr f FN(N). Price 1s 6d. [BM; Bodley; CUL; Wellcome; RCS; EdUL.
(2) 2nd ed. 1771. Pr f FN(N). Price 1s 6d. [Wellcome; CUL.
(3) For 3rd and 4th edd. see A478(1 and 2).

A460. ROWLEY, William, M.D. ESSAY ON THE CURE OF VENEREAL DISEASE, 2nd ed. 1771. Pr f FN(N). Price 1s. This is another issue of A458, with new matter at additional pp. 33–6. For 3rd ed. see A468. [RCS; CUL.

A461. ROWLEY, William, M.D. ESSAY ON THE INFLAMATION AND OTHER DISORDERS OF THE EYES, ARISING FROM THE SMALL POX. Pr f FN(N). Price 1s. Adv. *LC* 8–11.2.72, p. 143.

A462. ROWLEY, William, M.D. ESSAY ON THE MALIGNANT, ULCERATED SORE THROAT, 1788. Pr f EN et al. Price 3*s*. [BM; Bodley; RCS; EdUL.

A463. ROWLEY, William, M.D. ESSAY ON THE OPHTHALMIA, 1771. Pr f FN(N). Price 1*s*. [RCS; EdUL.

A464. ROWLEY, William, M.D. LETTER [TWO LETTERS] TO DR. WILLIAM HUNTER. See also A471(1 and 2).
(1) 1st ed. adv. *LC* 27–9.9.74, p. 311, as 'tomorrow w b p', price 1*s*, under the title (or description) *Letter to Dr. William Hunter...on the dangerous Tendency of Medical Vanity, occasioned by the Death of the late Lady Holland.*
(2) 2nd ed. listed (with A471(2)) in A482, 1790, as to be had of EN et al., under the title (or description) *Two Letters to Dr. William Hunter on the dangerous Tendency of Medical Vanity, Second Edition*, price 2*s*.

A465. ROWLEY, William, M.D. MEDICAL ADVICE, FOR THE USE OF THE ARMY AND NAVY, 1776. Pr f FN(N). [RCP.

A466. ROWLEY, William, M.D. MEDICAL ADVICE TO THE ARMY AND NAVY SERVING IN HOT CLIMATES. Listed in A482, 1790, as to be had of EN et al. Price 1*s*.

A467. ROWLEY, William, M.D. NEW AND SUCCESSFUL METHOD OF CURING THE CANCER OF THE BREASTS, 2nd ed. Adv. *LC* 26–8.10.80, p. 405, as pr f EN. Price 1*s* 6*d*. ? = A469(2); but the prices differ.

A468. ROWLEY, William, M.D. NEW METHOD OF CURING THE VENEREAL DISEASE, 3rd ed. 1772. Pr f FN(N). Price 1*s*. Previous edd. were A458 and A460. [Bodley.

A469. ROWLEY, William, M.D. PRACTICAL TREATISE ON DISEASES OF THE BREASTS OF WOMEN.
(1) 1st ed. 1772. Pr f FN(N) et al. Price 1*s* 6*d*. [RCP; Bodley (imperf.); RCS; EdUL.
(2) 2nd ed. 1777. Pr f FN(N). Price 1*s*. [BM.
(3) 3rd ed. Listed in A456, 1788, as one of the bks destroyed in the fire at Newbery's and to be reprinted.

A470. ROWLEY, William, M.D. RATIONAL PRACTICE OF PHYSIC, THE, 1793. S b EN et al. 4 vols, price £1 11*s* 6*d*. [Wellcome; BM; CUL; RCP.

A471. ROWLEY, William, M.D. SECOND LETTER TO DR. WILLIAM HUNTER. For the *First Letter* see A464(1 and 2).
(1) 1st ed. 1775. Pr f FN(N). Price 1s. [RCS; Bodley.
(2) 2nd ed. listed in A482, 1790, as to be had of EN et al. (together with A464(2)), price 2s.

A472. ROWLEY, William, M.D. SEVENTY FOUR SELECT CASES, WITH THE MANNER OF CURE...IN THE FOLLOWING DISEASES...
(1) 1st ed. 1779. Pr f FN(N). Price 1s 6d. [BM.
(2) 2nd ed. Listed in A462, 1788, as one of the bks destroyed in the fire at Newbery's and to be reprinted.

A473. ROWLEY, William, M.D. TRANSLATION INTO ENGLISH OF THE PRINCIPAL REFERENCES TO THE 66 PLATES OF SCHOLA MEDICINAE..., 1796. Pr f EN. [Wellcome; BM (imperf.); RCS; RCP.

A474. ROWLEY, William, M.D. TREATISE ON FEMALE, NERVOUS...DISEASES, 1788. Pr f EN et al. Price 7s 6d. [BM; CUL.

A475. ROWLEY, William, M.D. TREATISE ON 118 PRINCIPAL DISEASES OF THE EYES, 1790. Pr f EN et al. [Wellcome; MSL.

A476. ROWLEY, William, M.D. TREATISE ON THE REGULAR ...AND FLYING GOUT, 1792. Pr f EN et al. [Wellcome; BM; RCP.

A477. ROWLEY, William, M.D. TREATISE ON THE CAUSE AND CURE OF SWELLED LEGS, 1796. Pr f EN. Price 3s. [Wellcome; RCS; RCP.

A478. ROWLEY, William, M.D. TREATISE ON THE CURE OF ULCERATED LEGS. For 1st and 2nd edd. see A459(1 and 2).
(1) 3rd ed. 1774. Pr f FN(N). Price 1s 6d. [Wellcome; Bodley; RCP.
(2) 4th ed. 1786. Pr f EN. Price 2s. [Wellcome; RCP.

A479. ROWLEY, William, M.D. TREATISE ON THE MANAGEMENT OF FEMALE BREASTS.
(1) 1st ed. not traced.
(2) 2nd ed. 1790. Pr f EN et al. Price 2s 6d. [BM; Wellcome; RCS; RCP.

A480. ROWLEY, William, M.D. TREATISE ON THE PRINCIPAL DISEASES OF THE EYES.
(1) 1st ed. 1773. Pr f FN(N). [Wellcome; Bodley; RCS.

(2) 2nd ed. not traced.

(3) 3rd ed. listed in A462, 1788, as one of the bks destroyed in the fire at Newbery's and to be reprinted.

A481. ROWLEY, William, M.D. TREATISES. *LC* for 11–14.5.99, p. 458, adv. as s b EN et al. a 'new ed.' in 4 vols, price £1 11s 6d, of Rowley's *Treatises*...

A482. ROWLEY, William, M.D. TRUTH VINDICATED, 1790. Pr f EN et al. Price 1s 6d. [Wellcome; BM.

A483. RYSSEEG, F. TREATISE ON THE ORIGIN OF DISEASES, A, n.d. (not before 4.5.69). Adv. *MC&LA* 10.6.72. To be had of FN(N). Price 1s, plus medicine 3s 6d. [MSL.

A484. SADE, Jacques Francois Aldonce de. LIFE OF PETRARCH, COLLECTED BY MRS DOBSON.
(1) 3rd ed. 1797. Listed in J285, 1797, as pr f a s b EN and Vernor and Hood. Only copy seen by Vernor and Hood alone.
(2) 4th ed. 1799. 2 vols. Recorded by Wallis as pr by J. Maiden f EN, Vernor and Hood et al.

A485. SALMON, Thomas. UNIVERSAL TRAVELLER, THE.
Listed as pr f a s b JN in A172(2), 1765, 2 vols, fo, price £3.

A486. SAMSON, W. RATIONAL PHYSIC. 2nd ed. adv. *LC* 13–15.3.70, p. 251, as pr f FN(N). Price 2s 6d. The 1st ed. (1765) was by Fletcher, R. Davies and Cruttwell.

A487. SAUNIER, Jean de (Gapser de). GUIDE TO THE PERFECT KNOWLEDGE OF HORSES, 1769. Pr f N & C et al. Price 4s sewed, 5s bd. [BM; CUL.

A488. SCOTT, Sarah. HISTORY OF MECKLENBURGH. Welsh 267; *CBEL*, II, 645.
(1) 1st ed. 1762. Pr f JN. Price 5s. [Bodley; Bishop Percy's Lib. (Sotheby, 23.6.69, lot 467).
(2) 2nd ed. 1762. Pr f JN. Price 5s. [BM; Bodley.
(3) Listed as s b TC in A222(17), 1788, price 5s.

A488A. SCOTT, Sarah. TEST OF FILIAL DUTY, THE, 1772. S b TC. 2 vols, price 6s, or 5s in 1 vol, in the vell. manner. H&L, 6, p. 19. Adv. *LC* 4–7.1.72, p. 20.

A489. SEAMAN'S USEFUL FRIEND, THE, 1774. S b FN(N) et al. Price 1s 6d. [BM; EdUL.

A490. SEDGLY, Ben, and Timothy BECK. OBSERVATIONS ON MR. FIELDING'S ENQUIRY, 1751. Pr f JN et al. Price 1s 6d. [LUL.

A491. SENTIMENTAL FABLES. TRANSLATED FROM THE FRENCH, 1775. S b FN(N) et al. Welsh 215. [BM.

A492. SERAN DE LA TOUR, Abbé. LIFE OF SCIPIO AFRICANUS AND EPAMINONDAS, by R. Parry, 1787. Welsh 281 records its entry by TC at Stationers' Hall on 19.11.87. Pubd under the imprint of W. Richards. *CBEL*, II, 801.

A493. SERAO, Francesco. NATURAL HISTORY OF MOUNT VESUVIUS. Adv. *LC* 17–19.4.70, p. 371, as s b FN(N). Price 2s 6d sewed. Welsh 325.

A494. SHACKLEFORD, Ann. THE MODERN ART OF COOKERY IMPROVED. Welsh 305; A. W. Oxford 95.
(1) Ed. 1767, by JN and FN(N) in Times Bkshop Exhibn of Cookery Bks 1500–1954. Private Colln. Adv. *LC* 13–16.6.67, p. 575, price 3s, later 5s.
(2) Frequently listed and adv. 1768–71 as pr f or s b C & N. Price 3s.

A495. SHAKESPEARE, William. See Jaggard, *Shakespeare Bibliography*, 1911 (referred to as 'Jag.' in the following notes). *CBEL*, I, 539ff.

A496. SHAKESPEARE, Wm. WORKS...WITH NOTES...BY MR. THEOBALD, 1767. 8 vols. Pr f FN(N) et al. Price £1 8s. Jag. p. 502. The name of Newbery only appears in the General Title in vol. I. [BM; Bodley; EdUL.

A497. SHAKESPEARE, Wm. MR WILLIAM SHAKESPEARE, HIS COMEDIES..., 1767–8. Capell's ed. 10 vols. Adv. *LC* 20–3.2.68, p. 180, as pr f FN(N) et al. His name not in imprint. Priced 2 gns and listed as pr f EN in A378, 1781.

A498. SHAKESPEARE, Wm. PLAYS...WITH...NOTES BY SAMUEL JOHNSON, 1768. 8 vols. 8vo. Pr f FN* et al. Price £2 8s. Jag. p. 502; Courtney, p. 108. [BM; Bodley; DNS.

A499. SHAKESPEARE, Wm. PLAYS...WITH...NOTES BY SAMUEL JOHNSON AND GEORGE STEEVENS, 1773. 10 vols. 8vo. Pr f FN* et al. Jag. pp. 503–4. [BM (*ex* vol. v); Bodley; CUL; LUL; EdUL; UCL; AdE; DNS.

A500. SHAKESPEARE, Wm. WORKS...WITH NOTES...BY MR. THEOBALD, 1773. 8 vols. 12mo. Pr f FN* et al. Price £1 8s. Jag. p. 503; Courtney, p. 108. [BM; LL; UCL; EdUL.

A501. SHAKESPEARE, Wm. PLAYS...WITH...NOTES BY SAMUEL JOHNSON AND GEORGE STEEVENS, 1778. 2nd ed. 8vo. 10 vols. Pr f FN* et al. Price £3 10s. Jag. p. 504; Courtney, p. 109. [BM; Bodley; CUL; EdUL; AdE; DNS.

A502. SHAKESPEARE, Wm. Malone's SUPPLEMENT TO THE... PLAYS PUBLISHED IN 1778 BY SAMUEL JOHNSON AND GEORGE STEEVENS, 1780. Pr f FN* et al. 2 vols. 8vo. Price 18s in bds. Jag. p. 504. [BM; Bodley; EdUL; LL; UCL; AdE; NLA.

A503. SHAKESPEARE, Wm. PLAYS..., 1785. Johnson and Steevens's 3rd ed., revised and augmented by [Isaac Reed]. Pr f EN et al. 10 vols. 8vo. Price £3 in bds. Jag. pp. 504–5; Courtney, p. 109. [BM; Bodley; CUL; EdUL; AdE; DNS.

A504. SHAKESPEARE, Wm. PLAYS...FROM THE TEXT OF MR. MALONE'S EDITION, 1790–6. 7 vols. 12mo. EN's name only in vol. 1, 1790. Price £1 4s 6d. Jag. p. 505. [BM.

A505. SHAKESPEARE, Wm. PLAYS AND POEMS...TO WHICH ARE ADDED, AN ESSAY...BY EDMOND MALONE, 1790. Pr f EN et al. 10 (11) vols. 8vo. Price £3 17s in bds. Jag. p. 505. [BM; CUL; LUL; Rylands; EdUL; AdE; DNS.

A506. SHAKESPEARE, Wm. PLAYS...WITH...NOTES BY SAMUEL JOHNSON AND GEORGE STEEVENS...REVISED AND AUGMENTED BY [Isaac Reed], 1793. 4th ed. Pr f EN et al. 15 vols. 8vo. Price £6 15s in bds. There was a large paper issue of 25 copies. Jag. p. 506. [BM; Bodley; CUL; LUL; Rylands; LL; DNS.

A507. SHAKESPEARE, Wm. PLAYS AND POEMS, 1797. Steevens's Text. Pr f EN et al. 7 vols. 8vo. Some large paper copies at 7 gns. Jag. p. 507. [BPL(S), not seen; NN.

A508. SHAKESPEARE, Wm. PLAYS, 1797. Pr f EN et al. 6 vols. Jag. p. 507. [BPL(S), not seen.

A509. SHAKESPEARE, Wm. PLAYS, 1797. Steevens's Text. Pr f EN et al. 8 vols. 12mo. Price 2 gns. Jag. p. 507. [Bodley; EdUL.

A510. SHAKESPEARE, Wm. WORKS, 1798. Steevens's Text, Glossary etc by Nichols, Life by Rowe. Pr f EN et al. 9 vols. 12mo. Price 18*s* in bds, £1 7*s* on a superfine wove paper. Jag. p. 507. [BPL(S), not seen.

A511. SHAKESPEARE, Wm. AS YOU LIKE IT..., 1786. Pr f E. Newberry (*sic*) et al. Price 6*d.* Jag. p. 287. [BM.

A512. SHAKESPEARE, Wm. COMEDY OF ERRORS..., 1770. Pr f FN* et al. Price 6*d* sewed. Jag. p. 294. [BM; CUL.

A513. SHAKESPEARE, Wm. CYMBELINE..., 1770. Pr f FN* et al. Jag. p. 301. [BPL(S), not seen.

A514. SHAKESPEARE, Wm. CYMBELINE..., 1784. Pr f EN et al. Price 6*d.* Jag. p. 301. [BM.

A515. SHAKESPEARE, Wm. HAMLET..., 1782. Pr f EN et al. Price 6*d.* Jag. p. 309. [BM.

A516. SHAKESPEARE, Wm. JULIUS CAESAR. Adv. *LC* 16–18.5.86, p. 469, as pr f EN et al. Price 6*d.*

A517. SHAKESPEARE, Wm. [King] HENRY IV, [pt 1]..., 1785. Pr f EN et al. Price 6*d.* Jag. p. 329. [BM; LUL.

A518. SHAKESPEARE, Wm. KING HENRY VIII. Adv. *LC* 16–18.5.86, p. 469, as pr f EN et al. Price 6*d.*

A519. SHAKESPEARE, Wm. KING JOHN..., 1784. Pr f EN et al. Price 6*d.* Jag. p. 351. [LUL; BPL(S).

A520. SHAKESPEARE, Wm. KING LEAR..., 1786. Pr f EN et al. Price 6*d.* Jag. p. 358. [BM.

A521. SHAKESPEARE, Wm. KING RICHARD III. Adv. *LC* 19–22.3.85, p. 275, as to be had of EN et al. Price 6*d.*

A522. SHAKESPEARE, Wm. MACBETH..., 1770. Pr f FN* et al. Jag. p. 382. [BPL(S), not seen.

A523. SHAKESPEARE, Wm. MACBETH..., 1785. Pr f EN et al. Price 6*d.* Jag. pp. 383 and 726. [LUL; BPL(S).

A524. SHAKESPEARE, Wm. MEASURE FOR MEASURE..., 1784. Pr f EN et al. Price 6*d*. Not in Jag. [CUL.

A525. SHAKESPEARE, Wm. MERCHANT OF VENICE, 1783. Pr f EN et al. Price 6*d*. Jag. p. 395. [CUL (imperf.); BPL(S).

A526. SHAKESPEARE, Wm. MERRY WIVES OF WINDSOR. Adv. *LC* 19–22.3.85, p. 275, as to be had of EN et al. Price 6*d*.

A527. SHAKESPEARE, Wm. MUCH ADO ABOUT NOTHING. Adv. *LC* 16–18.5.86, p. 469, as pr f EN et al. Price 6*d*.

A528. SHAKESPEARE, Wm. OTHELLO..., 1784. Pr f EN et al. Price 6*d*. Jag. pp. 424 and 719. [BM (imperf.).

A529. SHAKESPEARE, Wm. ROMEO AND JULIET. Adv. as for A521. Price 6*d*.

A530. SHAKESPEARE, Wm. TAMING OF THE SHREW..., 1786. Pr f E. Newberry (*sic*) et al. Price 6*d*. Jag. p. 459. [BM.

A531. SHAKESPEARE, Wm. TEMPEST, THE..., 1785. Pr f EN et al. Price 6*d*. Jag. p. 464. [MB, not seen.

A532. SHAKESPEARE, Wm. TIMON OF ATHENS, n.d. [*ca.* 1770, *per* Jag. p. 472]. Pr f FN* et al. [BPL(S), not seen.

A533. SHAKESPEARE, Wm. TWELFTH NIGHT..., 1786. Pr f E. Newberry (*sic*) et al. Price 6*d*. ? not in Jag. [CUL, not seen.

A534. SHAKESPEARE, Wm. WINTER'S TALE..., 1785. Pr f EN et al. Price 6*d*. Jag. p. 491. [BM.

A535. SHARP, Samuel. LETTERS FROM ITALY, 3rd ed. [probably 1767]. S b F. Newberry (*sic*) (probably FN(N)) et al. Price 4*s* sewed, 5*s* bd. [BM; Bodley; LUL; LL; AdE.

A536. SHARPE, Gregory. SECOND ARGUMENT IN DEFENCE OF CHRISTIANITY, 1762. Pr f JN. Price 5*s*. Welsh 305. [BM (thick paper); Bodley; CUL; AdE.

A537. SHERIDAN, Thomas, and HENDERSON (   ). SHERIDAN AND HENDERSON'S PRACTICAL METHOD OF READING... ENGLISH POETRY, 1796. Pr f EN et al. Price 3*s* 6*d*. Welsh 299; *CBEL*, II, 252; Alston, VI, 426. [BM; CUL; AdE; NLSc; Sion; MH; CtY; MBAt.

A538. SHERIDAN, Thomas, and WALKER (   ). SHERIDAN AND WALKER'S PRONOUNCING DICTIONARY FOR THE POCKET. Listed in J131(4), 1799, as pr f EN. Price 3s 6d. Welsh 305. ? = A539.

A539. SHERIDAN, Thomas, and WALKER (   ). SHERIDAN AND WALKER'S PRONOUNCING DICTIONARY OF THE ENGLISH LANGUAGE. Listed in J273, 1797, as pr f EN. Price 3s 6d.

A540. SHERLOCK, Thomas, Bp of London. SERMON PREACHED AT...SALISBURY, OCTOBER 6, 1745, ON THE OCCASION OF THE REBELLION IN SCOTLAND. Adv. *GEP* 12–15.10.45 as pr a s b JN et al. There are at least 3 issues of this; I have not found one with JN's imprint. Welsh 304.

A541. SHERLOCK, Thomas, Bp of London. SEVERAL DISCOURSES PREACHED AT THE TEMPLE CHURCH. 7th ed. 3 vols. Price 9s. Adv. *LC* 9–11.6.76, p. 35, as pr f FN* et al.

A542. SHIRLEY, William. BIRTH OF HERCULES, THE, 1765. Forms the 2nd pt of Shirley's *Electra*, 1765, pp. 103–19.

A543. SHIRLEY, William. ELECTRA, 1765. To be had of JN et al. Price 5s, to non-subscribers 6s. [BM; Bodley; CUL.

A544. SIGNS OF DEATH. Welsh 197. Not identified.

A545. SLOANE, Sir Hans. ACCOUNT OF A MOST EFFICACIOUS MEDICINE FOR...THE EYES. A 'new ed.' adv. *LC* 23–6.3.71, p. 295, as s b C & N. Price 6d.

A546. SMART, Christopher. See Welsh 307–9. G. J. Gray, 'Biblio. of the Writings of C... S...', in *Transactions of the Bibliographical Soc.* VI (1903), 269ff. *CBEL*, II, 338–9 and V, 420, and see J338ff.

A547. SMART, Chris. HILLIAD, THE.
(1) Ed. 1753. S b JN et al. Price 2s. Welsh 31–3; Gray XXVIII; Rothschild 1875; *CBEL*, II, 338. [BM; Bodley; CUL; CambFL.
(2) Listed in A35(5), 1778, as pr f TC & Co et al. Price 2s.
(3) THE HILLIAD. BOOK THE SECOND. Adv. *PA* 10.5.53 as 'speedily w.b.p.'. Not traced, probably never pubd.

A548. SMART, Chris. (Ebenezer Pentweazle). HORATIAN CANONS OF FRIENDSHIP.

(1) 1st ed. 1750. S b JN. Price 1s. Welsh 282; Gray VIII; Rothschild 1867; *CBEL*, II, 338. [BM; Bodley; CUL; V&A.
(2) 2nd ed. 1750. S b JN. Price 1s. Not in Gray. [Bodley.
(3) Listed in A35(5), 1778, as pr f TC & Co. Price 1s.

A549. SMART, Chris. HYMN TO THE SUPREME BEING.
(1) Ed. 1756. Pr f JN. Price 6d. Gray XXXVI; Welsh 308; *CBEL*, II, 338. [BM; Bodley.
(2) Listed in A35(5), 1778, as pr f TC & Co. Price 6d.

SMART, Chris. HYMNS FOR THE AMUSEMENT OF CHILDREN. See J338.

A550. SMART, Chris. INDEX TO MANKIND. Gray XXI; *CBEL*, II, 338; *BUCOP*, 3, 208.
(1) Ed. 1751. Pr f TC. Price 1s. Rothschild 1872. [BM; Bodley; DNS.
(2) Issued bd up with *The Midwife*, 1753, and referred to in the TP to that work.
(3) Issued as an integral pt of Smart's *Nonpareil*, 1757.

A551. SMART, Chris. MRS MIDNIGHT'S WORKS COMPLEAT: INCLUDING HER MAGAZINE... Adv. *PA* 16.3.54 as pr f TC. Price 7s 6d. Almost certainly = A552.

A552. SMART, Chris. MIDWIFE, THE: OR, THE OLD WOMAN'S MAGAZINE, [1750]–3. S b [Pr f] TC. Issued in pts at 3d, the complete work 7s 6d, 3 vols. Welsh 268–9; *CBEL*, II, 339, 664 and 677; Gray XIII; *BUCOP*, 3, 208; Crane and Kaye, *Century of Brit. Newspapers*, 1927, no. 542; Rothschild 1869–70. [BM; Bodley; Roscoe (vol. I).

A553. SMART, Chris. NONPAREIL, THE. Welsh 277; Gray XIV; *CBEL*, II, 339, 677.
(1) Ed. 1757. Pr f TC. Price 3s. Rothschild 1880. [BM; Bodley; CUL; DNS.
(2) Listed in A172(2), 1765, as pr f a s b JN. Price 3s.
(3) Frequently listed as by C & N or TC up to 1788 (A222(17)), price 3s.

A554. SMART, Chris. NUT-CRACKER, THE. Not in Gray.
(1) 1st ed. 1751. Pr f JN et al. Price 1s 6d stitched in blue covers, 2s bd. Welsh 279; *CBEL*, II, 338 and 215. [BM.
(2) Ed. 1757. TC. Welsh 339.
(3) Ed. 1760. TC. *CBEL*, II, 219; Frank Hammond, Cat. 81 [1953] item 798, not seen.
(4) Ed. 1769. C & N. Price 1s 6d. *CBEL*, II, 226.

A555. SMART, Chris. OCCASIONAL PROLOGUE AND EPILOGUE TO OTHELLO. *CBEL*, II, 338.

(1) 1st ed. [1751]. S b TC. Price 6*d*. Gray xv; Rothschild 1871. [BM; Bodley.

(2) 2nd ed. [1751]. S b TC. Price 6*d*. Gray xvi. [BM; Bodley.

(3) 3rd ed. 1751. Adv. *GEP* 7–9.3.51 as pubd b TC. Price 6*d*. Gray xvii.

(4) Ed. 1781. TC. Recorded by Lyon.

A556. SMART, Chris. ODE ON ST. CECILIA'S DAY, TRANSLATED INTO LATIN FROM POPE.

(1) Hawkins, in *Life of Johnson*, 1787, wrote: 'When Smart published his Latin translation of Mr Pope's Ode on St Cecilia's Day, Mr Pope having read it, in a letter to Newbery the publisher of it returned his thanks to the author, with an assurance, that it exceeded his own original. This fact Newbery himself told me, and offered to show me the letter in Mr Pope's hand-writing.' No ed. by JN traced.

(2) Listed in A35(5), 1778, as pr f TC & Co. Price 2*s*.

A557. SMART, Chris. ON THE ETERNITY OF THE SUPREME BEING. *CBEL*, II, 338.

(1) 1st ed. 1750. Not by JN.

(2) 2nd ed. 1752. S b JN et al. Price 6*d*. Gray xi. [BM; Bodley.

(3) 3rd ed. 1756. S b JN et al. Price 6*d*. Welsh 308; Gray xii. [Bodley; Sotheby, 10.4.70, lot 622.

(4) Ed. 1761. ? JN. *CBEL*, II, 338.

(5) Listed in A35(5), 1778, as pr f TC & Co et al. Price 6*d*.

A558. SMART, Chris. ON THE GOODNESS OF THE SUPREME BEING. *CBEL*, II, 338.

(1) 1st ed. 1756. S b JN et al. Price 6*d*. Gray xxxiii; Rothschild 1877–8. [BM; Bodley.

(2) 2nd ed. 1756. S b JN et al. Welsh 308; Gray xxxiv. [BM; Bodley.

(3) Ed. 1761. ? JN. *CBEL*, II, 338.

(4) Listed in A35(5), 1778, as pr f TC & Co et al. Price 6*d*.

A559. SMART, Chris. ON THE IMMENSITY OF THE SUPREME BEING. *CBEL*, II, 338.

(1) 1st ed. 1751. S b JN et al. Price 6*d*. Gray xxii; Rothschild 1873. [BM; Bodley; CUL; Rylands; LGL.

(2) 2nd ed. 1753. Pr f JN et al. Price 6*d*. Gray xxiii. [BM; Bodley; CUL.

(3) 3rd ed. 1757. S b JN. Welsh 308; Gray xxiv (dates 1756). [Bodley; Sotheby, 10.4.70, lot 622.

(4) Ed. 1761. ? JN. *CBEL*, II, 338.

(5) Listed in A35(5), 1778, as pr f TC & Co et al. Price 6*d*.

A560. SMART, Chris. ON THE OMNISCIENCE OF THE SUPREME BEING. *CBEL*, II, 338.

(1) 1st ed. 1752. S b JN et al. Price 6*d*. Gray xxvi; Rothschild 1874. [BM; Bodley; DNS.

(2) 2nd ed. 1756. S b JN et al. Price 6d. Welsh 308; Gray xxvii. [BM; Bodley.
(3) Ed. 1761. ? JN. *CBEL*, ii, 338.
(4) Listed in A35(5), 1778, as pr f TC & Co et al. Price 6d.

A561. SMART, Chris. ON THE POWER OF THE SUPREME BEING. *CBEL*, ii, 338.
(1) 1st ed. 1754. S b JN et al. Price 6d. Gray xxx; Rothschild 1876. [BM; Bodley.
(2) 2nd ed. 1758. Pr f JN. Welsh 308; Gray xxxi. [Bodley; Sotheby, 10.4.70, lot 622.
(3) Ed. 1761. ? JN. *CBEL*, ii, 338.
(4) Listed in A35(5), 1778, as pr f TC & Co et al. Price 6d.

A562. SMART, Chris. POEMS ON SEVERAL OCCASIONS.
(1) 1st ed. 1752. S b JN. Price 10s 6d. Welsh 307; Gray xxv; *CBEL*, ii, 338. [BM; Bodley; CUL; V&A; LL; AdE; Roscoe; DNS.
(2) Listed in A637(2), vol. ii, 1768, as 'just pubd' by JN.
(3) Listed in A35(5), 1778, as pr f TC & Co et al. Price 10s 6d.

A563. SMART, Chris. POEMS OF THE LATE CHRISTOPHER SMART, 1791. S b F. Power & Co. Price 7s. Welsh 30 (footnote); Gray liv; *CBEL*, ii, 338. [BM; Bodley; RePL; CTrC; DNS.

A564. SMART, Chris. SOLEMN DIRGE, A, SACRED TO THE MEMORY OF...FREDERIC PRINCE OF WALES.
(1) 1st ed. 1751. Pr f TC. Price 6d. Welsh 223; Gray xviii; *CBEL*, ii, 338. [BM; Bodley.
(2) 2nd ed. 1751. Adv. *GEP* 16–18.4.51 as pr f TC. Price 6d. Gray xix.
(3) 3rd ed. 1751. ? TC. Adv. *London Daily Advertiser* 22.6.61. Gray xx.

A565. SMITH, Daniel, M.D. APOLOGY TO THE PUBLIC FOR COMMENCING THE PRACTICE OF PHYSIC.
(1) 1st ed. 1775. Pr f C & N. Price 6d. Noticed in *LM* Nov. 1775, p. 596.
(2) 2nd ed. [1775 or 1776]. Pr f C & N. Price 6d. [MSL; Wellcome; RCS.

A566. SMITH, Daniel, M.D. LETTER TO DR. CADOGAN.
(1) 1st ed. [1772]. Pr f C & N. Price 1s 6d. [RCP.
(2) 2nd ed. [1772 or 1773]. Pr f C & N. Price 1s 6d. [RSM.

A567. SMITH, Daniel, M.D. OBSERVATIONS ON DR WILLIAMS'S TREATISE UPON THE GOUT, n.d. 1702 or later. S b C & N et al. Price 1s. The *Treatise* was pubd 1772. [RSM.

A568. SMITH, Daniel, M.D. TREATISE ON HYSTERICAL AND NERVOUS DISEASES. Adv. *LC* 25–7.12.77, p. 621, as pr f C & N. Price 1s 6d.

A569. SMITH, Edmund. THALES. A MONODY. *CBEL*, II, 444.
(1) The BM copy 11630.b.3(17) is catalogued with date [1750]. The TP date has been cut off; the difference between this and no. (2) is not apparent. Welsh 309.
(2) Ed. 1751. Pr f JN. Price 6*d*. [BM; Bodley.

A570. SMITH, James. THE ART OF LIVING IN LONDON, 1768. Pr f F. Newbury (*sic*) (N) et al. Price 2*s*. *CBEL*, II, 146. [BM.

A571. SMITH, Thomas. COMPENDIOUS DIVISION.
(1) Ed. 1751. S b J. Newberry (*sic*). Price 1*s*. [RI; UCL.
(2) Adv. *LC* 28–30.3.58, p. 304, as s b G. Hawkins and JN. Price 1*s*.

A572. SMOLLETT, Tobias George. ADVENTURES OF RODERICK RANDOM, 9th ed. 1774. 2 vols, price 6*s*. Listed in A401(3), 1777, as pr f TC. His name not in the imprint of the Bodley copy.

A573. SPECTATOR, THE. *CBEL*, II, 603 (*sub* Addison); *BUCOP*, IV, 203.
(1) Ed. 1775. 8 vols. 8vo. Pr f FN(? N) et al. Price £2. (Communicated.) [ReU; TCD.
(2) Undated ed. 8 vols. 12mo. Pr f 'Newbery' et al. [BM (P.P.5250.ebi); Bodley.
(3) Ed. [1788]. 8 vols. 12mo. Pr f 'Newbury' (*sic*) et al. Price 1 gn. [Richnell; Bodley; CUL.
(4) Ed. 1789. 8 vols. 8vo. Pr f EN et al. [BM (*ex* vols I and II); Bodley; LGL.

A574. STAFFORD, Hugh. A TREATISE ON CYDER-MAKING.
(1) Welsh 310 says 2nd ed. was in 'F. Newbery's List, n.d.'. That ed. (1755) was by Henry and Cave. There was an ed. of 1753 by Cave.
(2) A 'new ed. with additions', 1769. Pr f FN(N). [CUL.

A575. STEVENS, George Alexander. SONGS, COMIC, AND SATYRICAL. *CBEL*, II, 328.
(1) 1st ed. 1772. S b FN(N) et al. Price 3*s* 6*d* bd, 3*s* sewed. Hugo 7. [BM; Bodley; CUL (imperf.); Oup; OEFL; EdUL.
(2) 2nd ed. 1782. S b EN et al. [CUL.

A576. STRAIGHT, Rev. John. SELECT DISCOVERIES ON MORAL AND RELIGIOUS SUBJECTS. Adv. *London Evening Post*, 29 Jan.–1 Feb. 1743 as s b JN et al. There was a 1741 ed. pr f J. Watts.

A577. STUDENT, THE. Afterwards THE STUDENT, OR THE OXFORD AND CAMBRIDGE MONTHLY MISCELLANY.
(1) Ed. 1750–1. Pr f JN et al. 2 vols, 12*s*. Monthly issues cost 6*d*. Welsh 310–12; Courtney p. 38; Chapman 135–6; Gray IX; *BUCOP*, IV, 235; *CBEL*, II, 214–15; Rothschild 1868. [BM; Bodley; CUL; LUL (vol. II); LL; OEFL; DNS (vol. I).
(2) Listed in A640(3), vol. IV, 1768, as pr f a s b N & C, 2 vols, price 12*s*.

A578. SYDENHAM, Thomas. THE ENTIRE WORKS OF DR THOMAS SYDENHAM...BY JOHN SWAN, M.D.
(1) 4th ed. 1763. Welsh 312 quotes from 'F. Newbery's List, about 1769'. This ed. was pubd by R. Cave.
(2) 5th ed. 1769. Pr f FN(N). Adv. in advance at 7s, later 7s 6d. [RCP; EdUL.

A579. SYDENHAM, Thomas. THE WORKS OF THOMAS SYDENHAM ON ACUTE AND CHRONIC DISEASES, 1788. Pr f EN et al. 2 vols. [BM; Wellcome; RCP; EdUL.

A580. TALBOT, Rev. William. NARRATIVE OF THE WHOLE OF HIS PROCEEDINGS RELATIVE TO JONATHAN BRITAIN, [1772]. S b TC et al. Price 6d. [Bodley; BM; CUL.

A581. TASSO, Torquato. JERUSALEM DELIVERED... TRANSLATED BY JOHN HOOLE. Welsh 237 and 313; *CBEL*, II, 471, 814.
(1) 1st ed. 1763. S b JN et al. Price 10s 6d sewed, 12s bd, 2 vols. [BM; Bodley.
(2) 2nd ed. 1764. Pr f JN et al. Price 5s sewed. [Only title leaves seen, Bodley (258.2.b.2, p. 135 for vol. II), Oup (for vol. I); A. R. Heath, Cat. II [1968] item 435.

A582. TATLER, THE; OR LUCUBRATIONS OF ISAAC BICKERSTAFF, ESQ. *BUCOP*, IV, 288.
(1) Ed. 1774. Pr f FN* et al. 4 vols. Price 10s. [Bodley; EdUL.
(2) A 'new ed.', 1786. Pr f EN et al. 6 vols. Price £1 11s 6d. [BM; EdUL; UCL; AdE.
(3) Ed. 1789. Pr f EN et al. 4 vols. [BM.
(4) Ed. 1797. Pr f EN et al. 4 vols. Price 8s per vol. in bds, 9s bd. [BM (large paper); LUL; Rylands.

A583. TEMPLEMAN, Peter. PRACTICAL OBSERVATIONS ON THE CULTURE OF LUCERNE, 1766. Pr f FN(N). Price 1s. Fussell, p. 47. [BM; LUL (imperf.); Wellcome.

A584. THEORY AND HISTORY OF EARTHQUAKES. Pr f a s b JN et al. Price 1s. Adv. *GEP* 6.4.50 (*per* Welsh 208). Possibly by Thos Sherlock, Bp of London.
(1) Undated ed. Pp. 62[63]. [BM (lacks last leaf); Bodley; Hodgsons, 16.12.60, lot 395.
(2) Another undated ed. (? issue). Pp. 66. [GeoM.

A585. THOMAS, Pascoe. A TRUE AND IMPARTIAL JOURNAL OF A VOYAGE TO THE SOUTH-SEAS...UNDER THE

COMMAND OF COMMODORE GEORGE ANSON, 1745. Pr a s b JN et al. Price 5s. Welsh 170; Sabin 95437; *CBEL*, II, 741. [BM; Bodley; EdUL; UCL.

A586. THOMPSON, Charles. TRAVELS OF THE LATE CHARLES THOMPSON, ESQ, 1744. Pr b JN et al. 3 vols, price 15s. Bodley's Cat. indicates that 'Charles Thompson' was a fictitious name. Welsh 316; *CBEL*, II, 745; Legg no. 23. Another issue of the same year under imprint of J. Robinson. [BM; Bodley; CUL; RePL; UCL; LL.

A587. THOMPSON, Charles. TRAVELS THROUGH TURKEY IN ASIA... Welsh 317. As to 'Charles Thompson' see A586.
(1) 1st ed. 1754. Pr f JN. 2 vols, price 6s. *CBEL*, II, 742. [BM.
(2) 2nd ed. adv. *PL* 12.2.60 as pr f JN. 2 vols, price 6s.
(3) 3rd ed. 1767. Pr f JN. 2 vols, price 6s. [BM.
(4) Listed in A222(17), 1788, as s b TC. Price 6s, 2 vols.

A588. THORNTON, Bonnell. THE BATTLE OF THE WIGS, 1768. S b FN(N) et al. Price 2s. *CBEL*, II, 383. [BM; Bodley; CUL; AdE; UCL.

A589. THOULIER D'OLIVET, Pierre Joseph. THOUGHTS OF CICERO.
(1) Ed. 1750 (1st trilingual ed.). Pr f JN et al. [BM; Bodley; LUL; UCL.
(2) Ed. 1751 (English text alone). Pr f JN et al. Price 2s 6d. [BM; Bodley.
(3) Listed in A640(3), vol. IV, 1768 as pr f a s b N & C. Price 2s 6d. Probably stock in hand of nos (1) or (2).
(4) Ed. 1773 (2nd trilingual ed.). Pr f C & N. Price 3s 6d. Welsh 332. [BM; Bodley.
(5) An English text ed. by Wishart listed in A640(3), vol. XIII, 1774, as pr f N & C. Price 2s 6d; also in J113(4), 1781 as pr f TC.

A590. TILLOTSON, John, Archbp. TWENTY DISCOURSES... ABRIDGED...BY D. HENRY. Welsh 317.
(1) 2nd ed. 1763. Adv. *LC* 21–4.1.69, p. 75, as pr f FN(N). But the ed. was pubd b Henry and Cave. As in 1769 FN(N) was about to publish the 3rd ed. it looks as if he had bought up the stock of the 2nd.
(2) 3rd ed. 1770. Pr f FN(N). Price 2s 6d. [Bodley.
(3) 4th ed. 1779. Pr f FN(N). [BM.

A591. TOLLENDAL, Thomas Arthur de (Count). MEMOIRS OF COUNT LALLY, FROM HIS EMBARKING FOR THE EAST INDIES, 1766. Pr f FN(N). Price 4s sewed, 5s bd. [BM; Bodley; Marchmont Bkshop, 1970.

A592. TOWNLEY, James. HIGH LIFE BELOW STAIRS. Welsh 319; *CBEL*, II, 445, 483; Nicoll 312, 397.

(1) 1st ed. 1759. Pr f JN et al. Price 1*s*. [BM; Bodley; CUL; AdE.

(2) 2nd ed. 1759. Not traced.

(3) 3rd ed. 1759. Pr f JN et al. Price 1*s*. 28 leaves. Pp. 54. [Bodley.

(4) Another 3rd ed. 1759. Pr f JN et al. Price 1*s*. 19 leaves. Pp. 35. [BM.

(5) 4th ed. 1759. Pr f JN et al. Price 1*s*. [Bodley.

(6) 5th ed. not traced.

(7) 6th ed. 1760. Pr f JN et al. Price 1*s*. [BM.

(8) 7th ed. 1763. Pr f JN. Price 1*s*. [Bodley; Colin Richardson, Cat. 115 [1960] item 1160.

(9) 8th ed. 1768. Pr f N & C. Price 1*s*. [BM; Bodley.

(10) 9th ed. 1775. Pr f C & N. Price 1*s*. [BM; Bodley.

A593. TRADER'S MAGAZINE, THE, AND MONTHLY TREASURY OF TRADE, COMMERCE, ARTS, MANUFACTURES AND MECHANICS. Adv. *LC* 31.12.74–3.1.75 as t.d.w.p. no. 1 (to be continued monthly), price 1*s*. Pr f the Authors; s b FN(N). No later number traced. Apparently unrecorded.

A594. TREATISE ON VIRTUES AND REWARDS... TRANSLATED FROM THE ITALIAN. Adv. *LC* 27–9.4.69, p. 407, as pr f FN(N) et al. Price 3*s* 6*d* sewed.

A595. TRUSLER, John. CHRONOLOGY; OR, THE HISTORIAN'S VADE-MECUM. Welsh 319.

(1) 5th ed. 1772. S b FN(N) et al. Price 1*s* 6*d* sewed. [Bodley; A. W. Laywood, Cat. 17 [1971] item 233.

(2) 7th ed. 1774. S b FN(N) et al. Price 1*s* 6*d*. [Exeter; Sotheby, 19.4.71, lot 18.

A596. UNHAPPY WIFE, THE, [IN] A SERIES OF LETTERS, BY A LADY, 1770. Pr f FN(N) et al. 2 vols, price 5*s* sewed. [BM.

A597. UNIVERSAL CHRONICLE, THE, OR WEEKLY GAZETTE. First issue Saturday, 8 April 1758. Welsh 37–9; *CBEL*, II, 715; *BUCOP*, IV, 426; S. Morison, *The English Newspaper*, pp. 137–9; Nichols, *Lit. Anecdotes*, III, 732, says that the paper was projected by JN. His name does not appear in the paper. [BM; Bodley, and see *BUCOP*.

A598. UNIVERSAL HARMONY OR, THE GENTLEMAN & LADIE'S SOCIAL COMPANION. *CBEL*, II, 210, 211, 212; *BUCM*, II, 1029. 1st ed. 1743, was pr f The Proprietors (copy in BM). No. (1) (below) seems to be only a re-issue of the sheets with new engvd FP and TP. There is evidence that some at least of the sheets had been used in an ed. of *The English Orpheus*

Universal Harmony

OR, THE

Gentleman & Ladie's

Social Companion.

CONSISTING

Of a great Variety of the Best & most Favourite
English & Scots Songs, Cantatas &c. &c.

With a Curious Design,
By way of Head piece,

Expressive of the sense of each particul.r Song

All neatly Engraved on Quarto CopperPlates,

And set to Music for the Voice, Violin, Hautboy, German & Common
Flute, with a Thorough Base for the Organ, Harpsich.d Spinet, &c.

By the Best Masters

The whole calculated to keep People in good Spirits, good
Health, & good Humour, to promote Social Friendship in all Comp.ys
and Universal Harmony in every Neighbourhood.

LONDON:
Printed for J. Newbery at y.e Bible & Crown, without Temple Bar. 1745.
S. Kitchin sculp.t

Fig. 35. Title-page of A598(1). (Reduced.)

382

pubd b Thos Kitchin in 1743. In a number of the plates in *Universal Harmony* traces of the erased words 'English Orpheus' are still to be seen at the head of the leaf.

(1) Ed. 1745 (probably 2nd ed.). Pr f JN (see Fig. 35). Price 7s 6d. Issued in pts, 5 songs in each, at 3d. Welsh 322 and 275. See Figure 13. [Roscoe; BM; CUL.

(2) Ed. 1746 (probably 3rd ed.). S b JN. Price 7s 6d. Apparently a further re-issue of the original sheets. [BM.

(3) In 1748 the work was adv. as s b J. Robinson; still adv. in 1770 (in A286(7)) as pr f N & C, price 7s 6d.

A599. UNIVERSAL HISTORY, AN, 1779–80. And THE MODERN PART OF AN UNIVERSAL HISTORY, 1780–4. Pr f FN (? FN(N)) et al.
I. THE ANCIENT PART. 18 vols. [BM; Bodley; EdUL; LL; Rylands; LGL.
II. THE MODERN PART. 42 vols. [BM; Bodley; EdUL; LL; Rylands; LGL.
III. MAPS AND CHARTS TO THE MODERN PART OF THE UNIVERSAL HISTORY. Adv. *LC* 20–3.1.87 as pr f EN et al. Price 12s half bd.

A600. UPHOLSTERER'S LETTER, THE, TO THE RT HONOURABLE WILLIAM PITT, ESQ; NOW LORD CHATHAM. TO WHICH ARE PREFIXED SOME PRELIMINARY REMARKS. Listed *LM* May 1768, p. 276, as by 'Newbery' (8vo, 31 pp.), and reviewed as 'a flippant composition'.

USONG. AN EASTERN NARRATIVE. See Haller, Albrecht.

A601. VANSITTART, Henry. LETTER TO THE PROPRIETORS OF EAST-INDIA STOCK, A, 1767. Pr f JN et al. Price 2s. Welsh 323. [BM; Bodley; LUL; LL; Rylands; AdE; LGL.

A602. VANSITTART, Henry. NARRATIVE OF THE TRANSACTIONS IN BENGAL, A, 1766. Pr f JN et al. 3 vols, price 18s. Welsh 323. [BM; Bodley; CUL; EdUL; AdE; UCL.

A603. VANSITTART, Henry. ORIGINAL PAPERS RELATIVE TO THE DISTURBANCES IN BENGAL, 1765. Pr f JN. 2 vols, price 7s sewed in marbled paper. Welsh 323. [BM.

A604. VATTEL, Emerich de. THE LAW OF NATIONS, 1760, vol. I. Pr f JN et al. Price 12s bd calf and lettered. Vol. II, 1759, was by J. Coote alone. Welsh 323–5; *CBEL*, II, 802. [BM; Bodley; CUL; EdUL; LGL.

A605. VENN, Henry. THE COMPLETE DUTY OF MAN. Welsh 325.
(1) 1st ed. 1763. Pr f JN et al. Price 5s. *CBEL*, II, 853. [BM.
(2) 2nd ed. 1765. Pr f JN et al. Price 5s. [BM.
(3) 3rd ed. 1779. Pr f C & N et al. [BM; CUL; EdUL.

A606. VOLTAIRE. The following very brief analysis of English edd. under the imprints of the Newbery family is based on, and owes almost everything to, Mr Hywel Berwyn Evans's valiant attempt to produce order out of chaos (*A Provisional Bibliography of English Editions and Translations of Voltaire*, in vol. VIII of Theodore Besterman's *Studies in Voltaire*, 1959). Particularly as regards the collected edd. an accurate bibliography seems almost impossible, as is any attempt to connect many of the newspaper adverts with known edd. Of the collected edd. Mr Evans says 'every set noted is incomplete and heterogeneous in the extreme'.

A607. VOLTAIRE. DRAMATIC WORKS, trans. Francklin. A 7-vol. ed. was adv. *LC* 9–11.4.65, p. 350, price 17s 6d sewed, 1 gn bd.
(1) Vol. I, 1761. Pr f JN et al. Welsh 223; Evans, p. 23. [BM; Bodley; DLC.
(2) Vol. II, 1761. Pr f JN et al. Welsh 223. [Bodley; Oup.
(3) Vols III and IV, 1762. JN et al. [Bodley; DLC.
(4) Vol. V, 1762. Pr f JN et al. Evans, p. 30. [Bodley; BmPL; DLC.
(5) Vols VI and VII, 1763. Pr f JN et al. Evans, p. 30. [Bodley (vol. VI); BmPL; DLC.
(6) Vols I and II, 1769. Pr f N & C. Evans, p. 29. [BmPL, not seen.
(7) Vols III and IV, 1771. Pr f C & N. Evans, p. 30. [BmPL, not seen.

A608. VOLTAIRE. GENUINE LETTERS BETWEEN THE ARCHBISHOP OF ANNECI AND MONS. DE VOLTAIRE, ON THE SUBJECT OF HIS PREACHING..., 1770. Pr f FN(N). Price 1s. Evans no. 76. [BM; DLC.

A609. VOLTAIRE. HENRIADE, THE, 1762. Pr f JN et al. Price 2s 6d sewed, 3s bd. Evans, p. 29, not seen. [BmPL; DLC.

A610. VOLTAIRE. HISTORY OF THE PARLIAMENT OF PARIS. Adv. *LC* 22–4.8.69, p. 187, as 'In the Press, and speedily w.b.p.' by FN(N).

A611. VOLTAIRE. MISCELLANEOUS POEMS, trans. T. Smollett. T. Francklin et al.
(1) Ed. 1764. Pr f JN et al. Evans, p. 29, not seen. [BmPL; DLC.
(2) 3rd ed. 1770. Pr f C & N et al. Evans, p. 29, not seen. [BmPL; DLC.

A612. VOLTAIRE. PUPIL OF NATURE, THE, 1771. Pr f TC. Price 2s sewed. Welsh 296; *CBEL*, II, 552 and 804; Evans no. 333. [BM; CUL; EdUL; GlaUL.

A613. VOLTAIRE. UNIVERSAL HISTORY. Adv. *LC* 28–30.6.57 as in the Press and speedily w.b.p. by JN. ? = Thos Nugent's trans. *An Essay on Universal History*, 2nd ed. 1759 (Evans 210–12).

A614. VOLTAIRE. WORKS. Trans. T. Smollett, T. Francklin et al. Welsh 326–7; Evans 1, pp. 16–20; *CBEL*, II, 37, 466, 804.
(1) 1st English ed. 1761–65. Pr f JN et al. A 25-vol. set. Monthly vols adv. at 2s, 2s 6d, 3s. [BM, 831.a.13–37; Wellcome (vols. 10, 15–17, 20, 21); Maggs Cat. 910 [1967] item 372, includes the 25 vols of the BM set.
(2) 2nd English ed. 1762–9. Pr f JN et al. 20 vols. Evans 25–8; *CBEL*, II, 37. [BmPL, not seen.
(2A) An ed. of 35 vols, price 5 gns, was listed in A172(2), 1765, as pr f JN. And *LC* for 9–11.4.65, p. 350, advtd as t.d.w.p. Vol. 35, pr f JN et al. 'which completes the work'.
(3) A 36-vol. set adv. *LC* 18–20.12.70, p. 587, as t.d.w.p. by C & N et al. Price £5 8s.
(4) Vol. 25 of the *Prose Works*, 1770, being vol. 35 of the *Works*. Pr f C & N et al. Evans, p. 24. [BM, 1341.d.6.
(5) 3rd English ed. Vols 1 (1770), 12 (1770), 13 (1771) and 25 (1770). Pr f C & N et al. Evans pp. 25, 27, 28. [BmPL, not seen.
(6) Vols 7 and 8, 1771. Pr f C & N et al. Evans 26. [BmPL, not seen.
(7) A 'new ed.', included in a 38-vol. set dated between 1761 and 1781. Evans 20–5. Pr f JN, C & N, FN(N) et al. [BM, 1341.c and d.

A614A. WALLIS, John. THE DUTY OF SEEKING ALL MEN'S SALVATION INCUMBENT ON ALL CHRISTIANS, 1740. S b 'Mr Newbury' (*sic*) et al. Legg 14. [BM; RePL.

A615. WARBLER'S DELIGHT, THE: OR, ENGLISH HARMONY. *CBEL*, II, 225 lists an ed. of [1767?]. Not in *BUCM* or Hirsch Cat.
(1) Adv. *LC* 14–16.1.66, p. 51, as t.d.w.p. by FN(N). Price 1s 6d.
(2) Adv. *LC* 17–20.1.67, p. 67, as t.d.w.p. by FN(N). Price 1s 6d neatly bd in red.

A616. WARD, Edward. THE LONDON SPY COMPLEAT IN 18 PARTS. THE FIRST VOLUME OF THE AUTHOR'S WRITINGS, 4th ed. 'revis'd', 1753. TC. Recorded by Algar. *CBEL*, II, 598.

A616A. WARD, Rev. Samuel. MODERN SYSTEM OF NATURAL HISTORY. See J376. Perhaps this should not have been included in the Juvenile section.

A617. WARNER, Ferdinando. SCHEME OF A FUND FOR THE BETTER MAINTENANCE OF THE WIDOWS AND CHILDREN OF THE CLERGY, 1752. Pr f JN et al. Price 6*d*. [BM; Bodley; CUL.

A618. WARTON, Thomas (the younger). LIFE OF SIR THOMAS POPE, THE, 1772. Pr f FN(? S) et al. Price 5*s* (adv. in 1771), 6*s* sewed in bds in 1772. *CBEL*, II, 385. [LL; BM; Bodley; CUL; Rylands; LGL; AdE.

A619. WARTON, Thomas (the younger). NEW-MARKET, A SATIRE, 1751. Pr f JN. Price 1*s*. Welsh 277; *CBEL*, II, 384. [Bodley.

A620. WARTON, Thomas (the younger) (edited). OXFORD SAUSAGE, THE. Welsh 280; *CBEL*, II, 223, 229, 232, 385.
(1) 'A new ed.' 1772. Pr f FN(N) et al. Price 2*s* sewed. [BM; EdUL; Renier.
(2) 'A new ed.' 1777. Pr f FN(N) et al. Price 2*s* sewed. Hugo 4035. [BM; DNS.
(3) Ed. 1789. EN [? et al.]. Hugo 34 describes as '12mo. With cuts said to be by Thomas Bewick'. There is no reason to suppose Bewick (born 1753) had anything to do with the wcts in 18th-cent. edd. of this book: the cuts (or most of them) in the 1st ed. (1764) being still used as late as J. Black's ed. of 1814. In 1815 Longman put out an ed. with redrawn cuts, stated in the TP to be by Thomas Bewick.
(4) 'A new ed.' undated. Pr f G. Robinson, EN and W. Jackson. Price 2*s* sewed. [Bodley (Gough Adds Oxford, 8vo 108); Quaritch (1964).
(5) Another undated 'New ed.'. Pr f G. Robinson, E. Newbury (*sic*) and W. Dawson & Co. Price 2*s* 6*d* sewed. [Bodley; CUL.

A621. WATERLAND, Daniel. COMMENTARY ON THE BOOKS OF THE OLD AND NEW TESTAMENTS. Dodd's *Commentary*, 1770 (no. A34(1) or (3)) is sometimes so described.

A622. WESTON, Richard. GARDENER'S AND PLANTER'S CALENDAR, THE.
(1) 1st ed. 1773. Pr f TC. 6 weekly pts at 6*d*, to be had bd 3*s* 6*d*. [BM; CUL; RHS; EdUL; AdE.
(2) 2nd ed. 1778. Pr f TC. Price 3*s* 6*d* in the vell. manner. [BM; Bodley; EdUL.

A623. WHITTELL, Thomas, and John DUMCOMBE. A TREATISE UPON THE DENDROMETER, [1768]. S b FN(N). Price 3*s* half bd. [BM; CUL; UCL; EdUL.

A624. WHITWORTH, Sir Charles. COLLECTION, A, OF THE SUPPLIES, AND WAYS AND MEANS.
(1) Ed. 1763. Pr f JN et al. Price 3s bd in red, 2s 6d sewed. Higgs 2966. [BM; LUL; NLA.
(2) Ed. 1764. Pr f JN et al. Price 3s. [BM.
(3) 'Second ed.', 1765. Pr f JN et al. Price 3s. Higgs 3499. [BM; LUL.

A625. WHITWORTH, Sir Charles. CONSIDERATIONS FOR THE MORE SPEEDY...EXECUTION OF THE ACT, FOR PAVING...THE CITY...OF WESTMINSTER, 1763. Pr f JN et al. Price 6d. [LGL; UCL.

A626. WHITWORTH, Sir Charles. SUCCESSION OF PARLIAMENTS, THE, 1764. Pr f JN et al. Price 3s. Higgs 3326. [BM; CUL; LUL.

A627. WILLIAMS, Aaron. THE UNIVERSAL PSALMODIST, [1770]. 4th ed. Pr f FN(S) et al. Price 4s. *BUCM*, II, 1082. [BM.

A628. WILLIS, Cecil, D.D. MATTER, THE, OF AGISTMENT TITHE OF UNPROFITABLE STOCK IN THE CASE OF THE VICAR OF HOLBEACH, n.d. Pr f FN(N). 1776 or after. Price 1s. [Bodley.

A629. WILLIS, Cecil, D.D. NATURE, THE, OF AGISTMENT TITHE... 2nd ed. 1778. Pr f FN(N). Price 3s. Presumably the 1st ed. was A628. [BM.

A630. WINCKELMANN, Johann Joachim. CRITICAL ACCOUNT OF THE SITUATION AND DESTRUCTION...OF HERCULANEUM..., 1771. Pr f C & N. Price 2s 6d. Welch 331. [BM; CUL; LUL; UCL; Rylands; AdE.

A631. WINDSOR, AND ITS ENVIRONS. Welsh 331.
(1) Ed. 1768. Pr f N & C et al. Price 1s. [BM; Bodley.
(2) Ed. 1774. Pr f C & N et al. Price 1s. [BM; Bodley; EdUL; AdE.

A632. WINSTANLEY, Rev. ( ). A USEFUL MEMORANDUM; OR, THE CHRISTIAN'S CONSTANT POCKET COMPANION. Adv. *PA* 8.12.52 as s b [J]N et al.

A633. WINTER, George. ANIMAL MAGNETISM, [1801]. S b E. Newberry (*sic*) et al. The Dedication is dated Bristol, May 1801. [BM; Bodley; CUL; AdE.

A634. WINTER, George. [NEW AND] COMPENDIOUS SYSTEM OF HUSBANDRY. Fussell p. 131.
(1) 1st ed. 1787, titled *a new and compendious*... S b Mrs E. Newberry (*sic*) et al. [BM; CUL; LUL; AdE; EdUL.
(2) 2nd ed. 1797, titled *a compendious*... Pr f Mrs E. Newberry (*sic*). Price 6s in bds. [BM; Bodley; LUL; AdE.

A635. WISE, Edward. THE REMARKABLE TRYAL OF THOMAS CHANDLER, 1751. S b JN et al. Price 1s. Legg no. 31. [BM; Bodley; RePL.

A636. WOLGAR'S COMPANION. Pr f EN. Price 3s. Listed *New British Dispensatory*, 1781.

A637. WONDERS OF NATURE AND ART, THE. Welsh 332.
(1) 1st ed. 1750 under the imprints of Corbett and Micklewright alone (4 vcls, 14s). By 1758 it was being listed as pr f a s b JN, and frequently thereafter. In 1763 a rival work, *The Beauties of Nature and Art*, was put out by J. Payne.
(2) 2nd ed. 1768. Pr f N & C. 6 vols, prices 18s and 1 gn, 15s in 1788. Listed as pr f F. Power & Co in 1789. In 1803 there was a shameless rehash by the Rev. Thos Smith, giving no acknowledgement of the earlier edd. [BM; Opie; Wellcome (vol. v).

A638. WOOD, Samuel. STRICTURES ON THE GOUT, 2nd ed. 1776. Pr f FN(N) et al. Price 1s 6d. [RSM.

A639. WOODFALL, William. SIR THOMAS OVERBURY: A TRAGEDY, 1777. S b FN(N). Price 1s 6d. Welsh 280; IAW 216; Nicoll 86–7, 317; *CBEL*, II, 457. [BM; Bodley; Hannas, Cat. 25 [1968] item 812.

A640. WORLD DISPLAYED, THE. Welsh 328 and 332–3; *CBEL*, II, 622 and 741; Courtney 98; Chapman 144; Osborne, Cat. 195. There are 2 forms of the title: 1. begins THE WORLD DISPLAYED; 2. begins A CURIOUS COLLECTION OF VOYAGES. The printing and publishing history of this work is often very obscure.
(1) *Editions dated in the period 1759–67, being 1st edd. and their re-issues.* About 31 vols. Pr f JN or JN and J. Hoey of Dublin. Price 1s 6d each vol. There is a prospectus for the 1st ed. in Oup. There is a 20-vol. set in Osborne. Details of the McKell set communicated. [BM; Bodley; Weedon; McKell.
(2) *Second edition.* 8 vols. 1760–8. Pr f JN or N & C. Vol. 1 dated 1760, all others 1768. [Vol. 1 McKell; all others Renier, not seen; EdUL Cat. 1918, vol. 3, p. 1280 records 'second edition, 20 vols, Lond, 1760'.
(3) *Third edition*, 1767–78. 21 vols. Pr f JN, or N & C or C & N. [BM; Renier; Weedon; Gardner. The BM copies are in the set 1424.b.1–20, which is described in the Catalogue as 'fourth edition'. In fact only vols I, II and XIV are of that edition.

(4) *Fourth edition.* Pr f C & N. The set of 20 vols was listed in 1781. Only vols I (1774), II (1777), XIV (1775) seen. No other volumes traced. [BM, in the set 1424.b.1–20.
(5) *An Edition of 1790.* CBEL, II, 741. Not traced.

A641. WORMS. A SHORT TRACT. Adv. *LC* 25–8.1.72 (and frequently later) as to be had gratis of Robt Witch, Chemist, at No. 17, in the Haymarket and of FN(N). Presumably a vermifuge, the tract issued in connection with the medicine.

A642. WOTY, William. SHRUBS OF PARNASSUS, THE, 1760. S b JN. Price 3s. Welsh 306; *CBEL*, II, 390. [BM; Bodley; CUL.

A643. XENOPHON. CYROPAEDIA, trans. Maurice Ashley. 4th ed. Pr f FN* et al. Adv. *LC* 17–19.2.78, p. 139. Price 6s in bds, 7s bd.

XENOPHON. See *Certain Ancient Tracts....* A79.

A644. YOUNGER BROTHER, THE, 1770, 1772. S b FN(N). Price 5s sewed, 2 vols. [BM.

NEWSPAPER ADVERTISEMENTS AS EVIDENCE FOR THE DATING OF BOOKS

Newspaper advertisements of books, when headed by slogans such as 'this day is [was] published', 'shortly will be published' and the like should, on the face of it, afford clear and unquestionable evidence as to dates of publication. Such phrases as these are the normal and usual headings to advertisements of books in the Press throughout the second half of the eighteenth century. And the evidence thus offered has been generally accepted without hesitation. So, to take an example, the first appearance of *A Little Pretty Pocket-Book* (J225) has been assigned to 1744 because, seemingly, it was advertised as 'This Day is publish'd According to Act of Parliament' in the *Penny London Morning Advertiser* on 18 June 1744; a like advertisement appeared in the *Daily Post*.[1]

Such acceptance would seem reasonable enough. But in point of fact these advertisements cannot, taken alone, be accepted as evidence of anything beyond the fact that the book named had already been, or was about to be, published;[2] it might be either of these, but the advertisement may give no clue as to which. 'This day was [or "is"] published' and its like will head an advertisement repeated over a number of weeks, months or even years.

To take some examples: the first edition of Bewick's *Quadrupeds*, 1790, was advertised in the *Newcastle Chronicle* for 17 and 24 April 1790 as 'to be published on Monday the 26th instant' and was advertised as 'this day is published' in the issues of the paper for 1 and 8 May. Lyle's *Art of Shorthand improved* (A311) was advertised in not less than six issues of the *London Chronicle* between 11 May and 15 June 1769 on each occasion as 'this day was published'. The second edition of the *Circle of the Sciences* was advertised in the *General Advertiser* as 'this day is published' on 14 April 1748 and 3 January 1749. The second edition of Brookes's *Introduction to Physic and Surgery* (A59(2)) was dated 1763 but was still being advertised as 'this day is published' as late as January 1769 (*London Chronicle*, 10–12 January). The 23rd edition of Lockman's *New History of England* (J231(12)) was dated 1794; it was advertised as 'this day was published' in the *London Chronicle* for 7–9 July 1795 and again as 'this day was published' on 10–12 December 1799 in the same paper. The later advertisement may possibly refer to a

[1] See, for instance, Muir, p. 59; Thwaite, pp. 1–2; *CBEL*, II, 561; Darton, pp. 1 etc.

[2] One might add 'or was in contemplation'; but this is debatable. The *London Chronicle* for 27–9 December 1764 advertised that 'On January 1st Mr Newbery intends to publish' certain books of one of which no edition dated before 1767 is known to have appeared. See the Introduction, at p. 11.

revised 23rd edition, but there is nothing to say so; it is described as 'corrected', but so is the edition dated 1794. The second edition of James Merrick's *Psalms* 1766 (A351), was advertised as 'this day was published' in the *London Chronicle* for 10–12 March 1768; and the sixth edition of Miller's *Abridgement of the Gardeners Dictionary*, 1771 (A358) was similarly advertised on 24–6 February 1778.

Nevertheless these advertisements may indicate the true year of publication, as against a false one on the title-page. Nichols (*Anecdotes*, III, 249) records that 'The Rule in general observed among Printers is, that when a Book happens not to be ready for Publication before November, the date of the ensuing year is used'. As examples of this rule, Elizabeth Newbery frequently published, in the *London Chronicle* and elsewhere, towards the end of December, lists of books 'just published' – usually juveniles 'for the Christmas Holidays' – some of which bear the date of the year just coming: *Flights of a Lady-Bird* (J136(1, 2)) advertised 'just published' 26–8 December 1786, dated in the imprint 1787; *Memoirs of Dick, the little Poney* (J241) 'just published' 21–4 December 1799, dated 1800; Wynne's *Tales for Youth* (J391(1)) 'just published' 19–21 December 1793, dated 1794. In these cases it seems obvious enough that the books were in the shops by Christmas, to catch the trade.

Brookes' and Collyer's *Dictionary of the World* (A62), issued in parts, has the title-page date 1772 but the first number of the part-issue was advertised as 'this day was published' in the *London Chronicle* for 21–3 October 1773. Here it may well be that the true date of issue of the first part was some time late in 1773, and that the general title-page to cover the complete work, dated, for reasons not apparent, 1772, was issued to subscribers on completion of the part-issues. The complete work was being advertised in March 1775 (*London Chronicle*, 11–14 March).

No doubt the regular newspaper reader of the period recognised these slogans for what they were intended to be: the customary signposts to advertisements of books, not to be taken literally. Although printed as a rule in very small lower-case italic type they did effectively spotlight the advertisements, as the present writer found when working through the files of the *London Chronicle*.

To repeat – it amounts to this, that the unsupported evidence of a newspaper advertisement cannot, as a rule, be relied on for dating purposes; but most certainly it must not be ignored. It may well be that the *Little Pretty Pocket-Book* did bear the date 1744 and did appear in (or near to) June of that year; but the evidence of the advertisements is not sufficient to prove it; it might have been published a year or two before, or even in 1745 or later.

Because of what I say above, the chronological list is confined to books dated in the title-page imprint or elsewhere, even though there may be extrinsic evidence to prove such a date a false one; or, by virtue of other evidence, datable.

As regards notices or reviews of books in periodicals such as the *London Magazine* or the *Gentleman's Magazine*, or their inclusion in the monthly lists of 'New Publications', these can be taken as reasonably certain indications of the year of issue, only bearing in mind that a review may be delayed for some months after actual publication. Books dated by this means are included in the chrono-logical list.

Mr William B. Todd, in an article 'The Use of Advertisements in Bibliographical Studies' (*The Library*, September 1953, pp. 174–87), has argued at length and powerfully that the evidence afforded by newspaper advertisements is superior to the evidence of title-pages, both as to names of publishers and dates of publication. He sums up:

Enough has been said, I believe, to convince even the most sceptical that the data provided in the book may be insufficient for an analysis of its production and certainly inadequate for any record of the circumstances attending its issue. As Macaulay once said of history, so I would say of bibliography, that the only true account of it is to be found in the newspapers, the daily record of events as they occur.

All very true – up to a point. But when the newspapers announce the publication of a book 'this day' over an extended period, as I have shown above, one comes to treat their evidence, on this matter at all events, with some caution.

APPENDIX 2
NOTES ON SOME BINDINGS

(1) BINDING IN THE VELLUM MANNER

The following note is based chiefly on information put at my disposal by Miss M. J. P. Weedon.

This binding (sometimes called 'Newbery's manner') consists of paper-covered boards, blue or green, very occasionally red, with vellum back-strips usually stained green or blue, a paper label on the spine (which has usually fallen off).

Vellum as a binding was no new thing at all, but by the second half of the eighteenth century seems to have become limited in its use in this country. *A General Description of all Trades*, 1747, says (at p. 26) concerning bookbinders:

This Art is divided into two principal Branches, *Velum* [sic]-*binding* used chiefly by the *Stationers*, of plain or white Paper-books for Accounts, &c And *Leather-binding*, for all Sorts of printed Books, &c.

Joseph Collyer's *The Parent's and Guardian's Assistant*, 1761, says (at p. 68):

Of this business [bookbinding] there are several sorts, as the calves leather binder, the vellum, and the sheep's leather binder...The Vellum Binder is chiefly employed in binding shop-books in vellum or parchment; he also rules paper for the account-books. This is the most profitable branch of binding both for the master and journeyman. [*Shop-book:* 'a shopkeeper's or mechanic's account book' – *OED*.]

There are indications that by 1768 binding in the conventional leather was running into difficulties. The following notice appeared in the *London Chronicle* for 21–4 May 1768 (p. 490):

The Booksellers of London to the Publick.

THE Scarcity of Leather has occasioned so great an increase in the Price of Binding, that the Booksellers find it impossible to serve their Customers at the usual Prices. They therefore think it their Duty to inform the Publick, that in their Opinion, no Method can be so effectual to restrain the exorbitant and repeated rise of that Commodity, as for Gentlemen to have their Books done up in Boards, or sewed in blue Paper; and hope for the future they will order them in that Manner, as at this Time, Leather can hardly be procured to answer one half of the necessary Demand.

The notice was repeated in the issue for 24–6 May.

A label inserted in the BM copy of Weston's *Gardener's... Calendar*, 1773,[1] reads:

The Purchasers of Books bound in the Vellum manner are desired to observe, that they are sewed much better than the Books which are bound in Leather; open easier at the Back, and are not so liable to warp in being read. If by any accident the covers should be stained or rubbed, they may be new covered for a Penny, an Advantage that can not be obtained in Leather; so that this method of binding is not only cheaper, but it is presumed will be found more useful.

The only Motive for trying the Experiment was, to adopt a Substitute for Leather, which was greatly enhanced in its Price, either by an increased Consumption, or Monopoly; how far that Purpose will be answered, must be submitted to the Determination of the Reader.

In the course of five Years, upwards of Fourteen Thousand Volumes have been sold bound in this Manner, and not One Hundred of them have been returned to be new covered; a sufficient Proof of its Utility and the Approbation of the Public. *St. Paul's Church-Yard*, Sept. 22, 1774.

Mr Michael Sadleir, in the 'Evolution of Publishers' Binding Styles, 1775–1900' (*Bibliographia* No. 1, 1930) records (at pp. 10–11) that

as early as 1761, one man at least had foreseen the supersession of the conventional leather binding by a style cheaper, less clumsy and (as matters turned out) directly prophetic of what was to come. In that year F. Newbery of St. Paul's Churchyard issued the following circular (a primitive version is recorded pasted into a book of that date, although the fuller version... is from a copy of Goldsmith's *Experimental Philosophy*, 2 vols., 1776, which latter work is actually bound – as recommended – in half green vellum and stout dark green paper boards)...

Mr Sadleir then quotes in full the first paragraph of the label of 22 September 1774; and his 'fuller version' (which he also quotes) is the second and third paragraphs of the label. I query whether his 'primitive version' is not in fact simply a copy of

[1] Also in a copy of Paterson's *Roads*, 2nd ed., 1772 (Sotheby, 29.7.68, lot 21). This copy is in the vellum manner binding.

the label from which the second and third paragraphs have been cut off. Apart from this there is a fatal flaw in Mr Sadleir's argument: neither of the two Francis Newberys was in business in St Paul's Church Yard in 1761. Francis the son was not, by all accounts, in any business at all until after his father's death in December 1767; Francis the nephew's place of business, until some time in 1768, was at The Crown in Pater Noster Row. So the 'circular' or 'label' inserted in the book of 1761 cannot be dated before 1768. Even if this argument were wrong the date of the book has nothing to do with the date of whatever was pasted in it. It follows that there is no connection between the date of the book and the date for the first use of the vellum manner binding dealt with in the 'circular'.

One piece of evidence would seem, on the face of it, to support the plea for a pre-1768 use of the vellum manner binding for printed books in a library: the BM copy of the *Art of Writing*, 2nd ed. 1748 (no. J72(2)) is bound in this way. It is not impossible that this was an early experiment in the manner, not at that time proceeded with. On the whole this seems unlikely; it was probably a case of the book being rebound in the new manner or (more likely) of unsold sheets being bound up in that way, in or after 1768. Much further evidence is to be found in newspaper advertisements and elsewhere in the years 1768 and after. The following pointers should be noted:

(1) Absence of advertisements or of other references to this manner of binding before 1768.

(2) An advertisement by Newbery & Carnan in the *London Chronicle* for 11–13 August (and later), 1768 of the *Wonders of Nature and Art*, 'neatly bound for a Library, in the Vellum Manner, and labelled on the Back, Price Eighteen Shillings, or One Guinea Calf lettered'.

(3) An advertisement by Newbery & Carnan in the same paper for 29 September–1 October 1768 of new editions of the *Historical Description of the Tower*, *Westminster Abbey*, and *St Paul's Cathedral*, 'neatly bound in the Vellum Manner, with a Register, and labelled on the Back, Price 2s 6d'.

(4) A similar advertisement on 15–17 November 1768 (and later) of La Condamine's *Extract from Observations made in a Tour through Italy*, 1768 (Newbery & Carnan), 'bound in the Vellum Manner, with a Register'. A note is added:

The increased consumption of Leather is perhaps the chief Cause of the high Price of that Commodity, the Method of binding here offered to the Public, if approved of and adopted, will lessen that Consumption, and of course reduce the Price.

That note could hardly have been written in respect of an already well-known and established method of binding.

(5) The third paragraph of the label of 22 September 1774, with its reference to sales in the previous five years.

The cumulative effect of the above facts would seem to establish beyond reasonable doubt that 1768 was the year in which the vellum manner binding for printed books for a library was first put to practical use in a commercial way. Also that it was a 'speciality' of Francis Newbery the son and Carnan, if not invented, then at all events first used, by them. And I am tempted to suggest that of these two it was probably Carnan, go-ahead and enterprising publisher and man of business, rather than Francis Newbery, the dilettante fine gentleman, who really exploited this manner of binding.

(2) BINDING IN DUTCH FLORAL BOARDS

This method of binding (for which a more correct description would be 'boards covered with Dutch floral paper') was used largely and extensively by the Newberys and Carnan, and by their English contemporaries, in the binding of books for children – but, so far as I know, only those books designed primarily for pleasure not for instruction and education.

In this country the method was certainly in use by 1740, when it was regularly used for Boreman's *Gigantick Histories*. Technically it seems to have been regarded as of small account. Joseph Collyer's *Parent's and Guardian's Assistant*, 1761, p. 68, says: 'The binding in sheep is chiefly employed in binding of school-books, and the little books in gilt paper for children, and requires no genius.'

Bernard C. Middleton's *History of English Craft Bookbinding Technique* (New York, 1963), at pp. 35–7, deals with the history and technical side of the method.[1] I quote from him the following passages:

These highly decorative papers were not marbled, but were printed by means of wooden or metal blocks or by engraved rollers. In use from about 1700, and known as 'Dutch Gilt' (or 'Dutch Flowered'), they were in fact manufactured in Germany and Italy, the misnomer possibly arising from the fact that the papers were imported into Holland and then exported by the Dutch to France and England, though not all of them came by that route.[2]

They were not nearly as much used in England as were marbled papers... They are found rather more often in use as wrappers for children's books published during the last quarter of the [eighteenth] century. Most of the papers used in England have floral designs coloured with green, red, blue and yellow, the gold providing highlights rather than predominating.

The only known manufacturer of the papers was named B. Moore. A sheet of his paper with the signature 'B. Moore, Newgate St. London 1763' is in the Victoria and Albert Museum, and in the Broxbourne Library there is a Scottish binding with Dutch gilt endpapers signed 'B. Moore, Newgate...1763'.

Mr Middleton quotes a passage from R. Dossie's *Handmaid to the Arts* (2nd ed., vol. I, 1764, p. 447) concerning this Mr Moore:

The society [The Society for the Encouragement of Arts, now The Royal Society of Arts] has accordingly given lately a bounty to Mr Moor (*sic*), of Newgate Street, who has established a manufacture of gilt and flowered paper, which exceeds greatly the foreign in beauty, and is sold at a cheaper rate than that can be afforded, even when the duty on importation is not paid.

[1] See also A. Haemmerle, *Buntpapier* (Callwey, München, 1961).
[2] Is not 'Dutch' merely an anglicised corruption of 'Deutsch'?

It is seldom now that any of the gilt remains on these bindings; sometimes traces can still be seen where the paper is lapped over on to the inside of the boards and is not overlaid by pastedown endpapers. But specimens of unused paper, not subjected to handling, on which the gilt is still present, are to be found. Two are in my possession; the paper is heavily and deeply impressed with designs of flowers, fruit and leaves of colour, red, yellow, orange, mauve, green. There is lettering on the edge of one of the papers, but, alas, illegible.

A representation of one of these specimens, in colour but not embossed, is given as a frontispiece to the present book.

(3) BINDING IN CANVAS (LINEN)

Used from about 1767 until early in the nineteenth century, 'canvas' (then described as 'linen') bindings were as a rule employed by the Newberys and others for school books, no doubt as being cheap and able to stand up to the inevitable rough usage. They are less uncommon than is generally supposed.

The following are in my possession: Greenwood's *London Vocabulary*, 15th ed., 1767 (Hawes, Clarke and Collins) and 22nd ed., 1802 (R. Baldwin and others); Lily's *Short Introduction to Grammar*, 1782; *The New Reading made Easy*, H. Goldney, 1790; *The Oxford Spelling Book*, B. Law and G. Robinson, n.d. I have also noted (among others) the following in this binding: Cordier's *Colloquia*, 5th ed., *ca.* 1768, printed for Newbery & Carnan (J85A(5)); Lenglet du Fresnoy's *Geography for Children*, 15th (1787), 17th (1793) and 20th (1799) edd., printed for E. Newbery (J212(2), (4) and (6)); *Exempla Minora . . . Printed at Eton, for the use of the lower Forms*, 1800; Florian's *Guide to the Study of the History of England*, printed for E. Newbery (J137).

More rarely books not of an educational nature are to be found so bound; they are probably exceptional; Dodsley's *Oeconomy of Human Life*, 12th ed., 1772; Ogilby and Morgan's *Traveller's Pocket Book*, 21st ed., printed for E. Newbery et al., 1782 (A392(1)).

An advertisement by Newbery & Carnan in the *London Chronicle* for 14–17 January 1769 of the 5th ed. of Cordier's *Colloquia* describes the book as:

Bound in linen and sewed in bands; by which Method it is much stronger than School Books are commonly bound . . . This Book having been advertised before, bound in the above manner, but some of them having been sold in Sheets to the Trade, who through Prejudice or Interest, bound them as School Books are usually done, we are determined, for the future, not to deliver any but what are bound, being convinced of the Preference that ought to be given to the Method.

And an advertisement in the same paper for 27–9 December 1768 of *An easy Guide to the English Language* (J98) says 'Bound in Linen and sewed in Bands, by which method it will last ten Times as long as the Spelling Books, which are bound in the common Manner'.

The subject is dealt with in *The Library*, June 1948, p. 40, and in Middleton's *History of English Craft Bookbinding Technique*, at p. 132.

APPENDIX 3

SOME PUBLISHERS, BOOKSELLERS AND PRINTERS WORKING IN THE NEIGHBOURHOOD OF PATER NOSTER ROW IN THE SECOND HALF OF THE EIGHTEENTH CENTURY

IN PATERNOSTER ROW

G. Allen, No. 59.
Allen & West, No. 15.
M. Allen, No. 15.
R. Baldwin, 'The Rose', No. 47.
Wm Baynes, No. 54.
J. Beecroft, 'The Bible and Crown', No. 23.
Wm Bent (successor to Wm Cumberlege), 'The Kings Arms', No. 34, also No. 55.
J. Bew, No. 28.
S. Bladon, No. 28, also No. 13.
Jas Buckland, 'The Buck', No. 57.
J. Bouquet, 'The White Hart'.
W. Button, No. 24; also Button & Son.
W. Button and T. Priestley.
J. Brownnell.
C. Cooke, No. 17.
J. Cooke, 'Shakespeare's Head', No. 17.
M. Cooper, 'The Globe'.
J. Coote, No. 16, and 'Kings Arms'.
Stanley Crowder, No. 12.
S. A. Cumberlege (successor to J. Hinton).
W. Dawson, No. 7.
Jas. Evans, No. 32.
T. Evans, No. 54, also No. 46.
J. Fielding.
Fielding and Walker, No. 20.
W. Goldsmith, No. 24, also No. 21.
Joseph Harden.
J. Harrison (also Harrison & Co), No. 18.
C. Hitch and L. Hawes.
Hawes, Clarke and Collins.
L. Hawes and Co, No. 32.
John Hinton, 'The Kings Arms', No. 34.
Alexander Hogg, 'The Kings Arms', No. 16.
Thomas Hurst, No. 32.
Wm Innys.

C. Johnson, No. 14.
M. Jones, No. 1.
Lee and Hurst, No. 32.
M. Lewis (or Lewes), No. 1.
Thomas Longman, No. 39; also Nos. 29 and 3.
J. MacGowan.
Mifflin.
J. Morgan.
F. Newbery, 'The Crown', No. 15.
J. Parsons, No. 21.
J. Payne, 'The Pope's Head'.
Richardson and Urquhart, No. 46.
J. Richardson.
George Robinson (also G. G. and J. Robinson), No. 25.
Robinson and Roberts, No. 25.
L. B. Seeley, No. 56.
S. Smith, No. 17, also No. 3.
R. Snagg, No. 29.
I. Souter, No. 1.
R. Stevens, 'The Pope's Head'.
D. Symonds.
H. D. Symonds, No. 20, also No. 23.
G. Terry.
H. Trapp.
John Walker, No. 44.
John Wheble, No. 24.
Henry Sampson Woodfall (also H. Woodfall), No. 1, Corner of Ivy Lane.
G. and T. Wilkie, No. 57.
West and Hughes.

IN ST PAUL'S CHURCH YARD

W. Anderson.
Carington Bowles, No. 69.
Thomas Bowles.
Carnan and Newbery, No. 65.
Alexander Donaldson, No. 48.

Etherington, 'Opposite the South Door of St Paul's'.

J. Fletcher, 'The Oxford Theatre in St Paul's Church Yard'.

Graham, No. 7.

W. Harris, No. 70.

John Hinton, 'Kings Arms'.

R. Griffiths, 'The Dunciad'.

Joseph Johnson, No. 72.

W. Johnson, 'The Golden Ball'.

Longman, Lukey & Co, No. 45.

J. Newbery, 'The Bible & Sun', No. 65.

W. Nicoll, 'The Paper Mill', No. 51.

C. Norris, 'Behind the Chapter House'.

R. Phillips, No. 71.

G. Riley, 'The City Library'.

John and Francis Rivington (also J. F. and Charles Rivington), No. 62.

Charles and Samuel Thompson, No. 75.

John Wilkie, No. 71.

G. and T. Wilkie.

IN LUDGATE STREET AND STATIONERS' COURT

T. Caslon, Stationers Ct.

B. Crosby, 4 Stat. Ct.

Crosby and Letterman, Stat. Ct.

Robt Horsfield, 5 Stat. Ct and 'The Crown', No. 22 L. St.

Anne Jefferies (successor to Eliz. Stevens), No. 2 Stat. Ct.

Wm Johnston, No. 16 L. St.

G. Kearsley, No. 11 L. St.

Bedwell Law, No. 5 Stat. Ct.

G. Lion.

W. March, No. 2 L. St.

F. Newbery and E. Newbery, No. 20 L. St.

J. Russel (successor to E. Stevens), No. 2 Stat. Ct.

Geo. Riley, 33 L. St.

Eliz. Stevens, No. 2 Stat. Ct.

Stonehouse, 'Yorick's Head', No. 16 L. St.

H. D. Symonds, opposite Stationers Hall, L. St.

Charles (or G.) Stalker, 4 Stat. Ct.

J. Wallis, 'Yorick's Head', No. 16 L. St.

N. Wills, Stat. Ct.

Thos. Wills, Stat. Ct.

IN LUDGATE HILL

W. Davis.

B. Dickinson.

T. Fox.

S. Hooper, No. 25.

Hooper and Davis.

E. Johnson, No. 3 (also Nos. 4, 5 and 16).

J. S. Jordan, No. 19.

Richard Manby.

R. Manby and H. S. Cox.

J. Rider.

C. and R. Ware.

IN AVE MARIA LANE

S. Birt.

Edward Cabe.

B. Dod, 'The Bible & Key'.

P. Davey.

Edward Johnson, No. 12.

Bedwell Law, No. 13.

C. Law, No. 13.

J. Scatcherd, No. 12.

Scatcherd and Whitaker.

J. Wheble.

IN STATIONERS' ALLEY, LUDGATE STREET

C. Hood, No. 8.

J. Wakelin and C. Hood, No. 8.

IN OLD BAILEY

G. Lister, No. 46.

J. Miller, No. 6.

IN MITRE COURT, ST PAUL'S CHURCH YARD

W. Tayler.

IN IVY LANE

G. Woodfall, No. 1.

The following additional abbreviations are used here:

Alm	Almanack	GM	*Gentleman's Magazine*
CC	*Circle of the Sciences*	HAB	*Housekeeper's Accompt Book*
Comp	Companion	Hist	History, historical
Dict	Dictionary	LCPB	*Ladies Complete Pocket-Book*
e a	et al	PB	Pocket Book

NOTE: The dates are, as a rule, those in the TP imprints, even though such dates may, on occasion, be false.

1740

Defence of the Author	JN e a	A111
Miscellaneous Works	JN e a	A362
Wallis: Duty of seeking all Men's Salvation	JN e a	A614A

1741

Knapp: Sett of New Psalm-Tunes. 2 ed.	JN e a	A286(1)

1742

Book of Common Prayer. Short Exposition	JN e a	A44
Johnson, Rev. S.: Christ's Presence	JN e a	A276
Explanation of Scripture	JN e a	A277
Loggon: History of the Brotherhood	JN e a	A305
Martin: Micrographia Nova	JN e a	A324
Merrick: Festival Hymns. 3 ed.	JN e a	J244

1743

Ingram: Essay on Gout	JN e a	A248
Martin: Course of Lectures	JN e a	A319

1744

Merrick: Dissertation on Proverbs	JN e a	A348
Heliocrene	JN e a	A354
Thompson: Travels of Chas Thompson	JN e a	A586

1745

Accomplish'd Housewife	JN	A1
CC Easy Spelling Dict	JN	J71
CC Grammar. 1 ed.	JN	J64(1)
Cordier: Colloquia. 2 ed.	JN	J85A(2)
Dict explaining difficult Terms	JN e a	A115
Flanders delineated	JN e a	A157(1, 2)
Gibson: Journal of late Siege	JN	A184
Mihles: Medical Essays	JN e a	A357

Thomas: Journal of a Voyage	JN e a	A585
Universal Harmony	JN	A598(1)

1745 or 1746

CC Spelling Book	JN	J70

1746

CC Arithmetic. 1 ed.	JN	J61(1)
CC Poetry. 1 ed.	JN	J68(1)
CC Rhetorick. 1 ed.	JN	J69(1)
CC Art of Writing	JN	J72(1)
Martin: Essay on Electricity	JN e a	A321
Supplement: containing Remarks	JN e a	A328
Mercurius Latinus	JN e a	A345
Universal Harmony	JN	A598(2)

1747

Knapp: Sett of New Psalms. 3 ed.	JN e a	A286(2)
Lovat, Simon Ld: Impartial Account. 2 ed.	JN e a	A310(1–3)

1748

CC Arithmetic. 2 ed.	JN	J61(2)
CC Chronology. 1 ed.	JN	J62(1)
CC Geography. 1 ed.	JN	J63(1)
CC Grammar. 2 ed.	JN	J64(2)
CC Logic. 1 ed.	JN	J66(1)
CC Poetry. 2 ed.	JN	J68(2)
CC Rhetoric. 2 ed.	JN	J69(2)
Cobden: Parable of the Talents	JN e a	A86
James: Dissertation on Fevers. 1 ed.	JN	A256(1)
Martin: Institutions of Language	JN e a	A322(1)
Newbery: Spelling Dict. 2 ed.	JN	J268(2)

1749

James: Dissertation on Fevers. 2 ed.	JN	A256(2)
London. All the royal Charters	JN	A307
Martin: Lingua Britannica	JN e a	A323(1)

1750

Boscawen, Ship.: Journal	TC	A46(1)
Burton: Attempt towards Eulogium	TC	A69
Caviller detected, The	JN	A77
Epistle on subject of Earthquakes	JN	A144
Knapp: Sett of New Psalms. 4 ed.	JN e a	A286(3)
LCPB for 1750	TC	A7(106)
Museum for young Gentlemen. 1 ed.	JN e a	J253(1)
Nouveau Magazin Francois	JN e a	A386
Raleigh: Interest of England	JN	A432
Smart: Horatian Canons. 1 and 2 ed.	JN	A548(1, 2)
Midwife (pts vol. 1)	TC	A552
Thoulier d'Olivet: Thoughts of Cicero	JN e a	A589(1)

1750–1

Student, The	JN e a	A577(1)

1751

Boscawen, Ship.: Journal. 2 ed.	TC	A46(2)
Brent: Interest improved	JN	A53(1)
Brookes: General Practice of Physic. 1 ed.	JN	A58(1)
Dicey: Hist Account of Guernsey	JN	A114(1, 2)
Epigrams, fresh gather'd	JN	A143
Index to Sermons	JN e a	A247
Lloyd: Progress of Envy	JN	A301(1)
More: Utopia	JN	A370(1)
Pretty Book for Children. 5 ed.	JN e a	J307(3)
Rolt: Monody	JN e a	A452
Two Hymns	JN	A454
Sedgly and Beck: Observations	JN e a	A490
Smart: Index to Mankind	TC	A550(1)
Midwife (pts vol. 1 and vol. 11)	TC	A552
Nutcracker. 1 ed.	JN e a	A554(1)
Occasional Prologue. 1–3 edd.	TC	A555(1–3)
On the Immensity. 1 ed.	JN e a	A559(1)
Solemn Dirge. 1 ed.	TC	A564(1)
Solemn Dirge. 2–3 edd.	? TC	A564(2, 3)
Smith: Thales	JN	A569(2)
Smith: Compendious Division	JN	A571(1)
Thoulier d'Olivet: Thoughts of Cicero	JN e a	A589(2)
Warton: Newmarket	JN	A619
Wise: Trial of Chandler	JN e a	A635

1751–2

Lilliputian Magazine (part issues)	TC	J219(1)

1752

Gobelin: Female Parricide	JN	A188
Knapp: Sett of New Psalms. 5 ed.	JN e a	A286(4)
LCBP for 1752	JN	A7(106B)
Martin: Philosophia Britannica, 2 ed. (2 vols)	JN e a	A326(2)
Muses Banquet	TC e a	A373A(1)
Newbery: Spelling Dict. 3 ed.	JN	J268(3)
Poetical Epistle	JN e a	A414
Pretty Book of Pictures	? JN	J308(1)
Smart: On the Eternity. 2 ed.	JN e a	A557(2)
On the Omniscience. 1 ed.	JN e a	A560(1)
Poems on several Occasions	JN e a	A562(1)
Warner: Scheme for a Fund	JN e a	A617

1753

Boyse: New Pantheon. 1 ed.	JN e a	A51(1)
Brookes: General Dispensatory. 1 ed.	JN e a	A56(1)
Gentleman's Pocket Library. 1 ed.	JN	A178(1)
Hardy: Complete System of Interest	JN e a	A211
Henry: Account of London and Westminster	JN	A219(1)
Description of St Paul's	JN	A221(1)
Description of The Tower	JN	A222(1)
Description of Westminster Abbey	JN	A223(1)
LCPB for 1753	JN	A7(106C)

More: Utopia	TC	A370(2)
Pocket Dict. 1 ed.	JN	J295(1)
Rolt: Memoirs of John Lindesay	JN	A451
Smart: Hilliad. 1 ed.	JN e a	A547(1)
Midwife. vol. III	TC	A552
On the Immensity. 2 ed.	JN e a	A559(2)
Ward: London Spy. 4 ed.	TC	A616

1754

Brookes: General Practice of Physic. 2 ed.	JN	A58(2)
Introduction to Physic. 1 ed.	JN	A59(1)
Considerations on Tidd's Aeolus	JN	A95
Fawkes: Description of Winter	JN e a	A151
Henry: Description of Tower	JN	A222(2)
Description of Westminster Abbey	JN	A223(2)
Knapp: New sett of Psalms. 6 ed.	JN e a	A286(5)
LCPB for 1754	JN	A7(106D)
Martin: Lingua Britannica. 2 ed.	JN	A323(3)
Racine: Religion	JN e a	A431
Smart: On the Power. 1 ed.	JN e a	A561(1)
Thompson: Travels thro' Turkey. 1 ed.	JN	A587(1)

1755

Boyce: Ode to Marquis of Hartington	JN e a	A48
CC Grammar. 3 ed.	JN	J64(3)
CC Logic. 2 ed.	JN	J66(2)
Gordon: Every young Man's Companion. 1 ed.	JN e a	J148A(1)
Henry: Curiosities of London	JN	A219(2)
Description of the Tower	JN	A222(3)
James: Dissertation on Fevers. 3 ed.	JN	A256(3)
Kidgell: The Card	JN	A282(1)
LCPB for 1755	JN	A7(106E)
New Testament adapted	JN	J35
Newbery: Spelling Dict. 5 ed.	JN	J268(5)
Nurse Truelove's New Year's Gift	JN	J270(2)
Pretty Book of Pictures	JN e a	J308(3)
Royal Primer	JN e a	J324(3)

1756

Elphinston: Analysis of French...	JN e a	A140
Gentleman's Pocket Library. 2 ed.	JN	A178(2)
Hill: British Herbal	JN e a	A229
Hist Account of Rise of Quakers	JN	A232
Horace: Works, trans. Smart. 1 ed.	JN	A241(1)
Infant Tutor. 4 ed.	JN	J186(3)
LCPB for 1756	JN	A7(107)
Newbery: Letters. 1 ed.	JN	J266(1)
Pretty Book for Children. 7 ed.	JN	J307(4A)
Rolt: New Dict of Trade	JN e a	A453(1)
Smart: Hymn to the Supreme Being	JN	A549(1)
On the Eternity. 3 ed.	JN e a	A557(3)
On the Goodness. 1 and 2 ed.	JN e a	A558(1, 2)
On the Omniscience. 2 ed.	JN e a	A560(2)

Tagg: Collection of pretty Poems. '54' and '55' edd.	JN	J346(1, 2)
Trapwit: Be Merry and Wise. 2 ed.	JN	J358(2)

1757

Abraham Aesop: Fables. 1 ed.	JN	J7A(1)
Bible abridged. 1 ed.	JN	J27(1)
Boyce: Poems	JN e a	A49
Byng, Admiral, Trial of	JN e a	A70
Gordon: Every young Man's Companion. 2 ed.	JN e a	J148A(2)
Henry: Description of the Tower	JN	A222(4)
LCPB for 1757	JN	A7(108)
Lindsay: Evangelical Hist	JN e a	A300
Newbery: Letters	JN	J266(1A)
Spelling Dict. 6 ed.	JN	J268(6)
New Hist of England by an Englishman	JN	J257
Plaisted: Journal from Calcutta. 1 ed.	JN	A408(1)
Pretty Poems	JN	J74(1)
Smart: Nonpareil	TC	A553(1)
Nutcracker	TC	A554(2)
On the Immensity. 3 ed.	JN	A559(3)

1758

Abraham Aesop: Fables	JN	J7A(2)
Brookes: General Practice of Physic. 3 ed.	JN	A58(3)
Compendious Hist of England. 1 ed.	JN	J76(1)
Dionysius Halicarnassensis: Roman Antiquities	JN e a	A123
Elmer: Tables of Weights	JN	A139(1)
Gibson: Atlas Minimus. 1 ed.	JN	J146A(1, 2)
James: Dissertation on Fevers. 4 ed.	JN	A256(4)
LCPB for 1758	JN	A7(109)
Martin: New Principles of Geography	JN	A325(1)
Museum for young Gentlemen. 2 ed.	JN e a	J253(3)
Newbery: Letters. 4 ed.	JN	J266(4)
Pocket Dict. 2 ed.	JN	J295(2)
Reeves: Art of Farriery. 1 ed.	JN e a	A434(1)
Smart: On the Power. 2 ed.	JN	A561(2)
Tagg: Collection of pretty Poems. '56' ed.	JN	J346(3)

?1758

John-the-Giant-Killer: Food for the Mind. 2 ed.	JN	J190B(2)

1759

Cordier: Colloquia. 4 ed.	JN	J85A(4)
Garrick: The Guardian. 1 and 2 edd.	JN	A173(1, 2)
Gordon: Every young Man's Companion. 3 ed.	JN e a	J148A(3)
Henry: Description of St Paul's	JN	A221(2)
John-the-Giant-Killer: Food for the Mind. 3 ed.	JN	J190B(3)
LCPB for 1759	JN	A7(110)
Martin: Philosophia Britannica. 2 ed. (3 vols)	JN e a	A326(3)
Supplement to Phil. Brit.	? JN e a	A329(1)
New Hist of England from Invasion	JN	J258(1A)
Newsreader's PB	JN	A385(1)
Penrose: Practice of Religion	JN	A403

Townley: High Life below Stairs. 1–4 edd.	JN e a	A592(1–5)
World displayed. 1 ed. vol. 1	JN	A640(1)

1760

Abraham Aesop: Fables. 3 ed.	JN	J7A(3)
Allen: Polite Lady. 1 ed.	JN	J8(1)
Anacreon [etc]	JN e a	A8(1)
Bible abridged	JN	J27(3)
Christian's Magazine. vol. 1	JN e a	A82
Grey: Apology for the Servants	JN	A203
Henry: Description of the Tower	JN	A222(5)
Infant Tutor. 5 ed.	JN	J186(4)
James: Treatise on Canine Madness	JN	A258
LCPB for 1760	JN	A7(111)
Lennox: Ladies' Museum	JN e a	A292
Little Pretty PB. 9 ed.	JN	J225(5)
Lockman: Cruel Sufferings	JN e a	A302
Museum for young Gentlemen. 3 ed.	JN	J253(4)
Newbery: Letters. 5 ed.	JN	J266(5)
Spelling Dict. 7 ed.	JN	J268(7)
Pretty Book for Children. 9 ed.	JN e a	J307(4B)
Short Hists for Improvement of Mind	JN	J334(1)
Smart: Nutcracker	TC	A554(3)
Tagg: Collection of pretty Poems. '57' ed.	JN	J346(4)
Townley: High Life. 6 ed.	JN e a	A592(7)
Vattel: Law of Nations. vol. 1	JN e a	A604
World displayed. 1 ed. vols 2–17	JN e a	A640(1)
2 ed. vols 1 and 1–20	JN e a	A640(2)
Woty: Shrubs of Parnassus	JN	A642

1761

Art of Poetry on a new Plan	JN	J16A(1)
Ascham: English Works	JN e a	A17
Campbell: Lives of the Admirals. 3 ed.	JN e a	A72
Christian's Magazine. vol. 11	JN e a	A82
Colman: Jealous Wife. 1–2 edd.	JN e a	A87(1, 2)
Conduct of a Rt Hon Gentleman. 1–2 edd.	JN	A94(1, 2)
Dodd: Magdalen Charity. 1 ed.	JN e a	A125(1)
Fawkes: Original Poems	JN e a	A152
Henry: Description of Westminster Abbey	JN	A223(3)
History of Greece by Q and A	JN e a	J165B(1)
James: Dissertation on Fevers. 5 ed.	JN	A256(5)
Johnson: Idler. 1st collected ed.	JN	A264(1)
Rambler. 5 ed.	JN e a	A273(1)
LCPB for 1761	JN	A7(112)
2 ed.	JN	A7(113)
3 ed.	JN	A7(114)
Lennox: Ladies Museum (issue for Jan. 1761)	JN e a	A292
New Hist of England from the Invasion	JN	J258(1B)
Newbery: Giles Gingerbread	JN	J267(1)
Pococke: Happiness of doing Good	JN e a	A410
Poetical Dict	JN e a	A412
Pretty Book for Children. 10 ed.	JN	J307(5A)

Smart: On the Eternity	? JN	A557(4)
On the Goodness	? JN	A558(3)
On the Immensity	? JN	A559(4)
On the Omniscience	? JN	A560(3)
On the Power	? JN	A561(3)
Telescope: Newtonian System. 1 ed.	JN	J348(1)
Trapwit: Be Merry. 5 ed.	JN	J358(5)
Voltaire: Dramatic Works	JN e a	A607
Works. vols 1–9	JN e a	A614
World displayed. 1 ed. vols 1, 2, 4–6, 8, 18–20	JN e a	A640(1)

1762

Art of Poetry on a new Plan	JN	J16A(2)
Brookes: General Gazeteer. 1 ed.	JN	A57(1)
Christian's Magazine. vol. 3	JN e a	A82
Dodd: Sermon on Job	JN e a	A128
Goldsmith: Citizen. 1 ed.	JN e a	A190(1, 2)
Life of Nash. 1–2 edd.	JN e a	A194(1, 2)
Henry: Description of the Tower	JN	A222(6)
Horace: Works, trans. Smart. 2 ed.	JN	A241(2)
Johnson: Idler. 2nd collected ed.	JN	A264(2)
Knapp: Sett of New Psalms. 7 ed.	JN e a	A286(6)
LCPB for 1762	JN	A7(115)
Milton: Familiar explanation, by Dodd	JN e a	A360
Montagu and Scott: Millenium Hall. 1 ed.	JN	A365(1)
Newbery: Spelling Dict. 8 ed.	JN	J268(8)
Plutarch's Lives abridged	JN	J294(1)
Pretty Book of Pictures	JN	J308(5)
Pretty Play-thing	JN	J309(3)
Scott: Hist Mecklenburgh. 1, 2 edd.	JN	A488(1, 2)
Telescope: Newtonian System. 2 ed.	JN	J348(2)
Voltaire: Dramatic Works. vols 3–5	JN e a	A607(3, 4)
Henriade	JN e a	A609
Works. vols 10–18	JN e a	A614(1)
Works. 2 ed. vols 2, 10, 11, 15–18	JN e a	A614(2)
World displayed. vol. 7, 1 ed.	JN e a	A640(1)

1762 or 1763

Nurse Truelove's Christmas Box	JN	J269(4)
Nurse Truelove's New Year's Gift	JN	J270(4)

1763

Bickerstaffe: Love in a Village. 1–3, 5–8 edd.	JN e a	A36(1–3, 5–8)
Brookes: General Practice of Physic. 4 ed.	JN	A58(4)
Introduction to Physic. 2 ed.	JN	A59(2)
Natural Hist	JN	A61(1)
Christian's Magazine. vol. 4	JN e a	A82
Colman: Jealous Wife. 3 ed.	JN e a	A87(3)
Compendious Hist of World	JN	J77(1)
Dissertation on the King's Evil. 1 ed.	JN	A124(1)
Dodd: Magdalen Charity. 2 ed.	JN	A125(2)
Reflections on Death. 1 ed.	JN	A127(1)
G., T.: Isle of Thanet. 1 ed.	JN e a	A172(1)

Guthrie: English Peerage	JN e a	A206
Henry: Curiosities of London and Westminster	JN	A219(3)
Hist of Lives of the Apostles	JN	J175(1)
Infant Tutor. 6 ed.	JN	J186(5)
Johnson: Rambler. 6 ed.	JN e a	A273(2)
LCPB for 1763	JN	A7(116)
Little pretty PB. 11 ed.	JN	J225(7)
Martial Review	JN	A318
Museum for young Gentlemen. 4 ed.	JN e a	J253(5)
Museum Rusticum. Pts for Sept. and Dec. 1763	JN e a	A374(1)
New Hist of England from the Invasion	JN	J258(2)
Newbery: Spelling Dict. 9 ed.	JN	J268(9)
Reeves: Art of Farriery. 2 ed.	JN e a	A434(2)
Tagg: Collection of pretty Poems. '58' ed.	JN	J346(5)
Tasso: Jerusalem delivered, trans. Hoole. 1 ed.	JN e a	A581(1)
Townley: High Life. 7 ed.	JN	A592(8)
Venn: Complete Duty of Man. 1 ed.	JN e a	A605(1)
Voltaire: Dramatic Works. vols 6 and 7	JN e a	A607(5)
Works. 1 ed. vols 19–22	JN e a	A614(1)
Works. 2 ed. vols 3, 4, 20–2, 26	JN e a	A614(2)
Whitworth: Collection of Supplies	JN e a	A624(1)
Act for Paving Westminster	JN e a	A625

1764

Annual Abstract of the Sinking Fund	JN e a	A10
Bible abridged. 5 and 6 edd.	JN	J27(5), J27(6)
Bible: New Testament abridged and harmonized	JN	J31
Bickerstaffe: Love in a Village. 10 ed.	JN e a	A36(10, 11)
Book of Common Prayer. Pleasant and useful Comp	JN	J40(1)
Boyse: New Pantheon. 3 ed.	JN e a	A51(3)
Christian's Magazine. vol. 5	JN e a	A82
Christian's Magazine. Supplement for 1763	JN e a	A82
Easter Gift	JN	J97(1A)
Francis: Reflections on David	JN	A169(1)
Giles Gingerbread	JN	J267(1A)
Goldsmith: Hist England in Series of Letters. 1 ed.	JN	J147(1)
Hist of Lives of the Martyrs	JN	J148(1)
Traveller. 1 ed.	JN	A199(1, 2)
Guthrie: Complete Index to General Hist	JN e a	A207(3)
General Hist of World. vols 1–8	JN e a	A207(1)
Henry: Description of Tower	JN	A222(7)
Description of Westminster Abbey	JN	A223(4)
Hist of Life of our Lord	JN	J174(2)
James: Dissertations on Fevers. 6 ed.	JN	A256(6)
LCPB for 1764	JN	A7(117)
LCPB for 1764. 3 ed.	JN	A7(119)
Meier: Merry Philosopher	JN	A342(1)
Merrick: Annotations on St John	JN e a	J243A(1, 2)
Montagu and Scott: Millenium Hall. 2 ed.	JN	A365(2)
Museum Rusticum. 1 ed. vols 1 and 2	JN e a	A374(1)
Museum Rusticum. 2 ed. vol. 1, no. 1	JN e a	A374(2)
Newbery: Letters. 6 ed.	JN	J266(6)
Spelling Dict. 10 ed.	JN	J268(10)

Parthenia	JN	A398(1)
Psalmanazar: Memoirs of * * * *. 1 ed.	JN e a	A429(1)
St James's Register	JN e a	A7(361)
Tasso: Jerusalem delivered. 2 ed.	JN e a	A581(2)
Voltaire: Miscellaneous Poems	JN e a	A611(1)
Works. 1 ed. vols 23, 24	JN e a	A614(1)
Works. 2 ed. vol. 23	JN e a	A614(2)
Whitsuntide Gift	JN	J380(1)
Whitworth: Collection of Supplies	JN e a	A624(2)
Succession of Parliaments	JN e a	A626
World displayed. 1 ed. vol. 10 (error for 11)	JN	A640(1)

1764 or 1765

Merrick: Letter to Joseph Warton	JN e a	A349
St James's Register corrected to 15.12.64. 2 ed.	JN e a	A7(362)

1765

Abraham Aesop. Fables. 5 ed.	JN	J7A(5)
Bible with commentary by Dodd	JN e a	A34(1)
Bickerstaffe: Daphne and Amintor	JN e a	A35(1, 2)
Love in a Village. 10 and 11 edd.	JN e a	A36(12, 13)
Maid of the Mill. 1–6 edd.	JN e a	A37(1–5)
Brookes: General Dispensatory. 2 ed.	JN e a	A56(2)
General Practice of Physic. 5 ed.	JN	A58(5)
Brown: Political Logic	FN(N)	A63
Christian's Magazine. vol. 6	JN e a	A82
Cooper: Elbow Chair	FN(N)	A96
Dodd: Reflections on Death. 2 ed.	JN	A127(3)
Truth of Christian Religion	JN	A131(1)
du Martre: Elements of Heraldry. 1 ed.	JN	A135(1)
G., T.: Isle of Thanet. 2 ed.	JN e a	A172(2)
Gessner: Death of Abel. 7 ed.	FN(N) e a	A183(2)
Giles Gingerbread	JN	J267(2)
Goldsmith: Traveller. 1–4 ed.	JN	A199(3–6)
Goody Two-Shoes. 1 ed.	JN	J167(1)
Gordon: Every young Man's Companion. 4 ed.	JN e a	J148A(4)
Grenville: Candid Refutation	FN(N)	A202
Guthrie: General Hist. vols 9, 10	JN e a	A207(1)
Henry: Curiosities of London	JN	A219(4)
Description of St Paul's	JN	A221(3)
Hist Description of Tower	JN	A222(8)
Jackson: Essay on Isinglass	JN	A250
LCPB for 1765	JN	A7(120)
LCPB for 1765. New ed.	JN	A7(121)
Lilliputian Magazine	JN	J219(3)
Meier: Merry Philosopher	JN e a	A342(2)
Merrick: Psalms translated. 1 ed.	JN e a	A351(1)
Museum Rusticum. vols 3–5	JN e a	A374(1)
Pocket Dict. 3 ed.	JN	J295(3)
Pretty Book of Pictures. 8 ed.	JN e a	J308(8)
Psalmanazar: Memoirs of * * * *. 2 ed.	JN e a	A429(2)
St James's Register corrected to 10.1.65. 3 ed.	JN e a	A7(363)
St James's Register corrected to 27.2.65. 4 ed.	JN e a	A7(364)

Shirley: Electra	JN	A543
Valentine's Gift	JN	J368(2)
Vansittart: Original Papers	JN	A603
Venn: Complete Duty of Man. 2 ed.	JN e a	A605(2)
Voltaire: Works. 1 ed. vol. 25	JN e a	A614(1)
Whitsuntide Gift	JN	J380(1)
Whitworth: Collection of Supplies. 2 ed.	JN e a	A624(3)

1766

Bickerstaffe: Daphne and Amintor. New ed.	JN e a	A35(3)
Brookes: Appendix to 5th ed. Gen. Practice of Physic	JN	A58(6)
General Gazeteer. 2 ed.	JN e a	A57(2)
Natural Hist. vol. 1	JN	A61(1A)
Christian's Magazine. vol. VII	JN e a	A82
Dict of the Bible	JN	A117(1)
Dodd: Magdalen Charity. 3 ed.	JN e a	A125(3)
Feriae Poeticae	JN e a	A156
Formey: Hist Philosophy. 1 ed.	FN(N)	A163(1)
Ecclesiastical Hist	JN e a	A164(1)
Elementary Principles	FN(N)	A165(1)
Genuine Collection of New Songs	FN(N)	A180
Giles Gingerbread	JN	J267(3)
Goldsmith: Vicar. 1–3 edd.	FN(N)	A200(1–4)
Goody Two-Shoes. 2, 3 edd.	JN	J167(2, 3)
Guthrie: General Hist. vol. XI	JN e a	A207(1)
Klopstock: Messiah. 2 ed.	JN e a	A284(1)
LCPB for 1766	JN	A7(122)
Merrick: Psalms translated. 2 ed.	JN e a	A351(2)
Museum Rusticum. vol. VI	JN e a	A374(1)
Museum Rusticum. 3 ed. vol. 1	JN e a	A374(3)
New Hist of England from the Invasion	JN	J258(4)
Newbery: Spelling Dict. 11 ed.	JN	J268(11)
Powys: Sermon	JN	A420
Public Ledger	FN(N)	A430
Rollin: Philosophy for Children	JN	J321(3)
St James's Register for 1766	JN and FN(N)	A7(365)
St James's Register for 1766. 3 ed.	JN and FN(N) e a	A7(367)
Telescope: Newtonian System. 3 ed.	JN	J348(3)
Templeman: Observations on Lucerne	FN(N)	A583
Tollendal: Memoirs of Count Lally	FN(N)	A591
Vansittart: Narrative of Transactions	JN e a	A602
Voltaire: Works. 2 ed. vols 5, 6, 14	JN e a	A614(2)
World displayed. 1 ed. vol. 15	JN	A640(1)

1767

Bible with Commentary by Dodd. vol. II	JN e a	A34(1)
Bickerstaffe: Love in a Village. New ed.	JN e a	A36(14)
Maid of the Mill. New ed.	JN e a	A37(6)
Bodmer: Noah	FN(N) e a	A43(1)
Byron: Voyage round the World. 1 and 2 edd.	JN & FN(N)	A71(1, 2)
Certain Ancient Tracts	JN e a	A79(1)
Christian's Magazine. Jan 1767 issue	JN e a	A82
Claparède: Considerations on Miracles	JN & FN(N)	A83
Costard: Hist of Astronomy	JN	A98(1)

Fairing. New ed.	JN	J110(2)
Garrick: Guardian. 3 ed.	JN	A173(3)
Genius	JN	A177
GM. vol. 37	FN(N)	A179
Goody Two-Shoes. 4 ed.	JN	J167(4)
Gough: Britannia	JN e a	A201
Guthrie: Gen. Hist. vol. 12	JN e a	A207(1)
Helvetius: Estimate of Manners of French	FN(N)	A217
Henry: Curiosities of London	JN	A219(5, 6)
Description of Tower	JN	A222(9)
Description of Westminster Abbey	JN	A223(5)
Johnson: Idler. 3 ed.	JN e a	A264(3)
Rambler. 7 ed.	JN e a	A273(3)
Kelly: Babler	JN e a	A281(1)
LCPB for 1767	JN	A7(123)
Lettres Portuguises	Newbery*	A298
Little Lottery Book. 6 ed.	JN	J223(2)
Little pretty PB	JN	J225(8)
Merrick: 2nd Pt. Annotations on John	JN e a	J243B
Montagu and Scott: Millenium Hall. 3 ed.	JN	A365(3)
Newbery: Essay on Fine Arts	? JN	A384
Letters. 7 ed.	JN	J266(7)
Original Pieces concerning the Protestants	FN(N) e a	A394
Pretty Book of Pictures. 9 ed.	JN e a	J308(9)
Public Ledger	FN(N)	A430
Reflections on Dissidents in Poland	FN(N) e a	A435
Richer: Great Events	FN(N)	A441(1)
St James's Register for 1767	JN & FN(N) e a	A7(368)
Shackleford: Cookery	JN & FN(N)	A494(1)
Shakespeare: Works (ed. Theobald)	FN(N) e a	A496
Thompson: Travels thro' Turkey. 3 ed.	JN	A587(3)
Twelfth-Day Gift	JN	J366(2)
Vansittart: Letter to the Proprietors	JN e a	A601
Voltaire: Works. 2 ed. vol. 9	JN e a	A614(2)
Whitsuntide Gift	JN	J380(2)
World displayed. 1 ed. vols 16, 17	JN	A640(1) (bb) and (dd)
World displayed. 3 ed. vols 1, 2 and 18	JN	A640(3) (a) (b) and (s)

?1767

Sharp: Letters from Italy. 3 ed.	FN(? N) e a	A535

1767 or 1768

Christian's Magazine. Suppl. to vol. VIII	FN jr & Co	A82
Fothergill: Two Discourses. 5 ed.	FN(? S) e a	A167(1)
Six-pennyworth of Wit.	JN	J336(1)

1768

Abraham Aesop: Fables. 6 ed.	C & N	J7A(6)
Berkshire. Copy of the Poll	N & C	A32
Bible	JN e a	A34(2)
Bible abridged	N & C	J27(7)
Bossuet: Universal Hist	C & N	A47(2)

Dawson: Answer to a Book	FN(N)	A106
Fairing	N & C	J110(3)
For Ever!	FN(N)	A160
Fothergill: Prayer of Agur	N & C e a	A166
Two Discourses. 6 ed.	FN(? S) e a	A167(2)
Gayton: Festivious Notes. 1 ed.	FN(N) e a	A176(1)
GM. vol. 38	FN(N)	A179
Gessner: Death of Abel. 9 ed.	FN(N) e a	A183(3)
Goldsmith: Traveller. 5 ed.	FN jr & Co	A199(7)
Goody Two-Shoes. 5 ed.	N & C	J167(5)
Henry: Description of the Tower	N & C	A222(10)
Jenner: Destruction of Niniveh	N & C	A260
La Condamine: Tour Thro' Italy	N & C	A287(1)
LCPB for 1768	JN	A7(124)
Le Roy: Attempts of Harrison and Le Roy	FN(N)	A293
Lilliputian Magazine	N & C	J219(4)
Little Lottery Book	N & C	J223(3)
Merrick: Annotations on Psalms	N & C e a	A347
Short Manual of Prayers. 2nd ed. (2 edd.)	Newbery & Co e a	A353(1, 2)
Needham: Hymns	N & C e a	A376
New Hist of England from the Invasion	FN & Co	J258(5)
Potter: Words of the Wise	FN(N)	J304(1)
Public Ledger	FN(N)	A430
Rawlins: Familiar Architecture	FN(N) e a	A433
Reply to a Pamphlet...Duke of Portland	FN(N) e a	A439
Richardson: Clarissa. 6 ed. vols I–v	FN* e a	A440(1)
Rollin: Ancient Hist of Egyptians. 5 ed.	N & C e a	A446(1)
Hist of Arts. 2 ed.	N & C e a	A447
Roman Hist. 3 ed.	N & C e a	A449
Shakespeare: Plays (ed. Johnson)	FN* e a	A498
Smith: Art of Living in London	FN(N) e a	A570
Tagg: Pretty Poems. '60' ed.	FN(S) and/or TC	J346(7)
Thornton: Battle of the Wigs	FN(N) e a	A588
Tom Thumb's Folio	N & C	J356(2)
Townley: High Life. 8 ed.	N & C	A592(9)
Upholsterer's Letter to Wm Pitt	Newbery*	A600
Whittell and Duncombe: Treatise on Dendrometer	FN(N) e a	A623
Windsor and its Environs	N & C e a	A631(1)
Wonders of Nature. 2 ed.	N & C	A637(1)
World displayed. 2 ed. vol. 19	JN	A640(2)
World displayed. 2 ed. vols 8, 10–12, 14, 20	N & C	A640(2)
World displayed. 3 ed. vols 3, 4	N & C	A640(3)

1769

Allen: Polite Lady. 2 ed.	N & C	J8(2)
Beccaria: Essay on Crimes. 2 ed.	FN(N)	A29(2)
Brookes: Explanation of Terms of Art	N & C	A55
CC Arithmetic. 3 ed.	N & C	J61(3)
CC Geography. 3 ed.	N & C	J63(3)
CC Grammar. 3 ed. with Additions	N & C	J64(4)
CC Logic. 3 ed.	N & C	J66(3)
CC Poetry. 3 ed.	N & C	J68(3)

CC Rhetoric. 3 ed.	N & C	J69(4)
Dawson: Answer to Letters	FN(N) e a	A107
Scriptural Right	FN(N)	A108
Utility of establishing Confessions	FN(N)	A109
Description of England. 1 ed. vols I–VIII	N & C	A112(1)
Dodd: Reflections on Death. 3 ed.	C & N	A127(4)
Sermon on Zechariah	FN(N)	A130
Fielding: Joseph Andrews abridged	FN(N)	J131(1)
Formey: Hist of Philosophy	FN(? S)	A163(1)
Franklin: Experiments on Electricity	FN(N)	A170(1)
Fruitless Repentance	FN(N)	A171
GM. vol. 39	FN(N)	A179
Giles Gingerbread	N & C	J267(4)
Goldsmith: Hist England in series of Letters	N & C	J147(2)
Gordon: Every young Man's Companion. 5 ed.	N & C e a	J148A(5)
Hart: Hymns etc. 6 ed.	FN(N) e a	A213(2)
Henry: Description historique de la Tour	N & C	A222(11)
Curiosities of London	N & C	A219(7)
Hist of Essex. vol. II	FN(N) e a	A146
Hist of Miss Somerville	N & C	A234(1)
Hoamchi-Vam: Bonze	FN(N) e a	A235
Infant Tutor	N & C	J186(6)
Jackson: Literatura Graeca	FN(N) e a	J190A
Jervey: Thoughts on Scurvy	FN(? S) e a	A261
Johnson: Life of Savage. 4 ed.	FN(N)	A267(1)
Junius: Political Contest. 1, 2 and 4 edd.	FN(N)	A280(1, 2, 4)
Political Contest being a continuation	FN(N)	A280(3)
Klopstock: Messiah. 3 ed.	FN(N) e a	A284(2)
Messiah. 4 ed. vols. 1 and 2	FN(N) e a	A284(3)
LCPB for 1769	N & C	A7(125)
Little Lottery Book	N & C	J223(4)
Massillon: Sermons	FN(N) e a	A333
Mother's Gift. 1 ed.	C & N	J251(1)
Parkhurst: Greek English Lexicon	FN(N) e a	A397
Pocket Herald	FN* e a	A409
Polyhymnia	FN(N)	A417
Pretty Book of Pictures. 10 ed.	N & C e a	J308(10)
Public Ledger	FN(N)	A430
Richardson: Clarissa. 6 ed. vol. VI	FN* e a	A440(1)
Pamela abridged	FN(N)	J316(1)
Rollin: Method of Teaching. 6 ed.	N & C e a	A448(1)
Royal Kalendar for 1769 (2 edd.)	FN(N) e a	A7(343, 344)
Saunier: Guide to Horses	N & C e a	A487
Short Hists for Improvement of Mind	N & C	J334(2)
Smart: Nutcracker	C & N	A554(4)
Stafford: Treatise on Cyder-making	FN(N)	A574(2)
Sydenham: Entire Works. 5 ed.	FN(N)	A578(2)
Voltaire: Dramatic Works. vols 1 and 2	N & C e a	A607(6)
Works. 2 ed. vols 24, 26	JN e a	A614(2)
Winlove: Moral Lectures	FN(N)	J382(1)
World displayed. 3 ed. vols 5 and 7	N & C	A640(3) (e) and (g)

1769 or **1770**
Duncan: Condemnation pronounced   C & N e a   A136

1770

Beccaria: Essay on Crimes. 3 ed.	FN(N)	A29(3)
Bible abridged	C & N	J27(8)
Bible with Commentary by Dodd	C & N e a	A34(1, 3)
Bodmer: Noah	FN(N) e a	A43(2)
Brother's Gift	FN(N)	J44(1)
CC Chronology. 3 ed.	N & C	J62(3)
Croxall: Fables. 9 ed.	FN(? N) e a	J87(1)
Curiosities of London and Westminster	FN(N)	J88(1)
Description of England and Wales. 1 ed. vols ix, x	N & C	A112(1)
Destruction of Trade	FN*	A113
Entertaining Fables	C & N	J103(2)
Favart: The Reapers	TC	A150
Fenelon: Telemachus abridged	TC	J113(2)
Filial Duty	FN(N)	J134(1)
GM. vol. 40	FN(N)	A179
Goldsmith: Hist England in Series of Letters	C & N	J147(3)
Traveller (var. edd.)	C & N	A199(8, 8A, 9, 10)
Vicar. 4 ed.	C & N	A200(5)
Goody Two-Shoes	C & N	J167(6)
Harper: Accomptant's Companion. 4 ed.	FN(N) e a	J153A(3)
Henry: Hist Description of St Paul's	C & N	A221(4)
Hist Description of Westminster Abbey	C & N	A223(6)
Hist of Essex. vols i and iii	FN(N) e a	A146
Horace: Works trans. Smart	C & N	A241(3)
James: Dissertation on Fevers. 7 ed.	FN(S)	A256(7)
New Roman Hist. 1 ed.	FN(N)	J263(1)
Kimber: James Ramble	FN(N)	A283
Knapp: Sett of New Psalms. 8 ed.	C & N e a	A286(7)
LCPB for 1770	N & C	A7(126)
Letters between Master Tommy...	C & N	J214(1, 1A)
Little female Orators. 1 ed.	TC	J222(1)
Little pretty PB	N & C	J225(9)
London Cries	TC	J233(1)
Lowe: Critical Spelling Book. 2 ed.	FN(N)	J234(2)
Mallet: Northern Antiquities	TC & Co	A314(1)
Margate Guide	C & N	A316(1)
Mother's Gift. 2 ed.	C & N	J251(2)
Museum for young Gentlemen. 6 ed.	N & C	J253(7)
New Hist of England from the Invasion	C & N	J258(6)
Newbery: Spelling Dict. 12 ed.	C & N	J268(12)
Pincot: Essay on artificial Stone	FN(N) e a	A407
Pratt: Art of Dressing the Hair	C & N e a	A422
Prevost d'Exiles: Memoirs of a Man of Quality	FN(N)	A426(2)
Public Ledger	FN(N)	A430
Reflections on the Ruins	FN(N) e a	A436
Robin Goodfellow	FN(N)	J320(2)
Rollin: Method of Teaching. 7 ed.	N & C e a	A448(2)
Rowly: Essay on ulcerated legs. 1 ed.	FN(N)	A459(1)
Royal Kalendar for 1770 (2 edd.)	FN(N) e a	A7(345, 346)

Shakespeare: Comedy of Errors	FN* e a	A512
Cymbeline	FN* e a	A513
Macbeth	FN* e a	A522
Tagg: Collection of pretty Poems	C & N	J346(8)
Telescope: Newtonian System. 4 ed.	C & N	J348(4)
Teltruth: Nat. Hist of Birds	FN(N)	J349(1B)
Tillotson: Twenty Discourses. 3 ed.	FN(N)	A590(2)
Trapwit: Be Merry	C & N	J358(7)
Twelfth-Day Gift. 2 ed.	C & N	J366(3)
Unhappy Wife	FN(N) e a	A596
Voltaire: Genuine letters	FN(N)	A608
Miscellaneous Poems. 3 ed.	C & N e a	A611(2)
Works. vol. 36	C & N e a	A614(4)
Works. 3 ed. vols 1, 12, 225	C & N e a	A614(5)
Williams: Universal Psalmodist. 4 ed.	FN(S) e a	A627
Winlove: Collection of Stories. 1 and 2 edd.	FN(N)	J381(1, 2)
Younger Brother. vol. 1	FN(N)	A644

1770 or 1771

Smart: Hymns for Amusement of Children. 1 ed.	TC	J338(1)

1771

Bickerstaffe: Love in a Village. New ed.	C & N e a	A36(15)
Blackrie: Disquisition on Medicines	FN(N) e a	A41
Book of Nature	TC	A45
Boyse: New Pantheon. 4 ed.	C & N e a	A51(4)
Brookes: General Practice of Physic. 6 ed.	C & N	A58(7)
Nat. Hist. 2 ed. vol. II	C & N	A61(2)(b)
Complete English Farmer	FN(N)	A90
Curiosities of London and Westminster	FN(N)	J88(2)
Description of England and Wales (repubd)	C & N	A112(2)
du Martre: Elements of Heraldry. 2 ed.	C & N	A135(2)
Dyche: English Dict. 14 ed.	FN* e a	A137(1)
Gayton: Festivious Notes. 2 ed.	FN(N) e a	A176(2)
GM. vol. 41	FN(N)	A179
Gessner: Death of Abel. 10 ed.	FN(N) e a	A183(4)
Giles: Miscellaneous Poems	FN(N) e a	A186
Henry: Hist Description of Tower	C & N	A222(12)
Hist of Essex. vol. IV	FN(N) e a	A146
John-the-Giant-Killer: Food for the Mind	TC and/or FN(S)	J190B(5)
Johnson: Rambler. 8 ed.	C & N e a	A273(4)
Klopstock: Messiah. 4 ed. vol. III	FN(N) e a	A284(3)
LCPB for 1771	C & N	A7(127)
Lady of Honour: Ladies PB for 1771	FN(N)	A7(175)
Martin: Philosophia Britannica. 3 ed.	C & N e a	A326(4)
Miller: Abridgement of Gardener's Dict. 6 ed.	FN* e a	A358
Paterson: Roads in G.B. 1 ed.	TC	A399(1)
Penny: Poems	FN* e a	A402
Potter: Curate of Coventry	FN(N)	A418
Public Ledger	FN(N)	A430
Reeves: Farriery. 3 ed.	C & N e a	A434(3)
Rowley: Essay on Gonorhoea	FN(N)	A458
Essay on Venereal Disease. 2 ed.	FN(N)	A460

Essay on Ophthalmia	FN(N)	A463
Essay on ulcerated Legs. 2 ed.	FN(N)	A459(2)
Royal Kalendar for 1771	FN(N) e a	A7(347)
Smart: Hymns for Amusement of Children. 2 ed.	TC	J338(2)
Sugar Plumb	FN(N)	J345(1)
Tea-Table Dialogues	TC	J347(1)
Voltaire: Pupil of Nature	TC	A612
Dramatic Works. vols 3 and 4	C & N	A607(7)
Works. vols 7 and 8	C & N e a	A614(6)
Works. 3 ed. vol. 13	C & N e a	A614(5)
Winckleman: Herculaneum	C & N	A630
World displayed. 3 ed. vol. 6	N & C	A640(3)

1771 or 1772

Falconer: Observations on Dr Cadogan on Gout. 1 ed.	FN(N) e a	A148(1)

1772

Abraham Aesop: Fables	C and/or N(S)	J7A(7)
Algarotti: Lady's Philosophy	FN(N)	A6
Bible abridged	C & N	J27(9)
Bible: Pocket Bible	FN(N)	J30(1)
Brookes: Nat. Hist. 2 ed. vols 1, 3–6	C & N	A61(2)
Brookes and Collyer: Dict of the World	C & N	A62
Bunyano: Prettiest Book	FN(N)	J48(1)
Dodd: Reflections on Death. 4 ed.	C & N	A127(5)
Falconer: Observations on Dr Cadogan on Gout. 2 and 3 edd.	FN(N) e a	A148(2, 3)
French Sheet Alm for 1772	TC e a	A7(70)
GM. vol. 42	FN(N)	A179
Goldsmith: Hist England in a Series of Letters	C & N	J147(4)
Goody Two-Shoes	C & N	J167(7)
Haller: Usong	FN(N) e a	A209
Harvest: Reasonableness of Subscription	FN(N)	A214
Hist of Essex. vols v and vi	FN(N) e a	A146
Hughes: Compleat Horseman	FN(N)	A245
Imprisonment for Debt	FN(N)	A246
Introduction to Study of Hist	TC	J188
Jacob: Complete Parish Officer. 16 ed.	FN* e a	A252
LCPB for 1772	C & N	A7(128)
Lilliputian Magazine	C & N	J219(5)
Littleton: Juvenile Trials. 1 ed.	TC	J229(1)
Middlesex Journal. nos 547–86	FN(N)	A356
New Hist of England from the Invasion	C & N	J258(7)
Newbery's Ladies PB for 1772	FN(N)	A7(273)
Paterson: Roads in GB. 2 ed.	TC	A399(2)
Travelling Dict. 1 ed.	TC	A401(1)
Perrault: Histories told by Mother Goose. 6 ed.	C & N e a	J279(2)
Public Ledger	FN(N)	A430
Rouppe: Observations on Diseases	C & N	A455
Rowley: Method of curing Venereal Disease. 3 ed.	FN(N)	A468
Diseases of Breasts of Women. 1 ed.	FN(N) e a	A469(1)
Royal Kalendar for 1772. (2 edd.)	FN(N) e a	A7(348, 349)
Scott: Test of filial Duty	TC	A488A

Smith: Letter to Dr Cadogan	C & N	A566
Stevens: Songs, comical... 1 ed.	FN(N) e a	A575(1)
Talbot: Narrative relative to Jonathan Britain	TC e a	A580
Tea-Table Dialogues	TC	J347(2)
Trusler: Chronology. 5 ed.	FN(N) e a	A595(1)
Tutor, The	FN(N)	J365(1)
Warton: Life of Pope	FN(? S) e a	A618
Oxford Sausage. New ed.	FN(N) e a	A620(1)
World displayed. 3 ed. vol. 8	C & N	A640(3)
Younger Brother. vol. 11	FN(N)	A644

1772–3

Middlesex Journal. nos 587–91	EN	A356
Smith: Letter to Dr Cadogan. 2 ed.	C & N	A566(2)

1773

Agreeable Companion	FN(N) e a	A4
Angelo, Master: Drawing School. 1 ed.	TC	J15(1)
Aulnoy: Mother Bunch's Tales	FN(N)	J17(1)
Bible, with notes by Bayly	FN* e a	A34(5)
Garrick: Guardian. 4 ed.	C & N	A173(4)
GM. vol. 43	FN(N)	A179
Gessner: Death of Abel. 11 ed.	FN* e a	A183(5)
Goldsmith: She Stoops. 1–5 edd.	FN(N)	A197(1–7)
Vicar. 5 ed.	C & N	A200(6)
Goody Two-Shoes	TC	J167(8)
Hey: Nature of obsolete Ordinances	C & N e a	A225
HAB for 1773	FN(N) e a	A242(1)
LCPB for 1773	C & N	A7(129)
Little female Orators	TC	J222(2)
London Companion. 1 ed.	TC	A308(1)
Marat: Philosophical Essay	FN(N) e a	A315
Monthly Chronicle	TC e a	A366
More, H.: Search after Happiness. 2 ed.	C & N e a	A369(2)
Mother's Gift. Second Part	C & N	J251(2A)
Newbery's Ladies PB for 1773	FN(N)	A7(274)
Paterson: Travelling Dict. 2 ed.	TC	A401(2)
Poetical Description of Beasts	TC	J298(1)
Poetical Description of Song Birds	TC	J299(1)
Public Ledger	FN(N)	A430
Register of Folly	FN(N) e a	A437
Rowley: Principal Diseases of the Eyes. 1 ed.	FN(N)	A480(1)
Royal Kalendar for 1773. (2 edd.)	FN(N) e a	A7(350, 351)
Shakespeare: Plays (ed. Johnson and Steevens). 1 ed.	FN* e a	A499
Works (ed. Theobald)	FN* e a	A500
Thoulier d'Olivet: Thought of Cicero	C & N	A589(4)
Weston: Gardener's Calendar. 1 ed.	TC	A622(1)
World displayed. 3 ed. vols 9, 10	C & N	A640(3)

1773 or 1774

Angelo, Master: Juvenile Sports	TC	J16(1)

1774–3

Henry: Account of all the Voyages	FN(N)	A218

1774

Abraham Aesop: Fables	TC &/or N(S)	J7A(8)
Angelo, Master: Drawing School. 2 ed.	TC	J15(2)
Boreman: 300 Animals. 11 ed.	FN(N) e a	J41(1)
Burrow, Reuben: Diary for 1774	TC	A7(20)
Cebes: Circuit of Human Life. 1 ed.	TC	J49B(1)
Chesterfield: Maxims	FN(N)	J53(1)
Coal-Heavers	C & N e a	A85
Colman, senr, and Thornton: Connoisseur. 6 ed.	FN(S) e a	A87A
Farmer's Lawyer. 1 ed.	FN(N) e a	A149(1)
Franklin: Experiments on Electricity. 5 ed.	FN(N)	A170(2)
GM. vol. 44	FN(N)	A179
Gibson: Atlas Minimus	C & N	J146A(4)
Goldsmith: Citizen. 3 ed.	C & N	A190(4)
Hist of Lives of the Martyrs	C & N	J148(3)
Traveller. 9 ed.	C & N	A199(12)
Goody Two-Shoes	N & C (Dublin reprint)	J167(8A)
Hart: Hymns. 8 ed.	FN(N)	A213(4)
Henry: Hist Description of Tower	C & N	A222(13)
Hey: Sermon	C & N e a	A226
Hist of Life of our Lord	C & N	J174(4)
Horace: Works, trans. Smart. 4 ed.	C & N	A241(4)
HAB for 1774	FN(N) e a	A242(2)
Johnson: Miscellaneous and fugitive Pieces	C & N e a	A271(1, 2)
LCPB for 1774	C & N	A7(130)
Ladies most elegant PB for 1774	FN(N) e a	A7(159)
Littleton: Juvenile Trials. 2 ed.	TC	J229(2)
More, H.: Inflexible Captive. 1–3 edd.	C & N e a	A368(1–3)
Search after Happiness. 3–5 edd.	C & N e a	A369(3–5)
Newbery: Spelling Dict. 13 ed.	C & N	J268(13)
Phipps and Lutwidge: Journal of Voyage	FN(N)	A405
Picture Exhibition	TC	J280(1)
Richardson: Clarissa. 7 ed.	FN* e a	A440(2)
Rollin: Ancient Hist of Egyptians. 6 ed.	C & N e a	A446(2)
Rowley: Cure of Ulcerated Legs. 3 ed.	FN(N)	A478(1)
Royal Kalendar for 1774	FN(N) e a	A7(352)
Seaman's useful Friend	FN(N) e a	A489
Tatler	FN* e a	A582(1)
Trader's Magazine	FN(N)	A593
Trapwit: Be merry	C & N	J358(8)
Trusler: Chronology. 7 ed.	FN(N) e a	A595(2)
Twelfth-Day Gift. 3 ed.	C & N	J366(4)
Valentine's Gift	C & N	J368(3)
Windsor and Environs	C & N e a	A631(2)
World displayed. 3 ed. vols 11–13, 4 ed. vol. 1	C & N	A640(3) and (4)

1774–8

Builder's Magazine. 1 ed.	FN(N)	A68(1)

1775

Allen: Polite Lady. 3 ed.	C & N	J8(3)
Beccaria: Essay on Crimes. 4 ed.	FN(N)	A29(4)

Bible abridged	C & N	J27(1)
'Cooper': New Hist England	FN(N)	J84(1)
Copper-Plate Museum	FN(N)	A97
Cries of London	FN(N)	J86(2)
Croxall: Fables. 10 ed.	FN(N) e a	J87(2)
Description of England and Wales. 2 ed.	C & N	A112(3)
Food for Poets	FN(N)	A158
GM. vol. 45	FN(N)	A179
Goody Two-Shoes	C & N	J167(9)
Griffin: Interest Tables	TC	A204
HAB for 1775	FN(N) e a	A242(3)
Hoyle: Games improved	FN(N) e a	A244(2)
LCPB for 1775	C & N e a	A7(131)
London Companion. 2 ed.	TC	A308(2)
Margate Guide. New ed.	C & N e a	A316(2)
Marra: Journal of Resolution's Voyage	FN(N)	A317
Milton: Paradise Lost. An 8 ed.	FN(N) e a	A361(1)
Modern Family Physician	FN(N)	A363
More, H.: Search after Happiness. 6 ed.	C & N e a	A369(6)
Mother's Gift. Third Part	C & N	J251(3)
Prestwich: Dissertation on Mineral...Poisons	FN(N)	A425
Rowley: 2nd Letter to Dr Hunter. 1 ed.	FN(N)	A471
Royal Kalendar for 1775. (2 edd.)	FN(N) e a	A7(354, 355)
Sentimental Fables	FN(N) e a	A491
Short Histories	C & N	J334(3)
Smart: Hymns for Amusement of Children. 3 ed.	TC	J338(3)
Smith: Apology for commencing. 1 ed.	C & N	A565(1)
Spectator	FN(? N) e a	A573
Sugar Plumb	FN(N)	J345(1A)
Townley: High Life. 9 ed.	C & N	A592(10)
Ward: Nat. Hist. vols 1–7	FN(N)	J376(1)
World displayed. 4 ed. vol. 14	C & N	A640(4)

1775 or 1776

Smith: Apology for commencing. 2 ed.	C & N	A565(2)

1776

Angelo, Master: Juvenile Sports. 2 ed.	TC	J16(2)
Aulnoy, Mother Bunch's Fairy Tales	FN(N)	J17(1A)
Bearde de l'Abbaye: Essays in Agriculture	TC	A25
Bickerstaffe: Love in a Village	C & N e a	A36(16)
Biographical Magazine. nos 1–10	FN(N)	A39
Burrow, Reuben: Diary or Sheet for 1776	TC e a	A7(22)
Lady's and Gent's Diary for 1776	TC	A7(25)
Cambridge Sheet (Alm)	TC e a	A7(31)
CC Geography. 4 ed.	C & N	J63(4)
CC Grammar. 4 ed.	C & N	J64(5)
CC Grammar and Rhetoric	C & N	J65
CC Logic, Ontology and Poetry	C & N	J67
CC Poetry. 4 ed.	C & N	J68(4)
Clermont: Professed Cook. 3 ed.	FN(N) e a	A84
Cordier: Colloquia. 7 ed.	C & N	J85A(7)
Cowley: Runaway. 1 and 2 edd.	C & N e a	A100(1, 2)

Cursory Observations	TC	A105
Dimsdale: Thoughts on Inoculation	C & N e a	A121
Drelincourt: Christian's Defence. 21 ed.	FN* e a	A132
Gentleman and Lady's Key	C & N	J145(3)
GM. vol. 46	FN(N)	A179
Goldsmith, John: G's Alm for 1776	TC e a	A7(76)
Comp to G's Alm	TC e a	A7(76A)
Goldsmith, O.: Hist Eng. in Series of Letters. 5 ed.	C & N	J147(6)
Survey of Philosophy. 1 ed.	C & N	A198(1, 2)
Henry: Curiosities of London	C & N	A219(10)
HAB for 1776	FN(N) e a	A242(4)
Infant Tutor	C & N	J186(7)
Letters between Master Tommy...	C & N	J214(2)
Littleton: Juvenile Trials. 3 ed.	TC	J229(3)
Jones: Cain Jones' Welsh Alm for 1776	TC	A7(95)
LCPB for 1776	C & N	A7(132)
Lives of British Admirals. pt 1	FN(N)	J230(1)
Moore, Fr.: Moore's Alm for 1776	TC e a	A7(243)
Vox Stellarum for 1776	TC e a	A7(265)
Museum for young Gentlemen. 8 ed.	N & C	J253(9)
New London Sheet Alm for 1776	TC e a	A7(217)
Nurse Truelove's Christmas Box	TC	J269(6)
Parker's Ephemeris for 1776	TC e a	A7(302)
Parker and White's Ephemeris for 1776	TC e a	A7(303)
Poor Robin's Alm for 1776	TC e a	A7(306)
Paterson: Roads in G.B. 3 ed.	TC	A399(3)
? Quin: Easy Introduction to Book-keeping	FN(N)	A430A
Remarks on West India Diseases	FN(N) e a	A421
Rider's Alm for 1776	TC e a	A7(319)
Rider's Alm for 1776. Comp to	TC e a	A7(320)
Rider's Sheet Alm...for 1776	TC e a	A7(335)
Rowley: Medical Advice	FN(N)	A465
Royal Kalendar for 1776	FN(N) e a	A7(356)
Royal Kalendar for 1776. New ed.	FN(N) e a	A7(357)
Royal Psalter. 3 ed.	N & C	J326(5)
Thumb: Bag of Nuts. 2 ed.	FN(N)	J353(2)
Ward: Nat. Hist. vols 8–12	FN(N)	J376(1)
Wing: Vincent's Wing's Sheet Alm for 1776	TC e a	A7(419)
Wood: Strictures on Gout. 2 ed.	FN(N) e a	A638

1776 or 1777

Willis: Matter of Agistment of Tithe	FN(N)	A628

1777

Abraham Aesop: Fables	TC &/or FN(S)	J7A(9)
Amusing Instructor	FN(N)	J12(1)
Andrews: Royal Alm for 1777	TC	A7(5)
Angelo, Master: Drawing School. 3 ed.	TC	J15(3)
Baldwin's Daily Journal for 1777	TC	A7(8)
Bath: Treatise on Diseases of the Liver	FN(N)	A24
Biographical Magazine. no. 15	FN(N)	A39
Boyse: New Pantheon. 5 ed.	C & N e a	A51(5)
Brother's Gift	FN(N)	J44(2)

Burrow: Diary or Sheet for 1777	TC	A7(23)
Lady's and Gent's Diary for 1777	TC	A7(26)
Cambridge Sheet (Alm) for 1777	TC	A7(32)
Chatter: Lilliputian Auction	TC	J52(2)
Chesterfield: Maxims	FN(N)	J53(2)
CC Arithmetic. 4 ed.	C & N	J61(4)
CC Logic. 4 ed.	C & N	J66(4)
CC Rhetoric. 4 ed.	C & N	J69(5)
Dict of the Bible. ? 2 ed.	C & N	A117(2)
Dodd: Reflections on Death	C & N	A127(6)
du Martre: Elements of Heraldry. 3 ed.	C & N	A135(3)
Dyche: English Dict. 16 ed.	FN* e a	A137(3)
Fables for Youth	TC	J106(1)
Fairing, The	(? C & N)	J110(4)
Giles Gingerbread	C & N	J267(5)
GM. vol. 47	FN(N)	A179
Goldsmith, J.: G's Alm for 1777	TC	A7(77)
G's Alm for 1777. Comp	TC	A7(78)
Goody Two-Shoes	C & N	J167(10)
Gordon: Every young Man's Comp. 6 ed.	N & C e a	J148A(6)
Hardy: Elements of Arithmetic. 2 ed.	FN(N) e a	A212
Hart: Hymns. 9 ed.	FN(N) e a	A213(5)
Henry: Description of St Paul's	C & N	A221(5)
Hill: Power of Water-Dock. 10 ed.	FN(N) e a	A230
Hist of Life of our Lord	C & N	J174(4A)
HAB for 1777	FN(N) e a	A242(5)
Johnson: Life of Savage. 4 ed.	FN(N)	A267(2)
LCPB for 1777	C & N e a	A7(133)
Ladies Town and Country Pocket Journal for 1777	FN(N)	A7(174A)
Lilliputian Magazine	C & N	J219(6)
Lives of British Admirals. pt II	FN(N)	J230(1)
Lockman: New Hist England. 18 ed.	TC & Co & FN* e a	J231(7)
Moore, Fr.: Vox Stellarum for 1777	TC	A7(266)
Museum for young Gentlemen	? C & N	J253(10)
New Hist England from the Invasion	C & N	J258(8)
New London Sheet (Alm) for 1777	TC	A7(218)
Paterson: Travelling Dict. 3 ed.	TC	A401(3)
Paths of Virtue exemplified	FN(N)	J277(1)
Perrault: Histories…by Mother Goose. 7 ed.	C & N e a	J279(3)
Poetical Description of Beasts	TC	J298(2–5)
Poor Robin's Alm for 1777	TC	A7(307)
Rider's Alm for 1777	TC	A7(321)
Sheet Alm for 1777	TC	A7(336)
Rowley: Diseases of the Breasts. 2 ed.	FN(N)	A469(2)
Royal Kalendar for 1777	FN(N) e a	A7(358)
Tagg: Pretty Poems	C & N	J346(9)
Twelfth-Day Gift. 4 ed.	C & N	J366(5)
Valentine's Gift	C & N	J368(4)
Warton: Oxford Sausage. New ed.	FN(N) e a	A620(2)
Wing: Almanack for 1777	TC	A7(420)
Woodfall: Sir Thomas Overbury	FN(N)	A639

World displayed. 3 ed. vols 15, 16	C & N	A640(3)
World displayed. 4 ed. vol. 2	C & N	A640(4)

1778

Adventurer	FN(? N) e a	A3(1)
Andrews: Royal Alm for 1778	TC	A7(6)
Arnold: Merchant and Owner's Friend	TC	A15
Arnold: Merchant and Seaman's Guardian	TC	A16
Baldwin's daily Journal for 1778	TC	A7(9)
Baretti: English Italian Dict	FN(? N) e a	A22(1)
Bible abridged	C & N	J27(11)
Bickerstaffe: Daphne and Amintor	C & N e a	A35(5)
Brookes: General Gazeteer. 4 ed.	TC e a	A57(4)
Burrow: Sheet Diary for 1778	TC	A7(30)
Lady's and Gent's Diary for 1778	TC	A7(27)
Diary for 1778	TC	A7(24)
Cambridge Sheet Alm for 1778	TC	A7(33)
Cervantes: Don Quixote abridged	FN(N)	J50(1B)
CC Chronology. 4 ed.	C & N	J62(4)
Cornwall Alm for 1778	TC	A7(44)
Devonshire Alm for 1778	TC	A7(58)
Dimsdale: Plan of the Dispensary	C & N e a	A119
Dorset Alm for 1778	TC	A7(62)
Essex Alm for 1778	TC	A7(66)
Gay: Fables	TC, FN* e a	A175(1A)
Glasse: Art of Cookery. New ed.	FN(? N) e a	A187(1)
GM. vol. 48	FN(N)	A179
Goldsmith's Alm for 1778	TC	A7(79)
Goldsmith, O.: Traveller	C & N	A199(14)
Traveller. 10 ed.	C & N	A199(15)
Hampshire Alm for 1778	TC	A7(90)
Henry: Hist Description of Tower	C & N	A222(14)
Hey: Substance of a Sermon	C & N e a	A227
HAB for 1778	FN(N) e a	A242(6)
James: Dissertation on Fevers. 8 ed.	FN(S)	A256(8)
John-the-Giant-Killer: Food for the Mind	C & N	J190B(6)
Kent Alm for 1778	TC	A7(96)
LCPB for 1778	C & N	A7(134)
Lancashire etc Alm for 1778	TC	A7(176)
Lincolnshire etc Alm for 1778	TC	A7(180)
Little female Orators	TC	J222(3)
Lockman: New Roman Hist. 9 ed.	TC & Co e a	J232(4)
Middlesex etc Sheet Alm for 1778	TC	A7(231)
Milton: Paradise Lost. 8 ed.	FN* e a	A361(2)
Paradise Lost	FN* e a	A361(3)
Montagu and Scott: Millenium Hall. 4 ed.	C & N	A365(4)
Moore's Alm for 1778	TC	A7(245)
Moore's Alm for 1778. Comp	TC	A7(246)
Moore: Vox Stellarum for 1778	TC	A7(267)
Museum for young Gentlemen. 9 ed.	N & C e a	J253(11)
New London Sheet Alm for 1778	TC	A7(219)
Norfolk Alm for 1778	TC	A7(275)
Northamptonshire etc Alm for 1778	TC	A7(286)

Northumberland etc Alm for 1778	TC	A7(292)
Oxfordshire etc Alm for 1778	TC	A7(298)
Paterson: Roads in G.B. 4 ed.	TC	A399(4)
Poor Robin's Alm for 1778	TC	A7(308)
Pretty Book of Pictures. 13 ed.	C & N e a	J308(13)
Reeves: Art of Farriery. 4 ed.	C & N e a	A434(4)
Rider's Alm for 1778	TC	A7(322)
Shakespeare: Plays ed Johnson and Steevens. 2 ed.	FN* e a	A501
Shropshire etc Alm for 1778	TC	A7(371)
Somersetshire etc Alm for 1778	TC	A7(377)
Staffordshire etc Alm for 1778	TC	A7(388)
Suffolk Alm for 1778	TC	A7(395)
Sussex Alm for 1778	TC	A7(400)
Telltruth: Nat. Hist of Birds	FN(N)	J349(2)
Nat. Hist of four-footed Beasts	FN(N)	J350(2)
Voltaire: Works. vols 1–3	C & N e a	A614(7)
Waters: Poetical Flower Garden	TC	J377(2)
Weston: Gardener's Calendar. 2 ed.	TC	A622(2)
Wheble's Most elegant PB for 1778	FN(N) e a	A7(409)
Willis: Nature of Agistment of Tithe. 2 ed.	FN(N)	A629
Wiltshire etc Alm for 1778	TC	A7(413)
Wing's Sheet Alm for 1778	TC	A7(421)
World displayed. 3 ed. vols 17–20	C & N	A640(3)
Yorkshire Alm for 1778	TC	A7(432)

1778 or 1779

Philomath: Alm for 1779	TC	A7(305)

1779

Andrews: Royal Alm for 1779	TC	A7(7)
Baldwin's Daily Journal for 1779	TC & Co	A7(10)
Builder's Magazine. 2 ed.	FN(N)	A68(2)
Burrow: Comp for Ladies Diary for 1779	TC	A7(29)
Lady's and Gent's Diary for 1779	TC	A7(28)
Cambridge Sheet (Alm) for 1779	TC	A7(34)
Collection of Pretty Poems	C & N	J74(7)
Cornwall Alm for 1779	TC	A7(45)
Court and City Register. New ed. corrected	Newbery*	A7(54A)
Cowley: Who's the Dupe? 1 and 2 edd.	C & N e a	A101(1, 2)
Devonshire Alm for 1779	TC	A7(59)
Dimsdale: Method of Inoculation. 7 ed.	C & N e a	A120
Dorsetshire Alm for 1779	TC	A7(63)
Essex etc Alm for 1779	TC	A7(67)
Fenelon: Telemachus	FN* e a	A153(3)
GM. vol. 49	FN(N)	A179
Gentleman's PB for 1779	TC	A7(72)
Gentlemen's PBs for 1779	TC	A7(75)
Gibson: Atlas Minimus	C & N	J146A(5)
Goldsmith's Alm for 1779	TC	A7(80)
Goldsmith: Deserted Village. 9 ed.	TC e a	A191(2)
Vicar. 6 ed.	C & N	A200(7)
Hampshire Alm for 1779	TC	A7(91)

HAB for 1779	FN(N) e a	A242(7)
Hoyle's Games improved	FN(N) e a	A244(3)
Johnson: Prefaces. vols I–IV	FN(N) e a	A272
Rambler. 9 ed.	TC, FN* e a	A273(5)
Poets	FN(? N) e a	A275(1)
Johnstone: Buthred	FN(N)	A278
Kent Alm for 1779	TC	A7(97)
LCPB for 1779	C & N e a	A7(135)
Lancashire etc Alm for 1779	TC	A7(177)
Letters between Master Tommy...	TC	J214(3)
Lincolnshire etc Alm for 1779	TC	A7(181)
Macbean: Dict of Bible	C & N	A312(2)
Middlesex Alm for 1779	TC	A7(232)
Moore: Comp to Moore's Alm for 1779	TC	A7(248)
Vox Stellarum for 1779	TC	A7(268)
New London Sheet Alm for 1779	TC	A7(220)
Norfolk Alm for 1779	TC	A7(276)
Northamptonshire etc Alm for 1779	TC	A7(287)
Northumberland etc Alm for 1779	TC	A7(293)
Oxfordshire etc Alm for 1779	TC	A7(299)
Pocket Dict. 4 ed.	C & N	J295(4)
Poetical Description of Birds	TC	J299(2)
Poor Robin's Alm for 1779	TC	A7(309)
Prince Arthur	FN(N)	A428
Rider's Alm for 1779	TC	A7(323)
Rider's Sheet Alm for 1779	TC	A7(338)
Rowley: 74 select Cases	FN(N)	A472
Shropshire etc Alm for 1779	TC	A7(372)
Somersetshire etc Alm for 1779	TC	A7(378)
Staffordshire etc Alm for 1779	TC	A7(389)
Suffolk Alm for 1779	TC	A7(396)
Sussex Alm for 1779	TC	A7(401)
Tea-Table Dialogues	TC	J347(3)
Telescope: Newtonian System. 5 ed.	C & N	J348(5)
Tillotson: Twenty Discourses. 4 ed.	FN(N)	A590(3)
Tom Thumb's Folio	C & N	J356(2A)
Venn: Complete Duty of Man	C & N e a	A605(3)
Voltaire: Works. vols 4, 5, 7–9, 11–15	C & N, FN(N) e a	A614
Wheble's Ladies PB for 1779	FN(N)	A7(410)
Wiltshire etc Alm for 1779	TC	A7(414)
Wing's Sheet Alm for 1779	TC	A7(422)
Wynne: Riley's Emblems. 3 ed. (2 issues)	FN(N) e a	J389(1, 2)
Yorkshire Alm for 1779	TC	A7(432)

1780

Alm Journal for 1780	TC	A7(2)
Alm Journal ruled for 1780	TC	A7(3)
Alm Memorandum Book for 1780	TC	A7(4)
Angelo, Master: Juvenile Sports	TC	J16(3)
Baldwin's Daily Journal for 1780	TC	A7(11)
Bible in Miniuture	EN	J28
Cambridge Sheet Alm for 1780	TC	A7(35)
Compendious Hist of World	TC	J76(4A)

'Cooper': New Hist of England. New ed.	FN(N)	J84(2)
Cornwall Alm for 1780	TC	A7(46)
Court and City Register. New ed. Corrected for 1780	Newbery* e a	A7(54B)
Court and City Register. Corrected to 20.4.79	FN* e a	A7(54C)
Devonshire Alm for 1780	TC	A7(60)
Dorsetshire Alm for 1780	TC	A7(64)
Essex etc Alm for 1780	TC	A7(68)
Fairing	TC	J110(4A)
Gentleman and Lady's Key	TC	J145(4)
GM. vol. 50	EN	A179
Gent's PB for 1780	TC	A7(73)
Goldsmith's Alm for 1780	TC	A7(81)
Goldsmith: Hist England in Series of Letters. 6 ed.	TC	J147(7)
Poetical and Dramatic Works	C & N e a	A196(1)
Goody Two-Shoes	C & N	J167(12)
Hampshire Alm for 1780	TC	A7(92)
Horace: Works trans. Smart	TC	A241(5)
HAB for 1780	FN(N) e a	A242(8)
Jenks: Prayers. 20 ed.	FN(? N) e a	A259(2)
Johnson: Index to Poets	FN(? N) e a	A265
Kent Alm for 1780	TC	A7(98)
LCPB for 1780	TC & Co e a	A7(136)
Ladies Diary Calendar without Aenigmas for 1780	TC	A7(146)
Ladies Diary with Aenigmas for 1780	TC	A7(147)
Ladies Diary for 1780. Comp to	TC	A7(148)
Ladies New Memorandum Book for 1780	TC	A7(165)
Lancashire etc Alm for 1780	TC	A7(178)
Lincolnshire etc Alm for 1780	TC	A7(182)
London Sheet Alm for 1780	TC	A7(210)
Margate Guide	TC e a	A316(3)
Melville: Fixible Air	EN e a	A343(1)
Middlesex etc Alm	TC	A7(233)
Moore: Alm for 1780	TC	A7(249)
Norfolk Alm for 1780	TC	A7(277)
Northamptonshire etc Alm for 1780	TC	A7(288)
Northumberland etc Alm for 1780	TC	A7(294)
Oxfordshire etc Alm for 1780	TC	A7(300)
Palmer: Female Stability	FN(N)	A396
Perrault: Mother Goose's Tales. 8 ed.	? TC	J279(4)
Rider's Alm for 1780	TC	A7(324)
Rider's Alm for 1780. Comp to	TC	A7(325)
Rider's Sheet Alm for 1780	TC	A7(339)
Shakespeare: Malone's Supplement to Johnson and Steevens	FN* e a	A502
Shropshire etc Alm for 1780	TC	A7(373)
Somersetshire etc Alm for 1780	TC	A7(379)
Staffordshire etc Alm for 1780	TC	A7(390)
Suffolk Alm for 1780	TC	A7(397)
Sussex Alm for 1780	TC	A7(402)
Voltaire: Works. vols 16–24, 26–8	C & N, FN(N) e a	A614(7)
Wheble's Ladies PB for 1780	FN(N)	A7(411)
Wiltshire etc Alm for 1780	TC	A7(415)
Wing's Sheet Alm for 1780	TC	A7(423)

Winlove: Lectures	? FN(N)	J382(3)
Yorkshire Alm for 1780	TC	A7(434)

1781

Baldwin's Daily Journal for 1781	TC	A7(12)
Brother's Gift	EN	J44(3)
Cambridge Sheet Alm for 1781	TC	A7(36)
Carnan: To the Rt Hon House of Commons	TC	A75
Cornwall Alm for 1781	TC	A7(47)
Devonshire Alm for 1781	TC	A7(61)
Dimsdale: Tracts on Inoculation	C & N e a	A122
Dorsetshire Alm for 1781	TC	A7(65)
Easter Gift	TC	J97(3)
Essex etc Alm for 1781	TC	A7(69)
Fenelon: Telemachus abridged	TC	J113(4)
Gent's Diary Calendar without Aenigmas for 1781	TC	A7(71)
GM. vol. 51	EN e a	A179
Gent's PB for 1781	TC	A7(74)
Goldsmith's Alm for 1781	TC	A7(82)
Goldsmith: Vicar	TC	A200(8)
Hampshire Alm for 1781	TC	A7(93)
HAB for 1781	EN e a	A242(10)
Johnson: Lives. 1 ed.	EN e a	A269(1)
Prefaces. vols v–x	EN e a	A272
Kent Alm for 1781	TC	A7(99)
LCPB for 1781	TC	A7(137)
Ladies Diary Calendar without Aenigmas for 1781	TC	A7(149)
Ladies Diary for 1781. Comp to	TC	A7(151)
Ladies New Memorandum Book for 1781	TC	A7(166)
Lancashire Alm for 1781	TC	A7(179)
Lincoln etc Alm for 1781	TC	A7(183)
List of all Fairs	TC	A91
Littleton: Juvenile Trials	TC	J229(4)
London Sheet Alm for 1781	TC	A7(211)
London Sheet Alm for 1781 with Court and City		
Kalendar	TC	A7(214)
Medical Museum. 2 ed.	? EN e a	A341(2)
Middlesex etc Alm for 1781	TC	A7(234)
Moore's Alm for 1781	TC	A7(250)
New British Dispensatory	FN(N)	A378
New Hist of England from the Invasion	TC	J258(9)
Norfolk Alm for 1781	TC	A7(278)
Northampton etc Alm for 1781	TC	A7(289)
Northumberland etc Alm for 1781	TC	A7(295)
Oxford etc Alm for 1781	TC	A7(301)
Paterson: Roads in England and Wales. 5 ed.	TC	A399(5)
Roads of Scotland. '5' ed.	TC	A400
Travelling Dict. 4 ed.	TC	A401(4)
Rickman: Journal of Capt Cook. 1 and 2 edd.	EN	A442(1, 2)
Rider's Alm for 1781	TC	A7(326)
Rider's Alm for 1781. Comp to	TC	A7(327)
Rider's Sheet Alm for 1781	TC	A7(340)
Shropshire etc Alm for 1781	TC	A7(374)

Smart: Occasional Prologue	TC	A555(4)
Somerset etc Alm for 1781	TC	A7(380)
Stafford etc Alm for 1781	TC	A7(391)
Suffolk Alm for 1781	TC	A7(398)
Sugar Plumb	EN	J345(2)
Sussex Alm for 1781	TC	A7(403)
Telltruth: Nat. Hist of four-footed Beasts	EN	J350(3)
Thumb: Bag of Nuts. 4 ed.	EN	J353(4)
Trapwit: Be Merry	TC	J358(9)
Voltaire: Works. vols 29–34	C & N, FN(N) e a	A614(7)
Wheble's Ladies PB for 1781	FN(N)	A7(412)
Whitsuntide Gift	TC	J380(3)
Wilts etc Alm for 1781	TC	A7(416)
Wing's Sheet Alm for 1781	TC	A7(424)
Winlove: Moral Lectures	EN	J382(4)
Wynne: Fables of Flowers	EN	J390
Riley's Emblems. 4 ed.	EN	J389(3)
Yorks Alm for 1781	TC	A7(435)

1782

Bailey: English Dict. 24 ed.	EN e a	A20
Baldwin's Daily Journal for 1782	TC	A7(13)
Bible abridged	TC	J27(12)
Brookes: General Gazeteer. 5 ed.	TC	A57(5)
Natural Hist. 3 ed. vol. II	TC	A61(3(c))
Cambridge Sheet Alm for 1782	TC	A7(37)
Cervantes: Don Quixote, trans. Smollett. 5 ed.	EN e a	A80
Cornwall etc Alm for 1782	TC	A7(48)
Croxall: Fables. 12 ed.	EN e a	J87(4)
Curiosities of London. vol. IV	EN	J88(3)
Giles Gingerbread	TC	J267(6)
GM. vol. 52	EN e a	A179
Goldsmith's Book Almanack for 1782	TC	A7(83)
Hampshire etc Alm for 1782	TC	A7(94)
Jacob: New Law-Dict. 10 ed.	? FN(S) e a	A255
LCPB for 1782	TC	A7(138)
Ladies Diary with Aenigmas for 1782	TC	A7(152)
Ladies New Memorandum Book for 1782	TC	A7(167)
Le Sage: Gil Blas abridged	EN	J213(2)
Lincoln etc Alm for 1782	TC	A7(184)
Little Robin Red Breast	EN	J226(1)
London Sheet Alm for 1782	TC	A7(212)
Mawe and Abercrombie: Every Man his own Gardener. 9 ed.	EN e a	A340(1)
Middlesex etc Alm for 1782	TC	A7(235)
Moore's Alm for 1782	TC	A7(251)
Moore's Alm for 1782. Comp to	TC	A7(252)
Museum for young Gentlemen. 10 ed.	TC	J253(12)
Nelson: Companion for the Festivals. 24 ed.	EN e a	A377(1)
New London Sheet Alm for 1782	TC	A7(223)
Norfolk etc Alm for 1782	TC	A7(279)
Northampton etc Alm for 1782	TC	A7(290)
Northumberland etc Alm for 1782	TC	A7(296)

Ogilby and Morgan: Beauties of G.B.	EN e a	A391
Traveller's PB. 21 ed.	EN e a	A392(1)
Partridge: Alm for 1782	TC	A7(304)
Poor Robin's Alm for 1782	TC	A7(312)
Rider's Alm for 1782	TC	A7(328)
Saunders's English Apollo for 1782	TC	A7(369)
Season on Seasons for 1782	TC	A7(370)
Shakespeare: Hamlet	EN e a	A515
Short Hists for Improvement of Mind	TC	J334(4)
Sister Witches	EN e a	J334A
Somerset etc Alm for 1782	TC	A7(381)
Stafford etc Alm for 1782	TC	A7(392)
Stevens: Songs, comical...	EN e a	A575(2)
Sussex etc Alm for 1782	TC	A7(404)
Valentine's Gift	TC	J368(5)
Wing, Tycho: Alm for 1782	TC	A7(418)
Wing's Sheet Alm for 1782	TC	A7(425)
Yorks etc Alm for 1782	TC	A7(436)

1783

Abraham Aesop: Fables	TC	J7A(10)
Baldwin's Daily Journal for 1783	TC	A7(14)
Cambridge Sheet Alm for 1783	TC	A7(38)
Chatter: Lilliputian Auction	TC	J52(3)
CC Geography. 5 ed.	TC	J63(5)
Cordier: Colloquia	TC	J85A(8)
Cornwall etc Alm for 1783	TC	A7(49)
Curiosities of London. vol. II	EN	J88(3)
Gay: Fables	TC, EN e a	A175(1B)
Gentleman and Lady's Key	TC	J145(5)
GM. vols 53, and 53 2nd pt	EN	A179
Goldsmith's Alm for 1783	TC	A7(84)
Goldsmith: Deserted Village. 10 ed.	TC e a	A191(3)
Hist of England in Series of Letters	TC	J147(8)
Goody Two-Shoes (2 edd.)	TC	J167(13, 14)
Henry: Hist Description of Westminster Abbey	TC	A223(7)
Hist of Little King Pippin	EN	J168(3)
HAB for 1783	EN e a	A242(11)
Infant Tutor	TC	J186(8)
J., S.: Tommy Playlove	EN	J189(1)
Johnson: Idler. 4 ed.	TC e a	A264(4)
Lives. New ed.	EN e a	A269(2)
LCPB for 1783	TC	A7(139)
Ladies Diary with Aenigmas for 1783	TC	A7(153)
Ladies most elegant PB for 1783	EN	A7(161)
Ladies new Memorandum Book for 1783	TC	A7(168)
Letters on the Medical Service	EN	A297
Lilliputian Magazine	TC	J219(8)
Lilliputian Masquerade	TC	J220(2)
Lincoln etc Alm for 1783	TC	A7(185)
Little Female Orators	TC	J225(10)
Little Pretty PB	TC	J222(4)
Lives of British Admirals	EN	J230(2)

London Alm for 1783	TC	A7(190A)
London Calendar or Court Register for 1783	TC e a	A7(202)
London Kalendar for 1783. Comp to	TC	A7(203)
London Kalendar for 1783. New ed. corrected	TC e a	A7(203A)
London Sheet Alm for 1783	TC	A7(213)
Middlesex etc Alm for 1783	TC	A7(236)
Moore's Alm for 1783	TC	A7(253)
Moore's Alm for 1783. Comp to	TC	A7(254)
Mother's Gift	TC	J251(4)
New London Sheet Alm for 1783	TC	A7(224)
New Royal Kalendar and Court Register for 1783	TC e a	A7(271)
Norfolk etc Alm for 1783	TC	A7(280)
Northampton etc Alm for 1783	TC	A7(291)
Northumberland etc Alm for 1783	TC	A7(297)
Picture Exhibition	TC	J280(2)
Poor Robin's Alm for 1783	TC	A7(313)
Richardson: Grandison abridged. New ed.	EN	J317(4)
Rider's Alm for 1783	TC	A7(329)
Shakespeare: Merchant of Venice	EN e a	A525
Somerset etc Alm for 1783	TC	A7(382)
Stafford etc Alm for 1783	TC	A7(393)
Sussex etc Alm for 1783	TC	A7(405)
Tagg: Pretty Poems	TC	J346(10)
Twelfth-Day Gift	TC	J366(6)
Wing's Sheet Alm for 1783	TC	A7(426)
Yorkshire etc Alm for 1783	TC	A7(437)

1784

Aulnoy: Mother Bunch's Fairy Tales	EN	J17(2)
Baldwin's Daily Journal for 1784	TC	A7(15)
Cambridge Sheet Alm for 1784	TC e a	A7(39)
Compendious Hist of England. 6 ed.	TC	J76(6)
Cornwall etc Alm for 1784	TC e a	A7(50)
Cries of London	EN	J86(3)
Curiosities of London. vol. III	EN	J88(3)
Defoe: Robinson Crusoe	TC	J93(2)
Fairing	TC	J110(5)
Fielding: Joseph Andrews abridged	EN	J131(2)
Tom Jones abridged	EN	J132(2)
GM. vol. 54	EN	A179
Glasse: Art of Cookery	EN e a	A187(2)
Goldsmith's Alm for 1784	TC e a	A7(85)
Goldsmith: Deserted Village. 11 ed.	TC e a	A191(4)
Hist England from earliest Times. 4 ed.	EN e a	A193(2)
Hart: Hymns. 10 ed.	EN e a	A213(6)
Henry: Hist Description of St Paul's	TC	A221(6)
Hist Description of Tower	TC	A222(15)
Hoppus: Practical Measuring. 11 ed.	EN e a	A239(1)
HAB for 1784	EN e a	A242(12)
Jacob: Every Man his own Lawyer. 9 ed.	EN e a	A253(2)
Johnson: Dict. 5 ed. F°	'MN' e a	A263(1)
Rambler. 10 ed.	TC, 'TN' e a	A273(6)
Kent etc Alm for 1784	TC e a	A7(100)

428

LCPB for 1784	TC e a	A7(140)
Ladies Diary with Aenigmas for 1784	TC e a	A7(154)
Ladies most convenient PB for 1784	EN	A7(162)
Ladies new Memorandum Book for 1784	TC e a	A7(169)
Lincoln etc Alm for 1784	TC e a	A7(186)
London Kalendar and Correct annual Register for 1784	TC e a	A7(197)
London Copper-plate Sheet Alm for 1784	TC e a	A7(192)
London Kalendar or Court Register for 1784	TC e a	A7(204)
London Calendar for 1784. Comp to	TC e a	A7(205)
Middlesex etc Alm for 1784	TC e a	A7(237)
Moore's Alm for 1784	TC e a	A7(255)
Moore's Alm for 1784. Comp to	TC e a	A7(256)
Moore, Francis: Vox Stellarum for 1784	TC	A7(269A)
Museum for young Gentlemen. 11 ed.	TC e a	J253(13)
New London Sheet Alm for 1784	TC e a	A7(225)
New Roman Hist	EN	J263(2)
Norfolk etc Alm for 1784	TC e a	A7(281)
Paterson: Roads in England and Wales. 6 ed.	TC	A399(6)
Poor Robin's Alm for 1784	TC e a	A7(314)
Rider's Alm for 1784	TC e a	A7(330)
Shakespeare: Cymbeline	EN e a	A513
King John	EN e a	A519
Measure for Measure	EN e a	A524
Othello	EN e a	A528
Somerset etc Alm for 1784	TC e a	A7(383)
Tea-Table Dialogues	TC	J347(4)
Telescope: Newtonian System. 6 ed.	TC	J348(6)
Ticklepitcher: Hobby Horse	EN	J354(3)
Wing's Sheet Alm for 1784	TC e a	A7(427)
Wynne: Choice Emblems. 5 ed.	EN	J389(4)
Yorks etc Alm for 1784	TC e a	A7(438)

1785

Allen: Polite Lady. 4 ed.	TC	J8(4)
Baldwin's Daily Journal for 1785	TC	A7(16)
Beccaria: Essay on Crimes, another 4 ed.	EN	A29(6)
Bible, New Hist of. 5 ed.	EN	A34(11)
Cambridge Sheet Alm for 1785	TC	A7(40)
'Cooper': New Hist of England	EN	J84(3)
Cornwall etc Alm for 1785	TC	A7(51)
Easter Gift	TC	J97(4)
Fortune-Teller	EN	J141(4)
Gay: Fables	TC, EN e a	A175(2)
GM. vol. 55	EN	A179
Goldsmith's Alm for 1785	TC	A7(86)
Goldsmith: She Stoops. New ed.	TC	A197(8)
Henry: Curiosities of London	TC	A219(11)
Journal of Capt Cook. New ed.	EN	A224
HAB for 1785	EN e a	A242(13)
Johnson: Dict. 6 ed. 4°	'MN' e a	A263(2)
Dict. 7 ed. F°	EN e a	A263(3)
Kent etc Alm for 1785	TC	A7(101)
LCPB for 1785	TC	A7(141)

429

Ladies Diary with Aenigmas for 1785	TC	A7(155)
Ladies new Memorandum Book for 1785	TC	A7(170)
Lincoln etc Alm for 1785	TC	A7(187)
London Kalendar and correct annual Register for 1785	TC	A7(198)
London Copper-Plate Sheet Alm for 1785	TC	A7(193)
London Calendar or Court Register for 1785	TC e a	A7(206)
Margate Guide	TC e a	A316(4)
Middlesex etc Alm for 1785	TC	A7(238)
Moore's Alm for 1785	TC	A7(257)
Moore's Alm for 1785. Comp to	TC	A7(258)
Moore, Francis: Vox Stellarum for 1785	TC	A7(269B)
New Hist of England from the Invasion	TC	J258(10)
New London Sheet Alm for 1785	TC	A7(226)
Norfolk etc Alm for 1785	TC	A7(282)
Ogilby and Morgan: Traveller's PB. 22 ed.	EN e a	A392(2)
Poor Robin's Alm for 1785	TC	A7(315)
Richardson: Clarissa. New ed.	EN e a	A440(3)
Rider's Alm for 1785	TC	A7(331)
Robin Goodfellow	EN	J320(4)
Shakespeare: King Henry IV, pt 1	EN e a	A517
Macbeth	EN e a	A523
Plays. Ed. Johnson and Steevens	EN e a	A503
Tempest	EN e a	A531
Winter's Tale	EN e a	A534
Somerset etc Alm for 1785	TC	A7(384)
Wing's Sheet Alm for 1785	TC	A7(428)
Yorks etc Alm for 1785	TC	A7(439)

1786

Baldwin's Daily Journal for 1786	TC	A7(17)
Bentick: Spelling and Explanatory Dict	TC	A30
Bible abridged	TC	J27(13)
Boreman: 300 Animals. New ed.	TC, EN e a	J41(3)
Brookes: General Gazeteer. 6 ed.	TC	A57(6)
Cambridge Sheet Alm for 1786	TC	A7(41)
Chesterfield: Maxims. New ed.	EN	J53(3)
'Cooper': Hist of France	EN	J83(1)
New Hist of England	EN	J84(4)
Cornwall etc Alm for 1786	TC	A7(52)
Croxall: Fables. 13 ed.	EN e a	J87(5)
Curiosities of London. vol. I	EN	J88(3)
Curiosities of London. vol. II	EN	J88(4)
GM. vol. 56	EN	A179
Goldsmith's Alm for 1786	TC	A7(87)
Goldsmith: Hist of England in Series of Letters	TC	J147(9)
Poetical Works. New ed.	TC, EN e a	A196(2)
She stoops. New ed.	EN	A197(9)
Traveller	? TC	A199(16)
Hist little King Pippin	EN	J168(4)
HAB for 1786	EN e a	A242(14)
Hoyle's Games improved. New ed.	EN e a	A244(4)
Johnson: Memoirs of King of Prussia	TC	A270
Juvenile Rambles	EN	J200(1)

Kent etc Alm for 1786	TC	A7(102)
LCPB for 1786	TC	A7(142)
Ladies Diary with Aenigmas for 1786	TC	A7(156)
Ladies New Memorandum Book for 1786	TC	A7(171)
Letters between Master Tommy...	TC	J214(4)
Lincoln etc Alm for 1786	TC	A7(188)
Little Moralists	EN	J224(1)
Littleton: Juvenile Trials	TC	J229(5)
London Kalendar and correct Register for 1786	TC	A7(199)
London Calendar or Court Register for 1786	TC e a	A7(207)
London Copper-Plate Sheet Alm for 1786	TC	A7(194)
Middlesex etc Alm for 1786	TC	A7(239)
Moore's Alm for 1786	TC	A7(259)
New Hist of Grecian States	EN	J261(1)
New London Sheet Alm for 1786	TC	A7(227)
Newbery: Letters	TC	J266(8)
Spelling Dict	TC	J268(14)
New Oxford Guide. 7 ed.	EN e a	A395(7)
Norfolk etc Alm for 1786	TC	A7(283)
Paterson: Roads in England and Wales. 7 ed.	TC	A399(7)
Poor Robin's Alm for 1786	TC	A7(316)
Puzzling Cap	EN	J312(2)
Rider's Alm for 1786	TC	A7(332)
Rowley: Treatise on ulcerated Legs. 4 ed.	EN	A478(2)
Shakespeare: As You Like It	EN e a	A511
King Lear	EN e a	A520
Taming of the Shrew	EN e a	A530
Twelfth Night	EN e a	A533
Smart: Hymns for Amusement of Children	TC	J338(4)
Somerset etc Alm for 1786	TC	A7(385)
Tatler. New ed.	EN e a	A582(2)
Tom Thumb's Folio	TC	J356(3)
Wing's Sheet Alm for 1786	TC	A7(429)
Yorks etc Alm for 1786	TC	A7(440)

1786–7

Flights of a Lady-Bird	EN	J136(1)
Little Wanderers	EN	J228(1)
Village Tatlers	EN	J370(1)

1786 or 1787

Adventures of a Silver Penny	EN	J3(1 &/or 2)
Hist of Tommy Titmouse	EN	J177(1)

1787

Baldwin's Daily Journal for 1787	TC	A7(18)
Berquin: Looking-Glass. 1 ed.	EN	J25(1)
Brother's Gift.	EN	J44(4)
Cambridge Sheet Alm for 1787	TC	A7(42)
Cornwall etc Alm for 1787	TC	A7(53)
Daily Journal or complete Accompt Book for 1787	TC e a	A7(54E)
Dodd: Reflections on Death	TC	A127(7)
du Martre: Elements of Heraldry. 4 ed.	TC	A135(4)

431

Newbery's Familiar Letter Writer	EN	J264(1)
Newbery's New Spelling Dict	EN	J265(1)
Norfolk etc Alm for 1788	TC	A7(285)
Ogilby and Morgan: Traveller's PB. 23 ed.	EN	A392(3)
Paltock: Peter Wilkins abridged	EN	J276(1)
Pleasing Reflections	EN	J293
Poor Robin's Alm for 1788	TC	A7(318)
Rider's Alm for 1788	TC	A7(334)
Rollin: Ancient Hist of Egyptians. 8 ed.	TC e a	A446(4)
Rowley: Malignant ulcerated sore Throat	EN e a	A462
Female nervous Diseases	EN e a	A474
Rural Felicity	EN	J327(1)
Somerset etc Alm for 1788	TC	A7(387)
Spectator	EN e a	A573(3)
Sugar Plumb	EN	J345(3)
Sydenham: Works	EN e a	A579
Ticklepitcher: Hobby Horse	EN	J354(4)
Trimmer: Facile Introduction	EN	J358A
Twelfth-Day Gift	TC	J366(7)
Village Tatlers	EN	J370(2)
Wing's Sheet Alm for 1788	TC	A7(431)
Wynne: Choice Emblems. 6 ed.	EN	J389(5)
Yorks etc Alm for 1788	TC	A7(442)

1789

Berquin: Looking-Glass	? EN	J25(2)
Blossoms of Morality. 1 ed.	EN	J39(1)
CC Logic. 5 ed.	Power	J66(5)
CC Rhetoric. 5 ed.	TC	J69(6)
Comical: Lecture upon Games. pts I and II	Power	J75(1, 2)
Defoe: Robinson Crusoe	Power	J93(4)
GM. vol. 59	EN	A179
Hawney: Complete Measurer. 16 ed.	EN e a	A216(1)
Henry: Description of Tower	Power	A222(18)
Hist of North America by 'Cooper'	EN	J169
Hist Prince Lee Boo	EN	J170(1)
Hist of South America by 'Cooper'	EN	J172
HAB for 1789	EN e a	A242(17)
J., S.: Hist Tommy Playlove	EN	J189(3)
Johnson: Rambler. 11 ed.	TC, EN e a	A273(7)
Ladies most elegant PB for 1789	EN	A7(163A)
LCPB for 1789	Administrators of TC	A7(145)
Melvill: Fixible Air	EN e a	A343(2)
Paterson: Roads in England and Wales. 8 ed.	Power	A399(8)
Paths of Virtue	EN	J277(3)
Pretty Book for Children	Exors of TC	J307(8)
Puzzling Cap	EN	J312(3)
Richardson: Grandison abridged	EN	J317(5)
Spectator	EN e a	A573(4)
Tatler	EN e a	A582(3)
Warton: Oxford Sausage	EN ? e a	A620(3)
Youthful Recreations	EN	J397(1)

1790

Adventures of a Bee	Power	J2
Aulnoy: Mother Bunch's Fairy Tales	EN	J17(3)
Baretti: English Italian Dict	EN e a	A22(2)
Brookes: Nat. Hist. 3 ed. vols I, III–V	Power	A61(3)
Campe: New Robinson Crusoe	EN	J49(1)
Cordier: Colloquia. 12 ed.	Power	J85A(10)
Daily Journal for 1790	Power	A7(57)
Fortnight's Tour	Power	J140
GM. vol. 60	EN	A179
Goldsmith: Hist England in Series of Letters	Power	J147(10)
Hoppus: Practical Measuring. 12 ed.	EN e a	A239(2)
HAB for 1790	EN	A242(18)
Hoyle's Games improved. New ed.	EN e a	A244(5)
Johnson: Idler. 5 ed.	Power	A264(6)
Lives. vols I and II	EN e a	A269(3)
Poets	EN e a	A275(2)
Ladies most elegant PB for 1790	EN	A7(164)
London Calendar or Court Register for 1790		
corrected	Power e a	A7(209C)
Milton: Paradise Lost. 9 ed. (Newton's ed.)	EN e a	A361(5)
Paradise Lost (from Tonson's ed.)	EN e a	A361(6)
Moral Sketches	EN	J247(1)
Museum for young Gentlemen. 12 ed.	Power e a	J253(15)
New Hist of England from the Invasion	Power	J258(11)
Plutarch's Lives abridged	Power	J294(3)
Rowley: 118 Diseases of the Eyes	EN e a	A475
Management of Female Breasts. 2 ed.	EN e a	A479(2)
Truth vindicated	EN e a	A482
Shakespeare: Plays and Poems, ed. Malone	EN e a	A505
Plays, Malone's text, vol. I only	EN e a	A504
Ticklepitcher: Hobby-Horse	EN	J354(5)
Valentine's Gift	Power	J368(6)
World displayed	? EN	A640(5)

1791

Bible abridged	Power	J27(14)
Boreman: 300 Animals. New ed.	EN, Power e a	J41(4)
Brookes: General Gazeteer. 7 ed.	Power e a	A57(7)
Nat. Hist. 3 ed. vol. VI	Power	A61(3(g))
'Cooper': New Hist of England. 8 ed.	EN	J84(6)
Cries of London	EN	J86(4)
GM. vol. 61	EN	A179
Goldsmith: Poetical and Dramatic Works. New ed.	Power e a	A196(3)
Vicar. 9 ed.	Power e a	A200(10)
HAB for 1791	EN e a	A242(19)
Johnson: Poets, vols III and IV	EN e a	A269(3)
Lenglet du Fresnoy: Geography. 16 ed.	EN e a	J212(3)
Lockman: New Roman Hist. 11 ed.	TC e a	J232(6)
London Calendar or Court Register for 1791 corrected	Power e a	A7(209D)
Masson: Elmina	EN	J237(1)
Mawe and Abercrombie: Every Man his own Gardener.		
13 ed.	EN e a	A340(5)
Mother Goose's Melody	Power	J250(2)

Nelson: Companion to the Festivals. 26 ed.	EN e a	A377(3)
Pinchard: Blind Child. 1 ed.	EN	J289(1)
Smart: Poems	Power e a	A563

1792

Berquin: Looking-Glass. New ed.	EN	J25(3)
'Cooper': Hist of France. 2 ed.	EN	J83(2)
Gay: Fables	EN e a	A175(5)
GM. vol. 62	EN	A179
HAB for 1792	EN e a	A242(20)
Johnson: Works	EN e a	A274(2)
Little Moralists	EN	J224(2)
Little Wanderers	EN	J228(3)
Murphy: Essay on Johnson. 1 ed.	EN e a	A373(1)
Newbery's New Spelling Dict	EN	J265(2)
Paterson: Roads in England and Wales. 9 ed.	Power	A399(9)
Pinchard: Dramatic Dialogues	EN	J290(1)
Puzzlewell: Collection of Riddles	EN	J311(1)
Rowley: Treatise on regular Gout	EN e a	A476
Visits of Tommy Lovebook	EN	J372

1793

Chesterfield: Maxims. New ed.	EN	J53(4)
Curiosities of London. vol. III	EN	J88(4C)
Curiosities of London. vol. IV	EN	J88(5)
Fielding: Joseph Andrews abridged	EN	J131(3)
Gay: Fables	EN e a	A175(6)
GM. vol. 63	EN	A179
Hamilton: Hist of Mayflower. 2 ed.	EN	A210
Hart: Hymns. 13 ed.	EN	A213(9)
Hist of Little King Pippin	EN	J168(5)
J., S.: Hist of Tommy Play-love	EN	J189(4)
Holiday Entertainment	EN	J180(3)
HAB for 1793	EN e a	A242(21)
Jones: Nat. Hist of Beasts	EN	J192(1)
Nat. Hist of Birds	EN	J193(1)
Nat. Hist of Fishes	EN	J194(1)
Rudiments of Reason	EN	J195
Lenglet du Fresnoy: Geography. 17 ed.	EN e a	J212(4)
Mavor: New Description of Blenheim. New ed.	EN e a	A337(1)
Murphy: Essay on Johnson. 2 ed.	EN e a	A373(2)
Museum for young Gentlemen, another 12 ed.	Power	J253(16)
New Roman Hist	EN	J263(3)
Paltock: Peter Wilkins abridged	EN	J276(2)
Pinchard: Blind Child. 2 ed.	EN	J289(2)
Poetical Blossoms	EN	J297
Rowley: Causes of great Number of Deaths	EN	A457
Rational Practice of Physic	EN e a	A470
Shakespeare: Plays (Johnson and Steevens, revised Isaac). 4 ed.	EN e a	A506
Sister's Gift	EN	J335(4)
Wynne: Choice Emblems. 7 ed.	EN	J389(6)
Youthful Jester	EN	J395(2)

1794

Anstey: New Bath Guide. New ed.	EN e a	A14
Beauties of Ancient Poetry	EN e a	A26
Berquin: Looking-Glass. New ed.	EN	J25(4)
'Cooper': New Hist of England. 9 ed.	EN	J84(7)
Dyche: New English Dict. 17 ed.	EN e a	A137(4)
Father's Gift	EN	J112(3)
Flights of a Lady-Bird	EN	J136(3)
Foundling	EN	J142(2)
GM. vol. 64	EN	A179
Hermit of the Forest	EN	J161(2)
Hist of Sinbad the Sailor	EN	J171(1)
Homeri Ilias ed Clarke. 12 ed.	EN e a	A237(2)
HAB for 1794	EN e a	A242(22)
Johnson: Poets	EN e a	A269(4)
Jones: New biographical Dict. 1 ed.	EN e a	A279(1)
Lenglet du Fresnoy: Geography. 18 ed.	EN e a	J212(4A)
Lockman: New Hist of England. 23 ed.	EN e a	J231(12)
Masson: Elmina	EN	J237(2)
Mawe and Abercrombie: Every Man his own Gardener.		
14 ed.	EN e a	A340(6)
Ogilby and Morgan: Traveller's PB. 24 ed.	EN e a	A392(4)
Pinchard: Blind Child	? EN	J289(4)
Two Cousins	EN	J291(1)
Puzzlewell: Riddles	EN	J311(2)
Wynne: Tales for Youth	EN	J391(1)

1795

Aulnoy: Mother Bunch's Fairy Tales	EN	J17(4)
Carter: Frugal Housewife	EN	A76(4)
Character of the Kings	EN e a	J51
Constantio and Selima	EN	J80
Dodd: Beauties of Hist	EN e a	J94(1)
Gaultier: Course of Geography	EN e a	J142B
GM. vol. 65	EN	A179
Goldsmith: Hist of England from earliest Times	EN	A193(5)
Hoppus: Practical Measuring. 13 ed.	EN e a	A239(3)
HAB for 1795	EN e a	A242(23)
Hurry: Mitchell's Tales	EN	J184
Jones: Nat. Hist of Fishes	EN	J194(2)
Lenglet du Fresnoy: Geography. Another 18 ed.	EN e a	J212(4B)
Little Moralists	EN	J224(3)
Locke: Essay concerning human Understanding	TC, FN e a	A301A
Milton: Paradise Lost	EN	A361(7)
New Hist of Grecian States	EN	J261(3)
Pinchard: Blind Child. 3 ed.	EN	J289(5)
Puzzlewell: Riddles. Pt Second	EN	J311(2A)
Puzzling Cap (2 edd.)	EN	J312(4, 5)
S., H.: Anecdotes of Mary	EN	J328
Ward: Nat. Hist of Fishes	EN	J376(6)

1796

Boyer: Dict Royal	EN e a	A50
Cries of London	EN	J86(5)

Curiosities of London. vol. 1	EN	J88(6A)
Dodd: Beauties of Hist. 2 ed.	EN e a	J94(2)
False Alarms	EN	J111(3)
Gaultier: Cours de Lectures, Premier Cours	EN e a	J143(1–4)
Jeu des Fautes	EN e a	J144
Gay: Fables	EN e a	A175(7)
GM. vol. 66	EN	A179
Glasse: Art of Cookery	EN e a	A187(3)
Hamilton: Hist of May-Flower. 2 ed.	EN	A210
Holiday Entertainment	EN	J180(4)
Hoyle's Games improved. New ed.	EN e a	A244(7)
Johnson: Works	EN e a	A274(3)
Mavor: Voyages. vols I–VII	EN	A335(1)
Juvenile Olio	EN	J239
Pinchard: Blind Child	? EN	J289(6)
Poems, Moral...	EN	A411
Puzzlewell: Riddles. Pt Second	EN	J311(3)
Riddles. Pt Third	EN	J311(4)
Rowley: Translation of References to Plates of Schola		
Medicinae	EN	A473
Treatise on swelled Legs	EN	A477
Sheridan and Henderson's Practical Method of Reading	EN e a	A537
Ticklepitcher: Hobby Horse	EN	J354(6)
Wakefield: Introduction to Botany. 1 ed.	EN e a	J375(1)
Youthful Portraits	EN	J396
Youthful Recreations	EN	J397

1797

Browne: Classical Dict	EN e a	J44A
Campe: New Robinson Crusoe	EN	J49(2)
Correspondence Historique	EN e a	A97A
Curiosities of London. vol. IV	EN	J88(7)
Fenn: Infant's Delight	EN	J116A
Infant's Friend. pt I	EN	J117
Infant's Friend. pt II	EN	J118
Force of Example	EN	J139
GM. vol. 67	EN	A179
Hist of Jacky Idle	EN	J166
Hist of Young Edwin	EN	J178(2)
Jacob: Law-Dict	EN e a	A254
Johnson: Poets abridged	EN	J191A
Lenglet du Fresnoy: Geography. 19 ed.	EN e a	J212(5)
Geography. 20 ed.	T. Newbury e a	J212(5A)
Mavor: Voyages. vols 8–20	EN	A335(1)
New Description of Blenheim. 4 ed.	EN e a	A337(2)
Mawe and Abercrombie: Every Man his own Gardener.		
15 ed.	EN e a	A340(7)
Moral Sketches	EN	J247(2)
New Children's Friend	EN	J255(1)
Palmer: Letters on several Subjects	EN	J273
Newly-invented Copy Book	EN	J274(1)
Paltock: Peter Wilkins abridged	EN	J276(3)
Pilkington: Edward Barnard	EN	J283

Obedience rewarded	EN e a	J285
Selector	EN	J333
Shakespeare: Plays and Poems, Steevens' text	EN e a	A507
Plays (6-vol. ed.)	EN e a	A508
Plays (8-vol. ed.)	EN e a	A509
Tatler	EN e a	A582(4)
Village Tatlers	EN	J370(3)
Winter: System of Husbandry. 2 ed.	EN	A634(2)
Youthful Jester	EN	J395(3)

1798

Bacon: New Abridgment of the Law. 5 ed.	EN e a	A18
Treatise on Leases	EN e a	A19
Berquin: Family Book	EN e a	J23
Livre de Famille	EN e a	J24
Looking-Glass. 7 ed.	EN	J25(7)
Chappell: Universal Arithmetic	EN e a	A80A
'Cooper': New Hist of England. 10 ed.	EN	J84(8)
Croxall: Fables. 16 ed.	EN e a	J87(8)
Curiosities of London. vol. 11	EN	J88(8)
Fenn: Parsing Lessons for elder Pupils	EN	J122
Parsing Lessons for young Children	EN	J123
Gaultier: Lectures graduées. vols I–IV	EN e a	J143(1–4A)
GM. vol. 68	EN	J179
Hawney: Complete Measurer. New ed.	EN e a	A216(2)
Helme: Instructive Rambles	EN e a	J155(1)
Hist of Sinbad the Sailor	EN	J171(2)
Hist of young Edwin	EN	J178(3)
Jones: Nat. Hist of Beasts	EN	J192(2)
Kendall: Keeper's Travels. 1 ed.	EN	J206(1)
The Sparrow	EN	J208
Le Sage: Gil Blas abridged	EN	J213(4)
Mavor: British Tourists. vols 1–5, 1 ed.	EN	A334(1)
Youth's Miscellany	EN	J240
Moral Amusement	EN e a	J246(1)
Music made easy	EN e a	A375
New Children's Friend. 2 ed.	EN e a	J255(2)
Pilkington: Historical Beauties. 1 ed.	EN e a	J284(1)
Scripture Histories	EN e a	J286
Tales of the Cottage	EN e a	J287(1)
Tales of the Hermitage	EN e a	J288(1)
Pinchard: Blind Child. 5 ed.	EN	J289(7)
Two Cousins	EN	J291(2)
Pratt: Pity's Gift. 1 and 2 edd.	EN e a	J305(1, 2)
S., H.: Davenport Family	EN	J329(3)
Shakespeare: Works, Steevens' text	EN e a	A510
Smythies: Hist of a Pin	EN	J341(1)
Wakefield: Introduction to Botany. 2 ed.	EN e a	J375(2)

1798 or 1799

Filial Duty	EN	J134(5)

1799

Aulnoy: Mother Bunch's Fairy Tales	EN	J17(5)
Beauties of the Poets. 6 ed.	EN e a	A28
Budget	EN	J46
Cries of London	EN	J86(6)
Curiosities of London. vol. 1	EN	J88(9)
Dodsley: Chronicles of the Kings. New ed.	EN e a	J95(1)
Enchanted Mirror	EN e a	J100(1)
English: Conversations	EN e a	J101
Faithful Mirror	EN e a	J102
False Alarms	EN	J111(4)
Fenn: Friend of Mothers	EN	J116
Some Hints to young Women	EN	A154
Toiles d'Araignées	EN e a	J129
Fielding: Joseph Andrews abridged	EN	J131(4)
Flights of a Lady-Bird	EN	J136(4)
Gaultier: Lectures graduées. vols v–vi	EN e a	J143A(7, 8)
GM. vol. 69	EN	A179
Hamlain	EN	J153
Helme: James Manners. 1 ed.	EN e a	J157(1)
Hermit of the Forest	EN	J161(3)
Hist Tommy Titmouse	EN	J177(2)
Johnson: Dict. 8 ed. 4°	EN e a	A263(4)
Jones: New Biographical Dict. 3 ed.	EN e a	A279(3)
Kendall: Canary Bird	EN	J204
Crested Wren	EN	J205
Keeper's Travels. 2 ed.	EN	J206(2)
Lenglet du Fresnoy: Geography. 20 ed.	EN e a	J212(6)
Little Moralists	EN	J224(4)
Memoirs of Danby Family	EN	J242
Moral Amusement	EN e a	J246(2)
Newbery: Thoughts on Taxation	D. Holt e a	A383
Peacock: Little Emigrant. 1 ed.	EN e a	J278(1)
Perrault: Histories by Mother Goose (the ed. dated '1719')	? EN e a	J279(5)
Pilkington: Biography for Girls. 1 ed.	EN e a	J282(1)
Historical Beauties. 2 ed.	EN e a	J284(2)
Tales of the Cottage	EN e a	J287(2)
Tales of the Hermitage	EN e a	J288(2)
Puzzlebrains: Christmas Amusement	EN	J310
Sade: Life of Petrarch by Dobson. 4 ed.	EN e a	A484(2)
Sister's Gift	EN	J335(5)
? Trimmer: Ladder to learning. Step the first	EN	J359(6)
? Trimmer: Silver Thimble	EN	J362(1)
Wynne: Choice Emblems. 9 ed.	EN	J389(8)
Young Gent's and Lady's Magazine. pts 1–11	EN e a	J393
Youthful Recreations	EN	J397(3)

1799–1800

Museum for young Gentlemen. 15 ed.	EN e a	J253(19)

1800

Adventures of a Silver Penny	EN	J3(3)

Butcher: Moral Tales	EN e a	J48A
Choice Scraps	EN	J55(3)
'Cooper': New Hist of England. 11 ed.	EN	J84(9)
Ducray-Dumenil: Little Mountaineers	EN e a	J96
Gay: Fables	EN e a	A175(8)
Goldsmith: Miscellaneous Works	EN e a	A195
Helme: James Manners. 2 ed.	EN e a	J157(2)
Holiday Entertainment	EN	J180(5)
Johnson: Poets	EN e a	A269(5)
Works	EN e a	A274(4)
Josse: Juvenile Biography	EN e a	J196
Julius	EN	J197
Juvenile Stories	EN e a	J202(2)
Kendall: Lessons of Virtue	EN	J207
Lockman: New Hist of England. 24 ed.	EN e a	J231(14)
Mason: Lady's Assistant. 8 ed.	EN e a	A331
Mavor: Histoire naturelle	EN e a	J238
Voyages. vols 1 and 21–5	EN e a	A335(2)
Milton: Poetical Works	EN e a	A359(3)
Newbery's Familiar Letter Writer. New ed.	EN	J264(2)
Newbery: Observations on Income Tax Act	Nicol	A382
Pleasant Tales	EN	J292
Poems, moral...	EN	A411(2)
Pratt: Pity's Gift. 3 ed.	EN e a	J305(3)
Sketches from Nature	EN	J337
Smith: Lucinda	EN	J339
Smythies: Hist of a Pin	EN	J341(2)
Somerville: Village Maid	EN e a	J343
Trimmer: Silver Thimble	EN	J362(2)
Winter: Animal Magnetism	EN e a	A633

1801–2

Winlove: Entertaining Stories	EN	J381(9)

1802

Peacock: Little Emigrant. 2 ed.	EN e a	J278(2)

1804

Ladies most elegant PB for 1804	EN	A7(164B)

1810

New Oxford Guide. 15 ed.	EN e a	A395(14)

1814

Thornton: Illustrations of School-Virgil	Newbery*	J352

1815

Newbery: Donum Amicis	[FN(S)]	A381

INDEX OF
PUBLISHERS, PRINTERS AND BOOKSELLERS
concerned with the books listed in Parts I and II (other than JN, FN(S), FN(N), EN and TC)

All worked in London except where otherwise stated. Some of the more long-lived firms changed the form of their names more than once over the years. Thus, e.g., Rivington will be found as Rivington & Co; Messrs R.; C. R.; J. R.; J. and J. R.; J. and F. R.; J. R. and Son; F. C. and J. R.; J. F. and C. R. In such a case as this all variants are gathered under 'Rivington'.

The names in this Index are only set out in the entries in the 'J' section of the Bibliography. They are, however, set out in the author's full notes, of which the entries in the 'A' section are abstracts. See the Preface, p. vii.

Little attempt has been made to analyse identical or closely allied names, e.g. under 'Woodfall, G.' are included one of that name who was working at Charing Cross in 1773, and one (a printer) in Pater Noster Row in 1799. They may be identical.

Baylis, —; T., J24, 129, 210
Baynes, W., A132(2)
Becket, T. & Co., J78(2)
    A3(1), 35(5), 36(16), 37(2–5), 57(3), 87(1–4),
        87A, 100(1, 2), 101(1, 2), 187(1, 2), 243(1, 2),
        244(2), 260, 265, 272, 273(4), 275(1), 291,
        358, 361(1–3), 440(1, 2), 573(1), 598, 599(I
        and II), 618
Becket, [T.] and De Hondt, [P. A.], A35(1, 3),
    36(13–15), 37(6), 57(2), 176(1, 2), 389, 588
Beecroft, —, A632
Beecroft, J., A137(1), 225, 226, 227, 361(1)
Beecroft, T., A20(1), 137(3), 153(3), 359(1),
    361(2, 3), 377(1)
Bell, — (of Oxford St), A299
Bell, J.; John (of The Strand), A595(1), 638
Bennett, J., A623
Bensley, —, A361(7)
Bent, —, A582(3)
Bent, J., A57(6, 7)
Bent, W., J87(5–8), 231(12, 13)
    A137(4), 175(2, 3, 5, 7, 8), 215(1, 2), 263(2, 3),
        269(3, 4), 274(1, 2), 275(2), 361(7), 373(1, 2),
        377(4)
Bentham, J. (Cambridge), A556(1), 557(2, 3),
    558(1, 2), 559(1, 2), 560(1, 2), 561(1)
Bew, J[ohn], J87(4–7)
    A7(160), 20(1, 2), 175(3, 4, 6), 187(1, 2, 2A),
        200(9), 215(1, 2), 237(1), 239(1, 2), 253(1–3),
        265, 269(1–3), 272, 273(5–7), 274(1), 275(1,
        2), 359(2), 361(2–6), 392(2, 3), 395(3–9), 491
Bickerstaff, R., J199A; A18, 19
Bigg, George, A286(7)
Binns, John (Leeds), J57
Birt, —; S., A44, 276, 277, 319, 322, 323(1, 2),
    326(2), 348, 357, 632
Bladon, R., A20(2)
Bladon, S[amuel], J231(3, 5), 232(2–6), 260(1, 2)
    A7(343–52, 354–9), 20, 36(17), 37(8), 50,
        137(1), 142, 174, 175(1A, 1B, 2–7), 200(9, 10),
        216(1), 243(1), 244(4–7), 252, 302(2), 377(4),
        392(2–4), 409, 487, 535, 595(1), 599(I, II,
        III), 627
Blakeney, J. (Windsor), A631(1, 2)
Blyth, F., A421
Bonner and Middleton (Bristol), A369(6)
Bonsor, H., J202(2)
Bonsor, J., J203, 287(3), 343
Booker, T. (? = T. Brooker), A7(209, 209C, D)
Boosey, —; T., J24, 142B, 143A(2, 4, 7, 8), 196,
    238
    A28, 216(2)
Bowen, —, A341(2)
Bowen, J., A175(1B), 263(1), 265, 269(1, 2), 272,
    275(1), 446(3), 599(II)
Bowles, —, A573(3)
Bowles, C., A391, 392(1, 2, 3)
Bowles, J. and T., A573(1), 599(I, II)
Bowles, T., A215(2), 599(III)

Bowles and Carver, A392(4)
Bowyer, W., A273(4)
Breadhower, Mr — (Gosport), A489
Brindley, —; J., A303, 584, 632
Bristow, W., A172(1, 2), 190(2), 341(1),
    430
Brooke, E., A255
Brooke, E. and R., A18, 19, 254
Brooker, T. (? = T. Booker), A7(208, 208A)
Brooks, S., A453(2)
Brotherton, —; J., A581(1), 632
Brotherton, R., A301A
Brown, Robert, A286(4, 5)
Brown, W., A254
Bryer, H., J292, 337, 362(2)
Buckland, —; J., J231(7, 9, 10)
    A20(1), 132(1), 175(1A, 1B, 2–4), 215(1, 2),
        259(1–3), 265, 269(1, 2), 272, 274(1), 275(1, 2),
        341(2), 377(1), 391, 392(1–3), 582(1–3), 627
Bull, Lewis (Bath), J57
Bulmer W. & Co, A240, 382
Burnett, G., A343(1, 2), 582(1, 2), 627
Burns, E., J250A, 254A
Bush, — (Ipswich), A299
Butterworth, J., A18, 19, 254
Bye and Law, A582(4)
Byfield and Hawksworth, A66
Cadell, —, A166, 167(1, 2), 573(3, 4), 582(3)
Cadell, J., A263(2)
Cadell, T., J87(1, 2, 4–7), 231(7, 9–13), 314(2)
    A3(1, 2, 3), 7(343–52, 354–9), 18, 19, 22(1, 2),
        80, 100(1, 2), 101(1, 2), 175(1A, B, 2–8),
        187(1, 2, 2A), 191(2, 4), 193(1–4), 196(1, 3),
        215(1, 2), 225, 226, 227, 254, 255, 263(1–3),
        264(4–6), 265, 269(1–4), 272, 273(4–7),
        274(1, 2), 275(1, 2), 337(1, 4), 340(1–5), 358,
        359(1, 2), 361(1–7), 368(1–3), 369(1–6),
        373(1, 2), 376, 440(1, 4), 567, 573(1), 582(1,
        2), 643
Cadell, T. (Bristol), A368(1–3), 369(2–6), 376,
    440(2, 3), 567, 599(I, II, III)
Cadell, Jr, A269(5)
Cadell, T., Jr, A193(6)
Cadell, [T.] and Davies [Davis], [W.], J87(8), 101,
    231(14)
    A3(3), 22(3), 50, 187(3), 263(4), 337(2, 3), 355,
        573(2), 582(4)
Cadell, [T.], Jr and [W.] Davis [Davies], A195,
    274(3, 4), 340(7, 8), 359(3)
Carnan, J. [& Co] (Reading), J243A(1, 2), 243B
    A136, 332, 347, 348(2), 349, 350, 351(1, 2),
        353(1, 2), 362, 545, 614A
Carnan, T. & Co, J231(6, 7), 232(4)
    A7(10, 136), 314, 398(2), 547(2), 548(3),
        549(2), 556(2), 557(5), 558(4), 559(5),
        560(4), 561(4), 562(3)
Carnan, T., Administrators or Executors of,
    J307(8); A7(145)
Carpenter & Co, J278(1, 2); A274(4), 359(3)

Caslon, T., J87(1, 2, 4), 148A(4, 6), 165B(1), 231(3, 5, 6, 7), 232(1–4), 260(1, 2)

A3(1), 7(54A, B, C, 343–52, 354–9), 20(1), 36(14–17), 37(2–6, 8), 43(2, 3), 51(4, 5), 56(3), 80, 84, 87A, 132(1), 137(1, 3), 153(3), 174, 175(1A, B), 183(3, 4), 187(1, 2), 243(1, 2), 244(2, 3), 252, 253(1), 255, 259(1, 2), 265, 269(1, 2), 272, 273(1–5), 275(1), 284(2, 3), 302(2), 358, 359(1), 361(1–3), 377(1), 391, 392(1), 409, 412, 446(1–3), 447, 448(1, 2), 449, 450, 541, 573(1), 582(1), 604

Cater, R., A301A

Cater, W., A255, 273(6)

Cave, —; R., A535, 574(1), 578(1), 590(1)

Cavell, W., A7(215)

Cawthorne, C., J95(1)

Chalmers, J., A213(9)

Champante and Whitrow, J43, 199A; A80A, 242(21–3), 299

Champion, F., A386

Chapelle, Mr, A303

Chapman, J., J389(3, 4)

Chase, W. (Norwich), A638

Clarendon Press, A350

Clark, John, A303

Clarke, Mr, A95

Clarke & Son, A269(5), 274(3, 4), 359(3)

Clarke, Charles, J101

Clarke, J., A302(1)

Clarke, W. [& Son], A7(208, 208A, 209, 209C, D), 18, 19, 187(2A, 3), 254, 269(4), 358

Clarke, W. and R. Collins, A358, 582(1)

Clements, R. (Oxford), A348(1)

Cole, B. Mr, A489, 623

Collins, — (Salisbury), A7(54A, B, C), 143, 319, 321

Collins, B[enjn] (Salisbury and occasionally London), J9(1), 21(4), 87(2, 4), 148A(1–4, 6), 190A, 253(1–3, 5, 7–9, 11), 279(2, 3), 301(1), 307(1, 2, 3, 4, 4B, 5A, 6), 308(1–3, 6, 8–10, 13, 14), 324(1, 2, 3, 5, 5A, B, C), 326(2, 5)

A7(10, 131, 133, 135, 136, 365, 368), 20(1), 51(1–5), 57(2), 173(1, 2), 190(2), 200(1, 2), 205, 207(1, 3), 215(1, 2), 229, 273(1–7), 274(1), 285, 286(1), 300(1, 2), 322, 323(1–3), 324, 326(1, 3, 4), 328, 329(1), 359(1), 361(1–3, 5), 373A, 427, 430, 434(1–4), 453(1), 554(1), 592(1, 3–5, 7, 8), 607(7), 611(2), 614(1, 2, 4–6)

Collins, B. C. (Salisbury), J87(5), 253(12, 13, 15, 17, 19), 279(5), 307(8), 324(5D)

A7(54E, 55, 57), 20(2), 51(6), 52, 274(2–4), 373(1, 2), 634(1)

Collins, S. (Salisbury), A93

Collyer, J[oseph], A43(1, 2), 183(2–4), 284(1–3)

Conant, J., A3(1)

Conant, N., A215(1, 2), 265, 269(1, 2), 272, 274(1, 2), 275(1, 2), 301A

Cook[e], Joshua (Sherborne), A285, 286(1)

Cook[e], A., A34(1), 125(3), 251

Cooper, —, A632

Cooper, M[ary], J165B(1), 232(1)

A48, 257, 326(1, 3), 329(1)

Cooper, T., A305, 324

Coote, J., J48(1)

A7(361–8), 34(2), 57(2), 72, 206, 207(1, 3), 291, 292, 390, 412, 604, 605(1, 2), 607(1, 2, 4–6), 609, 611(1), 614(1, 2)

Corbett, —, A637(1)

Corbett (Corbet), C., A7(361–8), 20(1), 132(1), 359(1), 361(1), 377(1, 3, 4), 391, 392(1)

Cornell, T., A7(209, 209C, D)

Corner, T., A7(208, 208A)

Cornish, J. D., J87(1, 2); A361(1–3)

Cowslade, — (Reading), see Smart and Cowslade

Cox, —, J352; A632

Craighton, Mr (Ipswich), A319

Creech, W. (Edinburgh), J13; A7(209C, D)

Cresch, W. (? = Creech) (Edinburgh), A7(209)

Crockatt, R., A307

Cropley, Wm, A54, 72

Crosby, B., J87(8); A187(3)

Crosby and Letterman, J253(19), 264(2); A331

Crouse Stephenson and Matchet (Norwich), A299

Crowder, —; J., J25(3–5, 7, 8), 28, 39(4), 207, 353(10), 355(5), 359(6), 391(1, 2), 397(3)

A337(3), 573(3, 4)

Crowder, S[tanley] [& Co], J87(1, 2, 4), 148A(2–4, 6), 165B(1), 231, 232(1–3), 260(1), 279(2, 3), 301(1), 307(4B, 5A, 6, 8), 308(6, 8–10, 13, 14)

A7(10, 54A, B, C, E, 55, 57, 131, 133, 135, 136, 343–52, 354–9, 361–8), 34(2), 51(2–6), 56(3), 57(2, 3, 5), 72, 101(1, 2), 132(1), 137(1, 3), 153(3), 175(1A, B), 187(1, 2), 206, 207(1, 3), 229, 243(1–3), 244(2–4), 252, 253(1), 255, 259(1), 265, 269(1, 2), 272, 273(1–4), 275(1), 286(6, 7), 291, 302(1, 2), 326(3), 329(1), 340(1), 358, 359(1), 361(1), 377(1, 3, 4), 390, 409, 412, 434(2–4), 440(1, 2), 446(1–3), 447, 448(1, 2), 449, 450, 453(2), 535, 573(1), 582(1), 599(1, II), 604, 605(1–3), 607(1, 2, 4–7), 609, 611(1, 2), 614(1–7), 627

Crowder and Hemsted, J28

Cruttwell (Crutwell), — (Bath), A230, 424A

Cruttwell, R[ichard] (Bath), A14, 148(2, 3), 242(1–23), 422, 424, 438, 443

Cruttwell (Crutwell), W. (Sherborne), A99, 242(1–8)

Cumberlege, S. A., A263(1), 377(1)

Cundee, J., J11, 48A, 96, 204, 241(2), 243, 281, 282(3), 364, 381(9), 389(8)

A380

Curtis, J. and T., A7(343–52), 409

Curtis, T., A7(354–9)

Cuthell, G., A274(4)

445

Cuthell, J., J94(3)
   A7(209, 209C, D), 50, 263(4), 269(5), 274(3)
Darton and Harvey, J24, 93(5), 94(2, 3), 95(1), 101, 108, 157(1, 2), 253(19), 255(2), 352, 375(1, 2)
   A3(3), 28, 137(4), 175(6), 274(2–4), 373(1, 2)
Davey, P., A302(1)
Davies, L., A193(4), 301A
Davies, R., A486
Davies, T., J87(1, 2)
   A3(1), 36(1, 2, 6–8), 87(1–4), 152, 206, 243(2), 244(2), 264(3), 265, 269(1, 2), 271, 272, 273(4), 275(1), 301A, 358, 361(1–3), 440(1, 3), 573(1), 581(1, 2), 582(1), 588, 607(1, 2, 4–6), 609, 611(1), 614(1, 2), 618
Davies, W., A187(1, 2), 193(6)
Davis, —; Mr, A7(54A, B, C), 95, 573(3, 4), 582(3)
Davis, C., A269(4, 5), 274(3, 4)
Davis, L., A3(2), 22(2), 34(1, 3, 4), 101(1, 2), 187(2A), 193(3), 215(1, 2), 263(1–3), 265, 269(1–3), 272, 274(1), 275(1, 2), 359(1, 2), 361(1–6), 429(2), 573(1)
Davis, Lockyer, A151
Davis, M., A242(3)
Davis, R., A7(361–8), 10, 11, 12, 34(1, 3, 4), 164(1), 374(1–3), 429(1), 543, 588, 625, 626
Davis, T., A402, 412
Davis, W., A34(5), 84, 243(2), 244(2, 3), 272, 274(3), 275(1)
Davis, [L.] and Reymers, [C.], A7(361–8), 10, 11, 12, 34(1), 125(1–3), 128, 152, 164(1), 374(1–3), 410, 429(1, 2), 625, 626
Davison, T., J84(9)
Davison, Thomas, A50, 381
Dawson, W. [& Co] (Oxford), A395(11, 13, 14), 620(5)
Deboffe, —, A97A
Debosse, —, A355
Debrett (Debret), J., A80, 187(2A, 3), 196(2, 3), 391, 392(1–4)
Deighton, J., A7(209, 209C, D), 50, 254, 269(5), 274(3, 4), 359(3)
Dell, H., A152
De Poggi, A. C., J143(1)
De Poggi, Mr's New Room, J142B
Dewick, J., J288
Dicey, C. (Northampton), A93
Dilly, —, A573(3, 4), 582(3, 4)
Dilly, C., J87(4, 5, 7, 8), 231(9–13)
   A3(3), 7(54A, B, C), 18, 19, 50, 57(5–7), 107, 215(1, 2), 237(1, 2), 244(7), 254, 255, 259(2, 3), 263(1–4), 269(1–4), 272, 273(6, 7), 274(1–3), 275(2), 359(2), 361(4–7), 373(1, 2), 582(2), 599(III)
Dilly, E. and C., J231(7)
   A259(1), 265, 272, 274(1), 333, 359(1), 361(1–3), 397, 573(1, 2), 582(1)
Dodd, —, A632

Dodsley, —; Messrs, A166, 167(1, 2), 303, 319, 341(2), 350, 351(1, 2), 438, 573(2–4), 582(3, 4)
Dodsley, J., A3(1–3), 43(1–3), 100(1, 2), 101(1, 2), 123, 136, 148(2, 3), 183(2–4), 215(1, 2), 260, 263(1–3), 265, 269(1–4), 272, 274(1–3), 275(1, 2), 284(1–3), 347, 348(2), 353(2), 358, 359(1, 2), 362(1–7), 373(1, 2), 394, 402, 435, 573(1), 580, 582(2), 601, 602
Dodsley, R., A43(1), 151, 556(1), 557(2), 559(2), 560(1)
Dodsley, R. and J., A17, 152, 581(1, 2)
Domville, B., A187(1, 2)
Domville, C., A244(4)
Domville, W., J218 (and the numbers there quoted)
   A34(5), 176(2), 186, 243(2, 3), 244(2, 3), 255, 300, 391, 392(1–3)
Dumville, see Domville
Donaldson, A., A7(202, 203A, 204)
Downes, — (Yarmouth), A299
Dulau, —; & Co, J196; A97A, 355
Durham, T., A43(1), 187(1, 2)
Dymott, R., A187(1, 2)
Easton, J., J100(1, 2); A210
Eddowes, J. (Shrewsbury), A7(95)
Edwards, —; I.; J., A269(3, 4), 274(3, 4), 275(2), 573(2, 4), 582(4)
Edwards's Manufactory and Music-shop, A375
Egerton, —; J.; T., J101; A263(4), 269(4, 5), 274(3, 4)
Egerton, J. & T.; T. and J., A20(2), 215(1, 2), 263(2, 3), 269(3), 274(1, 2), 275(2), 373(1, 2)
Elmsley (Elmsly), P., J142B, 144
   A22(1, 2), 50, 215(1, 2), 263(2, 3), 269(1–5), 274(1–4), 275(2), 355, 373(1, 2), 402
Elmsley and Bremner, J143, 143A(2, 4, 7, 8)
   A22(3), 97A, 263(4)
Etherington, C. (York), A638
Evans, J., A237(1, 2), 269(3, 4)
Evans, R. H., A269(5), 274(4)
Evans, T., A20(1), 22(1), 193(1, 2), 196(1), 215(1, 2), 254, 255, 263(1), 264(4, 5), 265, 269(1, 2), 272, 273(4, 6), 274(1–3), 275(1, 2), 340(1), 361(1–3), 373(1, 2), 377(3), 440(2), 541, 614(7), 627, 643
Faden, W[illiam], A70, 125(1–3), 126, 128, 130, 310(1–3), 333, 397, 410, 430, 543
Farley, S. (Bristol), A166, 167(1, 2), 368(1–3), 369(1–5), 376, 567, 580
Faulder, —; R., J101
   A3(3), 7(202, 203A, 204, 206–9, 209C, D), 50, 215(1, 2), 254, 263(4), 269(3–5), 274(1–4), 275(2), 373(1, 2), 377(3–5), 573(2, 4), 582(4)
Faulkener, G. (Dublin), A194(2)
Fell, J., A207(1, 3)
Fielding, J., A7(202, 203A), 20(1), 255, 377(1)
Fielding and Walker, J232(4); A137(3), 175(1A), 187(1, 2), 193(1)

446

Fletcher, J., J148A(2, 3); A54, 415, 580
Fletcher, J.; Mr (Oxford), J243A(1, 2), 243B
   A136, 260, 319, 324, 345, 347, 348(1, 2),
   349, 350, 351(1, 2), 353(1, 2), 395(1–9),
   618
Flexney, —; W., A3(1, 2), 7(54A, B, C), 132(1),
   137(1, 3), 149(1), 176(1, 2), 255, 359(1), 364,
   377(1, 3), 573(1, 3, 4), 582(1–3),
Fought, Henry, A627
Fox, —, A66
Fox, J., A80
Fox, W., A3(1, 2), 22(1), 187(1–3), 193(1), 215(1,
   2), 255, 263(1–3), 265, 269(1–4), 272, 273(5–
   7), 274(1–3), 275(1, 2), 359(1), 373(1, 2),
   440(3), 582(2), 599(1, 11), 614(7)
Francklin, R., A607(4, 5), 609, 611(1)
Frederic, T. (Bath), A136
Frederick, Mr — (Bath), A319, 321
Frederick, J. (Bath), A376
Frederick, W. (Bath), A7(365, 368), 166, 167(1,
   2), 173(1, 2), 190(2), 194(1, 2), 322, 323(1–
   3), 326(1, 3, 4), 328, 329(1), 369(1, 2), 422,
   580, 592(1, 3–5, 7, 8)
Frederic[k] and Bull (Bath), A368(1–3), 369(3–6)
Frederick and Taylor (Bath), A567
French, J., A491
Fry, H., J284A
Fuller, J., J248(1), 321(1); A252, 259(1), 489,
   604
Fuller, J., Jr, A582(1)
Galabin, H. L., J274
Galabin, J. W., A394
Gale and Curtis, J352
Gammage, Mr (Worcester), A166, 167(1, 2)
Gardener (Gardner), H. L., A175(1A, B, 2–8),
   215(2), 269(3–5), 274(3, 4), 275(2)
Gardiner, H., see Gardner, H.
Gardiner, W., A7(364)
Gardner (Gardiner), H., A50, 187(1–3), 377(1, 3,
   5), 446(3, 4)
Gardner, T., A557(3), 558(1, 2), 560(2)
Gardner, W. L., A377(4)
Gaselee, Mr (Gosport), A614A
Gedge, — (Bury), A299
Geisweiler, —, J196
Gill, W., A390
Gill, W. (Cambridge), A34(2)
Gilliver, —; L., A276, 277
Ginger, W.; & Son, J87(4, 5, 7, 8); A50
Gisbourne, W., A419
Goadby & Co (Sherborne), A634(1)
Godwin, J., A186
Goldney, H., A3(2), 196(1–3)
Goldsmith, —, A573(3, 4)
Goldsmith, G., A237(1, 2)
Goldsmith, W., J87(2, 4–7), 231(9–12), 314(2)
   A3(1–3), 7(355–9), 20(1, 2), 22(1, 2), 34(4), 80,
   87A, 137(1, 3, 4), 153(1, 3), 175(1A, B, 2–6),
   187(1, 2, 2A), 200(10), 215(1, 2), 216(1),

   239(1–3), 244(5, 6), 253(1–3), 259(1–3),
   263(1–3), 269(3, 4), 273(4–7), 274(1, 2),
   275(2), 340(1–5), 359(2), 361(4, 6, 7),
   373(1, 2), 437, 440(2, 3), 582(1, 2), 614(7),
   643
Gosnell, S., J177(2)
Grafton and Reddell (Birmingham), J37, 38(2)
Gretton, J., A206
Griffin, —, A438
Griffin, W., A35(1, 3), 36(1, 2, 6–8, 10–15), 37(2,
   6), 191(1), 192, 273(4), 393, 440(1, 2), 570,
   573(1)
Griffiths, R., A386, 589(1, 2)
Hall, J. (Margate), A316(1–4)
Hamilton, A., A72, 97, 291, 599(1, 11, 111)
Hamilton, S., A340(8)
Hand, J., A470, 481
Harding, Mr (Portsmouth), A489
Harding, J., A263(4), 269(5), 274(4)
Harlow, E., J142B
Harris, John, J381(9); A395
Harrison & Co, A270
Harrison, J., A281
Harrison, Owen, A597
Hart, J[ohannes], A74, 345
Hassell, L[ionel] (Chelmsford), A146, 436
Hassell, M. (Chelmsford), A146
Hatchard, —; J., J101, 102; A269(5), 274(4)
Hawes, —; & Co, J231(1, 3), 232(2), 260(1);
   A302(2), 326(4)
Hawes, L., A358, 582(1)
Hawes, [L.], Clarke, [W.], and Collins, [R.],
   J87(1, 2), 231(5, 6), 232(3), 260(2)
   A132(1), 137(1), 252, 273(4), 281, 361(1),
   446(1, 2), 447, 448(1, 2), 449, 450, 535,
   573(1), 627
Hawis, L., A301A.
Hawkins, —, A7(54A, B, C)
Hawkins, G., A7(346), 571(2), 617
Hayes, —, A264(5), 573(3, 4), 582(3)
Hayes, S., A3(2, 3), 20(1, 2), 57(6, 7), 187(2A),
   193(2–4), 215(1, 2), 237(1, 2), 239(1–3),
   263(1–3), 264(4, 6), 269(1–4), 273(7),
   274(1–3), 275(2), 373(1, 2), 377(4), 446(3, 4),
   579
Hazard, S. (Bath), J246(1)
Hearne, J., J352
Hemsted, —, J28
Henderson, C., A7(361–4), 10
Henry, D.; David; —, A170(1), 179 (years 1767–
   91), 535, 574(1), 590(1)
Heptinstall, T., J37
Hett, Richard, A407
Hildyard, J. (York), A557(2), 559(1, 2), 561(1)
Hind, —, A166, 167(1, 2)
Hinton, —, A7(54A, B, C)
Hinton, J., J87(1, 2)
   A132(1), 137(1, 3), 187(1, 2), 252, 273(4, 5),
   358, 573(1), 582(1)

Hitch, C. and Hawes, L., J165B(1), 232(1); A72, 323(3), 632

Hodges, —; J[ames], J148A(2), 253(1, 1A, 2), 279, 307(3, 4), 308(2, 3), 324(1, 2), 326(2)
   A229, 322, 323(1–3), 326(2), 431, 453(1), 617, 632

Hodson, —, J170(4)

Hoey, J. Jr (Dublin), A640(1)

Holt, D. (Newark), A383

Holton, Mr (Havant), A614A

Hookham, T., A7(209, 209C, D), 464, 464(2), 466, 471(2), 474, 475, 476, 479(2), 482

Hookham and Carpenter, A3(3), 573(2), 582(4)

Hookham & Co, A274(3)

Hooper, S., A175(1B)

Hopkins, —, J196

Horsfield, R., J87(2), 231(3, 5, 6), 232(2, 3), 260(1, 2)
   A132(1), 137(1), 175(1A, B), 252, 302(2), 446(1, 2), 447, 448(1, 2), 449, 450, 573(1), 582(1, 2)

Hotman, —, J196

Hughes, —, A7(54A, B, C)

Hughes, H., A275(1), 573(4)

Humphry, P., A489

Hurst, T., J11, 37, 129, 330, 330A, 331
   A28, 244(8), 269(5), 274(4), 331, 340(8), 377(5)

Jackson, Mr, A230

Jackson, W. (Oxford), A34(2), 87(1–4), 390, 395(1–9), 620(1, 2, 4)

Jackson, Fletcher and Cooke (Oxford), A337(1)

Jameson, R., A3(3), 215(2), 273(7), 274(1)

Jefferies, J., J248(1), 321(1)

Jeffery, E., A359(3)

Jefferys, T., A291

Jenkinson, J. (Huntingdon), A260

Johnson, E., A3(1), 7(54A, B, C), 132(1), 252, 259(1, 2), 359(1), 361(2, 3)

Johnson, J[oseph], J87(2, 4–8), 212(1–6), 232(5, 6), 236, 314(2), 352
   A3(3), 18, 19, 20(2), 22(1–3), 50, 57(5–7), 132(2), 137(3, 4), 153(1, 3), 175(1B, 2–8), 187(1–3), 195, 215(1), 216(1, 2), 212(4B), 237(1, 2), 239(1, 2, 3), 253(1, 2), 254, 255, 259(2, 3), 263(1–4), 269(1–5), 272, 274(1–4), 275(1, 2), 340(2–5, 7, 8), 359(2, 3), 361(4–7), 373(1, 2), 377(4), 392(2–4), 440(1, 3), 573(1–4), 582(1–4), 614(7), 627, 643

Johnson, J. & Co, A260, 535

Johnson and Payne, A107, 594

Johnston, —, A7(54A, B, C)

Johnston, E., J231(6); A361(1), 377(1), 446(3), 573(1), 582(1)

Johnston, S., J212(5A)

Johnston, T., J212(4A)

Johnston (Johnstone), W., J165B(1), 231(3, 5), 232(1, 3), 260(1, 2)

A57(2, 3), 72, 206, 252, 291, 301A, 302(1, 2), 326(4), 358, 440(1, 2), 446(1, 2), 447, 448(1, 2), 449, 450, 607(1, 2, 4–7), 609, 611(1, 2), 614(1–6)

Joliffe, J.; Mr —, A7(54A, B, C), 86, 230

Jones, G., A345

Jordan, J. S., A213(9)

Kay, —; J., J196, 231(14); A573(2)

Kay, T. (? = J. Kay), A331, 340(7, 8)

Kearsley, —, A66

Kearsley (Kearsly), C. and G.; G.; G. and C., J231(3), 232(2), 260(1)
   A7(343–52, 354), 34(5), 36(1, 2, 6–8, 10–12), 65, 149(1–3), 192, 196(1), 196A, 206, 243(1), 273(4), 274(2, 3, 4), 302(2), 311, 361(2, 3, 7), 364, 373(1, 2), 395(1, 2), 409, 412, 439, 444, 491, 604, 607(1, 4–6), 609, 611(1), 614(1, 2)

Kearsley, S. and J., A3(3)

Kearsly, J., A570

Keating, Mr (Stratford), A580

Keith, G., A20(1), 22(1), 153(3), 175(1A, B), 252, 253(1), 259(1, 2), 301A, 376, 453(1, 2), 582(1), 627

Keymer, W. (Colchester), A436

Kiernan, Chas, A591

Kincaid, A., & Co (Edinburgh), A87(1–4)

King and Son, A50

Kinnersly, T., A408(2)

Knapp, G. (Peterborough), A260

Knox, J., A80, 132(1), 137(3), 187(1, 2, 2A), 215(1, 2), 273(5–7), 274(1), 359(1, 2), 361(1–3, 5, 6), 377(1), 440(1–3), 446(2–4), 573(1, 3, 4)

Köpp, Henry, A451

Lackington & Co, A50, 263(4)

Lackington, Allen & Co, J94(3), 95(1), 238, 352
   A22(3), 269(5), 274(3, 4), 331, 340(8)

Lambert, Mr (Lewes), A489

Lane, W., A137(3, 4), 187(3)

Law, B[edwell]; & Co; & Son, J87(1, 2, 4–7), 148A(4), 165B(1), 231(3, 5–7, 9–12), 232(1–6), 260(1, 2), 314(2)
   A3(1–3), 7(54A, B, C, 343–52, 354–9), 20(1, 2), 22(1, 2), 50, 51(6), 57(2, 3, 5–7), 72, 80, 132(1), 137(3, 4), 149(2, 3), 153(1, 3), 175(1A, B, 2–7), 187(2A, 3), 193(1–4), 215(1, 2), 216(1), 237(1, 2), 239(1–3), 243(2, 3), 244(2–7), 252, 254, 255, 259(1–3), 263(1–3), 265, 269(1–4), 272, 273(1–7), 274(1–3), 275(1, 2), 302(2), 333, 340(1–5, 7), 359(1, 2), 361(1–7), 364, 373(1, 2), 377(1, 3, 4), 391, 392(1–4), 397, 409, 440(3), 446(1–4), 447, 448(1, 2), 449, 450, 541, 573(1–4), 582(1–4), 599(I, II, III), 604, 627, 643

Law, C., J87(8), 231(14), 278(1, 2); A175(8), 216(2), 274(4)

Lea, R., A175(8), 263(4), 269(5), 274(4), 331

Leach, D[ryden], A126, 156, 206, 497

450

269(1–3), 272, 274(1, 2), 275(1, 2), 358, 359(1, 2), 361(1–6), 373(1, 2), 573(1), 582(1, 2)
White, B. and B., A175(4–6), 237(1)
White, B. and J., A237(2), 274(3), 573(2), 582(4)
White, J., A18, 19, 274(4)
White, T. (Arundel), A489
Whittell, T., A623
Whittingham, C., J305(3); A175(8), 331
Whittingham, W. (Lynn, Norfolk), A85
Wicksteed, Trustees of, A239(1–3)
Wilkie, —, A582(3, 4)
Wilkie, G[eorge], J87(8), 231(9, 10, 13, 14)
  A28, 65, 175(8), 193(6), 195, 216(2), 243(3), 244(8), 263(4), 269(5), 274(4), 340(8), 359(3), 377(5)
Wilkie, G. and T., J87(7), 231(11, 12), 232(5, 6)
  A3(2, 3), 20(2), 50, 132(2), 137(4), 153(1), 175(2–7), 187(2A, 3), 210, 215(1, 2), 216(1), 237(1, 2), 239(2, 3), 244(6, 7), 254, 259(3), 269(3, 4), 273(7), 274(1–3), 275(2), 340(7), 359(2), 361(4–7), 373(1, 2), 377(3, 4), 392(2–4), 440(3), 582(2)
Wilkie, J., J232(4)
  A3(1), 20(1), 41, 137(3), 175(1A, B), 187(1, 2), 207(1, 3), 208, 225, 226, 227, 243(1, 2), 244(2, 3), 252, 259(2), 265, 269(1, 2), 272, 275(1), 300A, 306A, 368(1–3), 369(3–6), 377(1), 391, 392(1), 567, 582(1), 614(7)
Wilkie, T., A239(1), 244(4, 5)

Wilkie and Robinsons, J352
Williams, —, A7(54A, B, C)
Williams, R., A289
Williamson, R. (Liverpool), J148A(1)
Wilson, D., A41, 291
Wilson, J., A207(1, 3)
Wilson and Durham, A431
Wimpey, J.; Mr (Newbury), A111, 319, 362, 614A
Wingrave, F., A22(2, 3), 50, 464(2), 466, 471(2), 482
Wingrave, J., A475, 476, 479(2)
Witch, Robt, A641
Withy, R., J232(1), 165B(1); A207(1, 3)
Woodfall, —, J231(1)
Woodfall, G., J46, 131(4), 153, 209, 340; A4, 584
Woodfall, H., J148A(4–6), 165B(1), 231, 232(1, 2), 260(1)
  A72, 137(1, 3), 302(1, 2)
Woodfall, H. S., A20(1, 2), 137(4)
Woodfall, M., A149(1–3), 252, 253(1), 364, 444
Woodfall, W[illiam], J231(6), 232(3–6)
  A20(1, 2), 137(1, 3), 253(2, 3), 255, 639
Woodgate, H., J148A(2, 3); A229, 453(2)
Woodyer, J. (Cambridge), A226, 227, 228, 581
Wright, J., J374
Wright, T., A7(209, 209C, D), 573(4)
Wright, T. (Cambridge), A34(2)
Wright, W., A390
Wynn, —, A573(2)

The names in this Index are only set out in the entries in the 'J' section of the Bibliography. They are, however, set out in the author's full notes, of which the entries in the 'A' section are abstracts (see the Preface).

GENERAL INDEX

Numbers in italics refer to pages